D1632910

This Book Belongs To: BOB GUSTAFSON

TCP/IP
UNLEASHED

Third Edition

Karanjit S. Siyan, Ph.D.
Tim Parker, Ph.D.

SAMS 201 West 103rd Street, Indianapolis, IN 46290

TCP/IP Unleashed

Copyright © 2002 by Sams Publishing

All rights reserved. No part of this book shall be reproduced, stored in a retrieval system, or transmitted by any means, electronic, mechanical, photocopying, recording, or otherwise, without written permission from he publisher. No patent liability is assumed with respect to the use of the information contained herein. Although every precaution has been taken in the preparation of this book, the publisher and author assume no responsibility for errors or omissions. Nor is any liability assumed for damages resulting from the use of the information contained herein.

International Standard Book Number: 0-672-32351-6

Library of Congress Catalog Card Number: 2001096703

Printed in the United States of America

First Printing: March 2002

05   04   03   02   4   3   2   1

Trademarks

All terms mentioned in this book that are known to be trademarks or service marks have been appropriately capitalized. Sams Publishing cannot attest to the accuracy of this information. Use of a term in this book should not be regarded as affecting the validity of any trademark or service mark.

Warning and Disclaimer

Every effort has been made to make this book as complete and as accurate as possible, but no warranty or fitness is implied. The information provided is on an "as is" basis. The author and the publisher shall have neither liability nor responsibility to any person or entity with respect to any loss or damages arising from the information contained in this book or from the use of programs accompanying it.

ASSOCIATE PUBLISHER
Linda Engelman

ACQUISITIONS EDITOR
Dayna Isley

DEVELOPMENT EDITOR
Ginny Bess

MANAGING EDITOR
Charlotte Clapp

PROJECT EDITOR
Elizabeth Finney

COPY EDITOR
Paula Lowell

INDEXER
Larry Sweazy

PROOFREADER
Plan-it Publishing

TECHNICAL EDITOR
William Wagner

TEAM COORDINATOR
Lynne Williams

INTERIOR DESIGNER
Gary Adair

COVER DESIGNER
Alan Clements

PAGE LAYOUT
Rebecca Harmon

Contents at a Glance

Contents

Part X   Appendixes   1023

About the Author

Karanjit S. Siyan is Vice President of R&D for Higher Technology, a professional services company based in Hamden, Connecticut. He has authored international seminars on Solaris and SunOS, TCP/IP networks, PC Network Integration, Windows NT, Novell networks, and expert systems using Fuzzy Logic. He teaches advanced technology seminars in the United States, Canada, Europe, and the Far East. Dr. Siyan has published articles in *Dr. Dobbs Journal*, *The C Users Journal*, *Database Advisor*, and other research journals and is actively involved in Internet research. He has worked with computer networks for Unix, NetWare, Windows NT/2000, OS/2, and computer languages such as C/C++, Pascal, LISP, Algol, Ada, MSL, PL/1, Jovial, CMS-2, PL/SQL, Perl, VB, Java, and so on for many years. He has written compilers for a number of these languages. Karanjit holds a Ph.D in Computer Science, a master's degree in Electrical Engineering and Computer Science, and a bachelor's degree in Electronics and Electrical Communication Engineering. He is a member of IEEE and ACM, and his career achievements are recorded in Marquis' Who's Who in the World, Who is Who in America, Who's Who in Finance and Industry, and Who's Who in Science and Engineering.

Before working as an independent consultant, Dr. Siyan worked as a senior member of the technical staff at ROLM Corporation, and as a software developer on numerous projects. As part of his consulting work, Dr. Siyan has written a number of custom compiler and operating system development tools. His interests include Unix-based, NetWare-based, and Windows NT/2000-based networks. He is actively involved in the application of many computer science disciplines such as networks, operating systems, programming languages, databases, expert systems, and computer security. Dr. Siyan holds certification credentials for a number of commercial operating system products, and has written numerous books.

Dedication

To my wife for bringing so much joy in my life and to my parents for being there for me.

Acknowledgments

One of the more pleasurable tasks of being an author is to thank the people responsible for the success of a book. I want to thank all those close to me: Harpreet, Ahal Singh, Tejinder Kaur, Harjeet, Jagjit, Kookie, and Dolly. Special thanks to Mother, Saint Germain, El Morya Khan, Djwal Kul, Kuthumi Lal Singh, Kuan-Yin, Bhagwan Krishna, and Babaji. Without their spiritual support, this book would not have been possible.

I want to thank Bob Sanregret and Anders Amundson, who initially got me interested in writing teaching materials about computers. I also want to thank the many people at Higher Technology and Learning Tree for their help and support on various projects. In particular I would like to thank Philip Weinberg, Lenny Bernstein, Dr. David Collins, Eric Garen, and John Moriarty.

I want to thank Dayna Isley for keeping the project on track and Ginny Bess, the development editor. I want to also thank Elizabeth Finney and William Wagner for their help in developing this book.

Tell Us What You Think!

As the reader of this book, *you* are our most important critic and commentator. We value your opinion and want to know what we're doing right, what we could do better, what areas you would like to see us publish in, and any other words of wisdom you're willing to pass our way.

You can e-mail or write me directly to let me know what you did or didn't like about this book—as well as what we can do to make our books stronger.

Please note that I cannot help you with technical problems related to the topic of this book, and that due to the high volume of mail I receive, I might not be able to reply to every message.

When you write, please be sure to include this book's title and author as well as your name and phone or fax number. I will carefully review your comments and share them with the author and editors who worked on the book.

Email: `networking@samspublishing.com`

Mail: Mark Taber
            Associate Publisher
            Sams Publishing
            201 West 103rd Street
            Indianapolis, IN 46290 USA

Introduction

TCP/IP (Transmission Control Protocol/Internet Protocol) has become a de facto protocol not only for the Internet but also for intranets. On the intranet, TCP/IP was one choice among many, such as Novell's IPX/SPX, Microsoft's NetBIOS or NetBEUI, Apple's AppleTalk protocols. Although these other protocols can still be found on networks, TCP/IP has emerged as the dominant communications protocol.

What caused the change on intranets? It was gradual. As Windows NT/2000 and Novell NetWare servers evolved, they adopted TCP/IP. Microsoft included a TCP/IP stack with Windows 9x and NT/2000. One advantage of the adoption of a common protocol is that it promotes interoperability. For example, UNIX, Windows, and Macintosh computers can more seamlessly work together. The ability to connect seamlessly to the Internet, without having to convert network protocols, also helped move the momentum to TCP/IP. So today most networks, heterogeneous and Windows-specific, are TCP/IP based. IPX/SPX is a very small fraction of the market, and NetBEUI is used only on small, simple Windows networks.

The change has been for the better. TCP/IP is one of the most stable network protocols available, and it is evolving to meet the needs of the future. The security weaknesses of TCP/IP are well known and well researched. Standards such as IPSec have been created to make TCP/IP more secure. TCP/IP has been implemented on almost every type of hardware that needs to be networked. TCP/IP is an open standard, which means that all the specifications are published and readily available.

The growth of the Internet has helped push TCP/IP to the forefront of network protocols, of course. With the explosive growth of the World Wide Web, every computer now needs to understand TCP/IP in order to talk to an Internet service provider. And yet TCP/IP was in widespread use before the Web's popularity boost only a few years ago. Many of us were using TCP/IP for our e-mail, FTP, and Usenet services 20 years ago, working on old UNIX and CP/M systems that required us to understand more than how to click a few buttons in a GUI dialog box.

When the first edition of *TCP/IP Unleashed* and *Sams Teach Yourself TCP/IP in 14 Days* were published, they were in the minority: Books about TCP/IP were meant to be read by non-programmers or network administrators. Now, the shelves are crowded with TCP/IP books, many just derivatives of each other. The strange truth about TCP/IP is this: It is very simple, and at the same time very complex. If all you want to do is connect a Windows machine to a TCP/IP network, the steps are so simple they can be covered in a couple of pages of a book. Yet if you want to know the details behind TCP/IP's protocols and the utilities in the protocol suite, thousands of pages are required. Even more is necessary if you want to develop TCP/IP-based applications. So there's obviously a need for all levels of books. This edition of *TCP/IP Unleashed* tries to appeal to the person who needs to know about the protocols and tools involved in TCP/IP, how to add machines to a TCP/IP network, and what issues you need to be aware of, but skims only lightly across the developer's side of the protocol.

A lot of information is in this book: We cover all the basic TCP/IP protocols in detail. You'll see how the protocols are used and how TCP builds upon IP, which itself builds upon a network protocol. You'll see how all kinds of applications use the basic TCP and IP protocols. Tools you use on large networks every day, such as DNS (Domain Name System), NFS (Network File System), and NIS (Network Information Service) all use TCP as their basic protocol. Other protocols used by administrators, such as SNMP (Simple Network Management Protocol) and ARP (Address Resolution Protocol), all build on the basic TCP protocols, too. Even things as simple as your e-mail use TCP protocols such as SMTP (Simple Mail Transfer Protocol). TCP/IP is pervasive throughout all our computer tasks. Understanding the protocol and its underlying operation can help you understand your computer's services better.

Throughout this book we've tried to take a non-programmer's approach to the material. Each protocol in the TCP/IP family has its own chapter, and there is special emphasis on the IP and TCP protocols themselves with additional chapters dedicated to them. This book shows you how the TCP/IP protocol works, how it interacts with the other protocols in the TCP/IP family, what the protocol does for you and your network, and how you can implement it easily on your machine.

Where appropriate, we give you step-by-step guides to install and configure the protocol or service. We show you the commands you will use and the output you can expect. You'll see how to implement TCP/IP on many different operating systems including Windows 9x, Windows NT, Windows 2000, NetWare, and the widely used Linux system. You'll see information about firewalls and security. In short, everything we could think of about TCP/IP, with the exception of programming applications, is in this book. We hope you enjoy it.

Conventions Used in This Book

The following typographic conventions are used in this book:

- Code lines, commands, statements, variables, and any text you type or see onscreen appears in a mono typeface. **Bold mono** typeface is used to represent the user's input.

- Placeholders in syntax descriptions appear in an *italic mono* typeface. Replace the placeholder with the actual filename, parameter, or whatever element it represents.

- *Italics* highlight technical terms when they're being defined.

- The ➥ icon is used before a line of code that is really a continuation of the preceding line. Sometimes a line of code is too long to fit as a single line on the page. If you see ➥ before a line of code, remember that it's part of the line immediately above it.

- The book also contains Notes to help you spot important or useful information quickly. These notes contain tips and warnings as well. Some of these are helpful shortcuts to help you work more efficiently.

TCP/IP Fundamentals

PART

I

Introduction to Open Communications

by Mark A. Sportack

IN THIS CHAPTER

CHAPTER 1

Unarguably, TCP/IP (less commonly known as the Transmission Control Protocol/Internet Protocol) is the most successful communications protocol ever developed. The term *TCP/IP* is generically used to refer to a set of communication protocols, such as TCP for reliable delivery, UDP (User Datagram Protocol) for best-efforts delivery, IP for Internet Protocol, and other application services.

Evidence of the success of TCP/IP can be found on the Internet, the largest open network ever built. The Internet was specifically designed to facilitate defense-oriented research, and to enable the U.S. Government to continue communications despite the potentially devastating effects of a nuclear attack. TCP/IP was developed for this purpose.

Today, the Internet has grown into more commercial and consumer-oriented roles. Despite this radical change in its purpose, all of its original qualities (that is, openness, survivability, and reliability) continue to be essential. These attributes include reliable delivery of data with the use of explicit protocols such as TCP designed for that purpose, and the ability to automatically detect and avoid failures in the network. More importantly, though, TCP/IP is an open communications protocol. *Openness* means that communications are possible between *any* combination of devices, regardless of how physically dissimilar they might be.

This chapter explains how open communications emerged and the concepts that enable open data communications. It also introduces the two major models that make open communications a practical reality: the *Open Systems Interconnect* (OSI) *Reference Model* and the *TCP/IP Reference Model*. These models greatly facilitate the understanding of networks by dissecting them into their various functional components. These components are stratified into *layers*. A command of these layers, and the concept of open communications, will provide the context for a more meaningful examination of TCP/IP's various components and uses.

Evolution of Open Networks

Networks, originally, were highly proprietary connectivity solutions that were an integral part of an equally proprietary, bundled computing solution. Companies that automated their data processing or accounting functions during the primitive days before personal computers had to commit to a single vendor for a turnkey solution.

In such a proprietary, single-vendor environment, the application software executed only in an environment supported by a single operating system. The operating system could execute only within the safety of the same vendor's hardware products. Even the users' terminal equipment and connectivity to the computer were part of the same, one-vendor, integrated solution.

During the reign of single-vendor, integrated solutions, the *Department of Defense* (DoD) identified a need for a robust and reliable data communications network that could interconnect all of its computers, as well as the computers owned by affiliated organizations such as universities, think tanks, and defense contractors. This might not sound like a big deal, but it was. In the early days of computing, manufacturers developed very tightly integrated platforms of hardware, software, and networks. A user on one platform would be very hard-pressed to share data with a user on a different computing platform. The logic behind this was fairly simple: The *Department of Defense* manufacturers wanted captive audiences.

Forcing all of the DoD's subcontractors and affiliated research organizations to migrate to a single vendor's brand of equipment was utterly impractical. Consequently, a means of communicating between dissimilar platforms was needed. The result was the creation of the world's first open communications protocol: the *Internet Protocol* (IP).

An *open network*, therefore, is one that enables communications and resource-sharing between dissimilar computers. Openness is achieved through the collaborative development and maintenance of technical specifications. These specifications, which are also known as *open standards*, are made publicly available.

Layering the Communications Process

The key to enabling open communications lay in understanding all of the functions necessary for two end systems to communicate and share data with each other. Identifying these essential functions, and establishing the order in which they must occur, is the foundation for open communications. Two end systems can only communicate if they both agree on how to communicate. That is, they both must follow the same procedure for taking data from an application and packaging it for transit through a network. No detail, regardless of how small, can be taken for granted or left to chance.

Fortunately, there is a somewhat logical sequence of events that is necessary in a communications session. These events include, at a bare minimum, the following tasks:

- Data must be passed down from its application to a communications process (known as a *protocol*).

- The communications protocol must prepare the application data for transmission across some type of network. This usually means that the data must be broken down into more manageable pieces.

- The segmented data must then be enveloped in a data structure for passage through a network to a specific device (or devices). This means that the data must be wrapped in something that contains information that would enable any networked computing device to identify where that envelope of data came from, and where it was going. This structure can be a frame, a packet, or a cell, depending on the protocol being used.

- These frames or packets must be converted into the physical bits for transmission. These bits can be transmitted as pulses of light on a fiber-optic network (such as FDDI) or as electronic states (on or off) for transmission across an electronic network (such as Ethernet, or any other network that transmits data in the form of electricity over metallic wire).

At the destination, or recipient machine, this process is reversed.

Other functions, too, may be needed during the communications session. These functions enable the source and destination machines to coordinate efforts and ensure that the data arrives safely. These functions include the following:

- Regulating the flow of transmitted data so that the receiving machine, and/or the network, are not inundated.
- Checking the received data to ensure that it was not damaged in transit. This is done using checksums, such as the *Cyclic Redundancy Checksum* (CRC). CRC is a polynomial-based mathematical checksum that is able to detect errors in transmission.
- Coordinating the retransmission of any data that either failed to arrive at its destination, or arrived damaged.
- Lastly, the recipient of the data must reassemble the segments into a form that the receiving application can recognize. From the receiving application's perspective, the data should be exactly the same as what the transmitting application sent out. In other words, the two applications appear to be passing data directly between each other. This is known as *logical adjacency*.

Perhaps the best tool for explaining the concepts of layered communications, including logical adjacency, is the OSI Reference Model.

The OSI Reference Model

The *International Organization for Standardization* (ISO) developed the Open Systems Interconnection (OSI) Reference Model in 1978/1979 to facilitate the *open interconnection* of computer systems. An open interconnection is one that can be supported in a multivendor environment. This model established the global standard for defining the functional layers required for open communications between computers.

When the OSI Reference Model was developed almost 20 years ago, few commercial systems followed that model. Computer manufacturers at that time locked customers into proprietary, single-vendor architectures. Open communication was viewed as an invitation to competition. From the manufacturer's perspective, competition was undesirable. Consequently, all functions were integrated as tightly as possible. The notion of functional modularity, or layering, seemed antithetical to any manufacturer's mission.

It is important to note that the model has been so successful at achieving its original goals that it almost renders itself moot. The previous proprietary, integrated approach has disappeared. Open communications, today, are requisite. Curiously, very few products are fully OSI-compliant. Instead, its basic layered framework is frequently adapted to new standards. Nevertheless, the OSI Reference Model remains a viable mechanism for demonstrating the functional mechanics of a network.

Despite its successes, numerous misperceptions about the OSI Reference Model persist. Consequently, it is necessary to provide yet another overview of this model in this section. The overview identifies and corrects these misperceptions.

The first misperception is that the OSI Reference Model was developed by the *International Standards Organization* (ISO). It was not. The OSI Reference Model was developed by the International Organization for Standardization. This organization prefers to use a mnemonic abbreviation rather than an acronym. The mnemonic abbreviation is based on the Greek word, *isos*, which means equal or standard.

The OSI model categorizes the various processes necessary in a communications session into seven distinct functional layers. The layers are organized based on the natural sequence of events that occurs during a communications session.

Figure 1.1 illustrates the OSI Reference Model. Layers 1–3 provide network access, and Layers 4–7 are dedicated to the logistics of supporting end-to-end communications.

FIGURE 1.1

The OSI Reference Model.

OSI Reference Model Layer Description	OSI Layer Number
Application	7
Presentation	6
Session	5
Transport	4
Network	3
Data Link	2
Physical	1

Layer 1: The Physical Layer

The bottom layer is called the *Physical Layer*. This layer is responsible for the transmission of the bit stream. It accepts frames of data from Layer 2, the Data Link Layer, and transmits their structure and content, typically serially, one bit at a time. The Physical Layer is also responsible for the reception of incoming streams of data, one bit at a time. These streams are then passed on to the Data Link Layer for reframing.

The Physical Layer, quite literally, sees only 1s and 0s. It has no mechanism for determining the significance of the bits it transmits or receives. It is solely concerned with the physical characteristics of electrical and/or optical signaling techniques. This includes the voltage of the electrical current used to transport the signal (the line encoding and framing not to be confused with the data character coding and framing), the media type and impedance characteristics, and even the physical shape of the connector that is used to terminate the media.

A common misperception is that OSI's Layer 1 includes anything that either generates or carries the data communications signals. This is not true. It is a *functional* model only. The Physical Layer is limited to just the processes and mechanisms needed to place signals onto the transmission media, and to receive signals from that media. Its lower boundary is the physical connector that attaches to the transmission media. It does *not* include the transmission media, though the different LAN (Local Area Network) standards, such as 10BASET and 100BASET, do refer to the media type used.

Transmission media include any means of actually transporting signals generated by the OSI's Layer 1 mechanisms. Some examples of transmission media are coaxial cabling, fiber-optic cabling, and twisted-pair wiring. The confusion seems to stem from the fact that the Physical Layer does provide specifications for the media's performance. These are the performance characteristics that are required, and assumed to exist, by the processes and mechanisms defined in the Physical Layer.

Consequently, transmission media remain outside the scope of the Physical Layer and are sometimes referred to as *Layer 0* of the OSI Reference Model.

Layer 2: The Data Link Layer

The second layer of the OSI Reference Model is called the *Data Link Layer*. As all the layers do, it has two sets of responsibilities: transmit and receive. It is responsible for providing end-to-end validity of the data being transmitted, typically across a physical link.

On the transmit side, the Data Link Layer is responsible for packing instructions, data, and so forth into frames. A *frame* is a structure indigenous to the Data Link Layer that contains enough information to ensure that the data can be successfully sent across a physical link (such as a Local Area Network) to its destination.

Successful delivery means that the frame reaches its intended destination intact. Thus, the frame must also contain a mechanism to verify the integrity of its contents upon delivery.

Two things must happen for guaranteed delivery to occur:

• The originating node must receive an acknowledgment of each frame received intact by the destination node.

• The destination node, prior to acknowledging receipt of a frame, must verify the integrity of that frame's contents.

Numerous situations can result in transmitted frames either not reaching the destination or becoming damaged and unusable during transit. The Data Link Layer is responsible for detecting and correcting any and all such errors. The Data Link Layer is also responsible for reassembling any binary streams that are received from the Physical Layer back into frames. Given that both the structure and content of a frame are transmitted, however, the Data Link Layer isn't really rebuilding a frame. Rather, it is buffering the incoming bits until it has a complete frame.

Layers 1 and 2 are required for each and every type of communication, regardless of whether the network is a LAN or WAN. Typically, network cards inside computers implement the Layer 1 and Layer 2 functionality.

Layer 3: The Network Layer

The *Network Layer* is responsible for establishing the route to be used between the originating and destination computers. This layer lacks any native transmission error detection/correction mechanisms and, consequently, relies upon the link for reliable transmission service of the Data Link Layer. End-to-end reliability across several physical links is more of a function of the Transport Layer (Layer 4).

The Network Layer is used to establish communications with computer systems that lie beyond the local LAN segment. It can do so because it has its own routing addressing architecture, which is separate and distinct from the Layer 2 machine addressing. Such protocols are known as *routed* or *routable* protocols. Routable protocols include IP, Novell's IPX, and AppleTalk, although this book will focus exclusively on IP and its related protocols and applications.

Use of the Network Layer is optional. It is required only if the computer systems reside on different network segments that are separated by a router, or if the communicating applications require some service, feature, or capability of either the Network Layer or the Transport Layer. For example, two hosts that are directly connected to the same LAN may communicate well using just that LAN's communications mechanisms (Layers 1 and 2 of the OSI Reference Model).

> **Note**
>
> In modern networks, the requirement to connect two networks is so common that the Network Layer is no longer considered optional. Earlier protocols such as NetBEUI that do not provide an explicit network layer have to be handled as special cases in modern network design consisting of interconnected networks.

Layer 4: The Transport Layer

The *Transport Layer* provides a service similar to the Data Link Layer, in that it is responsible for the end-to-end integrity of transmissions. Unlike the Data Link Layer, however, the Transport Layer is capable of providing this function beyond the local LAN segment. It can detect packets that are discarded by routers and automatically generate a retransmit request. In other words, the Transport Layer provides true end-to-end reliability.

Another significant function of the Transport Layer is the resequencing of packets that may have arrived out of order. This can happen for a variety of reasons. For example, the packets may have taken different paths through the network, or some may have been damaged in transit. In any case, the Transport Layer is capable of identifying the original sequence of packets, and must put them back into that sequence before passing their contents up to the Session Layer.

Layer 5: The Session Layer

The fifth layer of the OSI Model is the *Session Layer*. This layer is relatively unused—many protocols bundle this layer's functionality into their transport layers.

The function of the OSI Session Layer is to manage the flow of communications during a connection between two computer systems. This flow of communications is known as a *session*. It determines whether communications can be uni- or bi-directional. It also ensures that one request is completed before a new one is accepted.

The Session Layer also may provide some of the following enhancements:

- Dialog control
- Token management
- Activity management

A session, in general, allows two-way communications (*full duplex*) across a connection. Some applications may require alternate one-way communications (*half duplex*). The Session Layer has the option of providing two-way or one-way communications: an option called *dialog control.*

For some protocols, it is essential that only one side attempt a critical operation at a time. To prevent both sides from attempting the same operation, a control mechanism, such as the use of *tokens*, must be implemented. When using the token method, only the side holding a token is permitted to perform the operation. Determining which side has the token and how it is transferred between the two sides is known as *token management.* The token management functions are used in the ISO session layer protocols.

> **Note**
>
> The use of the word "token" here should not be confused with Token Ring operation. Token management is a much higher level concept at Layer 5 of the OSI model. IBM's Token Ring operation belongs to Layers 2 and 1 of the OSI model.

If you are performing a one-hour file transfer between two machines, and a network crash occurs approximately every 30 minutes, you might never be able to complete the file transfer. After each transfer aborts, you have to start all over again. To avoid this problem, you can treat the entire file transfer as a single activity with checkpoints inserted into the datastream. That way, if a crash occurs, the session layer can synchronize to a previous checkpoint. These checkpoints are called *synchronization points.*

There are two types of synchronization points: major and minor synchronization points. A major synchronized point inserted by any communicating side must be acknowledged by the other communicating side, whereas a minor synchronization point is not acknowledged. That portion of the session that is between two major synchronization points is called a *dialog unit.* The operation of managing an entire activity is called *activity management.* An activity can consist of one or more dialog units.

TCP/IP networks do not have a general Session Layer protocol. This is because some of the characteristics of the Session layer are provided by the TCP protocol. If TCP/IP applications require special session services they provide their own. An example of such a TCP/IP application service is the Network File System (NFS), which implements its own Session Layer service—the Remote Procedure Call (RPC) protocol.

> **Note**
>
> The Network File System (NFS) protocol also uses its own Session Layer service: the External Data Representation (XDR) protocol.

Layer 6: The Presentation Layer

The *Presentation Layer* is responsible for managing the way that data is encoded. Not every computer system uses the same data-encoding scheme, and the Presentation Layer is responsible for providing the translation between otherwise incompatible data-encoding schemes, such as *American Standard Code for Information Interchange* (ASCII) and *Extended Binary Coded Decimal Interchange Code* (EBCDIC).

The Presentation Layer can be used to mediate differences in floating-point formats; number formats, such as one's complement and two's complement; and byte ordering; as well as to provide encryption and decryption services.

The Presentation Layer represents data with a common syntax and semantics. If all the nodes used and understood this common language, misunderstanding in data representation could be eliminated. An example of this common language is *Abstract Syntax Representation, Rev 1* (ASN.1), an OSI recommendation. In fact, ASN.1 is used by the Simple Network Management Protocol (SNMP) to encode its high-level data.

Layer 7: The Application Layer

The top layer in the OSI Reference Model is the *Application Layer*. Despite its name, this layer does not include user applications. Rather, it provides the interface between those applications and the network's services.

This layer can be thought of as the reason for initiating the communications session. For example, an email client might generate a request to retrieve new messages from the email server. This client application automatically generates a request to the appropriate Layer 7 protocol(s) and launches a communications session to get the needed files.

The Model's Usage

The vertical orientation of the stack is an acknowledgment of the functional flow of processes and data. Each layer has interfaces to its adjacent layers. In order to communicate, two systems must pass data, instructions, addresses, and so forth between the layers. The differences between the logical flow of communications and the actual flow of the session are illustrated in Figure 1.2.

FIGURE 1.2

Actual versus logical flow of layered communications.

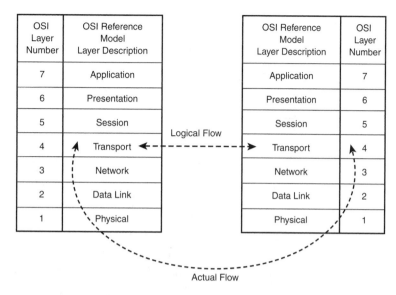

1

INTRODUCTION
TO OPEN
COMMUNICATIONS

> **Note**
>
> Although the Reference Model includes seven layers, not all layers are required for any given communications session. For example, communications across a single LAN segment can operate strictly at Layers 1 and 2 of the model, without requiring the other two communications layers.

Although communications flow vertically through the stack, each layer perceives itself to be capable of directly communicating with its counterpart layers on remote computers. To create this logical adjacency of layers, each layer of the originating machine's protocol stack adds a header. This header can be recognized and used by only that layer or its counterparts on other machines. The receiving machine's protocol stack removes the headers, one layer at a time, as the data is passed up to its application. This process is illustrated in Figure 1.3.

For example, segments of data are packaged by Layer 4 of an origination machine for presentation to Layer 3. Layer 3 bundles data received from Layer 4 into packets (that is, Layer 3 *packetizes* the segments), addresses them, and sends them to the destination machine's Layer 3 protocol by way of its own Layer 2. Layer 2 encases the packets with frames, complete with addressing that is recognized by the LAN. These frames are presented to Layer 1 for conversion into a stream of binary digits (bits) that are transmitted to the destination machine's Layer 1.

FIGURE 1.3

Use of layered headers to support logical adjacency.

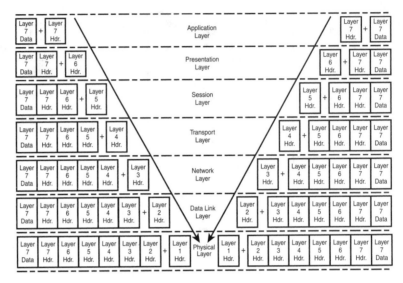

The destination machine reverses this flow of handoffs, with each layer stripping off the headers that were added by their counterparts on the origination machine. By the time the data reaches the destination machine's Layer 4, the data is back in the same form into which the originating machine's Layer 4 put it. Consequently, the two Layer 4 protocols appear to be physically adjacent and communicating directly.

> **Note**
>
> Please note that most of today's networking protocols use their own layered models. These models vary in the degree to which they adhere to the separation of functions demonstrated by the OSI Reference Model. It is quite common for these models to collapse the seven OSI layers into five or fewer layers. It is also common for higher layers to not correspond perfectly to their OSI-equivalent layers.

In fact, each Layer 3 passes the data down to Layer 2, which, in turn, converts the frames to a bit stream. After the destination computer's Layer 1 device receives the bit stream, it is passed up to the Data Link Layer for reassembly into a frame. After the frame's receipt is successfully completed, the framing is stripped off and the packet that was embedded in it is passed up to the recipient's Layer 3. It arrives in exactly the same form as that in which it was sent. To the Layer 3s, communications between them were virtually direct.

The fact that communication can appear to occur between adjacent layers (from the perspective of those layers) is a tribute to the success of the model.

Although the OSI Reference Model was originally intended as an architectural framework for open communications protocols, it has failed miserably in that capacity. In fact, the model has almost completely degenerated into just an academic construct. To its credit, the model is a marvelous device for explaining the concept of open communications, and the logical sequencing of necessary functions in a data communications session. A much more meaningful reference model is the TCP/IP Reference Model. This model describes the architecture of the IP suite of protocols, which are the focus of this book.

The TCP/IP Reference Model

Unlike the OSI Reference Model, the TCP/IP model focuses more on delivering interconnectivity than on rigidly adhering to functional layers. It does this by acknowledging the importance of a hierarchical arrangement of functions, but still leaving protocol designers ample flexibility for implementation. Consequently, the OSI Reference Model is significantly better at explaining the mechanics of inter-computer communications, but TCP/IP has become the internetworking protocol of choice in the marketplace.

The flexibility of the TCP/IP Reference Model is shown in Figure 1.4 in comparison with the OSI Reference Model.

FIGURE 1.4

Comparison of the OSI and TCP/IP Reference Models.

OSI Reference Model Layer Description	OSI Layer Number	TCP/IP Equivalent Layer Description
Application	7	Process/ Application
Presentation	6	Process/ Application
Session	5	Host-to-Host
Transport	4	Host-to-Host
Network	3	Internet
Data Link	2	Network Access
Physical	1	Network Access

The TCP/IP Reference Model, developed long after the protocol it explains, offers significantly more flexibility than its OSI counterpart because it emphasizes the hierarchical arrangement of functions, rather than strict functional layering.

Dissecting the TCP/IP Model

The TCP/IP protocol stack includes four functional layers: Process/Application, Host-to-Host, Internet, and Network Access. These four loosely correlate to the seven layers of the OSI Reference Model without compromising functionality.

The Process/Application Layer

The Application Layer provides protocols for remote access and resource sharing. Familiar applications such as Telnet, FTP, SMTP, HTTP, and many others all reside and operate in this layer and depend upon the functionality of the underlying layers. Similarly, any application (including homegrown and store-bought software) that requires communications over an IP network would also be described in this layer of the model.

The Host-to-Host Layer

The IP Host-to-Host Layer correlates loosely to the OSI Reference Model's Session and Transport Layers. The functions supported in this layer include segmenting application data for transport across a network, performing mathematical tests to determine the integrity of received data, and multiplexing streams of data (both transmitted and received) for multiple applications simultaneously. This implies that the Host-to-Host Layer is capable of identifying specific applications, and can resequence data that might have been received out of order.

The Host-to-Host Layer currently consists of two protocol entities: *Transmission Control Protocol* (TCP) and *User Datagram Protocol* (UDP). A third entity has been defined to accommodate the increasingly transaction-oriented nature of the Internet. This protocol entity is tentatively called *Transaction/Transmission Control Protocol* (T/TCP). However, most application services on the Internet use the TCP and UDP protocols for the Host-to-Host layer.

The Internet Layer

The Internet Layer of IPv4 consists of all the protocols and procedures necessary to allow data communications between hosts to traverse multiple networks. This means that the data-bearing packets must be routable. The Internet Protocol (IP) is responsible for making data packets routable.

The Internet Layer must also support other route management functions beyond just packet formatting. It must provide mechanisms for resolving Layer 2 addresses into Layer 3 addresses, and vice versa. These functions are provided by peer protocols to IP, which are described in Chapter 5, "ARP and RARP."

In addition, the Internet Layer must support routing and route management capabilities. These functions are also provided by external peer protocols, known as *routing protocols*. These protocols include Interior Gateway Protocols (IGP), and Exterior Gateway Protocols (EGP). These protocols are necessarily identified as peers because, even though they also reside at the Network Layer, they are not a native component of the IP suite of protocols. In fact, many of the routing protocols are capable of discovering and calculating routes in multiple routed protocol addressing architectures. Other examples of routed protocols with different address architectures include IPX and AppleTalk.

The Network Access Layer

The Network Access Layer consists of all the functions needed to physically connect to, and transmit over, a network. The OSI Reference Model breaks down this set of functions into two layers: the Physical Layer and the Data Link Layer. The TCP/IP Reference Model, due to its creation after its namesake protocols, lumps these two layers together because the various IP protocols stop at the Internet Layer. IP assumes that all the lower-level functions are provided by either a LAN or serial connection.

Summary

The basic network concepts presented in this chapter, their functions, and even their uses, are just the beginning. They are the proverbial building blocks that are explored in much greater detail throughout the remainder of this book. They have been presented to give you an appreciation for some of the fundamental terms and concepts of open networking.

Chapter 2, "TCP/IP and the Internet," builds on this framework by more closely examining the role of TCP/IP in the Internet, including the various mechanisms that are used to keep TCP/IP up-to-date. Both the OSI and TCP/IP Reference Models will be referred to throughout this book.

TCP/IP and the Internet

by Neal S. Jamison

TCP/IP allowed the Internet to evolve into what it is today, which subsequently has changed the way that we live and work in much the same way as its revolutionary forerunners such as the printing press, electricity, or the computer. This chapter discusses the development of the Internet, its caretakers, and future directions. It explores the process by which ideas go on to become standards, and it briefly introduces some of the more popular protocols and services, such as Telnet and HTTP (HyperText Transfer Protocol).

A History of the Internet

The progression of events that led to the Internet goes back to the beginning of time. Cave wall drawings, smoke signals, the Pony Express—all forms of communication that made our forefathers think there had to be a better way. Next came the telegraph, the telephone, and transatlantic wireless messages—now we're getting somewhere. Then the first computers were invented. Massive, heat-generating calculators less powerful than our smallest handheld calculators today, these giants helped win wars and calculate the census. But very few were in existence, and no one could afford them, much less house them.

By the 1960s, transistors had replaced vacuum tubes, and the size and cost of computers were falling as the power and intelligence of these machines were rising. About this time, a group of scientists was working to allow computers to communicate. Leonard Kleinrock, then a Ph.D student at MIT, conceptualized the underlying technology of "packet switching," and published a paper on the subject in 1961. At that time the *Advanced Research Projects Agency* (ARPA) was looking for ways to improve communication within its own agency (as well as for the military), and Kleinrock's work provided the spark they needed. ARPA issued a *request for quotes* (RFQ) to solicit bids for creating the first packet-switched network. A small acoustics firm from Massachusetts known as Bolt Beranek and Newman (BBN) was awarded the contract, and thus the ARPANET was born. The year was 1969.

The ARPANET

The original ARPANET consisted of four host computers—one each at UCLA, Stanford Research Institute, UC Santa Barbara, and the University of Utah. This small network, using the *Network Control Protocol* (NCP), provided its users with the ability to log in to a remote host, print to a remote printer, and transfer files. Ray Tomlinson, a BBN engineer, created the first e-mail program in 1971.

TCP/IP

In 1974, just five short years after the birth of the ARPANET, Vinton Cerf and Robert Kahn invented the *Transmission Control Protocol* (TCP). TCP/IP, which was designed to be independent of the underlying computer and network, replaced the limited NCP in the early 1980s, and allowed the ARPANET to grow beyond anyone's expectations by allowing other heterogeneous ARPANET-like networks (or internets) to intercommunicate. Thus the Internet was born.

> **Note**
>
> An internet (with a lowercase "i") is a network of heterogeneous computers. The Internet (with an uppercase "I") is THE network connecting millions of computers and users.

The Department of Defense helped to promote the use of TCP/IP by selecting it as their standard protocol and requiring its use and support by defense contractors. Around this same time, developers at the University of California at Berkeley released the newest version of their Unix operating system, 4.2BSD (Berkeley Software Distribution), which was made freely available to everyone. This was a boon for TCP/IP due to its tight integration into 4.2BSD. BSD Unix became the basis for other Unix systems, which explains the predominance of TCP/IP in the Unix world.

TCP/IP provided the reliability that the Internet needed to get off the ground, and researchers and engineers began to add protocols and tools to the TCP/IP suite. FTP, Telnet, and SMTP have been around since the beginning. Newer TCP/IP tools include IMAP (Internet Mail Access Protocol), POP (Post Office Protocol), and of course, HTTP.

The National Science Foundation (NSF)

Another network of great importance was the NSFNet. The National Science Foundation recognized the importance of work taking place with the ARPANET and decided to create a network of its own. The NSFNet connected a number of supercomputers with universities and government facilities. As NFSNet became more popular, the NSF increased the capability of the network by upgrading its "backbone" communication lines. Starting with 56k bit-per-second lines, progressing to T-1 (1.544Mbps) lines, and eventually to T-3 (43Mbps) lines, the NFSNet quickly became the fastest internet around.

Other networks that were created during this timeframe included the Because It's Time Network (BITNET) and the Computer Science Research Network (CSNET). The size of the ARPANET was still growing at an alarming rate, with the number of hosts doubling every year.

In the late 1980s and early 1990s, NFSNet replaced the older and slower ARPANET, becoming the official backbone of the Internet.

The Internet Today

In 1992, CERN (European Laboratory for Particle Physics) and Tim Berners-Lee demonstrated a concept called the World Wide Web (WWW), followed a year later by the release of a WWW client program called Mosaic. Together, these two events allowed the Internet to go from a text-only tool used by scientists and students to a graphical tool used today by many millions.

In April 1995, the NFSNet was retired and replaced with a competitive, commercial backbone. This relaxed the restrictions on connecting a host to the Internet, and opened it to a whole new type of user—the commercial user.

Point-to-Point Protocol (PPP) was created in 1994, and was becoming commonplace in 1995. PPP allowed TCP/IP over phone lines, which made it easier for home users to gain Internet access. This coincided nicely with an outcropping of *Internet service providers* (ISPs) who were willing and ready to connect home and business users, and the home-user boom was launched.

The Internet was (and still is!) growing at the alarming rate of 100 percent per year.

Today, a quick browse of the WWW allows us to see the significance of the evolution of the Internet. The Internet no longer is used only for academic and military communication and research. Today, we can shop and bank online. We can look up our favorite recipes or read books via the Web. The uses of the Internet today are endless.

RFCs and the Standardization Process

Throughout the evolution of the Internet, ideas and notes have been presented in the form of documents called *Requests for Comments* (RFCs). These documents discuss many aspects of Internet-related computing and computer communication. The first RFC (RFC 1), titled "Host Software," was written by Steve Crocker (a UCLA graduate student who wrote eight of the first 25 RFCs) in April 1969. These early RFCs provide fascinating reading to anyone interested in the history of the Internet. The documents that specify the Internet protocols, as defined by the IETF and IESG, are also published as RFCs.

The RFC Editor is the publisher of the RFCs and is responsible for the final editorial review of the documents. The Editor is discussed later in this chapter.

A good site for all types of RFC information is `http://www.rfc-editor.org/`.

> **Note**
>
> Jon Postel played a large role in the creation of the ARPANET, and thus the Internet. He participated in the creation of the Internet domain name system, which he administered for many years. That system is still in use today. Jon ran the *Internet Assigned Numbers Authority* (IANA) and was the RFC editor. Jon died in October 1998. RFC 2468 (Vinton Cerf, October 1998) is a tribute to Jon.

RFCs are the primary method for communicating new ideas on protocols, research, and standards. When a researcher comes up with a new protocol, research or tutorial on a topic, the researcher can submit this as an RFC document. Thus RFCs consist of Internet standards, proposals for new or revised protocols, implementation strategies, tutorials, collective wisdom, and so on.

Protocols that are to become standards in the Internet go through a series of states that describe their maturity levels. These levels are the proposed standard, draft standard, and standard. As each standard evolves, the amounts of scrutiny and testing increase. When a protocol completes this process, it is assigned a STD number, which is the number of the new standard.

As technology advances, some protocols are superseded by better ones or may be unused. These protocols are documented with the designation "historic." The results of early protocol research and development work are documented in some RFCs. These protocols are designated "experimental."

Protocols that are developed by other standards organizations, or by particular vendors and individuals, may be of interest or may be recommended for use in the Internet. The specifications of such protocols may be published as RFCs for the convenience and ease of distribution to the Internet community. These protocols are labeled "informational."

Sometimes protocols may achieve widespread implementation without the approval or involvement of the IESG. This may be because of the evolution of protocols in the marketplace or because of political reasons. Some of these vendor protocols may even become very important to the Internet community because business organizations may have deployed them within their intranets. The position of the IAB is that it strongly recommends that the standards process be used in the evolution of the protocol to maximize interoperability and to prevent incompatible protocol requirements from arising.

Not all the protocols are required to be implemented in all systems because there is such a variety of possible systems where a protocol implementation may not make sense. For example, Internet devices such as gateways, routers, terminal servers, workstations, and multi-user hosts have a different set of requirements. Not all of them require the same protocols.

Getting RFCs

RFCs can be obtained from several different repositories. You might want to start by referencing an RFC index. See the following section for a list of RFC indices.

You can obtain RFCs in several different ways, including via the Web, FTP, Telnet, and even e-mail. Table 2.1 lists several FTP-accessible RFC repositories.

TABLE 2.1 FTP-Accessible RFC Repositories

Site	*Login/Password Directory*
ftp.isi.edu	anonymous/name@host.domain/in-notes
wuarchive.wustl.edu	anonymous/name@host.domain/doc/rfc

Several of the RFC repositories also provide RFCs via e-mail. For example, you can send a mail message to nis-info@nis.nsf.net with a blank subject line and the text of the message reading "send rfc*nnnn*.txt" where *nnnn* is the desired RFC number.

As expected, many of these repositories also provide the documents over the Web. A good starting point for accessing RFCs via the Web is http://www.rfc-editor.org/.

See http://www.isi.edu/in-notes/rfc-retrieval.txt for more information on obtaining RFCs.

Indices of RFCs

A complete index of all RFC documents would take up far too many pages to include it here. However, several great indices are on the Web in ASCII text, HTML, and searchable format. These include the following:

- Text—ftp://ftp.isi.edu/in-notes/rfc-index.txt
- HTML—ftp://ftpeng.cisco.com/fred/rfc-index/rfc.html
- HTML by Protocol—http://www.garlic.com/~lynn/rfcprot.htm

An RFC search engine can be found at http://www.rfc-editor.org/rfcsearch.html.

Humorous RFCs

It may surprise you to learn that not all RFCs are of a serious nature. Table 2.2 lists several of the less serious RFCs.

TABLE 2.2 Humorous RFCs

RFC	Title
527	ARPAWOCKY
968	'Twas The Night Before Startup
1097	Telnet subliminal-message option
1121	Act one: the poems
1149	A standard for the Transmission of IP Datagrams on Avian Carriers
1300	Remembrances of Things Past
1438	IETF Statements of Boredom (SOBs)
1882	The 12 days of technology before Christmas
1925	The 12 networking truths
1927	Suggested additional MIME types for associating documents

2

TCP/IP AND THE INTERNET

A Brief Introduction to Internet Services

Without popular protocols and services such as HTTP, SMTP, and FTP, the Internet wouldn't be much more than a large number of computers connected into a worthless knot. This section briefly describes the popular (and most useful) of the Internet protocols and points you to other chapters in this book for more information.

Whois and Finger

Whois is the service and protocol that allows us to locate information about Internet hosts and domains. By querying any of the available Whois database servers, Whois clients can gather information such as host and domain points-of-contact, geographical addresses, and more. Whois is also used by some organizations as a form of online personnel directory. This is especially common at universities.

Whois can be found on well-known TCP port 43 and is specified by RFC 954.

Finger is the service/protocol that allows us to gather information about Internet users. By "fingering" someone, you can get their e-mail address, find out whether he or she has mail or is currently online, and even read a little about what he or she is working on. Due to the nature of this service, some host administrators choose to disable Finger. Finger listens on TCP port 79 and is specified by RFC 1288.

For more information on these services, refer to Chapter 29, "Whois and Finger."

File Transfer Protocol

File Transfer Protocol (FTP) is the service/protocol that enables the transfer of files across the Internet. It, too, is one of the earlier protocols, dating back to 1971. FTP is commonly used today for public file sharing (via anonymous FTP). FTP operates on well-known TCP ports 20 and 21 and is specified by RFC 959.

For more information) about FTP and other transfer protocols, see Chapter 30, "File Transfer Protocols."

Telnet

Telnet is the terminal emulation program for the Internet. Put in simple terms, Telnet allows you to log in to remote hosts without worrying about terminal compatibility. Telnet was one of the very first protocols and services in the early Internet (see RFC 15). Telnet operates on well-known TCP port 23 and is specified by RFC 854.

For more information about Telnet, see Chapter 31, "Using Telnet."

E-mail

Simple Mail Transfer Protocol (SMTP) is the Internet standard for e-mail. Many people use this protocol every day without even realizing it. SMTP is accompanied by other protocols and services, such as POP3 and IMAP4, which allow you to manipulate your mail on the mail server and download it to your local computer for reading. SMTP operates on well-known TCP port 25 and is specified in RFC 821.

For more information about SMTP and other e-mail-related protocols and services, see Chapter 35, "Internet Mail Protocols."

The World Wide Web

HTTP is the language of the World Wide Web. In fact, HTTP can be credited for the mid-1990s explosion of the Internet. HTTP clients (like Mosaic and Netscape) emerged that allowed us to "see" the Web for the first time. This was quickly followed by the appearance of Web servers presenting useful information. Today over six million HTTP-speaking Web sites are on the Internet. HTTP operates on well-known TCP port 80 and its current version, HTTP/1.1, is specified by RFC 2616.

For more information about HTTP and other Web-related services and protocols, refer to Chapter 36, "The HTTP (World Wide Web) Service."

USENET News

The *Network News Transfer Protocol* (NNTP) is the protocol/service used to post, transfer, and retrieve USENET news messages. USENET, a history lesson in itself, is an Internet-sized bulletin board system made up of newsgroups—discussion forums covering almost any subject possible. NNTP operates on well-known TCP port 119 and is specified by RFC 977.

For more information about NNTP, see Chapter 37, "The NNTP (Network News) Service."

Intranets and Extranets

After the commercialization of the Internet in 1991, corporations didn't take long to find new and improved ways to use the Internet and its services and technologies to save time, money, and gain strategic advantage. One of the largest applications of this technology to date may be the *intranet*.

Intranets

An *intranet* is a local network controlled by an organization that uses TCP/IP as its primary communication protocol. The application services on the intranet are based around the standard services available on the Internet, such as HTTP, FTP, TELNET, SSH, and so on.

Simply put, an intranet is a finite, closed network of computers that uses Internet technologies to share data. An intranet may be a subset of the Internet with access controls in place to keep out the uninvited. Or for that matter, an intranet doesn't have to be on the Internet at all.

Intranet Benefits

There are many benefits of implementing an organizational intranet. Due to the relatively low cost to implement and maintain, companies are realizing very high ROIs (return on investment). Benefits include the following:

- **Intranets are easy to use.** Because the user interface of the intranet is the Web browser, training costs are low to none.

- **Intranets facilitate the dissemination of information to employees.** Whether it is a one-page corporate memorandum or a 500-page telephone directory, intranets allow companies to share information with their employees with great efficiency.

- **Intranets reduce printing costs.** Not only is it logistically difficult to disseminate information in a large company or organization, it can also be very expensive.

- **Intranets add value to traditional documents.** Although looking up a name or product in a paper-based directory or catalog is not extremely difficult, it can be time consuming and tedious.

- **Intranets improve data accuracy.** Documents can become outdated soon after they are printed. Having copies of outdated and possibly inaccurate documents circulating can be dangerous.

These are just a few of the benefits of intranets. Companies that have deployed intranets have realized many more benefits than are listed here. By using Internet technologies and services such as "open source" Web server and browser software, all of these benefits can come at a relatively low cost.

Example Applications of the Intranet

The ways in which your intranet can be applied to making your organization more efficient and productive are just about endless. Here are some common uses of intranet technology:

- **Human Resources:** More and more companies are circulating job advertisements, maintaining databases of employee skills, distributing documents such as 401k forms, timesheets, expense reports, and even paycheck direct-deposit slips, all via the intranet.

- **Project Management:** Spreadsheets and Gantt charts can be posted on the intranet where they can be viewed and updated by project managers. Status reports can be posted to the intranet where they are available for managers to review and comment on.

- **Inventory Tracking:** Inventory databases can be made available online either in their raw data format or as value-added applications.

- **Office File Management:** A robust intranet server running open Web technologies can put your file server out of business.

Although Intranets are useful to corporate users, external clients can also benefit from using the corporate intranet. This has led to the creation of extranets, discussed in the next section.

Opening Our Intranets to Outsiders

Whereas intranets are intended to allow members of a company or organization to share information among themselves, an extranet goes one step further. *Extranets* are actually intranets that securely open their doors to an invited group of outsiders. One practical use of the extranet is to let companies share information with strategic partners, such as customers, shippers, or suppliers. In short, extranets are business-to-business networks.

Some uses of extranets follow:

- Conduct business using *Electronic Data Interchange* (EDI) or some other application.
- Collaborate with other organizations on projects.
- Share news or other information with partner organizations.

An example of an extranet in action is a major shipping company that allows a popular online bookseller access to its intranet so that the bookseller can arrange the shipping of its products to customers.

The Internet of Tomorrow

As the popularity and use of the Internet expands, so, too, does Internet technology. Several initiatives are underway to improve upon these technologies. Three of the most promising initiatives are

- The Next Generation Internet Initiative (NGI)
- Very high-speed Backbone Network Service (vBNS)
- Internet2 (I2)

Each of these is described in the following sections.

Next Generation Internet (NGI)

As called for by President Clinton in his 1998 State of the Union address, the *Next Generation Internet Initiative* is designed to fund and coordinate academia and federal agencies to design and build the next generation of Internet services.

For more information about the Next Generation Internet Initiative, refer to `http://www.ngi.gov/`.

vBNS

The National Science Foundation has launched an effort to create an experimental Wide Area Network (WAN) backbone of tremendous speed. This backbone network, implemented by MCI WorldCom, is known as the *very high-speed Backbone Network Service* (vBNS). vBNS will serve as a platform for testing new, high-speed Internet technologies and protocols. It currently links several supercomputer centers and network access points at OC-12 speeds (622Mbps) and higher. In February 1999, MCI WorldCom announced the installation of an OC-48 (2.5Gbps) link between Los Angeles and San Francisco, California.

For more information on vBNS, refer to `http://www.vbns.net/`.

Internet2 (I2)

Internet2 is a testing-ground network created to allow universities, government, and industry participants to collaboratively develop advanced Internet technologies. Internet2 partners connect using the Abilene network, which boasts very high speeds of up to 9.6Gbps. I2 also uses the vBNS network described in the previous section.

To learn more about I2, refer to `http://www.internet2.edu/`. For more information on Abilene, refer to `http://www.ucaid.edu/abilene/`.

Who's In Charge Anyway?

As large as the Internet has become and with all the high-technology initiatives going on to enhance it, you might think that the group in charge of the Internet stays very busy. Well, you are only partly correct: No one group is "in charge" of the Internet. There is no director or CEO, or even a president. The fact is that the Internet is still thriving under the 1960s anarchistic counterculture from which it was born. There are, however, several groups that help oversee the technologies of the Internet, the registration processes, and the other intricacies of running a major network.

The Internet Society (ISOC)

The *Internet Society* is a professional membership society with more than 150 organizational and 6,000 individual members in over 100 countries. Together, these organizations and members oversee the issues that affect the Internet and its future. The ISOC is made up of several of the groups responsible for Internet infrastructure standards, including the *Internet Architecture Board* (IAB) and the *Internet Engineering Task Force* (IETF).

The ISOC is on the Web at `http://www.isoc.org/`.

Internet Architecture Board (IAB)

Formerly known as the Internet Activities Board, the Internet Architecture Board is the technical advisory arm of the Internet Society. This small group (IAB members are nominated by the IETF and approved by the ISOC Board of Trustees) meets regularly to review and stimulate new ideas and proposals that need to be developed by the Internet Engineering Task Force and the Internet Engineering Steering Group.

The IAB Web site is at `http://www.iab.org/`.

Internet Engineering Task Force (IETF)

The Internet Engineering Task Force is an open community of network designers, vendors, and researchers concerned with the evolution of the Internet. The IETF meets only three times each year, and accomplishes most of its work via electronic mailing lists. The IETF is broken into working groups, with each group assigned to one specific topic. IESG working groups include the *Hypertext Transfer Protocol* (HTTP) and the *Internet Printing Protocol* (IPP) working group.

The IETF is open to anyone, and can be found on the Web at `http://www.ietf.org/`.

Internet Engineering Steering Group (IESG)

The Internet Engineering Steering Group is responsible for technical management of IETF activities and the Internet standards process. The IESG also ensures that everything goes according to the rules and procedures of the ISOC. The IESG gives final approval of specifications before they are adopted as Internet Standards.

You can locate more information about the IESG at `http://www.ietf.org/iesg.html`.

Internet Assigned Numbers Authority (IANA)

The Internet Assigned Numbers Authority is responsible for assigning IP addresses and managing the domain name space. IANA also controls IP protocol port numbers and other parameters. IANA operates under the auspices of ICANN.

Visit IANA at `http://www.iana.org/`.

Internet Corporation for Assigned Names and Numbers (ICANN)

The Internet Corporation for Assigned Names and Numbers was formed as part of an effort to internationalize the administration of domain names and IP address space. The goal of the ICANN is to help transition the policy administration of Internet domains and addresses from government to private-sector. Currently, ICANN is involved in the *Shared Registry System* (SRS) through which the Internet domain registration process is being opened to fair competition. See the next section, "The InterNIC and Other Registrars," for more information on the SRS.

For more information on ICANN, visit its homepage at `http://www.icann.org/`.

The InterNIC and Other Registrars

The InterNIC (short for Internet Network Information Center), operated by Network Solutions, Inc., has been the primary registrar for the top-level domains (`.com`, `.org`, `.net`, `.edu`) since 1993. The InterNIC is overseen by the *National Telecommunications & Information Administration* (NTIA), a subgroup of the Department of Commerce. The InterNIC has delegated some responsibility to other official registrars (such as the Department of Defense NIC, and the Asia-Pacific NIC). More recently there have been other initiatives that could break up the InterNIC even further. One such initiative, known as the *Shared Registry System* (SRS), strives to introduce fair and open competition to the domain registration process. Currently over 60 companies are acting as registrars under this initiative.

Table 2.3 lists some of the major registrars.

TABLE 2.3   Major Internet Registrars

Name	URL
InterNIC	`http://www.internic.net/`
Department of Defense NIC	`http://nic.mil/`
U.S. Federal Register	`http://nic.gov/`
Asia-Pacific NIC	`http://www.apnic.net`
RIPE (Réseaux IP Européens)	`http://www.ripe.net`
Council of Registrars (CORE)	`http://www.corenic.org/`
Register.com	`http://register.com`

The RFC Editor

The Requests for Comments are a series of notes and documents that, among other things, specify the standards of the Internet. For more information about RFCs, refer to the section "RFCs and the Standardization Process" earlier in this chapter.

The RFC Editor is the publisher of the Internet RFC documents and is responsible for the final editorial review of the documents.

For more information on the RFC Editor, see `http://www.rfc-editor.org/`.

The Internet Service Providers

The commercialization of the Internet in the 1990s was greeted by numerous Internet service providers just waiting to help millions of household and business users onto the Internet. *ISPs* are businesses that set up Internet servers within their office space or computer rooms. These servers are equipped with modems and run either the Point-to-Point Protocol (PPP) or the Serial Line Internet Protocol (SLIP). These protocols allow remote users to dial in from their personal computers and connect to the Internet.

For a fee, an ISP will provide a remote user with connectivity to the Internet. Most common ISPs also provide an email account on their server, and some even provide a UNIX shell account.

Larger, wholesaler ISPs can provide businesses and other ISPs with high-speed networks such as ISDN, fractional T-1, and even higher.

Internet.com provides a database of ISPs, searchable by telephone area code. Visit this ISP buyer's guide at `http://thelist.internet.com/`.

Summary

This chapter described the Internet through a look at its history, its evolution, and other related topics. Intranets and extranets, a modern use of Internet technology, were described as well.

The Request for Comments (RFC) process was explained, and links were provided to allow you to retrieve RFCs for further reading.

Some of the most popular Internet services, such as HTTP, Telnet, FTP, and SMTP, were described, and references were given to chapters later in this book to which you can turn for more information.

We looked into the organizations that have made the Internet what it is today and will continue to evolve it as technology and needs change. It's hard to tell what the future holds for the Internet. In just a few years, it has grown from a tiny experimental network used by a handful of scientists to a global internetwork of many millions of computers and users. One thing is for sure: With projects like the Next Generation Internet, I2, and vBNS, we've only just begun to see the capabilities and applications of this fascinating technology.

2

TCP/IP AND THE INTERNET

Overview of TCP/IP

by Rima S. Regas

CHAPTER 3

TCP/IP is everywhere. It's not something physical that can only be in one place at a time. It's a set of protocols that allows anyone with a computer, modem, and an Internet service provider to access and share information over the Internet. In fact, users of AOL's Instant Messenger service and ICQ (also owned by AOL) account for over 750 million messages per day. This is an incredible amount of traffic, and most of it is transmitted over the Internet.

It is TCP/IP that allows these millions of transactions per day to occur (it's actually well into the billions because many more things are going on than email and instant messaging), mostly without a hitch. And it shows no signs of letting up anytime soon. TCP/IP is a stable, well-established, complete set of protocols, and this chapter takes a close look at exactly what makes it tick.

Both TCP and IP, two separate protocols that work hand-in-hand, perform chores that manage and guide the general mobility of data packets over the Internet. They both use special headers that define each packet's contents and, if there is more than one, how many others should be expected. TCP concerns itself with making the connections to remote hosts. IP, on the other hand, deals with addressing so that messages are directed to where they are intended. The following section takes a look at the benefits of TCP/IP.

The Benefits of Using TCP/IP

TCP/IP enables cross-platform, or heterogeneous, networking. For example, a Windows NT/2000 network could contain Unix and Macintosh workstations or even networks mixed in it. TCP/IP also has the following characteristics:

- Good failure recovery
- The ability to add networks without interrupting existing services
- High error-rate handling
- Platform independence
- Low data overhead

Because TCP/IP was originally designed for Department of Defense–related purposes, what we now call features or characteristics were actually design requirements. The idea behind "Good Failure Recovery" was that if a portion of the network were disabled during an incursion or attack, its remaining pieces would still be able to function fully. Likewise is the capability of adding entire networks without any disruption to the services already in place. The ability to handle high error rates was built in so that if a packet of information got lost using one route, there would be a mechanism in place to ensure that it would reach its destination using another route. Platform independence means that the networks and clients can be Windows, Unix, Macintosh, or any other platform or combination thereof. The reason TCP/IP is so efficient lies in its low overhead. Performance is key for any network. TCP/IP is unmatched in its speed and simplicity.

TCP/IP Layers and Protocols

TCP and IP together manage the flow of data, both in and out, over a network. Whereas IP indiscriminately pumps packets into the ether, TCP is charged with making sure they get there. TCP is responsible for the following:

- Opening and closing a session
- Packet management
- Flow control
- Error detection and handling

Architecture

TCP/IP is the environment that handles all these operations and coordinates them with remote hosts. TCP/IP was created using the DoD (Department of Defense) model, which is made up of four layers instead of the seven that make up the OSI model.

The primary difference between the OSI and the TCP/IP layer formats is that the Transport Layer does not guarantee delivery at all times. TCP/IP offers the *User Datagram Protocol* (UDP), a more simplified protocol, wherein all the layers in the TCP/IP stack perform specific duties or run applications.

Application Layer

The Application Layer consists of protocols such as SMTP, FTP, NFS, NIS, LPD, Telnet, and Remote Login, all of which fall into areas that are familiar to most Internet users.

Transport Layer

The Transport Layer consists of UDP (User Datagram Protocol) and TCP, where the former delivers packets with almost non-existent checking, and the latter provides delivery guarantees.

Network Layer

The Network Layer is made up of the following protocols: ICMP, IP, IGMP, RIP, OSPF, EGP and BGP4. ICMP (Internet Control Message Protocol) is used for diagnostics and to report on problems with the IP layer and for obtaining information about IP parameters. IGMP (Internet Group Management Protocol) is used for managing multicasting. RIP, OSPF, EGP, and BGP4 are examples of routing protocols.

Link Layer

The Link Layer consists of ARP and RARP, and framing of data, which handle packet transmission.

Transmission Control Protocol (TCP)

Transmission Control Protocol (TCP) is a protocol that provides a reliable stream delivery and connection service to applications. TCP uses sequenced acknowledgment and is able to retransmit packets as needed.

The TCP header appears as follows:

16-bit	32-bit
Source Port	Destination Port
Sequence Number	
Acknowledgement Number (ACK)	
Offset Reserved U A P R S F	Window
Checksum	Urgent Pointer
Options and Padding	

The parts of the header are detailed in the following sections.

Source Port

The source port is the numerical value indicating the source port.

Destination Port

The destination port is the numerical value indicating the destination port.

Sequence Number

The sequence number is the number of the first data octet in any given segment.

Acknowledgement Number (ACK)

When the ACK bit is set, this field contains the next sequence number that the sender of the segment is expecting to receive. This value is always sent.

Data Offset

Data offset is the numerical value that indicates where the data begins, implying the end of the header by offset.

Reserved

Reserved is not used, but it must be off (0).

Control Bits

The control bits are as follows:

U(URG)	Urgent pointer field significant
A(ACK)	Acknowledgement field significant
P(PSH)	Push function
R(RST)	Reset connection
S(SYN)	Synchronize sequence numbers
F(FIN)	No more data

Window

The window indicates the number of octets the sender is willing to take. This starts with the packet in the ACK field.

Checksum

The checksum field is the 16-bit complement of the sum of all 16-bit words, restricted to the 1s column, in the header and text. If the result is an odd number of header and text octets, then the last octet is padded with zeros to form a 16-bit word that will checksum. Note that the pad is not sent as part of the segment.

Urgent (URG) Pointer

The URG pointer field shows the value of the URG pointer in the form of a positive offset of the sequence number from the octet that follows the URG data or points to the end of urgent data.

Options

Options may be sent at the end of a header, but must always be fully implemented and have a length that is any multiple of 8-bits. The two types of options are

- Type 1: A single octet of option-kind.
- Type 2: An octet of option-kind, an octet of option-length, and the actual option-data octets.

The option has a type, length and value field.

The length field includes the type, option length, as well as the value fields. The value field contains the data that makes up the options being sent. Table 3.1 shows how the octets are formatted in one of three classes. All the options are included in the checksum. An option can begin on any octet boundary as long as any remaining "dead" space is padded to meet the defined packet length.

> **NOTE**
>
> The list of options can be shorter than that designated by the data offset field because the contents of the header beyond the End-of-Option option must be padded with zeros (0).

TABLE 3.1 Formatted Octets

Class	Length	Description
0	-	End of options
1	-	No operation
2	4	Maximum segment size

The Class 0 option indicates the end of the option list, ending all options, but not each individual option. Only use this option if the end of the options list does not coincide with the end of the header.

The Class 1 option is used to align an option with a word boundary. Other than that this option does not contain any useful information. Its main purpose is for aligning and formatting.

The Class 2 option indicates the maximum segment size that it will receive. It can only be included in the initial request and in segments where the SYN item bit is set. If this option is not used, there is no size limit.

Internet Protocol (IP)

IP manages how packets are delivered to and from servers and clients.

The IP header appears as follows:

4-bit	8-bit	16-bit	32-bit	
Ver.	Header Length	Type of Service	Total Length	
Identification			Flags	Offset
Time To Live		Protocol	Checksum	
Source Address				
Destination Address				
Options and Padding				

Each field contains information about the IP packet that it carries. The descriptions in the following sections should be helpful.

Version Number

The version number indicates the version of IP that is in use for this packet. IP version 4 (Ipv4) is currently in widespread use.

Header Length

The header length indicates the overall length of the header. The receiving machine then knows when to stop reading the header and start reading data.

Type of Service

Mostly unused, the Type of Service field indicates the importance of the packet in a numerical value. Higher numbers result in prioritized handling.

Total Length

Total length shows the total length of the packet in bytes. The total packet length cannot exceed 65,535 bytes or it will be deemed corrupt by the receiver.

Identification

If there is more than one packet (an invariable inevitability), the identification field has an identifier that identifies its place in line, as it were. Fragmented packets retain their original ID number.

Flags

The first flag, if set, is ignored. If the DF (Do Not Fragment) flag is set, under no circumstances can the packet be fragmented. If the MF (More Fragments) bit is turned on (1), there are packet fragments to come, the last of which is set to off (0).

Offset

If the Flag field returns a 1 (on), the Offset field contains the location of the missing piece(s) indicated by a numerical offset based on the total length of the packet.

Time To Live (TTL)

Typically 15 to 30 seconds, TTL indicates the length of time that a packet is allowed to remain in transit. If a packet is discarded or lost in transit, an indicator is sent back to the sending computer that the loss occurred. The sending machine then has the option of resending that packet.

Protocol

The protocol field holds a numerical value indicating the handling protocol in use for this packet.

Checksum

The checksum value acts as a validation checksum for the header.

Source Address

The source address field indicates the address of the sending machine.

Destination Address

The destination address field indicates the address of the destination machine.

Options and Padding

The Options field is optional. If used, it contains codes that indicate the use of security, strict or loose source routing, routing records, and timestamping. If no options are used, the field is called *padded* and contains a 1. Padding is used to force a byte value that is rounded. Table 3.2 indicates the bit counts for the options available.

TABLE 3.2 Bit Counts

Class	Number	Option
0	0	End of option list
0	2	Military security
0	3	Loose source routing
0	7	Routing record*
0	9	Strict source routing
2	4	Timestamping

This option adds fields.

TCP/IP provides its services via a "stack" of translation layers, which are called, of all things, TCP/IP. Because TCP and IP are separate protocols, they require a common environment for translation services. As mentioned earlier in this chapter, the TCP/IP stack has four layers as opposed to the OSI's seven layers. In a nutshell, they are

- Application
- Transport
- Network
- Link

Each of these is discussed in the following sections.

Application Layer

The Application Layer combines a few services that the OSI separates into three layers. These services are end user-related: authentication, data handling, and compression. This is where email, Web browsers, telnet clients, and other Internet applications get their connections.

Transport Layer

Again, unlike OSI, this layer is not responsible for guaranteeing the delivery of packets. Its primary responsibility is managing the transfer between the source and the destination. The OSI guarantees that packets are checked and, if they don't match, are dumped and re-requested from the source.

Network Layer

The Network Layer deals strictly with packet-routing management. This layer is well-suited to making determinations on where to send packets based on the information it receives.

Link Layer

The Link Layer manages the connection of the network and provides packet I/O over the network, but not at the application level.

Now that you have a clear idea of what TCP/IP is and what it can do (although hands-on experience is as close as your nearest Internet-connected computer), the following section moves on to the tangible benefits that TCP/IP provides you.

Telnet

Telnet, short for TELecommunications NETwork, refers to both the application and the protocol itself, granting the name a dual role. Telnet provides users a way to log in and directly access their terminal across a network. This means actual, direct access to the remotely located computer. Telnet is provided on port 23.

Telnet requires that a Telnet server be located on the host machine, awaiting an authenticated login session from a remote location. Windows 9x/NT/2000, the BeOS, Linux, and other x86 platform–based operating systems require that a Telnet server be installed, configured, and running to accept incoming sessions. MacOS-based systems also require a Telnet server. Unix-based computers are the only systems that come with one and typically use an application called `telnetd` (the "d" denotes daemon, a server application). On the other end is a Telnet application that acts as an interface, either text-based or a GUI, for the session.

Note

Windows 2000 actually has a CLI Telnet application built in. If you click on a Telnet link or type `Telnet` in the console, it will appear. Therefore, Windows 2000 no longer requires the addition of a third-party Telnet server.

File Transfer Protocol (FTP)

Whereas Telnet facilitates a live connection to the remote host, FTP is more passive, allowing you to move files back and forth from remotely located servers. This utility is ideal for Webmasters or anyone requiring to move large files from one location to another with no previously established "hot" connection. FTP is typically operated in what is called Passive Mode, which loads directory trees to the client and then disconnects, but periodically "tickles" the server to maintain an open port.

> **Note**
>
> Various FTP servers will be configured based on the particular Webmaster's tastes. Some allow anonymous users to access all areas of the server without restriction. Others limit access to previously authenticated users only. Still others limit anonymous access to very short timeout periods. If the user is not active, the server automatically disconnects, forcing him to reconnect if he wants to continue using the server.

On Unix-based systems, these programs are typically named `ftpd` (again, "d" meaning daemon) and `ftp` (the client application). FTP's default ports are 20 (for data transfers) and 21 (for command transfers). This makes FTP unique among TCP/IP protocols because commands and data can be transferred simultaneously with the data being transferred in real time, a feature that other protocols do not share.

All operating systems have FTP clients and servers in one form or another. All MacOS-based FTP applications are graphically oriented. Most Windows-based ones now are as well. The benefits to using a graphical FTP client is that all the commands, usually entered by hand, are now managed by the client, reducing the possibility of error and making sessions quicker and easier. On the other hand, because FTP servers do not require much management after the initial setup, they don't require a GUI.

Trivial File Transfer Protocol (TFTP)

TFTP lives up to its name quite well. TFTP is the poor cousin of FTP in that it shares only a very small subset of the capabilities of FTP. It uses UDP, which, to use a similar metaphor, is TCP's poor relative. TFTP has no packet-monitoring capabilities and practically no error-handling capabilities. But then again, these limitations also reduce the process overhead. TFTP does not authenticate; it merely connects. As a built-in protection, TFTP can only move files that are publicly accessible.

Security is of great concern when employing TFTP. As a result, TFTP is typically used for embedded applications and copying configuration files for router configuration and in situations where space is of concern, and where security is handled in another fashion. TFTP is also used in a network computer environment where each machine is booted from a remote server and where TFTP can be easily embedded in the ROMs (Read Only Memory) on network cards.

Simple Mail Transfer Protocol (SMTP)

SMTP is the de facto standard for transferring email over networks, primarily the Internet. All operating systems have email clients that can use SMTP and most, if not all, Internet service providers use SMTP as their outgoing mail service. There are also SMTP servers for all operating systems including, but not limited to, Windows 9x/NT/2K, MacOS, Unix and variants, Linux, BeOS, and even AmigaOS.

SMTP is designed to provide a transport for email messages under various network environments. In fact, SMTP is not really concerned with *how* it travels, just with getting the message to its destination.

SMTP has robust mail handling features that allow mail to be automatically routed based on certain criteria. SMTP has the ability to immediately notify a user of a nonexistent email address and to return mail to the sender when the mail remains undeliverable for a period of time (set by the system administrator of the server that hosts the message). SMTP uses TCP port 25.

Network File System (NFS)

Sun Microsystems Inc. created NFS as an answer to problems with working in harmony across networks supporting many operating systems. NFS supports file sharing only and is now an integral part of many Unix-based operating systems. It is also well supported by most other operating systems.

NFS versions 1 and 2 used UDP as the primary transport protocol. Because UDP does not provide reliable delivery, reliable delivery had to be handled by NFS itself for unreliable links. Some of the early implementations of NFS had file corruption problems. Starting with NFS version 3, NFS can alternatively use TCP as the transport protocol. Actually, TCP support was available in NFS version 3 but was not optimized. With TCP as the transport protocol, NFS can use the reliability of TCP to provide better delivery over unreliable links. Consequently, NFS version 3 works better over WAN links and the Internet.

> **Note**
>
> An NFS version 4 has been proposed but most commercial implementations either implement NFS version 2 or version 3.

Pure NFS has no way of preventing various users from writing to a single file at the same time, allowing users to easily corrupt files at will without knowledge of other file activity. However, a file-locking mechanism implemented by a Network Lock Manager (NLM) protocol can be used in conjunction with NFS to enable file sharing and over-writing between multiple users.

NFS file access is seamless and transparent. After an NFS volume is mounted, it becomes part of the end user's system. There are no additional steps, beyond the export process, of course. Exporting is required to synchronize both server and clients to the NFS configuration. This system is neither simple nor administrator friendly.

SNMP

SNMP provides a simple level of router monitoring and management via various protocols, such as UDP, IPX, or IP. Simple is an important word to remember in any discussion of SNMP. SNMP is nothing if not simple. First of all, it only supports four commands—GET, GETNEXT, SET, and TRAP. The first two provide access to reporting information, and the third allows you to remotely control certain functions of the routers. The TRAP command enables devices to report on problems or events within the device.

Network devices supply their specific information via a *Management Information Base* (MIB). This data, which defines the device to the SNMP manager, is fed to the SNMP Management Station, which in turn identifies each device and stores its specific data. All SNMP-compliant devices are managed from this station. Each device runs an SNMP Agent that provides the client side of the operations for the device. When the Management Station requests a GET command for port conditions, the agent returns that information.

SNMP is not meant to manage all network devices to a high level of detail. This is simple, day-to-day management that allows you to pay close attention to your devices without having to load half a dozen management interfaces. SNMP uses the UDP transport protocol for sending messages.

3

OVERVIEW OF
TCP/IP

How TCP/IP Fits into Your System

You've seen what services TCP/IP provides and also that TCP/IP is flexible and accepted industry-wide. The Internet uses TCP/IP, so there are no apparent limitations to bandwidth or to the size of a network based on TCP/IP. You've seen all the things that make TCP/IP what it is and why it's so good.

The only reason you would consider using it is if you are not already. If you are using a Windows- or Unix-based network, the chances are high that you are already using TCP/IP. If you are using earlier versions of NetWare such as NetWare 2 or 3, you are likely running IPX/SPX. NetWare 3 added TCP/IP support at the server and an IPX-to-TCP/IP gateway for Internet connectivity. Starting with NetWare 4, there was better support for TCP/IP. NetWare 5 and higher allows IPX to be replaced by TCP/IP and fully supports TCP/IP.

The same is true if you are considering an upgrade from AppleShare over AppleTalk (pre-6.x). This does not pertain to AppleShare IP because that server suite already implements TCP/IP. But cost here is a factor. TCP/IP offers a wide range of capabilities, servers, services, clients, and so on at little or no cost.

You can spend large amounts of money to have a TCP/IP intranet installed, but you can achieve the same for little money. First, you would consider a server operating system, for example, Linux. It's free, or nearly so if you purchase a distribution. RedHat, Debian, Mandrake, and Caldera are the most popular distributions. Linux remains free, but if you purchase from RedHat, Debian, Mandrake, or Caldera, they also sell you their service and support, special installation software, and other bells and whistles that would not normally come with Linux.

> **Note**
>
> RedHat Linux is available free for download from its Web site if you don't want to spend $60, but it will take an extremely long time over an analog modem because RedHat consumes over 160MB of space. It takes less time to buy a distribution.

You could also use your existing operating systems, because a number of servers are available for MacOS, Windows 9x/NT/2000/XP, and others. Some are free. Others can range from $30 to $2,500, depending on what it is and what you are licensing. You could also rewire, but your existing media should be good enough, unless you plan on changing from a bookkeeper to a 3D specialty animation shop with 24-hour service!

The Intranet Concept

Three things drive TCP/IP as the protocol of choice in today's intranets: cost, speed, and extensibility. TCP/IP can be very inexpensive to implement. It can work alongside your older protocol (AppleTalk, IPX, and so on) until you migrate everything over; it works quickly and efficiently through solid and established protocols; and it can be added to on a whim via the convenience of packet switching.

The Internet is also a consideration because your company or network will now have access to this vast resource. Email is the most widely used application on the Internet today, far more even than browsing. Billions of messages are routed daily. Also, millions of Internet terminals allow people access to services that are posted to the Internet, such as sales data for a mobile workforce, an at-home workforce, or global communications.

There are many ways to connect to the Internet, but the dominant manner is dial-up and in some places DSL (Digital Subscriber Line) and Cable. Anyone with an analog modem can call an Internet service provider's modem and make a connection to the Internet. When connected, it's merely a matter of using the right resource. The dominant Data Link Layer protocol for dial-up is called Point-to-Point Protocol (PPP). An older protocol, Serial Line Interface Protocol (SLIP), allows you to make a serial connection to the Internet from a client. SLIP was later improved to provide compression of TCP/IP headers, and this led to a variation of SLIP called Compressed SLIP (CSLIP). Both SLIP and CSLIP have largely been replaced by PPP today.

Summary

As you have seen in this chapter, there are many issues to consider in moving a packet from one place to another. This is why TCP and IP are tied so closely together. They both perform critical jobs that make the Internet work as well as it does. You learned that TCP/IP works in layers, and that each layer performs a particular job. If any link in the chain fails, the whole thing collapses. Fortunately, this doesn't happen very often.

Reliability is a very good reason for making TCP/IP available on all operating systems, in one form or another.

TCP/IP, though, is scalable and mobile. If there's a situation where TCP/IP can be leveraged, then you probably won't be surprised to find that connectivity already exists. Remember to always take into account all the active protocols that your internetwork already uses and make sure that a transition to TCP/IP will not cause irreparable harm to user access. Other than that, it's a piece of cake.

Naming and Addressing

PART

II

Names and Addresses in an IP Network

by Mark A. Sportack

IN THIS CHAPTER

CHAPTER 4

A critical prerequisite to internetworking is having an efficient address architecture that is adhered to by all users of that internetwork. Address architectures can take many different forms. Network addresses are always numeric, but they can be expressed in base 2 (binary), base 10 (decimal), or even base 16 (hexadecimal) number systems. They can be proprietary, or open for all to see and implement. Address architectures can be highly scalable, or intentionally designed to serve only small communities of users.

This chapter examines the address architecture implemented by the Internet Protocol (IP). As IP has evolved substantially over the past 20 years, so has its address architecture. This chapter describes the evolution of the IP address architecture and explains critical concepts, including classful IP addresses, classless interdomain routing (CIDR) addresses, subnetwork addresses or masks, and variable-length subnet masking (VLSM).

IP Addressing

The *Internet Engineering Task Force* (IETF)—architects of both the Internet and IP—elected to use machine-friendly numeric addresses to identify IP networks and hosts. Thus, each network in the Internet would have its own unique numeric address—its network address. The administrator(s) of this network would also have to ensure that all the hosts in the network had their own unique host number.

The original version of IP, IP Version 4 (IPv4), uses a 32-bit binary (base 2) address. The address is commonly represented as four 8-bit decimal numbers separated by dots, also commonly referred to as dotted decimal notation. Each 8-bit number is called an *octet*. Binary numbers are machine friendly, but are not all user friendly. Thus, provisions were made to support the use of the more intuitive decimal (base 10) number system for internetwork addressing. The interrelationship between the binary and decimal number systems must be well understood because literally the entire IP address architecture is based on them. The relationship between binary and decimal numbers is examined in the next section, "Binary Versus Decimal Numbers."

The original 32-bit IPv4 address architecture meant that the Internet could support 4,294,967,296 possible IPv4 addresses—a number originally deemed ridiculously excessive. This number is arrived at by raising 2 to the power of 32. These addresses were squandered through a number of wasteful practices, including hoarding (but not using) large blocks of addresses, using classful addresses, assigning inappropriate subnet masks, and other practices. Thus, there is a shortage of addresses. Many of the more significant of these wasteful practices, and their subsequent fixes, will become more evident as you learn more about the IPv4 address architecture.

Note

A new version of IP is nearing completion. This version, IPv6, will feature radically different address architectures and use a colon hexadecimal representation. The IPv6 address will be 128 bits long, and use entirely new classifications that are designed to maximize their efficiency of use. Given that it will likely take several years for this new version of IP to be widely used, this book presents all examples using the IPv4 address architectures. Please see Chapter 12, "IP Version 6," for more information on IPv6.

Binary Versus Decimal Numbers

In a base 2, or binary, number, the value represented by a 1 is determined by its position. This is not unlike the all too familiar base 10 system, in which the right-most digit enumerates ones; the second digit from the right enumerates tens; the third digit from the right enumerates hundreds, ad infinitum. Each digit signifies a ten-fold difference from the digit to the right.

Whereas the base 10 number system provides ten digits to represent different values (0 through 9), the base 2 number system only supports two valid digits: 0 and 1. Their position, too, determines the value that they signify. The right-most position, in decimal terms, is equal to 1. The next position to the left is equal to 2. The next position, 4, then 8, and so on. Each position to the left is 2 times the value of the position to the right.

The decimal value of a binary number is calculated by summing the decimal values of the number's digits that are populated with ones. Mathematically, each octet of an IPv4 address (there are four of them) can have a maximum value of 255, in the base 10 number system. A binary number equal to 255 consists of 8 bits, with all bits set equal to 1. Table 4.1 demonstrates this relationship between binary and decimal numbers.

TABLE 4.1 Binary (11111111) Versus Decimal (255) Values of an Octet

Digit	8	7	6	5	4	3	2	1
Binary	1	1	1	1	1	1	1	1
Decimal Value of Digit	128	64	32	16	8	4	2	1

As you can see, each of the bits in the binary address is populated with a 1. Thus, calculating the decimal value of this binary number can be done by summing the decimal values of the eight columns: $128 + 64 + 32 + 16 + 8 + 4 + 2 + 1 = 255$.

Table 4.2 presents another example of the conversion between binary and decimal numbers. In this example, the fifth digit from the right is a zero. This position represents the decimal value 16. Thus, this binary number has a decimal value that is 16 less than 255: $128 + 64 + 32 + 8 + 4 + 2 + 1 = 239$.

TABLE 4.2   Binary (11101111) Versus Decimal (239) Values of an Octet

Position	8	7	6	5	4	3	2	1
Binary	1	1	1	0	1	1	1	1
Decimal	128	64	32	16	8	4	2	1

This relationship between binary and decimal numbers is the foundation for the entire IP address architecture. Remember that four binary octets are in each IPv4 address. Every other aspect of IP's address architecture, including subnetwork masking, VLSM, and CIDR, is based on these number systems. Thus, you must understand the relationship between these basic numbering systems, and conversion between them, before you can understand the various ways that IP addressing can be implemented.

IPv4 Address Formats

IP was standardized in September 1981. Its address architecture was as forward-looking as could be expected, given the state of computing at that time. The basic IP address was a 32-bit binary number that was compartmentalized into four 8-bit binary numbers, or octets.

To facilitate human usage, IP's machine-friendly binary addresses were converted into a more familiar number system: base 10. Each of the four octets in the IP address is represented by a decimal number, from 0 to 255, and is separated by dots (.). This is known as a *dotted-decimal* format. Thus the lowest possible value that can be represented within the framework of an IPv4 address is 0.0.0.0, and the highest possible value is 255.255.255.255. Both of these values, however, are reserved and cannot be assigned to individual end systems. The reason for this requires an examination of the way that the IETF implemented this basic address structure in its protocol.

The dotted-decimal IPv4 address was then broken down into classes, to accommodate large, medium, and small networks. The differences between the classes were the number of bits allocated to network versus host addresses. The five classes of IP addresses, identified by a single alphabetic character, are

- Class A
- Class B

- Class C
- Class D
- Class E

Each address consists of two parts: a network address and a host address. The five classes represent different compromises between the number of supportable networks and hosts.

Class A Addresses

The Class A IPv4 address was designed to support extremely large networks. Because the need for very large-scale networks was perceived to be minimal, an architecture was developed that maximized the possible number of host addresses, but severely limited the number of possible Class A networks that could be defined.

A Class A IP address uses only the first octet to indicate the network address. The remaining three octets enumerate host addresses. The first bit of a Class A address is always a 0. This mathematically limits the possible range of the Class A address to less than or equal to 127, which is the sum of $64 + 32 + 16 + 8 + 4 + 2 + 1$. The left-most bit's decimal value of 128 is absent from this equation. Thus, there can only ever be 127 possible Class A IP networks.

The last 24 bits (that is, three dotted-decimal numbers) of a Class A address represent possible host addresses. The range of possible Class A network addresses or host range is from 1.0.0.0 to 126.255.255.255.

Notice that only the first octet bears a network address number. The remaining three are used to create unique host addresses within each network number. As such, they are set to zeros when describing the range of network numbers.

4

> **Note**
>
> Technically, 127.0.0.0 is also a Class A network address, but it is reserved for loopback testing and cannot be assigned to a network. In retrospect, this design is poor because it wastes an entire class A address consisting of a large number of IP addresses.

Each Class A address can support 16,777,214 unique host addresses. This value is calculated by multiplying 2 to the 24th power and then subtracting 2. Subtracting 2 is necessary because IP reserved the *all zeros* address for identifying the network and the *all ones* address for broadcasting within that network. The proportion of network to host octets is presented in the following table.

> **Note**
>
> Class A is generally used for very large networks such as the original ARPANET. Most of the class A addresses are allocated and it is very difficult, if not impossible, to get a class A network address assignment from the InterNIC.

Class A Address Architecture

	Network Portion	Host Portion		
Octet	1	2	3	4

Class B Addresses

The Class B addresses were designed to support the needs of moderate- to large-sized networks. The range of possible Class B host addresses is from 128.1.0.0 to 191.255.255.255.

The mathematical logic underlying this class is fairly simple. A Class B IP address uses two of the four octets to indicate the network address. The other two octets enumerate host addresses. The first two bits of the first octet of a Class B address are 10. The remaining six bits may be populated with either ones or zeros. This mathematically limits the possible range of the Class B address space to less than or equal to 191, which is the sum of $128 + 32 + 16 + 8 + 4 + 2 + 1$.

The last 16 bits (2 octets) identify potential host addresses. Each Class B address can support 65,534 unique host addresses. This number is calculated by multiplying 2 to the 16th power, and subtracting 2 (values reserved by IP). Mathematically, there can be only 16,382 Class B networks defined.

The proportion of network to host octets is presented in the following table.

Class B Address Architecture

	Network Portion		Host Portion	
Octet	1	2	3	4

> **Note**
>
> Class B networks are popular in medium-sized networks. Many large organiza-
> tions have been assigned Class B addresses.

Class C Addresses

The Class C address space was intended to support lots of small networks. This address class can be thought of as the inverse of the Class A address space. Whereas the Class A space uses just one octet for network numbering, and the remaining three for host numbering, the Class C space uses three octets for networking addressing and just one octet for host numbering.

The first three bits of the first octet of a Class C address are 110. The first two bits sum to a decimal value of 192 (128 + 64). This forms the lower mathematical boundary of the Class C address space. The third bit equates to a decimal value of 32. Forcing this bit to a value of 0 establishes the upper mathematical boundary of the address space. Lacking the ability to use the third bit limits the maximum value of this octet to 255 – 32, which equals 223. Thus, the range of possible Class C host addresses is from 192.0.0.0 to 223.255.255.255.

The last octet is used for host addressing. Each Class C address can support a theoretical maximum of 256 unique host addresses (0 through 255), but only 254 are usable because 0 and 255 are not valid host numbers. There can be 2,097,150 different Class C network numbers.

> **Note**
>
> In the world of IP addressing, 0 and 255 are reserved host address values. IP
> addresses that have all of their host address bits set equal to 0 identify the local
> network. Similarly, IP addresses that have all their host address bits set equal to
> 255 are used to broadcast to all end systems within that network number, also
> known as a directive broadcast.

The proportion of network to host octets is presented in the following table.

Class C Address Architecture

	Network Portion			Host Portion
Octet	1	2	3	4

Class D Addresses

The Class D address class was created to enable multicasting in an IP network. The Class D multicasting mechanisms are used for applications that use a "push" technology to send a message to a group of nodes. A multicast address is a unique network address that directs packets with that destination address to predefined groups of IP addresses. Thus, a single station can simultaneously transmit a single stream of datagrams that gets routed to multiple recipients simultaneously. This is much more efficient than creating a separate stream for each recipient. Multicasting has long been deemed a desirable feature in an IP network because it can substantially reduce network traffic. IPv6 also uses multicasting for many aspects of its operation.

The Class D address space, much like the other address spaces, is mathematically constrained. The first four bits of a Class D address must be 1110. Presetting the first three bits of the first octet to ones means that the address space begins at 128 + 64 + 32, which equals 224. Preventing the fourth bit from being used means that the Class D address is limited to a maximum value of 128 + 64 + 32 + 8 + 4 + 2 + 1, or 239. Thus, the Class D address space ranges from 224.0.0.0 to 239.255.255.255.

This range may seem odd, as the upper boundary is specified with all four octets. Ordinarily, this would mean that the octets for both host and network numbers are being used to signify a network number. There is a reason for this! The Class D address space isn't used for internetworking to individual end systems or networks.

Class D addresses are used for delivering multicast datagrams within a private network to groups of IP-addressed end systems. Thus, there isn't a need to allocate octets or bits of the address to separate network and host addresses. Instead, the entire address space can be used to identify groups of IP addresses (Classes A, B, or C). Today, numerous other proposals are being developed that would allow IP multicasting without the complexity of a Class D address space.

The proportion of network to host octets is presented in the following table.

Class D Address Architecture

	Host Portion			
Octet	1	2	3	4

Class E Addresses

A Class E address has been defined but is reserved by the IETF for its own research. Thus, no Class E addresses have been released for use on the Internet. The first four bits of a Class E address are always set to ones, thus the range of valid addresses is from 240.0.0.0 to 255.255.255.255. Given that this class was defined for research purposes, and its use is limited to inside the IETF, examining it any further is not necessary.

Inefficiencies in the System

Historically, the large gaps between the IP address classes have wasted a considerable amount of potential addresses. Consider, for example, a medium-sized company that requires 300 IP addresses. A single Class C address (254 addresses) is inadequate. Using two Class C addresses provides more than enough addresses, but results in two separate networks within the company. This increases the size of the routing tables across the Internet—one table entry is required for each of the address spaces, even though they belong to the same organization.

Alternatively, stepping up to a Class B address provides all the needed addresses within a single domain, but wastes 65,234 addresses. Too frequently, a Class B was handed out whenever a network supported more than 254 hosts. Thus, the Class B address space approached depletion more rapidly than the other classes.

Perhaps the most wasteful practice was that address spaces were handed out upon request. Any organization that wanted an address space simply requested one, and had to fill out a form describing the number of networks and hosts within the network. No attempts to verify these claims were made. Consequently, many organizations locked up substantial portions of the IPv4 address space as a hedge against some unseen, unspecified, future need.

Fortunately, this is no longer the case. Numerous extensions to IP have been developed that are specifically designed to improve the efficiency with which the 32-bit address space can be used. Three of the more important of these are

- Subnet masks
- Variable Length Subnet Masks (VLSM)
- CIDR

These very different mechanisms were designed to solve different problems. Subnet masks, both fixed and variable length, were developed to accommodate the multiple logical networks that might exist within a physical site that connects to the Internet. Masks are covered in more detail in the section "Variable Length Subnet Masks (VLSM)," later in this chapter.

CIDR was developed to eliminate the inefficiency inherent in the original, rigid, address classes. This enabled routers to more efficiently aggregate many different network addresses into a single routing table entry.

It is important to note that these two mechanisms are not mutually exclusive; they can, and should, be used together.

Managing the Address Space

The Internet's stability is directly dependent on the uniqueness of publicly used network addresses. Thus, some mechanism was needed to ensure that addresses were, in fact, unique. This responsibility originally rested within an organization known as the InterNIC (Internet Network Information Center). This organization is now defunct and was succeeded by the Internet Assigned Numbers Authority (IANA). IANA, too, has been dismantled, and the new caretaker of the Internet's names and address numbers is the Internet Corporation for the Assignment of Names and Numbers (ICANN). ICANN is currently creating a competitive registry structure that will enable commercial entities to compete with each other in the registration of IP names and numbers.

One important goal is to ensure that duplication of publicly used addresses does not occur. Such duplication would cause instability on the Internet, and compromise its ability to deliver datagrams to networks using the duplicated addresses.

Although it is entirely possible for a network administrator to arbitrarily select unregistered IP addresses, this practice should not be condoned. Computers having such spurious IP addresses can only function properly within the confines of their network. Interconnecting networks with spurious addresses to the Internet incurs the risk of conflicting with an organization that has legitimate claim to that address space. Duplicated addresses will cause routing problems, and potentially hinder the Internet's ability to deliver datagrams to the correct network.

In a firewall environment, the private network can use non-unique addresses because network address translation is used so that the addresses on the private network are substituted with the address of the public interface on the firewall. In this case, the private addresses may be non-unique across the Internet. Certain addresses are reserved for private use. Specifically, one Class A address (10.0.0.0), 16 Class B addresses (172.16.0.0 – 172.31.0.0), and 256 Class C addresses (192.168.0.0 – 192.168.255.0) are designated for private use.

Special IP Addresses

There are certain special cases for IP addresses. RFC 1700 describes a special notation that can be used to express special IP addresses, as shown here:

```
IP-address ::= { <Network-number>, <Host-number> }
```

The previous notation defines an IP address as consisting of a network number and a host number. The `<Network-number>` corresponds to the *netid* and the `<Host-number>` corresponds to the *hostid* used earlier in this chapter.

If the notation "-1" is used, then the field contains all 1 bits, and a value of "0" means that the field contains all 0 bits.

The following special IP addresses have been defined:

- {`<Network-number>`, 0}
- {`<Network-number>`, -1}
- { -1, -1}
- {0, 0}
- {0, `<Host-number>`}
- {127, `<any>`}

Addresses of all zeros and all ones in the `<Host-number>` field cannot be assigned as individual IP addresses. This means that if *N* bits are in the host number field, you can have only $2**N$ IP address assignments.

These special addresses are discussed in the sections that follow. In addition to the previously listed special addresses, special addresses are to be used for broadcasting within subnets. The treatment of subnets is taken up in later chapters and is not discussed in this introductory chapter on IP addresses.

Addressing "This" Network

A *hostid* value of all 0s are never assigned to an individual TCP/IP host. An IP address with a *hostid* value of 0 indicates the network itself. This special address is described using the following type:

```
{<Network-number>, 0}
```

Consider, the IP address of 137.53.0.0. This is a class B network. Recall that in a Class B network, the <Network-number> is 16 bits (2 bytes or first two decimal numbers in the dotted decimal address), and the <Host-number> is the remaining 16 bits of the IP address. Therefore, the special address 137.53.0.0 refers to the Class B network 137.53.

The two Class B addresses 137.53.0.0 and 141.85.0.0 have a "0.0" for the *hostid* field. These addresses indicate all the nodes in that network. The {<Network-number>, 0} cannot be used as a source or destination IP address.

Directed Broadcast

The *hostid* value containing all 1s in the bit pattern indicates a *directed broadcast address*. A directed broadcast address can occur in the destination IP address of an IP datagram, but never as a source IP address. This special address is described using the following type:

```
{<Network-number>, -1}
```

A directed broadcast address will be seen by all nodes on that network. Therefore, for the network number 137.53, the broadcast address will be 137.53.255.255. The network number 137.53 is a Class B address and has 16 bits (2 bytes or first two decimal numbers in the dotted decimal address) in the hostid field. If 1s are used for the 16 bits of the *hostid*, they correspond to a decimal value of 255.255.

In the example of the network 137.53, the underlying network hardware supports broadcasts efficiently at the network hardware level. On other networks, such as point-to-point networks, hardware-level broadcast is not supported efficiently. In this case the broadcast has to be done by the IP protocol software by replicating the IP datagram across all possible links.

A directed broadcast is sent to a specific network identified in the <Network-number> field. Routers on the network configured to forward-directed broadcasts will send the IP datagram to the final router that connects the destination network <Network-number>. The destination network router will be obliged to send the IP datagram to all nodes on the network. If the destination network provides a hardware-level broadcast, it is used to broadcast the IP datagram.

Routers can be configured not to forward directed broadcasts in situations where broadcast to other networks is not to be permitted.

Limited Broadcasts

Another type of broadcast, called the *local broadcast,* is represented by the value of 255.255.255.255. This special address is described using the following type:

`{-1, -1}`

The limited broadcast can be used in local area networks, where a broadcast never crosses a router boundary.

In a directed broadcast, the sender must supply the value of the `<Network-number>`. If a broadcast is to be done over the local network, you can use the limited broadcast that does not require knowledge of the `<Network-number>`.

A limited broadcast address can never appear as a source IP address; it can appear only as a destination IP address.

All Zeros IP Address

An all zeros IP address is a special address of the following type:

`{0, 0}`

The `<Network-number>` field is 0, which means "this" network. The `<Host-number>` field is also 0, which means "this" node on the network. This address typically occurs when an IP node is trying to determine its IP address. An example of this is the BOOTP protocol, which can be used by nodes on a network to assign an IP address from a central BOOTP server.

When the IP node sends an initial request to the BOOTP server, the IP node does not know its IP address. It uses a value of 0.0.0.0 in the source IP address field to indicate that it could be "this" node (`<Host-number>` is 0) on "this" network (`<Network-number>` is 0). After the IP node learns its IP address, it does not use the 0.0.0.0 address.

The 0.0.0.0 address is also used in routing tables to indicate the network entry for the default router's (often called default gateway) IP address.

The IP address of 0.0.0.0 can only be used as a source IP address, and never as a destination IP address. Please note that some vintage systems still use an all-zero address as a local broadcast.

4

NAMES AND ADDRESSES IN AN IP NETWORK

IP Address on This Network

A `<Network-number>` value of 0 with the `<Host-number>` value of non-zero means the specific host number in "this" network.

`{0, <Host-number>}`

If a node on a network receives a packet whose destination IP address has the `<Network-number>` set to zero, but the `<Host-number>` matches the receiver's `<Host-number>` field, the receiver will accept the packet. The receiver interprets the `<Network-number>` value of zero to mean "this" network.

Software Loopback

The number 127 is reserved for the *loopback address*. The loopback address is the special address described by:

`{127, <any>}`

Any packet sent by a TCP/IP application to an IP address of 127.*X.X.X,* where *X* is a number from 0 to 255, results in the packet coming back to the application without reaching the network media. The packet is copied from the transmit to receive buffer on the same computer. This is why the IP address 127.*X.X.X* is called a loopback address. The software loopback address can be used as a quick check to see that the TCP/IP software is properly configured. For example, you can use this with the "ping" tool to test that the IP Layer software is functioning at some basic level. The "ping" tool sends an ICMP echo packet to a destination IP address. The IP Layer at that address responds to an ICMP echo packet with an ICMP reply packet.

Another useful aspect of the software loopback address is when a TCP/IP client and service are running on the same machine. You can access the service on the same machine by using the loopback address. For example, you can use the Telnet or FTP client to connect to the Telnet or FTP server on the same machine using the following typical commands to gain access:

- `telnet 127.0.0.1`
- `ftp 127.0.0.1`

Exception to IP Addressing

An important exception to the all 1s in the *hostid* field used for broadcast is TCP/IP software derived from 4.2 BSD Unix. Many commercial implementations were derived from BSD 4.2 Unix. If you are using old TCP/IP software, you may run into this exception.

BSD Unix used the convention of all 0s in the *hostid* field to indicate a broadcast address. At the time 4.2 BSD Unix was written, the RFCs were unclear about the convention used for broadcast addresses. This was clarified in later RFCs, which stated that all 1s in the *hostid* field should be used for broadcast addresses. 4.3 BSD Unix was modified to conform to the RFCs. Software derived from 4.2 BSD Unix, unless modified, may still use the all-0s broadcast convention. If hosts that use all-0s broadcast are placed on the same physical network as hosts that use all-1s broadcast, the broadcast mechanism will not work as expected. Symptoms of this will be failure of the TCP/IP applications on that network to work correctly.

The Emergence of Subnetworks

The Internet originally used a two-level hierarchy, consisting of only network and host addresses. Figure 4.1 demonstrates a rather small and simple two-level network. This hierarchy assumed that each site would have only a single network. Therefore, each site would only need a single connection to the Internet. Initially, these assumptions were safe. However, over time, networked computing matured and expanded. By 1985, it was no longer safe to assume that an organization would only have a single network, nor that it would be satisfied with a single connection to the Internet.

FIGURE 4.1

The Internet originally used a two-level hierarchy.

As sites began to develop multiple networks, it became obvious to the IETF that some mechanism was needed to differentiate between the multiple logical networks that were emerging within sites of the Internet's second tier. Otherwise, there could be no efficient way to route data to specific end systems in sites with multiple networks. This is illustrated in Figure 4.2.

FIGURE 4.2

The emergence of multiple networks per site violated the Internet's two-level hierarchy.

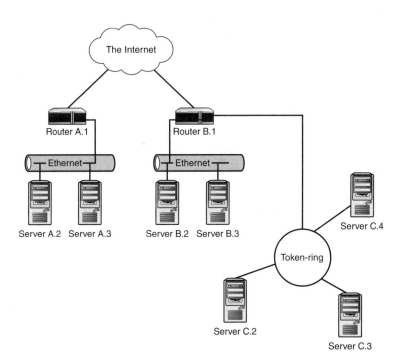

One answer was to give each logical network, or subnetwork, its own IP address range. This would work, but would be a tremendously inefficient use of the IP address space. It wouldn't take very long for this approach to threaten to completely consume the remaining unassigned IP address ranges. A more immediate impact would be the expansion of routing tables in the Internet's routers. Each network would require its own routing table entry. Clearly, a better approach was needed.

The answer was to organize these logical networks hierarchically, and route between them. Sites with multiple logical networks should, from the Internet's perspective, be treated as a single network. Thus, they would share a common IP address range. However, they would need their own unique range of subnetwork numbers.

Subnetting

In the mid-1980s, RFCs 917 and 950 were released. These documents proposed a means of solving the ever-growing problem posed by the relatively flat, two-level hierarchy of IP addressing. The solution was termed *subnetting*. The concept of subnetting is based on the need for a third level in the Internet's hierarchy. As internetworking technologies matured, their acceptance and use increased dramatically. As a result, it became normal for moderate and large-sized organizations to have multiple networks. Frequently, these networks were LANs. Each LAN may be treated as a subnet.

In such multiple-network environments, each subnetwork would interconnect to the Internet via a common point: a router. The actual details of the network environment are inconsequential to the Internet. They comprise a private network that is (or should be) capable of delivering its own datagrams. Thus, the Internet need only concern itself with how to reach that network's gateway router to the Internet. Inside the private network, the host portion of the IP address can be subdivided for use in identifying subnetworks.

Subnetting, as specified in RFC 950, enables the network number of any classful IP address (A, B, or C) to be subdivided into smaller network numbers. A subnetted IP address actually consists of three parts:

- Network address
- Subnetwork address
- Host address

The subnetwork and host addresses are carved from the original IP address's host address portion. Thus, your ability to subnet depends directly on the type of IP address being subnetted. The more host bits there are in the IP address, the more subnets and hosts you can create. However, these subnets decrease the number of hosts that can be addressed. You are, in effect, taking bits away from the host address to identify subnetwork numbers. Subnets are identified using a pseudo-IP address, known as a *subnet mask*.

A subnet mask is a 32-bit binary number that can be expressed in dotted-decimal form. The mask is used to tell end systems (including routers and other hosts) in the network how many bits of the IP address are used for network and subnetwork identification. These bits are called the *extended network prefix*. The remaining bits identify the hosts within the subnetwork. The bits of the mask that identify the network number are set to 1s and the host bits are set to 0s.

For example, a mask of 11111111.11111111.11111111.11000000 (255.255.255.192 in dotted-decimal notation) would yield 64 mathematically possible host addresses per subnet. The values of the right-most six bits, the ones set equal to zero, sum to 64 in the base 10 number system. Thus, you can uniquely identify 64 devices within this subnet. Only 62 of these addresses, however, are actually usable. The other two host addresses are reserved. The first host number in a subnet is always reserved for identifying the subnet itself. The last host number is also reserved, but is used for IP broadcasts within the subnet. Thus, you must always subtract 2 from the maximum number of hosts in a subnet to get the maximum number of *usable* host addresses per subnet.

The number of mathematically possible subnets, however, depends on what class of IP address is being subnetted. Each class reserves a different number of the available bits for the network number. Thus, each class offers a different number of bits that can be used for subnetting. Table 4.3 demonstrates the trade-off between the number of subnets and the number of hosts per subnet that can be carved from a Class B IP address. A

Class B address uses 16 bits for network number and 16 for host identification. As you peruse Table 4.3, you'll notice that the fewest number of bits you can allocate to the network prefix is 2, and the most is 14. The reason for this is simple. A network prefix of 1 bit will allow you to define only 2 subnet numbers: 0 and 1. Originally, the rules for subnetting prevented you from using a subnet address that consisted of all 0s, or all 1s. However, many commercial routers allowed the use of all 0s and all 1s for subnet addresses. A later RFC (1812), clarified this use. Today, the use of all 0s and all 1s are permitted for subnet addresses, notwithstanding the fact that many older books still refer to the use of all 0s and all 1s as not permissible.

Similarly, a network prefix of 2 bits only yields four usable subnet addresses. With a 2-bit binary subnet address field, the mathematically possible address combinations are 00, 01, 10, and 11.

TABLE 4.3 Subnetting a Class B Address Space

Number of Bits in Network Addresses Prefix	Subnet Mask	Number of Usable Subnet	Number of Usable Host Addresses, Per Subnet
2	255.255.192.0	4	16,382
3	255.255.224.0	8	8,190
4	255.255.240.0	16	4,094
5	255.255.248.0	32	2,046
6	255.255.252.0	64	1,022
7	255.255.254.0	128	510
8	255.255.255.0	256	254
9	255.255.255.128	512	126
10	255.255.255.192	1,024	62
11	255.255.255.224	2,048	30
12	255.255.255.240	4,096	14
13	255.255.255.248	8,192	6
14	255.255.255.252	16,384	2

Obviously, the more bits that are allocated to identifying a subnet number, the fewer remain for host identification, and vice versa.

Class C addresses, too, can be subnetted. Because a Class C address allocates 24 bits for network addressing, only 8 bits remain for apportioning between subnet and host addressing. The trade-offs between subnet and host addressing in a Class C network are presented in Table 4.4.

TABLE 4.4 Subnetting a Class C Address Space

Number of Bits in Network Prefix	Subnet Mask	Number of Usable Subnets Addresses	Number of Usable Hosts Addresses, Per Subnet
2	255.255.255.192	4	62
3	255.255.255.224	8	30
4	255.255.255.240	16	14
5	255.255.255.248	32	6
6	255.255.255.252	64	2

Although Tables 4.3 and 4.4 demonstrate the trade-offs between the numbers of possible subnets per mask, and hosts per subnet, they fall short of actually demonstrating how subnetting works. The best way to demonstrate subnetting is to actually subnet an IP address, which is done in the next section.

A Subnetting Example

Subnetting is, perhaps, the most difficult aspect of the IP address architecture to comprehend. This is largely because it really only makes sense when viewed in binary numbers, which isn't very intuitive. For example, you need to subnet the Class C address 193.168.125.0. This is your base address, the one to which the Internet would calculate routes. If you need to carve this into eight subnets, you would need at least three of the 8 host bits to create a unique extended network prefix for each of the eight subnets. These addresses would be 000, 001, 010, 011, 100, 101, 110, and 111. The last octet is split: 3 bits are added to the network number to form the extended network prefix, and the remaining 5 bits are used to identify hosts. Table 4.5 demonstrates how subnetworks are formed.

In Table 4.5, the extended network prefixes (which consist of the IP network address and the subnetwork address) are in bold. The subnet address is in bold italic. The host addresses are in normal typeface, and separated from the extended network prefix with a hyphen. This makes it easier to see how a basic IP network address can be subdivided into subnetworks.

4

NAMES AND ADDRESSES IN AN IP NETWORK

Table 4.5 Forming Subnets

Network #	Binary Address	Decimal Address
Base	11000001.10101000.01111101.00000000	193.168.125.0
Subnet 0	11000001.10101000.01111101.000-00000	193.168.125.0
Subnet 1	11000001.10101000.01111101.001-00000	193.168.125.32
Subnet 2	11000001.10101000.01111101.010-00000	193.168.125.64
Subnet 3	11000001.10101000.01111101.011-00000	193.168.125.96
Subnet 4	11000001.10101000.01111101.100-00000	193.168.125.128
Subnet 5	11000001.10101000.01111101.101-00000	193.168.125.160
Subnet 6	11000001.10101000.01111101.110-00000	193.168.125.192
Subnet 7	11000001.10101000.01111101.111-00000	193.168.125.224

Each subnetwork number is defined with the first three bits of the last octet. The decimal values of these digits are 128, 64, and 32, respectively. The starting IP address (in decimal) for each subnet is presented in the third column. Not surprisingly, these increment in multiples of 32 (the right-most bit of the subnet number).

> **Note**
>
> Subnets 0 and 7, although mathematically possible, even if defined on a router, were once not possible. They are now permissible. Their subnet addresses are 000 and 111, respectively.

Hosts in each subnet would be defined by incrementing the remaining five bits in the last octet. There are 32 possible combinations of 0s and 1s. The highest and lowest values are reserved, yielding a usable maximum of 30 hosts per subnet. A device with an IP address of 193.168.125.193 would be the first host defined in Subnet 6. Subsequent hosts would be numbered up to 193.168.125.222, at which point the subnet would be fully populated. No further hosts could be added.

Variable Length Subnet Masks (VLSM)

Although subnetting proved a valuable addition to the Internet addressing architecture, it did suffer from one fundamental limitation: You were limited to a single subnet mask for an entire network. Thus, after you selected a subnet mask (which dictated the number of hosts you could support per subnet number) you couldn't support subnets of a different size. Any requirement for larger-sized subnets meant you had to change the size of the subnet mask for the entire network. Needless to say, this could be a complicated and time-consuming affair.

A solution to this problem arose in 1987. The IETF published RFC 1009, which specified how a subnetted network could use more than one subnet mask. Ostensibly, each subnet mask would be a different size. Otherwise, they wouldn't be different masks—their network prefix would be identical. The new subnetting technique was, therefore, called VLSM.

VLSM enables a more efficient use of an organization's IP address space, by enabling the network's administrator(s) to customize the size of a subnet mask to the specific requirements of each subnet. To illustrate this point, assume a base IP address of 172.16.0.0. This is a Class B address, which uses a 16-bit network number. Extending the network prefix by 6 bits results in a 22-bit extended network prefix. Mathematically, there are 64 usable subnet addresses and 1,022 usable host addresses per subnet.

This subnetting scheme would make sense if the organization needed more than 30 subnets populated with more than 500 hosts per subnet. However, if the organization consisted of a few large sub-organizations with more than 500 hosts each, and many smaller sub-organizations with just 40 or 50 host devices each, the majority of possible IP addresses would be wasted. Each organization, regardless of need, would be allocated a subnet with 1,022 host addresses. The smaller organizations would each waste approximately 950 host addresses. Given that a subnetted network could only use a single mask, of fixed and predetermined length, such address waste could not be avoided.

As a purely mathematical exercise, subnetting was an ideal solution to a vexing problem: the rapid depletion of the finite IP address space. Enabling networks to redefine the host field of an IP address into subnetwork and host addresses would greatly reduce the amount of wasted IP addresses. Unfortunately, in a real-world setting, the need for subnets is not homogeneous. It is not realistic to expect an organization, or its networks, to be divided into uniformly-sized subcomponents. It is much more likely that there will be organizations (and subnetworks) of all sizes. Thus, using a fixed-length subnet mask would result in wasted IP host addresses in each subnet defined, as was shown in the previous example.

4

NAMES AND ADDRESSES IN AN IP NETWORK

Note

The size of an extended network prefix can be identified using a slash (/) followed by the number of bits used for the network and subnetwork addressing. Thus, 193.168.125.0/27 identifies a specific Class C address, with 27 bits used for the extended network prefix. This is also called Binary count notation.

The solution to this dilemma was to allow an IP address space to be subnetted flexibly, using different-sized subnet masks. Using the previous example, a network administrator could carve up a base IP address into different subnet masks. The few large organizations could continue to use the 22-bit extended network prefix, whereas the smaller organizations could be given a 25- or 26-bit extended network prefix. The 25-bit prefix would enable the creation of 126 host subnets, and the 26-bit prefix would permit subnets with up to 62 hosts each. This solution is VLSM.

Classless Interdomain Routing (CIDR)

CIDR is a relatively recent addition to the IP address architecture. It was born of the crisis that accompanied the Internet's explosive growth during the early 1990s.

As early as 1992, the IETF became concerned with the Internet's ability to continue to scale upward in response to demand for Internet use. Their specific concerns were

- The exhaustion of the remaining unassigned IPv4 network addresses. The Class B space was in particular danger of depletion.
- The rapid, and substantial, increase in the size of the Internet's routing tables as a result of its growth.

All indications were that the Internet's rapid growth would continue, as more commercial organizations came online. In fact, some members of the IETF even predicted a "Date of Doom." This date, March 1994, was the projected date of the depletion of the Class B address space. Absent any other mechanism for addressing, the Internet's scalability would be seriously compromised. More ominously, the Internet's routing mechanisms might collapse under the weight of their ever-growing routing tables before the Date of Doom.

The Internet was becoming a victim of its own success. The IETF decided that, to avoid the collapse of the Internet, both short- and long-term solutions would be needed. In the long term, the only viable solution was a completely new IP, with greatly expanded address space and address architectures. Ultimately, this solution became known as IPng (Internet Protocol: Next Generation) or, more formally, as IP Version 6 (IPv6).

The more pressing, short-term needs were to slow down the rate of depletion of the remaining unassigned addresses. The answer was to eliminate the inefficient classes of addresses in favor of a more flexible addressing architecture. The result was CIDR. In September 1993, the plans for CIDR were released in RFCs 1517, 1518, 1519, and 1520.

CIDR had several key features that were invaluable in staving off depletion of the IPv4 address space. These features are

- The elimination of classful addressing
- Enhanced route aggregation
- Supernetting

The net effect of these innovations was the obsolescence of class-based addressing. Such addresses may still be found in use, but classless addresses (regardless of the negative connotation!) are much more efficient.

Classless Addressing

Mathematically, the IPv4 address space still held a substantial number of available addresses. Unfortunately, many of these potential addresses were squandered because they were locked into assigned blocks, or classes, of assigned addresses. Eliminating classes wouldn't necessarily recover the addresses locked into those address spaces that were already assigned, but it would enable the remaining addresses to be used much more efficiently. Ostensibly, this stopgap effort would buy the time needed for IPv6 to be developed and deployed.

Enhanced Route Aggregation

CIDR enables Internet routers (or any CIDR-compliant router) to more efficiently aggregate routing information. In other words, a single entry in a routing table can represent the address spaces of many networks. This greatly reduces the size of the routing tables needed in any given internetwork, and directly translates into an increased scalability.

CIDR was implemented in the Internet during 1994–1995, and was immediately effective in containing the expansion of the Internet routers' routing tables. It is doubtful that the Internet would have continued to grow had CIDR not been implemented.

Supernetting

Another benefit of CIDR is the ability to supernet. *Supernetting* is nothing more than using contiguous blocks of Class C address spaces to simulate a single, albeit larger, address space. If you were to obtain enough contiguous Class C addresses, you could redefine the allocation of bits between network and host identification fields, and simulate a Class B address.

Supernetting is designed to alleviate the pressure on the rapidly depleting Class B address space by offering a more flexible alternative. The previous class-based address

4

NAMES AND
ADDRESSES IN AN
IP NETWORK

architecture suffered from a tremendous disparity between its Class B and Class C net-works. Networks that required more than the 254 hosts offered by a Class C had two choices, neither of which was highly desirable. These choices were

- Using multiple Class C addresses (which would have necessitated routing between the network domains)
- Stepping up to a Class B address, with its 65,534 usable host addresses

The simpler solution, frequently, was to use the Class B even though it wasted tens of thousands of IP addresses.

How CIDR Works

CIDR was a dramatic break from tradition in that it completely abandoned the rigid classes of addresses. The original IPv4 address architecture used an 8-bit network num-ber for Class A addresses, a 16-bit network number for Class B addresses, and a 24-bit number for Class C addresses. CIDR replaced these categories with a more generalized network prefix. This prefix could be of any length, rather than just 8, 16, or 24 bits. This allows CIDR to craft network address spaces according to the size of a network, rather than force-fitting networks into presized network address spaces.

Each CIDR-compliant network address is advertised with a specific bit mask. This mask identifies the length of the network prefix. For example, 192.125.61.8/20 identifies a CIDR address with a 20-bit network address. The IP address can be any mathematically valid address, regardless of whether that address was originally part of the Class A, B, or C range! CIDR-compliant routers look at the number after the / to determine the network number. Thus, the former Class C address 192.125.61.8 previously had a network num-ber of 192.125.61 and a host number of 8. With a Class C address, you could provide addresses for a maximum of 254 hosts within the network. Using CIDR, the architectural limitations of the 8-bit boundaries between address components is eliminated. To better understand how this works, translating the decimal number to binary is necessary.

In binary, this network portion of this address is 11000000.01111101.00111101. The first 20 bits of this example identify the network number. Table 4.6 demonstrates the split of this address between network and host numbers.

TABLE 4.6   A 20-bit CIDR Network Number

	Network Number	*Host Number*
Binary Address	11000000.01111101.0011	1101.00001000

Notice that the split between the network and host portions of the address falls in the middle of the third octet. The bits that aren't allocated to network number are used to identify hosts. Thus, an IPv4 address with a 20-bit network prefix has 12 bits left for host identification. Mathematically, this translates to 4,094 usable host addresses. Because none of the left-most bits are preset (which previously established the address class), virtually the entire range of addresses can be used in a CIDR network. Thus, a 20-bit network prefix can be assigned a value that was previously reserved for Class A, B, or C networks.

Public Address Spaces

If your WAN will not be directly interconnected with the Internet, or to any other network, internetwork addresses could be arbitrarily selected. Generally speaking, arbitrarily selecting internetwork addresses is shortsighted and a gross dereliction of duties. That being said, Request for Comment (RFC) 1597 was released in May 1993, and posited a plan to the contrary.

Requests for Comment (RFC) 1597 and 1918

RFC 1597 was made obsolete by RFC 1918 in February 1996. However, this new RFC only made extremely minor changes to the original specification. The most substantial of these changes was the abandonment of alphabetic classes, such as A, B, and C. Instead, RFC 1918 posited the use of the new CIDR-compliant addressing. As explained in the previous section, CIDR does not use class-based addresses. Instead, the number of bits reserved for the network number are identified with a slash (/) followed by the number of bits. Thus, a Class A address of 10 is identified as 10/8 because only 8 bits are used to designate network numbers. More significantly, a host address can be established on any bit boundary, as opposed to the previous classful addresses, which required the address to be created in multiples of 8 bits.

Three ranges of addresses that could be used for internal networking purposes only were identified and reserved. These ranges include one each of IPv4's Class A, B, and C addresses. They are as follows:

- 10.0.0.0–10.255.255.255
- 172.16.0.0–172.31.255.255
- 192.168.0.0–192.168.255.255

These ranges were reserved by IANA for use in private networks. One stipulation of RFC 1597 was that these addresses couldn't be used when directly accessing the Internet. Companies that used these addresses and subsequently found the need to access

4

NAMES AND
ADDRESSES IN AN
IP NETWORK

the Internet faced a tough decision. They could renumber all their devices, to comply with IANA, or they could use a proxy server or a *network address translator* (NAT) as an intermediary between their intranet and the Internet. Using such devices would enable the company to keep their spurious addressing without compromising access to, and from, the Internet.

If you choose to implement RFC 1597's reserved addresses for your intranet, you must consider the long-term implications of that decision. Over time, you may need to inter-connect with other company networks through an extranet, or to the Internet itself. In either event, you may not be able to guarantee the uniqueness of any given made-up address.

Finally, if you implement one of the address ranges reserved for private networks in RFC 1918, you must still guarantee the uniqueness of each device's address within your private network domain. The addresses won't be unique globally, but they must be unique locally.

Private Network Addresses

In order to reduce the need for new IP addresses, RFC 1597 on Address Allocation for Private Internets was issued in March 1994. The authors of this RFC suggest a scheme for IP address assignments for private networks. Private networks are those not connected to the network or those that have hosts and services that have limited interaction with the connected Internet. Hosts on the network can be classified into the following categories:

- Hosts that do not require access to hosts in other enterprises or the Internet at large.
- Hosts that need access to a limited set of outside services such as email, FTP, netnews, remote login, and so on, which can be handled by an application-level gateway.
- Hosts that need Network Layer access outside the enterprise. This is provided via IP connectivity and includes router devices or hosts that are visible to the outside world.

Hosts within the first category can use IP addresses that are unique within the private network, but may not be unique across the Internet. Because there is no packet exchange with these hosts outside the private network, the duplicate IP address problem will never be seen.

For hosts in the second category that are insulated from the external Internet by an application-level gateway, having unique IP addresses across the Internet is unnecessary. This is because the application-level gateway hides the IP addresses of these hosts from the external network.

Hosts in the third category require IP addresses that are globally unique across the Internet.

If proper documentation on the network is maintained, identifying hosts in category 1 and 2 is relatively easy. These hosts do not need Network Layer connectivity outside the organization's network.

RFC 1597 gives the following examples of hosts in categories 1 and 2:

- A large airport that has many arrival/departure displays individually addressable via TCP/IP. It is very unlikely that these displays need to be directly accessible from other networks.

- Large organizations like banks and retail chains are switching to TCP/IP for their internal communication. Local workstations like cash registers, money machines, and equipment at clerical positions rarely need to have such connectivity.

- For security reasons, many enterprises use application-layer gateways (for example, firewalls) to connect their internal network to the Internet. The internal network usually does not have direct access to the Internet, and only one or more firewall hosts are visible from the Internet. In this case, the internal network can use non-unique IP numbers.

- If two enterprises communicate over their own private link, usually only a very limited set of hosts are reachable from the other enterprise over this link. Only those hosts need globally unique IP numbers.

- Interfaces of routers on an internal network usually do not need to be directly accessible from outside the enterprise.

Based on the request of the authors of RFC 1597, the ICANN has reserved the following three blocks of the IP address space for private networks that can be assigned for hosts in categories 1 and 2:

- 10.0.0.0 to 10.255.255.255—1 Class A network
- 172.16.0.0 to 172.31.255.255—16 Class B networks
- 192.168.0.0 to 192.168.255.255—256 Class C networks

An enterprise that decides to use IP addresses out of the previously listed address space can do so without any coordination with ICANN or an Internet registry. This address space can thus be used by many enterprises and would reduce the need for assigning new network numbers. Addresses within this private address space will be unique within the enterprise, but not unique across the network.

If an enterprise needs globally unique address space for applications and devices that are connected at the IP Layer, they will have to obtain such addresses from an Internet registry. The ICANN will not assign IP addresses from the private IP address space.

Because private addresses have no global meaning, routing information about private networks should not be propagated outside the enterprise. Routers in networks not using private address space, such as those of Internet Service Providers (ISPs), should have their filters set to reject routing information about private networks. Filtering out private address information should not be reported as a routing protocol error.

In order to use private address space, an enterprise needs to determine which hosts do not need to have Network Layer connectivity. If the configuration of the hosts change and Network Layer connectivity is needed to external networks, globally unique addresses must be assigned. That is, the IP address of these hosts must be changed from the private address space to the public address space. If an organization does not keep proper track of changing requirements for hosts, the organization can accidentally create a situation of duplicate IP address problems. Perhaps for this and other reasons, RFC 1627 was issued in July 1994.

The authors of RFC 1627 titled "Network 10 Considered Harmful (Some Practices Shouldn't be Codified)" argue that the recommendations in RFC 1597 reduce network reliability, security, and are costly in terms of potential problems. For example, if two organizations that are using private address spaces need to connect directly, at least one of them will have to change its IP address assignments. RFC 1627 states that "RFC 1597 gives the illusion of remedying a problem, by creating formal structure to a long-standing informal practice. In fact, the structure distracts us from the need to solve these very real problems and does not even provide substantive aid in the near-term." Additionally, RFC 1627 states that the ICANN has overstepped their mandate in recommending RFC 1597 without the benefit of the usual, public review and approval by the IETF or IAB.

So what should you, the network designer, do in the midst of this controversy about using private addresses? If you plan on using the recommendations of RFC 1597, do so with great care. Ensure that you have proper documentation and an understanding of which services are visible or non-visible to the outside world. Read RFC 1627 and understand the objections it raises.

Internet Class C Address Allocation

The Class C addresses from 192.0.0 through 223.255.245 have been divided into eight blocks of addresses. Regional authorities are responsible for allocation of these blocks. Table 4.7 shows this address allocation.

TABLE 4.7   Class C Address Allocation

Address range	Region
192.0.0-193.255.255	Multi-regional. Includes addresses before the region-based address allocation scheme was introduced.
194.0.0-195.255.255	Europe
196.0.0-197.255.255	Used when there is a need to assign IP addresses not based on region.
198.0.0-199.255.255	North America
200.0.0-201.255.255	Central and South America
202.0.0-203.255.255	Pacific Rim
204.0.0-205.255.255	Used when there is a need to assign IP addresses not based on region.
206.0.0-207.255.255	Used when there is a need to assign IP addresses not based on region.
208.0.0-223.255.255	Available for assignment.

The IP address allocation information in Table 4.7 can be useful if you have a protocol trace of packets coming into your network and you want to determine the region of the world from which the packets are originating.

Configuring IP Addresses

Hosts on a TCP/IP network need to be configured using proper IP addresses. The actual configuration procedure depends on the operating system. The configuration procedure can be classified into the following categories:

- Command-line–based
- Menu interface
- Graphical User Interface–based
- Obtained dynamically when host boots from a central server

Table 4.8 shows examples of operating systems that fit into these categories.

TABLE 4.8   Configuring IP Address and Other Parameters for Hosts

Method	*Operating System/Protocol*
Command line	Unix, VMS, Router devices, MS-DOS
Menu interface	Router devices, Unix, NetWare servers, MS-DOS
Graphical User Interface	Unix, Microsoft Windows products
Dynamically assigned	DHCP and BOOTP protocols. Available on almost all major operating system platforms.

Many systems offer a command that can be executed to modify the IP address. In these systems, the command line is often placed in the startup script for the operating system. The Menu interface is built using the extended line-drawing character set. You are prompted to enter the IP address and other IP parameters. The Graphical User Interface is for systems that offer a pixel-based graphical view. Examples of these are X-Windows and Microsoft Windows operating systems. The dynamically assigned IP address is used in conjunction with BOOTP or DHCP protocol. A device on starting up requests its IP address and other parameters from a central server that can deliver this information using either the BOOTP or the DHCP protocol.

The IP address information for the host is recorded in a number of places. When the IP address information is entered, it is cached in memory and available for use by the TCP/IP software. Alternatively, this information may also be recorded on a system file in the operating system. IP addresses of other systems can be discovered by consulting a special file, usually called the "hosts" file or by using the DNS protocol. The DNS service is typically used to determine a host's IP address given its symbolic DNS name (see Chapter 1, "Introduction to Open Communications"). In some systems, proprietary protocols can be used to discover an IP address on a network. An example of this is the WINS service used in Microsoft's operating systems.

IP Version 6 Addresses

As noted earlier in this chapter, the 32-bit address space for IP addresses is running out as the Internet continues to grow. Notwithstanding RFC 1597, every IP network connection on the Internet requires a unique IP address. Some devices have more than one network connection, which results in the rapid consumption of assignable IP addresses.

It is estimated that the 32-bit IP addresses (also called IP version 4 addressing) can provide over 2,100,000 networks and over a total of 3,720 million hosts. However, the IP address space allocation scheme is not very efficient because new network numbers are generally required to connect networks through Network Layer relay devices such as routers.

IP addresses are fast becoming a scarce resource. To overcome this problem, the IETF has studied methods for overcoming the address space problem and making improvements to the protocol so that it can run more efficiently over newer networking technologies. After studying a variety of proposals for solving limitations of the current IP protocol (called IP version 4 (IPv4), after the version number field value of 4 in the IP header), the IETF has decided on the "IP Next Generation" protocol known as IPng or IP version 6 (IPv6). One of the design goals of IPv6 was to support at least one billion networks. To support this design criterion, IPv6 uses 128-bit addresses. This is four times the bit size of IPv4 addresses. IPv6 uses the concept of network numbers and host numbers, but extends this to several levels. The hierarchical addressing in IPv6 can support more efficient routing. The IPv6 address can contain an IPv4 address. This is done by using 32-bit IPv4 addresses in the lower bits of the IPv6 address and adding a fixed prefix of 96 bits. The 96-bit prefix consists of 80 zero bits followed by 16 zero or 16 one bits.

Unregistered IPv4 addresses can be used in IPv6 by adding a unique registered modifier so that the overall IPv6 address is unique.

IPv6 is designed to interoperate with IPv4 systems. This allows a period of coexistence of the two IP systems. The goal is to have current IPv4 systems replaced by IPv6 systems. Routers with both IPv6 and IPv4 support could be used to relay information between networks running the IPv4 protocol and the newer IPv6 protocol.

IPv6 includes support for mobile portable systems. This permits portable computer and other device users to connect anywhere within the network without having to perform manual configuration. Mobile systems will be automatically connected when joining the network at a new attachment point. In addition to automatic configuration for mobile systems, regular workstations are self-configuring. IPv6 supports encryption at the Internet Layer and better support for real-time traffic. Real-time data traffic requires that there be some guarantee of the maximum delay in transmitting datagrams across the network.

Because IPv6 addresses are 128 bits long, using dotted-decimal notation is not a convenient notation for writing IPv6 addresses. If the dotted-decimal notation were used for writing IPv6 addresses, you would have to write a string of 16 decimal numbers separated by dots!

Consider the following bit pattern representation of an IPv6 address:

```
01011000 00000000 00000000 11000000

11100011 11000011 11110001 10101010

01001000 11100011 11011001 00100111

11010100 10010101 10101010 11111110
```

You will notice that 128 bits are in the IPv6 address, and that writing it as a bit pattern is not very convenient. If the dotted-decimal notation were being used, this IPv6 address would be written as the following:

```
88.0.0.192.227.195.241.170.72.227.217.39.212.149.170.254
```

As you can see from the previous dotted-decimal value, it is not a compact notation. The designers chose to use a *colon hexadecimal notation* to write out the bit patterns. The hexadecimal values are written as 16 bits separated by the colon (:) character. The previous IPv6 address is written as the following:

```
5800:00C0:E3C3:F1AA:48E3:D927:D495:AAFE
```

Using the colon hexadecimal notation requires fewer digits and separation characters. The *colon hexadecimal notation* specifies two shorthand techniques that you can use to reduce the number of characters that you have to write.

The first technique is that you can skip leading zeros. Consider the following IPv6 address:

```
48A6:0000:0000:0000:0000:0DA3:003F:0001
```

By skipping the leading zeros, you can write this as the following simplified address:

```
48A6:0:0:0:0:DA3:3F:1
```

Note that 0000 is replaced by 0; 0DA3 is replaced by DA3; 0001 is replaced by 1. In each case, leading zeros are skipped to reduce the number of characters that you have to write.

The second technique uses *zero compression,* in which a single string of repeated zeros is replaced by a double colon (::). In the previous IPv6 address, there is a string of four 0s (0:0:0:0). These can be replaced by "::". The previous IPv6 address can therefore be written as the following:

```
48A6::DA3:3F:1
```

To expand the zero-compressed IPv6 address, align whatever is to the left of the colon with the left 16-bit words of the IPv6 address. Next, align whatever is to the right of the double colon with the right 16-bit words of the IPv6 address. Fill the remaining 16-bit words of the IPv6 address with 0s. As an example, consider the following zero-compressed IPv6 address:

```
5400:FD45::FFFF:3AFE
```

In the expanded form, this IPv6 address becomes the following:

```
5400:FD45:0:0:0:0:FFFF:3AFE
```

You can use the double colon only once in the notation so as to produce an unambiguous interpretation. The following IPv6 notation is illegal, because the number of zeros that were compressed is ambiguous.

```
5400::45A1::23A6
```

The third technique is to use the double colon either as a prefix or suffix. Consider the following IPv6 representation of the IPv4 address 170.1.1.1:

```
0:0:0:0:0:0:AA01:101
```

This can be represented as the following:

```
::AA01:101
```

Summary

A solid understanding of IP's address architecture is a prerequisite to appreciating the fundamentals of internetworking with IP. The basics presented in this chapter should help you better appreciate the mechanics of internetworking with the IP. Many of the architectural devices presented in this chapter, including CIDR, subnet masking, and VLSM, are so widely used that not understanding them will compromise your ability to support and design internetworks. This chapter also gave you an understanding of private addresses and when to use them. The structure of IPv6 addresses was also presented.

In the subsequent chapters of this Part, other aspects of naming and addressing in IP networks are examined. These aspects include how IP addresses are correlated to local area network hardware addresses, as well as how user-friendly names are resolved into IP addresses.

4

NAMES AND ADDRESSES IN AN IP NETWORK

ARP and RARP

by Tim Parker

CHAPTER 5

IP addresses are the common identifiers for machines under TCP/IP, although the IP address alone is not enough to get a datagram to its target. Instead, the network system itself is involved, and the behavior of the network is usually specific to the network operating system and hardware type. In order to gain a good understanding of the manner in which data is routed from a source to a destination machine, you need to understand how a network interworks with its constituent machines. This chapter starts with a look at a typical network system, in particular Ethernet, and presents a look at how TCP/IP provides for a conversion of an IP address to a data link–specific address that the network can find. The conversion of IP address to data link address is performed by the Address Resolution Protocol (ARP). A complementary protocol called Reverse Address Resolution Protocol (RARP) converts data link addresses to IP addresses.

Using Addresses

The purpose of an IP address is to help TCP/IP deliver a datagram to the proper destination. The three terms commonly used that relate to addressing are name, address, and route.

A *name* is a specific identification of a machine, a user, or an application. It is usually unique and provides an absolute target to which a datagram is to be delivered. An *address* typically identifies where the target is located, usually as its physical or logical location in a network. A *route* tells the system how to get a datagram to the correct address. Be careful when using the term address because it is often generically used with communications protocols to refer to many different things. It can mean the destination, a port of a machine, a memory location, an application, and more. In general, each layer of the OSI model has its own address. For example, the Data Link Layer address for Ethernet networks is the Ethernet hardware address that is unique for each network card, and the Network Layer address is the IP address for a TCP/IP node.

The recipient's login name is usually the key to the whole delivery process. From the username and machine name, a network software package called the *name server* resolves the address and the route, hiding that aspect of TCP/IP routing and delivery from the application. Besides making the addressing and routing transparent to the application, using a name server has another primary advantage: It gives the system or network administrator a lot of freedom to change the network as required, without having to update each user's machine individually. As long as an application can access a name server somewhere on the network, applications and users can ignore routing changes.

Subnetwork Addressing

When you send a piece of data to another machine, you usually do it with the IP address. Whereas TCP/IP is designed to work with IP addresses, the actual network software and hardware is not. Instead, the network hardware uses a physical address encoded into the network hardware that identifies each machine. Making the correspondence between the IP address and a physical address is not normally part of the TCP/IP protocol's responsibility, so a number of special protocols have been developed for this task. These protocols are discussed in the next section, but first this section looks at the structure of the network's physical address.

On a single local area or wide area network, several pieces of information are necessary to ensure the correct delivery of datagrams. The primary pieces are the physical address and the data link address of the destination machine. These are important enough to warrant a closer look at each.

Physical Addresses

Each device on a network has a unique *physical address*, sometimes called the *hardware address* or *Data Link Layer address*. For networking hardware, the addresses are usually encoded into the network interface card. The physical address is sometimes user-settable through switches or software. More often, they are not modifiable by users at all because a unique number is encoded into the card's Programmable Read-only Memory (PROM); manufacturers often work together to ensure there is no possibility of duplication of physical addresses. On any given network, there can be only one occurrence of each address; otherwise, the name server will have no way of unambiguously identifying the target machine. The length of the physical address varies depending on the networking system. For example, Ethernet and several other network schemes use 48 bits in each address. For communications to occur, two physical addresses are required: one each for the sending and receiving devices.

The IEEE is now handling the task of assigning universal physical addresses for subnetworks (a task previously performed by Xerox, which originally developed Ethernet). For each subnetwork, the IEEE assigns an *organization unique identifier* (OUI) that is 24-bits long, enabling the organization to assign the other 24 bits however it wants. Actually, two of the 24 bits assigned as an OUI are control bits, so only 22 bits identify the subnetwork. The format of the organization unique identifier is shown in Figure 5.1. The combination of 24 bits from the OUI and 24 locally assigned bits is called a *media access control* (MAC) address. Both the OUI and the local address are programmed into the network card. When a packet of data is assembled for transfer across an internetwork, there will be two sets of MACs—one from the sending machine and one for the receiving machine.

5

ARP AND RARP

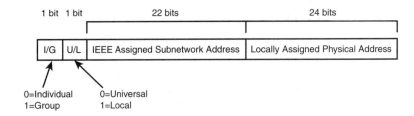

FIGURE 5.1

The structure of the organization unique identifier.

The least significant bit of the address (the lowest bit number or the bit to the left in the structure) is called the *individual* or *group* address bit. If the bit is set to 0, the rest of the address refers to an individual address; a setting of 1 means that the rest of the address field identifies a group address that needs further resolution. If the entire OUI is set to 1, all stations on the network are assumed to be the destination. This is a special convention supported by the OUI.

The second bit in the OUI structure is called the *local* or *universal* bit. If the second bit is set to 0, it has been set by the universal administration body. This is the setting for IEEE-assigned OUIs. If the second bit has the value of 1, the OUI has been locally assigned and would cause addressing problems if decoded as an IEEE-assigned address. Usually, a structure that has the second bit set to 1 is kept within a local or wide area network and not passed to other networks that may follow the IEEE addressing format.

> **Note**
>
> Older protocols such as DECNet Phase IV used locally assigned addresses where the locally assigned physical address was set to the DECNet network address.

The remaining 22 bits in the OUI structure make up the physical address of the subnetwork, as assigned by the IEEE. The second set of 24 bits identifies local network addresses and is administered locally. If an organization were to run out of physical addresses (about 16 million addresses are possible from 24 bits), the IEEE could assign a second subnetwork address.

Logical Link Control Address

The IEEE Ethernet standards use another address called the Link Layer address (usually abbreviated as LSAP for *link service access point*). The Data Link Layer in IEEE networks is divided into an upper layer called the Logical Link Control (LLC) and a lower layer that contains the hardware dependencies called the MAC (Media Access Control) layer. The LLC layer protocol addresses are called Service Access Points (SAPs) or Logical Service Access Points (LSAPs).

The LSAP identifies the type of link protocol used in the Data Link Layer. As with the physical addresses, a datagram will carry both sending and receiving LSAPs.

Network Frames

The layout of information in each transmitted packet of data differs depending on the protocol used by the network. However, it is instructive to examine one to see how the addresses previously mentioned, as well as other related information, are added to the datagram before it is sent out over the network. We can use Ethernet as an example because of its wide use with TCP/IP. It is quite similar to other systems as well, although the exact structures of the headers may differ. Remember that this is the way the network protocols package the TCP/IP-constructed headers, and has little to do specifically with TCP/IP. A typical Ethernet frame (the term for a network-ready datagram) is shown in Figure 5.2.

FIGURE 5.2
*The structure of
an Ethernet frame.*

Preamble	Recipient Address	Sender Address	Type	Data	CRC
64 Bits	48 Bits	48 Bits	16 Bits	Variable Length	32 Bits

The preamble is 64 bits used primarily to synchronize the communication process and account for any random noise in the first few bits that are sent. The preamble is ignored as far as addressing and routing are concerned. At the end of the preamble's field is a sequence of bits called the *start frame delimiter* (SFD), which indicates that the frame follows immediately.

The recipient and sender addresses in the Ethernet frame structure use the IEEE 48-bit format, followed by a 16-bit type indicator that is used to identify the type of protocol used. The actual data (which is the assembled TCP/IP datagram) follows the type indicator. The Data field is between 64 and 1,500 bytes in length with standard Ethernet. If the data is less than 64 bytes in length, it is padded with zeroes until it is 46 bytes long. Padding to a minimum data length of 64 bytes is done to ensure that Ethernet collisions can be easily detected.

At the end of the Ethernet frame is the *cyclic redundancy check* (CRC) checksum count, used to ensure that the frame's contents have not been modified during the transmission process. Each machine along the transmission route calculates a CRC value for the frame and compares it to the value at the end of the frame. If the two match, the frame data is considered valid and can be sent farther along the network or into the subnetwork; if they differ, a modification to the frame must have happened, the frame is discarded, and a retransmit request may be sent.

5

ARP AND RARP

In some protocols related to Ethernet, such as the IEEE 802.3, the overall layout of the frame is the same but slight variations in the contents are used. With 802.3, the 16 bits used by Ethernet to identify the protocol type are replaced with a 16-bit value for the length of the data block. Also, a new field appends the data area itself.

IP Addresses

As mentioned before, TCP/IP uses a 32-bit address to identify any machine on a network and the network to which it is attached. IP addresses identify a machine's connection to the network, not the machine itself; this is an important distinction. Whenever a machine's location on the network is moved, the IP address must sometimes be changed, too, depending on the way in which the network is set up. The IP address is the set of numbers many people see on their workstations or terminals, such as 128.40.8.72, which uniquely identifies the device. IP addresses are four sets of 8 bits, for the total 32 bits. IP addresses are assigned only by the *Network Information Center* (NIC), although if a network is not connected to the Internet that network can determine its own numbering. The decimal notation used for IP addresses is properly called *dotted-quad notation* or just the *dotted-decimal notation*.

Four formats are used for the IP address, depending on the size of the network. The four formats, Class A through Class D, are shown in Figure 5.3. The class is identified by the first few bit sequences, shown in the figure as one bit for Class A and up to four bits for Class D. The class can be determined from the first three (high-order) bits. In fact, in most cases, the first two bits are enough, because there are few Class D networks.

FIGURE 5.3

The four IP address class structures.

Class A | 0 | Network (7 bits) | Local Address (24 bits)

Class B | 10 | Network (14 bits) | Local Address (16 bits)

Class C | 110 | Network (21 bits) | Local Address (8 bits)

Class D | 1110 | Multicast Address (28 bits)

Class A addresses are for large networks that have many machines. The 24 bits for the local address (also frequently called the host address) are needed in these cases. The network address is kept to seven bits, which limits the number of networks that can be identified.

Class B addresses are for intermediate-sized networks, with 16-bit local or host addresses and 14-bit network addresses.

Class C networks have only eight bits for the local or host address, limiting the number of devices to 256. There are 21 bits for the network address.

Finally, Class D networks are used for multicasting purposes, when a general broadcast to more than one device is required.

From an IP address, a network gateway can determine whether the data is to be sent out to the Internet (or other internetwork) or remain in the local area network. If the network address portion of the destination address is the same as the address of the network to which the sender is connected (directly connected network), the destination is on the directly connected network and the internetwork is avoided. All other network addresses are routed to a router (historically called the gateway on the Internet) so that they can leave the local network (*indirect host*).

It is possible for a machine (especially a router) to have more than one IP address if it is connected to more than one network. These machines are called *multihomed* because they have a unique address for each network to which they are connected. Two networks can have the same network address if they are connected by a gateway, which is an addressing problem because the gateway must be able to differentiate which network the physical address is on. This problem is handled by a special protocol—the *Address Resolution Protocol* (ARP)—that deals only with address resolution.

Overview of the Address Resolution Protocol

In order to send datagrams from one machine to another on a local or wide area network, the sender needs to know the destination machine's physical address, if it is not known. There needs to be some method to resolve the IP addresses (provided by applications) into the physical addresses of the hardware connecting each machine to the network.

The brute-force method of providing an IP address to physical address resolution is to build a table of conversions on each machine. Then, when an application sends data to another machine, the software can examine the conversion table for the physical address. This method has a variety of problems associated with it, which is why almost no one does it. The primary disadvantage is the need to constantly update the tables of addresses on each machine whenever there is a change.

The Address Resolution Protocol was developed to help solve this problem. ARP's task is to convert IP addresses to physical addresses (network and local) and in doing so, eliminate the need for applications to know anything about physical addresses. Put in its simplest terms, ARP is a conversion table of IP addresses and their corresponding physical addresses. This is called an *ARP table*. The ARP table is usually built dynamically, although static entries can be manually added for troubleshooting and fixing ARP corruption table problems.

The layout of an ARP table is shown in Figure 5.4. ARP also maintains a cache of entries in memory, called an *ARP cache*. Usually the ARP cache is searched for a match, then the ARP table is checked if one is not found in the cache. Dynamically generated ARP cache entries are timed-out after the ARP cache timeout has been exceeded, whereas static entries are not meant to be timed out. Static entries being timed-out indicates a corruption problem in the ARP cache tables.

FIGURE 5.4

The ARP table layout, whereby each row in the table represents one device in the cache.

	IF INDEX	PHYSICAL ADDRESS	IP ADDRESS	TYPE
Entry 1				
Entry 2				
Entry 3				
Entry n				

The ARP Cache

Each row in the ARP cache corresponds to one device, with the following four pieces of information stored for each device:

- IF Index—The physical port (interface)
- Physical Address—The physical address of the device
- IP Address—The IP address corresponding to the physical address
- Type—The type of entry to which this line corresponds

The type has one of four possible values. A value of 2 means the entry is invalid; a value of 3 means the mapping is dynamic (the entry may change); a value of 4 means static (the entry doesn't change); and a value of 1 means none of the above.

When ARP is handed an IP address to discover the corresponding physical address, it searches the ARP cache and ARP table for a match. If it finds one, it returns the physical address to whoever supplied the IP address. If ARP doesn't find a match for an IP address, it sends a message out on the network. The message, called an *ARP request*, is a broadcast that is received by all devices on the local network.

The ARP request contains the IP address of the intended recipient device. If a device recognizes the IP address as belonging to it, the device sends a reply message containing its physical address back to the machine that generated the ARP request, which places the information into its ARP table and cache for future use. In this manner, ARP can determine the physical address for any machine based on its IP address.

The layout of an ARP request or ARP reply is shown in Figure 5.5. When an ARP request is sent, all fields in the layout are used except the Recipient Hardware Address (which the request is trying to identify). In an ARP reply, all the fields are used.

FIGURE 5.5

The ARP request and reply layout.

Hardware Type (16 bits)	
Protocol Type (16 bits)	
Hardware Address Length	Protocol Address Length
Operation Code (16 bits)	
Sender Hardware Address	
Sender IP Address	
Recipient Hardware Address	
Recipient IP Address	

The fields in the ARP request and reply can have several values. The remainder of this section presents a look at each of the fields in a little more detail to show their uses.

Hardware Type

The hardware type identifies the type of hardware interface. Legal values are

Type	Description
1	Ethernet
2	Experimental Ethernet
3	X.25
4	Proteon ProNET (Token Ring)
5	Chaos
6	IEEE 802.X
7	ARCnet
8	Hyperchannel
9	Lanstar
10	Autonet Short Address
11	LocalTalk
12	LocalNet
13	Ultra link
14	SMDS
15	Frame Relay
16	Asynchronous Transmission Mode (ATM)
17	HDLC
18	Fibre Channel
19	Asynchronous Transmission Mode (ATM)
20	Serial Line
21	Asynchronous Transmission Mode (ATM)

Protocol Type

The protocol type identifies the type of protocol the sending device is using. With TCP/IP, these protocols are usually an EtherType, for which the legal values are as follows:

Decimal	Description
512	XEROX PUP
513	PUP Address Translation
1536	XEROX NS IDP
2048	Internet Protocol (IP)
2049	X.75
2050	NBS

Decimal	Description
2051	ECMA
2052	Chaosnet
2053	X.25 Level 3
2054	Address Resolution Protocol (ARP)
2055	XNS
4096	Berkeley Trailer
21000	BBN Simnet
24577	DEC MOP Dump/Load
24578	DEC MOP Remote Console
24579	DEC DECnet Phase IV
24580	DEC LAT
24582	DEC
24583	DEC
32773	HP Probe
32784	Excelan
32821	Reverse ARP
32823	AppleTalk
32824	DEC LANBridge

If the protocol is not EtherType, other values are allowed.

Hardware Address Length

Hardware address length is the length of each hardware address in the datagram, given in bytes. For Ethernet networks, this value is set to 4 bytes.

Protocol Address Length

Protocol address length is the length of the protocol address in the datagram, given in bytes. For the IP protocol, the protocol address length is set to 4 bytes.

Operation Code (Opcode)

The Opcode indicates whether the datagram is an ARP request or an ARP reply. If it is an ARP request, the value is set to 1. If the datagram is an ARP reply, the value is set to 2.

5

ARP AND RARP

Sender Hardware Address

The sender hardware address is the hardware address of the sending device.

Sender IP Address

The sender IP address is the IP address of the sending device.

Recipient Hardware Address

The recipient hardware address is the hardware address of the recipient device.

Recipient IP Address

The recipient IP address is the IP address of the recipient device.

Details of ARP Operation

As an IP packet is sent through the network layers of nodes in a TCP/IP internet, the routing component of the Network Layer determines the IP address of the next router.

The routing component of the Network Layer determines whether the IP datagram is to be sent to a host on the local network or a host on a different network segment.

If the sender host determines that the destination is on the local network, it needs to find the destination's hardware address. If the destination is on a remote network (different network than the local network) then the sender needs to find the hardware address of the router port to which the IP datagram is to be forwarded.

For broadcast networks ARP is used to find the hardware address of the target node which is either the node on the local network or the router port on the local network.

ARP is implemented as part of the IP module in networks that need address resolution such as broadcast LANs (Ethernet, Token Ring and so on). The ARP protocol is directly encapsulated by the Data Link Layer protocol; it is not encapsulated by the IP protocol. This means that the ARP protocol cannot be routed; that is, it cannot cross a router boundary.

Before sending the ARP request, the ARP module tries to find the target address in its local cache, also called the ARP cache table. The ARP cache table keeps pairs of entries of IP addresses and the corresponding hardware address.

If the target IP address is found in the ARP cache table, it looks up the corresponding hardware address and returns it to the ARP module. The ARP module returns the hardware address to the network driver that made the request for discovering the target node's hardware address. The network driver then transmits a Data Link Layer frame containing the IP datagram with the target node's hardware address placed in the destination hardware address field. In the scenario just discussed, an ARP request is never generated, because the target node's hardware address was discovered in the local cache.

What happens if the ARP cache does not contain the target node's hardware address? In this case, the ARP module generates a Data Link Layer frame containing the ARP request to discover the target node's hardware address. The ARP request is broadcast at the Data Link Layer to all nodes on the local network segment. As mentioned earlier, the ARP request/replies are confined to the local network segment and do not cross router boundaries.

When an ARP request is received, the Data Link Layer at the target node gives the packet to the Address Resolution module. The ARP request is broadcast at the Data Link level, so all nodes on the local network will receive it. However, only the node whose IP address corresponds to the Target IP address will respond with an ARP reply.

The steps performed by the ARP module at the receiving node are outlined here:

1. First, the node checks to see whether it recognizes the hardware type in the Hardware Type field of the ARP request packet. If it does recognize the hardware type, it optionally checks the hardware length Hlen in the ARP request packet.

2. The node then answers this question, "Do I speak the protocol in the Protocol Type field in ARP request packet?" If the answer is yes, the node optionally checks the protocol length Plen in the ARP request packet.

3. The Set Merge_flag is set to *false.*

4. If the pair <protocol type, sender protocol address> is already in the node's translation table, it updates the sender hardware address field of the entry with the new information in the packet and sets the Merge_flag to true.

5. The node then answers the question, "Am I the target protocol address?" This means "Is my IP address the same as that in the Target IP address field?" If the answer is yes, then the following occurs: If the merge flag is false, add the triplet <protocol type, sender protocol address, sender hardware address> to the translation table.

6. Finally, the node answers the question, "Is the Operation field value a request?" If the answer is yes, swap the hardware and protocol fields, putting the local hardware and protocol addresses in the sender fields. See the Operation field to ARP reply. Send the packet to the (new) target hardware address on the same hardware on which the request was received.

5

ARP AND RARP

In the algorithm just described, the <protocol type, sender protocol address, sender hardware address> triplet is merged into the ARP cache table before the Operation field is examined in step 4. This step only occurs if a node has an entry for the sender's IP address in their ARP cache table.

Note that only the ARP cache table for nodes that have an entry for the sender IP address are modified.

Updating or adding ARP cache entries is done because the upper layers of the target node are likely to respond to the ARP request sender; when the target generates a Data Link Layer frame, it will consult its ARP cache table and discover that it already knows the hardware address of the sender. Thus an ARP request to discover the sender's hardware address is not required.

Also note also that if the target node already has an entry in its ARP cache table for the <protocol type, sender protocol address> pair, then the new hardware address replaces the old address. This could occur in any of the following situations:

- New network hardware was added in the ARP request sender to replace the existing one. In this case the hardware address of the node is different.

- The IP addresses were reassigned. The ARP request sender is another node that was assigned the IP address that is in the ARP cache table of the target. The hardware address of the ARP sender is different because it is a different node.

- There is a duplicate address problem. Another node claims to have the same IP address as the one in the target node's ARP cache table.

Although the first two situations are normal, the last situation of duplicate IP addresses is an error condition and is examined in detail in the sections on duplicate IP addresses in this chapter.

The ARP Protocol Design

In theory, the length fields HLen and PLen in the ARP packet format are redundant, because the length of the hardware address and the protocol address can be determined by the value of the Hardware Type and Protocol Type fields. For instance, the Hardware Type field having a value of 1 indicates an Ethernet frame, and this implies an HLen value of 6 octets because Ethernet addresses are 6 octets long. Similarly, if the Protocol Type field indicates an IP protocol, the PLen value is 4 octets because IP addresses are 4 octets long.

The redundant HLen and PLen fields are included for optional consistency checking, and for the use of network monitoring tools.

The Operation field is used to determine whether this is a request or a reply to a previous request. Using a two-octet field is excessive considering the number of the operation codes that have been assigned thus far. In retrospect, a one-octet field would have been sufficient.

The Sender HA and Sender IP address fields are needed because these fields are potentially recorded in the ARP cache tables of the receiving nodes. In the ARP request the Target HA has no meaning because its value is not known. Note that the answer is actually returned in the Sender HA field in the ARP reply. The Target HA is included for completeness and network monitoring.

The Target IP field is necessary in the ARP request so that a machine can determine whether or not it is the target node and therefore needs to send a reply. The Target IP field is not necessarily needed in the ARP reply if one assumes a reply is only provoked by a request. It could be used for network monitoring, and to simplify the ARP request/reply processing algorithm.

Network Monitoring with ARP

ARP can be used by a monitoring device to gain knowledge about the higher level protocol activity by just examining the ARP frame headers. For example, the network-monitoring device can determine which protocols are in use by examining the Protocol Type field value. A monitoring device could be designed along the lines suggested in this section.

When the monitoring device receives an ARP packet, it can enter the protocol type, sender protocol address, and sender hardware address in a table. Additionally, it can determine the length of the hardware and protocol address from the HLen and PLen fields of the ARP packet. Note that ARP requests are broadcast at the Data Link level, and a monitor receives all ARP requests.

If the Operation field indicates an ARP reply packet, and the target protocol address matches the protocol address of the monitor, the monitor sends an ARP reply like any other target node. The monitor will not receive any other ARP replies because an ARP reply is sent directly to the requesting host.

Timeouts in the ARP Cache Table

ARP cache tables are often implemented with a timeout mechanism. Entries in the ARP cache table may have timestamp values associated with them. The following is a discussion of some of the timeout issues associated with ARP tables.

If a node is moved it is usually shut down before moving. Shutting down a node clears its ARP cache table so old entries will not cause confusion. Other nodes on the network will generally not be aware that a particular node has moved or been shut down.

If the node has been moved to a location on the same network segment, the ARP cache information about the moved node will still be valid because the IP address and hardware address of the moved node will not have changed.

If the node has been shut down, other nodes will not be able to reach this node. They will use their ARP cache information to access the node but be unable to make the connection. An implementation could use the failure to initiate a connection to a node to delete the information in the ARP cache table about the node. It could also try accessing the node by sending a few more ARP requests before giving up.

If the node has been moved to a location on a different network segment, it is behind a router boundary. Because IP addresses contain information about the network segment they are attached to, the IP address of the moved node must change even though its hardware address remains the same. Recall that ARP transmissions do not go beyond a router boundary. For all practical purposes the new node can be assumed to be shut down or unavailable.

An ARP implementation typically updates the timestamps when the address resolution entry is used for transmitting packets to a node. The timestamps are also updated when ARP requests are received from a node whose entry exists in the ARP cache table. If no packets are received from a node for a suitable length of time, called the ARP timeout value, the address resolution entry is discarded.

An ARP implementation may also have an independent process (also called a *daemon* process). This independent process checks the ARP cache table periodically and times-out old entries. In many TCP/IP implementations, a default timeout of 15 minutes is used, and in some implementations this value can be configured by a system administrator.

As a refinement, it is also possible for the ARP daemon to first send an ARP request to the node directly. If an ARP reply is not seen after a few retransmissions, the ARP entry is discarded. In this situation, the ARP request is sent directly and *not broadcast* because the hardware address of the node is known from the ARP cache table. This refinement is common in Linux implementations.

Many TCP/IP implementations allow you to make manual entries in the ARP cache table. Normally, there is no need to make manual entries in the ARP table, as the dynamic ARP operation determines the IP address and hardware associations. ARP entries made manually are not timed out and can be used to fix problems with incorrect entries in the ARP table because of duplicate IP address problems or malfunctioning software. The tool used to view or make changes in the ARP table depends on the operating system: It can be a command-line tool or a graphical tool. A tool called ARP is available on both Windows NT/2000 and UNIX systems. The following shows the syntax for the ARP command for Windows 2000:

```
ARP -s inet_addr eth_addr [if_addr]
ARP -d inet_addr [if_addr]
ARP -a [inet_addr] [-N if_addr]

-a      Displays current ARP entries by interrogating the current
        protocol data. If inet_addr is specified, the IP and Physical
        addresses for only the specified computer are displayed. If
        more than one network interface uses ARP, entries for each ARP
        table are displayed.
-g      Same as -a.
inet_addr   Specifies an internet address.
-N if_addr  Displays the ARP entries for the network interface specified
        by if_addr.
-d      Deletes the host specified by inet_addr. inet_addr may be
        wildcarded with * to delete all hosts.
-s      Adds the host and associates the Internet address inet_addr
        with the Physical address eth_addr. The Physical address is
        given as 6 hexadecimal bytes separated by hyphens. The entry
        is permanent.
eth_addr    Specifies a physical address.
if_addr     If present, this specifies the Internet address of the
        interface whose address translation table should be modified.
        If not present, the first applicable interface will be used.
Example:
> arp -s 157.55.85.212  00-aa-00-62-c6-09 .... Adds a static entry.
> arp -a                 .... Displays the arp table.
```

ARP in Bridged Networks

Networks can be interconnected by using bridge devices that operate at OSI layer 2 and routers that operate at OSI layer 3. Bridges extend the range of LANs. ARP operation on LANs requires special discussion, which is the focus of this section.

When a TCP/IP connection fails, the TCP protocol, which is responsible for reliable delivery, attempts to recover from the failure by retransmitting packets. If the failure was caused by a physical link failure and other paths to the destination are available, the IP datagrams get routed around the failed link. If TCP is unable to recover from the failure, recovery continues at the lower layers. At the lower layers, the ARP module attempts to recover from the connection by broadcasting ARP requests. If the target node is on the local network segment, this is viable technique for recovering from failure. However, a complication arises when the several nodes start sending ARP request broadcasts. This could happen when a central host is no longer available because of host or link failure.

If 100 stations are connected to a central host on the network, and the connection to the host goes down, all 100 stations will start transmitting ARP broadcasts simultaneously. On some systems, ARP requests are sent every second. One hundred stations sending ARP broadcasts results in 100 broadcast packets being sent every second. This broadcast traffic will cause a significant amount of network traffic that would affect the network availability to other nodes on the network.

Broadcast traffic could even slow down nodes not currently accessing the network. This is because the network board and the associated software driver must examine every broadcast packet. In the case of ARP requests, the ARP module will also be executed for every broadcast request. Processing even 50 ARP requests/second can take a fair amount of processing power and have a significant slowdown effect on a node. As a result all nodes on the network will appear to slow down.

The repeated ARP broadcasts create further complications in a bridged network. Network segments separated by bridges are considered to be part of the same MAC domain. ARP requests/replies must be transmitted across these bridges. Propagation of broadcast traffic across bridges can have a multiplying effect and the network traffic could increase even more. Creating a large or complex network topology using bridges is therefore not desirable under these conditions.

Duplicate Addresses and ARP

IP addresses on a network must be unique. How do you ensure this uniqueness? You ensure it by proper documentation and assignment of IP addresses. Because of the human element involved in assigning IP addresses, inadvertently assigning nodes on a network with the same IP address is possible. When this happens, chaos and confusion ensues. Networked applications work intermittently or sometimes mysteriously stop working altogether.

To help you understand the effect of duplicate IP addresses, the following sections discuss two scenarios:

- Duplicate IP addresses at TCP/IP clients
- Duplicate IP addresses at TCP/IP servers

Duplicate IP Addresses at TCP/IP Clients

Consider the situation where two TCP/IP clients called "workstation 1" and "workstation 2" access a central TCP/IP server at IP address 144.19.74.102. The server's hardware address is 080020021545.

Workstations 1 and 2 are using the same IP address of 144.19.74.1. Their hardware addresses are 0000C0085121 and 0000C0075106, respectively.

Workstation 1 starts an FTP session with the TCP/IP server. Before the FTP session starts, workstation 1 will issue an ARP broadcast request to discover the hardware address of the TCP/IP server. On receiving the ARP request, the TCP/IP server will add an entry for the ARP request sender (workstation 1) in its ARP cache table, and send an ARP reply to the sender. On receiving the ARP reply, workstation 1 will add an entry for the TCP/IP server in its local ARP cache table. At this point the ARP cache tables for the TCP/IP server and workstation 1 are as follows:

TCP/IP server:

IP Address	Hardware Address
144.19.74.1	0000C0085121

Workstation 1:

IP Address	Hardware Address
144.19.74.102	080020021545

In the second phase, workstation 2 attempts to establish a TCP/IP session (perhaps another FTP session) to the same TCP/IP server.

Before making the connection, workstation 2 must discover the TCP/IP server's hardware address. It attempts to do just that by sending an ARP request. On receiving the ARP request, the TCP/IP server will want to add an entry for the ARP request sender (workstation 2) in its ARP cache table, and send an ARP reply to the sender. The TCP/IP server will find that there is already an entry for 144.19.74.1 in its ARP cache table. As per RFC 826 on the Address Resolution Protocol, the TCP/IP server must replace the existing entry with the new one. Most TCP/IP implementations will perform this replacement silently without issuing any warning of a potential duplicate IP address problem. Some TCP/IP implementations will issue a warning of a potential duplicate IP address problem. The TCP/IP server will reply to the ARP request from workstation 2. On receiving the ARP reply, workstation 2 will add an entry for the TCP/IP server in its local ARP cache table. At this point the ARP cache tables for the TCP/IP server and workstation 2 are as follows:

TCP/IP server:

IP Address	Hardware Address
144.19.74.1	0000C0075106

5

ARP AND RARP

Workstation 2:

IP Address	Hardware Address
144.19.74.102	080020021545

When the TCP/IP server wants to send data to workstation 1, it will look up the hardware address of workstation 1 at IP address 144.19.74.1 in its local ARP cache table and send the data to this hardware address. Unfortunately, this is workstation 2's hardware address, and the data will be sent to workstation 2. Workstation 1 on not receiving expected data will try to resend its last transmission, and the TCP/IP server will continue sending the response to workstation 2. Workstation 1 will therefore "hang" waiting for a response. It will eventually time-out, or the workstation may have to be rebooted to recover from the error. In any case, an application that was working fine some time ago may suddenly stop working, much to the consternation of the user and system administrator alike!

Workstation 2 on receiving unexpected data destined for workstation 1 will probably reject it, optionally generate an error message, and continue with its session with the TCP/IP server. Alternatively, workstation 2 can become confused with unexpected data and also "hang."

If the user at workstation 1 reboots the "hung" computer and tries to reconnect to the TCP/IP server, the ARP cache entry for workstation 2 at the TCP/IP server will be replaced with that for workstation 1. This will cause workstation 2 to "hang," and the situation could repeat until the users give up in frustration.

If the users at workstations 1 and 2 are not in communication with each other about the problems they are experiencing, each will experience his or her side of the story—that is, the workstation "hangs" unexpectedly in the middle of accessing the TCP/IP server. If the users do not access the TCP/IP server at the same time, they will never experience this problem and the duplicate IP address problem will go undetected. If the users experience the problem occasionally, they may dismiss the problem as a fluke on the network and never report it. Again, the problem will go undetected.

Duplicate IP Addresses at TCP/IP Servers

Consider the situation where there are two TCP/IP servers called "server 1" and "server 2." They are both set to the duplicate IP address of 144.19.74.102. The servers' hardware addresses are 080020021545 and AA0004126750, respectively.

A workstation with the IP address 144.19.74.1 tries to access the TCP/IP server at 144.19.74.102. The workstation's hardware address is 0000C0085121.

The workstation tries to connect with server 2. Before making the TCP/IP connection, the workstation will issue an ARP broadcast request to discover the hardware address of the TCP/IP server. There are two TCP/IP servers at the same target IP address of 144.19.74.102. On receiving the ARP request, both servers 1 and 2 will add an entry for the ARP request sender (workstation) in their local ARP cache tables, and send an ARP reply to the sender. Two responses are sent on the network. The workstation accepts the first ARP reply and silently ignores the second response. If server 2's ARP reply reaches the workstation first, the workstation will add an entry for server 2 in its local ARP cache table. At this point the ARP cache tables for the servers and the workstation are as follows:

Server 1:

IP Address	Hardware Address
144.19.74.1	0000C0085121

Server 2:

IP Address	Hardware Address
144.19.74.1	AA0004126750

Workstation:

IP Address	Hardware Address
144.19.74.102	080020021545

The workstation will then continue interacting with server 2, instead of server 1 as it had originally intended. If server 2 does not have the expected service, the connection will fail, and the user will experience an error message about the service not being supported at the server. This would be puzzling to the user, especially if the user had successfully accessed services at server 1 on prior occasions.

If server 2 has the service that the workstation expects, the user will attempt to log on to that service. If the service is Telnet or FTP, a user login and password will be required. If the user is not alert, he or she may not notice that the FTP server or Telnet server name/version number reported on the screen is different from the one he or she expects. If the user does not have a logon account with the same name and password as server 1, logon will be denied. If the logon account and password are the same on both servers, the user will log on to the wrong server. The user may not find the files or data he or she is expecting because he or she has logged on to the wrong server.

If the server is a *multihomed* host (a server with multiple network connections) that acts as a router, there may be the possibility of even more confusion because packets destined to outside networks may not follow the expected route or may not get delivered because the wrong server has accepted the packets for delivery.

The ARP Duplicate Address Test

Many TCP/IP implementations broadcast an ARP request on startup. The ARP request is sent with the Target IP field in the ARP request set to that of the node that is starting up.

The purpose of this initial ARP request is to discover whether any nodes have a duplicate IP address. If an ARP reply is received, another node (the one generating the ARP reply) has the same IP address as that of the node that is booting up. The node that is starting up should report the duplicate IP address in a suitable manner. It is even possible for the node responding to the ARP request to do an extra check on the Sender IP field in the ARP request packet to see whether it is the same as its own IP address. If the Sender IP and Target IP address fields match, the responding node can generate a suitable alert about a duplicate IP address problem.

The initial ARP frame can only discover duplicate IP address problems on the same network segment. Because ARP packets do not cross router boundaries, they cannot detect duplicate IP address problems for network segments connected by routers.

Another function of the initial ARP broadcast is for nodes that have an entry for the node that is starting up to update their ARP cache table. If the node that is starting up has a different hardware address (because the network hardware was changed), all nodes receiving the ARP broadcast discard the old hardware address and update their ARP cache tables with the new hardware address.

Proxy ARP

Earlier in this chapter, you saw that two networks connected through a gateway can have the same network address. The gateway has to determine to which of the networks the physical address or IP address of an incoming datagram corresponds. The gateway can do this with a modified ARP called *Proxy ARP* (sometimes called Promiscuous ARP).

Proxy ARP creates an ARP cache consisting of entries from both networks. The gateway has to manage the ARP requests and replies that cross the two networks. By combining two ARP caches into one, Proxy ARP adds flexibility to the resolution process and prevents excessive request and reply ARP datagrams whenever an address has to cross a network gateway.

Reverse Address Resolution Protocol

If a device doesn't know its own IP address, there is no way to generate ARP requests and ARP replies. This is often the case when a device such as a diskless workstation is on the network. The only address the device is aware of is the physical address set on the network interface card.

A simple solution is the *Reverse Address Resolution Protocol* (RARP), which works as the reverse of ARP. RARP sends out the physical address of a destination and expects back an IP address. The reply containing the IP address is sent by a RARP server, a machine that can supply the information. Although the originating device sends the message as a broadcast, RARP rules stipulate that only the RARP server can generate a reply. Many networks assign more than one RARP server, both to spread the processing load and to act as a backup in case of problems.

RARP is often used in "diskless stations" that do not have local storage. Modern diskless stations may actually have a local disk, but this disk is used for speeding up the operation of the operating system and not for storing TCP/IP-related parameters, which are kept at a remote server. For example, the local disk may only be used for holding a local swap area needed to implement the operating system's virtual memory mechanism.

Diskless stations also have a copy of the operating system image kept on remote servers. On startup the diskless station downloads a copy of the operating system image from the remote server to its memory. Before the diskless station can download its operating system image using TCP/IP file transfer protocols, it needs an IP address. This IP address cannot be a random value; it must be unique and have the same prefix as the IP addresses of other nodes on that network segment. For example, if other stations on the network have IP addresses like 199.245.180.1, 199.245.180.5, 199.245.180.7, then the common prefix is "199.245.180". The diskless station must also have the same common prefix. A common prefix is needed because information on how to route to a network segment is embedded as a prefix value in the IP address.

The diskless station typically obtains its IP address by sending a request to servers on that network segment. Because it does not know the address information of the remote server, this request is sent as a Data Link Layer broadcast. One mechanism to obtain IP addresses from remote servers is the Reverse Address Resolution Protocol (RARP). The protocol is called Reverse ARP, because the information it seeks is opposite to that sought by the ARP protocol.

Diskless stations are used to reduce hardware costs, simplify node configuration and upgrades by keeping critical information in a central location, and reduce the possibility of viruses being introduced because the users cannot easily introduce programs through diskless workstations.

RARP Operation

In RARP operation, the node that wants to discover its IP address (called the RARP client) broadcasts a request called the RARP request. The RARP request is broadcast at the Data Link Layer because the RARP client does not know the address (hardware or IP address) of the remote server. The remote server that processes the RARP request is called the RARP server. All nodes on the network segment will receive the RARP request broadcast, but only the nodes acting as RARP servers will respond.

If there is more than one RARP server, all RARP servers will attempt to process the RARP request. The RARP client will typically accept the first response it receives and silently ignore the rest.

The RARP server keeps a table of the IP address for nodes on the network segment. This table is indexed by a unique identifier that is specific to each machine. This unique identifier is sent in the RARP request. For diskless stations this unique identifier must be some hardware-specific parameter that it can easily read. The identifier cannot be a value stored in local storage because diskless stations do not have a local disk available for this purpose. The RARP designers (see STD 38, RFC 903) decided to use the hardware addresses as unique identifiers because they are unique for a network segment and can be easily read by the network drivers.

When a RARP server receives a RARP request, it consults its table of IP address and hardware address bindings (see Figure 5.6). If it finds an entry in the RARP table that matches the hardware address found in the RARP request, it returns the corresponding IP address in a RARP reply. The RARP reply is not broadcast because the RARP server looks up the hardware address of the RARP client from the RARP request.

The RARP request and reply packets use the same packet format as ARP packets. The difference between ARP and RARP is the values that are placed in the fields. When RARP packets are in an Ethernet frame, an EtherType value of 8035 hex is used.

FIGURE 5.6

*RARP operation.
(Courtesy of
Learning Tree)*

RARP Operation

• RARP uses same packet structure as ARP

The RARP request fields are filled in as follows.

RARP Request:

> Data Link Destination Hardware Address = *Broadcast*
>
> Data Link Source Hardware Address = RARP client HA
>
> DataLink EtherType = 8035 hex
>
> Operation = 3 (RARP Request)
>
> Sender HA = RARP client HA
>
> Sender IP = Undefined; Usually 0.0.0.0 used
>
> Target HA = RARP client HA
>
> Target IP = Undefined

RARP Reply:

> Data Link Destination Hardware Address = RARP client HA
>
> Data Link Source Hardware Address = RARP server HA
>
> DataLink EtherType = 8035 hex

5

ARP AND RARP

>Operation = 4 (RARP Reply)
>
>Sender HA = RARP server HA
>
>Sender IP = RARP server IP address
>
>Target HA = RARP client HA
>
>Target IP = RARP client IP address; This is the answer

The Target HA address field in the RARP request is set to that of the RARP client. This is done as a convenience for the RARP server that does not then have to modify this field, because it contains the RARP client hardware address in the RARP reply.

The network driver can examine the EtherType field and know that this is a RARP packet (EtherType = 8035 hex) and send the request to the RARP module. The Operation code fields used for RARP are 3 for RARP request and 4 for RARP reply. These fields could also be used to distinguish an ARP packet from a RARP packet. However, this approach is not very efficient because the ARP module would have to examine the Operation field first, and if this indicated a RARP packet, the ARP module would then send it to the RARP module. By using the EtherType field protocol, demultiplexing can be done efficiently at a lower layer.

Note

In many implementations RARP is not automatically provided by the ARP or IP module. It must be run as a separate process, such as a daemon process, on the computer that is to act as a RARP server.

RARP Storms

If the RARP server is unavailable because of a hardware link failure or because the RARP server is down, RARP clients will be unable to boot up. RARP clients will continually send out RARP broadcast requests. If many RARP clients simultaneously send out RARP request broadcasts, then a heavy network traffic load results.

The situation of not receiving a RARP reply is more serious than not receiving an ARP reply. Not receiving an ARP reply means that a particular host and its services are not available. The ARP client can still try to access other nodes on the network. However, if there is no RARP reply, the RARP client cannot boot up. Many RARP clients continue to send RARP broadcast requests indefinitely in the hope that the RARP server may eventually become available. The situation of repeated RARP broadcast requests is therefore more serious than that of ARP requests because it can result in greater network traffic.

Primary and Backup RARP Servers

To make the availability of RARP services more reliable, multiple RARP servers can be used. With multiple RARP servers, all servers would attempt to answer to the RARP broadcast request simultaneously. Only one of the RARP replies is used by the RARP client; all other RARP replies are discarded as to not use up network bandwidth. One scheme to prevent multiple RARP replies is to designate one of the RARP servers as a primary and all others as secondary RARP servers.

On receiving a RARP request, the primary RARP server will respond to the request. The secondary servers do not respond, but note the arrival time of the RARP request. If the primary does not respond within a timeout interval, the secondary RARP server assumes that the primary RARP server is down, and responds to the RARP request.

If there are multiple secondary RARP servers, all secondary servers will attempt to respond at the same time. A refinement of this scheme is to have secondary RARP servers wait for a random time interval before responding. If the primary server is functioning normally, there will be no additional delays in sending the RARP reply. If the primary server is down, there may be a small random delay before one of the secondary RARP server responds.

Using the ARP Command

Most implementations of TCP/IP (but not all) provide a way for you to check the ARP cache. Both UNIX and Windows NT/2000/XP implement the arp command. The arp command shows you all the entries in the machine's cache. To see the cache contents, issue the command with the -a (for all) option:

```
$ arp -a
brutus <205.150.89.3> at 0:0:d2:03:08:10
```

In this case, one machine called brutus has the IP address 205.150.89.3 and the MAC (Media Access Control) address 0:0:d2:03:08:10.

The arp command is seldom used except when a network administrator is trying to resolve the problem of duplicate IP addresses. If there are two machines with the same address (but with different MACs), they will show up in the ARP cache.

Summary

In this chapter, you have seen the address resolution protocols in common use: ARP, Proxy ARP, and RARP. The chapter started off with a look at how Ethernet frames are

5

ARP AND RARP

assembled on top of the TCP/IP datagrams. With all these layers of complexity in inter-networking, you should be getting a good idea of how TCP/IP functions and how data is passed over networks to destination machines.

DNS: Name Services

by Rima S. Regas and
Karanjit S. Siyan, Ph.D.

IN THIS CHAPTER

In the early ARPANET when the network was small, users on a network were required to maintain a HOSTS configuration file. This file contained all the information the workstation needed in order to communicate with the other systems on the network. Problems were prevalent, however, because each machine's HOSTS file needed to be updated separately, by hand. There was little or no automated configuration, making updates tedious and time-consuming.

A HOSTS file contains information about which IPs are assigned to what name. When the computer needed to locate another computer on the network, it would look at the local HOSTS file. If the computer did not have an entry in the HOSTS file, it essentially did not exist. *Domain Name System* (DNS) changed this situation drastically. DNS allowed systems administrators to use a server as a DNS host. When the computers on the network needed to locate another server, for example, they would look to the HOSTS file.

Today, the HOSTS file is still used, but typically only to prevent a machine on a LAN from using the DNS to look up a local machine. It's much faster this way. In a nutshell, the computer's networking software is directed to look in the local HOSTS file before using the default DNS server. If a match is there, the client software proceeds to communicate with the remote host directly, greatly reducing the time involved in discovering the IP number via DNS.

Domain Name System: The Concept

The technique used to give IP addresses names is *mnemonic*. The term is used to indicate that names are easier to recall than numbers. Although most people have an amazing capacity for remembering phone numbers, addresses, amounts, and other life-related figures, simply far too many IP numbers are in existence to make remembering easy. Hence the naming format. For example, C|Net's domain name is www.cnet.com. There is no vertical slash and there is no capitalization. In comparison to the name of the site, it's rather sterile. It works, though. Mnemonically, it's a perfect match for the site's name. C|Net is one of the largest and most visited sites in the world.

Before there was DNS, the idea was to have a system that would translate a name into its given number. When you translate or resolve a Web site's domain name (for example, www.cnet.com) and find its IP number, (it is 204.162.80.181, in case you were wondering), the IP number is the actual address. This is how the correct Internet content is delivered to your Web browser. This process requires a network of systems called DNS, or Domain Name Service (system, if you talk to certain people), servers.

Part of the job of maintaining a DNS system on the Internet involves providing the primary root domain servers to which the rest of the DNS servers would look to find the top-level domains registered on the Internet. DNS information is distributed across many DNS servers. If your DNS server cannot resolve the domain name to an IP address, that server contacts another DNS server that is expected to know more information about the name to be resolved. If that DNS server is unable to resolve the domain name, it can return a referral to another DNS server that might know the answer. This process is repeated until a timeout is reached. An error is then returned to the initiating IP and, if the client is capable, an error message is displayed. In the case of a Web site that cannot be found, the browser will display an error message stating that it was unable to locate the server or there was a DNS error.

The referral mechanism described in the previous paragraph is typically used by DNS servers when they query other DNS servers. This type of DNS query is called an *iterative* query. The DNS resolver, which is another name for a DNS client, resides on the node that issues the DNS query. The DNS resolver does not issue an iterative query. Instead, the DNS resolver issues another type of query called a *recursive* query. In a recursive query, the node issuing the query to the DNS server expects that DNS server to return the final answer or a response indicating that the name could not be resolved. When a DNS server receives a recursive query it does not return a referral to another DNS server; it is expected to do iterative queries to obtain the final answer.

Hierarchical by virtue of its organizational structure, DNS cascades from the top-level DNS root servers and propagates names and IPs to servers located all around the world. An example that clearly shows how the system is hierarchical is as simple as a DNS server that does not have a translation stored locally. When it cannot find the IP in its own databases, it seeks out another DNS server to see whether it has the IP address, and so on until it either times out or finds it. The following section takes a closer look at the structure because there is another, more important aspect to the hierarchy.

DNS Hierarchical Organization

In the original RFC #819 (Request For Comments) document published in 1982, Zaw-Sing Su and Jon Postel laid out the concepts and plans for the DNS. Here's an example of the language they used.

> The set of domains forms a hierarchy. Using a graph theory representation, this hierarchy may be modeled as a directed graph. A directed graph consists of a set of nodes and a collection of arcs, where arcs are identified by ordered pairs of distinct nodes [1]. Each node of the graph represents a domain. An ordered pair (B, A), an arc from B to A, indicates that B is a subdomain of domain A, and B is a simple name unique within A.

This is not very easily understood, if comprehensible at all, so we will go through the concepts in a simpler fashion. The principle is simple. You have a top-level domain, like COM or EDU. COM and EDU domains represent the highest domain level and cannot be super-seded. There is, however, one exception. In truth, there should be a period after COM (COM.). That period is an even higher domain than COM called the root domain. Top-level domains (such as COM, EDU, and ORG) are referred to as a Naming Universe because they contain the domains and subdomains that are placed below them in the hierarchy, much like the roots of a tree.

From the top level you move into the intermediate domains or the second-level domains. Examples of intermediate domains include coke.com, whitehouse.gov, and disney.com. These can be registered, but are usually only done so to cover a range of related domain names. Registering a complete domain in a subdomain, or Endpoint domain as Su and Postel referred to it, is common. Examples of these are www.coke.com, www.whitehouse.gov, and www.disney.com. Of course, these are all representational of domains in the InterNIC registration system. Other systems outside the United States use different conventions to indicate location and country of origin. For example, www.bbc.co.uk indicates that the BBC's Web site is a commercial concern (CO, which is similar to COM) and is located in the United Kingdom (UK).

Figure 6.1 shows Su and Postel's original Domain Hierarchy figure illustrating the branching possibilities.

FIGURE 6.1

An illustration of the original domain hierarchy.

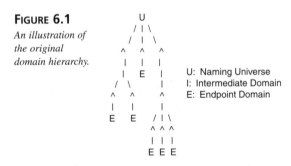

Subdomains can be just about anything. Examples of this are www.netscape.com, home.netscape.com, and www1.netscape.com. All of these could be very different places on the Internet and often will contain different information. Of course, all of these could point to one site and one page if the Webmaster so chose. That is the case with the Netscape site; it can be reached by all the listed URLs.

Note

As another example, Webopædia chose to also register webopedia.com as a sub-domain because many people had trouble with the classic greek character æ.

Delegating Authority

DNS is arranged in a way that allows servers subordinate to the root name servers to take over control of a given domain. A good example of this would be a local ISP that hosts Web sites for people and companies. When Company X registers its domain name (www.companyx.com) with InterNIC, it declares the Primary and Secondary DNS servers of its ISP as its DNS servers. InterNIC puts the information into its .COM root server and allows it to propagate.

Note

DNS servers periodically synchronize their local database with various other databases on other DNS servers and check for new entries on the root servers. This process is commonly referred to as *propagation*. Domain name registration is by no means instantaneous, but a newly registered domain name will propagate in roughly three to four days, making it available around the world.

In order for this system to work there needed to be a way of determining where a machine was located on the network. This need gave rise to the system hierarchy, a means of categorizing each machine in relation to its function. For example, if the machine in question was located at an educational institution, it would be located in the top-level domain known as .EDU. If the site was commercial or civilian in nature, it would be placed in the .COM top-level domain, and so on. This concept forms the root of the DNS hierarchy, but not the root name servers (we'll get to more on that shortly).

DNS Distributed Database

The DNS distributed database architecture is quite powerful. As previously stated, authority is delegated to other servers that are better positioned to handle the traffic for a domain or subdomain. The manner in which the information is propagated to the servers is via a thorough distribution plan.

Each domain has an owner assigned to it. This is defined as part of the domain's *Start of Authority* (SOA), which is covered a little later in greater detail. The top-level domain, for example COM., delegates authority for a domain name, such as disney.com, to the DNS servers specified to act as the primary DNS server. This relieves the top-level domain controller from being burdened with handling every single DNS query on the Internet.

After an SOA is associated with a domain controller, it can delegate subdomain control to other DNS servers, and so on. This is the manner in which delegation is distributed down the DNS server hierarchy from the topmost level to the bottom.

Domains and Zones

Domains and zones are often paired together, but there is a subtle difference. A zone is the primary domain in a naming universe that is delegated to another DNS server for administrative purposes. Whereas Disney.com is a zone, www.disney.com is a host in that zone. A zone can consist of a single domain or several subdomains. For example, Disney could have subdomains called east-coast.Disney.com and west-coast.Disney.com. If these subdomains are delegated, they will form a separate zone called east-coast.Disney.com and west-coast.Disney.com, which will have their own DNS servers. If these subdomains are not delegated, they are part of the zone Disney.com and are handled by the DNS servers for the Disney.com server.

Administrative duties are delegated to the primary DNS server. The primary DNS server for Disney's site is huey.disney.com and its IP is 204.128.192.10. Because Huey is designated the primary DNS for Disney, it is also the primary DNS for the zone of Disney.com. The designated owner for this server is root@huey.disney.com, which is shown in the SOA as root.huey.disney.com.

> **Note**
>
> Be aware that a properly formatted SOA will change the administrator's email address to all periods, removing the @ symbol common to all email addresses. Some companies like to format email addresses with a separator preceding the @. This is problematic because, for example, an administrator's email address that is formatted as host.admin@example.com would be shown in the SOA as host.admin.example.com. Any system attempting to resolve that would assume host@admin.example.com and would receive a DNS error (assuming that it is not a valid address).

Internet Top-Level Domains

There are a number of top-level domains (TLD), the most familiar of which are COM, EDU, GOV, MIL, NET, and ORG. There are, however, many, many more. Most of the unfamiliar ones are located in other countries. Each country has its own two-letter TLD. UK is the TLD for the United Kingdom (actually, the official TLD is GB, but this is not commonly used), NZ for New Zealand, JP for Japan, and so on. An example of a TLD in use would be www.bbc.co.uk.

> **Note**
>
> More domains are involved in foreign addresses than in the States. The CO indicates a commercial concern, much like the InterNICs COM.

> **Caution**
>
> There is nothing to prevent people from registering domains in other countries even though the server would not even be near the country indicated in the URL.

Choosing a Name Server

You can select a name server on many platforms, such as Windows NT/2000/XP, UNIX, NetWare, Macintosh, and so on. Windows NT/2000 comes with DNS server implementations. Apple has a free DNS server called MacDNS. UNIX systems have the ever-present and reliable BIND to fall back on. There are, however, still a number of powerful third-party DNS servers available.

A good site to evaluate DNS servers is Dave Central (www.davecentral.com) and Tucows (www.tucows.com, and be prepared to select a local server affiliate). They generally review just about every piece of software that comes through there and give you a good idea of what is available.

Name Service Resolution Process

When a client, such as a browser, puts in a request for a URL, it is passed to the local DNS server, which tries to parse the name into an IP address. If it is successful, it passes the data onward, completing the next leg of the journey, and takes the next request. If the server is unable to locate the address, it has two options, depending on the way the server is configured. Those two are Recursive and Iterative.

Recursive Queries

Recursive queries are the most typical. If the query comes into the server and the A record is located in the cache for the server, no additional searching is needed. If not, it must ask another server, so it moves up the ladder. This is where the *Time to Live* (TTL) comes in. If finding the A record takes too long, the query sputters out and dies in the process. The originating DNS server returns an `address not found` error.

Iterative Queries

Iterative queries are forced to stay local for several reasons, the most common being that another DNS server is not available. The recursion feature may have been turned off in the DNS server you are accessing, but it is unlikely. The server will do its best to locate the best match it can possibly find in its cache. If it is not there, it's not there. An error is returned.

Caching

As the DNS server goes about its business throughout the day, it picks up resources and stores them. These are Resource Records (RRs) that contain information about queried URLs. The TTL also comes into play here. The server will only cache as much as it is allocated and as long as it is valid.

Reverse Resolution (Pointer) Queries

The typical query is forward looking, trying to match a URL with an IP. Reverse resolution is just the opposite, trying to match an IP to a URL. Several utilities will perform this type of lookup for you, but the best one for Windows is CyberKit from Luc Niejens, a freeware network utility that you can download at `www.ping.be/cyberkit/`.

DNS Security

Clients can make secure updates to a dynamic DNS server so that their records are automatically updated without administrator intervention.

Resource Records (RR)

All the DNS resource records have a similar format. Although many shortcut notations and abbreviations can be found in DNS files, these examples use the simplest nomenclature to eliminate confusion and ambiguity.

The first field in any DNS record is always either an IP address or a hostname. If it is missing, the name or address from the previous record is implied. *Note that all names and addresses end with a trailing "dot"(.).* This signifies that the name or address is absolute rather than relative. *Absolute* addresses, also called *fully qualified domain names*, are relative to the root, whereas *relative* addresses are relative to a default domain (which may or may not be the root). This field may, optionally, be followed by a Time-to-Live (TTL) value, which indicates the length of time that the information in this field should be considered valid.

The second field indicates the address type. In today's DNS databases, the string "IN" most likely indicates an Internet address. This field is present for historical purposes and compatibility with older systems.

The third field is a string that indicates the type of resource record. This field is followed by optional parameters that are specific to the RR.

Start of Authority (SOA)

An SOA record indicates that this DNS name server is the best source of information for the data within this DNS domain. SOA records serve to identify the email contact for the zone, to identify that changes have been made to a zone's database file, and to set timers on how often other servers update their copies of the zone information.

The record stores the name of the DNS system and the name of the person who is responsible for it. Here is an example of an SOA at the top of an RR:

```
; Start of Authority (SOA) record
dns.com.  IN SOA dns1.dns.com. owner.dns.com. (
        00000001  ; serial # (counter)
          10800   ; refresh (3 hours)
           3600   ; retry (1 hour)
         604800   ; expire (1 week)
          86400)  ; TTL (1 day)
```

A couple of things to note here are that the owner is listed as owner.dns.com, which should be read as owner@dns.com. Also, there is an opening parenthesis following that. It is closed in the last line after the TTL value. This is important because the record is formatted this way to ease reading. This could easily be shown like the following and still be valid:

```
Dns.com. IN SOA dns1.dns.com. owner.dns.com.
➥(0000001 10800 3600 604800 86400)
```

The semicolon (;) is the comment operator here. Anything that comes after that will be ignored. The last item of note is that all numerical values are shown in seconds. The sub-items are discussed in the following sections.

Serial Number

The *Serial Number* value identifies the active revision of the DNS database. When the database gets updated, this must be incremented so that secondary servers will know that they must update their database.

The Serial Number controls DNS zone transfers between primary and secondary DNS name servers. The secondary name server contacts a primary name server periodically and requests the serial number of the primary's zone data. If the primary zone's serial number is larger than the secondary's, the secondary's zone data is out of date and the secondary transfers a new copy of the zone data from the primary. The transfer of information from a primary to a secondary server is called a *zone transfer*.

The serial number value can be a simple counter, but more typically a timestamp value is used, because the timestamp when the change was done will always increase with newer changes to the primary server database.

Refresh

Refresh tells any secondary name servers how often to check for updated information (10,800 seconds is three hours).

The number in the Refresh Interval field specifies how often the secondary DNS name servers check the zone data of the primary DNS name servers. The default refresh interval is three hours; if your secondaries accept notification of changes, you can safely increase it to a long value (a day or more) to reduce the polling. This feature is particularly valuable over slow or on-demand lines.

Retry

If the secondary name server is unable to contact the primary name server, it will re-attempt a connection every *retry* seconds (3600 seconds is one hour).

The Retry Interval field determines how often a secondary server should try to reconnect after a failed connection. The Retry Interval usually is shorter than the Refresh Interval. The default value is 60 minutes.

Expire

If a secondary name server cannot contact the primary name server for *expire* seconds, the secondary will stop answering any queries about this domain. The theory here is that at some point, the data is so old as to be possibly harmful, and no answer is better than a bad answer (604,800 seconds is one week).

The Expire Time field refers to the amount of time the secondary server's data is good. If a secondary DNS name server fails to contact the primary DNS name server, the secondary's data might be invalid. The default value is three days, and it must exceed both the Minimum Default TTL and Retry values.

TTL

The *TTL* (time-to-live) value is returned with all responses to database queries, and tells the requester (or other servers) how long the information can safely be cached (86,400 seconds is one day). This TTL value is the default value for all records in the file; it may be overridden by a TTL value provided with a given RR.

The Minimum Default TTL (time-to-live) has the greatest effect on DNS traffic. It controls how long a receiving server can cache the data. Each query response is sent with a TTL value. The default value is 24 hours. If you anticipate making major changes to your DNS zone, you should temporarily set this to a short interval, like one hour, and then wait the previous minimum value before making your changes. After you verify the correctness of your changes, you should increase the TTL back up to its previous value. Following this procedure enables your changes to propagate through the Internet much more efficiently and reduces the time during which stale DNS data may lurk in other servers' caches.

Address (A) Resource Records

The A records contain an IP address to be associated with the hostname in the first field of the record.

The A records are the most common type of resource records you can expect to find in zone data files. The A record maps a hostname to its IP address.

Name Server (NS) Resource Records

The NS records contain the address of the name server(s) for this domain. In this example, there are two name servers with the `foo.com` DNS information.

The NS record identifies an authoritative DNS server for the DNS domain. You should always have at least two of these for any domain. An NS record has two fields.

Canonical Name Records (CNAME)

The CNAME records contain an alias hostname to associate with the hostname in the first field of the record. Although a single A record and many CNAME records can be assigned to a single system, care must be taken. Some mailers, for example, do unpredictable things when asked to resolve an MX hostname that uses a CNAME record rather than an explicit A record.

You can use CNAME records to hide the implementation details of your network from the clients that connect to it. For alias names, you can use shortened forms of the hostnames. The hostname `public1.business.com`, for example, might have an alias of `www.business.com`.

Pointer (PTR) Records

Pointer records map an IP address to a hostname in the DNS reverse lookup domain (in-addr.arpa). The pointer record specifies the IP Address and the Host Name corresponding to that IP address. For the hostname, you use the FQDN. Many Internet sites deny access to computers that do not have matching Address and Pointer records as a security measure, so be sure to keep your PTR records synchronized with your A records.

The reverse lookup query is sometimes called a PTR query and can also be used to discover the organization responsible for an IP address, because the result of a pointer query contains the FQDN, and the FQDN includes the domain name.

Delegated Domains

Delegated domains remove the primary responsibility of administration for a domain from one server to a subservient one. The ICANN has administrative control over `.COM`. and delegates all domains registered under it to their respective controllers. In reality, most sites are hosted, which means the server space is sold to someone and the site owner does not have to maintain the hardware. That job is for the hosting service. Control of the domains that reside on hosted sites are often delegated to the DNS server administrator for the DNS servers of the host. There is, however, a free DNS server on which you can request space at `http://soa.granitecanyon.com`.

Hardware Information (HINFO) Record

The HINFO record identifies a host's hardware type and operating system. The Internet standard abbreviations for identifying the operating system of a host are published in the Assigned Numbers RFC (RFC 1700 at the time of this writing) under the System Names List. Abbreviations for the hardware type of hosts also are defined in the Assigned Numbers RFC. The CPU Type identification number is in the Machine Names List. For a small sample of the types specified in the Assigned Numbers RFC, see Table 6.1.

The names are up to 40 characters long and contain uppercase letters and digits, including a hyphen (-) and a slash (/). The names must begin with a letter and end with a letter or digit. Some people choose not to provide this on publicly accessible DNS servers because it reveals information about a computer system that might make it easier for someone to break into a system, perhaps by attacking known security flaws for a particular system type. If you do use HINFO records, be sure to keep up with CERT security advisories for your systems.

TABLE 6.1 RFC 1700 Standard Codes for Common Operating Systems

APOLLO	OPENVMS	TANDEM
AIX/370	OS/2	UNIX
DOMAIN	PCDOS	UNIX-BSD
DOS	SCO-OPEN-DESKTOP-2.0	UNIX-PC
INTERLISP	SCO-OPEN-DESKTOP-3.0	UNKNOWN
ITS	SCO-UNIX-3.2V4.0	VM
LISP	SCO-UNIX-3.2V4.1	VM/370
MSDOS	SCO-UNIX-3.2V4.2	VMS
MULTICS	SUN	WANG
MVS	SUN-OS-3.5	WIN32
NONSTOP	SUN-OS-4.0	X11R3
APOLLO	IBM-RS/6000	SUN-4/200
APPLE-MACINTOSH	INTEL-386	SUN-4/390
APPLE-POWERBOOK	M68000	SYMBOLICS-3600
CRAY-2	MAC-II	UNKNOWN
DECSTATION	MAC-POWERBOOK	VAX
DEC-VAX	MACINTOSH	VAX-11/725
DEC-VAXCLUSTER	MICROVAX	VAXCLUSTER
DEC-VAXSTATION	PDP-11	VAXSTATION
IBM-PC/AT	SILICON-GRAPHICS	
IBM-PC/XT	SUN	

Integrated Services Digital Network (ISDN) Record

The ISDN record maps the hostname to an ISDN address. The ISDN phone number also can include the Direct Dial In (DDI) number. An ISDN subaddress is optional. ISDN records have several possible uses. The ISDN resource records can provide simple documentation of the correct addresses to use in static configurations of ISDN dial-up applications. In the future, they also may be used automatically by Internet routers.

Mailbox (MB) Record

The MB record identifies a mailbox for the indicated host. You must provide the Mailbox name and the fully qualified domain name (FQDN) of the host that contains the mailbox. This record type is considered experimental and should not be used unless you are part of the Internet experiment.

Mailgroup (MG) Record

The MG record identifies a mailbox that is a member of the group mailing list in the given DNS domain name. You must type the mailbox name as a FQDN (Fully Qualified Domain Name). This record type is considered experimental and should not be used unless you are part of the Internet experiment.

Mail Information (MINFO) Record

The MINFO record provides information about a mailing list or mailbox. It has two fields: the Responsible Mailbox DNS field, which contains the fully qualified domain name (FQDN) of the mailbox that is responsible for the mailing list identified in the resource record; and the Error Mailbox DNS field, which contains the FQDN of the mailbox that is to receive error messages related to the mailing list. Although you can associate these records with a simple mailbox, they usually are used with a mailing list that uses different mailing addresses for administrative matters, such as subscriptions (usually the responsible mailbox), and for error messages, like `mail not deliverable` (the error mailbox).

Mail Rename (MR) Record

The MR record renames a given mailbox. Type the FQDN of the new mailbox name in the Replacement Mailbox DNS Name field. You can use an alias name if a mailbox is moved from one host to another. This record type is considered experimental and should not be used unless you are part of the Internet experiment.

Mail Exchange (MX) Record

An MX record indicates the hostname of a server that will process or forward mail for a given domain or host. The hostname of the mail exchanger must be a FQDN. The MX record format consists of the following fields:

- **For Domain.** Enter the host or domain name for which the mail exchanger will process mail.
- **Mail Exchange Server DNS Name.** Enter the FQDN of the mail exchange server.
- **Preference Number.** Enter the preference number of that particular mail exchanger.

The Preference Number is a number from 0 to 65,535 that indicates the mail exchange server's priority with respect to the other mail exchange servers for that destination. Lower preference numbers have higher priority, the highest priority being a preference number of 0. The absolute value of the preference is not significant except in relation to other mail exchanger values for the same destination. A mailer attempts delivery to the mail exchange server with the lowest preference number first. If delivery fails, the mail exchange server with the next highest preference number is tried next. If two or more mail exchange servers share the same preference number, the mailer must decide which one to try first. All mail exchange servers with a given preference number are tried before the mailer moves up to the next highest preference number, however. One normally uses a preference of 10 for the best mail server, with less preferred mail exchangers identified at 20, and then 30, or some similar scheme. Doing so enables you to insert a new mail exchanger between or before your existing mailers if needed.

Mail Exchange lookups are not recursive. After an MX record identifies the best destination for mail to a host, the only other lookup performed is for the A record of the mail exchanger. MX records for the mail exchanger itself are ignored unless the mail is addressed directly to that particular mail exchanger.

Responsible Person (RP) Record

The RP record indicates who is responsible for the device identified by the specified DNS name. Although the SOA record indicates who is responsible for a zone and gives the best point of contact for DNS-related issues, different people usually are in charge of various hosts within a domain. The RP record enables you to indicate who should be contacted if a problem arises associated with something that has a DNS name. Typical problems might be that an important server has become unavailable or that another site is noticing suspicious activity from a host.

An RP record requires an email address and the FQDN to check for text records with more information. The email address is in standard DNS domain name format, with a period for the at symbol (@) used in most email addresses. The DNS text reference is a DNS domain name that acts as a pointer to a TXT resource record. You can use the Text resource record to which the RP record points to provide free-format information about the contact, such as full name and phone or pager number.

Route Through (RT) Record

The RT record identifies an intermediate host that routes packets to a destination host that does not have direct connectivity itself. The Intermediate Host DNS Name must be a FQDN of an intermediate host that will accept packets for the destination. An intermediate host functions like a mail exchange server, in that there can be only one level of indirection, which means that the path to an intermediate host cannot be through another intermediate host.

Text (TXT) Record

The TXT record contains information in straight text form, often a name and phone number of a contact or other relevant information. The text string must be less than 256 characters in length.

Well Known Service (WKS) Record

The WKS record describes the services provided by a particular protocol on a particular interface, identified by the IP address. The services include Telnet and FTP. The Access Protocol indicates the protocol for the available service. This record generally isn't used and should be avoided (RFC 1123).

X25 Record

The X25 record is similar to the A resource record, but maps the hostname to an X.121 address rather than an IP address. X.121 addresses are the standard form of addresses for X.25 networks. The PSDN (Public Switched Data Network) address begins with the four-digit DNIC (Data Network Identification Code) specified in X.121 guidelines established by the International Telephone and Telegraph Consultative Committee. Do not use the national prefixes as part of the address. The X25 resource record is designed for use in conjunction with the RT (route through) resource record.

Summary

In this chapter you learned that a hierarchical structure controls the Domain Name System for the Internet. This system is expressly available to make names the primary form of addressing for the Internet's resources. You also learned that DNS uses a number of methods to determine the IP number of a domain name. It is important to remember that, like anything, the system can fail. If this material is not clear to you or you find yourself confused by its structure, allow your ISP to handle it. This is, after all, the way a Web site is reached or a resource located under another protocol.

WINS

by Kurt Hudson

IN THIS CHAPTER

The *Windows Internet Name Service* (WINS) is also called the NetBIOS Name Service because it handles the resolution of NetBIOS names to IP addresses. The Network Basic Input/Output System (NetBIOS) was invented by IBM and co-developed by IBM and Microsoft. Later, Microsoft acquired NetBIOS to use in its now obsolete LANManager product. Today, NetBIOS lives on in Microsoft network operating system products earlier than Windows 2000 (that is, NT 5.0). Networks running Windows 3.x, Windows 95, Windows 98, and Windows NT 4.0 or earlier utilize NetBIOS networking. Anyone supporting a network running those operating systems should familiarize himself with NetBIOS name resolution, especially WINS.

This chapter describes the configuration process for, and limitations of, NetBIOS names. NetBIOS name resolution techniques such as LMHOSTS files and WINS are discussed. A special emphasis is placed on WINS name resolution, WINS client and server configuration, and WINS administration.

> **Note**
>
> Microsoft has stripped NetBIOS out of Windows 2000 products. The company says that its future operating systems will only support NetBIOS naming for backward compatibility, but will not be dependent upon NetBIOS naming. For this reason, WINS is discussed for Windows 9x and Windows NT. Although a Windows 2000 server can be configured as a WINS server, this would normally be done for backward compatibility only.

NetBIOS

Microsoft considers NetBIOS an *Application Programming Interface* (API). Essentially, an API is a layer of separation between components. The NetBIOS Layer resides between the Application and Transport Layers in the Microsoft TCP/IP protocol stack, as shown in Figure 7.1.

FIGURE 7.1

NetBIOS in Microsoft's TCP/IP protocol stack.

Application
— NetBIOS —
Transport
Internetwork
Network Interface

The function of NetBIOS is to provide independence between the Application and Transport Layers. The goal is to allow an application developer to write a network-enabled program without having to understand the underlying protocol. In addition, the NetBIOS Layer allows multiple transport protocols to be used with that application. The developer needs only to write the application to function with the NetBIOS Layer, not the specific protocol.

> **Note**
>
> Microsoft also includes an API called Windows Sockets (also known as WinSocks), which resides between the Application Layer and Transport Layer, like NetBIOS. NetBIOS and WinSocks are not integrated; they are two different paths of communication. WinSocks was created to allow Microsoft TCP/IP to utilize existing Internet utilities (primarily written for UNIX systems), which utilize the Sockets interface.

When a Microsoft network operating system is installed, the setup program requests that a computer name be configured. The computer name that is configured is actually the NetBIOS name. The NetBIOS name must be unique on the network; no other computer should be using the name that is entered. The maximum length of the NetBIOS name is 15 characters, and it cannot contain the following characters or symbols:

- backslash (\)
- space ( )
- hyphen (-)
- single quotation mark (')
- at sign (@)
- percent sign (%)
- exclamation point (!)
- ampersand (&)
- period (.)

All Microsoft network operating systems (prior to Windows 2000) that utilize TCP/IP have a NetBIOS computer name and a hostname. The hostname is configured through the properties of the TCP/IP protocol. By default, the hostname and the NetBIOS computer name are identical for the system. You should leave these two names the same; otherwise, an additional level of complexity is added when troubleshooting. For example, utilities such as ping query the hostname, but mapping a drive to a Microsoft server utilizes the NetBIOS name. If the two names are different, troubleshooting a failed connection would be a little more difficult because each name and connection would have to be considered separately.

However, if the computer will be used on the Internet, the TCP/IP hostname has some additional character limitations that should be kept in mind when assigning the NetBIOS computer name. It can only include A–Z, a–z, 0–9, and the – (dash), and the first and last characters of the TCP/IP hostname must be alphanumeric (that is, A–Z, a–z, or 0–9).

On Microsoft operating systems, the NetBIOS name is the computer name, as shown in Figure 7.2. The figure illustrates the NetBIOS name for a Windows 98 computer, which applies identically to a Windows 95 system.

FIGURE 7.2

The NetBIOS name is the computer name.

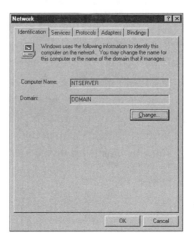

To access this configuration dialog box, you can right-click the Windows 95/98 Network Neighborhood icon and select Properties from the resulting context menu. Then, click the Identification tab on the Network dialog box. In Windows NT 4, the same procedure applies except the tab is named General, which appears by default.

The TCP/IP hostname is part of the TCP/IP configuration on Microsoft operating systems, as illustrated in the Microsoft Windows NT screen shot shown in Figure 7.3. The configuration settings for TCP/IP in Windows 95/98 are covered in Chapter 23, "Configuring TCP/IP for Windows 95 and Windows 98." The TCP/IP configuration settings for Windows NT are described in Chapter 25, "Configuring TCP/IP for Windows NT."

FIGURE 7.3

TCP/IP hostname configuration in Windows NT Server.

NetBIOS is such an integral part of the Microsoft network configuration that the TCP/IP protocol for Microsoft operating systems is known by the acronyms NBT and NetBT. NBT and NetBT both stand for NetBIOS over TCP/IP. The networking components in a Microsoft operating system will not function correctly if NetBIOS is removed from the system.

NetBIOS Name Resolution

Just like hostnames, NetBIOS names must be resolved to IP addresses when used on a TCP/IP network. There are several ways in which a NetBIOS name can be resolved to an IP address. Microsoft operating systems use the following methods of resolving NetBIOS names to IP addresses:

- *Name cache*—Microsoft clients maintain a NetBIOS name cache that contains the computer names and IP addresses that the client previously resolved. You can view the contents of the name cache by typing **NBTSTAT -c** at the command prompt of a Microsoft networked operating system using TCP/IP.

- *WINS server*—The WINS server maintains a database of computer names to IP addresses. Clients query the WINS server to obtain computer-name-to-IP-address resolution. This is also referred to as a *NetBIOS Name Server* (NBNS).

- *Broadcast*—A Microsoft client can broadcast a name query on the local segment to determine whether a system on that segment owns the computer name the client is attempting to resolve.

- *LMHOSTS file*—A static file that can be posted centrally or on individual systems. This file is a list of IP addresses and their corresponding computer names.

- *HOSTS file*—Another static file that can be posted centrally or on individual systems. This file, maintained in the same format as the 4.2 Berkeley Software Distribution (BSD) UNIX\etc\hosts ASCII text file, is a list of Internet hostnames and *Fully Qualified Domain Names* (FQDN) and their corresponding IP addresses.

- *DNS server*—The DNS server can be used by the WINS clients for WINS name resolution. This option, configured on the client system, allows NetBIOS name resolution to be routed through a DNS server, instead of a WINS server.

The order in which the client system attempts to resolve a NetBIOS name is determined by its NetBIOS node type. The four NetBIOS node types are

- *B-node*—This is called a Broadcast node because a computer configured as a B-node only broadcasts on the local segment for NetBIOS name resolution. Actually, Microsoft systems use an enhanced B-node, meaning they will check for an LMHOSTS file entry if the name is not discovered on the local segment.

- *P-node*—Systems configured for point-to-point (P-node) call a WINS server for name resolution, but do not broadcast on the local segment.

- *M-node*—Mixed node (M-node) systems first broadcast on the local segment, and then they contact a WINS server for name resolution.

- *H-node*—Hybrid node (H-node) systems contact WINS servers first for name resolution. If no answer is provided, the H-node system will broadcast on the local segment.

All Microsoft clients first check the name cache before they attempt any other form of NetBIOS name resolution. The default node type for Microsoft operating systems is either B-node or H-node. Enhanced B-node is the default for all systems that are not configured with a WINS server address. H-node is the default for all systems that are configured with the address of a WINS server. Client configuration is explained later in this chapter.

Modifying Node Type Via the Registry

If you want to modify the NetBIOS node type to point-to-point or mixed, you will have to edit the Windows Registry. For more information on configuring TCP/IP in Windows NT (including modification of the NetBIOS node type), see the Microsoft support Web site at http://www.microsoft.com or obtain a copy of the Microsoft TechNet CD. The article that describes Windows 95/98 settings is titled "MS TCP/IP and Windows 95 Networking." The article that describes TCP/IP settings for Windows NT can be found by searching for "Q120642." These articles also describe many other configuration parameters for Microsoft TCP/IP.

There are actually several types of NetBIOS names that each Microsoft operating system may use. These name types are made unique by appending a hexadecimal identifier to the computer name of the system. Each unique name describes a type of service that the computer supports. For example, every Microsoft network operating system has a workstation name, which allows it to communicate on the network. If the operating system also provides services on the network, such as file sharing or printer sharing, it will have a server name as well. Table 7.1 lists the common NetBIOS name types a Microsoft operating system may use.

TABLE 7.1   NetBIOS Names with Hexadecimal Identifiers

NetBIOS Name and Hex ID	*Description*
Computer name[00h]	Workstation service on a WINS client
Computer name[03h]	Messenger service on a WINS client
Computer name[20h]	Server service on a WINS client
User name[03h]	The registered user name of the currently logged-on user
Domain name[1Bh]	Indicates the Primary Domain Controller (PDC) functioning as the Domain Master Browser

As Table 7.1 implies, each Microsoft operating system on the network typically registers multiple NetBIOS computer names on the network. Name registration is handled in one of two ways: If the system is a WINS client, it registers each of its NetBIOS names with the WINS server. If the system is not a WINS client, it broadcasts the names on the local segment. If another system does not respond to the registration broadcast informing the system that those names are already in use, the names are considered registered. If another computer on the local segment was already using any of those NetBIOS names, the system attempting to register them would automatically remove itself from the network by shutting down its networking services. Then, it would be up to the system administrator to configure a different NetBIOS name for one of these systems.

Dynamic NetBIOS Name Resolution

WINS is the only dynamic method of resolving NetBIOS names to IP addresses on Microsoft TCP/IP networks. A WINS server receives name registration requests from WINS clients when they start up. When WINS clients shut down, they send a name release to the WINS server. This way, the WINS database is kept current with the names of computers active on the network.

WINS is a server service that is run on Windows NT servers. The service uses an Access database to store the name registration information and provide name resolution services.

Benefits of Using WINS

There are several ways in which a WINS server improves NetBIOS name resolution on a Microsoft network. The following list describes the benefits of using WINS:

- WINS reduces name resolution broadcast traffic. WINS clients contact the WINS server directly instead of broadcasting for name resolution on the local segment.
- WINS clients can reach WINS servers on remote segments. Routers typically filter broadcast traffic, so broadcasts for name resolution are limited to the local subnet. WINS clients contact the WINS server via a directed request to the WINS server IP address. Although allowing a router to forward name resolution broadcasts by enabling UDP ports 137 and 138 is possible, it is not recommended because of the resulting increase in network traffic.
- WINS is dynamic. WINS clients register with the WINS server when they start up. An administrator does not have to type in the IP address to NetBIOS name resolutions.
- WINS offers better browse list maintenance. Microsoft systems maintain large browse lists, which are lists of resources available on the network such as shared files and printers. The WINS server helps to document the available resources on the network by collecting the various NetBIOS names from each computer. If the network relied only on broadcast traffic, the browse lists would be incomplete on multisegment networks.

How WINS Works

A WINS server gathers and maintains a central database of the NetBIOS names that are active on the network. The WINS server handles name registration, name release, and name resolution requests from WINS clients. As previously stated, the WINS server relies on the WINS clients to register their names with the WINS server when those clients start up. The clients are also expected to release their names when they shut down. Because all WINS clients register and release their names through the WINS server, the WINS server can accurately provide IP address to NetBIOS name resolution when clients request it.

Name Registration

WINS clients are required to register their NetBIOS names with the WINS server when they start up. The name registration request is sent directly to the WINS server, and the WINS server either registers the name or refuses the name registration.

If the name is not in use by another system, the WINS server will register the name and send an acknowledgment packet to the client system. The acknowledgment packet contains the registered name and the *Time To Live* (TTL) for that name. The TTL is the amount of time that the name will be reserved for that client until that name is either reregistered or released. If the WINS client does not renew the name before the TTL expires, the name will be removed from the WINS database and made available for another system to register. The TTL ensures that systems that register names and then shut down abnormally, or lose power, do not occupy NetBIOS names when they are no longer on the network.

If a WINS client attempts to register a NetBIOS name that is already in use in the WINS database, the WINS server returns a wait for acknowledgment packet to the client. The WINS server then verifies that the name is actually in use on the network by sending a challenge packet to the listed owner of that computer name. If the WINS server receives a response from the system that originally registered the name, the WINS server denies the second computer's request to register that name. Should the previously registered owner of the name not respond, the WINS server queries it two more times. If the previous owner does not respond to all queries, the WINS server releases the name and gives it to the requesting computer.

> **Note**
>
> If the WINS client does not receive a response from its primary WINS server during the startup process after three tries, one of the alternate or secondary WINS servers will be contacted. If the primary and secondary WINS servers fail to respond, the WINS client uses a broadcast to register its NetBIOS name.

Name Renewal

The TTL is used by the WINS client to determine when the NetBIOS name should be renewed with the WINS server. The default TTL for a WINS name is six days, or 518,400 seconds. WINS clients attempt to renew their name after one-eighth of the TTL has expired. If the WINS server cannot be contacted at that time, the client will attempt to contact a secondary or alternate WINS server to renew the name. After the name has been renewed, the client will wait until half the TTL has passed before attempting to renew the name again. If the client is unsuccessful in all of its attempts to renew the name, the NetBIOS name will be released.

Name Query and Response

As explained earlier, WINS clients default to the Hybrid NetBIOS node type, which means these clients query the WINS server when they need name resolution services. For example, if a WINS client is attempting to contact the computer named HOSTX, the WINS client first checks its name cache for an existing name resolution. If a mapping is not found in the local name cache, the WINS client contacts the WINS server to determine the IP address for HOSTX. If the primary WINS server cannot be located after three repeated requests, the WINS client attempts to call a secondary WINS server. If all WINS servers are unavailable, or any responding WINS server does not have a mapping for the NetBIOS name, the WINS client will broadcast for name resolution on the local subnet.

Name Release

WINS clients are required to provide name release requests when they shut down. These name release requests are sent directly to the WINS server for each name the client has registered. The name release packet includes the NetBIOS name and corresponding IP address that is being released.

The server responds to the WINS client's name release request with a name release request response packet. This response packet can either be a positive or negative acknowledgment. If the WINS server finds a conflict in the database, such as the computer attempting to release the name is not the computer that registered the name, then the response packet will be negative. This does not make any difference to the WINS client that is shutting down because it ignores the contents of the release response packet and shuts down whether the response is negative or positive.

Configuring WINS Clients

Configuring a Windows NT or Windows 95 computer to use WINS is a matter of entering the IP address of the WINS server. Both operating systems can be configured for WINS via the TCP/IP protocol properties dialog box (using the WINS Configuration tab in Windows 95 and Windows 98 and the WINS tab in Windows NT). Figure 7.4 illustrates the WINS configuration for a Windows 98 system.

To enable WINS resolution on the client, you need only enter the IP address of a single WINS server. If you want the client to have access to multiple WINS servers, you can enter additional IP addresses into the configuration dialog box. On Windows NT systems you can enter a primary and secondary WINS server only through the interface. By default, the secondary WINS server is only contacted when the client cannot find the primary WINS server on the network.

FIGURE 7.4

Configuring WINS in Windows 98.

The following operating systems can be configured as WINS clients:

- Windows NT Server 4.0, 3.5x
- Windows NT Workstation 4.0. 3.5x
- Windows 95/98
- Windows for Workgroups 3.11 with Microsoft TCP/IP-32
- Microsoft Network Client 3.0 for MS-DOS
- LAN Manager 2.2c for MS-DOS

As previously described, configuring a client with a WINS address automatically changes the node type from B-node to H-node. You can confirm this change by typing **IPCONFIG /ALL** at the command prompt of a Windows NT system. To check the IP configuration of a Windows 95/98 system, you must type **WINIPCFG** at the command prompt. To see the node type, click the More Info button on the resulting dialog box.

Configuring WINS for Proxy Agents

Windows 95, Windows 98, and Windows NT can be configured to provide WINS proxy services. When a WINS client is configured to provide WINS proxy services, it is called a WINS Proxy Agent. The WINS Proxy Agent contacts the WINS server for name resolution on behalf of non-WINS clients on the local segment. This allows non-WINS clients to benefit from WINS NetBIOS name resolution services.

The process is not much different from the normal WINS name resolution process. When a non-WINS client broadcasts for name resolution on the local subnet, the WINS Proxy Agent receives the request and forwards it to the WINS server. If the WINS server is able to provide a mapping for the NetBIOS name to IP address, the WINS Proxy Agent forwards the answer to a non-WINS client.

One important item that you should keep in mind when configuring systems to be WINS Proxy Agents is that they increase network traffic because they repeat name resolution requests. Microsoft recommends that you have no more than two WINS Proxy Agents per subnet where non-WINS clients exist. If all the computers on a network were configured as WINS Proxy Agents, a single broadcast for name resolution would be repeated once for every computer on the network.

Configuring NT 4 Systems

To configure a Windows NT 4 system to be a WINS Proxy Agent, you must complete the following steps:

1. Open REGEDIT.EXE or REGEDT32.EXE to edit the Windows NT 4 Registry.
2. Locate the Parameters sub-key in the following path: HKEY_LOCAL_MACHINE\ SYSTEM\CurrentControlSet\Services\NetBT.
3. Double-click the EnableProxy key and set its value to 1.
4. Close the Registry Editor.
5. Restart the computer.

Configuring Windows 95 and Windows 98 Systems

To configure a Windows 95 or Windows 98 computer to be a WINS Proxy Agent, do the following:

1. Open REGEDIT.EXE to edit the Windows 95/98 Registry.
2. Locate the MSTCP sub-key in the following path: HKEY_LOCAL_MACHINE\SYSTEM\CurrentControlSet\Services\VxD.
3. Highlight the MSTCP sub-key by clicking it once.
4. Select Edit, New, and String Value from the Registry Editor toolbar.
5. Type **EnableProxy** as the new value.
6. Double-click the new EnableProxy string value to open the Edit String dialog box.
7. Enter 1 as the Value data and click OK.
8. Close the Registry Editor and reboot the system.

Installing a WINS Server

The WINS server service can be installed on a Windows NT server. After it is installed, the Windows NT server becomes a WINS server. The WINS server service software ships as part of the Windows NT Server software, but is not part of the default NT Server installation.

To install the WINS server service on a Windows NT 4 system:

1. Right-click the Network Neighborhood icon and select Properties from the resulting context menu. The Network dialog box opens.
2. Click the Services tab.
3. Click the Add button.
4. From the list of services, select the Windows Internet Name Service and click OK.
5. You are asked for the path to the Windows NT source files. Ensure that the path is correct, and then click OK.
6. When the service is done installing, click Close and restart the computer as requested.

After the system restarts:

1. Confirm installation by opening the Control Panel (click Start, choose Settings, then choose Control Panel).
2. Double-click the Services icon in the Control Panel to view a list of installed services.

If the Windows Internet Name Service was successfully installed, it will be part of this list. The Windows Internet Name Service should be near the end of the list of installed services. From this interface, you can stop, start, pause, and configure the startup configuration for the WINS service and many others.

WINS Administration and Maintenance

After the WINS server service is installed, the WINS Manager application should appear under the Administrative Tools section of the Windows NT Start menu. Click Start, Programs, Administrative Tools, and then select WINS Manager.

The WINS Manager application allows you to perform several administrative tasks on the WINS server. For example, you can add static mappings to the WINS database for non-WINS clients. You can also back up the WINS database, configure WINS replication partners, and view the WINS database from the WINS Manager application.

Adding Static Entries

If you have non-WINS clients on your network and you want the WINS server to be able to resolve the non-WINS client's computer names to IP addresses, you can configure static mappings. A static mapping is one that you add to the WINS database manually to allow WINS clients to resolve the IP address to the NetBIOS name of non-WINS clients. To add a static mapping, follow these steps:

1. Open WINS Manager.

2. Click the Mappings menu and select Static Mappings.

3. Click Add Mappings.

4. In the Add Static Mappings dialog box, type the Name and IP address for the computer you want to statically add to the database.

5. Choose the correct name type for the computer. You can choose from the following options:

   Unique—Used for a single computer name to IP address mapping.

   Group—Used as a "Normal Group" name. The IP address of individual members of a group is not stored because broadcast name packets are used to communicate with group members.

   Domain Name—Used for entering a Domain Name. This option is for listing Windows NT domain controllers.

   Internet Group—Enables you to group resources, such as printers, for browsing purposes.

   Multihomed—Used to support computers that have multiple IP addresses, but only one computer name. Typically, these systems have multiple network cards, but use a single computer name. This entry supports such a configuration by mapping multiple IP addresses to the same NetBIOS computer name.

6. Click Add.

7. Repeat the process for each additional entry you require. When you are finished, click Close.

Because the Domain Name, Internet Group, and Multihomed entries allow for more than one entry, an additional dialog box appears when these categories are selected. All of these options allow for a maximum of 25 total entries each. WINS client computers will be unable to register names that have been statically configured on the WINS server.

Maintaining the WINS Database

Several maintenance tasks can be performed on the WINS database; these tasks include backing up the database, restoring the database, compressing the database, and reconciling database records.

You can view the records of the WINS database from the WINS Manager. To view the WINS database records, click the Mappings menu and select Show Database. You have the option of viewing all database entries or just those of the selected owner. An owner is a WINS server. When multiple WINS servers are connected as replication partners, each partner can view the database records of the other. The configuration of WINS replication partners is detailed later in this chapter. You can also sort the database entries by IP Address, Computer Name, Expiration Date, Version ID, or Type (see Figure 7.5).

FIGURE 7.5

The WINS database.

In the Mappings window, you can determine whether the entries are active or static. If an entry is static, then the S column has a check mark in it. Likewise, if an entry is active, then the A column has a check mark in it. Entries that do not have check marks for active or static cannot be verified and are awaiting removal.

Initiating Scavenging

When the database records seem to be incorrect, you can try to get the WINS server to reconcile the entries. For example, if you notice that computer names no longer on the network remain in the WINS database, you can initiate scavenging through the WINS server. After you initiate scavenging, the database should be cleared of names that were released or entries that were added by other WINS servers. If you notice that several entries need to be removed prior to the automatic scavenging of the database, you might want to initiate scavenging via the Mappings menu in the WINS manager.

Purging the Database

Sometimes the WINS database maintains entries that should have been purged. The database is supposed to remove entries that have expired, but occasionally an entry will remain in the database after it should have been removed. If you have tried initiating scavenging and still see entries that should be removed, there are a couple of ways to purge database entries manually. You can purge the entire database by selecting Delete Owner from the Show Database dialog box. Follow these steps:

1. From the WINS Manager application, click Mappings, and then click Show Database. The Show Database dialog box appears.

2. From the Show Database dialog box, select the Owner window, then click the name or IP address of the WINS computer that you want to purge.

3. Click the Delete Owner button.

4. Confirm this action by clicking Yes in the WINS Manager warning dialog box. The message tells you that entries cannot be reconciled by this WINS database until those entries are rebuilt.

Of course, purging the entire database removes all the entries in the database. After the database is purged, each WINS client must re-register its name with the WINS database. This is done automatically if the computers on the network are rebooted.

Another way to clear entries from the WINS database is to remove the specific records individually. The WINSCL.EXE utility allows you to remove specific, individual records from the WINS database. You can obtain this utility from the Windows NT 4.0 Resource Kit, which is sold in bookstores. You can also purchase the Windows NT 4.0 Resource Kit CD directly from Microsoft.

Controlling Automatic Intervals

The WINS database automatically performs many database maintenance tasks at set intervals. You can modify the interval for these automated activities via the WINS Server Configuration dialog box. To access this dialog box, click the Server menu in the WINS Manager application, and then select Configuration (see Figure 7.6).

FIGURE 7.6

The WINS Server Configuration dialog box.

You can manage the following intervals via the WINS Server Configuration section:

- *Renewal Interval*—The time-to-live for a registered name. A WINS client must renew its name before this time interval expires. By default, the entry is set at 144 hours (six days).

- *Extinction Interval*—The time span (default 144 hours) between the release of a name and the expiration of that name. When this time period has elapsed, the computer name is marked as *extinct*.

- *Extinction Timeout*—The time between the marking of an entry as *extinct* and its actual removal from the database. The extinction timeout is 144 hours by default.

- *Verify Interval*—Entries that came from other WINS servers are verified every 576 hours (24 days) by default. Only the entries from other WINS servers are verified in this manner.

Advanced WINS Server Configuration

If you click the Advanced button on the WINS Server Configuration dialog box, you can access the Advanced WINS Server Configuration dialog box. In this dialog box, you can control WINS server logging, backup, and other options. The following options are available:

- *Logging Enabled*—A log of database changes is kept in the `%system_root%/system32/wins` folder by default. This file is used by WINS to recover transactions after a failure.

- *Log Detailed Events*—Causes WINS to log every WINS action in detail. If you are experiencing difficulty with WINS server registration, you might want to enable this option. Because this option slows down the WINS server, it should only be enabled when you are troubleshooting registration problems. Detailed events can be found in the System Log of the Event Viewer application.

- *Replicate Only With Partners*—By default the WINS server does not replicate with other WINS servers that are not listed as replication partners. If this option is deselected, the WINS server can be configured to push or pull entries to or from an unlisted WINS server.

- *Backup On Termination*—Backs up the WINS database each time the WINS Manager application is closed.

- *Migrate On/Off*—Allows WINS clients to overwrite static entries. This option is used when static entries have been configured for non-WINS clients and those clients are then made WINS clients. This option allows the new WINS clients to dynamically register their computer names (overwriting their existing static entries). Select this option when upgrading non-Windows NT computer systems to Windows NT.

- *Starting Version Count*—The value used to track the version of the latest database. If the WINS database becomes corrupt beyond repair, you can set this version number to zero to refresh the database.

- *Database Backup Path*—The location for database backups. It is used for restoration in the event of a WINS or system failure. One caveat: Do not specify a network directory to back up the WINS database to; in the event of a network outage, you may be unable to access or restore the WINS database.

Backing Up the WINS Database

Every 24 hours the WINS database is automatically backed up. However, you must specify a backup directory for this action to occur. Follow these steps:

1. Click the Mappings menu and select Back Up Database.
2. Type (or select by browsing) the location for the backup directory.
3. Click OK.

Backing Up the WINS Registry Entries

As part of routine WINS maintenance, you should also plan on backing up the Registry Entries for the WINS server by following these steps:

1. Open REGEDIT.EXE or REGEDT32.EXE to edit the Windows NT 4 Registry.
2. Locate the WINS key in the following path:
   HKEY_LOCAL_MACHINE\SYSTEM\CurrentControlSet\Services\.
3. Click the Registry menu and select Save Key. The Save Key dialog box appears.
4. Type (or select by browsing) the location for the backup directory or use the same backup directory from the previous section and click Save.
5. Close the Registry Editor.

Restoring the WINS Database

If you find that WINS is no longer functioning properly, suspect that the WINS database is corrupt. WINS automatically restores the database if it determines that the database is corrupt. You can stop and restart the WINS service in hopes that the corruption will be detected by following these steps:

1. Open the Control Panel (click Start, choose Settings, then choose Control Panel).
2. Double-click the Services icon.
3. Highlight the Windows Internet Name Service from the list of services.
4. Click Stop.
5. Click Start.

If WINS detects the database corruption and restores the database, you can look in the Event Viewer application to confirm the restoration. If WINS does not detect the corruption and restore the database after a restart, you can restore the database manually. To do so, follow these steps:

1. Click the Mappings menu and select Restore Database.
2. Type (or select) the location of the backup.
3. Click OK.

If the option to restore the database is grayed out, the WINS database has never been backed up. In this case, you would have to delete the WINS database (Delete Owner) as described earlier and rebuild it. To rebuild a deleted database, all clients must reregister with WINS. This happens automatically when the client systems are rebooted.

Compressing the WINS Database

Whenever the WINS database (`wins.mdb`) reaches a size of 30MB or more, you should compress it. To compress the WINS database manually use the `JETPACK.EXE` utility from a command prompt. The WINS database is located in the `C:\WINNT\SYSTEM32\WINS` directory by default. Be sure to stop the WINS service before compacting the database, and restart the service when it is complete. Here is the command-line structure for compacting the WINS database:

```
jetpack wins.mdb temporary_name.mdb
```

You can perform the entire process from the command line. The full command syntax to stop the WINS service, compact the database, and restart the WINS service is as follows:

```
net stop wins
Jetpack wins.mdb temp1.mdb
net start wins
```

You can type any temporary name for the temporary database file. The temporary file is automatically deleted by the system when the compression is complete.

WINS Replication Partners

On networks with multiple WINS servers, having the WINS servers share their databases with one another is often wise. Sharing the databases ensures maximum name resolution capabilities for each WINS server because they have access to the mappings of all WINS servers. WINS servers that share their databases with each other are called *replication partners*.

The replication process is done as a push or pull operation. When the replication is configured as a push, the replication is done whenever a certain number (set by the administrator) of changes to the database have occurred. Pull replication is configured on a schedule, which is also set by the administrator.

Typically, only pull replication is configured on slow wide area network links because it can be scheduled around peak usage periods. Push and pull replications are typically configured for local area networks where connections are usually fast. The push ensures that too many changes do not occur to the database before an update is issued. In addition, the pull system ensures updates are issued on a regular basis no matter how few changes have occurred.

To configure database replication, open the WINS Manager application, click the Server menu, and then choose Replication Partners (see Figure 7.7).

FIGURE 7.7

WINS replication partners.

The Replication Partner dialog box allows you to configure pull and/or push replication partners. The Replicate Now button starts both push and pull replication. The Push with Propagation option sends changes to replication partners and triggers a chain reaction, which not only updates the replication partner, but also any and all replication partners configured under that partner.

WINS Implementation Recommendations

Although only one WINS server is required to implement WINS on the network, Microsoft recommends that you implement a minimum of two WINS servers. The second WINS server provides a level of fault tolerance in the event that the first WINS server fails. In addition to fault tolerance, a second WINS server could provide some load balancing. To ensure that the load is equally balanced between the WINS servers, configure half of the clients to access one WINS server primarily and the other half to access the other WINS server primarily. Then, configure the opposite WINS server as a secondary or alternate for each WINS client to get the benefits of fault tolerance. In addition, be sure that the WINS servers act as replication partners.

In order to handle the load properly, you should add additional WINS servers for every 10,000 WINS clients served. If you want to increase the performance of a single WINS server, you can turn off logging. If the WINS server crashes, you will lose recent changes to the database, but the server performs better with logging off. If you want to increase performance by adding hardware to the WINS server, consider using a multiprocessor system. Microsoft states that WINS servers perform up to 25% better with each additional processor.

Integrating WINS and DNS Name Resolution Services

In addition to using a WINS server, the Microsoft clients can contact a DNS server for NetBIOS name resolution. Windows NT 4.0 systems have an Enable DNS for Windows Resolution check box (see Figure 7.8) to allow you to enable this feature. If this option is enabled, the WINS client calls the DNS server to resolve NetBIOS names after failing to resolve the name via the WINS server, broadcast, or LMHOSTS/HOSTS file.

Microsoft DNS servers can also be configured to use WINS to help with name resolution (see Figure 7.9). The Microsoft DNS server only calls the WINS server to resolve the host part of a computer on the network. This means that the DNS server must be able to resolve the domain name and any sub-domain names before contacting the WINS server.

FIGURE 7.8

Enabling the WINS client to contact the DNS server.

FIGURE 7.9

Enabling the DNS server to contact the WINS server.

DHCP Serving WINS Options

A DHCP server can be configured to provide more than just an IP address and subnet mask to a DHCP client. The DHCP client can also receive WINS options from the DHCP server. Specifically, the DHCP client can be configured with a primary and secondary WINS server address and a NetBIOS node type.

The four types of NetBIOS nodes were described earlier in this chapter. Remember, the NetBIOS node types are the B-node, P-node, M-node, and H-node options. Figure 7.10 shows the configuration dialog box for implementing these options on a Microsoft DHCP server. You will learn more about configuring DHCP in Chapter 8, "Automatic Configuration."

NOTE

IP addresses configured in primary and secondary WINS servers take priority over corresponding parameters previously configured via DHCP.

FIGURE 7.10

DHCP servers can provide WINS configuration options.

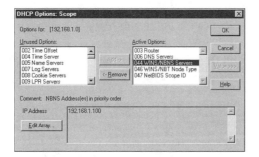

7

WINS

NetBIOS Name Resolution Via LMHOSTS

The LMHOSTS file can also perform NetBIOS name to IP address resolution. However, the LMHOSTS file must be manually created and maintained. Essentially, it is a static mapping file that matches computer names to IP addresses. Microsoft has included sample LMHOSTS files in the Windows NT and Windows 95/98 operating systems. You can find the LMHOSTS.SAM file under the C:\WINDOWS directory in Windows 95/98 operating systems. In Windows NT operating systems, the LMHOSTS.SAM is in the C:\WINNT\SYSTEM32\DRIVERS\ETC directory.

The LMHOSTS.SAM file describes in detail how to create an LMHOSTS file. However, in order for the LMHOSTS file to be active it must have the name LMHOSTS without a file extension. Figure 7.11 illustrates a sample LMHOSTS file.

FIGURE 7.11

LMHOSTS file example.

In addition to mapping IP addresses to NetBIOS computer names, the LMHOSTS file has special predefined tags, which allow for added functionality. For instance, an entry in the LMHOSTS file followed by a #PRE tag is placed in the NetBIOS name cache when the computer starts up. This increases the speed of name resolution because Microsoft clients always check the name cache before attempting any other type of name resolution.

Table 7.2 lists the special tags that can be set in an LMHOSTS file.

TABLE 7.2 LMHOSTS Tags and Descriptions

LMHOSTS Tag	*Description*
#PRE	Entries with a #PRE tag are preloaded into the NetBIOS name cache.
#DOM:domain_name	#DOM identifies the domain name. This entry is essential for domain controller activity such as database synchronization and browsing.
#INCLUDE<*filename*>	#INCLUDE<*filename*> sets alternate files to be used for name resolution. These files can be the LMHOSTS files on remote computers and can be referenced with a UNC path. If you use a remote computer's LMHOSTS file, you must have already provided a mapping to that computer for this entry to work.
#BEGIN_ALTERNATE #END_ALTERNATE	#BEGIN_ALTERNATE and #END_ALTERNATE allow multiple #INCLUDE entries to exist in an LMHOSTS file. This enables the LMHOSTS file to parse multiple remote LMHOSTS files as if they were local entries.
#MH	#MH is for multihomed computers that may have multiple IP addresses mapping to a single computer name.
#comment	Comments can be placed in the LMHOSTS file after any entry or as a standalone line.

The #PRE tag is probably the most significant LMHOSTS file tag because it can have the greatest impact on the speed of name resolution on the network. The second most important tag is #DOM, which identifies the domain controllers. Implementing the #PRE and #DOM entries in the LMHOSTS file on all domain controllers improves the performance of administrative communications between domain controllers. In addition, if client computers have LMHOSTS files that add the domain controller's IP addresses into their name cache, the login process is faster because the client system already has a mapping for the domain controller's IP address.

Note

The HOSTS file and LMHOSTS file are very similar. The focus of the LMHOSTS file is NetBIOS name resolution and the focus of the HOSTS file is hostname resolution, as explained in Chapter 6, "DNS: Name Services."

Summary

NetBIOS names are used in Microsoft networks prior to Windows 2000. On a TCP/IP network, these NetBIOS names, like hostnames, must be resolved to IP addresses in order for communication to take place between two computers. There are a few different methods for resolving IP addresses to NetBIOS names, but the only dynamic method is to use WINS.

WINS functions as a client/server application built in to Microsoft operating systems. The WINS client registers its NetBIOS name and IP address with the WINS server when it starts up. A WINS client releases its name from the WINS server when the WINS client shuts down. This allows the WINS server to maintain a current database of NetBIOS names in use on the network. When WINS clients want to contact other computers on the network, they call the WINS server for NetBIOS name to IP address resolution.

In order for a client system to become a WINS client, the IP address of at least one WINS server must be entered for the client. The entry is made in the TCP/IP configuration dialog box for the WINS client. The IP addresses of multiple WINS servers can be configured on a WINS client system to provide fault tolerance. The WINS client will contact an alternate or secondary WINS server when the primary WINS server is unavailable.

Non-WINS clients can also take advantage of WINS services. WINS Proxy Agents help non-WINS clients to utilize WINS services. WINS Proxy Agents take local subnet name resolution broadcasts and forward them to the WINS server. WINS Proxy Agents return the WINS server response to the non-WINS clients. This means that non-WINS clients can benefit from WINS server name resolution via a WINS Proxy Agent.

Many maintenance and administrative tasks are automatically accomplished by a WINS server. However, you must set the WINS server to perform backups via the WINS Manager application. The WINS server can automatically restore a corrupted database (if there is a backup) after it is restarted. However, database restoration can be done manually through the WINS Manager application. The WINS server database can be compressed through the command-line utility JETPACK.EXE.

WINS replication partners are WINS servers that are configured to exchange WINS database information. WINS replication partners can be push partners and/or pull partners. Pull partners are best for slow WAN links. On fast LAN connections you can enable both push and pull to ensure that your WINS databases have the most current information.

LMHOSTS files can help with NetBIOS name resolution in several ways. Although they are not dynamic, like WINS, and must be manually maintained, they do provide some benefits. Entries in the LMHOSTS files can be added directly to the NetBIOS name cache by tagging them with #PRE. In addition, domain controllers can be identified in the LMHOSTS file by the tag #DOM.

Automatic Configuration

by Karanjit S. Siyan, Ph.D.

CHAPTER 8

Configuring TCP/IP parameters for each workstation on a large network can be a difficult and time-consuming task, particularly when the TCP/IP parameters, such as IP addresses and subnet masks, need to be changed. The changes can occur because of a major restructuring of the network or because the network has a large number of mobile users with portable computers that can be connected to any of the network segments. The network connections can be direct physical connections or wireless connections. Because the TCP/IP parameters for computers depend on the network segment they connect to, appropriate values must be set up whenever a computer is connected to a different network segment.

Understanding the consequences of TCP/IP parameter changes requires knowledgeable network administrators. Several auto-configuration protocols, such as Boot Protocol (BOOTP) and Dynamic Host Configuration Protocol (DHCP), have been developed by the Internet Engineering Task Force (IETF) for TCP/IP internetworks.

Dynamic Configuration Using BOOTP

BOOTP is designed to use User Datagram Protocol (UDP) and Internet Protocol (IP) to carry configuration information for computers wanting to configure themselves. Computers making the request are called *BOOTP clients*, and computers that respond to the BOOTP client requests are called *BOOTP servers* (see Figure 8.1).

The purpose of the BOOTP client request is to discover the IP parameter settings for the computer running the BOOTP client.

BOOTP is discussed in RFC 951 on the "Bootstrap Protocol" and is updated by RFC 2132, RFC 1532, RFC 1542, and RFC 1395. The following sections describe the operation of BOOTP.

BOOTP Request/Reply IP Addresses

The BOOTP messages are encapsulated in a UDP header that identifies the port number used by the BOOTP processes. The UDP datagram is encapsulated in an IP header. What source and destination IP address values are used in the IP header? This is an interesting question because when the BOOTP client makes its request, it must use a source and destination IP address. Typically, the BOOTP client does not know its IP address; it uses a source IP address value of 0.0.0.0. If the BOOTP client knows its IP address, it uses this address in the BOOTP client request.

FIGURE 8.1
*BOOTP clients
and servers.*

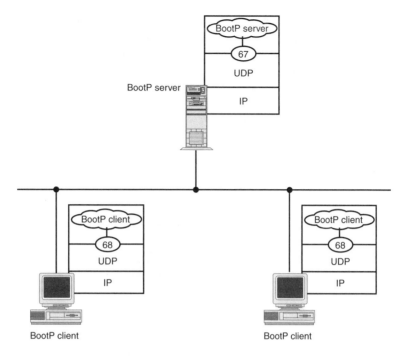

Does the BOOTP client know the IP address of the BOOTP server? Typically, no. This is especially true in situations where the BOOTP client is a diskless workstation and has no way of knowing the BOOTP server address. In situations where the workstation can be configured with the BOOTP server address, the BOOTP client can use the BOOTP server address.

When the BOOTP client does not recognize the BOOTP server's IP address, it uses a limited IP broadcast. The IP limited broadcast has the following value:

255.255.255.255

Note

The limited or local broadcast address is received by all IP nodes including BOOTP servers on the local network.

8

AUTOMATIC
CONFIGURATION

What if the BOOTP server is on a different IP subnet, beyond a router boundary? A limited broadcast cannot cross a router boundary. In this case, the router must be configured with a BOOTP relay agent that checks to see whether the UDP destination port number of 67 is being used in the limited broadcast datagram. (UDP port 67 is reserved for BOOTP/DHCP.) If this is the case, the limited broadcast is forwarded to the router's network interfaces (see Figure 8.2).

FIGURE 8.2

Forwarding of BOOTP messages across a router boundary.

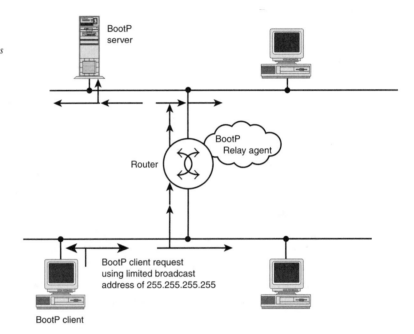

When the BOOTP server is on the local network, it can respond to the BOOTP client request message. Does the BOOTP reply message from the BOOTP server use the IP address of the client? In other words, can the BOOTP server send a directed reply? The answer depends on the BOOTP server implementation.

A problem is associated with sending a directed BOOTP reply to the BOOTP client. The BOOTP server knows the BOOTP client's IP address by looking it up in its BOOTP configuration database. Why can't the BOOTP server use this IP address to send a directed reply to the BOOTP client? The answer to this question lies in the fact that when the BOOTP server sends an ARP request message to discover the hardware address of the BOOTP client, the BOOTP client is unable to respond. Why? The answer is because the BOOTP client does not know its IP address yet. The BOOTP server knows the hardware address of the BOOTP client from the Data Link Layer header in the BOOTP client message. A BOOTP server implementation may add an entry in the ARP cache table for the BOOTP client (see Figure 8.3). If it does, the BOOTP server can use a directed reply.

> **Note**
>
> The BSD Unix BOOTP implementation uses the ARP modification technique.

Figure 8.3

Adjusting of the ARP cache table by a BOOTP server.

If a BOOTP server does not adjust the ARP cache table, it must broadcast its reply.

Handling the Loss of BOOTP Messages

BOOTP uses UDP and IP protocols. These protocols cannot guarantee delivery of BOOTP messages. As a result BOOTP messages can become lost, delayed, duplicated, or delivered out of sequence. Because IP provides only a checksum to guard against errors in the IP header and not the data field, a BOOTP implementation may require that the UDP checksum be enabled. The UDP checksum can guard against error in the entire BOOTP message.

8

Automatic Configuration

A BOOTP client sends requests using the IP Don't Fragment (DF) flag set to 1 to simplify the processing of BOOTP replies, and in case it does not have enough memory to reassemble fragmented datagrams.

BOOTP uses a timeout and retransmission policy to handle message loss. When a BOOTP client sends its request, it also starts a timer. A BOOTP reply within the timeout interval cancels the timer, but if the timer expires before a BOOTP reply is received, the BOOTP retransmits its request.

When BOOTP clients start at the same time, they can flood the network with BOOTP broadcast requests. To prevent this from occurring, the BOOTP specification recommends using a random delay starting with a random timeout interval from zero to four seconds. Successive retransmissions cause the doubling of the random timeout interval until a large value, such as 60 seconds, is reached. When this upper limit is reached, the random timeout interval is not doubled, but random time delays within this interval are still used. Randomization is used to avoid simultaneous BOOTP client requests that could overload the server and cause packet collisions in an ethernet network. Doubling the random timeout interval avoids overloading the network with too many BOOTP client broadcast requests.

BOOTP Message Format

Figure 8.4 shows the BOOTP message format, and Table 8.1 discusses the meanings of the fields in the BOOT message.

Figure 8.4

BOOTP message format.

Numbers in parenthesis ( ) represent octets

TABLE 8.1   DHCP Fields

Field	Octets	Description
op	1	Message op code (message type). A value of 1 means it is a BOOTREQUEST message, and a value of 2 means it is a BOOTREPLY message.
htype	1	Hardware address type. The values are the same as those used for the ARP packet format. For example, a value of 1 is used for 10 Mbps ethernet.
hlen	1	Hardware address length in octets. Ethernet and token-ring hardware address length is 6 bytes.
hops	1	Set to zero by the BOOTP client. This is optionally used by relay agents running on routers when they forward BOOTP messages.
xid	4	Transaction ID. A randomly generated number chosen by the BOOTP client when it generates a BOOTP message. The BOOTP server uses the same Transaction ID in its BOOTP messages to the client. The Transaction ID enables the BOOTP clients and servers to associate BOOTP messages with the corresponding responses.
secs	2	Filled by the BOOTP client. It is the seconds elapsed since client started trying to boot.
unused	2	Not used.
ciaddr	4	The BOOTP client's IP address. It is filled by the BOOTP client in a BOOTPREQUEST message to verify the use of previously allocated configuration parameters. If the client does not recognize its IP address, this field is set to 0.
yiaddr	4	The BOOTP client's "your IP address." Returned by the BOOTP server.
siaddr	4	The server's IP address. Inserted by the BOOTP client if the client wants to contact a BOOTP server. The BOOTP server's IP address may have been initialized as part of the TCP/IP configuration database at the BOOTP client. The value returned by the BOOTP server may be the address of the next server to contact as part of the boot process. For example, this may be the address of a server that holds the operating system boot image.
giaddr	4	The IP address of the router that runs the BOOTP relay agent.
chaddr	16	The BOOTP client's hardware address. A value of 16 octets is used to enable different network hardware types. Ethernet and token-ring hardware use only 6 octets.
sname	64	An optional server hostname if recognized by the BOOTP client. It is a null-terminated string.

8

AUTOMATIC
CONFIGURATION

TABLE 8.1 continued

Field	Octets	Description
file	128	The boot filename. It is a null-terminated string. If the BOOTP client wants to boot with an image of the operating system downloaded from a network device, it can specify a generic name, such as "unix," for booting a UNIX image.
		The BOOTP server can hold more specific information about the exact operating system image needed for that workstation. This reply from the BOOTP server contains the fully qualified directory pathname.
vendor	64	An optional vendor-specific area. This could be hardware type/serial on request, or "capability"/remote file system handle on reply. This information may be set aside for use by a third phase bootstrap or kernel.

Phases of the BOOTP Procedure

Contrary to what might be suggested by its name, BOOTP is not used for actually transferring the operating system image to the BOOTP client. The transfer of the operating system image is handled by a separate protocol called Trivial File Transfer Protocol (TFTP), which runs on the UDP transport. Diskless workstations need to download the operating system image. Other workstations that are only using BOOTP to assign IP addresses from a central location don't download the operating system image.

Figure 8.5 shows the phases of the complete bootstrap procedure required to download an operating system image. In step 1, the BOOTP client makes a request to obtain the IP configuration image. In step 2, the BOOTP server returns the IP configuration information and the name of the operating system image file to download. In step 3, the BOOTP client passes a request to obtain the operating system image to the TFTP client. In step 4, the TFTP client issues a request to the TFTP server to obtain the operating system image. In step 5, the TFTP server returns a series of data packets containing the operating system image. After obtaining the operating system image, the BOOTP loads the operating system image in memory and initializes itself.

Keeping the BOOTP phase separate from the transfer of the operating system image has the advantage that the BOOTP server need not run on the same machine that stores the operating system images (TFTP server). Additionally, it enables BOOTP to be used in situations where only the configuration image is needed from the BOOTP server and there is no need to transfer the operating system image.

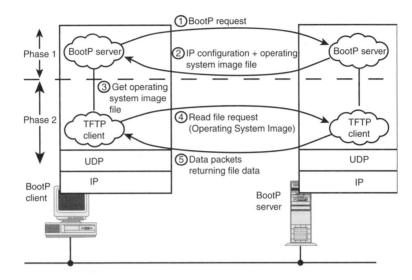

FIGURE 8.5

Typical bootstrap procedure.

There may be situations in which an administrator may want to set up a workstation to boot up with a different operating system type depending on the user. In this case, the BOOTP request message can contain a generic label in the filename field, such as "unix," to download a Unix operating system image or "default" to download some other default operating system image. On seeing the generic name of the operating system image that has been requested, the BOOTP server can consult its configuration database and map the generic name to its fully qualified filename and return this name in the BOOTP reply. The BOOTP client can pass this fully qualified name to its local TFTP client for downloading the operating system image.

The Vendor Specific Area Field

The BOOTP message format describes several common IP parameters. Many vendors need to describe additional parameters for their devices. The *Vendor Specific Area* field in BOOTP messages is used for these additional parameters.

The Vendor Specific Area field in the BOOTP message contains vendor-specific data for the BOOTP client. This field is optional, and its usage depends on the type of additional configuration information needed by the BOOTP client. The first four octets contain a "magic cookie" value that defines the format of the rest of the vendor field. These four octets are expressed using a dotted-decimal notation—they should not be confused as IP addresses. The magic cookie value of 99.130.83.99 (hexadecimal dotted notation 63.82.53.63) is an arbitrary agreed-upon value that specifies a standard format for the vendor-specific area. The magic cookie value is followed by a list of items. Each item is identified by the following:

- A 1-octet tag field or type field
- An optional 1-octet length field that specifies the length of the data field that follows
- A multi-octet data field

The BOOTP item tags were defined in RFC 1497 on "BOOTP Vendor Information Extensions." With the introduction of the DHCP protocol, the BOOTP vendor extensions and the DHCP options field now have a common format. This common format is described in RFC 2132 in "DHCP Options and BOOTP Vendor Extensions." Common examples of the vendor-specific tag values are listed in Table 8.2.

TABLE 8.2   Common Vendor-Specific Tags for BOOTP

Tag	*Length*	*Meaning (octets)*
0	-	Used only for padding. The pad option can be used to cause subsequent fields to align on word boundaries.
1	4	Subnet Mask field.
2	4	Time Offset field. Specifies time offset of the client's subnet in seconds from Coordinated Universal Time (UTC). The offset is expressed as a signed 32-bit integer.
3	N	Router option. Specifies a list of IP addresses for routers on the client's subnet. Routers should be listed in order of preference. The minimum length for the router option is 4 octets, and the length must always be a multiple of 4.
4	N	Time Server option. Specifies a list of RFC 868 time servers available to the client. Servers should be listed in order of preference. The minimum length for the router option is 4 octets, and the length must always be a multiple of 4.
5	N	Name Server option. Specifies a list of Internet Engineering Note (IEN) 116 name servers available to the client. Servers should be listed in order of preference. The minimum length for the router option is 4 octets, and the length must always be a multiple of 4.
6	N	Domain Name Server option. Specifies a list of Domain Name System (STD 13, RFC 1035) name servers available to the client. Servers should be listed in order of preference. The minimum length for the router option is 4 octets, and the length must always be a multiple of 4.

TABLE 8.2 continued

Tag	Length	Meaning (octets)
7	N	Log Server option. Specifies a list of MIT-LCS UDP log servers available to the client. Servers should be listed in order of preference. The minimum length for the router option is 4 octets, and the length must always be a multiple of 4.
8	N	Cookie Server option. Specifies a list of RFC 865 cookie servers available to the client. Servers should be listed in order of preference. The minimum length for the router option is 4 octets, and the length must always be a multiple of 4.
9	N	LPR Server option. Specifies a list of RFC 1179 line printer servers available to the client. Servers should be listed in order of preference. The minimum length for the router option is 4 octets, and the length must always be a multiple of 4.
10	N	Impress Server option. Specifies a list of Imagen Impress servers available to the client. Servers should be listed in order of preference. The minimum length for the router option is 4 octets, and the length must always be a multiple of 4.
11	N	Resource Location Server option. Specifies a list of RFC 887 Resource Location servers available to the client. Servers should be listed in order of preference. The minimum length for the router option is 4 octets, and the length must always be a multiple of 4.
12	N	Host Name option. Specifies the name of the client. The name may or may not be qualified with the local domain name. See RFC 1035 for character set restrictions. Minimum length of the data field is 1 octet.
13	2	Boot File Size option. Specifies the length in 512-octet blocks of the default boot image for the client. The file length is specified as an unsigned 16-bit integer.
128-254	Undefined	Reserved for site-specific options. Interpretation depends on implementation.
255	-	End option. Marks the end of valid information in the vendor field. Subsequent octets should be filled with the pad option.

8

AUTOMATIC
CONFIGURATION

Dynamic Configuration Using DHCP

Dynamic Host Configuration Protocol (DHCP) is an extension of the BOOTP protocol that provides greater flexibility in IP address management. DHCP can be used for the dynamic configuration of essential TCP/IP parameters for hosts (workstations and servers) on a network. The DHCP protocol consists of two elements:

- A mechanism for allocating IP addresses and other TCP/IP parameters
- A protocol for negotiating and transmitting host-specific information

The TCP/IP host requesting the TCP/IP configuration information is called the *DHCP client*, and the TCP/IP host that supplies this information is called a *DHCP server*.

The DHCP protocol is described in RFC 2131 on "Dynamic Host Configuration Protocol." The following sections discuss the operation of DHCP.

Understanding IP Address Management with DHCP

DHCP uses the following three methods for IP address allocation:

- Manual allocation
- Automatic allocation
- Dynamic allocation

In the manual allocation method, the DHCP client's IP address is set manually by the network administrator at the DHCP server, and DHCP is used to convey to the DHCP client the value of the manually configured IP address.

In the automatic allocation method, no manual assignments of IP addresses need to be made. The DHCP client is assigned an IP address when it first contacts the DHCP server. The IP address assigned using this method is permanently assigned to the DHCP client and is not reused by another DHCP client.

In the dynamic allocation method, DHCP assigns an IP address to a DHCP client on a temporary basis. The IP address is on loan or "leased" to the DHCP client for a specified duration. On the expiry of this lease, the IP address is revoked, and the DHCP client is required to surrender the IP address. If the DHCP client still needs an IP address to perform its functions, it can request another IP address.

The dynamic allocation method is the only one of the three methods that affords automatic reuse of an IP address. An IP address need not be surrendered by the DHCP client on the expiry of the lease. If the DHCP client no longer needs an IP address, such as when the computer is being gracefully shut down, it can release the IP address to the DHCP server. The DHCP server then can reissue the same IP address to another DHCP client making a request for an IP address.

The dynamic allocation method is particularly useful for DHCP clients that need an IP address for temporary connection to a network. For example, consider a situation where 300 users have portable computers on a network and a class C address has been assigned to a network. This enables the network to have 253 nodes on the network (255–2 special addresses = 253). Because computers connecting to a network using TCP/IP are required to have unique IP addresses, all the 300 computers cannot be simultaneously connected to the network. However, if at most only 200 physical connections are on the network, using a class C address by reusing IP addresses that are not in use should be possible. Using DHCP's dynamic IP address allocation, IP address reuse is possible.

Dynamic IP address allocation is also a good choice for assigning IP addresses to new hosts that are being permanently connected and where IP addresses are scarce. As old hosts are retired, their IP addresses can be immediately reused.

> **Note**
>
> Regardless of which of the three methods of IP address allocation is used, you can still configure IP parameters at a central DHCP server once, instead of repeating the TCP/IP configuration for each computer.

The DHCP IP Address Acquisition Process

Upon contacting a DHCP server, a DHCP client goes through several internal states during which it negotiates the use of an IP address and the duration of use. How a DHCP client acquires the IP address can best be explained in terms of a state transition diagram (also called a finite state machine). Figure 8.6 shows the state transition diagram that explains the interaction between the DHCP client and DHCP server.

8

AUTOMATIC CONFIGURATION

FIGURE 8.6

DHCP state transition diagram showing DHCP client/server interaction.

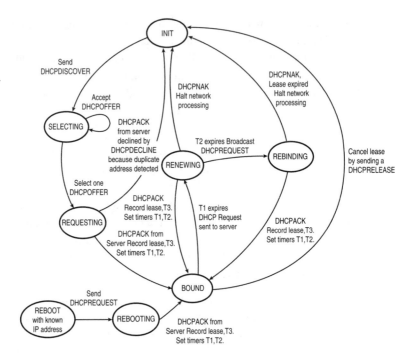

When the DHCP client is first started, it begins in the INIT (initialize) state. At this point the DHCP client does not recognize its IP parameters, and so sends a DHCPDISCOVER broadcast. The DHCPDISCOVER is encapsulated in a UDP/IP packet. The destination UDP port number is set to 67 (decimal), the same as that for a BOOTP server, because the DHCP protocol is an extension of the BOOTP protocol. A local IP broadcast address of 255.255.255.255 is used in the DHCPDISCOVER packet. If DHCP servers are not on the local network, the IP router must have DHCP-relay agent support to forward the DHCPDISCOVER request to other subnetworks. DHCP-relay agent support is discussed in RFC 1542.

Before sending the DHCPDISCOVER broadcast packet, the DHCP client waits for a random time interval between 1 to 10 seconds. This is to prevent DHCP clients from starting at the same time if they are powered up at the same time (as sometimes happens after a power failure).

After sending the DHCPDISCOVER broadcast, the DHCP client enters the SELECTING state. In this state, the DHCP client receives DHCPOFFER messages from the DHCP servers that have been configured to respond to the DHCP client. The time period over which the DHCP client waits to receive DHCPOFFER messages is implementation dependent. The DHCP client must select one DHCPOFFER response if it receives multiple DHCPOFFER responses. After selecting a DHCPOFFER message from a server, the DHCP client sends a DHCPREQUEST message to the selected DHCP server. The DHCP server responds with a DHCPACK.

The DHCP client may optionally perform a check on the IP address sent in the DHCPACK to verify that the address is not in use. On a broadcast network, the DHCP client can send an ARP request for the suggested IP address to see whether there is an ARP response. An ARP response would imply that the suggested IP address is already in use, in which case the DHCPACK from the sever is ignored, a DHCPDECLINE is sent, and the DHCP client enters the INIT state and retries to get a valid unused IP address. When the ARP request is broadcast on the local network, the client uses its own hardware address in the sender hardware address field of the ARP packet, but sets a value of 0 in the sender IP address field. A sender IP address of 0 is used rather than the suggested IP address, so as not to confuse ARP caches on other TCP/IP hosts (in case the suggested IP address is already in use).

When the DHCPACK from the DHCP server is accepted, three timer values are set, and the DHCP client moves into the BOUND state. The first timer, T1, is the lease renewal timer; the second timer, T2, is the rebinding timer; and the third timer, T3, is the lease duration. The DHCPACK always returns the value of T3, which is the duration of the lease. The values of timers T1 and T2 can be configured at the DHCP server, but if they are not set, default values are used based on the duration of the lease. The following list shows the default values used for T1 and T2:

> T1 = renewal timer
> T2 = rebinding timer
> T3 = duration of lease
> T1 = 0.5 x T3
> T2 = 0.875 x T3

The actual time at which the timer values expire is computed by adding to the timer value, the time at which the DHCPREQUEST that generated the DHCPACK response was sent. If the time at which the DHCP request was sent was T0, then the expiration values are computed as follows:

> Expiration of T1 = T0 + T1
> Expiration of T2 = T0 + T2
> Expiration of T3 = T0 + T3

8

AUTOMATIC
CONFIGURATION

> **Note**
>
> RFC 2131 recommends that a "fuzz" factor be added to the timers T1 and T2 to prevent several DHCP clients from expiring their timers at the same time.

At the expiration of timer T1, the DHCP client moves from the BOUND state to the RENEWING state. In the RENEWING state a new lease for the allocated IP address must be negotiated by the DHCP client from the DHCP server that originally allocated the IP address. If the original DHCP server does not renew the release, it sends a DHCP-NAK message, and the DHCP client moves into the INIT state and tries to obtain a new IP address. If the original DHCP server sends a DHCPACK message, this message contains the new lease duration. The DHCP client sets its timer values and moves to the BOUND state.

If the timer T2 expires while DHCP client is waiting in the RENEWING state for a DHCPACK or DHCPNAK message from the original DHCP server, the DHCP client moves from the RENEWING state to the REBINDING state. The original DHCP server may not respond because it's down or a network link is down. Note from the previous equations that T2 > T1, so the DHCP client waits for the original DHCP server to renew the release for a duration of T2-T1.

At the expiration of a timer T2, a broadcast DHCPREQUEST is sent on the network to contact any DHCP server to extend the lease, and the DHCP client is in the REBIND-ING state. A broadcast DHCPREQUEST is sent because the DHCP client assumes, after spending T2-T1 seconds in the RENEWING state, that the original DHCP server is not available, and the DHCP client tries to contact any configured DHCP server to respond to it. If a DHCP server responds with a DHCPACK message, the DHCP client renews its lease (T3), sets the timers T1 and T2, and moves back to the BOUND state. If no DHCP server is able to renew the release after the expiration of timer T3, the lease expires and the DHCP client moves to the INIT state. Note that by this time, the DHCP client has tried to renew the lease, first with the original DHCP server and then with any DHCP server on the network.

When the lease expires (timer T3 expires), the DHCP client must surrender the use of its IP address and halt network processing with that IP address.

The DHCP client does not always have to wait for the expiration of the lease (timer T3) to surrender the use of an IP address. It could voluntarily relinquish control of an IP address by canceling its lease. For example, a user with a portable computer may connect to the network to perform a network activity. The DHCP server on the network may set the duration of the lease for one hour. Assume that the user finishes the network tasks in

30 minutes, and now wants to disconnect from the network. When the user gracefully shuts down his computer, the DHCP client sends a DHCPRELEASE message to the DHCP server to cancel its lease. The surrendered IP address is now available for use by another DHCP client.

If DHCP clients are run on computers that have a disk, the IP address allocated can be stored on the disk, and when the computer reboots, it can make a request for the same IP address. This is shown in Figure 8.6 in the state labeled "REBOOT with known IP address."

DHCP Packet Format

The DHCP packet format is shown in Figure 8.7. The DHCP messages use a fixed format for all the fields, except the options field that has a minimum size of 312 octets. Readers who are familiar with the BOOTP protocol recognize that with the exception of the flags field and the options field, the message formats for DHCP and BOOTP are identical. In fact the DHCP server can be configured to answer BOOTP requests. The configuration details are operating system–specific.

FIGURE 8.7
DHCP packet format.

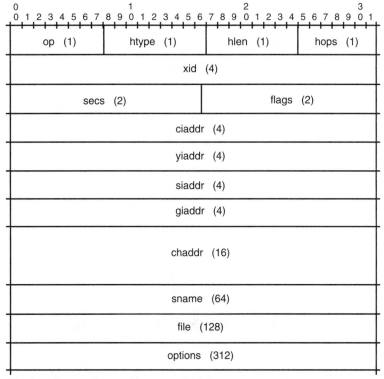

Numbers in parentheses ( ) represent octets

8

AUTOMATIC
CONFIGURATION

Table 8.3 provides an explanation of the fields used in the DHCP protocol. Only the left-most bit of the DHCP options field is used (see Figure 8.8). The other bits in the options field must be set to 0.

FIGURE 8.8

DHCP options field.

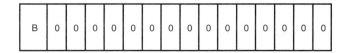

B = 1   Broadcast

B = 0   Unicast

TABLE 8.3   DHCP Fields

Field	Octets	Description
op	1	Message op code (message type). A value of 1 means it is a BOOTREQUEST message, and a value of 2 means it is a BOOTREPLY message.
htype	1	The hardware address type. The values are the same as that used for the ARP packet format. For example, a value of 1 is used for 10 Mbps ethernet.
hlen	1	The hardware address length in octets. Ethernet and token-ring hardware adders length is 6 bytes.
hops	1	Set to 0 by the DHCP client. This is optionally used by relay agents running on routers when they forward DHCP messages.
xid	4	A Transaction ID. A randomly generated number chosen by the DHCP client when it generates a DHCP message. The DHCP server uses the same Transaction ID in its DHCP messages to the client. The Transaction ID enables the DHCP clients and servers to associate DHCP messages with the corresponding responses.
secs	2	Filled by the DHCP client. It is the seconds elapsed since client started trying to boot.
flags	2	Used to indicate whether this is a broadcast message. If so, the leftmost bit has a value of 1. All other bits must remain zero.
ciaddr	4	The DHCP client's IP address. It is filled by the DHCP client in a DHCPREQUEST message to verify the use of previously allocated configuration parameters. If the client does not know its IP address, this field is set to 0.
yiaddr	4	The DHCP client's "your IP address" returned by the DHCP server.

TABLE 8.3   continued

Field	Octets	Description
siaddr	4	The server's IP address. If the DHCP client wants to contact a specific DHCP server, it inserts the server's IP address in this field. The DHCP server's IP address may have been discovered in prior DHCPOFFER and DHCPACK messages returned by the server. The value returned by the DHCP server may be the address of the next server to contact as part of the boot process. For example, this may be the address of a server that holds the operating system boot image.
giaddr	4	The IP address of the router that runs the relay agent.
chaddr	16	The DHCP client's hardware address. A value of 16 octets is used to enable different network hardware types. Ethernet and token-ring hardware use only 6 octets.
sname	64	An optional server hostname if known by the DHCP client. It is a null-terminated string.
file	128	The boot filename. It is a null-terminated string. If the DHCP client wants to boot with an image of the operating system downloaded from a network device, it can specify a generic name, such as "unix," for booting a Unix image in a DHCPDISCOVER. The DHCP server can hold more specific information about the exact operating system image needed for that workstation. This image name can be returned as a fully qualified directory path name in the DHCPOFFER message from the DHCP server.
options	312	An optional parameters field.

Most of the DHCP messages sent by the DHCP server to the DHCP client are *unicast messages* (messages sent to a single IP address). This is because the DHCP server learns about the DHCP client's hardware address in messages sent by the DHCP client to the server. The DHCP client may request that the DHCP server respond with a broadcast address by setting the leftmost bit in the options field to 1. The DHCP client will do this if it does not know its IP address yet. The IP protocol module in DHCP client rejects a received datagram if the destination IP address in the datagram does not match the IP address of the DHCP client's network interface. If the IP address of the network interface is not known, the datagram still is rejected. However, the IP protocol module accepts any IP broadcast datagram. Therefore, to ensure that the IP protocol module accepts the DHCP server reply when the IP address is not yet configured, the DHCP client requests that the DHCP server reply use broadcast messages instead of unicast messages.

The options field is variable in length, with the minimum size extended to 312 octets, so that the total minimum size of a DHCP message is 576 octets, which is the minimum IP datagram size a host must be prepared to accept. If a DHCP client needs to use larger size messages it can negotiate this using the Maximum DHCP message size option. Because the sname and file fields are quite large and may not always be used, DHCP options may be further extended into these fields by specifying the Option Overload option. If present, the usual meanings of the sname and file fields are ignored, and these fields are examined for options. Options are expressed using the Type, Length, Value (T-L-V) format.

Figure 8.9 shows that in DHCP, the option consists of a 1-octet Type field, followed by a 1-octet Length field. The value of the Length field contains the size of the Value field. The different DHCP messages themselves are expressed using a special Type value of 53. The option values that describe the DHCP messages are shown in Figure 8.10.

FIGURE 8.9

Option format for DHCP messages.

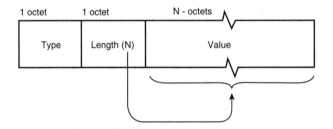

FIGURE 8.10

Option values for the DHCP messages.

	1 octet	1 octet	1 octet
DHCPDISCOVER	53 Type	1 length	1 value
DHCPOFFER	53 Type	1 length	2 value
DHCPREQUEST	53 Type	1 length	3 value
DHCPDECLINE	53 Type	1 length	4 value
DHCKACK	53 Type	1 length	5 value
DHCPNAK	53 Type	1 length	6 value
DHCPRELEASE	53 Type	1 length	7 value

DHCP Protocol Trace

This section describes the DHCP message format for packets captured on a real-life network. Because the DHCP protocol and its packet format are a superset of BOOTP, only DHCP traces are discussed in this chapter. In fact, the DHCP client and servers use the same port number assignments for the BOOTP client and BOOTP servers. That is, DHCP client uses UDP port number 68, and DHCP server uses UDP port number 67. Most protocol analyzers will attempt to decode DHCP and BOOTP messages in the same format.

DHCP Trace with Directed Reply from DHCP Server

Figures 8.11 and 8.12 show a DHCP client broadcast request and a DHCP server reply. The DHCP server reply is a directed reply. A directed reply was possible because this implementation of the DHCP server made a direct entry in the ARP cache table at the server to add an entry for the DHCP client.

The DHCP broadcast request has the following parameters:

op = 1
htype = 1
hlen = 6
hops = 0
xid = 826E7769 (hex)
secs = 0
flags = 0
ciaddr = 0.0.0.0
yiaddr = 0.0.0.0
siaddr = 0.0.0.0
giaddr = 0.0.0.0
chaddr = 00A024ABD1E6 00000000000000000000
sname = 0 (64 octets)
file = 0 (128 octets)
options = 0 (312 octets)

FIGURE 8.11

DHCP broadcast request.

```
Packet Number : 4                    7:28:11 PM
Length : 346 bytes
ether: ==================== Ethernet Datalink Layer ====================
        Station: 00-A0-24-AB-D1-E6 ----> FF-FF-FF-FF-FF-FF
        Type: 0x0800 (IP)
   ip: ===================== Internet Protocol =====================
        Station:0.0.0.0 ---->255.255.255.255
        Protocol: UDP
        Version: 4
        Header Length (32 bit words): 5
        Precedence: Routine
                Normal Delay, Normal Throughput, Normal Reliability
        Total length: 328
        Identification:       0
        Fragmentation allowed, Last fragment
        Fragment Offset: 0
        Time to Live: 128 seconds
        Checksum: 0x39A6(Valid)
  udp: ===================== User Datagram Protocol ====================
        Source Port: BOOTPC
        Destination Port: BOOTPS
        Length = 308
        Checksum: 0xA382(Valid)
Data:
  0: 01 01 06 00 82 6E 77 69 00 00 00 00 00 00 00 00 |.....nwi........
 10: 00 00 00 00 00 00 00 00 00 00 00 00 00 A0 24 AB |..............$.
 20: D1 E6 00 00 00 00 00 00 00 00 00 00 00 00 00 00 |................
 30: 00 00 00 00 00 00 00 00 00 00 00 00 00 00 00 00 |................
 40: 00 00 00 00 00 00 00 00 00 00 00 00 00 00 00 00 |................
 50: 00 00 00 00 00 00 00 00 00 00 00 00 00 00 00 00 |................
 60: 00 00 00 00 00 00 00 00 00 00 00 00 00 00 00 00 |................
 70: 00 00 00 00 00 00 00 00 00 00 00 00 00 00 00 00 |................
 80: 00 00 00 00 00 00 00 00 00 00 00 00 00 00 00 00 |................
 90: 00 00 00 00 00 00 00 00 00 00 00 00 00 00 00 00 |................
 A0: 00 00 00 00 00 00 00 00 00 00 00 00 00 00 00 00 |................
 B0: 00 00 00 00 00 00 00 00 00 00 00 00 00 00 00 00 |................
 C0: 00 00 00 00 00 00 00 00 00 00 00 00 00 00 00 00 |................
 D0: 00 00 00 00 00 00 00 00 00 00 00 00 00 00 00 00 |................
 E0: 00 00 00 00 00 00 00 00 00 00 00 00 63 82 53 63 |............c.Sc
 F0: 35 01 01 3D 07 01 00 A0 24 AB D1 E6 0C 06 54 50 |5..=....$.....TP
100: 4E 54 57 00 37 07 01 0F 03 2C 2E 2F 06 FF 00 00 |NTW.7....,./....
110: 00 00 00 00 00 00 00 00 00 00 00 00 00 00 00 00 |................
120: 00 00 00 00 00 00 00 00 00 00 00 00             |............
```

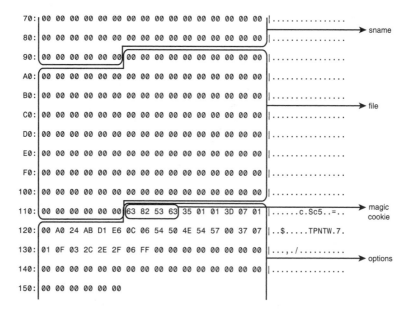

The DHCP directed reply has the following parameters:

    op = 2
    htype = 1
    hlen = 6
    hops = 0
    xid = 826E7769 (hex)
    secs = 0
    flags = 0
    ciaddr = 0.0.0.0
    yiaddr = 199.245.180.41
    siaddr = 199.245.180.10
    giaddr = 0.0.0.0
    chaddr = 00A024ABD1E6 00000000000000000000
    sname = 0 (64 octets)
    file = 0 (128 octets)
    options: magic cookie = 63 82 53 63 (hex)

8

AUTOMATIC
CONFIGURATION

FIGURE 8.12

DHCP directed reply.

```
Packet Number : 5              7:28:11 PM
Length : 594 bytes
ether: =================== Ethernet Datalink Layer ==================
       Station: 00-00-C0-DD-14-5C ----> 00-A0-24-AB-D1-E6
       Type: 0x0800 (IP)
   ip: ===================== Internet Protocol =====================
       Station:199.245.180.10 ---->199.245.180.41
       Protocol: UDP
       Version: 4
       Header Length (32 bit words): 5
       Precedence: Routine
              Normal Delay, Normal Throughput, Normal Reliability
       Total length: 576
       Identification: 47444
       Fragmentation allowed, Last fragment
       Fragment Offset: 0
       Time to Live: 128 seconds
       Checksum: 0x8739(Valid)
  udp: ==================== User Datagram Protocol ==================
       Source Port: BOOTPS
       Destination Port: BOOTPC
       Length = 556
       Checksum: 0x0000(checksum not used)
Data:
   0: 02 01 06 00 82 6E 77 69 00 00 00 00 00 00 00 00  |.....nwi........
  10: C7 F5 B4 29 C7 F5 B4 0A 00 00 00 00 00 A0 24 AB  |...).........$.
  20: D1 E6 00 00 00 00 00 00 00 00 00 00 00 00 00 00  |................
  30: 00 00 00 00 00 00 00 00 00 00 00 00 00 00 00 00  |................
  40: 00 00 00 00 00 00 00 00 00 00 00 00 00 00 00 00  |................
  50: 00 00 00 00 00 00 00 00 00 00 00 00 00 00 00 00  |................
  60: 00 00 00 00 00 00 00 00 00 00 00 00 00 00 00 00  |................
  70: 00 00 00 00 00 00 00 00 00 00 00 00 00 00 00 00  |................
  80: 00 00 00 00 00 00 00 00 00 00 00 00 00 00 00 00  |................
  90: 00 00 00 00 00 00 00 00 00 00 00 00 00 00 00 00  |................
  A0: 00 00 00 00 00 00 00 00 00 00 00 00 00 00 00 00  |................
  B0: 00 00 00 00 00 00 00 00 00 00 00 00 00 00 00 00  |................
  C0: 00 00 00 00 00 00 00 00 00 00 00 00 00 00 00 00  |................
  D0: 00 00 00 00 00 00 00 00 00 00 00 00 00 00 00 00  |................
  E0: 00 00 00 00 00 00 00 00 00 00 00 00 63 82 53 63  |............c.Sc
  F0: 35 01 02 36 04 C7 F5 B4 0A 33 04 00 00 0E 10 3A  |5..6.....3.....:
 100: 04 00 00 07 08 3B 04 00 00 0C 3C 01 04 FF FF FF  |.....;....<.....
 110: 00 06 04 C7 F5 B4 0A 0F 0C 6B 69 6E 65 74 69 63  |.........kinetic
 120: 73 2E 63 6F 6D FF 00 00 00 00 00 00 00 00 00 00  |s.com..........
 130: 00 00 00 00 00 00 00 00 00 00 00 00 00 00 00 00  |................
 140: 00 00 00 00 00 00 00 00 00 00 00 00 00 00 00 00  |................
 150: 00 00 00 00 00 00 00 00 00 00 00 00 00 00 00 00  |................
 160: 00 00 00 00 00 00 00 00 00 00 00 00 00 00 00 00  |................
 170: 00 00 00 00 00 00 00 00 00 00 00 00 00 00 00 00  |................
 180: 00 00 00 00 00 00 00 00 00 00 00 00 00 00 00 00  |................
 190: 00 00 00 00 00 00 00 00 00 00 00 00 00 00 00 00  |................
 1A0: 00 00 00 00 00 00 00 00 00 00 00 00 00 00 00 00  |................
 1B0: 00 00 00 00 00 00 00 00 00 00 00 00 00 00 00 00  |................
 1C0: 00 00 00 00 00 00 00 00 00 00 00 00 00 00 00 00  |................
 1D0: 00 00 00 00 00 00 00 00 00 00 00 00 00 00 00 00  |................
 1E0: 00 00 00 00 00 00 00 00 00 00 00 00 00 00 00 00  |................
 1F0: 00 00 00 00 00 00 00 00 00 00 00 00 00 00 00 00  |................
 200: 00 00 00 00 00 00 00 00 00 00 00 00 00 00 00 00  |................
 210: 00 00 00 00 00 00 00 00 00 00 00 00 00 00 00 00  |................
 220: 00 00 00 00
```

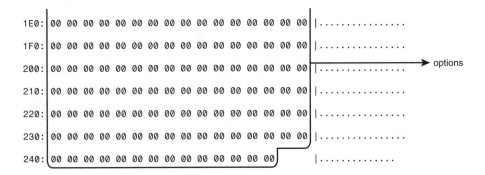

DHCP Trace with Broadcast Reply from DHCP Server

Figures 8.13 and 8.14 show a DHCP client broadcast request and a DHCP server reply. However, unlike the trace discussed in the preceding section, the DHCP server reply is sent as a broadcast reply. A directed reply was not possible because this implementation of the DHCP server does not make a direct entry in the ARP cache table.

The DHCP broadcast request has the following parameters:

op = 1
htype = 1
hlen = 6
hops = 0
xid = 826E7769 (hex)
secs = 0
flags = 0
ciaddr = 0.0.0.0
yiaddr = 0.0.0.0
siaddr = 0.0.0.0
giaddr = 0.0.0.0
chaddr = 00A024ABD1E6 00000000000000000000
sname = 0 (64 octets)
file = 0 (128 octets)
options = 0 (312 octets)

FIGURE 8.13

DHCP broadcast request.

```
Packet Number : 6              7:28:11 PM
Length : 346 bytes
ether: ==================== Ethernet Datalink Layer ===================
        Station: 00-A0-24-AB-D1-E6 ----> FF-FF-FF-FF-FF-FF
        Type: 0x0800 (IP)
   ip:  ====================== Internet Protocol ======================
        Station:0.0.0.0 ---->255.255.255.255
        Protocol: UDP
        Version: 4
        Header Length (32 bit words): 5
        Precedence: Routine
                Normal Delay, Normal Throughput, Normal Reliability
        Total length: 328
        Identification:   256
        Fragmentation allowed, Last fragment
        Fragment Offset: 0
        Time to Live: 128 seconds
        Checksum: 0x38A6(Valid)
  udp:  ==================== User Datagram Protocol ===================
        Source Port: BOOTPC
        Destination Port: BOOTPS
        Length = 308
        Checksum: 0x8EB0(Valid)
Data:
   0: 01 01 06 00 01 4E AB 33 00 00 00 00 00 00 00 00 |.....N.3........
  10: 00 00 00 00 00 00 00 00 00 00 00 00 00 A0 24 AB |..............$.
  20: D1 E6 00 00 00 00 00 00 00 00 00 00 00 00 00 00 |...............
  30: 00 00 00 00 00 00 00 00 00 00 00 00 00 00 00 00 |...............
  40: 00 00 00 00 00 00 00 00 00 00 00 00 00 00 00 00 |...............
  50: 00 00 00 00 00 00 00 00 00 00 00 00 00 00 00 00 |...............
  60: 00 00 00 00 00 00 00 00 00 00 00 00 00 00 00 00 |...............
  70: 00 00 00 00 00 00 00 00 00 00 00 00 00 00 00 00 |...............
  80: 00 00 00 00 00 00 00 00 00 00 00 00 00 00 00 00 |...............
  90: 00 00 00 00 00 00 00 00 00 00 00 00 00 00 00 00 |...............
  A0: 00 00 00 00 00 00 00 00 00 00 00 00 00 00 00 00 |...............
  B0: 00 00 00 00 00 00 00 00 00 00 00 00 00 00 00 00 |...............
  C0: 00 00 00 00 00 00 00 00 00 00 00 00 00 00 00 00 |...............
  D0: 00 00 00 00 00 00 00 00 00 00 00 00 00 82 00 00 |...............
  E0: 00 00 00 00 00 00 00 00 00 00 00 00 63 82 53 63 |............c.Sc
  F0: 35 01 03 3D 07 01 00 A0 24 AB D1 E6 32 04 C7 F5 |5..=....$...2...
 100: B4 29 36 04 C7 F5 B4 0A 0C 06 54 50 4E 54 57 00 |.)6......TPNTW.
 110: 37 07 01 0F 03 2C 2E 2F 06 FF 00 00 00 00 00 00 |7....,./........
 120: 00 00 00 00 00 00 00 00 00 00                   |...........
```

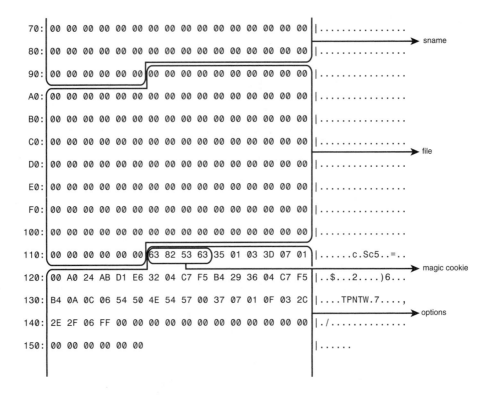

The DHCP broadcast reply has the following parameters:

op = 2

htype = 1

hlen = 6

hops = 0

xid = 826E7769 (hex)

secs = 0

flags = 0

ciaddr = 0.0.0.0

yiaddr = 0.0.0.0

siaddr = 199.245.180.10

giaddr = 0.0.0.0

chaddr = 00A024ABD1E6 0000000000000000000000

sname = 0 (64 octets)

file = 0 (128 octets)

options: magic cookie = 63 82 53 63 (hex)

FIGURE 8.14

DHCP broadcast reply.

```
Packet Number : 7              7:28:11 PM
Length : 594 bytes
ether: =================== Ethernet Datalink Layer ===================
        Station: 00-00-C0-DD-14-5C ----> FF-FF-FF-FF-FF-FF
        Type: 0x0800 (IP)
    ip: ===================== Internet Protocol =====================
        Station:199.245.180.10 ---->255.255.255.255
        Protocol: UDP
        Version: 4
        Header Length (32 bit words): 5
        Precedence: Routine
                Normal Delay, Normal Throughput, Normal Reliability
        Total length: 576
        Identification: 47445
        Fragmentation allowed, Last fragment
        Fragment Offset: 0
        Time to Live: 128 seconds
        Checksum: 0x0358(Valid)
   udp: ==================== User Datagram Protocol ====================
        Source Port: BOOTPS
        Destination Port: BOOTPC
        Length = 556
        Checksum: 0x0000(checksum not used)
Data:
    0: 02 01 06 00 01 4E AB 33 00 00 00 00 00 00 00 00 |.....N.3........
   10: 00 00 00 00 C7 F5 B4 0A 00 00 00 00 00 A0 24 AB |..............$.
   20: D1 E6 00 00 00 00 00 00 00 00 00 00 00 00 00 00 |................
   30: 00 00 00 00 00 00 00 00 00 00 00 00 00 00 00 00 |................
   40: 00 00 00 00 00 00 00 00 00 00 00 00 00 00 00 00 |................
   50: 00 00 00 00 00 00 00 00 00 00 00 00 00 00 00 00 |................
   60: 00 00 00 00 00 00 00 00 00 00 00 00 00 00 00 00 |................
   70: 00 00 00 00 00 00 00 00 00 00 00 00 00 00 00 00 |................
   80: 00 00 00 00 00 00 00 00 00 00 00 00 00 00 00 00 |................
   90: 00 00 00 00 00 00 00 00 00 00 00 00 00 00 00 00 |................
   A0: 00 00 00 00 00 00 00 00 00 00 00 00 00 00 00 00 |................
   B0: 00 00 00 00 00 00 00 00 00 00 00 00 00 00 00 00 |................
   C0: 00 00 00 00 00 00 00 00 00 00 00 00 00 00 00 00 |................
   D0: 00 00 00 00 00 00 00 00 00 00 00 00 00 00 00 00 |................
   E0: 00 00 00 00 00 00 00 00 00 00 00 00 63 82 53 63 |............c.Sc
   F0: 35 01 06 FF 00 00 00 00 00 00 00 00 00 00 00 00 |5...............
  100: 00 00 00 00 00 00 00 00 00 00 00 00 00 00 00 00 |................
  110: 00 00 00 00 00 00 00 00 00 00 00 00 00 00 00 00 |................
  120: 00 00 00 00 00 00 00 00 00 00 00 00 00 00 00 00 |................
  130: 00 00 00 00 00 00 00 00 00 00 00 00 00 00 00 00 |................
  140: 00 00 00 00 00 00 00 00 00 00 00 00 00 00 00 00 |................
  150: 00 00 00 00 00 00 00 00 00 00 00 00 00 00 00 00 |................
  160: 00 00 00 00 00 00 00 00 00 00 00 00 00 00 00 00 |................
  170: 00 00 00 00 00 00 00 00 00 00 00 00 00 00 00 00 |................
  180: 00 00 00 00 00 00 00 00 00 00 00 00 00 00 00 00 |................
  190: 00 00 00 00 00 00 00 00 00 00 00 00 00 00 00 00 |................
  1A0: 00 00 00 00 00 00 00 00 00 00 00 00 00 00 00 00 |................
  1B0: 00 00 00 00 00 00 00 00 00 00 00 00 00 00 00 00 |................
  1C0: 00 00 00 00 00 00 00 00 00 00 00 00 00 00 00 00 |................
  1D0: 00 00 00 00 00 00 00 00 00 00 00 00 00 00 00 00 |................
  1E0: 00 00 00 00 00 00 00 00 00 00 00 00 00 00 00 00 |................
  1F0: 00 00 00 00 00 00 00 00 00 00 00 00 00 00 00 00 |................
  200: 00 00 00 00 00 00 00 00 00 00 00 00 00 00 00 00 |................
  210: 00 00 00 00 00 00 00 00 00 00 00 00 00 00 00 00 |................
  220: 00 00 00 00                                     |....
```

8

AUTOMATIC
CONFIGURATION

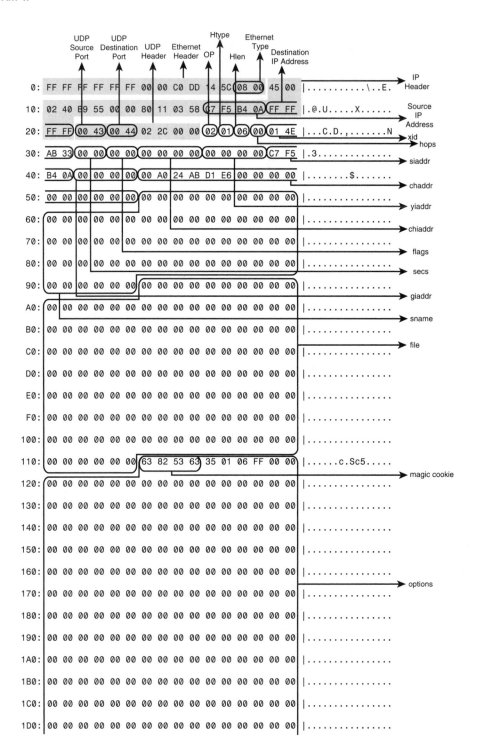

```
          UDP       UDP                        Htype   Ethernet
         Source  Destination  UDP    Ethernet           Type
          Port      Port     Header   Header  OP         Destination
                                              Hlen        IP Address

  0:  FF FF FF FF FF FF 00 00 C0 DD 14 5C 08 00 45 00   |...........\..E.     IP
                                                                              Header
 10:  02 40 B9 55 00 00 80 11 03 58 C7 F5 B4 0A FF FF   |.@.U.....X......     Source
                                                                              IP
 20:  FF FF 00 43 00 44 02 2C 00 00 02 01 06 00 01 4E   |...C.D.,........N     Address
                                                                           → xid
 30:  AB 33 00 00 00 00 00 00 00 00 00 00 00 00 C7 F5   |.3..............  → hops
                                                                           → siaddr
 40:  B4 0A 00 00 00 00 00 A0 24 AB D1 E6 00 00 00 00   |........$.......
                                                                           → chaddr
 50:  00 00 00 00 00 00 00 00 00 00 00 00 00 00 00 00   |................
                                                                           → yiaddr
 60:  00 00 00 00 00 00 00 00 00 00 00 00 00 00 00 00   |................
                                                                           → chiaddr
 70:  00 00 00 00 00 00 00 00 00 00 00 00 00 00 00 00   |................
                                                                           → flags
 80:  00 00 00 00 00 00 00 00 00 00 00 00 00 00 00 00   |................
                                                                           → secs
 90:  00 00 00 00 00 00 00 00 00 00 00 00 00 00 00 00   |................
                                                                           → giaddr
 A0:  00 00 00 00 00 00 00 00 00 00 00 00 00 00 00 00   |................
                                                                           → sname
 B0:  00 00 00 00 00 00 00 00 00 00 00 00 00 00 00 00   |................
                                                                           → file
 C0:  00 00 00 00 00 00 00 00 00 00 00 00 00 00 00 00   |................
 D0:  00 00 00 00 00 00 00 00 00 00 00 00 00 00 00 00   |................
 E0:  00 00 00 00 00 00 00 00 00 00 00 00 00 00 00 00   |................
 F0:  00 00 00 00 00 00 00 00 00 00 00 00 00 00 00 00   |................
100:  00 00 00 00 00 00 00 00 00 00 00 00 00 00 00 00   |................
110:  00 00 00 00 00 00 63 82 53 63 35 01 06 FF 00 00   |......c.Sc5.....
                                                                           → magic cookie
120:  00 00 00 00 00 00 00 00 00 00 00 00 00 00 00 00   |................
130:  00 00 00 00 00 00 00 00 00 00 00 00 00 00 00 00   |................
140:  00 00 00 00 00 00 00 00 00 00 00 00 00 00 00 00   |................
150:  00 00 00 00 00 00 00 00 00 00 00 00 00 00 00 00   |................
160:  00 00 00 00 00 00 00 00 00 00 00 00 00 00 00 00   |................
                                                                           → options
170:  00 00 00 00 00 00 00 00 00 00 00 00 00 00 00 00   |................
180:  00 00 00 00 00 00 00 00 00 00 00 00 00 00 00 00   |................
190:  00 00 00 00 00 00 00 00 00 00 00 00 00 00 00 00   |................
1A0:  00 00 00 00 00 00 00 00 00 00 00 00 00 00 00 00   |................
1B0:  00 00 00 00 00 00 00 00 00 00 00 00 00 00 00 00   |................
1C0:  00 00 00 00 00 00 00 00 2C 00 00 00 00 00 00 00   |................
1D0:  00 00 00 00 00 00 00 00 00 00 00 00 00 00 00 00   |................
```

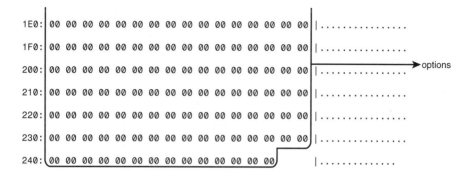

```
1E0: 00 00 00 00 00 00 00 00 00 00 00 00 00 00 00 00  |...............
1F0: 00 00 00 00 00 00 00 00 00 00 00 00 00 00 00 00  |...............
200: 00 00 00 00 00 00 00 00 00 00 00 00 00 00 00 00  |...............
210: 00 00 00 00 00 00 00 00 00 00 00 00 00 00 00 00  |...............
220: 00 00 00 00 00 00 00 00 00 00 00 00 00 00 00 00  |...............
230: 00 00 00 00 00 00 00 00 00 00 00 00 00 00 00 00  |...............
240: 00 00 00 00 00 00 00 00 00 00 00 00 00 00         |..............
```
→ options

Summary

Both BOOTP and DHCP solve the important problem of automatic configuration of IP parameters, such as IP addresses and subnet masks, for individual devices on the network. Both protocols are client/server based and use the same UDP port numbers. The DHCP protocol is designed to replace the older BOOTP protocol and is a superset of the BOOTP message format.

A major advantage of DHCP is that IP addresses can be leased on a time basis. This enables a more flexible reuse of IP addresses where IP addresses do not have to be permanently allocated to a station based on their hardware addresses. The BOOTP IP address allocation is less flexible than that of DHCP because IP addresses are associated with the hardware address of a network interface.

8

AUTOMATIC
CONFIGURATION

IP and Related Protocols

PART

III

IN THIS PART

Overview of the IP Family of Protocols

by Mark A. Sportack and Karanjit S. Siyan, Ph.D.

TCP/IP has become a catch-all phrase that describes IP-based communications. Despite its popularity, few people realize that it is really a whole family of protocols, each with its own set of capabilities and limitations. This chapter examines the architecture, functionality, and uses of the various protocols within the IP family of protocols.

The purpose of this chapter is to establish the framework for discussing the details of TCP/IP. Later chapters describe the components of the TCP/IP family of protocols in more detail. Even though some of the information has been presented earlier, its review here will help you establish an overview of the TCP/IP protocol.

The TCP/IP Model

When TCP/IP was developed, it was described in terms of its own Reference Model that describes the stratification of its functions. TCP/IP's model was developed long after the protocol suite itself was developed. Consequently, the model couldn't guide the development of the protocols, and anomalies were rampant!

The TCP/IP Reference Model is discussed in Chapter 1, "Introduction to Open Communications."

The TCP/IP Suite of Protocols

Although they are frequently identified as just "TCP/IP," several different component protocols actually exist within the IP suite of protocols. These include:

- *IP*—The Internet Layer protocol.
- *TCP*—The reliable Host-to-Host Layer protocol.
- *UDP*—The best-effort Host-to-Host Layer protocol.
- *ICMP*—A multilayer protocol designed to facilitate control, testing, and management functions within an IP network. The various ICMP protocols span the Host-to-Host Layer and the Process/Application Layer.

The relationship between these protocols is illustrated in Figure 9.1.

> **Note**
>
> The applications that reside at the Process/Application Layer (such as Telnet, FTP, and many others) must also be considered a native component of the IP suite of protocols. However, because these are applications rather than protocols, they are not addressed in this chapter.

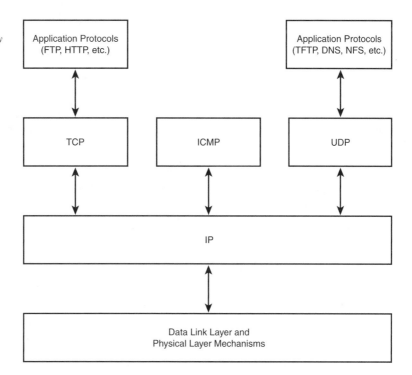

FIGURE 9.1
TCP/IP is actually a suite of related protocols, rather than just a single protocol.

Understanding the Internet Protocol (IP)

The Internet Protocol has become the dominant internetworking protocol in the world. Other contenders, such as OSI, AppleTalk, and even IPX have ultimately lost out to IP due to its openness. Despite this success in the marketplace, IP remains a mostly misunderstood protocol. Its functionality is defined by the amount of data that resides in its header structure. The IP header structure, and its resulting capability set, were originally defined in a series of RFCs and other openly published documents that date back to the creation of the IETF. RFC 791, published in September of 1981, is generally accepted as the foundation document for today's version of IP.

IP is continuously evolving, thanks to the ceaseless efforts of the IETF. Many new features and capabilities have been added through subsequent RFCs. All, however, build upon the basis established in RFC 791. Architecturally speaking, the current version of IP is version 4 (IPv4). A new version, version 6, will eventually replace IPv4, but IPv4 is the current standard that is broadly supported. For additional information on IPv6, please see Chapter 12, "IP Version 6."

The IPv4 Header

Figure 9.2 illustrates the structure of the IP header, as well as the sizes of its fields.

FIGURE 9.2

The structure of an IP header reveals the many fields that support IP's capabilities.

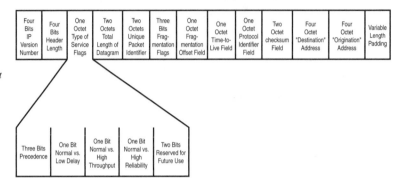

The IP header has the following sizes and fields:

- *Version*—The first 4 bits of the IP header identify the operating version of IP; for example, version 4 or version 6.

- *Internet Header Length*—The next 4 bits of the header contain the length of the header, expressed in multiples of 32.

- *Type of Service*—The next octet contains a series of flags that can be used to specify precedence (that is, absolute priority relative to other IP packets), delay, throughput, and reliability parameters for that packet of data. The precedence flag is 3 bits long whereas the delay, throughput, and reliability flags are each 1 bit in length. The remaining 2 bits are reserved for future use.

- *Total Length*—This 16-bit field contains the total length of the IP packet measured in octets. Valid values can range up to 65,535 octets.

- *Identifier*—Each IP packet is given a unique 16-bit identifier, which is used to identify the fragments of a datagram.

- *Fragmentation Flags*—The next field contains three 1-bit flags that indicate whether fragmentation of the packet is permitted, and if it is used. The first bit is reserved and always set equal to 0. The second bit indicates whether that packet's data can be fragmented. If this bit is equal to 0, the contents can be fragmented. If it is equal to 1, it cannot be fragmented. The third bit has significance only if the second bit was set to 0. If that bit was equal to 0 (and the data can be segmented across multiple packets), this bit indicates whether this particular packet is the last in the series of the fragment, or whether the receiving application can expect additional fragments. A 0 indicates that this packet is the last one.

- *Fragment Offset*—This 8-bit field measures the offset of the fragmented contents relative to the beginning of the entire packet. This value is measured in 64-bit increments.

- *Time-to-Live (TTL)*—The IP packet cannot be permitted to roam the WAN in perpetuity. It must be limited to a finite TTL. The 8-bit TTL field is incremented by one for each hop the packet makes. After reaching its maximum limit, the packet is assumed to be undeliverable. An ICMP message is generated and sent back to the source machine and the undeliverable packet is destroyed.

- *Protocol*—This 8-bit field identifies the protocol that follows the IP header, such as VINES, TCP, UDP, and so forth.

- *Checksum*—The Checksum field is a 16-bit error-checking field. The destination computer, and every gateway node in the network, will recompute the mathematical calculation on the packet's header as the source computer did. If the data survived the trip intact, the results of these two calculations are identical. This field also informs the destination host of the amount of incoming data.

- *Source IP Address*—The source address is the IP address of the source computer.

- *Destination IP Address*—The destination address is the IP address of the destination computer.

- *Padding*—Extra zeros are added to this field to ensure that the IP header is always a multiple of 32 bits.

These header fields reveal that IPv4's Internet Layer is inherently connectionless: The packet forwarding devices in the network are free to determine the ideal path for each packet to take through the network. It also doesn't provide any of the acknowledgments, flow control, or sequencing functions of higher-level protocols such as TCP. Nor can IP be used to direct the data contained in an IP datagram to the appropriate destination application. These functions are left to higher-level protocols, such as TCP and UDP.

What Does IP Do?

The header information of an IP packet contains all the information necessary to enable some critical network functions. These functions include

- Addressing and routing
- Fragmentation and reassembly
- Detection and correction of data damaged in transit

Addressing and Routing

One of the more obvious capabilities of IP is that it enables packets to be delivered to a specific destination. The destination IP address is used by routers and switches in the network that intervenes the source and destination machine pairs, to identify the optimal path through that network.

Similarly, IP packets also bear the IP address of the source machine. Thus, the destination machine may contact the source machine should the need arise.

Fragmentation and Reassembly

Sometimes segments of application data don't fit cleanly inside a single IP packet constrained by the Maximum Transmission Unit (MTU) size of the underlying network. In this case the IP packet must be fragmented and split across two or more packets. When this occurs, IP must be able to reconstruct the original data segment, regardless of how many packets were required to get it to its destination.

It is important to note that the source and destination machine must understand, and adhere to, the exact procedure for fragmenting data segments. Otherwise, reassembling data that was fragmented into multiple packets for delivery through a network would be impossible. The delivered data has been successfully reassembled when it has been restored to the exact form it was in on the source machine, before it was fragmented. The fragmentation flags in the IP header are used to identify fragmented data segments.

Note

Reassembling fragmented data segments is quite different than resequencing data that has arrived out of order. Resequencing is a function of TCP.

Compensating for Damaged Packets

The last major function of IP is to detect and compensate for any datagrams whose payload may have been damaged or lost in transit. There are many ways that a packet can become damaged: *Radio frequency interference (RFI)* and *electromagnetic interference (EMI)* are two of the more obvious. A packet is considered damaged when it arrives at its destination with a different bit pattern than the source machine created.

A packet may be lost for many reasons. For one thing, network congestion may result in a packet exceeding its time-to-live (TTL). The router that detects the expiration of the

TTL would simply discard that packet. Alternatively, a packet may become so corrupted in transit by either EMI or RFI that its header information becomes meaningless. In such cases, the packet would also likely be discarded.

Whenever an IP packet becomes undeliverable or unusable, the source machine must be notified. The IP header contains the source machine's IP address to facilitate this notification. Thus, although IP does not contain the mechanisms to coordinate a retransmission, it plays an integral role in the notification of a source machine about the possible need to retransmit.

IP Conclusions

Despite these capabilities, IP must be acknowledged as just an internetworking protocol. To be useful, it must be accompanied by both a transport protocol (Layer 4 of the OSI Reference Model) and a Data Link Layer protocol (Layer 2 of the OSI Reference Model). Although Data Link Layer architectures are outside the scope of this book, the remainder of this chapter focuses on two of the transport protocols that rely upon IP for internetworking. These are TCP and UDP.

Understanding the Transmission Control Protocol (TCP)

TCP is the transport layer (Layer 4 of the OSI Reference Model) protocol that uses IP to provide reliable delivery of application data. TCP establishes a connection-oriented session between two or more hosts. It can support multiple data streams, as well as coordinate flow and error control and even the reordering of packets that may have been received out of order. The Transmission Control Protocol was also developed through a series of open published IETF documents. The development of TCP culminated in RFC 793 in September of 1981. As with RFC 791 IP, RFC 793 TCP has been augmented over the past 18 years, but it has never been completely superceded. Thus, the contents of that RFC remain TCP's core.

TCP Header Structure

As with IP, the functionality of TCP is limited by the amount of information that it carries in its header. Thus, understanding the mechanics and capabilities of TCP requires an appreciation for the contents of its header. Figure 9.3 illustrates the structure of the TCP header, as well as the sizes of its fields.

FIGURE 9.3

The structure of
a TCP header
demonstrates that
it relies upon
several fields to
function properly.

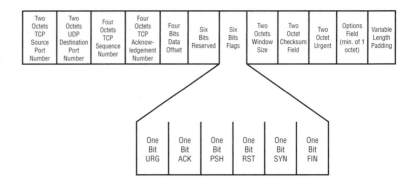

The TCP protocol header is a minimum of 20 octets and contains the following fields:

- *TCP Source Port*—The 16-bit source port field contains the number of the port that initiates the communications session. The source port and source IP address function as the packet's return address.

- *TCP Destination Port*—The 16-bit destination port field is the address of the port for which the transmission is destined. This port contains the interface address of the application on the recipient's computer to which the packet's data will be passed.

- *TCP Sequence Number*—The 32-bit sequence number is used by the receiving computer to reconstruct the fragmented data back into its original form. In a dynamically routed network, it is quite possible for some of the packets to take different routes and, consequently, to arrive out of order. This sequencing field compensates for this inconsistency of delivery.

- *TCP Acknowledgment Number*—TCP uses a 32-bit acknowledgment (ACK) of the first octet of data contained in the next expected segment. It may seem counter-intuitive to acknowledge something that hasn't occurred yet, but a source TCP/IP machine that receives an ACK knows that all the data up to, but not including, that specified segment has been received. The number used to identify each ACK is the sequence number of the packet being acknowledged. This field is only valid if the ACK flag (see Flags, later in this list) is set.

- *Data Offset*—This 4-bit field contains the size of the TCP header, measured in a 32-bit data structure known as a "word."

- *Reserved*—This 6-bit field is always set to zero. It is reserved for an as-yet unspecified future use.

- *Flags*—The 6-bit flag field contains six 1-bit flags that enable the control functions of urgent field, acknowledgment of significant field, push, reset connection, synchronize sequence numbers, and finished sending data. The flags, in their order of appearance in the string, are *URG*, *ACK*, *PSH*, *RST*, *SYN*, and *FIN*. Given the preceding description of their functions, these mnemonic abbreviations should be self-apparent.

- *Window Size*—This 16-bit field is used by the destination machine to tell the source host how much data it is willing to accept, per TCP segment.

- *Checksum*—The TCP header also contains a 16-bit error-checking field known as a "Checksum." The source host calculates a mathematical value, based upon the segment's contents. The destination host performs the same calculation. If the content remained intact, the result of the two calculations is identical, thereby proving the validity of the data.

- *Urgent*—The Urgent field is an optional 16-bit pointer that points to the last octet of urgent data within the segment. This field is only valid if the URG flag was set. If that flag is not set, the Urgent field is pre-empted with Padding. Segments of data that are identified as urgent are treated to expedited handling by all TCP/IP devices that lie in the network intervening the source and destination machines.

- *Options*—A variable length field of at least 1 octet identifies which options, if any, are valid for the TCP segment. If no options are set, this 1-octet field is set equal to 0, which indicates the end of the Options field. A value of 1 in this octet indicates that no operation is required. A value of 2 indicates that the next four octets contain the source machine's *Maximum Segment Size* (MSS). The MSS is the greatest number of octets that the data field can be, as agreed to by the source and destination machines.

- *Data*—Although not technically a part of the TCP header, it is important to recognize that segments of application data follow the Urgent and/or Options fields, but precede the Padding field. The field's size is the largest MSS that can be negotiated between the source and destination machines. Segments may be smaller than the MSS, but never larger.

- *Padding*—Contrary to any indication of superfluousity that its name might suggest, padding always serves a mathematical purpose in data communications. That purpose is to ensure predictability of spacing, timing, or sizing. Extra zeros are added to this field to ensure that the TCP header is always a multiple of 32 bits.

What Does TCP Do?

TCP provides several important functions in a communications session. It can best be thought of as the liaison between multiple applications and the network. Its functions include

- Multiplexing data from multiple applications to and from the network
- Testing received data for integrity

- Resequencing application data that may have arrived out of order
- Acknowledging successful receipt of transmitted data
- Rate-adaptive flow control (via the TCP window size)
- Timing functions
- Coordinating the retransmission of data that was damaged or lost in transit

Multiplexing Data Streams

TCP is the interface between a user's applications and the network's myriad communications protocols. Because it would be virtually unheard of for any user to be limited to just one application, TCP must be able to simultaneously accept data from multiple applications, bundle them into segments of data, and pass these segments off to IP. Similarly, TCP must be able to receive data for multiple applications at the same time.

TCP keeps track of which incoming packets must be forwarded to which applications through the use of *port numbers*. Thus, it is really useful if both the source and destination machines agree on a common set of port numbers for their application base. Unfortunately, there is such a tremendous amount of applications that can run on IP that it would be virtually impossible to get any sort of consistency of numbers on an ad hoc basis. Consequently, IANA, and now ICANN, have stepped up to regulating at least a portion of the available port numbers.

Simplifying ICANN's task is that many applications are so common that they are regarded as *well known*. As such, ICANN can assign port numbers to these applications, and anyone can reasonably expect any IP-capable host to recognize them. Examples of well-known port numbers include

- Port 80 (the Hypertext Transfer Protocol, or HTTP)
- Port 119 (Network News Transfer Protocol, or NNTP)
- Port 69 (Trivial File Transfer Protocol, or TFTP)

It would be impossible to list all the well-known port numbers here because there are 1,024 of them (ranging from 0 to 1,023). For a complete list of the well-known port numbers for both TCP and UDP, please refer to RFC 1700.

Because the port number field contains a 16-bit binary number, there are 65,535 mathematically possible port numbers. Whereas numbers 0 through 1023 are regarded as well known, anything greater than 1023 is generally regarded as a *high port number* or *temporary port number*, or *ephemeral port number*. The high port numbers are not regulated by ICANN. Thus, applications that are not well known (including homegrown applications or shrink-wrapped software) are not precluded from using IP for their communications needs. They can arbitrarily select one of the high port numbers that is not in use.

TCP maintains both the source and destination application's port number in each TCP segment. Another term that is frequently used is *socket*, although there is no discrete socket field in the TCP header. A socket is the concatenation of a host's IP address and the port number of a specific application that resides on that host. Thus, a socket describes a unique host and application pair. A ":" separates the two numbers. For example, socket 10.1.1.9:666 identifies the application port number 666 (the port number for DOOM) on host 10.1.1.9.

> **Note**
>
> The term *socket* also refers to a programming data structure that is used to keep track of the IP address and port number pair just described. The set of system calls that use the socket data structure are called the *sockets interface*. The sockets interface was popularized in BSD Unix, and is also sometimes called BSD Sockets interface. The implementation of BSD sockets for the Windows operating system is called Windows Sockets or WinSock. WinSock is usually implemented as a Dynamic Link Library (DLL).

Testing for Data Integrity

TCP performs a mathematical operation on each segment of data that is encapsulated in a TCP segment, and places the result of that operation in the Checksum field of the TCP header. Upon arrival at its intended destination, performing the same mathematical operation on the received data should yield the same result as was stored in the TCP header. If it does, the data can reasonably be assumed to have arrived intact. Otherwise, a request is sent back to the source machine for another copy of that segment of data.

Resequencing

It is not uncommon for segments of data to arrive out of sequence at their destination. There are many reasons for this. For example, in a highly used network, it is possible that the routing protocols selected different routes through the network. This could result in segments arriving out of sequence. Alternatively, packets could be lost or damaged in transit. Thus, the sequence of data that is needed by the recipient application would be thrown off. Regardless, the destination machine's TCP protocol would buffer the received segments of data until it could resequence them into the correct order.

This task is accomplished by examining the contents of the TCP Sequence Number field in the TCP header. Resequencing is simply a matter of mathematically sorting the received segments, based on this field.

Flow Control

The source and destination machines in a TCP session are known as *peers*. Each peer has the capability to control the flow of data that is streaming into its physical input buffers. The mechanism that is used is the size of the TCP *window*. A window size is communicated between a source and destination machine via the TCP header. Any machine that is becoming backlogged with incoming data may throttle back the rate at which the transmitting machine can transmit, simply by informing that machine of its new window size. If a machine's buffers fill up completely, it will send an acknowledgment of the last received data segment with a new window size of 0. This effectively halts transmission until that congested machine can clear its buffers. Each segment that it processes must be acknowledged and, with this acknowledgment, comes another opportunity to restart transmissions by re-establishing a window size greater than 0.

Although this simple mechanism can effectively regulate the flow of data between two machines, it can only help ensure that these end systems aren't overwhelmed with incoming data. Window size, by itself, does not take into account any congestion that may exist on the network. Congestion on the network would mean that each transmitted segment takes longer than usual to actually reach its destination. Therefore, congestion management must be a function of time on the network. TCP implements congestion management through the use of timers.

Timing Mechanisms

TCP uses timing mechanisms for several critical functions. Each time a segment is transmitted, a timer is set. If that timer expires (that is, decrements to 0) before an acknowledgment is received, the segment is assumed to be lost. Consequently, it is retransmitted. This timer can also be used to manage network congestion indirectly by slowing the rate of transmission whenever a timeout occurs. In theory, transmission of segments is throttled back until timeouts cease occurring. Thus, TCP can't quite manage congestion on a network, but it can decrease its own contribution to that congestion.

Acknowledging Receipt

A destination TCP machine must acknowledge the receipt of a specific data segment (as identified by its sequence number), if the ACK flag is set. Given that TCP is almost always used in a reliable mode, it would be unusual for the ACK flag to not be set.

Data segments whose transmission is not acknowledged are assumed to be lost in transit, and are re-sent. The retransmission must be coordinated between the source and destination machines.

Understanding the User Datagram Protocol (UDP)

The User Datagram Protocol is IP's other Host-to-Host Layer protocol (which corresponds to the Transport Layer of the OSI Reference Model). UDP provides a basic, low-overhead, data transmission known as "datagrams." To appreciate just how simple a mechanism UDP is, you need only compare RFC 768 (the original specification describing UDP's functionality, data structures, and mechanisms) to almost any other RFC. RFC 768 is svelte: a mere three pages in length. Many other RFCs require three pages just for their tables of content!

The simplicity of datagrams makes UDP inappropriate for some applications, but perfect for more sophisticated applications that can provide their own connection-oriented functionality. Other possible uses for UDP include exchanges of such data as forwarding routing table contents, system messages, network monitoring data, and so forth. These types of exchanges do not require flow control, acknowledgments, reordering, or any of the functionality that TCP provides.

Generally speaking, UDP is used in applications that are broadcast oriented, or message based, or that do not require the full reliability that TCP provides. More recently, UDP has also found use in real-time applications such as Voice over IP (VoIP) where the reliability and retransmissions of TCP for lost message segments is excessive overhead that is not needed and that would add to the overall delay in transmitting packets.

UDP Header Structure

Figure 9.4 illustrates the structure of the IP header, as well as the sizes of its fields.

FIGURE 9.4

The structure of a UDP header demonstrates its utter simplicity in form and function.

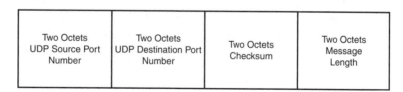

The UDP protocol header has the following structure:

- *UDP Source Port Number*—The 16-bit source port is the connection number on the source computer. The source port and source IP address function as the packet's return address.

- *UDP Destination Port Number*—The 16-bit destination port is the connection number on the destination computer. The UDP Destination Port is used to forward the packet to the correct application after the packet arrives at the intended destination machine.

- *UDP Checksum*—The Checksum is a 16-bit error-checking field that is calculated based upon the contents of the segment. The destination computer performs the same mathematical function as the originating host. A discrepancy in the two calculated values indicates that an error has occurred during the transmission of the packet.

- *UDP Message Length*—The Message Length field is also 16-bits in length, and informs the destination computer of the size of the message. This provides another mechanism for the destination computer to use in determining the message's validity.

> **Note**
>
> It is important to note that though both TCP and UDP use 16-bit port numbers, they occupy different address spaces. That is, a TCP port number of 2000 is quite distinct from a UDP port number of 2000.

What Does UDP Do?

Not much! UDP was deliberately designed to be an efficient and minimal transport protocol. This is directly reflected in its header structure. It contains just enough information to forward the datagram to the appropriate applications (that is, port numbers), and perform some error-checking.

UDP does not provide any of the more advanced functions that TCP supports. There are no timing mechanisms, flow control or congestion management mechanisms, acknowledgments, provisions for expedient delivery of urgent data, and so on. UDP, quite literally, makes a best-effort attempt to deliver a datagram. If that effort fails for any reason, the datagram is discarded and no attempt is made at retransmission.

TCP Versus UDP

TCP and UDP are very different transport layer protocols that were designed to do different things. Their one commonality is that they both utilize IP as their Network Layer protocol. The major functional difference between TCP and UDP is reliability. TCP is reliable and UDP is a simple, best-effort datagram delivery mechanism. This fundamental difference implies that TCP is much more complex, and requires a substantial amount of overhead to function, whereas UDP is simple and efficient.

UDP is frequently criticized for being unreliable because it possesses none of TCP's reliability mechanisms. There is some truth to UDP being unreliable because UDP possesses none of TCP's mechanisms for acknowledging receipt of a datagram, resequencing datagrams received out of order, or even requesting a retransmission for a packet received damaged. In other words, there are no guarantees that a UDP datagram will ever reach its destination intact! Thus, UDP is best suited for small transmissions (that is, individual packets), whereas TCP is used to regulate a stream of transmitted data that spans multiple packets.

It is imperative to balance this description of UDP's unreliability with an explanation of its benefits. UDP is a minimal and frugal transport layer protocol. It is capable of operating much faster than TCP. Thus, it is well suited for the ever-emerging, time-sensitive applications such as Voice over IP (VoIP) and real-time video conferencing.

UDP is also well suited to many other functions in a network, such as transporting routing table updates between routers, or transporting network management/monitoring data. Such functions, although critical to the network's operability, could actually experience detrimental effects if forced to use the reliable delivery mechanisms of TCP. Thus, being an unreliable protocol does not mean that UDP is a useless protocol. It just means that it was designed to support different application types than TCP.

Summary

The TCP/IP suite of protocols (including UDP and ICMP) have served the communications needs of a rapidly expanding base of users and applications for over 20 years. During that time, these protocols have been updated constantly to keep pace with technological innovation as well as the Internet's evolution from a semi-private research mechanism to a public, commercial infrastructure.

The commercialization of the Internet precipitated an unprecedented growth in the Internet's user population and a shift in its demographics. This, in turn, has created the need for more addresses and Internet Layer support for new types of service. Thus, IPv4's limitations have driven the development of a completely new version of the protocol. This new version is called IP Version 6 (IPv6) but is also commonly referred to as Internet Protocol: Next Generation (IPng). IPv6 is explored in more detail in Chapter 12.

9

OVERVIEW OF THE
IP FAMILY OF
PROTOCOLS

The Internet Protocol

by Karanjit S. Siyan, Ph.D.

The Internet Protocol (IP) provides the first level of abstraction that provides a virtual view of the network where all nodes are treated as IP nodes. IP provides an abstract view of the network, a logical view wherein the network is viewed as an idealized network possessing properties that are described in this chapter.

Because of the abstraction layer that IP provides, protocols above the IP layers—such as the TCP and UDP protocols—can treat the network as an IP-only network. In reality, the network may not be an IP-only network; it may support other protocols besides TCP/IP. The IP node's network connections are identified by the 32-bit value known as the IP address. IP provides connectionless services to upper-layer services. The connectionless service is implemented using datagrams that contain the source and destination IP addresses and other parameters needed for IP operation. This chapter provides a strong conceptual understanding of how IP works in real-life networks.

IP Abstraction

The IP layer relies on the underlying network hardware for its transmission. This means that IP datagram is encapsulated by the frames of the underlying network, such as Ethernet, Token Ring, or X.25.

The upper-layer protocols, such as TCP and UDP, need not be aware of the network hardware encapsulation and the underlying hardware. Upper-layer protocols may expect a certain quality of service, such as throughput and delay factors. These are called *Quality of Service* (QoS) parameters. The upper layers pass the QoS parameters along with the data to the IP layer. The IP layer may attempt to map the QoS parameters to services provided by the underlying network hardware. The underlying network hardware may or may not be able to supply this service.

Figure 10.1 shows that the IP host has three network connections. These connections are for Ethernet, Token Ring, and X.25 networks. In this example, IP runs on each of the three network connections. These network connections are identified by a unique 32-bit identifier called the *IP address*. The IP layer presents to the upper layers an abstraction for each of the three networks. This abstraction is independent of the physical attributes of the networks, such as address size, maximum transmission unit (MTU) size, network bandwidth, maximum data transmission rate, and so on. The MTU size is the maximum size of the data field for the underlying physical network. Because the data field contains IP datagrams for TCP/IP networks, the MTU size is also the maximum size of the IP datagram that can be carried on a physical network.

In the example network in Figure 10.1, the MTU size of the Ethernet network is 1500 bytes. The MTU size is 4440 for the IEEE 802.5, 4 Mbps Token Ring network; it is

17940 for the IEEE 802.5, 16 Mbps network. For the X.25 network, the MTU size is negotiated as an option and can range from 64 bytes to 4 KB. IP networks are required to process datagrams of at least 576 bytes in size. Because the smallest IP datagram that all routers must process is 576 bytes, the lower values are not used as MTU sizes in an X.25 network carrying TCP/IP data.

Regardless of the MTU size and speed differences of the networks, the IP layer translates these networks into a common logical IP network that is independent of physical differences.

FIGURE 10.1

IP abstraction. (Courtesy Learning Tree)

- **IP Layer**
  - Provides powerful logical abstraction
  - Hides Physical Layer dependency

- **Upper layer processes see a logical IP network**

PAD = packet assembler/disassembler

The abstract IP network is connectionless. Each datagram is independently routed. It is possible, therefore, for successive datagrams to be transmitted along different paths (see Figure 10.2).

FIGURE 10.2

Independent routing of IP datagrams.

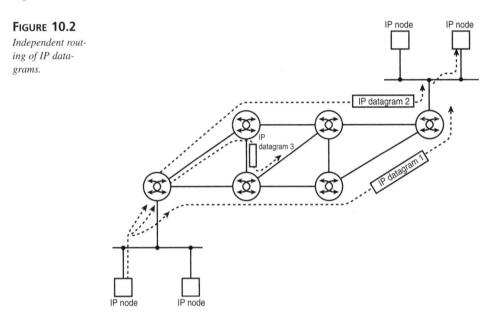

Because of the difference in time delays along the paths, datagrams arriving at the destination in a different sequence from that in which they were sent is possible. The IP layer makes no attempt to solve the problem of ensuring that datagrams are delivered to applications in the destination host in the correct order. Nor does it make any attempt to ensure that the datagrams are delivered reliably to the destination. Delivering datagrams in the proper order is called *sequencing*. The sequencing problem and the problem of reliable data delivery are solved by an upper-layer protocol such as TCP.

Because IP does not attempt to solve the sequencing and reliable data delivery problem, mapping IP onto a variety of network hardware is easy. Upper-layer protocols can add additional levels of reliability as needed by applications.

It is important to realize that the IP network in itself, without the assistance of any higher-level protocols, is inherently unreliable. The IP network uses a best-effort delivery method; that is, it tries to do the best job it can delivering the IP datagram, but it cannot guarantee delivery of the datagram. This is why IP is almost always used in conjunction with upper-layer protocols, which provides added functionality.

The IP service is connectionless, and each datagram is routed independently of others. Each datagram includes the sender and destination IP address. Intervening IP routers use the destination address to forward the IP datagram to the correct destination.

IP abstraction enables datagrams to be transmitted regardless of the MTU size of the network. IP nodes can fragment a large datagram when needed. The following sections explain this concept in greater detail.

IP Datagram Size

IP was designed to accommodate a variety of network hardware types. As pointed out earlier, different networks have different restrictions on the maximum data size that can be transmitted by the Data Link Layer frame. Table 10.1 lists the MTU size of the different hardware types.

TABLE 10.1 MTU Sizes

Network Type	MTU (octets)
Ethernet	1500
IEEE 802.3	1492
Token Ring	4440 to 17940 (actual size depends on the Token Holding Time)
FDDI	4352
IEEE 802.4	8166
SMDS	9180
X.25	1007 (ARPANET via DDN Standard X.25) 576 (for Public Data Networks, but can be increased by negotiation)

Token Ring MTU sizes shown in Table 10.1 depend on the Token Holding Time (THT), which is approximately 8.58 ms (milliseconds). For a 4 Mbps transmission rate, the maximum Token Ring frame size is computed as follows:

Maximum Token Ring
frame size (@ 4Mbps)

$$= 8.58 \text{ ms} \times 4 \text{ Mbps}$$

$$= 8.58 \times 4 \times 1024 \times 1024$$

$$= 36000 \text{ bits}$$

$$= 36000 \div 8 \text{ octets} = 4500 \text{ octets}$$

10

THE INTERNET
PROTOCOL

In the previous calculations 1 Mbps is actually 1 Kbps × 1 Kbps = 1024 × 1024 bps.

The largest Token Ring frame header is computed as follows:

MAC Header	= 15 octets
Routing Information field	= 30 octets
LLC header	= 4 octets
SNAP header	= 5 octets
MAC trailer	= 6 octets
Total frame header	= 60 octets
MTU size for Token Ring @ 4 Mbps	= Maximum Frame size – Token Ring frame header size
	= 4500 – 60 = 4440 octets

For Token Ring at 16 Mbps, the maximum Token Ring frame size is computed as follows:

Maximum Token Ring frame size @ 16 Mbps	= 8.58 ms × 16 Mbps
	= 8.58 × 16 × 1024 × 1024
	= 144000 bits
	= 144000 ÷ 8 octets = 18000 octets
MTU size for Token Ring @ 16 Mbps	= Maximum Frame size – Token Ring frame header size
	= 18000 – 60 = 17940 octets

The FDDI MTU size in Table 10.1 is computed as follows:

Maximum FDDI frame size using the 4B/5B encoding	= 4500 octets

Largest FDDI frame header is computed as follows:

MAC Header	= 16 octets
LLC header	= 4 octets
SNAP header	= 5 octets
MAC trailer	= 7 octets (approximately)
Total frame header	= 32 octets

To accommodate future expansion, it is recommended that 148 octets be allocated for the FDDI frame header.

MTU size for FDDI @ 100 Mbps	= Maximum Frame size – Adjusted FDDI frame header size
	= 4500 – 148 = 4352 octets

The IP datagram can be up to 65536 bytes long. Most networks do not have an MTU size that is as big as 65536 bytes. The IP layer at the sender usually limits the size of the datagram to not exceed that of the MTU size of the local network. If an IP datagram must traverse intervening networks, the IP datagram cannot exceed the MTU size of the networks if the IP datagram is to be delivered in one whole piece. IP networks do not have any efficient mechanism to determine beforehand the MTU sizes of the intervening networks. If they did, the sender could send an IP datagram that does not exceed the MTU size of the intervening networks. Instead, IP networks depend on the fragmentation mechanism to deliver arbitrarily sized datagrams to any network.

IP Fragmentation

If an IP datagram exceeds the MTU size of the network it must traverse, it cannot be sent in one whole piece. The IP datagram must be broken into smaller fragments that do not exceed the MTU size of the network. This process is called *fragmentation*. Each fragment of the original datagram is sent as an IP datagram. The IP header carries sufficient information to identify the fragment. This information is used by the destination host in assembling the fragments.

Figure 10.3 illustrates the process of sending an IP datagram across networks. In this example, network B's MTU size is smaller than the datagram size. Router R1 detects this fact and fragments the IP datagram into smaller IP datagrams that do not exceed the MTU size of network B. The fragmented datagrams are routed independently and arrive at host C. Though the MTU size of network C can accommodate the original datagram, the router R2 at the boundary between networks B and C makes no attempt at reassembling the fragments to form the original datagram. Reassembly of the IP datagram fragments is performed by the destination IP module and never by intervening routers.

FIGURE 10.3

IP datagram fragmentation. (Courtesy Learning Tree)

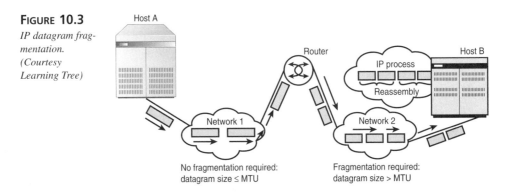

What happens in Figure 10.3 when host C needs to reply to host A? Host C will adjust the datagram size to not exceed the MTU size of network C. The datagram from host C can be delivered to host A without any fragmentation. However, the intervening routers will not attempt to combine multiple datagrams into a larger datagram to increase the efficiency of transmission.

> **Note**
>
> In IP networks, only fragmented datagrams are assembled at the destination. Whole datagrams are never combined into a larger datagram to increase efficiency of transmission.

IP Datagram Format

The IP datagram format contains an IP header and the IP data from upper-layer protocols (see Figure 10.4). The IP header is designed to accommodate the features of the IP layer.

From what you have learned about the IP layer in the previous sections, the IP header must contain at least the following information:

- IP address of source and destination. This is needed because IP is a connectionless protocol, and complete source and destination address information must be included with every datagram.

- Quality of service. This field is needed to specify the type of service expected from the underlying network.

- Fragmentation information. Because the IP datagram can get fragmented on a network boundary, there should be fields that help identify the fragment within the original datagram.

- Datagram size. IP datagrams can be of variable size. For this reason, there should be a field identifying the total length of the IP datagram.

- IP header size. IP datagrams can include optional fields that specify the IP options used for security, source routing, and so on. This causes the IP header size to be of variable length. For this reason the actual IP header size must be indicated in the IP header.

FIGURE 10.4

IP datagram format.

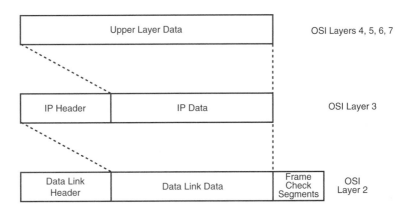

The following section discusses the details of the actual IP header format.

IP Header Format

The IP header has a minimum length of 20 octets. If IP options are specified in the IP datagram, the header length may be longer. Figure 10.5 shows the fields and structure of the IP header.

> **Note**
>
> The IP header format is discussed in detail in RFC 791 and RFC 1122. RFC 1349 describes the use of the Type of Service (TOS) field in the IP header in detail.

10

THE INTERNET PROTOCOL

FIGURE 10.5

IP header.

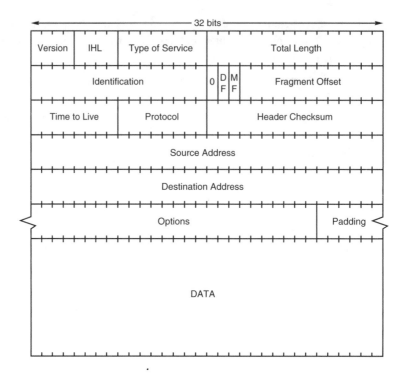

The Version Field

In Figure 10.5, the *Version* field is four bits long and indicates the format of the IP header. This enables future IP packet structures to be defined. The current version number is 4, and this IP is called IPv4. The next generation of IP has a version number value of 6 and allows for 128-bit IP addresses. For this reason it is called IPv6. Chapter 12 contains more information about IPv6. Table 10.2 shows the other possible values of the version number field.

> **Note**
>
> Version number values of 7, 8, and 9 were assigned to experimental and proposed IP protocols to solve the limitation of the 32-bit IP address problem. These protocols have been superseded by Ipv6.

TABLE 10.2   IP Version Number Values

IP Version	Meaning
0	Reserved
1–3	Unassigned
4	IPv4
5	Stream IP Datagram Mode (Experimental IP)
6	IPv6. Also called IPng.
7	TP/IX: The Next Internet
8	The "P" Internet Protocol
9	TUBA
10–14	Unassigned
15	Reserved

The Version field is used by the sender, receiver, and any intervening routers to determine the format of the IP header. IP software is required to check the Version field to ensure that the IP header format is the one it expects. For example, if the IP software can only process version 4 datagrams, it will reject datagrams that have a different value than 4 in the Version field.

The following is an explanation of some of the entries that you see in Table 10.2:

- The Stream IP protocol is an experimental protocol used to provide end-to-end guaranteed service across an internet. Stream IP is described in RFC 1819.

- The TP/IX, "P" Internet protocol, and TUBA were all at one time contenders for the replacement of IPv4. They are no longer serious contenders and are relegated to historical status, because IPv6 is the approach that has been adopted as a replacement for IPv4.

- The "P" Internet protocol is a new protocol with advanced features and variable-length addresses. It was later merged with Simple Internet Protocol (SIP). SIP uses 64-bit addressing and was merged with IP Address Encapsulation (IPAE), which describes how the transition between IPv4 and longer addressing would be achieved. SIP is described in RFC 1710.

- The TP/IX protocol (refer to Table 10.2) is an older protocol that became the basis of the Common Architecture for the Internet (CATNIP) that integrates IPv4 with Internet Packet Exchange (IPX) and the OSI Connectionless Network Protocol (CLNP). The CATNIP protocol is primarily of historical interest. CATNIP is described in RFC 1707.

10

THE INTERNET PROTOCOL

- TUBA stands for TCP and UDP with Bigger Addresses. TUBA is based on CLNP. TUBA is described in RFC 1347, RFC 1526, and RFC 1561.

The Internet Header Length Field

The *Internet Header Length* (IHL) field is the length of the header in 32-bit words. This field is 4 bits long and is required because the IP header contains a variable-length options field. All other fields have a fixed length. The options field is padded, if necessary, to be a multiple of 32-bit words. Typically, most IP headers do not have any options listed. Excluding the options field, the IP header length is 20 octets. The typical IHL value is, therefore, five 32-bit words. The maximal internet header is 60 octets and specifies the use of IP options. In this case the IHL value will be fifteen 32-bit words.

The Type of Service Field

The *Type of Service* (ToS) field informs the networks of the QoS desired, such as precedence, delay, throughput, and reliability. The meaning of this 8-bit field is shown in Figure 10.6.

FIGURE 10.6

Type of Service field for IP packets.

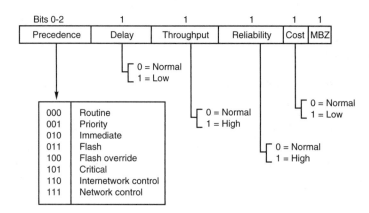

The first three bits deal with the Precedence value associated with the IP datagram. The *Precedence* field reflects the military origin of IP networks (the Department of Defense, which is discussed presently). The following are the meanings of some of the precedence values:

- Flash. ASAP (As Soon As Possible). Maximum priority on all circuits.
- Immediate. Within four hours.
- Priority. Same day.
- Routine. Within one day.

The Precedence values are 3 bits long. Table 10.3 lists the possible values and meanings of the precedence field.

TABLE 10.3   Precedence Values

Precedence	Meaning
000	Routine
001	Priority
010	Immediate
011	Flash
100	Flash-override
101	Critical
110	Internetwork control
111	Network control

The Precedence field was intended for Department of Defense applications of the Internet protocols. The use of non-zero values in this field is outside the scope of the IP standard specification. The IP layer must provide a means for the transport layer to set the TOS field of every datagram that is sent; the default is all 0 bits. The IP layer should pass received TOS values up to the transport layer.

> **Note**
>
> Vendors should consult the Defense Information Systems Agency (DISA) for guidance on the IP Precedence field and its implications for other protocol layers. Vendors should note that the use of precedence most likely will require that its value be passed between protocol layers in much the same way as the TOS field is passed.

The 4 bits that follow the Precedence field are a code for types of service. These codes are interpreted as shown in Table 10.4.

TABLE 10.4   Types of Service Codes

TOS code	Meaning
1000	Minimum delay
0100	Maximum throughput
0010	Maximum reliability
0001	Minimum monetary cost
0000	Normal service

The last bit of the TOS field must be zero. This 1-bit field is called the must be zero (MBZ) field and is reserved for future use. IP protocols participating in Internet experiments may make use of this field. Routers and recipients of datagrams ignore the value of this field. This field is copied on fragmentation, which results in all the IP datagram fragments having the same type of service.

Most IP implementations and routing protocols—RIP, HELLO, and so on—ignore the Type of Service field. Although the TOS field has been little used in the past, it is expected to play an increasing role with routing protocols such as OSPF that could make use of the TOS field. The TOS field is expected to be used to control two aspects of router operations: routing and queuing algorithms. The TOS field also may be mapped into link-layer sharing of serial lines by different classes of TCP traffic.

The TOS field can be used as a hint to the routing algorithms to select the most appropriate path. If a router knows of more than one possible route to a destination, it can use the TOS field to select the route that more closely matches the TOS field value. For example, a router may know of two paths to a destination: one with a high-delay and high-throughput connection such as a satellite link, and one with a low-delay and low-throughput connection such as a leased line. If the application traffic carries interactive user keystrokes, the requirement is one of low delay but not very high throughput. Consequently, the router should select the leased-line connection for routing this type of traffic. If the application traffic requires a high volume of file data transfer, throughput is important and the high delay is not so critical. In this case, the satellite link with high throughput is the best route.

> **Note**
>
> RFC 1349 describes the use of the TOS field in detail.

The Total Length Field

The *Total Length field* contains the length of the IP header and data in bytes. This field is 16 bits long, which limits the datagram to a maximum size of 65535 octets. This number is the maximum value that can be represented by 16 bits and consists of 16 ones:

1111111111111111

The preceding number is equal to $2^{16}-1$, a decimal value of 65535.

Datagrams that are as long as 65535 octets are impractical for most hosts and networks. Most networks have an MTU size that is far less than 65535 octets. It also is not efficient to design the communication buffers where IP datagrams can be as large as 65535 octets. Typical datagram size for most networks and hosts seldom exceeds 16 KB.

All IP nodes must be prepared to receive datagrams of at least 576 bytes whether they arrive whole or in fragments. The minimum size of 576 bytes is based on 512 bytes of data plus 64 bytes of protocol overhead.

Datagrams that are larger than the MTU size of the underlying network must be fragmented because they cannot be otherwise sent through the underlying network whose MTU size is too small to transmit the datagram.

The Identification Field

The *Identification field* is set uniquely for each datagram, and is the datagram number. Each sending side numbers the datagram starting with some initial value (see Figure 10.7). Most IP implementations use a global memory counter that is incremented with each IP datagram that is sent. If you capture network traffic from hosts that have been up for some time, such as server computers, you will see Identification field values that start from a seemingly arbitrary initial value. This is because the hosts have been sending IP datagrams in previous network sessions, and the Identification field is incremented for each IP datagram that is sent.

FIGURE 10.7
Identification field values.

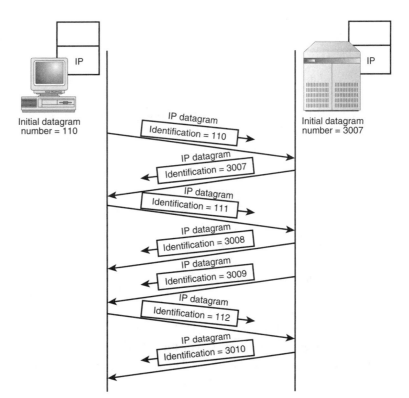

The identification field is 16 bits long. This allows for datagrams to be numbered from 0 to 65535.

The Identification field is used primarily to identify IP datagram fragments as belonging to a particular original IP datagram. The Identification field is used in conjunction with the fragment flags Don't Fragment (DF), More Fragments (MF), and Fragment Offset fields to reassemble the datagram. These flags are discussed in the sections that follow.

Fragmentation Flags and Fragment Offset Fields

The DF flag set to 1 means that the datagram should not be fragmented. This may be done if the sender knows that the receiver may not have sufficient capability to reassemble the fragments into the original datagram. An example of this is a bootstrap program running in the ROM of a computer that downloads data from a server machine. If the entire data is designed to fit inside a datagram, the sender can set the DF flag to 1. Another reason for setting the DF flag is in the situation where the sender wants to eliminate the delays caused by reassembly of IP datagram fragments at the receiver. If the DF flag is set to 0, it indicates that a router or host may fragment the IP datagram.

The MF flag set to 1 indicates to the receiver that more fragments are to come. An MF set to 0 indicates that it is the last fragment. For complete IP datagrams, the MF flag will always be set to 0 to indicate that there are no more fragments to this datagram.

In the ideal situation, the MTU size of all the networks that an IP datagram needs to traverse should have an MTU size that is larger than the largest IP datagram to be transmitted by a sender. In this case, there is no need to perform any fragmentation. Even if the smallest MTU size along a path is known, you should realize that successive datagrams may follow a different path and, therefore, encounter a different smallest MTU size. (This is because each IP datagram is routed independently of other datagrams.)

How is an IP datagram fragmented? Consider the situation in Figure 10.8 where a host on network A is sending IP datagrams to a host on network C. There is an intervening network B that the IP datagrams must traverse. The MTU sizes of networks A, B, and C are 1500, 525, and 4470 octets, respectively. Router Ra joins networks A and B, and router Rc joins networks B and C. Typically host A will send IP datagrams that fit inside the MTU size of network A. In this example, assume that an IP datagram with an Identification value of 5 and a size of 1500 octets is sent by host A. When the router Ra encounters this IP datagram, it will fragment the IP datagram before it can forward the datagram to network B because the MTU size of network B is smaller than the datagram size. The fragment size is selected so that it will fit inside the MTU size of network B (525 bytes). The *offset*, the start of the data field relative to the original unfragmented data, is placed in the Fragment Offset field of each IP datagram fragment.

FIGURE 10.8

Fragmentation example.

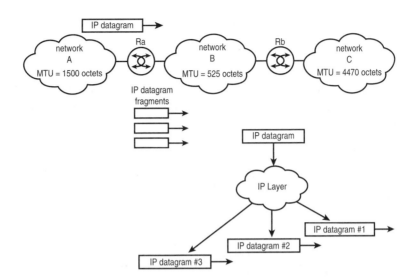

The Fragment Offset field indicates the position of the fragment's data relative to the start of the original datagram. (The specifics of the value of this field are discussed shortly.) The Fragment Offset field is 13 bits long. If you study the IP header format in Figure 10.5, you will notice that only 13 bits are used because some of the other bits are used for the DF and MF flags.

Because the IP datagram can be up to 65535 octets long, this field is not sufficiently long to describe offset values greater than 8192 octets. For this reason, the Fragment Offset field is extended by appending three 0 bits:

    fragment_offset_value000

The resulting fragment offset value is always a multiple of 8 bytes. Therefore, the fragment offset always describes fragments in units of 8-byte groups. The fragment offset value must be multiplied by 8 to get the actual offset of the fragment. This means that all fragments except the very last must be a multiple of 8. In addition the fragments must fit inside the MTU size of the network. In the example of the 1500-octet IP datagram, consider the situation where you decided to fragment as shown next because the MTU size of the network is too small:

Fragment 1 size	= 525 octets
Fragment 2 size	= 525 octets
Fragment 3 size	= 450 octets
IP datagram size	= 1500 octets

10

THE INTERNET PROTOCOL

However, 525 bytes is not a multiple of 8. You also must take into account the size of the IP header (a minimum of 20 octets), which must also fit within the MTU size. With an MTU size of 525, subtracting the typical size of an IP header of 20 octets yields 505 octets for the fragment size. This number also is not a multiple of 8. The next smallest fragment size that is divisible by 8 is 504. Therefore, you can select the IP fragment size to be 504 octets. Figure 10.9 shows the breakdown of the original IP datagram into the following fragments:

Fragment 1	= 504 octets
Fragment 2	= 504 octets
Fragment 3	= 492 octets
IP datagram	= 1500 octets

FIGURE 10.9

Fragmentation of the original IP datagram.

Each fragment must have its own IP header. The Identification field value in the fragmented IP datagrams have the value belonging to the original fragmented IP datagram. This identifies the IP fragment as belonging to a specific original IP datagram. The flag settings and fragment offset values of the fragmented IP datagrams (see Figure 10.10) are as follows:

Fragment 1:

Total Length	= 504 octets
Identification	= 5
DF flag	= 0
MF	= 1
Fragment Offset	= 0

Fragment 2:

Total Length	= 504 octets
Identification	= 5
DF flag	= 0
MF	= 1
Fragment Offset	= 63 8-octet words (504 octets)

Fragment 3:

Total Length	= 492 octets
Identification	= 5
DF flag	= 0
MF	= 0
Fragment Offset	= 126 8-octet words (1008 octets)

For the receiver to reassemble the IP datagram, it must obtain all fragments starting with the IP datagram fragment with a fragment offset value of 0, and going onto the highest fragment offset value. The receiver uses the size of each fragment (Total Length field of the IP datagram header), the fragment offset value, and the MF flag to determine whether it has received all the fragments. How does a receiver know that the last fragment has been received? The last fragment has an MF flag value set to 0. The first fragment is identified by an MF flag set to 1 and a fragment offset set to 0. All other intermediate fragments will have an MF flag set to 1 and a non-zero fragment offset value.

10

THE INTERNET PROTOCOL

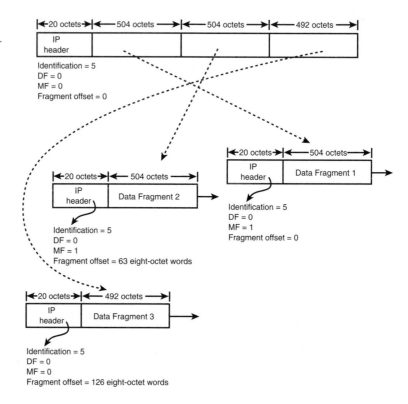

FIGURE 10.10

IP datagram fragments.

After an IP datagram has been fragmented, the individual pieces travel to the destination along potentially separate paths. The IP fragments are reassembled at the receiver and never at an intervening router. This fact leads to the following issues:

- IP fragments travel from their point of fragmentation to the destination.
- Despite intervening networks having a larger MTU size than the fragment size, the fragments will be carried in small size packets, which results in poor protocol efficiency.
- Excessive fragmentation leads to excessive network traffic.

If a fragment is lost, the original datagram cannot be reassembled. Despite successful transmission of the remaining fragments, the original datagram must be discarded. In this case, upper-layer protocols such as TCP ensure that the original datagram is present, but this datagram will be fragmented again at the point where the IP datagram exceeds the MTU size.

The receiving IP node starts a reassembly timer upon receiving the first IP fragment. If this timer expires before all the other fragments arrive, the IP node discards the remaining fragments even though they were received correctly. As the number of fragments increases, so does the possibility of losing an IP datagram. This is because a loss of a single fragment results in the loss of the entire datagram. When the reassembly timer expires, an Internet Control Message Protocol (ICMP) message is sent to the sender announcing that the reassembly timer has expired. A monitoring device such as a protocol analyzer can be used to alert you to this problem.

The decision to reassemble the IP datagram at the receiver, while creating the problems described previously, has the advantage of keeping the router implementation simple. The IP routers do not have to be concerned about storing and reassembling the IP fragments. If there are several networks with a small MTU size, reassembling the IP fragments at intervening routers would be somewhat wasteful because the reassembled IP datagram would have to be fragmented before traversing a network with a small MTU size.

The TTL field

The *Time To Live* (TTL) is measured in seconds and represents the maximum time an IP datagram can live on the network. It should be decremented at each router by the amount of time taken to process the packet. When the TTL field becomes 0, the TTL timer expires. The intent is that TTL expiration causes a datagram to be discarded by a router, but not by the destination host. Hosts acting as routers by forwarding datagrams must follow the previously discussed behavior for TLL routing. The TTL field has two functions:

- Limits the lifetime of TCP segments
- Terminates Internet routing loops

When the TTL timer expires, an ICMP message announcing this fact is sent to the source.

Although TTL is measured in seconds, it is difficult for routers to estimate the exact transit time for IP datagrams on a network segment. Routers could note the time an IP datagram spends inside the router by noting the time when a datagram arrives and the time when it leaves the router. Because of the extra processing required to do so, many routers do not attempt to estimate the time an IP datagram spends inside a router and simply decrease the TTL value by 1. Because of this, the TTL field has some attributes of a hop count. Some earlier implementers mistakenly set the TTL value to 16 because 16 is infinity for RIP (Routing Information Protocol). TTL is independent of RIP metrics, however.

Other considerations for TTL fields are the following:

- A host must not send a datagram with a TTL value of 0, and a host must not discard a datagram just because it was received with a TTL less than 2.

- An upper-layer protocol may want to set the TTL to implement an expanding scope search for some Internet resource. This is used by some diagnostic tools and is expected to be useful for locating the "nearest" server of a given class using IP multicasting, for example. A particular transport protocol also may want to specify its own TTL boundary on maximum datagram lifetime.

- A fixed value must be at least big enough for the Internet *diameter*, the longest possible path. A reasonable value is about twice the diameter, which enables continued Internet growth.

- The IP layer must provide a means for the transport layer to set the TTL field of every datagram that is sent. When a fixed TTL value is used, that value must be configurable. Unfortunately, most implementations do not enable the initial TTL value to be set. A default value of 32 or 64 is very common.

The Protocol Field

The *Protocol field* is used to indicate the upper-layer protocol that is to receive the IP data. The Protocol field is used for multiplexing/demultiplexing of data to upper-layer protocols. For example, TCP has a Protocol field value of 6, UDP has a value of 17, and ICMP has a value of 1. When IP sees a Protocol field value of 6, it knows that the IP header encapsulates TCP data that must be delivered to the TCP module. If IP sees a Protocol field value of 17, it knows that this must be delivered to the UDP module. Similarly, when IP sees a Protocol field value of 1, it knows that this must be delivered to the ICMP module.

Table 10.5 shows the Protocol field values for IP.

TABLE 10.5   Protocol IDs

Protocol ID	Abbreviation	Meaning
0		(Reserved)
1	ICMP	Internet Control Message
2	IGMP	Internet Group Management
3	GGP	Gateway-to-Gateway
4	IP	IP in IP (encapsulation)
5	ST	Stream
6	TCP	Transmission Control

TABLE 10.5   Continued

Protocol ID	Abbreviation	Meaning
7	UCL	UCL
8	EGP	Exterior Gateway Protocol
9	IGP	Any private interior gateway
10	BBN-RCC-MON	BBN RCC Monitoring
11	NVP-II	Network Voice Protocol
12	PUP	PUP
13	ARGUS	ARGUS
14	EMCON	EMCON
15	XNET	Cross Net Debugger
16	CHAOS	Chaos
17	UDP	User Datagram
18	MUX	Multiplexing
19	DCN-MEAS	DCN Measurement Subsystems
20	HMP	Host Monitoring
21	PRM	Packet Radio Measurement
22	XNS-IDP	XEROX NS IDP
23	TRUNK-1	Trunk-1
24	TRUNK-2	Trunk-2
25	LEAF-1	Leaf-1
26	LEAF-2	Leaf-2
27	RDP	Reliable Data Protocol
28	IRTP	Internet Reliable Transaction
29	ISO-TP4	ISO Transport Protocol Class4
30	NETBLT	Bulk Data Transfer Protocol
31	MFE-NSP	MFE Network Services Protocol
32	MERIT-INP	MERIT Internodal Protocol
33	SEP	Sequential Exchange Protocol
34	3PC	Third Party Connect Protocol
35	IDPR	Inter-Domain Policy Routing Protocol
36	XTP	XTP
37	DDP	Datagram Delivery Protocol

10

THE INTERNET PROTOCOL

TABLE 10.5 Continued

Protocol ID	Abbreviation	Meaning
38	IDPR-CMTP	IDPR Control Message Transport Protocol
39	TP++	TP++ Transport Protocol
40	IL	IL Transport Protocol
41	SIP	Simple Internet Protocol
42	SDRP	Source Demand Routing Protocol
43	SIP-SR	SIP Source Route
44	SIP-FRAG	SIP Fragment
45	IDRP	Inter-Domain Routing Protocol
46	RSVP	Reservation Protocol
47	GRE	General Routing Encapsulation
48	MHRP	Mobile Host Routing Protocol
49	BNA	BNA
50	SIPP-ESP	SIPP Encap Security Payload
51	SIPP-AH	SIPP Authentication Header
52	I-NLSP	Integrated Net Layer Security TUBA
53	SWIPE	IP with Encryption
54	NHRP	NBMA Next Hop Resolution Protocol
55–60		(Unassigned)
61		(Any host internal protocol)
62	CFTP	CFTP
63		(Any local network)
64	SAT-EXPAK	SATNET and Backroom EXPAK
65	KRYPTOLAN	Kryptolan
66	RVD	MIT Remote Virtual Disk Protocol
67	IPPC	Internet Pluribus Packet Core
68		(Any distributed file system)
69	SAT-MON	SATNET Monitoring
70	VISA	VISA Protocol
71	IPCV	Internet Packet Core Utility

TABLE 10.5 Continued

Protocol ID	Abbreviation	Meaning
72	CPNX	Computer Protocol Network Executive
73	CPHB	Computer Protocol Heart Beat
74	WSN	Wang Span Network
75	PVP	Packet Video Protocol
76	BR-SAT-MON	Backroom SATNET Monitoring
77	SUN-ND	SUN ND PROTOCOL-Temporary
78	WB-MON	WIDEBAND Monitoring
79	WB-EXPAK	WIDEBAND EXPAK
80	ISO-IP	ISO Internet Protocol
81	VMTP	VMTP
82	SECURE-VMTP	SECURE-VMTP
83	VINES	VINES
84	TTP	TTP
85	NSFNET-IGP	NSFNET-IGP
86	DGP	Dissimilar Gateway Protocol
87	TCF	TCF
88	IGRP	IGRP
89	OSPFIGP	OSPFIGP
90	Sprite-RPC	Sprite RPC Protocol
91	LARP	Locus Address Resolution Protocol
92	MTP	Multicast Transport Protocol
93	AX.25	AX.25 Frames
94	IPIP	IP-within-IP Encapsulation Protocol
95	MICP	Mobile Internetworking Control Pro.
96	SCC-SP	Semaphore Communications Sec. Pro.
97	ETHERIP	Ethernet-within-IP Encapsulation
98	ENCAP	Encapsulation Header

10

THE INTERNET PROTOCOL

TABLE 10.5 Continued

Protocol ID	Abbreviation	Meaning
99		(Any private encryption scheme)
100	GMTP	GMTP
101–254		(Unassigned)
255		(Reserved)

Header Checksum Field

The *Header Checksum* is used for the IP header only. The 1's complement of each 16-bit value making up the header is added (excluding the Header Checksum field). Then the 1's complement of the sum is taken. This field is recomputed at each router because the TTL field is decremented at the router, and this results in the modification of the IP header.

It is quite simple to compute the checksum, and experimental evidence indicates that it is adequate in detecting errors in transmitting the datagram.

Source and Destination IP Addresses

The *Source Address* and *Destination Address* are the 32-bit IP addresses of the source and destination nodes. These are sent in every IP datagram because the IP network is a connectionless network, and each IP datagram must include the sender and destination IP addresses.

The routers use the destination IP address value to perform the routing for each IP datagram.

IP Options

IP implements facilities for indicating the security of a datagram, source routing information, and timestamp information. Because these facilities are infrequently used, they are implemented as optional fields called *IP options*.

The IP options are as follows:

- Security
- Record Route
- Strict Source Routing
- Loose Source Routing
- Internet Timestamp

The IP options must be handled by all IP nodes, and may optionally appear in IP datagrams near the end of the IP header. Their transmission in any particular datagram is optional, but their implementation is not. For example, in environments that need a high level of security, the Security option may be required in all IP datagrams.

The option field is variable in length, and values must be multiples of 32-bit words. Zero pad values may be added to make the options field size multiples of 32-bit words. The two formats for IP option values (see Figure 10.11) are

- Option format 1. A single octet of option-type.
- Option format 2. An option-type octet, an option-length octet, and the actual option-data octets. The option-length octet contains the overall size of this option including the octet-type, option-length, and option-data fields.

FIGURE 10.11

Option formats.

The option-type octet is the first octet that occurs in an option specification. In option format 1 the option-type octet is the only octet, and in option format 2 it is followed by two other fields. The option-type consists of the following three fields (see Figure 10.12):

- Copied flag (1 bit)
- Option-class (2 bits)
- Option-number (5 bits)

FIGURE 10.12

Option octet.

The Copied flag controls how routers process the options field during fragmentation. When set to 1, the Copied flag indicates that the options should be copied into all IP datagram fragments. When set to 0, the Copied flag indicates that the options should be copied into the first IP fragment and not into all IP datagram fragments.

The Option-class field is 2 bits long and can have a value from 0 to 3. The meanings of these values are listed in Table 10.6.

TABLE 10.6 Option-Class Field Values in Option-Type Octet

Code	Meaning
0	Network control
1	Reserved for future use
2	Debugging and measurement
3	Reserved for future use

The class field is used to determine the general category of the option. The categories are for network control and debugging. The Option-number field is 5 bits long and enables the specification of up to 32 options for a given option category. Table 10.7 lists the different options that have been defined.

TABLE 10.7 IP Options

Option-class	Option-number	Length	Meaning
0	0	-	End of Option list. This option occupies only 1 octet and has no length octet. It is used if options do not end at an end of header.
0	1	-	No Operation. This option occupies only 1 octet; it has no length octet. It is used to align octets in a list of options.
0	2	11	Basic Security. This is used to carry Security, Compartmentation, User Group (TCC), and Handling Restriction Codes compatible with DoD requirements.
0	3	variable	Loose Source Routing. Used to route the IP datagram based on information supplied by the source.
0	5	variable	Extended Security. Used for specifying additional security.
0	7	variable	Record Route. Used to trace the route an IP datagram takes.
0	8	4	Stream ID. Used to carry the 16-bit SATNET stream identifier through networks that do not support the stream concept. It is now obsolete.

TABLE 10.7 Continued

Option-class	Option-number	Length	Meaning
0	9	variable	Strict Source Routing. Used to route the IP datagram based on information supplied by the source.
2	4	variable	Internet Timestamp. Used to record time-stamps along the route. This is currently the only option defined for the debugging and measurement category of option-class.

The following sections explain the different IP option types in greater detail.

End of Option List and the No Operation Options

The End of Option List and the No Operation options are the only single octet options. The End of Option list (refer to Table 10.7) is a 1-octet option consisting of all zeros (see Figure 10.13).

FIGURE 10.13

The End of Option list.

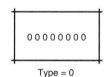

Type = 0

This option indicates the end of the option list, which may not coincide with the end of the internet header according to the IHL field. This option is used at the end of all options, and not at the end of each option. This option need only be used if the end of the options would not otherwise fall on a 32-bit boundary.

The No Option list (refer to Table 10.7) is a 1-octet option consisting of the following bit pattern (see Figure 10.14).

FIGURE 10.14

The No Option list.

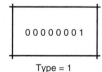

Type = 1

10

THE INTERNET PROTOCOL

The No Operation option may be used between options to align the beginning of a subsequent option on a 32-bit boundary.

The Security Option

The Security option provides a way for hosts to send security, compartmentation, handling restrictions, and closed user group parameters. The two types of Security options are

- Basic Security. Used to indicate security-level designations Confidential, Unclassified, Secret, and so on.

- Extended Security. Used to specify additional security per the needs of a military organization.

These are discussed in the following sections.

Basic Security Option

Figure 10.15 shows the Basic Security option format. It is characterized by an octet-type code of 130. The codes define protection authorities that have various rules concerning the treatment of the IP datagram. These protection authorities include the U.S. National Security Agency (NSA), Central Intelligence Agency (CIA), and Department of Energy (DOE).

FIGURE 10.15

Basic Security Option format.

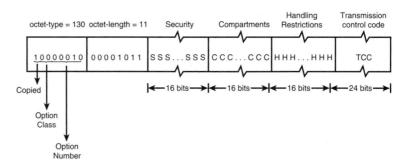

The Security field is 16 bits long and specifies one of 16 levels of security, 8 of which are reserved for future use. The security code values are described in Table 10.8. Some of the code values have meanings that are internal to the various protection authorities.

Table 10.8 Security Code Values for IP Options

Code	Meaning
00000000 00000000	Unclassified
11110001 00110101	Confidential
01111000 10011010	EFTO
10111100 01001101	MMMM
01011110 00100110	PROG
10101111 00010011	Restricted
11010111 10001000	Secret
01101011 11000101	Top Secret
00110101 11100010	Reserved for future use
10011010 11110001	Reserved for future use
01001101 01111000	Reserved for future use
00100100 10111101	Reserved for future use
00010011 01011110	Reserved for future use
10001001 10101111	Reserved for future use
11000100 11010110	Reserved for future use
11100010 01101011	Reserved for future use

The Compartments field is 16 bits long, and an all-zero value is used when the information transmitted is not compartmented. Other values for the compartments field may be obtained from the Defense Intelligence Agency.

The Handling Restrictions field is 16 bits long. The values represent control and release markings and are alphanumeric digraphs that are defined in the Defense Intelligence Agency Manual (DIAM) 65-19, "Standard Security Markings."

The Transmission Control Code (TCC) field is 24 bits long and is used to segregate traffic and define controlled communities of interest among subscribers. The TCC values are trigraphs and are available from the Defense Communication Agency (DCA).

Extended Security Option

The Extended Security option is used for specifying additional security requirements (see Figure 10.16). It is characterized by an octet-type code of 133.

Commercial routers may not support IP security options.

Record Route Option

The Record Route option is used by the sender to record the IP addresses of the routers that forward the IP datagram to the destination. The list of routers actually visited is recorded.

FIGURE 10.16

Extended Security option.

The Record Route option begins with the Option-type code of value 131 (see Figure 10.17). The second octet is the option length (the length of the entire option). The Record Data field contains slots for a list of IP address values. The third octet is the pointer into the Route Data field and indicates the start of the next slot to be processed. The pointer is relative to this option, and the smallest value for the pointer is 4. If the pointer value is greater than the Octet-length, there are no empty slots in the Record Data field; that is, the Record Data field is full. If the Record Data list is full, a router forwards the datagram without inserting itself in the list.

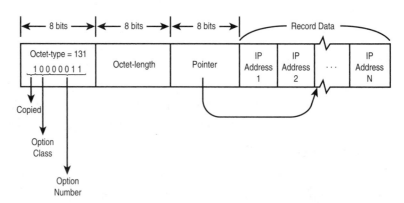

FIGURE 10.17

Record Route option.

If the pointer is not greater than the Octet-length, the Record Data list is not full and empty slots are available. The router inserts its IP address at the position specified by the pointer field and increments the pointer field value by 4, the size of the IP address. The recorded address is the IP address of the network interface of the router through which this datagram is being forwarded.

Both sender and receiver have to agree that record route information will be used and processed. The sender adds the Record Route option and sufficient slots for the IP addresses to the IP datagram. The receiver agrees to process the list of IP addresses recorded in the Record Data field. If the receiver has not agreed to process the record route data, then this information is ignored by the receiver.

Strict and Loose Source Routing

In source routing, the sender supplies the path to reach the destination. The path consists of a list of IP addresses of the routers that must be visited. Normally, the path to reach the destination is decided by the routers based on the optimal path determined by routing protocols. In source routing, the sender dictates the path that a datagram must follow in arriving at the destination. The source routing facility is useful in testing a particular path even when you know that the routers would not normally select that path. This also gives you the flexibility of routing datagrams through networks that are known to work reliably. The disadvantage of source routing is the presumption that you know the topology of the network and the list of routers that are used for forwarding a datagram. In a complex network, the topology and the actual path an IP datagram must follow may not be easy to determine.

The two types of source routing are

- Strict source routing
- Loose source routing

In the Strict Source Routing option (see Figure 10.18), the sender includes a sequence of IP addresses that must be followed exactly in forwarding the datagram. The path between two successive IP addresses in the source route list can only be a single physical network segment. A single physical network segment can consist only of layers 1 (repeater) and 2 (bridge) devices, but not layer 3 (router) devices. If routers cannot follow the strict sequence of IP addresses, the datagram is rejected.

In the Loose Source Routing option (see Figure 10.19), the sender also includes a sequence of IP addresses that must be followed in forwarding the datagram. However, the path between two successive IP addresses may include any number of routers. Figure 10.20 shows the comparison between strict and loose source routing.

10

THE INTERNET PROTOCOL

FIGURE 10.18
Strict source routing.

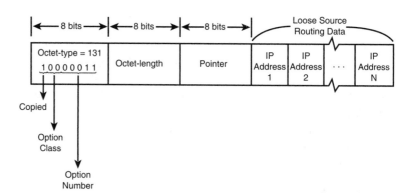

FIGURE 10.19
Loose source routing.

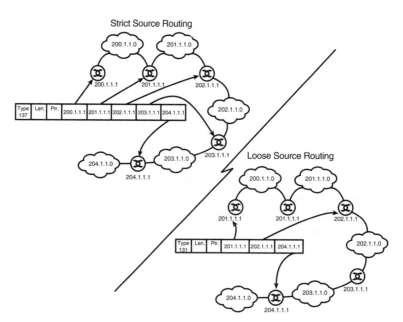

FIGURE 10.20
Strict versus loose source routing.

In both the Strict and Loose Source Routing options, the routers overwrite the source address in the option with their local IP addresses. When a datagram arrives at its destination, the IP address list contains the actual route that was taken. This list is like the one produced by the Record Route option. For this reason the Loose Source Routing option is also called the *Loose Source and Record Route* (LSRR) option, and the Strict Source Routing option is called the *Strict Source and Record Route* (SSRR) option.

As you examine the formats of the record route, strict source routing, and loose source routing in Figures 10.17, 10.18, and 10.19, notice that the option format is very similar. The Pointer field acts like an index into the IP address list. The Octet-length field indicates the number of IP address slots. When a route finishes processing an IP address, it advances the Pointer index to the next available IP address slot. Because IP addresses are 4 octets long, the Pointer field value is incremented by 4 to advance it to the next IP address slot.

When the Pointer field value is greater than the Octet-length field value, the IP address list has been processed or exhausted. In this case, the IP datagram is forwarded as usual by information in the router's routing table, without the help of the information in the IP option fields. If the Pointer is not greater than the Octet-length field value, the IP address list has not been fully processed (see Figure 10.21). In this case, the router uses the Pointer field index to obtain the value of the next router address to which it must forward the datagram. Additionally, the router then places the IP address of the network interface through which the datagram is forwarded in the IP address slot pointed to by the Pointer field index. This is done for the purpose of recording the actual route that was taken. The Pointer field index is advanced to the next IP address slot by incrementing it by 4.

FIGURE 10.21

Use of Pointer and Octet-length field.

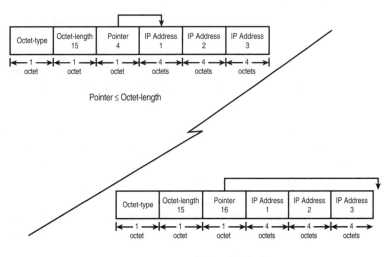

Pointer ≤ Octet-length

Pointer > Octet-length

10

THE INTERNET PROTOCOL

The Route Data field consists of a series of IP addresses. Each IP address is 4 octets long. If the Pointer value is greater than the Octet-length field, the source route is empty and the recorded route is full. The routing is based on the destination address field of the IP datagram.

Internet Timestamp

The Internet Timestamp option is used to record the timestamps at which the IP datagram is received at each router. The router's IP address and time at which the IP datagram is received by a router is recorded. The timestamps are measured as the number of milliseconds since midnight, Universal Time Coordinated (m). UTC was formerly called Greenwich Mean Time (GMT) and is the time at 0 degrees longitude.

In addition to timestamps, the IP addresses of the router can also be recorded using the Internet Timestamp option. Figure 10.22 shows the format of the Internet Timestamp option.

FIGURE 10.22

Internet Timestamp option.

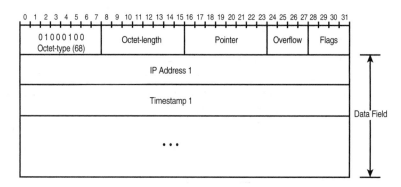

The Option-type is 68, and the Option-length is the number of octets in the option counting all the fields. Each entry in the data field of the Timestamp option contains two 32-bit values: the IP address of the router and the timestamp that it recorded.

The Octet-length specifies the amount of space reserved in the data field for the IP addresses and timestamps. The Pointer field is an index into the data field and points to the next unused slot. The index value in the Pointer field is measured from the beginning of the option. The smallest legal value of the Pointer field is 5. When the Pointer value is greater than the Octet-length field value, the timestamp area is full. The sender must create the Timestamp option with a large enough data area to hold all the timestamp information expected. The size of this option is not changed when the IP datagram is in transit. The sender must initialize the data area with zero values.

The Overflow field is 4 bits long and contains the number of routers that could not supply the timestamp because the data field was too small. The maximum value in the Overflow field is 15 routers. If there is insufficient room for a full timestamp to be inserted in the data area, or the overflow count exceeds 15, then the IP datagram is considered to be in error and is discarded. In either case an ICMP parameter problem message is sent to the sender.

The Flags field controls the format of the information in the data field. It can have three values whose codes are described in Table 10.9.

TABLE 10.9   IP Timestamp Option Flag Values

Flag Value	Meaning
0	Timestamps only, stored in consecutive 32-bit words. IP addresses are omitted.
1	Each timestamp is preceded with the IP address of the registering entity (router). This format is shown in Figure 10.20.
3	The IP address fields are specified by the sender. An IP module (router) only registers its timestamp if its IP address matches the next specified IP address.

The Timestamp values are right-justified, with 32-bit values measured in milliseconds since midnight UTC. If the time is not available in milliseconds or cannot be provided with respect to midnight UTC, then any time value, such as local time, may be inserted in the Timestamp field provided the high-order bit of the Timestamp field is set to 1. Setting the high-order bit of the Timestamp field to 1 indicates the use of a nonstandard value.

Routers may be set to the local time, and their clocks may not be synchronized. Because of differences in the routers' clock values, the Timestamp values should be treated as approximate values.

The Timestamp option is not copied upon fragmentation and is carried only in the first IP datagram fragment.

Network Byte Order

The Physical Layer transmits the bits in the order in which they are received from the upper layers. The bits that constitute the transmitted data may be stored in a different way on each computer. For example, not all computers store 32-bit integer values (such as IP addresses) in the same way. Some computers store the low-order bytes of the 32-bit integer in lower-memory addresses. This storage method is called *little endian*, and

10

THE INTERNET
PROTOCOL

the computers are called little endian computers. The other method is the *big endian* method in which the high-order bytes are stored in lower-memory addresses.

Some computers, especially the older 16-bit computers, store data in units of 16 bits with lower-order bytes stored in lower-memory addresses, but with the bytes swapped in the 16-bit word.

Because of differences in storage of data bytes, you cannot directly copy the data from one IP node to another. The TCP/IP protocols define a *network standard byte order* that is used for storing binary fields in internet packets. All IP nodes must represent the data in packets using this network standard byte order. Before sending a packet, an IP node converts its local data representation to the network standard byte order. On receiving the IP packet, an IP node converts the network standard byte order to the local data representation for that IP node. In most TCP/IP implementations, conversion between the network standard byte order to the node-specific representation is handled by the TCP/IP application programming interfaces and support routines.

The network standard byte order specifies that integers with the most significant byte are sent first; this is the *big endian* style. This means that if you examine an internet packet header field in transit, you see integer values with the most significant byte near the beginning of the packet and the least significant byte near the end of the packet.

TCP/IP protocol headers are often laid out as 32-bit words (refer to Figure 10.5). The order of transmission of the octets in the header is the normal order in which they are read in English (from left to right). For example, in Figure 10.23 the octets are transmitted in the order in which they are numbered.

FIGURE 10.23

Transmission order of bytes.

Whenever an octet represents a numeric value, the left-most bit in the diagram is the high-order or most significant bit (MSB). That is, the bit labeled 0 is the most significant bit. For example, Figure 10.24 represents the value 170 (decimal).

FIGURE 10.24

Significance of bits.

Whenever a multi-octet field represents a numeric quantity, the left-most bit of the entire field is the most significant bit. When a multi-octet quantity is transmitted, the most significant octet is transmitted first.

IP Trace

The following sections present you with protocol decodes of IP packets captured on a real-life network. You should study this protocol decode after briefly reviewing the previous sections that describe the meaning of the IP fields. Figure 10.25 shows the summary protocol trace of the first 50 packets captured in a Telnet session. Because this chapter discusses only the IP protocol, only selected packets in this Telnet trace will be discussed.

FIGURE 10.25

Telnet trace.

```
No.  Source        Destination    Layer  Size  Summary
  1  0000C024282D  FFFFFFFFFFFF   arp    0064  Req by 144.19.74.44 for 144.19.74
  2  0000C024282D  FFFFFFFFFFFF   arp    0064  Req by 144.19.74.44 for 144.19.74
  3  0000C0A20F8E  0000C024282D   arp    0064  Reply 144.19.74.201=0000C0A20F8E
  4  0000C024282D  0000C0A20F8E   tcp    0064  Port:6295 ---> TELNET SYN
  5  0000C0A20F8E  0000C024282D   tcp    0064  Port:TELNET ---> 6295 ACK SYN
  6  0000C024282D  0000C0A20F8E   telnt  0069  Cmd=Do; Code=Echo; Cmd=Do; Code=S
  7  0000C0A20F8E  0000C024282D   tcp    0064  Port:TELNET ---> 6295 ACK
  8  0000C0A20F8E  0000C024282D   telnt  0064  Cmd=Do; Code=;
  9  0000C024282D  0000C0A20F8E   telnt  0064  Cmd=Won't; Code=;
 10  0000C024282D  0000C0A20F8E   telnt  0067  Cmd=Will; Code=Echo; Cmd=Will; Co
 11  0000C0A20F8E  0000C024282D   tcp    0064  Port:TELNET ---> 6295 ACK
 12  0000C024282D  0000C0A20F8E   telnt  0072  Cmd=Do; Code=Suppress Go Ahead; C
 13  0000C0A20F8E  0000C024282D   telnt  0070  Cmd=Do; Code=Terminal Type; Cmd=D
 14  0000C0A20F8E  0000C024282D   tcp    0064  Port:TELNET ---> 6295 ACK
 15  0000C024282D  0000C0A20F8E   telnt  0072  Cmd=Will; Code=Terminal Type; Cmd
 16  0000C0A20F8E  0000C024282D   tcp    0064  Port:TELNET ---> 6295 ACK
 17  0000C0A20F8E  0000C024282D   telnt  0064  Cmd=Subnegotiation Begin; Code=Te
 18  0000C024282D  0000C0A20F8E   telnt  0071  Cmd=Subnegotiation Begin; Code=Te
 19  0000C0A20F8E  0000C024282D   tcp    0064  Port:TELNET ---> 6295 ACK
 20  0000C0A20F8E  0000C024282D   telnt  0067  Cmd=Do; Code=Echo; Cmd=Will; Code
 21  0000C024282D  0000C0A20F8E   telnt  0069  Cmd=Won't; Code=Echo; Cmd=Don't;
 22  0000C0A20F8E  0000C024282D   tcp    0064  Port:TELNET ---> 6295 ACK
 23  0000C0A20F8E  0000C024282D   telnt  0104  Data=..Linux 1.3.50 (ltreec1.ltre
 24  0000C024282D  0000C0A20F8E   tcp    0064  Port:6295 ---> TELNET ACK
 25  0000C0A20F8E  0000C024282D   telnt  0064  Data=..
 26  0000C024282D  0000C0A20F8E   tcp    0064  Port:6295 ---> TELNET ACK
 27  0000C0A20F8E  0000C024282D   telnt  0073  Data=ltreec1 login:
 28  0000C024282D  0000C0A20F8E   tcp    0064  Port:6295 ---> TELNET ACK
 29  0000C024282D  0000C0A20F8E   telnt  0064  Data=u
 30  0000C0A20F8E  0000C024282D   tcp    0064  Port:TELNET ---> 6295 ACK
 31  0000C0A20F8E  0000C024282D   telnt  0064  Data=u
 32  0000C024282D  0000C0A20F8E   tcp    0064  Port:6295 ---> TELNET ACK
 33  0000C024282D  0000C0A20F8E   telnt  0064  Data=s
 34  0000C0A20F8E  0000C024282D   tcp    0064  Port:TELNET ---> 6295 ACK
 35  0000C0A20F8E  0000C024282D   telnt  0064  Data=s
 36  0000C024282D  0000C0A20F8E   tcp    0064  Port:6295 ---> TELNET ACK
 37  0000C024282D  0000C0A20F8E   telnt  0064  Data=e
 38  0000C0A20F8E  0000C024282D   tcp    0064  Port:TELNET ---> 6295 ACK
 39  0000C0A20F8E  0000C024282D   telnt  0064  Data=e
 40  0000C024282D  0000C0A20F8E   tcp    0064  Port:6295 ---> TELNET ACK
 41  0000C024282D  0000C0A20F8E   telnt  0064  Data=r
 42  0000C0A20F8E  0000C024282D   tcp    0064  Port:TELNET ---> 6295 ACK
 43  0000C0A20F8E  0000C024282D   telnt  0064  Data=r
 44  0000C024282D  0000C0A20F8E   tcp    0064  Port:6295 ---> TELNET ACK
 45  0000C024282D  0000C0A20F8E   telnt  0064  Data=1
 46  0000C0A20F8E  0000C024282D   tcp    0064  Port:TELNET ---> 6295 ACK
 47  0000C0A20F8E  0000C024282D   telnt  0064  Data=1
 48  0000C024282D  0000C0A20F8E   tcp    0064  Port:6295 ---> TELNET ACK
 49  0000C024282D  0000C0A20F8E   telnt  0064  Data=..
 50  0000C0A20F8E  0000C024282D   tcp    0064  Port:TELNET ---> 6295 ACK
```

Notice that the first three packets of this Telnet trace are ARP packets. The use of ARP to resolve hardware addresses is discussed in Chapter 5, "ARP and RARP."

The Ethernet header for all the IP datagrams contains an EtherType value of 800 hex. This EtherType value indicates that the Ethernet frame encapsulates an IP datagram.

The Protocol field in the IP headers of all the datagrams has a value of 6. This indicates that the IP datagram encapsulates a TCP packet.

IP Datagram #1: IP Packet with Flags = 0, MF = 0, DF = 0

Figure 10.26 shows the first IP datagram (packet # 4 in Figure 10.25) sent from the source at 199.245.180.44 to the Telnet host at 199.245.180.201. As you examine the IP header, you will notice the following parameter values:

> Version: 4
>
> Header Length (32 bit words): 5
>
> TOS: 0 (Precedence: Routine, Normal Delay, Normal Throughput, Normal Reliability)
>
> Total length: 44
>
> Identification: 1
>
> Flags: 0, DF = 0, MF = 0 (Fragmentation allowed, Last fragment)
>
> Fragment Offset: 0
>
> Time to Live: 100 seconds
>
> Protocol: 6 (TCP)
>
> Checksum: 0xA1AF(Valid)
>
> Source IP address: 144.19.74.44
>
> Destination IP address: 144.19.74.201

The Version field value is 4, so the format of the IP datagram is IPv4.

The Header Length is 5 words (20 octets). This is the minimum size of the IP datagram, so there are no IP options.

The Total Length of this IP datagram is 44 octets. The Ethernet header and CRC checksum is 18 octets long. Adding these two gives an Ethernet packet size of 62 octets. An additional 2 octets of pad are added to bring the total Ethernet frame size to 64 octets.

FIGURE 10.26

IP datagram 1.

```
Packet Number : 4              6:38:38 PM
Length : 64 bytes
ether: ==================== Ethernet Datalink Layer ====================
       Station: 00-00-C0-24-28-2D ----> 00-00-C0-A2-0F-8E
       Type: 0x0800 (IP)
   ip: ==================== Internet Protocol ====================
       Station:144.19.74.44 ---->144.19.74.201
       Protocol: TCP
       Version: 4
       Header Length (32 bit words): 5
       Precedence: Routine
               Normal Delay, Normal Throughput, Normal Reliability
       Total length: 44
       Identification:      1
       Fragmentation allowed, Last fragment
       Fragment Offset: 0
       Time to Live: 100 seconds
       Checksum: 0xA1AF(Valid)
  tcp: ================= Transmission Control Protocol =================
       Source Port: 6295
       Destination Port: TELNET
       Sequence Number: 25784320
       Acknowledgement Number: 0
       Data Offset (32-bit words): 6
       Window: 4096
       Control Bits: Synchronize Sequence Numbers (SYN)
       Checksum: 0x4A87(Valid)
       Urgent Pointer: 0
       Option:MAXIMUM SEGMENT SIZE
               Option Length: 4
               Maximum Segment Size : 1024
```

This IP datagram has an Identification field value of 1 and a TTL value of 100 seconds. The TTL value of 100 seconds is the default TTL value that is used by the host at 199.245.180.44 for all IP datagrams that it sends.

The TOS value is 0, so this IP datagram should be treated with routine precedence, normal delay, normal throughput, and normal reliability.

The fragmentation Flags field has a value of 0, so the flags DF = 0, and MF = 0. This datagram could be fragmented, and this is the last fragment. The Fragment Offset value of 0 indicates that this is also the first fragment. A datagram that is the first and last fragment has no other fragments—this is a complete unfragmented datagram.

The Protocol field value has a code of 6, indicating that the IP datagram is carrying a TCP message.

The Checksum value is A1AF (hex) and is valid.

IP Datagram #2: Response IP Packet with Flags = 0, MF = 0, DF = 0

Figure 10.27 shows the second IP datagram (packet #5 in Figure 10.25) that is sent in response to the IP datagram discussed in the preceding section. This datagram is sent from the Telnet host at 199.245.180.201 to the Telnet client at 199.245.180.44. As you examine the IP header, notice the following parameter values:

Version: 4

Header Length (32 bit words): 5

TOS: 0 (Precedence: Routine, Normal Delay, Normal Throughput, Normal Reliability)

Total length: 44

Identification: 21410

Flags: 0, DF = 0, MF = 0 (Fragmentation allowed, Last fragment)

Fragment Offset: 0

Time to Live: 64 seconds

Protocol: 6 (TCP)

Checksum: 0x720E (Valid)

Source IP address: 144.19.74.201

Destination IP address: 144.19.74.44

The Version field value is 4, so the format of the IP datagram is IPv4.

The Header Length is 5 words (20 octets). This is the minimum size of the IP datagram, so there are no IP options.

The Total Length of this IP datagram is 44 octets. The Ethernet header and CRC checksum is 18 octets long. Adding these two gives an Ethernet packet size of 62 octets. An additional 2 octets of pad are added to bring the total Ethernet frame size to 64 octets.

FIGURE 10.27

IP datagram 2.

```
Packet Number : 5              6:38:38 PM
Length : 64 bytes
ether: ==================== Ethernet Datalink Layer ====================
       Station: 00-00-C0-A2-0F-8E ----> 00-00-C0-24-28-2D
       Type: 0x0800 (IP)
  ip: ===================== Internet Protocol =====================
       Station:144.19.74.201 ---->144.19.74.44
       Protocol: TCP
       Version: 4
       Header Length (32 bit words): 5
       Precedence: Routine
              Normal Delay, Normal Throughput, Normal Reliability
       Total length: 44
       Identification: 21410
       Fragmentation allowed, Last fragment
       Fragment Offset: 0
       Time to Live: 64  seconds
       Checksum: 0x720E(Valid)
  tcp: ================= Transmission Control Protocol =================
       Source Port: TELNET
       Destination Port: 6295
       Sequence Number: 1508167651
       Acknowledgement Number: 25784321
       Data Offset (32-bit words): 6
       Window: 30719
       Control Bits: Acknowledgement Field is Valid (ACK)
              Synchronize Sequence Numbers (SYN)
       Checksum: 0xB8AE(Valid)
       Urgent Pointer: 0
       Option:MAXIMUM SEGMENT SIZE
              Option Length: 4
              Maximum Segment Size : 1024
```

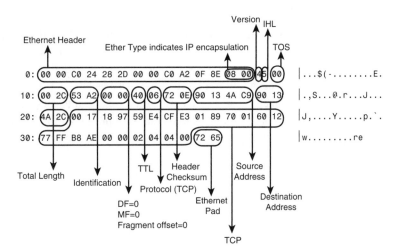

This IP datagram has an Identification field value of 21410. Notice that this Identification value is different from that sent by the Telnet client. The Identification value starts from a large number because the Telnet host has sent many IP datagrams prior to this session.

Another interesting item to note is that the TTL value is 64 seconds. This is the default TTL value that is used by the Telnet host at 199.245.180.201 for all IP datagrams that it sends. Notice that this TTL value is different from that sent by 199.245.180.44. Different TCP/IP implementations use different initial TTL values.

The TOS value is 0, which indicates that this IP datagram should be treated with routine precedence, normal delay, normal throughput, and normal reliability.

The fragmentation Flags field has a value of 0, so the flags DF = 0, and MF = 0. This datagram could be fragmented, and this is the last fragment. The Fragment Offset value of 0 indicates that this is also the first fragment. A datagram that is the first and last fragment has no other fragments—this is a complete unfragmented datagram.

The Protocol field value has a code of 6, so the IP datagram is carrying a TCP message.

The Checksum value is 720E (hex) and is valid.

IP Datagrams #3 and #4: Observing the Identification Field

Figures 10.28 and 10.29 show the next two IP datagrams that are exchanged between the Telnet client at 199.245.180.44 and the Telnet host at 199.245.180.201.

It is instructive to examine the Identification field value in these datagrams. The datagram in Figure 10.28 is the second datagram sent from the Telnet client to the Telnet host. The identification field in this datagram is 2, which is one more than that of the datagram sent in Figure 10.26. The datagram in Figure 10.28 is the second datagram sent from the Telnet host to the Telnet client. The identification field in this datagram is 21411, which is one more than that of the previous datagram sent in Figure 10.27. This example shows that the Identification fields are maintained separately by each sending side.

FIGURE 10.28

IP datagram 3.

```
Packet Number : 6            6:38:38 PM
Length : 69 bytes
ether: ==================== Ethernet Datalink Layer ====================
        Station: 00-00-C0-24-28-2D ----> 00-00-C0-A2-0F-8E
        Type: 0x0800 (IP)
   ip: ===================== Internet Protocol =====================
        Station:144.19.74.44 ---->144.19.74.201
        Protocol: TCP
        Version: 4
        Header Length (32 bit words): 5
        Precedence: Routine
                Normal Delay, Normal Throughput, Normal Reliability
        Total length: 49
        Identification:      2
        Fragmentation allowed, Last fragment
        Fragment Offset: 0
        Time to Live: 100 seconds
        Checksum: 0xA1A9(Valid)
  tcp: ================= Transmission Control Protocol =================
        Source Port: 6295
        Destination Port: TELNET
        Sequence Number: 25784321
        Acknowledgement Number: 1508167652
        Data Offset (32-bit words): 5
        Window: 4096
        Control Bits: Acknowledgement Field is Valid (ACK)
                Push Function Requested (PSH)
        Checksum: 0x18A9(Valid)
        Urgent Pointer: 0
telnt: ======================= Telnet Protocol =======================
        Command: Do
        Option Code: Echo
        Command: Do
        Option Code: Suppress Go Ahead
        Command: Will
        Option Code:
```

FIGURE 10.29

IP datagram 4.

```
Packet Number : 7                6:38:38 PM
Length : 64 bytes
ether: ================== Ethernet Datalink Layer ==================
        Station: 00-00-C0-A2-0F-8E ----> 00-00-C0-24-28-2D
        Type: 0x0800 (IP)
  ip: ===================== Internet Protocol =====================
        Station:144.19.74.201 ---->144.19.74.44
        Protocol: TCP
        Version: 4
        Header Length (32 bit words): 5
        Precedence: Routine
               Normal Delay, Normal Throughput, Normal Reliability
        Total length: 40
        Identification: 21411
        Fragmentation allowed, Last fragment
        Fragment Offset: 0
        Time to Live: 64   seconds
        Checksum: 0x7211(Valid)
  tcp: ================= Transmission Control Protocol =================
        Source Port: TELNET
        Destination Port: 6295
        Sequence Number: 1508167652
        Acknowledgement Number: 25784330
        Data Offset (32-bit words): 5
        Window: 30710
        Control Bits: Acknowledgement Field is Valid (ACK)
        Checksum: 0xCEB7(Valid)
        Urgent Pointer: 0
```

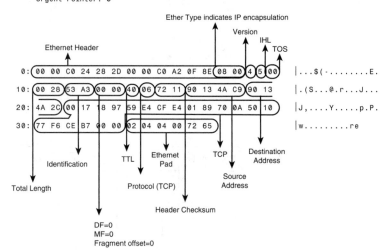

IP Datagram #5: Datagram with DF = 1

Figure 10.30 shows an IP datagram that is sent from the Telnet host at 199.245.180.201 to the Telnet client at 199.245.180.44. As you examine the IP header, notice the following parameter values:

Version: 4

Header Length (32-bit words): 5

TOS: 0 (Precedence: Routine, Normal Delay, Normal Throughput, Normal Reliability)

Total length: 43

Identification: 21412

Flags: 0, DF = 1, MF = 0 (Fragmentation not allowed, Last fragment)

Fragment Offset: 0

Time to Live: 64 seconds

Protocol: 6 (TCP)

Checksum: 0x320D (Valid)

Source IP address: 144.19.74.201

Destination IP address: 144.19.74.44

The field values are similar to those discussed in earlier IP datagrams. The difference is in the fragmentation Flags field, which has the DF flag set to 1. This means that the Telnet host is requesting that this datagram should not be fragmented.

FIGURE **10.30**

IP datagram 5.

```
Packet Number : 8              6:38:39 PM
Length : 64 bytes
ether: ==================== Ethernet Datalink Layer ====================
        Station: 00-00-C0-A2-0F-8E ----> 00-00-C0-24-28-2D
        Type: 0x0800 (IP)
   ip: ====================== Internet Protocol ======================
        Station:144.19.74.201 ---->144.19.74.44
        Protocol: TCP
        Version: 4
        Header Length (32 bit words): 5
        Precedence: Routine
                Normal Delay, Normal Throughput, Normal Reliability
        Total length: 43
        Identification: 21412
        Fragmentation not allowed, Last fragment
        Fragment Offset: 0
        Time to Live: 64   seconds
        Checksum: 0x320D(Valid)
  tcp: ================= Transmission Control Protocol =================
        Source Port: TELNET
        Destination Port: 6295
        Sequence Number: 1508167652
        Acknowledgement Number: 25784330
        Data Offset (32-bit words): 5
        Window: 30710
        Control Bits: Acknowledgement Field is Valid (ACK)
                Push Function Requested (PSH)
        Checksum: 0xA9AE(Valid)
        Urgent Pointer: 0
telnt: ======================= Telnet Protocol =======================
        Command: Do
        Option Code:
```

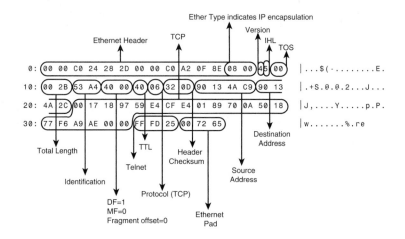

Summary

The Internet Protocol provides a logical view of the network regardless of the different network technologies used to build the physical network. The logical network is independent of Physical Layer addresses, MTU size, and any other differences. Upper-layer protocols, such as the TCP and UDP, treat the network as an IP-only network. The IP network provides connectionless services to upper-layer services. The connectionless service is implemented using datagrams that contain the source and destination IP addresses and other parameters needed for IP operation. An important aspect of IP operation is that datagrams in transit are fragmented as needed by routers to ensure that the datagrams can be transmitted in the packet size of the underlying networks. When IP fragmentation takes place, the receiver is responsible for assembling the IP datagram fragments into the original datagram.

The Transport Protocols

by Karanjit S. Siyan, Ph.D.

The TCP/IP transport protocols correspond to the Transport Layer of the OSI model. The TCP/IP protocol suite defines two standard transport protocols: TCP and UDP. TCP (Transmission Control protocol) implements a reliable data-stream protocol, whereas UDP (User Datagram protocol) implements an unreliable data-stream protocol.

Both TCP and UDP run on top of the Internet protocol and build on the services provided by IP (see Figure 11.1). IP provides a connectionless datagram service between two computers. By using TCP and UDP, you can deliver data not just to a remote computer, but to an application process running on the remote computer. These application processes are identified by port numbers. TCP can ensure that data is delivered reliably to the destination by providing a connection-oriented service. UDP, on the other hand, is connectionless and cannot guarantee delivery of data. However, UDP is useful in many applications, such as those where data needs to be sent to a particular application running on a machine, or in situations where application data needs to be broadcasted or multicasted.

Although Chapter 3, "Overview of TCP/IP" gave you some overview details about TCP and UDP, this chapter presents this information in considerably more detail.

FIGURE 11.1

TCP and UDP.

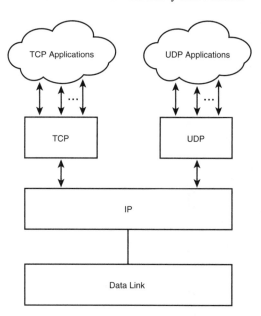

The Transmission Control Protocol (TCP)

The TCP protocol provides a very important service in the TCP/IP protocol suite because it provides a standard general-purpose method for reliable delivery of data. Rather than inventing their own transport protocol, applications typically use TCP to provide reliable delivery of data because the TCP protocol has reached considerable maturity and many improvements have been made to the protocol to improve its performance and reliability.

TCP provides end-to-end reliability between an application process running on one computer system to another application process running on another computer system (see Figure 11.2). TCP provides this reliability by adding services on top of IP. IP is connectionless and does not guarantee delivery of packets. TCP assumes that IP is inherently unreliable, so TCP adds services to ensure end-to-end delivery of data. Because TCP has very few expectations on the services provided by the network, TCP can run across a large variety of hardware. All that TCP asks for is that some kind of simple, unreliable datagram service be provided at the lower layer. Sometimes networks such as X.25 provide sophisticated connection-oriented services at the Network Layer. In this case, the IP datagrams are transmitted on an X.25 virtual circuit, and the TCP protocol packets are encapsulated inside the IP datagrams.

TCP is the primary transport protocol used to provide reliable, full-duplex, virtual-circuit connections. The most common use of TCP is to run it over IPv4 or IPv6, although several experimental projects have been done to run TCP on other Network Layer protocols.

FIGURE 11.2
End-to-end TCP reliability.

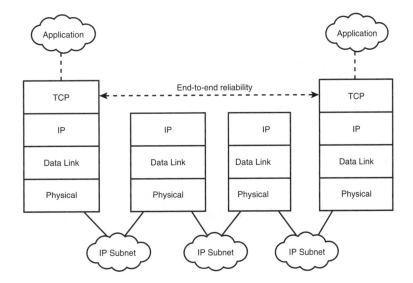

Although IP is implemented on hosts and routers, TCP is typically implemented on hosts only to provide reliable end-to-end data delivery. Today, many routers are not just routers—they also provide other services that make them easy to configure and manage. For example, many commercial routers can also implement TCP or UDP to provide remote login and network-management facilities. Even though TCP and UDP are implemented in routers, the transport protocols are not used by routing services and messages.

The TCP protocol is described in RFC 792 (STD 7), "Transmission Control Protocol." The UDP protocol is described in RFC 768 (STD 6), "User Datagram Protocol." RFC 1122 (STD 3), "Requirements for Internet Hosts—Communication Layers," contains important additions. Both the TCP and UDP protocol status is recommended. But in actual practice, all TCP/IP devices—unless they are pure routers—will implement TCP and UDP. In most implementations, UDP logic is embedded in the TCP module and is not separate from the TCP implementation.

The following section discusses the features of TCP.

TCP Features

TCP has the following noteworthy features:

- Basic data transfer
- Reliability
- Flow control
- Multiplexing
- Connections
- Precedence and security

Basic Data Transfer

Basic data transfer is the capability of TCP to transfer a continuous stream of octets in each direction. The octets are sent among application processes running on remote systems that use TCP. The application processes then group a set of bytes that need to be sent/received into a message *segment*. Message segments can be of arbitrary length. Ultimately, the messages have to be sent in IP datagrams that are limited by the MTU size of a network interface. However, at the TCP level, there is no real restriction on message size because the details of accommodating the message segments in IP datagrams is the task of the IP Layer. For reasons of efficiency in managing messages, TCP connections typically negotiate a maximum segment size.

Messages sent by TCP have an octet stream orientation (see Figure 11.3). TCP keeps track of each octet that is sent/received. The TCP has no inherent notion of a block of data, unlike other transport protocols, which typically keep track of the Transport Protocol Data Unit (TPDU) number and not the octet number. TCP can be used to provide multiple virtual-circuit connections between two TCP hosts.

FIGURE 11.3

TCP octet stream orientation. (Courtesy Learning Tree)

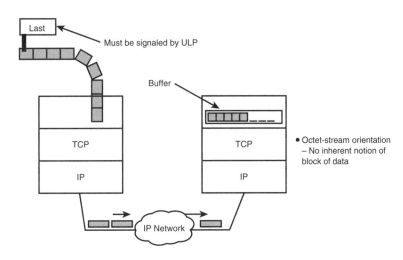

Last

Must be signaled by ULP

Buffer

TCP

TCP

IP

IP

IP Network

• Octet-stream orientation
  – No inherent notion of block of data

Application processes that use TCP send data in whatever size is convenient for sending. For example, an application can send data that is as little as one octet or as big as several kilo-octets. TCP numbers each octet that it sends. The octets are delivered to the application processes at the receiving end in the order in which they are sent. This process is called *sequencing* of octets.

An application can send data to TCP a few octets at a time. TCP buffers this data and sends these octets either as a single message or as several smaller message segments. All that TCP guarantees is that data arrives at the receiver in the order in which it was sent. For example, if an application sends 1,024 octets of data over a period of ten seconds, the data can be sent across the network in a single TCP packet of 1,024 octets, or in four TCP packets of 256 octets, or in any combination of octets.

Because TCP sends data as a stream of octets, there is no real end-of-message marker in the data stream. To ensure that all the data submitted to the TCP module has been transmitted, a *push* function is required to be implemented by TCP. The push causes the TCP promptly to send any data that it has received from an application up to that point.

The actual data that is sent by TCP is treated as an unstructured stream of octets. TCP does not contain any facility to superimpose an application-dependent structure on the data. For example, you cannot tell TCP to treat the data as a set of records in a database and to send one record at a time. Any such structuring must be handled by the application processes that communicate by using TCP.

Reliability

One of the most important features of TCP is reliable end-to-end data delivery. In order to provide reliability, TCP must recover from data that is damaged, lost, duplicated, or delivered out of order by the Network Layer. TCP uses the Positive Acknowledgment Retransmission (PAR) scheme for achieving reliability. Figure 11.4 shows the PAR scheme, where all data and acknowledgments are received as expected. This figure shows that data is sent only after previously sent data has been acknowledged. Figure 11.5 shows how the PAR scheme recovers from lost data.

FIGURE 11.4

PAR scheme under normal operation.

FIGURE 11.5

PAR scheme illustrating recovery from lost data.

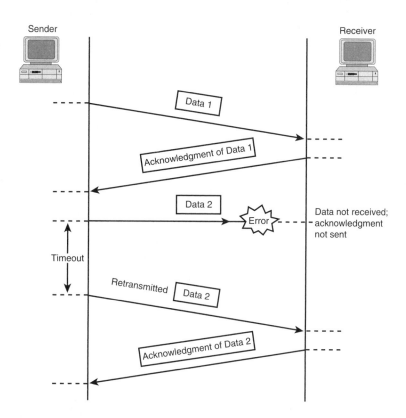

TCP implements PAR by assigning a sequence number to each octet that is transmitted and by requiring a positive acknowledgment (ACK) from the receiving TCP module. If the ACK is not received within a time-out interval, the data is retransmitted. At the receiver TCP module, the sequence numbers are used to correctly order segments that may have arrived out of order and to eliminate duplicates. Corruption of data is detected by using a checksum field filed in the TCP packet header. Data segments that are received with a bad checksum field are discarded. Unless a physical break in the link causes physical partitioning of the network, TCP recovers from most Internet communications system errors.

Flow Control

Computers that send and receive TCP data segments can operate at different data rates because of differences in CPU and network bandwidth. As a result, it is quite possible for a sender to send data at a much faster rate than the receiver can handle. TCP implements a flow control mechanism that controls the amount of data sent by the sender. TCP uses a sliding window mechanism for implementing flow control. Figure 11.6 illustrates the sliding window flow control used in TCP. The stream of data in TCP is numbered at the octet level. The number assigned to an octet is called the *sequence number.*

FIGURE 11.6

*TCP Sliding
Window flow con-
trol. (Courtesy
Learning Tree)*

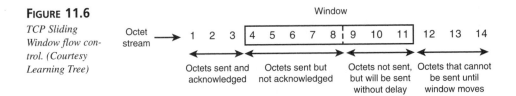

The receiver TCP module sends back to the sender an acknowledgment that indicates a range of acceptable sequence numbers beyond the last segment successfully received. This range of acceptable sequence numbers is called a *window*. The window, therefore, indicates the number of octets that the sender can transmit before receiving further permission.

In Figure 11.6, the window range is from sequence numbers 4 through 11. In this example, octets 1 through 3 have been sent and acknowledged. Octets 4 through 11, which are in the window range, may have been sent or are waiting to be sent, but they have not been acknowledged yet. The sender TCP is not required to send a TCP segment that is equal to the window size. The window size indicates the maximum number of unacknowledged octets that TCP can send. In Figure 11.6, octets 4 through 8 have been sent; octets 9 through 11, which are within the window range, have not been sent, but they can be sent without delay. Octets 12 and beyond cannot be sent because they are to the right of the window range. To summarize, the TCP flow control mechanism exhibits the following properties:

- Octets that are to the left of the window range have already been sent and acknowledged.
- Octets in the window range can be sent without any delay. Some of the octets in the window range may already have been sent, but they have not been acknowledged. Other octets may be waiting to be sent.
- Octets that are to the right of the window range have not been sent. These octets can be sent only when they fall in the window range.

The left edge of the window is the lowest numbered octet that has not been acknowledged. The window can advance; that is, the left edge of the window can move to the right when an acknowledgment is received for data that has been sent. The TCP packet containing the acknowledgment contains information about the window size that the sender should use.

The window size reflects the amount of buffer space available for new data at the receiver. If this buffer space size shrinks because the receiver is being overrun, the receiver will send back a smaller window size. In the extreme case, it is possible for the receiver to send a window size of only one octet, which means that only one octet can be sent. This situation is referred to as the *silly window syndrome,* and most TCP implementations take special measures to avoid it. See "Avoiding the Silly Window Syndrome," later in this chapter.

A TCP module sending back a window size of zero indicates to the sender that its buffers are full and no additional data should be sent. TCP includes mechanisms to shrink window size when the receiver experiences congestion of data and to expand window size as the congestion problem clears.

The goal of the sliding window mechanism is to keep the channel full of data and to reduce to a minimum the delays experienced by waiting for acknowledgments.

Multiplexing

TCP enables many processes within a single computer to use the TCP communications services simultaneously; this is called TCP *multiplexing*. Because these processes may be communicating over the same network interface, they are identified by the IP address of the network interface. However, you need more than the IP address of the network interface to identify a process because all processes that are using the same network interface on a computer have a common IP address.

TCP associates a port number value for applications that use TCP. This association enables several connections to exist between application processes on remote computers because each connection uses a different pair of port numbers. Figure 11.7 shows several connections being multiplexed over TCP.

The binding of ports to application processes is handled independently by each computer. In many computer systems, a *logger* or *super daemon* process watches over the port numbers that are identified or well known to other computer systems.

Connections

Before application processes can send data by using TCP, they must establish a connection. The connections are made between the port numbers of the sender and the receiver nodes. A TCP connection identifies the end points involved in the connection. The end point (see Figure 11.8) is formally defined as a pair that includes the IP address and port number:

(IP address, port numbers)

The *IP address* is the internetwork address of the network interface over which the TCP/IP application communicates. The *port* number is the TCP port number that identifies the application. The *end point* contains both the IP address and port numbers because port identifiers are selected independently by each TCP, and they may not be unique. By concatenating the unique IP address with port numbers, a unique value for the end point is created.

FIGURE 11.7

TCP Multiplexing.

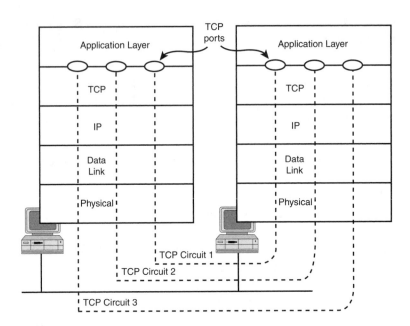

FIGURE 11.8

TCP end point.

A TCP connection is established between two end points (see Figure 11.9). The TCP connection is identified by the parameters of both end points, as follows:

(IP address1, port number1, IP address2, port number2)

These parameters make it possible to have several application processes connect to the same remote end point. Figure 11.9 shows that several application processes connect to the same remote end point (199.11.23.1, 2001). The TCP module at 199.11.23.1 can keep the different TCP connections separate because TCP uses both the local and remote end points to identify the connection. In Figure 11.9, the end point (199.11.23.1, 2001) is the same, but the end points at the other end of the connection are different. This difference enables TCP to keep these connections separate.

FIGURE 11.9

TCP connection between end points. (Courtesy Learning Tree)

Figure 11.9 also illustrates that TCP can support multiple connections concurrently. These connections are multiplexed over the same network interface.

A connection is fully specified by the pair of end points. A local end point can participate in many connections to different foreign end points. A TCP connection can carry data in both directions; that is, it is *full duplex*.

In relationship to TCP connections, it is also helpful to define the notion of a half association and a full association. A *half association* is an end point that also includes the transport protocol name, as follows:

(TransportProtocol, IP address, port number)

The half associations in Figure 11.9 are, therefore, the following:

(tcp, 199.21.32.2, 1400)

(tcp, 196.62.132.1, 21)

A *full association* consists of two half associations and is expressed by the following ordered pair:

(TransportProtocol, IP address1, port number1, IP address2, port number2)

The *TransportProtocol* is listed only once because it has to be the same on both parts of the half association. The concept of half and full associations is useful when dealing with different transport protocols. As an example, the full association in Figure 11.9 is listed as follows:

> (tcp, 199.21.32.2, 1400, 196.62.132.1, 21)

A full association consisting of source and destination IP addresses, and source and destination port numbers uniquely identifies a TCP connection.

TCP Host Environment

TCP is implemented as a protocol module that interacts with the computer's operating system. In many operating systems, the TCP module is accessed like the file system of the operating system. The BSD Sockets interface that is implemented on Unix systems and the more recent Winsock interface implemented by Microsoft's proprietary operating systems are based on this file system model.

The TCP module depends on other operating system functions to manage its data structures and services. The actual interface to the network is typically controlled by a device driver module. TCP does not interact directly with the device driver module. Instead, TCP calls the IP module, which in turn calls on the device driver module (see Figure 11.10).

FIGURE 11.10

TCP module interaction with network.

Offloading the processing of the TCP/IP protocol stack modules to a front-end processor is also possible. The front-end processor acts as a dedicated protocol communications device that executes the protocol modules (see Figure 11.11). There has to be a mechanism for communication between the host and its front-end processor. Typically, this mechanism is provided by a file system interface.

FIGURE 11.11
Offloading TCP processing.

From an abstract viewpoint, applications will interface with the TCP module with the following system calls:

- OPEN to open a connection
- CLOSE to close a connection
- SEND to send data on an open connection
- RECEIVE to receive data from an open connection
- STATUS to find information about a connection

These system calls are implemented just like calls from user programs on the operating system. For example, the calls to open and close a connection are like the calls to open and close a file. The call to send or receive data is like the call to write or read from a file.

The TCP system calls can interact with other TCP modules anywhere on an internet system. The TCP system calls must be passed parameters for executing the system call. Examples of such parameters are IP addresses, type of service, precedence, security, application port number, and so on.

TCP Connection Opening and Closing

A connection is specified in the OPEN call on the local port. The parameters supplied are the destination end point. The return from the system call contains a short integer value called the *handle*, by which the user refers to the connection in subsequent calls. Information about the connection is stored in a data structure called a *Transmission Control Block* (TCB), and the handle is used to access the information in the TCB.

TCP identifies two types of OPEN calls:

• Active OPEN

• Passive OPEN

In an active OPEN call, the connection establishment is to be actively initiated. An active OPEN call translates to a TCP message that is generated to contact another end point.

A passive OPEN call signals an intent to receive an active OPEN connection; it does not generate any TCP message segment. A passive OPEN request means that the process wants to accept incoming connection requests rather than attempting to initiate a connection. Often the process requesting a passive OPEN call will accept a connection request from any caller. Alternatively, a passive OPEN call can specify that it can accept a connection only from a specific end point.

Processes that issue passive OPENs and wait for matching active OPENs from other processes can be informed by the TCP when connections have been established (see Figure 11.12).

If two processes issue active OPENs to each other at the same time, they will be correctly connected (see Figure 11.13). Using two active OPENs to set up a TCP connection is useful in distributed computing, where components can act asynchronously with respect to each other.

FIGURE 11.12
Active and passive OPENs for setting up TCP connections.

Passive Open
Issued by Receiver

Active Open

Receiver in
Listening State

Acknowledgment of Active Open

Passive Open

TCP Connection Opened

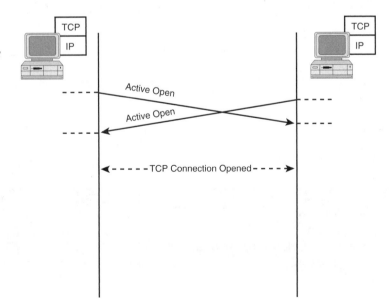

FIGURE 11.13
Using only active OPENs for setting up TCP connections.

Active Open

Active Open

TCP Connection Opened

TCP Message Format

Figure 11.14 shows the TCP packet structure. Like most TCP/IP protocols, the TCP header is using a 32-bit word format.

FIGURE 11.14

TCP packet structure.

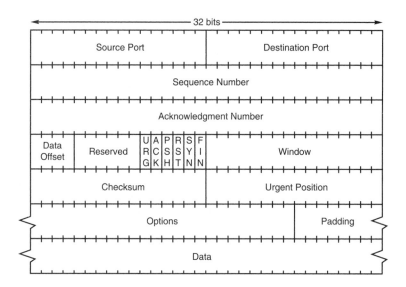

The following sections define the individual fields in the TCP header.

Source and Destination Port Number Fields

The Source Port and Destination Port number fields (refer to Figure 11.14) are used to identify the end point processes in the TCP virtual circuit. Source and Destination Port numbers are needed in defining associations between processes. Some port numbers are well-known port numbers, others have been registered, and still others are dynamically assigned.

The Assigned Number RFC, which is issued periodically as a different numbered RFC, contains a description of some of the well-known port numbers.

> **Note**
>
> Port numbers in the range of 0–1,023 are called *well-known port numbers* and are administered by IANA. Port numbers greater than 1,023 can be registered but are not controlled by IANA. These port numbers are, therefore, called

registered port numbers. Not all port numbers at 1,024 and greater are registered. Some are assigned on an as-needed basis and are called *transient port
numbers.* Transient port numbers are allocated within a TCP implementation.
The actual algorithm used to allocate transient port numbers is implementation-
dependent.

TCP modules are free to associate any port number with application processes, with the
restriction that well-known ports are reserved for special applications. In many operating
systems, application processes can "own" ports. These ports are allocated on a random
basis as long as they are greater than 1,023. Some implementations use a hashing function that takes into account the process name when allocating port numbers. Typically,
the high-order bits of the port number are associated with the process name.

Sequence and Acknowledgment Number Fields

Transmission by TCP is made reliable via the use of sequence numbers and acknowledgment numbers. Conceptually, each octet of data is assigned a sequence number. The
sequence number of the first octet of data in a message segment is sent in the TCP
header for that segment and is called the *segment sequence number.*

When a message segment is sent by the receiver, it also carries an acknowledgment number, which is the sequence number of the next expected data octet of transmission. TCP
transmissions are full duplex. At any time, a TCP module is both a sender for the data
that it is sending and a receiver for data from other senders.

When the TCP needs to transmit a segment, it puts a copy of the segment into its transmission queue and starts a timer. When the acknowledgment for that data is received
before the timer expires, the segment is deleted from the queue. If the acknowledgment
is not received before the timer expires, the segment is retransmitted from its copy in the
transmission queue.

The 32-bit Sequence Number field (refer to Figure 11.14) is the number of the first byte
of data in the current message. If the SYN flag field is set to 1, this field defines the
initial sequence number (ISN) to be used for that session, and the first data offset is
ISN+1. A 32-bit value is used to avoid using old sequence numbers that already may
have been assigned to data that is in transit on the network.

The Acknowledgment Number field is used to indicate the sequence number of the next
byte expected by the receiver. TCP acknowledgments are cumulative. That is, a single
acknowledgment can be used to acknowledge a number of prior TCP message segments.
After a connection is established, the acknowledgment number is always sent.

An acknowledgment by TCP guarantees only that the TCP module has received the data. The acknowledgment does not guarantee that the data has been delivered to the application running on top of TCP. An acknowledgment indicates that the receiving TCP has taken the responsibility to deliver the data to the application. It is possible that other system errors in the TCP module and the application interface may prevent the data from being delivered to the application.

Data Offset Field

The Data Offset field is the number of 32-bit words in the TCP header (refer to Figure 11.14). This field is needed because the TCP options field could be variable in length. Without TCP options, the Data Offset field is five words (20 octets). The TCP header, even if it includes options, is an integral number of 32 bits.

The only TCP option that has been defined is the Maximum Segment Size (MSS) option. This option is used at the start of a TCP connection. When this option has been specified, the Data Offset field value is six words (24 octets).

The Reserved fields that follow the Data Offset field must be set to 0.

The Flags Field

The Flags field in the TCP header (refer to Figure 11.14) have the following meanings:

- The ACK flag being set indicates that the Acknowledgment Number field is valid.
- The SYN flag is used to indicate the opening of a virtual-circuit connection.
- The FIN flag is used to terminate the connection.
- The RST bit is used to reset the virtual circuit due to unrecoverable errors. When an RST is received in a TCP segment, the receiver must respond by immediately terminating the connection. A reset causes both sides immediately to release the connection and all its resources. As a result, transfer of data ceases in both directions, which can result in loss of data that is in transit. A TCP RST is not the normal way to close a TCP connection; it indicates an abnormal condition. To close a TCP connection normally, use the FIN flag. The reason for a reset can be a host crash or delayed duplicate SYN packets.
- When the PSH flag is set, it tells TCP immediately to deliver data for this message to the upper-layer process.
- The URG flag is used to send out-of-band data without waiting for the receiver to process octets already in the stream.

TCP connections are opened by using the three-way-handshake procedure. The SYN and the ACK flags are used to indicate the following packets:

SYN = 1 and ACK = 0	Open connection packet
SYN = 1 and ACK = 1	Open connection acknowledgment
SYN = 0 and ACK = 1	Data packet or ACK packet

The procedures to establish connections utilize the synchronize (SYN) control flag and involves an exchange of three messages termed the three-way handshake (see Figure 11.15).

FIGURE 11.15
TCP SYN flag use. (Courtesy Learning Tree)

TCB= Transmission Control Block

A connection is initiated by the rendezvous of an arriving segment containing a SYN and a waiting TCB entry. The arriving TCP segment is generated by an active OPEN, and the waiting TCB entry is created by a passive OPEN. The matching of an active and a passive OPEN results in the creation of a connection. The SYN flag is set to 1 to indicate that sequence numbers have been synchronized in both directions. In Figure 11.15, the active OPEN generates a TCP segment with the following flags:

ULSYN = 1, ACK = 0

When the receiving TCP that has issued a passive OPEN receives an active OPEN, it acknowledges this active OPEN with the following TCP flags:

SYN = 1, ACK = 1

This acknowledgment of the active OPEN packet is sometimes called the passive OPEN packet. The ACK = 1 flag indicates that the Acknowledgment Number field contains valid data.

Figure 11.16 illustrates the general mechanism of the three-way handshake.

FIGURE 11.16

Three-way hand-shake. (Courtesy Learning Tree)

Step 1	Step 2	Step 3
Source	**Destination**	**Source**
May I open? SEQ=X ACK=0 *Begin data transmission option* send Z octets	Yes. You may. SEQ=Y ACK=X+1+Z	SEQ=X+1+Z ACK=Y+1 *Continue data transmission*

In Step 1 (see Figure 11.16), the active OPEN is sent with a Sequence Number value of X. As an option, additional data can be sent with the active OPEN packet. This additional data (Z octets) may contain authentication information, such as user name and password, for the service being requested. In most TCP/IP applications, authentication information is sent after the connection is established. But in some networks, such as those in which TCP/IP is run on X.25 networks, authentication information may be sent as part of the OPEN connection request. The Sequence and Acknowledgment Number fields are set as follows:

Sequence Number = X

Acknowledgment Number = 0

In Step 2, the receiver responds with an Acknowledgment Number set to X+1+Z, the next expected octet number. The initial Sequence Number (Y), which is used by the destination, is also sent. The Sequence and Acknowledgment Number fields are set as follows:

Sequence Number = Y

Acknowledgment Number = X + 1 + Z

In Step 3, the source acknowledges that it has received the Sequence Number value from the receiver. The Sequence and Acknowledgment Number fields are set as follows:

Sequence Number = X + 1 + Z

Acknowledgment Number = Y + 1

Why is the third step necessary in the three-way handshake? This step is often a source of puzzlement and confusion. You use the third step to complete the handshake to inform the receiver that its initial sequence number has been received by the source that opens the TCP connection. Without this acknowledgment, there is no way to ensure that the sender knows about the initial receiver sequence number. The following summarizes the three steps involved in the three-way handshake:

- Step 1: Source sends its initial SEND sequence number (ISS).

- Step 2: Receiver acknowledges reception of ISS by sending an acknowledgment number that is 1 greater than ISS or the amount of data sent by the source. Receiver sends its initial RECEIVER sequence number (IRS).

- Step 3: Source sends an acknowledgment number to acknowledge that it has received the receiver ISN.

To ensure that TCP does not send a segment containing a sequence number that is the duplicate of an old segment on the network, TCP has the notion of a *maximum segment lifetime (MSL)*. MSL is the time that must elapse before assigning any sequence numbers upon starting up or recovering from a crash (in which memory of sequence numbers previously used was lost). In the TCP specification, MSL is taken to be two minutes. If a TCP implementation can retain memory of sequence numbers in use, then it need not wait for the MSL duration because it can start using sequence numbers larger than those recently used.

In TCP, because every octet is numbered, sequence numbers are consumed rapidly. If message octets are sent at the rate of 2 Mbps, it takes about 4.5 hours to use up 2^{32} octets of sequence numbers. Because the maximum segment lifetime in the net is not likely to exceed a few tens of seconds, this amount of time is adequate protection for rates that escalate to 10s of Mbps. At 100 megabits/sec, the MSL time is 5.4 minutes, which is still greater than the two minutes assumed by the TCP specification in RFC 793.

How is the value of an ISN selected? RFC 793 suggests the use of an initial sequence number (ISN) generator to select a new 32-bit ISN. One possibility is that this generator is bound to a 32-bit time clock whose low-order bit is incremented roughly every four microseconds. If this is the case, the ISN cycles approximately every 4.55 hours. It is unlikely that segments will stay in the network more than 4.55 hours; therefore, you can reasonably assume that ISNs will be unique.

After a TCP connection has been established, the ACK flag is always set to 1 to indicate that the Acknowledgment Number field is valid. Data transmission then takes place with messages being exchanged by both sides in a full-duplex fashion until the TCP connection is ready to be closed.

When a TCP connection is ready to close, the FIN control flag is issued. In TCP, a connection is not automatically closed when TCP sends a FIN flag. Both sides of the connection must send a FIN flag and agree to close the connection. This kind of FIN close is called a *graceful close* because it ensures that the connections are not abruptly closed. Consider what would happen if one side of the connection closed the connection without informing the other side. The other side may still continue sending data that is never acknowledged because the connection is closed. This scenario would result in the loss of data. The TCP graceful close mechanism illustrated in Figure 11.17 prevents the loss of data due to premature closing of a TCP connection.

FIGURE 11.17

TCP FIN flag use (the graceful close). (Courtesy Learning Tree)

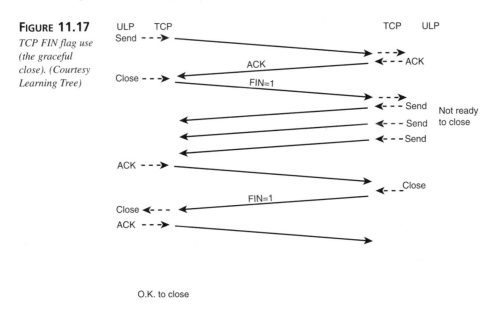

O.K. to close

ULP=Upper Layer Protocol

Another point to note about the use of TCP flags in sending messages is how the PSH flag is used. The PSH flag was initially designed to inform TCP that it must act upon the data that it has received so far. When an application issues a series of SEND calls without setting the PSH flag, the TCP can aggregate the data internally without sending it. Similarly, when a series of segments is received without the PSH bit, a TCP can queue the data internally without passing it to the receiving application. The PSH bit is not a record marker and is independent of segment boundaries. Some implementations incorrectly think of the PSH as a record marker, however. The transmitter should collapse successive PSH bits when it packetizes data to send the largest possible segment.

A TCP can implement PSH flags on SEND calls. If PSH flags are not implemented, then the sending TCP must do the following:

1. It must not buffer data indefinitely.
2. It must set the PSH bit in the last buffered segment (for example, when there is no more queued data to be sent).

RFC-793 erroneously implies that a received PSH flag must be passed to the Application Layer. Passing a received PSH flag to the Application Layer is now optional.

An application program is logically required to set the PSH flag in a SEND call whenever the program needs to force delivery of the data to avoid a communications deadlock. A TCP should send a maximum-size segment whenever possible to improve performance, however. This means that on the sender side, a PSH may not result in the segment's being immediately transmitted.

When the PSH flag is not implemented on SEND TCP calls (or when the application/TCP interface uses a pure streaming model), responsibility for aggregating any tiny data fragments to form reasonable-size segments is partially borne by the Application Layer. Generally, an interactive application protocol must set the PSH flag, at least in the last SEND call in each command or response sequence. A bulk transfer protocol such as FTP should set the PSH flag on the last segment of a file or when necessary to prevent buffer deadlock. Figure 11.18 illustrates the use of the PSH flag.

FIGURE 11.18

TCP PSH flag use. (Courtesy Learning Tree)

At the receiver, the PSH bit forces buffered data to be delivered to the application (even if less than a full buffer has been received). Conversely, the lack of a PSH avoids unnecessary wake-up calls to the application process. Avoiding these calls can be an important performance optimization for large time-sharing hosts.

TCP contains a mechanism to send out-of-band data by using the URG flag. The URG flag is used in conjunction with the Urgent Pointer field to "jump the queue" for sending data and to communicate an important message to the receiver. This feature enables the sender to send interrupt signals to the receiver without these signals ending up in the normal data queue at the receiver.

Consider what would happen if such a mechanism did not exist. Suppose that you want to interrupt the processing of user data that is sent. If the urgent message ends up in the normal data queue for TCP at the receiver, it may never be read because data that is ahead of the urgent message in the queue will have to be processed before the urgent message is detected. In many cases, the urgent message may arrive too late. Also, the urgent message may never be read if the application process that is supposed to read the message is hung up.

When the URG flag is set, the Urgent Pointer field is valid (see Figure 11.19). RFC 1122 states that the urgent pointer points to the sequence number of the LAST octet (not LAST+1) in a sequence of urgent data, and that RFC 793 describes it incorrectly as LAST+1.

FIGURE 11.19

TCP URG flag.
(Courtesy
Learning Tree)

- Used for sending *out-of-band* data
  - Without waiting for receiver to process octets already in the stream

- Has meaning only if URG=1

- Urgent pointer indicates the last octet of the urgent message

A TCP implementation must support a sequence of urgent data of any length. A TCP layer must inform the Application Layer asynchronously whenever the TCP layer receives an urgent pointer with no previous pending urgent data, or whenever the urgent pointer advances in the data stream. There must be a way for the application to learn how much urgent data remains to be read from the connection or at least to determine whether more urgent data remains to be read. Although the urgent mechanism may be used for any application, it is normally used to send interrupt-type commands to a Telnet program. The asynchronous, or out-of-band, notification enables the application to go into urgent mode by reading data from the TCP connection. This allows control commands to be sent to an application whose normal input buffers are full of unprocessed data.

Window Field

The Window field is used to implement flow control and is used by the receiver. The receiving TCP reports a "window" to the sending TCP. This window specifies the number of octets—starting with the acknowledgment number—that the receiving TCP is currently prepared to receive.

Checksum Field

The checksum field is 1's complement of the 1's complement sum of all the 16-bit words in the TCP packet. A 96-bit pseudoheader (see Figure 11.20) is prepended to the TCP header for checksum computation. The pseudoheader is used to identify whether the packet has arrived at the correct destination. The pseudoheader gives the TCP protection against misrouted segments. The pseudoheader has the protocol ID (6 for TCP), source, and destination IP address. Because the TCP header contains the source and destination port number, this describes the connection between the end points. Between the IP and TCP headers, there is sufficient information to identify completely the *full association* formed by the TCP connection.

The TCP Length field in the pseudoheader is the TCP header length plus the data length in octets. (This field is not an explicitly transmitted quantity; it is computed.) This field does not count the 12 octets of the pseudoheader.

Options Field

The TCP Options field may occupy space at the end of the TCP header and is a multiple of eight bits in length. The Options field is included in the checksum. An option may begin on any octet boundary. The two formats for an option are

- Case 1: A single octet of option-kind.
- Case 2: An octet of option-kind, an octet of option-length, and the actual option-data octets.

FIGURE **11.20**

Pseudoheader in
TCP checksum.

In Case 2, the option-length counts the two octets of option-kind and option-length as well as the option-data octets. The actual list of options may be shorter than the Data Offset field implies. The content of the header beyond the End-of-Option list must be zero-padded.

Currently, the defined options include the following:

Kind	Length	Meaning
0	-	End-of-Option list
1	-	No-Operation
2	4	Maximum Segment Size

Options with the option-kind value of 0 (End-of-Option list) and 1 (No-Operation) are examples of the Case 1 format option. The TCP options are shown in Figure 11.21.

The End-of-Option list indicates the end of the option list that may not coincide with the end of the TCP header according to the Data Offset field. The End-of-Option list is used at the end of all options, but not at the end of each option. You need to use this option only if the end of the options would not otherwise coincide with the end of the TCP header.

The No-Operation option code may be used between options to align the beginning of a subsequent option on a word boundary. Because there is no guarantee that TCP senders will use this option, TCP receivers must be prepared to process options even if they do not begin on a word boundary.

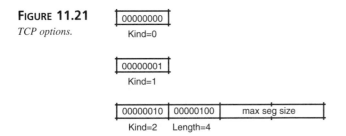

FIGURE 11.21
TCP options.

Currently, the only specific option carrying any real information is the Maximum Segment Size (MSS). The MSS can be negotiated only at the start of the TCP connection when the sequence numbers are being synchronized. This synchronization occurs when the SYN flag is set to 1. Typically, each TCP sends a MSS option informing the remote TCP about its MSS. If the MSS option is not used, any segment size is allowed.

Cumulative ACKs in TCP

Compared to transport protocols in other protocol suites, TCP is unusual as far as the meaning of the sequence numbers is concerned. In most transport protocols, the sequence number refers to the number of a packet. Not so in TCP. In TCP, sequence numbers refer to octets. Every octet is numbered in TCP. TCP sends octets in segments of variable length. When an acknowledgment is not received, segments are retransmitted. There is no guarantee that a retransmitted segment will be exactly the same as the original transmission. A retransmitted segment may contain additional data because the sending application may have generated additional data since the original transmission. The acknowledgment number cannot, therefore, refer to the segment that was sent.

In TCP, the acknowledgment number indicates the position in the data stream up to which data has been received and acknowledged by the remote TCP module. More specifically, an acknowledgment number value refers to the next octet number that needs to be sent. The acknowledgment number corresponds to the left edge of the TCP window.

TCP acknowledgment numbers are cumulative in the sense that an acknowledgment number indicates how much of the data stream has been accumulated so far. It is possible for a single acknowledgment number to acknowledge octets received in multiple data segments. Figure 11.22 shows that the three segments sent by the sender are acknowledged by a single acknowledgment number.

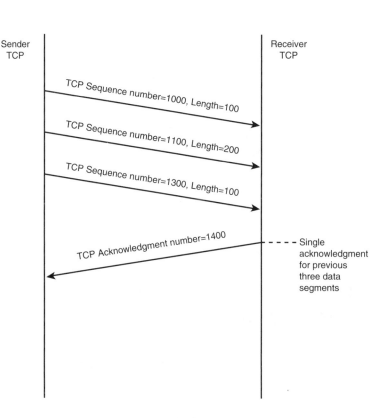

FIGURE 11.22

Single acknowledg-ment for multiple data segments.

Many TCP implementations try to minimize the number of separate acknowledgment segments that need to be sent. For example, a TCP implementation may try to send a single acknowledgment for every two TCP data segments that are received.

Because TCP segments are ultimately encapsulated in IP datagrams, there is no guarantee that they will arrive in order at the destination. The receiver TCP uses the sequence numbers of the octets in the segments to construct a continuous stream of octets. The receiver acknowledges the longest continuous prefix octet stream that it has received so far. If there is a gap in the octet stream that represents data not received, the received TCP can acknowledge only data up to the gap.

Cumulative acknowledgments have the advantage in that lost acknowledgments do not force retransmission. Therefore, even if one acknowledgment is lost in transmission, subsequent acknowledgments will acknowledge all the data that has been received so far. However, cumulative acknowledgments are not efficient when there is a gap representing lost data and when data after the gap has been received. Data received after the gap cannot be acknowledged unless the missing data in the gap is received. The sender does not receive information about the successful transmission of data after the gap because the receiver can acknowledge only data prior to the gap. This situation is illustrated in Figure 11.23. In this figure, segments SEG2 and SEG3 have been successfully received. However, segment SEG1 has been lost in transmission.

FIGURE 11.23

A TCP sender does not know about successful transmissions. (Courtesy Learning Tree)

• **Acknowledgments**

  – Refer to *byte position* in stream and *not* packet number
  – Are *cumulative*
    -- Advantage: Lost acknowledgments need not force
      retransmissions
    -- Disadvantage: Sender does not know about successful
      transmissions

Even though segments SEG2 and SEG3 have been successfully received, the loss of segment SEG1 represents a gap in the data stream at the receiver. The sender cannot advance the window because it does not receive acknowledgment about SEG1. There is no mechanism for the receiver to tell the sender that it has received segments SEG2 and SEG3 successfully. At this point, the following two situations can arise:

1. The sender will time-out and send segments SEG1, SEG2, and SEG3. In this case, segments SEG2 and SEG3 are sent needlessly because they were previously sent successfully. Retransmission of segments SEG2 and SEG3 is inefficient and adds to additional network traffic.

2. The sender will time-out and send only segment SEG1 and wait for acknowledgment to come back before deciding on sending additional data. When the receiver receives SEG1, it sends a cumulative acknowledgment packet that acknowledges correct reception of segment SEG1 and the previously sent segments SEG2 and SEG3. Although this scenario may appear to be more efficient, you should take into account that the sender has to wait for an acknowledgment of SEG1 before sending SEG2 and SEG3. This wait means that the sender is not taking advantage of its large window size and is sending only a segment at a time.

Adaptive Time-Outs in TCP

TCP was originally designed to run over WAN links; later on, TCP adapted for LANs also. Therefore, TCP has an advantage over those protocols that have their origins in LANs only. This advantage means that TCP has sophisticated algorithms that adjust to the wide variance in time delays that are encountered in sending messages over WAN links. LANs, on the other hand, typically do not exhibit such wide variances in time delays.

An interesting fact to note about IP is that even if the IP layers send the same message over the same path at two different times, the time delay to reach the destination is probably different because of the following factors:

- WAN links typically send messages serially, one at a time. If the WAN link is busy sending other messages, the message has to wait in a queue. This process leads to uncertainties in time delay.

- Routers connecting the WAN links may be flooded with bursts of traffic. The IP datagrams that a router receives may have to wait in a queue until the time the router can resolve the route for the datagram. Even after its route is determined, the datagram may have to queue up for a network interface over which it is to be routed to become available. In the worst case, the datagrams arrive at a rate that fills the available router memory, in which case the router will have to drop datagrams that it cannot store in its memory. This scenario can happen because there is no pre-allocation of memory for individual TCP connections in an IP datagram network.

The IP Layer is so designed that each IP datagram is routed independently. Successive TCP segments in a connection may not be sent on the same path and may experience different delays as they traverse different sets of routers and links.

When TCP sends a message, it waits for acknowledgments to come back before it can advance its window. How long should it wait? The time it should wait is called the *time-out interval*. Because of the wide variance in time delays between successive transmissions in TCP, it uses an adaptive time-out. The algorithm for this adaptive time-out is called the *adaptive retransmission algorithm*. This algorithm is described in the following steps:

1. Measure the elapsed time between sending a data octet with a particular sequence number and receiving an acknowledgment that covers that sequence number. This measured elapsed time is the round-trip time (RTT). Based on the RTT, compute a smoothed round-trip time (SRTT) as

SRTT = ($\alpha \times$ SRTT) + ((1 − $\alpha \times$ RTT)

α is the weighting factor whose value is between 0 and 1 ($0 \leq \alpha < 1$). The SRTT is an estimated time-out. The SRTT computation, therefore, takes into account its old SRTT value and the new RTT value and takes a weighted average of these two. When $\alpha = 0.5$, SRTT is just the simple average of old SRTT and the following RTT values:

SRTT = (SRTT + RTT) ÷ 2, when $\alpha = 0.5$

When α is less than 0.5, a greater weight is given to the actual round-trip time (RTT). When α is greater than 0.5, a greater weight is given to the preceding estimated smoothed round-trip time (SRTT).

When $\alpha = 0$ or almost 1, you have the two extremes. When $\alpha = 0$, SRTT is always set to RTT; and when α is almost 1, a fixed SRTT is used with little deference to the actual RTT. Needless to say, the two extremes are seldom used in actual practice, but they are useful for understanding the nature of the weighted average.

2. The SRTT is then used to compute the retransmission time-out (RTO) by using the following:

RTO = min[UBOUND,max[LBOUND,($\beta \times$ SRTT)]]

UBOUND is an upper boundary on the time-out (for example, 1 minute), and LBOUND is a lower boundary on the time-out (for example 1 second). These values ensure that the RTO will fall between LBOUND and UBOUND. β is a delay variance factor that changes the sensitivity of the delay. If β is set to 1, RTO will be set to SRTT unless the SRTT value is below LBOUND or above UBOUND. This value ($\beta = 1$)will make TCP sensitive to packet loss and will not cause TCP to wait for a long time before retransmitting. However, small delays may cause unnecessary retransmissions. To make TCP less susceptible to small delays, a larger β value can be used. RFC 793 suggests using a value from 1.3 to 2.0.

In 1987, Karn and Partridge published a paper, "Improving Round-Trip Estimates in Reliable Transport Protocols," in the Proceedings of ACM SIGCOMM '87. Although not issued as an RFC, this paper influenced several TCP implementations, particularly the BSD UNIX implementation of TCP. This algorithm has since become known as *Karn's algorithm*. RFC 1122 recommends that Karn's algorithm be used in conjunction with Van Jacobson's slow start algorithm for congested networks. Van Jacobson's slow start algorithm is discussed in the section "Minimizing Impact of Congestion in TCP" in this chapter. Karn's algorithm takes into account the fact of retransmitted segments and is described next.

When retransmissions take place in Karn's algorithm, the SRTT value is not adjusted. Instead, a backoff strategy is used to adjust the time-out by a factor. The idea is that if a retransmission takes place, something drastic happened on the network, and the time-out should be increased sharply to avoid further retransmissions. The timer backoff strategy is implemented by using a simple equation such as the following:

$$\text{Backoff TIMEOUT} = \Gamma \times \text{TIMEOUT}$$

This equation is used until some previously decided upon upper boundary is reached. Typically, Γ is set to 2 so that this algorithm behaves like a binary exponential backoff algorithm. The Backoff TIMEOUT does not affect the SRTT that is used in normal computation. When an acknowledgment is received for a segment that does not require retransmission, TCP measures the RTT value and uses this value to compute the SRTT and the RTO values.

Minimizing Impact of Congestion in TCP

When congestion occurs in a network, TCP can respond with adjusting the time-out and retransmitting when acknowledgments are not received within the time-out interval. However, retransmissions can add to the problems of an already congested network by increasing the amount of data already being processed by the network. If retransmissions increase to a point that the retransmitted data being added to the network approaches the storage capacity of the network, then a condition called *congestion collapse* is imminent. When a network is experiencing congestion, a method is needed to stop or slow down additional data from being added to the network.

In 1988, Van Jacobson published a paper on "Congestion Avoidance and Control" in Proceedings ACM SIGCOMM'88. This paper outlines a technique for responding to congestion by reducing the amount of data sent by the sender. Routers that detect congestion can send the ICMP Source Quench message to the sender. The sender passes this message to the TCP module, which is alerted to a congestion condition.

> **Note**
>
> Techniques such as the Jacobson's slow start algorithm can deal successfully with congestion by adjusting the TCP window size dynamically.

Jacobson's slow start algorithm tries to avoid congestion by automatically adjusting the TCP window size, and it is implemented in all modern TCP implementations. In fact, Jacobson's algorithm, along with Karn's algorithm, is required to be implemented as per RFC 1122.

In Jacobson's slow start algorithm, TCP keeps track of a second limit called the *congestion window size*. The actual window size that is used is the smaller of the congestion window size and the TCP receiver window size.

Actual window size = min {congestion window size, TCP window size}

Under normal network conditions when there is no congestion, the congestion window size is the same as the TCP window size, which means that the actual window size is the same as the TCP window size. When congestion is detected, such as when there is a loss of segment, Jacobson's algorithm reduces the congestion window size by half. At every successive loss of a segment, the congestion window is again reduced by half. This process results in a rapid exponential decrease in window size. If the loss continues, the TCP window size is reduced to one segment, which means that only one datagram is transmitted at a time. At the same time, Karn's algorithm is used to double the time-out value before retransmitting. This dramatic reduction is called *exponential backoff* or *multiplicative decrease*.

Jacobson's algorithm uses a slow start to recover from congestion. If an acknowledgment is received for a segment, the algorithm increases the congestion window size by one segment. Because the initial window size for a severely congested network is 1, when an acknowledgment is received, the congestion window size becomes 2. This process means that TCP can now send two segments. If the acknowledgments for these segments come back, the congestion window size becomes 4, which enables TCP to send four segments. When the acknowledgments for these segments come back, the congestion window size becomes 8. This process continues until the congestion window size is equal to the receiver window size. Because of the exponential increase in congestion window size, it takes only $\log_2(N)$ successful transmissions before TCP can send N segments.

If the congestion window size increases too rapidly, it can add to network traffic before the network has completely recovered from congestion. If congestion is experienced again, the congestion window size will shrink rapidly. This alternating increase and decrease in congestion window size causes the congestion window size to oscillate rapidly. Jacobson's algorithm prevents too rapid an increase in congestion window size by using the *congestion avoidance* technique. In this technique, when the congestion window size becomes one-half the original TCP window size, the congestion window size is increased by one segment only if all the segments sent so far have been acknowledged.

Avoiding the Silly Window Syndrome

Early TCP implementations exhibited a pathological condition called the *Silly Window Syndrome (SWS)*. This condition was so named because the TCP transmission took place one octet at a time under certain conditions. Therefore, a TCP segment consists of one octet only, and each octet is individually acknowledged. The SWS can occur when any of the following is true:

- The application at the receiver reads data one octet at a time from a buffer that is full, and the receiver TCP sends a window size of 1 in an acknowledgment to the sender (see Figure 11.24).

- The application at the sender generates data one octet at a time, and the sender TCP sends this data immediately (see Figure 11.25).

FIGURE 11.24

Silly Window Syndrome caused by receiver.

In Figure 11.24, because the receiver sends a window size of 1 octet, the sender responds by sending only one octet of data. As soon as this octet is received, the receiver application reads just one octet of data, and the receiver TCP again advertises a window size of 1. And the cycle continues.

In Figure 11.25, the sender application sends only one octet of data. The sender TCP does not wait to see whether other data is accumulated but sends this one octet immediately. As the sender application continues to generate data one octet at a time, each octet is sent immediately.

FIGURE 11.25
Silly Window Syndrome caused by sender.

In both situations, the overhead of sending the data is enormous because of the following reasons:

- A large number of small packets is generated.

- Each packet is processed separately by each of the Data Link, IP, and TCP Layers at the sender and the receiver. Intervening routers must process the packets at the Data Link and IP Layers.

- There is a large computational overhead in each of the protocol layers because each packet must be individually routed, checksummed, and encapsulated/decapsulated. Each packet must also have its sequence and acknowledgment numbers computed, and must be handled by send/receive buffers.

- The ratio of the protocol headers to actual payload (data delivered) is high; that is, protocol efficiency is low. As a result, data throughput is low.

- As each octet segment is individually acknowledged, the delays for each octet accumulate to a significant value, and the data throughput is low. For 1,000 octets sent in 1,000 packets over a link with 50 ms delay, total delay is $1,000 \times 50$ ms = 5 seconds. Assuming that the time to transmit the packet to the link is small compared to the delay of the link, the overall throughput is only 1,000 octets $\times$ 8 bits/octet $\div$ 5 seconds = 1,600 bps.

To avoid the SWS on the receiver side, TCP implementations use the following mechanisms:

- Delay advertising. If the receive window size is smaller than a given size, the receiver delays advertising the window size until the receiver window size is at least equal to the following:

    min (0.5 × Receiver buffer size, Maximum Segment Size)

- Delay acknowledgments. Acknowledgments that contain the receiver window size computed in the previous bullet are delayed. This delay reduces network traffic by decreasing the number of acknowledgments. Recall that TCP acknowledgments are cumulative, so a later acknowledgment can acknowledge all data received so far. The risk here is that the delaying of acknowledgments can cause the sender to time-out and retransmit segments. To prevent this occurrence, ACKs are delayed to a maximum of 500 milliseconds, after which they must be sent. Many implementations delay acknowledgments by no more than 200 milliseconds. Additionally, the receiver should acknowledge every other data segment to ensure that the sender has a sufficient number of round-trip time estimates to implement its adaptive time-out algorithm.

Rather than delaying the acknowledgment, you can use another approach. In this approach, the acknowledgment is not delayed, but it is sent immediately without advertising an increase in window size until the prespecified limit has been reached. This approach is not recommended by the TCP standards, however.

To avoid the SWS on the sender side, TCP implementations use the Nagle avoidance algorithm. The basic ideas behind Nagle's SWS avoidance algorithm include the following:

- The sender sends the first data segment. After the first data segment, the sender does not immediately send short size segments even if the sender application sets the PSH flag.
- Data is sent only if the following is true:
    1. There is sufficient data to send to fill a maximum-size segment.
    2. An acknowledgment arrives while waiting for data to send.
    3. A preset time-out occurs.

If an application rapidly generates data, it will rapidly fill up the sender TCP buffer to the maximum segment size. TCP will send the maximum segment size without delay. Also, when an acknowledgment is received, the segment data in the buffer is sent without delay even if it is smaller than the maximum segment size.

If the application slowly generates data, segments will be sent when successive acknowledgments are received. Meanwhile, the sender TCP buffer will accumulate data.

The Nagle avoidance algorithm can be disabled for real-time applications that require minimum delay and send large bursts of data at a time.

Dealing with Dead TCP Connections

When a remote computer crashes or the network links are down, the TCP connections will break. How does TCP detect a connection that is dead and release its resources? An ICMP message may arrive informing TCP that the destination is unreachable. TCP retries a few times by retransmitting segments before reporting the condition to the application. What if TCP does not receive any ICMP messages because they are lost in transmission? TCP then retries for a first threshold number of retransmissions, after which TCP notifies IP to check whether a dead router or route is the problem. IP tries to recompute the route to the destination. Meanwhile, TCP retries for a second threshold number of transmissions, after which TCP declares that the connection is dead. On detecting a dead connection, TCP must release all resources such as TCB (transmission control buffers) associated with the connection.

When neither end point has sent data for a long time, the connection is maintained in the idle state. In the idle state, the connection consumes resources to maintain the connection even if the network or one of the other end points is down. Some TCP implementations send a keep-alive TCP message, which periodically checks to see whether the connection is alive. When a keep-alive TCP message is sent, an acknowledgment is expected from the receiver. The suggested default for the keep-alive timer is two hours. In some TCP implementations, the default is much smaller (for example, 10–15 minutes). The keep-alive timers should be set to what makes sense for the majority of applications running on a TCP host. Keeping this timer too short will generate excessive traffic, and keeping the timer value too long will not quickly alert TCP that the connection is dead.

TCP Finite State Machine

Figure 11.26 shows the behavior of the TCP as a finite state machine. A *finite state machine* is a logical model for the behavior of a system whose internal state changes with the occurrence of specified events. The boxes represent the state of the machine, and the arrows represent the transition from one state to another. The labels on the arrows represent the event that caused the transition between the states and the response of TCP to that event in the following format:

> *event*
> ‾‾‾‾‾
> *response*

In Figure 11.26, an *x* for the *response* indicates that no special response occurs.

Each end point of a TCP connection starts from the closed state. Arrows from this closed state are shown to indicate that a connection can occur by an active OPEN or a passive OPEN.

An active OPEN causes TCP to create a TCB and send a SYN flag segment and enter into the SYN SENT state. When a SYN flag and ACK flag are sent by the other end point, TCP sends an acknowledgment to complete the three-way handshake and enters the CONNECTION ESTABLISHED state.

When a passive OPEN is issued by an end point, it creates a TCB and enters into the LISTEN state. When TCP receives a SYN flag in this state (active OPEN request), it sends the flag's sequence number and the SYN and ACK flags in a TCP segment and enters the SYN RCVD state. When TCP receives an ACK or SYN flag from the other end point, the connection moves to the CONNECTION ESTABLISHED state.

FIGURE 11.26

TCP finite state machine.

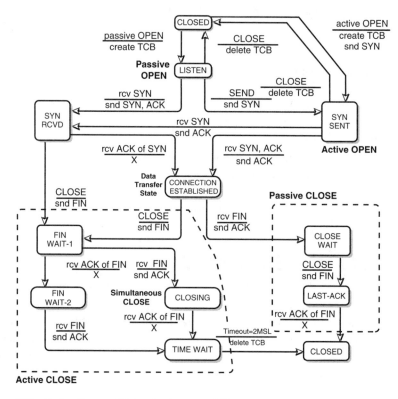

MSL = Maxium Segment Lifetime (2 minutes per RFC 793)

TCB = Transmission Control Buffer (contains state information on the TCP end point)

The TIME WAIT state is entered upon closing the connection to ensure that there is a delay of twice the MSL (maximum segment lifetime) time interval. This state is used to avoid duplicate segment numbers. See the earlier discussion in the section "The Flags Field" on avoiding duplicate sequence numbers.

The FIN WAIT-1 and FIN WAIT-2 states show the graceful close mechanism of TCP. Both sides have to agree on closing the connection before a connection is closed.

TCP Traces

The Telnet protocol uses TCP, and it is a good candidate for studying its protocol trace to examine the behavior of TCP. Figure 11.27 shows a complete Telnet trace of a user who performs the following activities:

1. Logs on to a Telnet server

2. Executes various commands at a Telnet server

3. Logs off from the Telnet server

FIGURE 11.27

Telnet trace.

No.	Source	Destination	Layer	Size	Summary
1	0000C024282D	FFFFFFFFFFFF	arp	0064	Req by 144.19.74.44 for 144.19.74
2	0000C024282D	FFFFFFFFFFFF	arp	0064	Req by 144.19.74.44 for 144.19.74
3	0000C0A20F8E	0000C024282D	arp	0064	Reply 144.19.74.201=0000C0A20F8E
4	0000C024282D	0000C0A20F8E	tcp	0064	Port:6295 ---> TELNET SYN
5	0000C0A20F8E	0000C024282D	tcp	0064	Port:TELNET ---> 6295 ACK SYN
6	0000C024282D	0000C0A20F8E	telnt	0069	Cmd=Do; Code=Do; Cmd=Do; Code=S
7	0000C0A20F8E	0000C024282D	tcp	0064	Port:TELNET ---> 6295 ACK
8	0000C0A20F8E	0000C024282D	telnt	0064	Cmd=Do; Code=;
9	0000C024282D	0000C0A20F8E	telnt	0064	Cmd=Won't; Code=;
10	0000C0A20F8E	0000C024282D	telnt	0067	Cmd=Will; Code=Echo; Cmd=Will; Co
11	0000C0A20F8E	0000C024282D	tcp	0064	Port:TELNET ---> 6295 ACK
12	0000C024282D	0000C0A20F8E	telnt	0072	Cmd=Do; Code=Suppress Go Ahead; C
13	0000C0A20F8E	0000C024282D	telnt	0070	Cmd=Do; Code=Terminal Type; Cmd=D
14	0000C0A20F8E	0000C024282D	tcp	0064	Port:TELNET ---> 6295 ACK
15	0000C024282D	0000C0A20F8E	telnt	0072	Cmd=Will; Code=Terminal Type; Cmd
16	0000C0A20F8E	0000C024282D	tcp	0064	Port:TELNET ---> 6295 ACK
17	0000C0A20F8E	0000C024282D	telnt	0064	Cmd=Subnegotiation Begin; Code=Te
18	0000C024282D	0000C0A20F8E	telnt	0071	Cmd=Subnegotiation Begin; Code=Te
19	0000C0A20F8E	0000C024282D	tcp	0064	Port:TELNET ---> 6295 ACK
20	0000C0A20F8E	0000C024282D	telnt	0067	Cmd=Do; Code=Echo; Cmd=Will; Code
21	0000C024282D	0000C0A20F8E	telnt	0069	Cmd=Won't; Code=Echo; Cmd=Don't;
22	0000C0A20F8E	0000C024282D	tcp	0064	Port:TELNET ---> 6295 ACK
23	0000C0A20F8E	0000C024282D	telnt	0104	Data=..Linux 1.3.50 (ltreec1.ltre
24	0000C024282D	0000C0A20F8E	tcp	0064	Port:6295 ---> TELNET ACK
25	0000C0A20F8E	0000C024282D	telnt	0064	Data=..
26	0000C024282D	0000C0A20F8E	tcp	0064	Port:6295 ---> TELNET ACK
27	0000C0A20F8E	0000C024282D	telnt	0073	Data=ltreec1 login:
28	0000C024282D	0000C0A20F8E	tcp	0064	Port:6295 ---> TELNET ACK
29	0000C024282D	0000C0A20F8E	telnt	0064	Data=u
30	0000C0A20F8E	0000C024282D	tcp	0064	Port:TELNET ---> 6295 ACK
31	0000C0A20F8E	0000C024282D	telnt	0064	Data=u
32	0000C024282D	0000C0A20F8E	tcp	0064	Port:6295 ---> TELNET ACK
33	0000C024282D	0000C0A20F8E	telnt	0064	Data=s
34	0000C0A20F8E	0000C024282D	tcp	0064	Port:TELNET ---> 6295 ACK
35	0000C0A20F8E	0000C024282D	telnt	0064	Data=s
36	0000C024282D	0000C0A20F8E	tcp	0064	Port:6295 ---> TELNET ACK
37	0000C024282D	0000C0A20F8E	telnt	0064	Data=e
38	0000C0A20F8E	0000C024282D	tcp	0064	Port:TELNET ---> 6295 ACK
39	0000C0A20F8E	0000C024282D	telnt	0064	Data=e
40	0000C024282D	0000C0A20F8E	tcp	0064	Port:6295 ---> TELNET ACK
41	0000C024282D	0000C0A20F8E	telnt	0064	Data=r

```
 42 0000C0A20F8E  0000C024282D  tcp    0064  Port:TELNET ---> 6295 ACK
 43 0000C0A20F8E  0000C024282D  telnt  0064  Data=r
 44 0000C024282D  0000C0A20F8E  tcp    0064  Port:6295 ---> TELNET ACK
 45 0000C024282D  0000C0A20F8E  telnt  0064  Data=1
 46 0000C0A20F8E  0000C024282D  tcp    0064  Port:TELNET ---> 6295 ACK
 47 0000C0A20F8E  0000C024282D  telnt  0064  Data=1
 48 0000C024282D  0000C0A20F8E  tcp    0064  Port:6295 ---> TELNET ACK
 49 0000C024282D  0000C0A20F8E  telnt  0064  Data=..
 50 0000C0A20F8E  0000C024282D  tcp    0064  Port:TELNET ---> 6295 ACK
 51 0000C0A20F8E  0000C024282D  telnt  0064  Data=..
 52 0000C024282D  0000C0A20F8E  tcp    0064  Port:6295 ---> TELNET ACK
 53 0000C0A20F8E  0000C024282D  telnt  0068  Data=Password:
 54 0000C024282D  0000C0A20F8E  tcp    0064  Port:6295 ---> TELNET ACK
 55 0000C024282D  0000C0A20F8E  telnt  0064  Data=u
 56 0000C0A20F8E  0000C024282D  tcp    0064  Port:TELNET ---> 6295 ACK
 57 0000C024282D  0000C0A20F8E  telnt  0064  Data=s
 58 0000C0A20F8E  0000C024282D  tcp    0064  Port:TELNET ---> 6295 ACK
 59 0000C024282D  0000C0A20F8E  telnt  0064  Data=e
 60 0000C0A20F8E  0000C024282D  tcp    0064  Port:TELNET ---> 6295 ACK
 61 0000C024282D  0000C0A20F8E  telnt  0064  Data=r
 62 0000C0A20F8E  0000C024282D  tcp    0064  Port:TELNET ---> 6295 ACK
 63 0000C024282D  0000C0A20F8E  telnt  0064  Data=1
 64 0000C0A20F8E  0000C024282D  tcp    0064  Port:TELNET ---> 6295 ACK
 65 0000C024282D  0000C0A20F8E  telnt  0064  Data=p
 66 0000C0A20F8E  0000C024282D  tcp    0064  Port:TELNET ---> 6295 ACK
 67 0000C024282D  0000C0A20F8E  telnt  0064  Data=w
 68 0000C0A20F8E  0000C024282D  tcp    0064  Port:TELNET ---> 6295 ACK
 69 0000C024282D  0000C0A20F8E  telnt  0064  Data=..
 70 0000C0A20F8E  0000C024282D  tcp    0064  Port:TELNET ---> 6295 ACK
 71 0000C0A20F8E  0000C024282D  telnt  0064  Data=....
 72 0000C024282D  0000C0A20F8E  tcp    0064  Port:6295 ---> TELNET ACK
 73 0000C0A20F8E  0000C024282D  telnt  0113  Data=Last login: Wed May 28 18:33
 74 0000C024282D  0000C0A20F8E  tcp    0064  Port:6295 ---> TELNET ACK
 75 0000C0A20F8E  0000C024282D  telnt  0073  Data=Linux 1.3.50...
 76 0000C024282D  0000C0A20F8E  tcp    0064  Port:6295 ---> TELNET ACK
 77 0000C0A20F8E  0000C024282D  telnt  0064  Data=..
 78 0000C024282D  0000C0A20F8E  tcp    0064  Port:6295 ---> TELNET ACK
 79 0000C0A20F8E  0000C024282D  telnt  0069  Data=Power, n:..
 80 0000C024282D  0000C0A20F8E  tcp    0064  Port:6295 ---> TELNET ACK
 81 0000C0A20F8E  0000C024282D  telnt  0119  Data=.The only narcotic regulated
 82 0000C024282D  0000C0A20F8E  tcp    0064  Port:6295 ---> TELNET ACK
 83 0000C0A20F8E  0000C024282D  telnt  0064  Data=..
 84 0000C024282D  0000C0A20F8E  tcp    0064  Port:6295 ---> TELNET ACK
 85 0000C0A20F8E  0000C024282D  telnt  0069  Data=ltreec1:~$
 86 0000C024282D  0000C0A20F8E  tcp    0064  Port:6295 ---> TELNET ACK
 87 0000C024282D  0000C0A20F8E  telnt  0064  Data=l
 88 0000C0A20F8E  0000C024282D  tcp    0064  Port:TELNET ---> 6295 ACK
 89 0000C0A20F8E  0000C024282D  telnt  0064  Data=l
 90 0000C024282D  0000C0A20F8E  tcp    0064  Port:6295 ---> TELNET ACK
 91 0000C024282D  0000C0A20F8E  telnt  0064  Data=s
 92 0000C0A20F8E  0000C024282D  tcp    0064  Port:TELNET ---> 6295 ACK
 93 0000C0A20F8E  0000C024282D  telnt  0064  Data=s
 94 0000C024282D  0000C0A20F8E  tcp    0064  Port:6295 ---> TELNET ACK
 95 0000C024282D  0000C0A20F8E  telnt  0064  Data=
 96 0000C0A20F8E  0000C024282D  tcp    0064  Port:TELNET ---> 6295 ACK
 97 0000C0A20F8E  0000C024282D  telnt  0064  Data=
 98 0000C024282D  0000C0A20F8E  tcp    0064  Port:6295 ---> TELNET ACK
 99 0000C024282D  0000C0A20F8E  telnt  0064  Data=-
100 0000C0A20F8E  0000C024282D  tcp    0064  Port:TELNET ---> 6295 ACK
101 0000C0A20F8E  0000C024282D  telnt  0064  Data=-
102 0000C024282D  0000C0A20F8E  tcp    0064  Port:6295 ---> TELNET ACK
103 0000C024282D  0000C0A20F8E  telnt  0064  Data=a
104 0000C0A20F8E  0000C024282D  tcp    0064  Port:TELNET ---> 6295 ACK
105 0000C0A20F8E  0000C024282D  telnt  0064  Data=a
106 0000C024282D  0000C0A20F8E  tcp    0064  Port:6295 ---> TELNET ACK
107 0000C024282D  0000C0A20F8E  telnt  0064  Data=l
108 0000C0A20F8E  0000C024282D  tcp    0064  Port:TELNET ---> 6295 ACK
109 0000C0A20F8E  0000C024282D  telnt  0064  Data=l
110 0000C024282D  0000C0A20F8E  tcp    0064  Port:6295 ---> TELNET ACK
111 0000C024282D  0000C0A20F8E  telnt  0064  Data=..
112 0000C0A20F8E  0000C024282D  tcp    0064  Port:TELNET ---> 6295 ACK
113 0000C0A20F8E  0000C024282D  telnt  0064  Data=..
114 0000C024282D  0000C0A20F8E  tcp    0064  Port:6295 ---> TELNET ACK
115 0000C0A20F8E  0000C024282D  telnt  0067  Data=total 7..
116 0000C024282D  0000C0A20F8E  tcp    0064  Port:6295 ---> TELNET ACK
```

```
117 0000C0A20F8E  0000C024282D  telnt  0130  Data=drwxr-xr-x   3 user1     user
118 0000C024282D  0000C0A20F8E  tcp    0064  Port:6295 ---> TELNET ACK
119 0000C0A20F8E  0000C024282D  telnt  0131  Data=drwxr-xr-x  19 root      root
120 0000C024282D  0000C0A20F8E  tcp    0064  Port:6295 ---> TELNET ACK
121 0000C0A20F8E  0000C024282D  telnt  0138  Data=-rw-r--r--   1 user1     user
122 0000C024282D  0000C0A20F8E  tcp    0064  Port:6295 ---> TELNET ACK
123 0000C0A20F8E  0000C024282D  telnt  0132  Data=-rw-r--r--   1 user1     user
124 0000C024282D  0000C0A20F8E  tcp    0064  Port:6295 ---> TELNET ACK
125 0000C0A20F8E  0000C024282D  telnt  0130  Data=-rw-r--r--   1 user1     user
126 0000C024282D  0000C0A20F8E  tcp    0064  Port:6295 ---> TELNET ACK
127 0000C0A20F8E  0000C024282D  telnt  0132  Data=-rw-r--r--   1 user1     user
128 0000C024282D  0000C0A20F8E  tcp    0064  Port:6295 ---> TELNET ACK
129 0000C0A20F8E  0000C024282D  telnt  0134  Data=drwxr-xr-x   2 user1     user
130 0000C024282D  0000C0A20F8E  tcp    0064  Port:6295 ---> TELNET ACK
131 0000C0A20F8E  0000C024282D  telnt  0064  Data=l
132 0000C024282D  0000C0A20F8E  tcp    0064  Port:6295 ---> TELNET ACK
133 0000C0A20F8E  0000C024282D  telnt  0068  Data=treec1:~$
134 0000C024282D  0000C0A20F8E  tcp    0064  Port:6295 ---> TELNET ACK
135 0000C024282D  0000C0A20F8E  telnt  0064  Data=p
136 0000C0A20F8E  0000C024282D  tcp    0064  Port:TELNET ---> 6295 ACK
137 0000C0A20F8E  0000C024282D  telnt  0064  Data=p
138 0000C024282D  0000C0A20F8E  tcp    0064  Port:6295 ---> TELNET ACK
139 0000C024282D  0000C0A20F8E  telnt  0064  Data=s
140 0000C0A20F8E  0000C024282D  tcp    0064  Port:TELNET ---> 6295 ACK
141 0000C0A20F8E  0000C024282D  telnt  0064  Data=s
142 0000C024282D  0000C0A20F8E  tcp    0064  Port:6295 ---> TELNET ACK
143 0000C024282D  0000C0A20F8E  telnt  0064  Data=
144 0000C0A20F8E  0000C024282D  tcp    0064  Port:TELNET ---> 6295 ACK
145 0000C0A20F8E  0000C024282D  telnt  0064  Data=
146 0000C024282D  0000C0A20F8E  tcp    0064  Port:6295 ---> TELNET ACK
147 0000C024282D  0000C0A20F8E  telnt  0064  Data=-
148 0000C0A20F8E  0000C024282D  tcp    0064  Port:TELNET ---> 6295 ACK
149 0000C0A20F8E  0000C024282D  telnt  0064  Data=-
150 0000C024282D  0000C0A20F8E  tcp    0064  Port:6295 ---> TELNET ACK
151 0000C024282D  0000C0A20F8E  telnt  0064  Data=a
152 0000C0A20F8E  0000C024282D  tcp    0064  Port:TELNET ---> 6295 ACK
153 0000C0A20F8E  0000C024282D  telnt  0064  Data=a
154 0000C024282D  0000C0A20F8E  tcp    0064  Port:6295 ---> TELNET ACK
155 0000C024282D  0000C0A20F8E  telnt  0064  Data=l
156 0000C0A20F8E  0000C024282D  tcp    0064  Port:TELNET ---> 6295 ACK
157 0000C0A20F8E  0000C024282D  telnt  0064  Data=l
158 0000C024282D  0000C0A20F8E  tcp    0064  Port:6295 ---> TELNET ACK
159 0000C024282D  0000C0A20F8E  telnt  0064  Data=x
160 0000C0A20F8E  0000C024282D  tcp    0064  Port:TELNET ---> 6295 ACK
161 0000C0A20F8E  0000C024282D  telnt  0064  Data=x
162 0000C024282D  0000C0A20F8E  tcp    0064  Port:6295 ---> TELNET ACK
163 0000C024282D  0000C0A20F8E  telnt  0064  Data=..
164 0000C0A20F8E  0000C024282D  tcp    0064  Port:TELNET ---> 6295 ACK
165 0000C0A20F8E  0000C024282D  telnt  0064  Data=..
166 0000C024282D  0000C0A20F8E  tcp    0064  Port:6295 ---> TELNET ACK
167 0000C0A20F8E  0000C024282D  telnt  0133  Data= F    UID   PID  PPID PRI NI
168 0000C024282D  0000C0A20F8E  tcp    0064  Port:6295 ---> TELNET ACK
169 0000C024282D  0000C0A20F8E  telnt  0140  Data= 0    0    1     0  30 15
170 0000C024282D  0000C0A20F8E  tcp    0064  Port:6295 ---> TELNET ACK
171 0000C0A20F8E  0000C024282D  telnt  0143  Data= 0    0    2     1  30 15
172 0000C024282D  0000C0A20F8E  tcp    0064  Port:6295 ---> TELNET ACK
173 0000C0A20F8E  0000C024282D  telnt  0140  Data= 0    0    8     1  30 15
174 0000C024282D  0000C0A20F8E  tcp    0064  Port:6295 ---> TELNET ACK
175 0000C0A20F8E  0000C024282D  telnt  0140  Data= 0    0    24    1  30 15
176 0000C024282D  0000C0A20F8E  tcp    0064  Port:6295 ---> TELNET ACK
177 0000C0A20F8E  0000C024282D  telnt  0140  Data= 0    0    38    1  30 15
178 0000C024282D  0000C0A20F8E  tcp    0064  Port:6295 ---> TELNET ACK
179 0000C0A20F8E  0000C024282D  telnt  0140  Data= 0    0    40    1  30 15
180 0000C024282D  0000C0A20F8E  tcp    0064  Port:6295 ---> TELNET ACK
181 0000C0A20F8E  0000C024282D  telnt  0140  Data= 0    1    42    1  30 15
182 0000C024282D  0000C0A20F8E  tcp    0064  Port:6295 ---> TELNET ACK
183 0000C0A20F8E  0000C024282D  telnt  0140  Data= 0    0    44    1  30 15
184 0000C024282D  0000C0A20F8E  tcp    0064  Port:6295 ---> TELNET ACK
185 0000C0A20F8E  0000C024282D  telnt  0139  Data= 0    0    46    1  30 15
```

```
186 0000C024282D   0000C0A20F8E   tcp     0064   Port:6295 ---> TELNET ACK
187 0000C0A20F8E   0000C024282D   telnt   0140   Data=  0     0     49      1   30 15
188 0000C024282D   0000C0A20F8E   tcp     0064   Port:6295 ---> TELNET ACK
189 0000C0A20F8E   0000C024282D   telnt   0140   Data=  0     0     51      1   30 15
190 0000C0A20F8E   0000C024282D   tcp     0064   Port:6295 ---> TELNET ACK
191 0000C0A20F8E   0000C024282D   telnt   0140   Data=  0     0     53      1   30 15
192 0000C024282D   0000C0A20F8E   tcp     0064   Port:6295 ---> TELNET ACK
193 0000C0A20F8E   0000C024282D   telnt   0140   Data=  0     0     57      1   30 15
194 0000C024282D   0000C0A20F8E   tcp     0064   Port:6295 ---> TELNET ACK
195 0000C0A20F8E   0000C024282D   telnt   0140   Data=  0     0     61      1   30 15
196 0000C024282D   0000C0A20F8E   tcp     0064   Port:6295 ---> TELNET ACK
197 0000C0A20F8E   0000C024282D   telnt   0140   Data=  0     0     62      1   30 15
198 0000C024282D   0000C0A20F8E   tcp     0064   Port:6295 ---> TELNET ACK
199 0000C0A20F8E   0000C024282D   telnt   0140   Data=  0     0     63      1   30 15
200 0000C024282D   0000C0A20F8E   tcp     0064   Port:6295 ---> TELNET ACK
201 0000C0A20F8E   0000C024282D   telnt   0140   Data=  0     0     64      1   30 15
202 0000C024282D   0000C0A20F8E   tcp     0064   Port:6295 ---> TELNET ACK
203 0000C0A20F8E   0000C024282D   telnt   0140   Data=  0     0     65      1   30 15
204 0000C024282D   0000C0A20F8E   tcp     0064   Port:6295 ---> TELNET ACK
205 0000C0A20F8E   0000C024282D   telnt   0131   Data=  0     0    145      1   30 15
206 0000C024282D   0000C0A20F8E   tcp     0064   Port:6295 ---> TELNET ACK
207 0000C024282D   0000C0A20F8E   telnt   0064   Data=.
208 0000C024282D   0000C0A20F8E   tcp     0064   Port:TELNET ---> 6295 ACK
209 0000C0A20F8E   0000C024282D   telnt   0136   Data=  0     0    258     44   29 15
210 0000C0A20F8E   0000C024282D   telnt   0064   Cmd=;
211 0000C024282D   0000C0A20F8E   telnt   0064   Data=.
212 0000C0A20F8E   0000C024282D   telnt   0064   Data=.
213 0000C0A20F8E   0000C024282D   tcp     0064   Port:TELNET ---> 6295 ACK
214 0000C024282D   0000C0A20F8E   tcp     0064   Port:6295 ---> TELNET ACK
215 0000C0A20F8E   0000C024282D   telnt   0071   Data=..ltreec1:~$
216 0000C024282D   0000C0A20F8E   tcp     0064   Port:6295 ---> TELNET ACK
217 0000C024282D   0000C0A20F8E   telnt   0064   Data=l
218 0000C0A20F8E   0000C024282D   tcp     0064   Port:TELNET ---> 6295 ACK
219 0000C0A20F8E   0000C024282D   telnt   0064   Data=l
220 0000C024282D   0000C0A20F8E   tcp     0064   Port:6295 ---> TELNET ACK
221 0000C024282D   0000C0A20F8E   telnt   0064   Data=o
222 0000C0A20F8E   0000C024282D   tcp     0064   Port:TELNET ---> 6295 ACK
223 0000C0A20F8E   0000C024282D   telnt   0064   Data=o
224 0000C024282D   0000C0A20F8E   tcp     0064   Port:6295 ---> TELNET ACK
225 0000C024282D   0000C0A20F8E   telnt   0064   Data=g
226 0000C0A20F8E   0000C024282D   tcp     0064   Port:TELNET ---> 6295 ACK
227 0000C0A20F8E   0000C024282D   telnt   0064   Data=g
228 0000C024282D   0000C0A20F8E   tcp     0064   Port:6295 ---> TELNET ACK
229 0000C0A20F8E   0000C024282D   telnt   0064   Data=o
230 0000C0A20F8E   0000C024282D   tcp     0064   Port:TELNET ---> 6295 ACK
231 0000C0A20F8E   0000C024282D   telnt   0064   Data=o
232 0000C024282D   0000C0A20F8E   tcp     0064   Port:6295 ---> TELNET ACK
233 0000C024282D   0000C0A20F8E   telnt   0064   Data=u
234 0000C0A20F8E   0000C024282D   tcp     0064   Port:TELNET ---> 6295 ACK
235 0000C0A20F8E   0000C024282D   telnt   0064   Data=u
236 0000C024282D   0000C0A20F8E   tcp     0064   Port:6295 ---> TELNET ACK
237 0000C024282D   0000C0A20F8E   telnt   0064   Data=t
238 0000C0A20F8E   0000C024282D   tcp     0064   Port:TELNET ---> 6295 ACK
239 0000C0A20F8E   0000C024282D   telnt   0064   Data=t
240 0000C024282D   0000C0A20F8E   tcp     0064   Port:6295 ---> TELNET ACK
241 0000C024282D   0000C0A20F8E   telnt   0064   Data=..
242 0000C0A20F8E   0000C024282D   tcp     0064   Port:TELNET ---> 6295 ACK
243 0000C0A20F8E   0000C024282D   tcp     0064   Port:TELNET ---> 6295 ACK FIN
244 0000C024282D   0000C0A20F8E   tcp     0064   Port:6295 ---> TELNET ACK FIN
245 0000C0A20F8E   0000C024282D   tcp     0064   Port:TELNET ---> 6295 ACK
```

Packets 1 through 3 in Figure 11.27 deal with ARP resolution. ARP resolution is discussed in Chapter 5, "ARP and RARP." The actual Telnet trace begins from packet 4.

The following sections examine only the TCP aspect of the Telnet trace in Figure 11.27 and not the Telnet application data. The packet numbers in the following traces correspond to the packet numbers in Figure 11.27. For this reason, the entire trace of the

Telnet session is reproduced in Figure 11.27 for your reference, even though the trace itself is somewhat long.

TCP Open Connection Three-Way Handshake Trace

Figures 11.28 through 11.30 show the three TCP packets involved in the three-way handshake that is used to open a TCP connection.

FIGURE 11.28

OPEN TCP connection request: sending the initial sender sequence number (ISS).

```
Packet Number : 4              6:38:38 PM
Length : 64 bytes
ether: ================== Ethernet Datalink Layer ==================
        Station: 00-00-C0-24-28-2D ----> 00-00-C0-A2-0F-8E
        Type: 0x0800 (IP)
  ip: ===================== Internet Protocol =====================
        Station:144.19.74.44 ---->144.19.74.201
        Protocol: TCP
        Version: 4
        Header Length (32 bit words): 5
        Precedence: Routine
              Normal Delay, Normal Throughput, Normal Reliability
        Total length: 44
        Identification:      1
        Fragmentation allowed, Last fragment
        Fragment Offset: 0
        Time to Live: 100 seconds
        Checksum: 0xA1AF(Valid)
  tcp: ================= Transmission Control Protocol =================
        Source Port: 6295
        Destination Port: TELNET
        Sequence Number: 25784320
        Acknowledgement Number: 0
        Data Offset (32-bit words): 6
        Window: 4096
        Control Bits: Synchronize Sequence Numbers (SYN)
        Checksum: 0x4A87(Valid)
        Urgent Pointer: 0
        Option:MAXIMUM SEGMENT SIZE
                Option Length: 4
                Maximum Segment Size : 1024
```

The OPEN connection request TCP packet has the following flags and sequence number and represents Step 1 in the three-way handshake:

e number = 25784320 (ISS)

Acknowledgment Number = 0 (not valid because ACK = 0)

Another interesting thing to note about the OPEN connection option is that the Data Offset field is 6, which indicates the existence of a TCP option. This option is the MSS option (option-kind = 2) with the following hex codes:

02 04 04 00

These codes translate to the following TCP option values:

Option:	MAXIMUM SEGMENT SIZE
Option Length:	4
Maximum Segment Size:	1,024

The source port, destination port, and window size of this initial packet are as follows:

Source Port:	6295
Destination Port:	23 (standard Telnet server port)
Window:	4,096

The source port represents the port on which the Telnet client is listening to receive data from the Telnet server. The destination port is the port on the Telnet server that is being contacted for opening a connection. The window is the number of octets that the Telnet client can receive; that is, it is the size of the Telnet client computer's TCP receive buffer.

Figure 11.29 shows the acknowledgment of the OPEN connection request TCP packet by the receiver. This is Step 2 in the three-way handshake:

SYN = 1

ACK = 1

All other TCP flags set to 0

Sequence Number = 1508167651 (IRS)

Acknowledgment Number = 25784321 (ISS + 1)

FIGURE 11.29

*Acknowledgment
of OPEN connec-
tion request: send-
ing the initial
receiver sequence
number (IRS).*

```
Packet Number : 5              6:38:38 PM
Length : 64 bytes
ether: ==================== Ethernet Datalink Layer ====================
       Station: 00-00-C0-A2-0F-8E ----> 00-00-C0-24-28-2D
       Type: 0x0800 (IP)
  ip:  ====================== Internet Protocol ======================
       Station:144.19.74.201 ---->144.19.74.44
       Protocol: TCP
       Version: 4
       Header Length (32 bit words): 5
       Precedence: Routine
             Normal Delay, Normal Throughput, Normal Reliability
       Total length: 44
       Identification: 21410
       Fragmentation allowed, Last fragment
       Fragment Offset: 0
       Time to Live: 64  seconds
       Checksum: 0x720E(Valid)
  tcp: ================= Transmission Control Protocol =================
       Source Port: TELNET
       Destination Port: 6295
       Sequence Number: 1508167651
       Acknowledgement Number: 25784321
       Data Offset (32-bit words): 6
       Window: 30719
       Control Bits: Acknowledgement Field is Valid (ACK)
             Synchronize Sequence Numbers (SYN)
       Checksum: 0xB8AE(Valid)
       Urgent Pointer: 0
       Option:MAXIMUM SEGMENT SIZE
               Option Length: 4
               Maximum Segment Size : 1024
```

The packet in Figure 11.29 is sent by the Telnet server to synchronize its sequence number and contains the server's initial sequence number. Another interesting thing to note
about the OPEN connection option is that the Data Offset field is 6, which indicates the
existence of a TCP option. This option is the MSS option (option–kind = 2) with the following hex codes:

02 04 04 00

These codes translate to the following TCP option values:

Option:	MAXIMUM SEGMENT SIZE
Option Length:	4
Maximum Segment Size:	1,024

In this example, both the Telnet client and server use the same MSS size, but this situation does not always have to exist. The source port, destination port, and window size of the OPEN connection acknowledgment packet are as follows:

Source Port:	23 (standard Telnet server port)
Destination Port:	6295
Window:	30,719

The source port represents the port on which the Telnet server is listening to receive data from the Telnet client. The destination port is the port on the Telnet client that made the request for opening a connection. The window is the number of octets that the Telnet server can receive; that is, it is the size of the Telnet server computer's TCP receive buffer. Note that this number is larger than that of the Telnet client.

Figure 11.30 shows the last step in the three-way handshake. In this step the Telnet server's sequence number received by the Telnet client is being acknowledged. This packet has the following flags and sequence numbers:

ACK = 1

PSH = 1

All other TCP flags set to 0

Sequence Number = 25784321 (ISS + 1)

Acknowledgment Number = 1508167652 (IRS + 1)

FIGURE 11.30

Acknowledgment of initial receiver sequence number (IRS).

```
Packet Number : 6              6:38:38 PM
Length : 69 bytes
ether: ==================== Ethernet Datalink Layer ====================
       Station: 00-00-C0-24-28-2D ----> 00-00-C0-A2-0F-8E
       Type: 0x0800 (IP)
   ip: ==================== Internet Protocol ====================
       Station:144.19.74.44 ---->144.19.74.201
       Protocol: TCP
       Version: 4
       Header Length (32 bit words): 5
       Precedence: Routine
             Normal Delay, Normal Throughput, Normal Reliability
       Total length: 49
       Identification:     2
       Fragmentation allowed, Last fragment
       Fragment Offset: 0
       Time to Live: 100 seconds
       Checksum: 0xA1A9(Valid)
  tcp: ================= Transmission Control Protocol =================
       Source Port: 6295
       Destination Port: TELNET
       Sequence Number: 25784321
       Acknowledgement Number: 1508167652
       Data Offset (32-bit words): 5
       Window: 4096
       Control Bits: Acknowledgement Field is Valid (ACK)
               Push Function Requested (PSH)
       Checksum: 0x18A9(Valid)
       Urgent Pointer: 0
telnt: ==================== Telnet Protocol ====================
       Command: Do
       Option Code: Echo
       Command: Do
       Option Code: Suppress Go Ahead
       Command: Will
       Option Code:
```

The PSH flag is set to suggest to TCP that it should send the data. Nagle's avoidance technique is used to prevent the Silly Window Syndrome (SWS). See the earlier section "Avoiding the Silly Window Syndrome" for details on Nagle's algorithm to avoid SWS.

Another interesting thing to note about the OPEN connection option is that the Data Offset field is 5, which indicates no TCP options.

The source port, destination port, and window size of this initial packet are as follows:

Source port: 6295

Destination port: 23 (standard Telnet server port)

Window: 4,096

The source port represents the end point of the TCP connection on the Telnet client. The destination port represents the end point of the TCP connection on the Telnet server. The window is the number of octets that the Telnet client can receive; that is, it is the size of the Telnet client computer's TCP receive buffer.

TCP Normal Data Mode Trace

In packet 6 (refer to Figure 11.30), which concludes the three-way handshake and acknowledges the TCP receiver's IRS, nine octets of Telnet data are sent:

FF FD 01 FF FD 03 FF FB 1F

How do you know that nine octets of Telnet data have been sent? Examine the IP header field to determine the size of the IP datagram (refer to Figure 11.30). The IP datagram is 49 octets. Of these 49 octets, 20 octets (Header Length = 5 words) are taken up by the IP header, and 20 octets (Data Offset = 5 words) are taken up by the TCP header. What remains is 49 – 20 – 20 = 9 octets for the Telnet data.

Packet 6 represents the start of data transmission mode in the TCP trace. Packet 7 (see Figure 11.31) contains an acknowledgment of this data from the Telnet server. The Telnet server at this point does not have any data to send and, therefore, sends only an acknowledgment.

Note that this packet has the following flags and sequence numbers:

ACK = 1

All other TCP flags set to 0

Sequence Number: 1508167652

Acknowledgment Number: 25784330

Note that the acknowledgment number that is sent back contains the acknowledgment for the nine octets of Telnet client data:

ISN from Telnet client = 25784321

Telnet data = 9

Acknowledgment Number data 　　 = ISN from Telnet client + Telnet
　　　　　　　　　　　　　　　　= 25784321 + 9
　　　　　　　　　　　　　　　　= 25784330

FIGURE 11.31

*Acknowledgment
packet.*

```
Packet Number : 7              6:38:38 PM
Length : 64 bytes
ether: ==================== Ethernet Datalink Layer ====================
       Station: 00-00-C0-A2-0F-8E ----> 00-00-C0-24-28-2D
       Type: 0x0800 (IP)
  ip:  ===================== Internet Protocol =====================
       Station:144.19.74.201 ---->144.19.74.44
       Protocol: TCP
       Version: 4
       Header Length (32 bit words): 5
       Precedence: Routine
             Normal Delay, Normal Throughput, Normal Reliability
       Total length: 40
       Identification: 21411
       Fragmentation allowed, Last fragment
       Fragment Offset: 0
       Time to Live: 64  seconds
       Checksum: 0x7211(Valid)
  tcp: ================= Transmission Control Protocol =================
       Source Port: TELNET
       Destination Port: 6295
       Sequence Number: 1508167652
       Acknowledgement Number: 25784330
       Data Offset (32-bit words): 5
       Window: 30710
       Control Bits: Acknowledgement Field is Valid (ACK)
       Checksum: 0xCEB7(Valid)
       Urgent Pointer: 0
```

One second after the acknowledgment packet is sent, the Telnet server sends a response
to the Telnet client data in packet 8 (see Figure 11.32). If the Telnet server had been
ready to send this response right away, it could have done so in packet 7. TCP will delay
sending acknowledgments to avoid sending small packets, but the maximum delay

according to the TCP standard is 500 milliseconds (see the discussion in the previous section "Avoiding the Silly Window Syndrome"). You know that one second has transpired between packets 7 and 8 by examining the timestamps that are displayed on the first line in the protocol decodes. These timestamps indicate the time that a packet was captured by using a protocol analyzer.

The amount of application data that is sent in packet 8 is computed as before:

IP Total Length – IP Header Length – TCP Data Offset

= 43 – 20 – 20 = 3 octets

FIGURE 11.32

TCP data transmission.

```
Packet Number : 243          6:39:12 PM
Length : 64 bytes
ether: ================== Ethernet Datalink Layer ====================
       Station: 00-00-C0-A2-0F-8E ----> 00-00-C0-24-28-2D
       Type: 0x0800 (IP)
   ip: ===================== Internet Protocol =====================
       Station:144.19.74.201 ---->144.19.74.44
       Protocol: TCP
       Version: 4
       Header Length (32 bit words): 5
       Precedence: Routine
            Normal Delay, Normal Throughput, Normal Reliability
       Total length: 40
       Identification: 21533
       Fragmentation allowed, Last fragment
       Fragment Offset: 0
       Time to Live: 64   seconds
       Checksum: 0x7197(Valid)
  tcp: ================= Transmission Control Protocol ==================
       Source Port: TELNET
       Destination Port: 6295
       Sequence Number: 1508170215
       Acknowledgement Number: 25784420
       Data Offset (32-bit words): 5
       Window: 30719
       Control Bits: Acknowledgement Field is Valid (ACK)
            No More Data from Sender (FIN)
       Checksum: 0xC450(Valid)
       Urgent Pointer: 0
```

TCP Graceful Close Trace

Packets 217 through 242 (refer to Figure 11.27) show the Telnet client transmitting the logout command one character at a time to the Telnet server. Packets 243 through 245 illustrate the graceful close mechanism. In packet 243 (see Figure 11.33), the Telnet server that receives the logout command requests a close of the TCP connection by setting the FIN flag to 1. This flag indicates that the Telnet server has no more data to send.

FIGURE 11.33

Graceful close request issued by Telnet server.

```
Packet Number : 243          6:39:12 PM
Length : 64 bytes
ether: ==================== Ethernet Datalink Layer ====================
       Station: 00-00-C0-A2-0F-8E ----> 00-00-C0-24-28-2D
       Type: 0x0800 (IP)
   ip: ===================== Internet Protocol =====================
       Station:144.19.74.201 ---->144.19.74.44
       Protocol: TCP
       Version: 4
       Header Length (32 bit words): 5
       Precedence: Routine
             Normal Delay, Normal Throughput, Normal Reliability
       Total length: 40
       Identification: 21533
       Fragmentation allowed, Last fragment
       Fragment Offset: 0
       Time to Live: 64  seconds
       Checksum: 0x7197(Valid)
  tcp: ================= Transmission Control Protocol =================
       Source Port: TELNET
       Destination Port: 6295
       Sequence Number: 1508170215
       Acknowledgement Number: 25784420
       Data Offset (32-bit words): 5
       Window: 30719
       Control Bits: Acknowledgement Field is Valid (ACK)
                     No More Data from Sender (FIN)
       Checksum: 0xC450(Valid)
       Urgent Pointer: 0
```

In packet 244 (see Figure 11.34), the Telnet client responds by setting the FIN flag to 1, thereby indicating that the client is ready to close the connection and that it has no more data to send. Note that in this implementation, the window size is set to 0 to indicate that TCP at the Telnet client will not accept any more data.

FIGURE 11.34

Graceful close request agreed upon by Telnet client.

```
Packet Number : 244           6:39:12 PM
Length : 64 bytes
ether: ==================== Ethernet Datalink Layer ====================
       Station: 00-00-C0-24-28-2D ----> 00-00-C0-A2-0F-8E
       Type: 0x0800 (IP)
ip:    ===================== Internet Protocol =====================
       Station:144.19.74.44 ---->144.19.74.201
       Protocol: TCP
       Version: 4
       Header Length (32 bit words): 5
       Precedence: Routine
              Normal Delay, Normal Throughput, Normal Reliability
       Total length: 40
       Identification:   117
       Fragmentation allowed, Last fragment
       Fragment Offset: 0
       Time to Live: 100 seconds
       Checksum: 0xA13F(Valid)
tcp:   ================= Transmission Control Protocol =================
       Source Port: 6295
       Destination Port: TELNET
       Sequence Number: 25784420
       Acknowledgement Number: 1508170216
       Data Offset (32-bit words): 5
       Window: 0
       Control Bits: Acknowledgement Field is Valid (ACK)
              No More Data from Sender (FIN)
       Checksum: 0x3C4F(Valid)
       Urgent Pointer: 0
```

In Figure 11.35, the Telnet server acknowledges the reception of the FIN flag from the Telnet client. At this point, the TCP modules at the Telnet client and the server will release the resources associated with the TCP connection.

FIGURE **11.35**

*Acknowledgment
of graceful close
request from
Telnet client.*

```
Packet Number : 245        6:39:12 PM
Length : 64 bytes
ether: ==================== Ethernet Datalink Layer ====================
       Station: 00-00-C0-A2-0F-8E ----> 00-00-C0-24-28-2D
       Type: 0x0800 (IP)
   ip: ===================== Internet Protocol =====================
       Station:144.19.74.201 ---->144.19.74.44
       Protocol: TCP
       Version: 4
       Header Length (32 bit words): 5
       Precedence: Routine
              Normal Delay, Normal Throughput, Normal Reliability
       Total length: 40
       Identification: 21534
       Fragmentation allowed, Last fragment
       Fragment Offset: 0
       Time to Live: 64  seconds
       Checksum: 0x7196(Valid)
  tcp: ================= Transmission Control Protocol =================
       Source Port: TELNET
       Destination Port: 6295
       Sequence Number: 1508170216
       Acknowledgement Number: 25784421
       Data Offset (32-bit words): 5
       Window: 30718
       Control Bits: Acknowledgement Field is Valid (ACK)
       Checksum: 0xC450(Valid)
       Urgent Pointer: 0
```

The User Datagram Protocol (UDP)

There are a number of applications for which the robustness of TCP is not required. Instead, what is needed is a transport protocol that can identify the applications on the computers and provide a rudimentary error check. The User Datagram Protocol (UDP) provides these capabilities.

Unlike TCP, which is connection oriented, UDP (as its name suggests) operates in the datagram mode. UDP makes no attempt to create a connection. Data is sent by encapsulating it in a UDP header and passing the data to the IP Layer. The IP Layer sends the UDP packet in a single IP datagram unless fragmentation is required. UDP does not attempt to provide sequencing of data; therefore, it is possible for data to arrive in a different order from which it was sent. Applications that need sequencing services must either build their own sequencing mechanism as part of the application or use TCP instead of UDP. In many LAN environments, the chance of data being received out of sequence is small because of small predictable delays and simple network topology.

UDP is useful in applications that are command/response oriented and in which the commands and responses can be sent in a single datagram. There is no overhead involved in opening and then closing a connection just to send a small amount of data. Another advantage of UDP is for applications that require broadcast/multicast. In TCP, if a broadcast has to be sent to 1,000 stations, the sender has to open 1,000 connections, send data on each connection, and then close the 1,000 connections. The overhead of opening these connections, maintaining them (resource utilization), and then closing them is high. If UDP is used, the sender can send the data to the IP module requesting a broadcast/multicast distribution. The underlying network's broadcast/multicast capability may be used in sending the data.

UDP provides a rudimentary form of optional error checking over the integrity of the data. If the underlying network is known to be reliable, the UDP checksums can be disabled, which will speed up UDP processing.

The features of UDP are summarized as follows:

- UDP has a provision for identifying application processes by using UDP port numbers.
- UDP is datagram oriented with no overhead for opening, maintaining, and closing a connection.
- UDP is efficient for broadcast/multicast applications.
- There is no sequencing of data. Data cannot be correctly guaranteed for delivery.
- UDP uses optional error checksum of data only.
- UDP is faster, simpler and more efficient than TCP; however, it is also less robust then TCP.

UDP provides unreliable, connectionless delivery services over TCP. UDP is regarded as a Transport Layer protocol. As a Transport Layer protocol, UDP is somewhat of a paradox because the function of a Transport Layer is to provide end-to-end data integrity, which is something UDP does not do. Despite this drawback, a large number of practical applications are built around UDP. These applications include the following:

- TFTP (Trivial File Transfer Protocol)
- DNS (Domain Name System)
- NFS (Network File System) version 2
- SNMP (Simple Network Management Protocol)
- RIP (Routing Information Protocol)

- Many services that broadcast data, such as WHOD (Who daemon on Unix servers)

The upcoming sections explore UDP in greater detail.

UDP Header Format

The UDP header has a fixed length of eight octets. The format of the UDP header is shown in Figure 11.36.

FIGURE **11.36**

UDP header format.

The Source Port is a 16-bit field. This field is optional. When meaningful, it indicates the following:

- The port number of the sending process.
- The source port number is the port to which a reply should be addressed in the absence of any other information.
- When set to 0, the field indicates that the source port number is not used.

The Destination Port field identifies the process at the destination IP address. This process is to receive the UDP data being sent. Like TCP, UDP performs demultiplexing of data to the destination process by using port number values. If UDP receives a datagram with a port number that is not in use (no UDP application associated with the port), UDP generates an ICMP port unreachable error message and rejects the datagram.

The Length field is the length of this UDP packet in octets. This length includes the UDP header and its data. The minimum value of the Length field is 8 and indicates a zero-size data field.

The checksum field is the 16-bit 1's complement of the 1's complement sum of a pseudoheader of information from the IP header, the UDP header, and the data, padded with zero octets at the end (if necessary) to make a multiple of two octets. The checksum procedure is the same as is used in TCP.

The pseudoheader, which is prefixed conceptually to the UDP header, contains the source address, the destination address, the protocol (UDP protocol number is 17), and the UDP length (see Figure 11.37). This information provides protection against mis-routed datagrams. The pseudoheader has a fixed size of 12 octets. The information in the UDP pseudoheader completely specifies the half association of the destination, even though no connection is being set up.

FIGURE 11.37

UDP pseudo-header used in checksum calculations.

If the computed checksum is 0 (zero), it is transmitted as all 1s (the equivalent in 1 in complement arithmetic). Therefore, an all-0 checksum will never be generated by the preceding calculation, and it is used to indicate a special condition: An all 0 transmitted checksum value means that checksums are not being used. Another way of looking at this situation is that 0 has two representations if you use 1's complement arithmetic: all 0s, and all 1s. All 1s is used for calculated checksum, and all 0s indicates that checksumming is disabled. An application running on a reliable IP network, such as a LAN, may want to disable the extra overhead of generating checksums on transmission and verifying them on receiving the UDP datagram.

The UDP protocol runs on top of IP. The IP checksum is done only over the header, whereas the UDP checksum is done over the UDP header and data. The UDP checksum is needed for guaranteeing the integrity of the data field.

UDP Layering and Encapsulation

UDP runs on top of IP, as you can see in Figure 11.38. Applications that run on top of UDP are associated with a UDP port number. The UDP port number is in a different address space than the TCP port number address space. Thus it is possible to have a TCP port number of 1017 and a UDP port number of 1017 to refer to separate application processes.

Figure 11.39 shows how UDP data is encapsulated in an IP header, which in turn is encapsulated by the Data Link layer. The protocol number assigned to UDP is 17.

There is a strong degree of coupling between UDP and IP because of the necessity of the UDP layer to know the IP address for the pseudoheader. Recall that the pseudoheader is used as part of the UDP checksum. The implication here is that the UDP module must be able to determine the source and destination IP addresses and the Protocol field from the IP header. One possible UDP/IP interface would return the whole IP datagram, including all of the IP header, in response to a RECEIVE operation issued by a UDP application. This interface then would enable UDP to pass a full IP datagram, complete with header, to the IP to send. The IP Layer then would verify certain fields for consistency and would compute the IP header checksum.

FIGURE 11.38

UDP protocol layering.

FIGURE 11.39

UDP encapsulation.

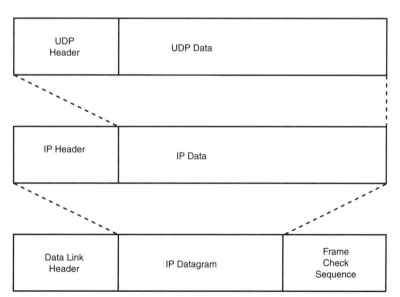

UDP Trace

Figures 11.40 and 11.41 show two UDP packets: one generated by the Unix WHOD (Who daemon) and another generated by the RIP protocol.

The WHOD UDP source and destination port numbers are 513. The RIP UDP source and destination port numbers are 520. Both UDP protocol decodes show a nonzero checksum, which means that checksums are in use.

FIGURE **11.40**

*UDP packet for
the WHOD
process.*

```
Packet Number : 2            10:57:22 PM
Length : 130 bytes
ether: ==================== Ethernet Datalink Layer ===================
        Station: 00-00-C0-BB-E8-73 ----> FF-FF-FF-FF-FF-FF
        Type: 0x0800 (IP)
   ip:  ==================== Internet Protocol =====================
        Station:199.245.180.15 ---->199.245.180.255
        Protocol: UDP
        Version: 4
        Header Length (32 bit words): 5
        Precedence: Routine
               Normal Delay, Normal Throughput, Normal Reliability
        Total length: 112
        Identification:   296
        Fragmentation allowed, Last fragment
        Fragment Offset: 0
        Time to Live: 64  seconds
        Checksum: 0x805B(Valid)
  udp:  ==================== User Datagram Protocol ====================
        Source Port: WHO
        Destination Port: WHO
        Length = 92
        Checksum: 0x086A(Valid)
Data:
   0: 01 01 00 00 31 EE A4 F5 00 00 00 00 67 61 74 65  |....1.......gate
  10: 6B 65 65 70 65 72 00 00 00 00 00 00 00 00 00 00  |keeper..........
  20: 00 00 00 00 00 00 00 00 00 00 00 00 00 00 00 00  |................
  30: 00 00 00 00 00 00 00 00 31 EE 7F 85 63 6F 6E 73  |........1...cons
  40: 6F 6C 65 00 72 6F 6F 74 00 00 00 00 31 EE 80 10  |ole.root....1...
  50: 00 00 24 36                                       |..$6
```

FIGURE **11.41**

*UDP packet for
the RIP process.*

```
Packet Number : 4              10:57:57 PM
Length : 70 bytes
ether: ==================== Ethernet Datalink Layer ==================
       Station: 00-00-C0-A2-0F-8E ----> FF-FF-FF-FF-FF-FF
       Type: 0x0800 (IP)
   ip: ===================== Internet Protocol =====================
       Station:144.19.74.201 ---->144.19.255.255
       Protocol: UDP
       Version: 4
       Header Length (32 bit words): 5
       Precedence: Routine
              Normal Delay, Normal Throughput, Normal Reliability
       Total length: 52
       Identification:    30
       Fragmentation allowed, Last fragment
       Fragment Offset: 0
       Time to Live: 64  seconds
       Checksum: 0x0FAC(Valid)
  udp: ===================== User Datagram Protocol ==================
       Source Port: ROUTER
       Destination Port: ROUTER
       Length = 32
       Checksum: 0xFE96(Valid)
  rip: ================= Routing Information Protocol =================
       Command: Response
       Version: 1
       Family ID: IP
          IP Address: 144.19.0.0
          Distance: 1
```

Also, note that the IP Protocol field is set to 17 to indicate that UDP is being encapsulated.

Summary

TCP and UDP are standard Transport Layer protocols that are implemented for IP networks. All nonrouter devices that implement the TCP/IP protocol suite are used to implement TCP. Pure router devices do not implement TCP or UDP. However, most commercial routers provide network management and remote logon capability. These services require the use of the Transport protocols TCP and UDP. In many TCP implementations, UDP is implemented as part of the TCP module, even though UDP is separate from TCP conceptually.

By using TCP and UDP, you can deliver data not just to a remote computer, but to an application process running on the remote computer. These application processes are identified by port numbers. TCP can ensure that data is delivered reliably to the destination by providing a connection-oriented service. UDP, on the other hand, is connectionless and cannot guarantee delivery of data. However, UDP is useful in many applications such as those in which data needs to be sent to a particular application running on a machine, or in situations in which application data needs to be broadcasted or multicasted.

IP Version 6

by Tim Parker

IN THIS CHAPTER

CHAPTER 12

When IP version 4 (the current release) was developed, the use of a 32-bit IP address seemed more than adequate to handle projected use of the Internet. With the accelerated growth rate of the Internet, though, that 32-bit IP address has proven to be a problem. To counter this limit, IP Next Generation, also known as IP version 6 (IPv6), is under development.

Before the finalization of the IP version 6 (IPv6) protocol several proposals were studied. The most popular of these proposals were TUBA (TCP and UDP with Bigger Addresses), CATNIP (Common Architecture for the Internet), and SIPP (Simple Internet Protocol Plus). None of these three meet all the proposed changes for version 6, but a compromise or modification based on several of these proposals was made.

What does IP Next Generation have to offer? This list of changes tells you the main features of IPv6 in a nutshell:

- 128-bit network address instead of 32-bit
- More efficient IP header with extensions for applications and options
- Optional fields added as optional headers after a fixed base header
- A flow label for quality-of-service requirements
- Prevention of intermediate fragmentation of datagrams
- Better support for mobile stations
- Automatic assignment of IPv6 addresses based on MAC addresses
- Built-in security for authentication and encryption

The next sections look at IPv6 in a little more detail to highlight the changes, as well as network programmers and network administrators. In the following section, the IPv6 header format is examined.

IPv6 Datagram

As already mentioned, the header for IP datagrams with version 6 has been modified. The changes are mostly to provide support for the new, longer 128-bit IP addresses and to move optional fields to extension headers. The basic layout of the IPv6 header is shown in Figure 12.1. For comparison, the older IP version 4 header layout is shown in Figure 12.2.

The version number in the IP datagram header is four bits long and holds the release number, which is 6 with IPv6. The Priority field is four bits long and holds a value indicating the datagram's priority. The priority, which is used to define the transmission order, is set first with a broad classification, then with a narrower identifier within each class. (See the upcoming "Priority Classification" section for more information.)

Figure 12.1

The IPv6 header layout.

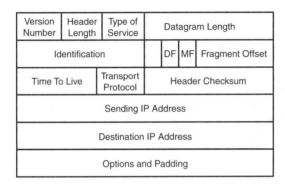

Version Number	Priority	Flow Label		
Payload Length		Next Header	Hop Limit	
Sending IP Address				
Destination Address				

Figure 12.2

The IPv4 header layout.

Version Number	Header Length	Type of Service	Datagram Length		
Identification			DF	MF	Fragment Offset
Time To Live		Transport Protocol	Header Checksum		
Sending IP Address					
Destination IP Address					
Options and Padding					

The Flow Label field is 24 bits long. It is combined with the source machine IP address to provide flow identification for the network. For example, if you are using a Unix workstation on the network, the flow will be different from that of another machine such as a Windows machine. This field can be used to identify flow characteristics and provide some adjustment capabilities. The field can also be used to help identify target machines for large transfers, in which case a cache system becomes more efficient at routing between source and destination. Flow labels are discussed in more detail later in this chapter in the section "Flow Labels."

The Payload Length field is a 16-bit field used to specify the total length of the IP datagram, given in bytes. The total length is exclusive of the IP header itself. The use of a 16-bit field limits the maximum value in this field to 65,535, but there is a provision to send large datagrams using an extension header. (See "IP Extension Headers," later in this chapter.)

The Next Header field is used to indicate which header follows the IP header when other applications want to piggyback on the IP header. Several values have been defined for the Next Header field, as shown in Table 12.1. The Next Header is an 8-bit field that identifies the type of header immediately following the IPv6 basic header. The header that immediately follows can be the protocol type value identifying a transport protocol such as TCP (6) or UDP (17), or it can be a value identifying an IPv6 extension header. IPv6 extension headers are used to specify IPv6 options and other information.

Figure 12.3 shows the use of the Next Header field to specify a TCP message that follows immediately, and extension headers. A Next Header value of 59 indicates no next header; that is, no encapsulation of any other protocol or data.

Figure 12.3

Use of Next Header field.

IPv6 header Next Header = TCP (6)	TCP header + data

Basic IPv6 header encapsulating TCP segment

IPv6 header Next Header = Routing (43)	Routing header Next Header = TCP (6)	TCP header + data

Basic IPv6 header, and routing header encapsulating TCP segment

IPv6 header Next Header = Routing (43)	Routing header Next Header = Fragment (44)	Fragment header Next Header = TCP (6)	fragment of TCP header + data

Basic IPv6 header, routing header, and fragmentation header encapsulating TCP segment

Table 12.1   IP Next Header Field Values

Value	Description
0	Hop-by-hop options
4	IP
6	TCP
17	UDP
43	Routing
44	Fragment
45	Interdomain Routine
46	Resource Reservation
50	Encapsulating Security
51	Authentication
58	ICMP
59	No next header
60	Destination options

The Hop Limit field determines the number of hops that the datagram will travel. With each forwarding, the number is decremented by one. When the Hop Limit field reaches zero, the datagram is discarded. The Hop Limit field prevents old datagrams from circulating around the network endlessly, which could occur if a routing loop is created. The initial value of the Hop Limit is set by the sender. The Hop Limit is similar to the TTL field in the IPv4 header. The difference is that in IPv4, the TTL field is measured in seconds and in IPv6, the Hop Limit is measured in hops. Actually, even in IPv4, the TTL for all practical considerations has the property of a hop count because routers decrease the TTL value by 1 instead of the time it takes to process the datagram. In reality, protocols such as TCP use large sequence number fields (see Chapter 11, "The Transport Protocols") to guard against the resurgence of old packets.

Finally, the sender and destination IP addresses in 128-bit format are placed in the header. The new IP address format is discussed in more detail later in this chapter in the section "128-Bit IP Addresses."

Priority Classification

The Priority Classification field in the IPv6 header first divides the datagram into one of two categories: congestion-controlled and non–congestion-controlled. Non–congestion-controlled datagrams are always routed as a priority over congestion-controlled datagrams. Subclassifications of non–congestion-controlled datagram priorities (priority 8 through 15) are available for use.

If the datagram is congestion-controlled, it is sensitive to congestion problems on the network. If congestion occurs, the datagram can be slowed down and held temporarily in caches until the problem is alleviated. Within the broad congestion-controlled category are several subclasses that further refine the priority of the datagram. The subcategories of congestion-controlled priorities are listed in Table 12.2.

TABLE 12.2   Priorities for Congestion-Controlled Datagrams

Priority	*Description*
0	No priority specified
1	Background traffic
2	Unattended data transfer
3	Unassigned
4	Attended bulk transfer
5	Unassigned
6	Interactive traffic
7	Control traffic

12

IP VERSION 6

Non–congestion-controlled traffic has priorities 8 through 15. Priority values 8 to 15 are used to specify the priority of traffic that does not back off in response to congestion, such as real-time packets being sent at a constant rate.

Examples of each of the primary subcategories may help you see how the datagrams are prioritized. Routing and network management traffic that is considered highest priority is assigned category 7. Interactive applications such as Telnet and Remote X sessions are assigned as interactive traffic (category 6). Transfers that are not time-critical, such as Telnet sessions, but are still controlled by an interactive application like FTP, are assigned as category 4. Email is usually assigned as category 2, whereas low-priority material such as news is set to category 1.

Flow Labels

As mentioned earlier, the Flow Label field new to the IPv6 header can be used to help identify the sender and destination of a number of IP datagrams. By employing caches to handle flows, the datagrams can be routed more efficiently. Not all applications will be able to handle flow labels, in which case the field is set to a value of zero.

A simple example may help show the usefulness of the Flow Label field. Suppose a PC running Windows is connected to a Unix server on another network and sending a large number of datagrams. By setting a specific value of the flow label for all the datagrams in the transmission, the routers along the way to the server can assemble an entry in their routing caches that indicates which way to route each datagram with the same flow label. When subsequent datagrams with the same flow label arrive, the router doesn't have to recalculate the route; it can simply check the cache and extract the saved routing information. This speeds up the passage of the datagrams through each router.

To prevent caches from growing too large or holding stale information, IPv6 stipulates that the cache maintained in a routing device cannot be kept for more than six seconds. If a new datagram with the same flow label is not received within six seconds, the cache entry is removed. To prevent repeated values from the sending machine, the sender must wait six seconds before using the same flow label value for another destination.

IPv6 allows flow labels to be used to reserve a route for time-critical applications. For example, a real-time application that has to send a number of datagrams along the same route and needs as rapid a transmission as possible (such as is needed for video or audio) can establish the route by sending datagrams ahead of time, being careful not to exceed the six-second timeout on the interim routers.

128-Bit IP Addresses

Probably the most important aspect of IPv6 is the ability to provide for longer IP addresses. Version 6 increases the IP address from 32 bits to 128 bits. This will enable an exponential increase in the number of addresses to be assembled.

The new IP addresses support three kinds of addresses: unicast, multicast, and anycast. These are described here:

- *Unicast addresses* are meant to identify a particular machine's interface. This will make it possible for a PC, for example, to have several different protocols in use, each with its own address. Thus, you could send messages specifically to a machine's IP interface address and not the NetBEUI interface address.

- A *multicast address* identifies a group of interfaces, enabling all machines in a group to receive the same packet. This will be similar to multicasts in version 4 IP. Multicast addresses provide more flexibility for defining groups. Your machine's interfaces could belong to several multicast groups.

- An *anycast address* will identify a group of interfaces on a single multicast address. In other words, more than one interface can receive the datagram on the same machine.

We will look at the three types of addresses in a little more detail later in this chapter in the section "Unicast, Multicast, and Anycast Headers."

The IP header also changes considerably with version 6, providing lots more information and flexibility. In addition, the handling of fragmentation and reassembly is changed, to provide more capabilities for IP. Also proposed for IPv6 is an authentication and encryption scheme that can ensure that the data has not been corrupted between sender and receiver, as well as that the sending and receiving machines are who they claim they are.

12

IP VERSION 6

Note

The authentication and encryption scheme is part of the IPSec (IP Security) proposal.

IP Extension Headers

IPv6 has the provision to enable additional optional headers to be added to the IP header. This may be necessary when a simple routing to the destination is not possible, or when special services, such as authentication, are required for the datagram. The additional information required is packaged into an extension header and appended to the IP header.

IPv6 defines several types of extension headers identified by a number that is placed in the Next Header field of the IP header. The currently accepted values and their meanings were shown in Table 12.1. Several extensions can be appended onto one IP header, with each extension's Next Header field indicating the next extension. Extension headers are appended in ascending order, as show in the following:

1. IPv6 header
2. Hop-by-Hop Options header
3. Destination Options header
4. Routing header
5. Fragment header
6. Authentication header
7. Encapsulating Security Payload header
8. Destination Options header
9. Upper-Layer header

The ordering of the extension headers makes it easier for routers to analyze the extensions, stopping the examination when it gets past router-specific extensions.

Hop-by-Hop Headers

Extension type 0 is hop-by-hop, which is used to provide IP options to every machine the datagram passes through. The options included in the hop-by-hop extension have a standard format of a type value, a length, and a value (except for the Pad1 option, which has a single value set to zero and no Length or Value field). Both the Type and Length fields are a single byte in length, whereas the Value field's length is variable and indicated by the length byte.

The three types of hop-by-hop extensions defined so far are Pad1, PadN, and Jumbo Payload. The Pad1 option is a single byte with a value of zero, no length, and no value. It is used to alter the order and position of other options in the header when necessary, dictated usually by an application. The PadN option is similar except there are N zeros placed in the value field, and a calculated value for the length.

The Jumbo Payload extension option is used to handle datagram sizes in excess of 65,535 bytes. The Length field in the IP header is limited to 16 bits, hence the limit of 65,535 for the datagram size. To handle larger datagram lengths, the IP header's Length field is set to zero, which redirects the routers to the extension to pick up a correct length value. The Length field can be defined in the extension header using 32 bits, which yields datagrams in excess of 4 billion bytes!

The Hop-by-Hop Options header is identified by a Next Header value of 0 in the IPv6 header, and has the format shown in Figure 12.4.

FIGURE 12.4

IPv6 Hop-by-Hop Options header.

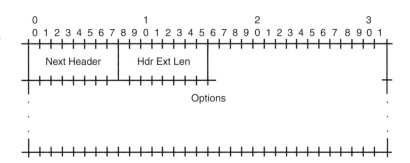

The fields in the Hop-by-Hop Options header have the following meaning:

- Next Header. An 8–bit selector that identifies the type of header immediately following the routing header.
- Hdr Ext Len. An 8–bit unsigned integer. This is the length of the routing header in 8–octet units, excluding the first 8 octets.
- Options. This is a variable–length field, such that the complete Destination Options header length is an integer multiple of 8 octets. The option values are encodes using the Type-Length-Value (TLV) format.

In addition to the Pad1 and PadN options, the Jumbo Payload option is defined for use with the hop-by-hop option (see Figure 12.5).

FIGURE 12.5

IPv6 Jumbo Payload option.

The alignment requirement for the Jumbo Payload option is *4n + 2*. This means that the start of the option must be a multiple of 4 octets plus 2 from the start of the header.

The Jumbo Payload option is used to send IPv6 packets with payloads longer than 65,535 octets. The Jumbo Payload Length field is 32 bits wide and represents the length of the packet in octets, excluding the IPv6 header but including the Hop-by-Hop Options header; it must be greater than 65,535. If a packet is received with a Jumbo Payload option containing a Jumbo Payload Length less than or equal to 65,535, an ICMP Parameter Problem message, Code 0, is sent to the packet's source, pointing to the high-order octet of the invalid Jumbo Payload Length field.

In addition, the Payload Length field in the IPv6 header must be set to zero in every packet that carries the Jumbo Payload option. If a packet is received with a valid Jumbo Payload option present and a non-zero IPv6 Payload Length field, an ICMP Parameter Problem message, Code 0, is sent to the packet's source, pointing to the Option Type field of the Jumbo Payload option.

Routing Headers

A routing extension can be appended onto the IP header when the sending machine wants to control the routing of the datagram instead of leaving it to the routers along the path. This type of routing is called *source routing*. The routing extension, which includes fields for each IP address along the desired route, can be used to give routes to the destination.

The IPv6 routing extension header (see Figure 12.6) is used to specify one or more intermediate routers that an IPv6 datagram must visit on its way to the destination. This header is used to implement the idea of the source routing option that is also specified in IPv4. The IPv6 routing extension header is identified by the Next Header value of 43 in the IPv6 basic header.

FIGURE 12.6

IPv6 routing extension header.

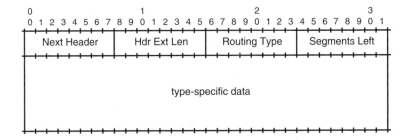

The fields in the IPv6 routing extension header have the following meaning:

- Next Header. This is an 8-bit selector that identifies the type of header that immediately follows the routing header. It can be another IPv6 extension header as part of a chain of IPv6 extension headers, or an upper-layer transport protocol.

- Hdr Ext Len. This is an 8-bit unsigned integer that indicates the length of the routing header in 8-octet units, excluding the first 8 octets.

- Routing Type. This field is an 8-bit identifier of a particular routing header variant. Currently a routing type of 0 is defined in the IPv6 specification (RFC 1883). Other values can be used to identify alternative routing header formats.

- Segments Left. This field is an 8-bit unsigned integer and specifies the number of route segments remaining. The number of remaining route segments is the number of explicitly listed intermediate nodes that still need to be visited before reaching the final destination.

- Type-specific data. This is a variable-length field whose format is determined by the Routing Type. The length of the field is such that the complete routing header length is an integer multiple of 8 octets.

If a node encounters a routing header with an unrecognized Routing Type value, it processes the packet based on the value of the Segments Left field. If Segments Left is zero, the node ignores the routing header and proceeds to process the next header in the packet. The next header is identified by the Next Header field in the routing header. If Segments Left is non-zero, the node must discard the packet and send an ICMP Parameter Problem, Code 0, message to the packet's destination indicated by the Source Address field, and pointing to the unrecognized Routing Type.

Figure 12.7 shows a routing header for Routing Type 0. Note that the first 32 bits of this header are the same as shown in Figure 12.6. The Type-specific data field contains a list of router addresses that allow the source to override the route that might have been otherwise followed by the IPv6 datagram as determined by the routing protocol running at the router.

FIGURE 12.7

Routing Type 0, IPv6 routing header.

The fields in the IPv6 type 0 routing extension header have the following meaning:

- Next Header. An 8-bit selector that identifies the type of header immediately following the routing header.
- Hdr Ext Len. An 8-bit unsigned integer. This is the length of the routing header in 8-octet units, excluding the first 8 octets. For the Type 0 routing header, the Hdr Ext Len is equal to two times the number of addresses in the header, and must be an even number less than or equal to 46.
- Segments Left. An 8-bit unsigned integer. This is the number of route segments remaining. It's maximum legal value is 23 for Route Type 0.
- Reserved. An 8-bit reserved field that is initialized to zero for transmission and ignored on reception.
- Strict/Loose Bit Map. A 24-bit bitmap, numbered 0 to 23, left-to-right. Each bit corresponds to a segment of the route, and indicates whether or not the next destination address must be a neighbor of the preceding address. A bit value of 1 means strict source routing; that is, the next destination address must be a neighbor. A bit value of 0 means loose source routing; that is, the next destination address need not be a neighbor.
- Address[1..n]. This is a vector of 128-bit addresses, numbered 1 to n.

Fragment Headers

The fragment header can be appended to an IP datagram to allow a machine to fragment a large datagram into smaller parts. Part of the design of IPv6 was to prevent subsequent fragmentation, but in some cases fragmentation must be allowed in order to pass the datagram along the network.

Unlike IPv4, fragmentation in IPv6 is performed only by source nodes, and not by routers along a packet's delivery path. An IPv6 source node knows the path MTU size to the destination. IPv6 nodes implement Path MTU Discovery as defined in RFC 1191 on "Path MTU Discovery" to discover the path MTU to the destination.

An IPv6 source will insert the fragment header if it has to send packets that are larger than the path MTU to the destination. The fragment header is identified by a Next Header value of 44 in the immediately preceding header. Figure 12.8 shows the format of the fragment header.

FIGURE 12.8

IPv6 fragment extension header.

The fields in the fragmentation header have the following meanings:

- Next Header. This is an 8-bit selector that identifies the type of header that immediately follows the routing header. It can be another IPv6 extension header as part of a chain of IPv6 extension headers, or an upper-layer transport protocol.

- Reserved. An 8-bit reserved field that is initialized to zero for transmission and ignored on reception.

- Fragment Offset. A 13-bit unsigned integer that indicates the offset, in 8-octet units, of the data following this header. Offsets are measured relative to the start of the Fragmentable Part of the original packet.

- Res. A 2-bit reserved field that is initialized to zero for transmission and ignored on reception.

- M flag. This field is set to 1 for more fragments, and 0 for the last fragment.

- Identification. This is a 32-bit field. For every packet that is to be fragmented, the source node generates an Identification value. The Identification must be different than that of any other fragmented packet sent recently with the same Source Address and Destination Address.

Authentication Headers

The authentication header is used to ensure that no alteration was made to the contents of the datagram, and that the datagram originated at the machine shown in the IP header. By default, IPv6 uses an authentication scheme called Message Digest 5 (MD5). Other authentication schemes can be used as long as both ends of the connection agree on the same scheme.

The authentication header consists of a *security parameters index* (SPI), which, when combined with the destination IP address, defines the authentication scheme. The SPI is followed by authentication data, which with MD5 is 16 bytes long. MD5 starts with a key (padded to 128 bits if it is shorter), then appends the entire datagram. The key is then tagged at the end, and the MD5 algorithm is run on the whole. To prevent problems with hop counters and the authentication header itself altering the values, they are zeroed for the purposes of calculating the authentication value. The MD5 algorithm generates a 128-bit value that is placed in the authentication header. The steps are repeated on the receiving end. Both ends must have the same key value, of course, for the scheme to work.

The datagram contents can be encrypted prior to generating authentication values using the default IPv6 encryption scheme, called *Cipher Block Chaining* (CBC), part of the *Data Encryption Standard* (DES).

12

IP VERSION 6

The fields of the authentication header (see Figure 12.9) have the following meaning:

- Next Header. An 8-bit selector that identifies the type of header immediately following the routing header.
- Length. This field is 8 bits wide and specifies the length of the Authentication Data field in 32-bit words. It's minimum value is 0 words, which is used only in the special case when no authentication algorithm is used.
- Reserved. This field is 16 bits wide and is reserved for future use. It must be set to all zeros by the sender. The value is included in the Authentication Data calculation, but is otherwise ignored by the recipient.
- Security Parameters Index (SPI). This is a 32-bit pseudo-random value identifying the security association for this datagram. The Security Parameters Index value 0 is reserved to indicate that no security association exists. The set of Security Parameters Index values in the range 1 through 255 are reserved to the Internet Assigned Numbers Authority (IANA) for future use. A reserved SPI value will not normally be assigned by IANA unless the use of that particular assigned SPI value is openly specified in an RFC.
- Authentication Data. This is a variable-length field, but is always an integral number of 32-bit words and contains the calculated authentication data for this packet.

FIGURE 12.9

*IPv6 authentica-
tion header.*

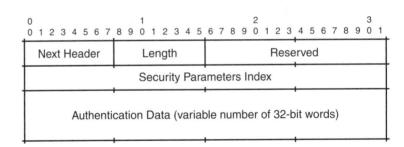

IPv6 Encrypted Security Payload Header

The IPv6 Encrypted Security Payload (ESP) header is used for providing integrity and confidentiality of IP datagrams. It may be used to provide authentication, depending on which is used. Non-repudiation and protection from traffic analysis are not provided by ESP. The IPv6 authentication header can provide non-repudiation if used with certain authentication algorithms.

The IP authentication header can be used in conjunction with ESP to provide authentication. An application requiring integrity and authentication without confidentiality should use the authentication header instead of ESP.

ESP encrypts data to be protected and places the encrypted data in the data portion of the Encapsulating Security Payload. This mechanism may be used to encrypt either a transport-layer segment or an entire IP datagram.

ESP has two modes of operation:

- Tunnel-mode ESP
- Transport-mode ESP

In Tunnel-mode ESP, the original IP datagram is placed in the encrypted portion of the Encapsulating Security Payload and that entire ESP frame is placed within a datagram having unencrypted IP headers. The information in the unencrypted IP headers is used to route the secure datagram from origin to destination. An unencrypted IP routing header might be included between the IP header and the Encapsulating Security Payload.

In Transport-mode ESP, the ESP header is inserted into the IP datagram immediately prior to the transport-layer protocol header. In this mode bandwidth is conserved because there are no encrypted IP headers or IP options.

ESP may appear anywhere after the IP header and before the final transport-layer protocol. The header immediately preceding an ESP header must contain the value 50 in its Next Header field. ESP consists of an unencrypted header followed by encrypted data. The encrypted data includes both the protected ESP header fields and the protected user data, which is either an entire IP datagram or a transport-layer protocol. A high-level diagram of a secure IP datagram is shown in Figure 12.10.

FIGURE 12.10

IPv6 Encrypted Security Payload header.

Layout of ESP header

Format of ESP Header

Encryption and authentication algorithms, and the precise format of the Opaque Transform Data associated with them are known as *transforms*. The ESP format is designed to support new transforms in the future to support new or additional cryptographic algorithms.

The SPI field (refer to Figure 12.10) is a 32-bit pseudo-random value identifying the security association for this datagram. If no security association has been established, the value of the SPI field is set to 0. An SPI is similar to the Security Association Identifier (SAID) used in other security protocols. SPI values from 0 through 255 are reserved by the Internet Assigned Numbers Authority (IANA) for future use. The SPI is the only mandatory transform-independent field.

Multiple IP Addresses per Host

Apart from the potential problem of running out of IP addresses, why are we bothering to develop a radically different IP structure? As you can probably determine from the makeup of the IP headers, a lot of features are embedded in this new version. One of the more important ideas with IPv6 has to be the potential for more than one IP address per host machine.

With today's TCP/IP systems, almost every host has a single IP address. The exceptions tend to be machines that act as gateways, routers, firewalls, proxy servers, and Network Address Translators (NATs). Single-homed machines allow a number of advantages: By counting the number of IP addresses on a network, we know the number of machines there are. With single IP addresses per host, configuring networks is easier than it would be with multiple hosts. For users, remembering a single IP address for FTP and Telnet purposes is easier than remembering a bunch of different addresses. DNS and other services require a single IP address for mapping purposes, and these services will have to be changed with IPv6. But we are moving to a multiple-address per host model with IPv6 for a number of good reasons.

One of the most useful advantages for multiple addresses is on multiuser machines. If you share a workstation with four other users (who may be on diskless workstations or other devices), for example, having a separate IP address for each user would be handy. This would make connecting to their filesystem easier, as well as providing better tracking and billing. Having a single IP address per user allows some of the encryption technologies that are enabled by IPv6 to be used with a different encryption key for each user, enhancing security.

Encryption is an important advantage of multiple host addresses, as well. Consider that most servers today can be reached with a variation of their domain name (ftp.microsoft.com for FTP daemons; http://www.miscrosoft.com for the World Wide Web, for example), and all these services are run from a single host with the same security built into IP. With IPv6, you could have a different IP address for each service (although the names could map to the same alphabetical names for convenience) but could involve different encryption or authentication methods based on the IP address. For example, one address could lead to `http://www.microsoft.com` and involve little encryption and authentication, but another address that maps to `ftp.microsoft.com` could require strict authentication to ensure only valid systems are allowed to transfer files. Although this type of handling based on the service is possible with IP today, IPv6 adds a lot more capability. On the downside, there will need to be many more addresses mapped to names.

TCP port numbers can be added more easily with IPv6 than with the current IP. For example, if you want to reach TCP port 14 on a server, you need to address the system with the IP address and port number (such as 205.150.89.1:14). As a user, you need to know the port number to specify it. The TCP port could easily be resolved with multiple addresses in IPv6. One address could lead to one FTP port with wider protection than a second address leading to another FTP port, for example.

Multiple addresses work well when subnetworks are merged. If your company has two LANs, one for research and development and another for management, and you happen to manage the R&D group, your machine needs an IP address on both networks. Your machine may act as a type of router in some cases, and you often have to specify which LAN you want to work with. With IPv6, IP addresses can be assigned so that you can send information on both LANs at once, or can move data between the two without much hassle (essentially eliminating a router).

Unicast, Multicast, and Anycast Headers

Unicast addresses are supported in a number of variations, including a global unicast address that goes to all providers, a site-specific unicast address for a particular network, and a version of unicast that is compatible with IPv4 machines. The specifications for IPv6 allow for other types of unicast addresses in the future, as they are needed.

The global unicast address is used for connecting to every provider on the Internet. The format of this global, or provider-based, unicast address is shown in Figure 12.11.

In Figure 12.11, the first three bits are set to 010 and identify the unicast as a provider-based type. The REG ID (Registry ID) field is the Internet address registry that assigns the Provider ID (PROV ID), which subsequently grants IP addresses to customers

(PROV ID is the ISP in most cases). SUBSC ID allows multiple subscribers (customers) to be identified in the provider's network, and SUBNET ID allows a specific address to be used. Finally, INTF ID is the interface ID, which can be used to identify a particular subscriber interface.

FIGURE **12.11**

The provider-based unicast header layout.

010	REG ID	PROV ID	SUBSC ID	SUBNET ID	INTF ID

A site-specific, or local-user, unicast address is used only within a network or subnetwork, so it needs less information. The header for a local-user unicast is shown in Figure 12.12. The INTF ID is an interface ID on the network or subnetwork. A slight variation of the local-user unicast address adds a Subnet ID to the header, removing space from the INT ID field. When used, the Subnet ID field can be used to specify a particular subnet on a network.

FIGURE **12.12**

The local-user unicast header layout.

1111111010	0	INTF ID

Finally, the unicast address with embedded IPv4 addresses is shown in Figure 12.13. This has the IPv4 address appended to the end of the unicast header and can be used by the older version of IP.

FIGURE **12.13**

The embedded IPv4 unicast header layout.

80 Bits	16 Bits	32 Bits
000...000	FFFF	IP v4 Address

Anycast addresses use the same layout as unicast headers, and in most cases cannot be distinguished from unicast broadcasts.

Multicast headers have the layout shown in Figure 12.14.

FIGURE **12.14**

The multicast header layout.

1111111	OOOT (Flags)	Scope	Group ID

The leading eight bits of 1s identify the header as a multicast. The Flags field has four bits that lead with three zeros (reserved bits for future use) and a trailing bit that can be either a zero for a permanently assigned multicast address or a one for a non-permanent multicast address. The Scope field is four bits that can be used to limit the multicast reach. Legal values for the Scope field are shown in Table 12.3. Finally, the Group ID identifies a particular multicast group.

TABLE 12.3   Legal Values for the Multicast Scope Field

Value	Description
0	Reserved
1	Node-local
2	Link-local
3,4	Unassigned
5	Site-local
6,7	Unassigned
8	Organization-local
9,A,B,C,D	Unassigned
E	Global
F	Reserved

Transition from IPv4 to IPv6

Although IPv6 is technically superior to the current version of IP (IPv4), potential problems exist with implementing IPv6 worldwide. Simply switching from the old IP version to the newer on a single date is impossible, so the rollout must be managed in such a manner as to provide compatibility for both versions for a while. Because the establishment of IPv6 worldwide is expected to take several years, transition becomes a very important issue.

One problem with changing from IPv4 to IPv6 is the simple fact that IPv4 is embedded in many layers of the TCP/IP suite and within many applications as well. To switch over to IPv6, every application, driver, and TCP stack that uses IP has to be converted. This amounts to hundreds of thousands of changes, involving millions of lines of code. Spread over thousands of vendors, it is unlikely that all will change their code within a specific timespan. Again, this means that IPv4 and IPv6 must coexist for quite a while.

All current machines (hosts computers, routers, bridges, and so on) use IPv4. As machines are converted to run IPv6 (either through a software or hardware update), all these machines will likely need two sets of IP software, one for the old version and one for the new release. In some cases, that's going to be very difficult to implement because of memory or performance problems, so some devices may have to be one version of IP or the other (or be replaced with more powerful devices).

Conversion software must be developed for applications that can't or won't be updated to IPv6. For example, some devices and applications that communicate using IPv4 and yet need to talk to IPv6 systems will need to have a conversion or translation application sitting between the two parts. This adds more overhead to the system and slows down performance, but it may be the only way to handle some legacy software and hardware.

Translation between IPv4 and IPv6 may not seem like a big problem, but it could be. The primary issue is header translation, where even the slightest problem causes loss of data. IPv6 is based on IPv4, but the headers are very different. Any information in an IPv6 header that is not supported in IPv4 (such as priority classification) will be lost when converted. Conversely, a packet leaving an IPv4 host that is converted to IPv6 will have a lot of information missing from the header, some of it potentially important.

Address mapping (converting IPv4 IP addresses to IPv6 IP addresses and vice versa) will require some special handling. If you have a host that has several IP addresses under IPv6 but only one IP address under IPv4, a converter, router, or other forwarding device that converts from one version of IP to another must have a large table of mappings. This will become impractical in large organizations, and when converting from IPv4 to IPv6, may result in incorrect destinations. An IPv4 IP address can be embedded in an IPv6 header, but this may cause routing problems for IPv6-based systems.

Some TCP/IP services are going to need drastic overhauls for the change to IPv6. DNS, for example, holds a mapping of common names to IP addresses. When IPv6 rolls out, DNS is going to have to handle both versions of IP, as well as resolve multiple IP addresses for each host. You may have a PC with 10 IP addresses under IPv6 (different IP addresses for different services on your machine, for example). Broadcasting is a problem with IPv4 at the moment because there are many times when a LAN- or WAN-wide broadcast is sent with IPv4 (for example, ARP uses data-link layer broadcast). IPv6 reduces broadcasting because of the multicast feature, which is designed to permit a multicast to travel on a LAN or WAN only once. Resolving the two broadcast systems during a conversion is again going to be a problem.

There's a lot more involved in converting an entire network infrastructure from IPv4 to IPv6. A lot of technical issues need to be worked on to provide maximum flexibility as companies and networks convert from one version of IP to another. The process is not easy, and is expected to take years, but the end result should be a network based entirely on IPv6 (although it seems likely that many older devices will not be able to upgrade to IPv6, and hence will need a translator of some sort). For most people, the change from IPv4 to IPv6 will be transparent: The network administrators will take care of the conversion for you. For those involved in network management, though, the conversion from IPv4 to IPv6 promises to be an experience.

Summary

Although IPv6 is going to take a number of years to gain widespread usage, it will eventually happen. Whether you make a change all at once or employ a gradual change-over, eventually you will need to implement IPv6. For most users, especially those connecting through an ISP, the actual time of changeover is quite a long way away. For companies, though, the advantages IPv6 offers will tend to make the changeover faster. Compatibility between IPv6 and IPv4 is built in, so there will be support for the older IP system for quite a while.

Internetworking with IP

PART

IV

Routing in IP Networks

by Mark A. Sportack

In This Chapter

One of the most critical functions in an interconnected IP network is routing. *Routing* is the process of discovering, comparing, and selecting paths through the network to any destination IP address. Typically, the routing function is embodied in special-purpose devices called *routers*. Technological advances, however, are rapidly blurring the distinctions between traditional routers, LAN switches, and even network-attached hosts. Today, all three types of devices are capable of discovering, comparing, and selecting routes. Thus, routing must be regarded as a function rather than as a physical device.

The essence of routing exists in the form of highly specialized network protocols that enable routers (regardless of which type of physical device that may be) to perform their vital functions. These functions include

- Sharing information about locally connected hosts and networks
- Comparing potentially redundant paths
- Converging upon an agreement of a network's topology

Examining the mechanics of these basic functions in an IP network will provide the context for a more in-depth examination of three of the more commonly encountered dynamic IP routing protocols, which is provided in Chapters 14 through 16.

The Fundamentals of Routing

Routers can route in two basic ways. They can use preprogrammed *static* routes, or they can dynamically calculate routes using any one of a number of dynamic routing protocols. Dynamic routing protocols are used by routers to discover routes. Routers then forward packets (or datagrams) over those routes. Routers that are statically programmed are incapable of discovering routes; they lack any mechanism for communicating routing information with other routers. Statically programmed routers can only forward packets using routes defined by a network administrator.

In addition to static programming of routes, there are two basic categories of dynamic routing protocols:

- Distance-vector
- Link-state

The primary differences between these types of dynamic routing protocols lie in the way they discover and calculate new routes to destinations.

Two Functional Classes of Dynamic Routing Protocols

Many ways exist to classify routing protocols, including by operational characteristics such as their field of use, the number of redundant routes to each destination supported, and so on. This book classifies routing protocols by the way they discover and calculate routes. However, referencing them by their field of use is still sometimes useful; that is, categorizing them by the role they perform in an internetwork. For example, there are two functional classes of dynamic routing protocols: Interior Gateway Protocols (IGPs) and Exterior Gateway Protocols (EGPs).

Perhaps the easiest way to explain this is that IGPs are used *within* autonomous systems, such as intranets, whereas EGPs are used *between* autonomous systems. An autonomous system is a collection of networks that is self-contained, usually administered by a single administrator or group of administrators. *Border Gateway Protocol* (BGP—an EGP) is the protocol used to calculate routes across the Internet. The Internet, from a routing perspective, is nothing more than a backbone transport for a global collection of privately owned and operated autonomous systems.

The specific protocols covered in this book are identified as either IGPs or EGPs.

13

ROUTING IN IP
NETWORKS

Static Routing

Static, or preprogrammed, routes are the simplest form of routing. The tasks of discovering routes and propagating them throughout a network are left to the internetwork's administrator(s).

A router that is programmed for static routing forwards packets out of predetermined ports. After the relationship between a destination address and a router port is configured, there is no longer any need for routers to attempt route discovery or even communicate information about routes to that destination. It is possible, however, for a router to use static routes for certain destinations and dynamically route to others.

There are many benefits to using static routes. For instance, statically programmed routes can make for a more secure network: There can be only a single path into, and out of, a network connected with a statically defined route. That is, of course, unless multiple static routes are defined.

Another benefit is that static routing is much more resource-efficient. It uses far less bandwidth across the transmission facilities, doesn't waste any router CPU cycles trying to calculate routes, and requires less memory. In some networks, you might even be able to use smaller, less expensive routers by using static routes. Despite these benefits, there are some inherent limitations to static routing of which you must be aware.

Static routes are sometimes used for small networks whose topology seldom changes. An example of such a network is two sites connected by a point-to-point link.

Static routes can also be used for troubleshooting and temporary fixes to routing problems. For instance, if you know that the routing entries in a table are corrupt, overriding these incorrect entries with static routes that contain the correct route paths might be useful.

Generally speaking, mixing static routing with dynamic routing is not a good idea. Doing so can cause static routes to be in conflict with dynamically computed routes. In this case, static routes will be used even if the dynamic routes are more efficient.

Drawbacks to Static Routing

In the event of a network failure, or other source of topology change, the onus is on the network administrator to manually accommodate the change. Figure 13.1 illustrates this point.

FIGURE 13.1

A simple internetwork with static routes.

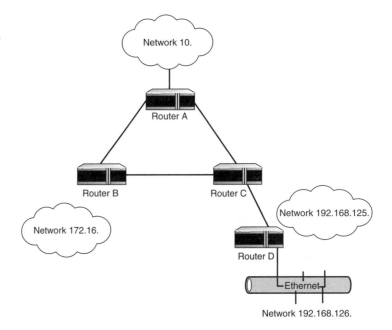

In this simple example, the networks' administrators have collaborated on a scheme for distributing routing information that they believe will minimize their workload as well as network traffic loads. The internetwork is relatively small, consisting of three different networks, one of which supports a small, isolated network. Such networks are called *stub* networks. Each network uses its own address space and a different dynamic routing protocol. Given the innate incompatibility of the three different routing protocols, the administrators chose not to redistribute routing information between their networks. Rather, they aggregated the routes into network numbers, and statically defined paths for them. The routing tables of the three gateway routers are summarized in Table 13.1. Router D connects a small, stub network to the other networks. As such, this router uses its serial port as a default gateway for all packets addressed to any IP address that does not belong to 192.168.126.

TABLE 13.1 Statically Defined Routes

Router	Destination	Next Hop
A	172.16.0.0	B
A	192.168.125.0	C
A	192.168.126.0	C
B	10.0.0.0	A
B	192.168.125.0	C
B	192.168.126.0	C
C	10.0.0.0	A
C	172.16.0.0	B
C	192.168.126.0	D

13

ROUTING IN IP
NETWORKS

In this scenario, Router A will forward all packets addressed to any hosts within the 172.16 network address space to Router B. Router A will also forward all packets addressed to hosts within networks 192.168.125 and 192.168.126 to Router C. Router B will forward all packets addressed to any hosts within the 192.168.125 and 192.168.126 address spaces to Router C. Router B will forward packets addressed to hosts within network 10 to Router A. Router C forwards all packets destined for network 10 to Router A, and 172.16 to Router B. Additionally, Router C forwards packets addressed to 192.168.126 to Router D—its stub network. This network is a stub because it is literally a dead-end in the network. There is only one way in and one way out. This small network is completely dependent upon its link to Router C, and Router C itself, for connectivity to all the internetworked hosts.

In this example, a failure will result in unreachable destinations despite the fact that an alternate path is available for use. In Figure 13.2, the transmission facility between Gateway Routers A and C has failed.

FIGURE 13.2

A link failure in a statically programmed internetwork can disrupt communications.

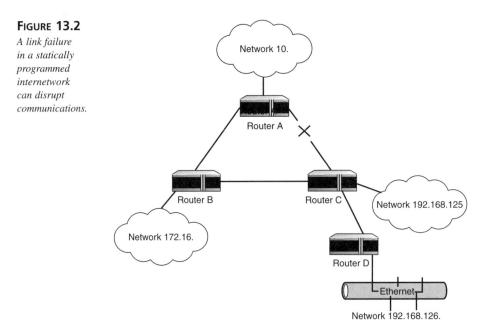

The effect of this failure is that end systems in networks 10 and 192.168 are unable to communicate with each other, even though a valid route exists through Router B! The effects of this type of failure on the routing tables are summarized in Table 13.2.

TABLE 13.2 Static Routes with a Failed Link

Router	Destination	Next Hop
A	172.16.0.0	B
A	192.168.125.0	C—unreachable
A	192.168.126.0	C—unreachable
B	10.0.0.0	A
B	192.168.125.0	C
B	192.168.126.0	C
C	10.0.0.0	A—unreachable
C	172.16.0.0	B

The lack of any dynamic mechanism prevents Routers A and C from recognizing the link failure. They are not using a routing protocol that would otherwise discover and test the qualities of the links to known destinations. Consequently, Routers A and C cannot discover the alternate path through Router B. Although this route is valid and usable, their programming prevents them from discovering, or using, it. This situation will remain constant until the network administrator(s) takes corrective action manually.

Benefits of Static Routing

At this point, you might be wondering what possible benefit there is in statically defined routes. Static routing is good only for very small networks that have a single path to any given destination. In such cases, static routing can be the most efficient routing mechanism because it doesn't consume bandwidth trying to discover routes or communicate with other routers.

As networks grow larger, and add redundant paths to destinations, static routing becomes a labor-intensive liability. Any changes in the availability of routers or transmission facilities in the WAN must be manually discovered and programmed in. WANs that feature more complex topologies that offer multiple potential paths absolutely require dynamic routing. Attempts to use static routing in complex, multipath WANs will defeat the purpose of having that route redundancy.

There are instances where statically defined routes would be desirable, even in large or complex networks. For example, static routes can be configured to enhance security. Your company's connection to the Internet could have a statically defined route to a security server. No ingress would be possible without having first passed whatever authentication mechanisms the security server provides.

Alternatively, statically defined routes might be extremely useful in building extranet connections using IP to other companies with which your employer does a lot of business. Lastly, static routes might be the best way to connect small locations with stub networks to your WAN. The point is that static routes can be quite useful. You just need to understand what they can and can't do.

Distance-Vector Routing

In routing based on distance-vector algorithms, also sometimes called Bellman-Ford algorithms, the algorithms periodically pass copies of their routing tables to their immediate network neighbors. Each recipient adds a *distance vector*, or its own distance "value," to the table and forwards it on to their immediate neighbors. This process occurs omnidirectionally between immediately neighboring routers. This step-by-step process results in each router learning about other routers, and developing a cumulative perspective of network "distances."

13

ROUTING IN IP
NETWORKS

The cumulative table is then used to update each router's routing tables. When completed, each router has learned approximate information about the "distances" to networked resources. It does not learn anything specific about other routers, or the network's actual topology.

Drawbacks to Distance-Vector Routing

Distance-vector routing can, under certain circumstances, actually create routing problems for distance-vector protocols. For example, a failure or other change in the network requires some time for the routers to *converge* on a new understanding of the network's topology. During the convergence process, the network may be vulnerable to inconsistent routing, and even infinite loops. Safeguards exist to contain many of these risks, but the fact remains that the network's performance is at risk during the convergence process. Thus, older distance-vector protocols that are slow to converge may not be appropriate for large, complex WANs.

Even in smaller networks, distance-vector routing protocols may be problematic at worst, or suboptimal, at best. This is because the simplicity that is this genre's strength can also be a source of weakness. For example, Figure 13.3 presents an internetwork with specific geographic locations.

Figure 13.3

An internetwork using a distance-vector routing protocol.

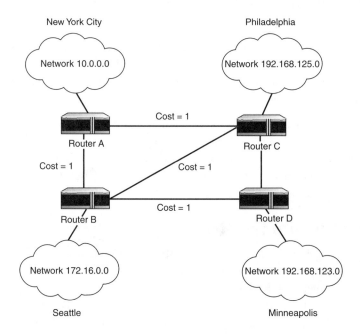

In this example, network 1 is located in New York, 2 is in Seattle, 3 is in Philadelphia, and 4 is in Minneapolis. The distance-vector routing protocol uses a statically assigned cost of 1 for each hop, regardless of the distance of the link or even its bandwidth. Table 13.3 summarizes the number of hops to each of the destination network numbers. In this table, you will notice that routers do not have to create separate entries in their routing tables for every known end-system. Your network can perform such host-based routing, but it will likely perform much better if you perform only network-based routing. Network-based routes are those routes based on just the network portion of an IP address; the host identifier is truncated.

In theory, the same path can be used to get to all the hosts or end-systems on any given network. Thus, nothing is gained by creating separate entries for each host address.

TABLE 13.3   The Number of Hops with the Distance-Vector Protocol

Router	Destination	Next Hop	Number of Hops to Destination
A	172.16.0.0	B	1
A	192.168.125.0	C	1
A	192.168.253.0	B or C	2
B	10.0.0.0	A	1
B	192.168.125.0	C	1
B	192.168.253.0	D	1
C	10.0.0.0	A	1
C	172.16.0.0	B	1
C	192.168.253.0	D	1
D	10.0.0.0	B or C	2
D	172.16.0.0	B	1
D	192.168.125.0	C	1

13

ROUTING IN IP
NETWORKS

In any internetwork with redundant routes, using a distance-vector protocol rather than static routes is better. This is because distance-vector routing protocols can automatically detect and correct most failures in the network. Unfortunately, they aren't perfect. For instance, consider the routing table entries for Gateway Router A. This is the New York Gateway. From its perspective, the Minneapolis Gateway is two hops away, regardless of whether it goes through Philadelphia or Seattle. This router would be indifferent to accessing Minneapolis through either Philadelphia or Seattle.

If all the variables in the network were held constant, (including such things as traffic levels, the bandwidth of each link, and even transmission technology) the geographically shortest path would incur the least amount of propagation delay. Thus, logic dictates taking the shorter route, through Philadelphia. In reality, such logic is beyond the abilities of simple distance-vector protocols. Distance-vector protocols aren't exactly limited by this because propagation delay is often the least significant of the factors driving the performance of a route. Bandwidth and traffic levels can both have much more noticeable effects on the performance of a network.

Benefits of Distance-Vector Routing

Distance-vector protocols are generally very simple protocols that are easy to understand, configure, maintain, and use. Consequently, they are quite useful in very small networks that have few, if any, redundant paths and no stringent network performance requirements. The epitome of the distance-vector routing protocol is *Routing Information Protocol* (RIP). RIP uses a single distance metric to determine the next best path to take for any given packet: cost. RIP has been widely used for decades, and has only recently warranted updating. For more information on RIP, see Chapter 15, "Routing Information Protocol (RIP)."

Link-State Routing

Link-state routing algorithms, known cumulatively as *Shortest Path First* (SPF) protocols, maintain a complex database of the network's topology. Unlike distance-vector protocols, link-state protocols develop and maintain a full knowledge of the network's routers, as well as how they interconnect. This is achieved via the exchange of *Link-State Advertisements* (LSAs) with other routers in a network.

Each router that has exchanged LSAs then constructs a topological database using all received LSAs. An SPF algorithm is then used to compute reachability to networked destinations. This information is used to update the routing table. This process is capable of discovering changes in the network topology that were caused by component failure or network growth.

In fact, the LSA exchange is triggered by an event in the network, rather than running periodically. This can greatly expedite the convergence process because there is no need to wait for a series of arbitrary timers to expire before the networked routers can begin to converge!

If the internetwork depicted in Figure 13.3 were to use a link-state routing protocol, the concerns about connectivity between New York and Minneapolis would be rendered moot. Depending on the actual protocol employed, and the metrics selected, it is highly likely that the routing protocol would be able to discriminate between the two paths and try to use the best one. The summarized contents of the gateways' routing tables are presented in Table 13.4.

TABLE 13.4 Hop Counts in a Link-State Network

Router	Destination	Next Hop	Number of Hops to Destination
A	172.16.0.0	B	1
A	192.168.125.0	C	1
A	192.168.253.0	B	2
A	192.168.253.0	C	2
B	10.0.0.0	A	1
B	192.168.125.0	C	1
B	192.168.253.0	D	1
C	10.0.0.0	A	1
C	172.16.0.0	B	1
C	192.168.253.0	D	1
D	10.0.0.0	B	2
D	10.0.0.0	C	2
D	172.16.0.0	B	1
D	192.168.125.0	C	1

13

ROUTING IN IP
NETWORKS

As is evident in this table's routing entries for the New York-to-Minneapolis routes, a link-state protocol would remember both routes. Some link-state protocols may even provide a means to assess the performance capabilities of these two routes, and bias toward the better performing one. If the better performing path, for example the route through Philadelphia, were to experience operational difficulties of any kind (including congestion or component failure), the link-state routing protocol would detect this change and begin forwarding packets through Seattle.

Drawbacks to Link-State Routing

Despite all of its features and flexibility, link-state routing raises two potential concerns:

- During the initial discovery process, link-state routing protocols can flood the network's transmission facilities, thereby significantly decreasing the network's ability to transport data. This performance degradation is temporary, but can be very noticeable. Whether or not this flooding process will impede a network's performance noticeably will depend on two things: the amount of available bandwidth, and the number of routers that must exchange routing information. Flooding in large networks with relatively small links (such as low-bandwidth DLCIs on a Frame Relay network) will be much more noticeable than a similar exercise on a small network with large-sized links (such as T3s).

- Link-state routing is both memory and processor intensive. Consequently, more fully configured routers are required to support link-state routing than distance-vector routing. This can tend to increase the cost of the routers configured for link-state routing.

These flaws are hardly fatal in the link-state approach to routing. The potential performance impacts of both can be addressed, and resolved, through foresight, planning, and engineering.

Benefits of Link-State Routing

The link-state approach to dynamic routing can be quite useful in networks of any size. In a well-designed network, a link-state routing protocol will enable your network to gracefully weather the effects of unexpected topological change. Using events, such as changes, to drive updates (rather than fixed-interval timers) enables convergence to begin that much quicker after a topological change.

The overheads of the frequent, time-driven updates of a distance-vector routing protocol are also avoided. This allows more bandwidth to be used for routing traffic instead of network maintenance, provided you design your network properly.

A side benefit of the bandwidth efficiency of link-state routing protocols is that they facilitate network scalability better than either static routes or distance-vector protocols. Taking into account the limitations of static routes and distance-vector protocols, it is easy to see that link-state routing is best in larger, more complicated networks or in networks that must be highly scalable. It may be challenging to initially configure a link-state protocol in a large network, but it is well worth the effort in the long run. For more information on link-state routing, see Chapter 16, "Open Shortest Path First (OSPF)."

Convergence in an IP Network

One of the most fascinating aspects of routing is a concept known as *convergence*. Quite simply, whenever there is a change in a network's topology, or shape, all the routers in that network must develop a new understanding of the changed network topology. This process is both collaborative and independent; the routers share information with each other, but must independently calculate the impacts of the topology change on their own routes. Because they must mutually develop an agreement of the new topology independently from different perspectives, they are said to *converge* upon this consensus.

Convergence is necessary because routers are intelligent devices capable of making their own routing decisions. This is simultaneously a source of strength and vulnerability. Under normal operating conditions, this independent and distributed intelligence is a tremendous advantage. During changes in the network's topology, the process of converging on a new consensus of the network's shape may actually introduce instability and routing problems.

Accommodating Topological Changes

Unfortunately, the independent nature of routers can also be a source of vulnerability whenever a change occurs in the network's topology. Such changes, by their very nature, change a network's topology. Figure 13.4 illustrates how a change in the network is, de facto, a change in its topology.

FIGURE 13.4

A four-gateway internetwork.

Figure 13.4 features another fairly simple, four-node internetwork with some route redundancy. The routing tables of the four routers are summarized in Table 13.5. For the sake of this example, consider this table to be preconvergence routing table information.

TABLE 13.5 Preconvergence Routing Table Contents

Router	*Destination*	*Next Hop*	*Number of Hops to Destination*
A	172.16.0.0	B	1
A	192.168.125.0	C	1
A	192.168.253.0	B or C	2
B	10.0.0.0	A	1
B	192.168.125.0	A or D	2
B	192.168.253.0	D	1
C	10.0.0.0	A	1
C	172.16.0.0	A or D	2
C	192.168.253.0	D	1
D	10.0.0.0	B or C	2
D	172.16.0.0	B	1
D	192.168.125.0	C	1

If packets sent by Router C to server 192.168.253.2 suddenly become undeliverable, it is likely that an error occurred somewhere in the network. This could have been caused by a seemingly infinite number of different, specific failures. Some of the more common suspects include

- The server has failed completely (due to a hardware, software, or electrical failure).
- The LAN connection to the server has failed.
- Router D has experienced a total failure.
- Router D's serial interface port to Router C has failed.
- The transmission facility between Gateway Routers C and D has failed.
- Router C's serial interface port to Router D has failed.

Obviously, the new network topology can't be determined until the exact location of the failure has been identified. Similarly, the routers can't attempt to route around the problem until the failure location has been isolated. If any of the first two scenarios occurred, server 192.168.253.2 would be completely unavailable to all the users of the internetwork, regardless of any route redundancy that may have been built in to the network.

Similarly, if router D had failed completely, all the LAN-attached resources at that location would be isolated from the rest of the network. If, however, the failure was either a partial failure of that router, or elsewhere in the network, there might still be a way to reach hosts located within network 192.168.255. Finding a new route to network 192.168.255 requires the network's routers to recognize, and agree, on what piece of the network failed. Subtracting this component from the network, in effect, changes the network's topology.

To continue with the example, assume that Router D's serial interface port to Router C has failed. This renders the link between C and D unusable. The new network topology is illustrated in Figure 13.5.

FIGURE 13.5

The link between routers C and D is unusable.

Routers using a dynamic routing protocol would quickly determine that server 192.168.253.2 was unreachable through their current, preferred route. Individually, none of the routers would be able to determine where the actual failure occurred, nor could they determine whether any viable alternate routes still existed. However, by sharing information with each other, a new composite picture of the network can be developed.

Note

For the purposes of this chapter, this example uses an intentionally generic method of convergence. More specific details about each routing protocol's convergence characteristics are presented in Chapters 14 through 16.

The routing protocol used in this internetwork is relatively simple. It limits each router to just exchanging routing information with its immediate neighbors, although it supports the recording of multiple routes per destination. Table 13.6 summarizes the pairs of immediately adjacent routers illustrated in Figure 13.5.

TABLE 13.6   Routers That Share Routing Information with Immediate Neighbors

Router	*A*	*B*	*C*	*D*
A	—	yes	yes	no
B	yes	—	no	yes
C	yes	no	—	yes
D	no	yes	yes	—

The entries in Table 13.6 that contain the word *yes* indicate a physically adjacent pair of routers that would exchange routing information. The entries that contain a dash denote the same router: A router cannot be adjacent to itself. Lastly, those entries that contain the word *no* indicate nonadjacent routers that cannot directly exchange routing information. Such routers must rely upon their adjacent neighbors for updates about destinations on nonadjacent routers.

From this table, it is apparent that, because they are not directly connected to each other, Routers A and D must rely on Routers B and C for information about each other's destinations. Similarly, Routers B and C must rely on Routers A and D for information about each other's destinations.

Figure 13.6 pictorially demonstrates this sharing of routing information between immediate neighbors.

The important implication in this scenario is that, because not every router is immediately adjacent to every other router, more than one routing update may be required to fully propagate new routing information that accommodates the failed link. Thus, accommodating topological change is an iterative and communal process.

For the sake of simplicity, assume that convergence occurs within two routing table updates in this example. During the first iteration, the routers are starting to converge on a new understanding of their topology. Routers C and D, due to the unusable link between them, cannot exchange routing information. Consequently, they invalidate this route, and all destinations that use it. The contents of the four routers' routing tables *during* the convergence process are summarized in Table 13.7. Please note that the contents of some routing tables may reflect the mistaken belief that the link between Routers C and D is still valid.

FIGURE 13.6

Immediate neighbors sharing routing data.

Autonomous System #1
Network 10.0.0.0

Autonomous System #3
Network 192.168.125.0

Router A

Router C

Router B

Router D

Ethernet

Autonomous System #2
Network 172.16.0.0

Server 192.168.253.2

User Desktop

= Exchange of Routing Information

TABLE 13.7   Midconvergence Routing Table Contents

Gateway Router	Destination	Next Hop	Number of Hops to Destination
A	172.16.0.0	B	1
A	192.168.125.0	C	1
A	192.168.253.0	B or C	2
B	10.0.0.0	A	1
B	192.168.125.0	A or D	2
B	192.168.253.0	D	1
C	10.0.0.0	A	1
C	172.16.0.0	A only (D failed)	2
C	192.168.253.0	D—invalid route	not reachable
D	10.0.0.0	B or C	2
D	172.16.0.0	B	1
D	192.168.125.0	C—invalid route	not reachable

In Table 13.7, Routers C and D have invalidated the route between them. Routers A and B, however, still believe that their routes through this link are viable. They must await a routing update from either Router C or D before they can recognize the change in the internetwork's topology.

Table 13.8 contains the contents of the four routers' routing tables *after* they have converged on a new topology. Remember, this depiction of the convergence process is intentionally generic, and not indicative of any particular routing protocol's mechanics.

TABLE 13.8   Postconvergence Routing Table Contents

Router	Destination	Next Hop	Number of Hops to Destination
A	172.16.0.0	B	1
A	192.168.125.0	C	1
A	192.168.253.0	B only	2
B	10.0.0.0	A	1
B	192.168.125.0	A only	2
B	192.168.253.0	D	1
C	10.0.0.0	A	1
C	172.16.0.0	A only	2
C	192.168.253.0	A	3
D	10.0.0.0	B only	2
D	172.16.0.0	B	1
D	192.168.125.0	B only	3

As evident in Table 13.8, all the routers in the internetwork eventually agree that the link between C and D is unusable, but that destinations in each autonomous system are still reachable via an alternate route.

Convergence Time

It is virtually impossible for all routers in a network to simultaneously detect a topology change. In fact, depending on the routing protocol in use, as well as numerous other factors, there can be a considerable time delay before all the routers in that network reach a consensus, or agreement, on what the new topology is. This delay is referred to as *convergence time*. The important thing to remember is that convergence is not immediate. The only uncertainty is how much time is required for convergence to occur.

Some factors that can exacerbate the time delay inherent in convergence include

- A router's distance (in hops) from the point of change.
- The number of routers in the network that use dynamic routing protocols.
- Bandwidth and traffic load on communications links.
- A router's load.
- Traffic patterns vis-à-vis the topological change.
- The routing protocol used.

The effects of some of these factors can be minimized through careful network engineering. For example, a network can be engineered to minimize the load on any given router or communications link. Other factors, such as the number of routers in the network, must be accepted as risks inherent in a network's design. However, it may be possible to engineer the network such that fewer routers need to converge. By using static routes to interconnect stubs to the network, you reduce the number of routers that must converge. This directly reduces convergence times. Given these factors, clearly the two keys to minimizing convergence times are

- Selection of a routing protocol that can calculate routes efficiently.
- Designing the network properly.

Calculating Routes in IP Networks

As demonstrated through the examples in the preceding section, convergence is absolutely critical to a network's ability to respond to operational fluctuations. The key factor in convergence is communications between the routers in the network. Routing protocols are responsible for providing this function. Specifically, these protocols are designed to enable routers to share information about routes to the various destinations within the network.

Unfortunately, all routing protocols are not created equal. In fact, one of the best ways to assess the suitability of a routing protocol is to evaluate its abilities to calculate routes and converge relative to other routing protocols. It should be obvious from the preceding list of factors that convergence times may be difficult for you to calculate with any degree of certainty. Your router vendor may be able to assist you with this process, even if it only provides you with general estimates.

A routing protocol's convergence ability is a function of its ability to calculate routes. The efficacy of a routing protocol's route calculation is based upon several factors:

- Whether or not the protocol calculates, and stores, multiple routes to each destination.
- The manner in which routing updates are initiated.
- The metrics used to calculate distances or costs.

Each of these specific functions, and how they contribute to the overall operating efficiency of a routing protocol, is examined in the following sections.

Storing Multiple Routes

Some routing protocols attempt to improve their operational efficiency by recording only a single route (ideally, the best route) to each known destination. The drawback to this approach is that, when a topology change occurs, each router must calculate a new route through the network for the impacted destinations.

Other protocols accept the processing overheads that accompany larger routing table sizes, and store multiple routes to each destination. Under normal operating conditions, maintaining multiple routes enables the router to balance traffic loads across multiple links. If, or when, a topology change occurs, the routers already have alternate routes to the impacted destinations in their routing tables. Having an alternate route already mapped out does not necessarily accelerate the convergence process. It does, however, enable networks to more gracefully sustain topology changes.

Initiating Updates

Some routing protocols use the passing of time to initiate routing updates. Others are event-driven. That is, they are initiated whenever a topological change is detected. Holding all other variables constant, event-driven updates will result in shorter convergence times than will timed updates.

Timed Updates

A timed update is a very simple mechanism. Time is decremented in a counter as it elapses. When a specified period of time has elapsed, an update is performed regardless of whether a topological change has occurred. This has two implications:

- Many updates will be performed unnecessarily, which wastes bandwidth and router resources.
- Convergence times can be needlessly inflated if route calculations are driven by the passing of time.

Distance Vector routing protocols generally use timed updates.

Event-Driven Updates

Event-driven updates are a much more sophisticated means of initiating routing updates. Ostensibly, an update is only initiated when a change in the network's topology has been detected. Given that a topology change is what creates the need for convergence, this approach is obviously the more efficient one.

You can select an update initiator simply by selecting a routing protocol; each protocol implements either one or the other. Thus, this is one factor that must be considered when selecting a routing protocol.

Link-state routing protocols generally use event-driven updates.

Routing Metrics

Another important mechanism that is determined by the routing protocol is metric(s). A wide disparity exists in terms of both the number and the type of metrics used.

Quantity of Metrics

Simple routing protocols support as few as one or two routing metrics. More sophisticated protocols can support five or more metrics. It is safe to assume that the more metrics exist, the more varied and specific they are. Thus, the greater the variety of available metrics, the greater your ability to tailor the network's operation to your particular needs. For example, the simple distance-vector protocols use a euphemistic metric: distance. In reality, that distance is not at all related to geographic mileage, much less the physical cable mileage that separates source and destination machines. Instead, it usually just counts the number of hops between those two points.

Link-state protocols may afford the ability to calculate routes based on several factors:

- Traffic load
- Available bandwidth
- Propagation delay
- The network cost of a connection (although this metric tends to be more of an estimate than an actual value)

Most of these factors are highly dynamic in a network; they vary by time of day, day of week, and so on. The important thing to remember is that as they vary, so does the network's performance. Therefore, the intent of dynamic-routing metrics is to allow optimal routing decisions to be made using the most current information available.

Static Versus Dynamic Metrics

Some metrics are simplistic and static, whereas others are highly sophisticated and dynamic. Static metrics usually offer the ability to customize their values when they are configured. After this is done, each value remains a constant until it is manually changed.

Dynamic protocols enable routing decisions to be made based upon real-time information about the state of the network. These protocols are only supported by the more sophisticated link-state or hybridized routing protocols.

Summary

Routing is the function that enables users and end-systems to communicate within, and across, IP networks. However, there are many ways to calculate and compare routes. The differences are more than academic or philosophic—they can directly impact the performance and functionality of your IP network. This chapter provided a generic overview of the various ways that routing can be performed, as well as the benefits and limitations of each. The next three chapters build on this overview of IP routing, with specific details about how the RIP, OSPF, and BGP operate.

Gateway Protocols

by Tim Parker

CHAPTER 14

TCP/IP was developed primarily to support internetwork traffic on the network that eventually became the Internet. To that end, TCP/IP was designed with a layered architecture, which specifically works well across networks. As a datagram passes from network to network along the internetwork, it passes through machines that act as routers into each network.

The routers determine whether the datagram is for the local network to which the gateway leads, and if so, removes it from the internetwork backbone and routes it through the local network. If the datagram is to be passed on to other routers further down the internetwork, the router performs that function. In order to correctly forward datagrams on to other routers, each route has to have an up-to-date table of destinations that are used by the routing software. This chapter looks at how internetwork routers handle the routing of information between themselves. Special protocols have been developed specifically for different kinds of routers.

Gateways, Bridges, and Routers

When a router receives a datagram from an internetwork, it performs a simple check of the message's destination address, which is contained in the TCP Protocol Data Unit. If the network portion of the IP address for the destination machine matches the network's IP address, the router knows the datagram is for a machine on its directly connected network and passes the datagram into the network for delivery. If the datagram's IP address reveals that the datagram is not for the directly connected network, the datagram is passed on to the next router on the internetwork.

Moving messages from machine to machine on a small network is easy because each machine can be aware of the IP addresses of every other machine on the network. With a large network or several networks tied together into an internetwork, the complexity increases enormously. For very large internetworks, such as the Internet, it would be impossible for a single router to hold all the valid IP addresses of every machine on the Net. For this reason, several special devices were developed to simplify the routing of datagrams from network to network, across an internetwork, or through a wide area network. These devices are called gateways, bridges, and routers. They vary in purpose, as the following definitions show:

- A *gateway* is a machine that performs protocol translations. Gateways operate at OSI layers 4 to 7. Typically, they operate at Layer 7, such as email gateways.

- A *bridge* is a machine that connects two or more networks that use the same protocol. A bridge operates at Layer 2 of the OSI model. Lately, a new class of devices called Layer 2 switches have become available that can be used as replacements for bridges. Bridges are aware of Data Link Layer addresses but not IP addresses of the Network Layer.

- A *router* is a machine that forwards datagrams around a network. Routers operate at Layer 3 of the OSI model. Commercial routers may perform other non-Layer 3 functions. Examples are routers that combine routing functions with a bridge, routers that perform network address translation (NAT) functions, and routers that perform security-related functions such as packet filtering.

> **Note**
>
> In the earlier Internet literature, the term *gateways* was commonly used to refer to devices that are now called routers. This usage is unfortunate because it causes some confusion. The modern terminology for the older gateway devices is routers.

Gateway

A gateway is a device that can convert protocols. This is necessary if the gateway is acting as an interface between the Internet (using TCP/IP) and a local area network (using Novell NetWare, for example). The gateway has to convert the NetWare IPX/SPX packets to TCP/IP datagrams, and vice versa, for the two networks to be able to exchange data. Gateways can perform translations between many different protocols, often servicing more than two protocols at the same time, depending on the network connections. Gateways may also have to perform conversion of file formats or handle encryption and decryption, depending on the network systems.

Bridge

Bridges are easily thought of as a link between two or more networks. Often, a leased high-speed line is used to connect one LAN to another, as would be the case of a multinational company with offices in separate locations. Both networks may use the same protocol (such as TCP/IP), but need a fast routing system between the two over a high-speed telecommunications line. A bridge handles the routing of datagrams from one LAN to another. Bridges can handle many LANs at the same time, but they all must use the same protocol.

Router

Routers operate more or less at the network level. Their function is to forward datagrams to their destination. Some routers can perform protocol conversions, like a gateway, when there are optional routes to a destination.

14

GATEWAY
PROTOCOLS

Autonomous System

The term *autonomous system* is often used when talking about networks attached to the Internet and other internetworks. An autonomous system is one in which the structure of the local area network to which it is attached is not visible to the rest of the internetwork. Usually, a border router leads into the local area network and all traffic for that network goes through the border router. This hides the internal structure of the local area network from the rest of the internetwork, which both simplifies handling of datagrams and adds security.

Gateway Protocols: The Basics

As mentioned earlier in this chapter, having a single router hold the entire Internet routing table is practically impossible, so most routers handle only a specific section of the internetwork and rely on neighboring gateways to know more about their own attached networks. This results in a common problem, though, when a lack of information results in incomplete routing decisions. For this reason, default routes are used.

Routing protocols exchange routing and status information between gateways. Several router protocols are designed for fast, reliable data transfer with a minimum of overhead. Before looking at the protocols, distinguishing between two types of gateways used on the Internet (and most other internetworks, too) is necessary. The gateway types are called core and non-core.

Core gateways are machines administered by the *Internet Network Operations Center* (INOC) and form part of the backbone of the Internet. As noted earlier, even though these machines are called gateways, they are actually routers. Core gateways were first developed for ARPAnet, where they were called *stub gateways*. *Non-core gateways* are administered by groups outside the Internet organization that are connected to the Internet but administered by the owning company or organization. Typically, corporations and educational institutions that reside on the Internet use non-core gateways. Back in ARPAnet days, any gateway not under direct control of ARPAnet (any non-core gateway in current terminology) was called a *nonrouting gateway*.

The change to the Internet structure and its growing number of core gateways required the development of a protocol to enable the core gateways to communicate with each other. This is the *Gateway-to-Gateway Protocol* (GGP), which is usually used only between core gateways. GGP is used primarily to spread information about the non-core gateways attached to each core gateway, allowing each core gateway to update its routing tables.

Some local area or wide area networks have more than one router within them. For example, you may have a large network that has so much Internet-bound traffic that two routers are used to handle the shared load. On the other hand, if you have two distinct LANs that are part of a larger corporate-wide area network, you may set up the local area networks so each has its own router. If two routers are used in a LAN or WAN and they can talk to each other, they are considered interior neighbors. If the routers don't talk to each other directly (they belong to different autonomous systems), they are called *exterior gateways* or *border routers*. When default routes are required, it is up to the exterior gateways to route messages between autonomous systems.

Within a single local or wide area network, routing information is usually transferred between interior gateways through the *Routing Information Protocol* (RIP). Some systems use a less common protocol called HELLO. Both HELLO and RIP are *Interior Gateway Protocols* (IGPs) designed specifically for interior neighbors to communicate with each other. Messages between two exterior gateways are usually handled through the *Exterior Gateway Protocol* (EGP).

The RIP, HELLO, and EGP protocols all rely on a frequent transfer of a status datagram between gateways to update routing tables. The three gateway protocols are not independent but share a relationship. EGP is used between gateways of autonomous systems, whereas RIP and HELLO (both IGPs) are used within the network itself. GGP is used between core gateways on the Internet.

Interior and Exterior Gateway Protocols

The details of the protocols used in router communications are not really important to users or developers because few applications use the routing protocols directly.

Gateway-to-Gateway Protocol

Core gateways need to know what is happening to the rest of the Internet in order to route datagrams properly and efficiently. This includes routing information and the characteristics of attached subnetworks. A common example of using this type of information occurs when one gateway is particularly slow processing a heavy load and it is the only access method to a subnetwork; other gateways on the network can tailor the traffic to better offload the gateway.

GGP is used primarily to exchange routing information. It is important not to confuse routing information (containing addresses, topology, and details on routing delays) with algorithms used to make routing decisions. Routing algorithms are usually fixed within a gateway and not modified by GGP. A core gateway talks to other core gateways by sending out GGP messages, waiting for replies, and then updating routing tables if the reply has specific information in it.

GGP is a called a *vector-distance protocol*, meaning that messages tend to specify a destination (vector) and the distance to that destination. For a vector-distance protocol to be effective, a gateway must have complete information about all the gateways on the internetwork; otherwise, computing an efficient route to a destination is impossible. For this reason, all core gateways maintain a table of all the other core gateways on the Internet. This is a fairly small list and can easily be handled by the gateways.

> **Note**
>
> The routing protocol used on the Internet to communicate reachability information amongst the core Internet routers is the Border Gateway Protocol (BGP). The current version of BGP is version 4. BGP4 is required for supporting CIDR (Classless Internet Domain Routing), which summarizes routing entries.

The Exterior Gateway Protocol

The Exterior Gateway Protocol is used to transfer information between non-core neighboring gateways. Non-core gateways contain all routing information about their immediate neighbors on the internetwork and the machines attached to them, but they lack information about the rest of the Internet.

For the most part, EGP is restricted to information about the LAN or WAN the gateway serves. This prevents too much routing information from passing through the local or wide area networks. EGP imposes restrictions on the non-core gateways about the machines it communicates with about routing information.

Because core gateways use GGP and non-core gateways use EGP, but they both reside on the Internet, there must be some method for the two to communicate with each other. The Internet enables any autonomous (non-core) gateway to send "reachability" information to other systems, which must also go to at least one core gateway. If there is a larger autonomous network, one gateway usually assumes the responsibility for handling this reachability information.

As with GGP, EGP uses a polling process to keep gateways aware of their neighbors and to continually exchange routing and status information with all of their neighbors. EGP is a *state-driven protocol*, meaning it depends on a state table containing values that reflect gateway conditions and a set of operations that must be performed when a state table entry changes.

Interior Gateway Protocols

Several interior gateway protocols are in use, the most popular of which are RIP and HELLO (mentioned earlier in this chapter), and a third protocol called *Open Shortest Path First* (OSPF). No single protocol has proven dominant, although RIP and OSPF are probably the most common IGP protocols. The specific choice of an IGP is made on the basis of network architecture.

Both the RIP and HELLO protocols calculate distances to a destination, and their messages contain both a machine identifier and the distance to that machine. In general, messages tend to be long because they contain many entries for a routing table. Both RIP and HELLO are constantly connecting between neighboring gateways to ensure the machines are active.

The Routing Information Protocol version 1 uses a broadcast technology. This means that the gateways broadcast their routing tables to other gateways on the network at intervals. This is also one of RIP's problems because the increased network traffic and inefficient messaging can slow down networks. RIP version 2 uses multicast for sending routing table updates. Multicast is more efficient than broadcast because only the RIP routers that are part of the multicast group will process the message.

The HELLO protocol is different from RIP in that HELLO uses time instead of distance as a routing factor. This requires the gateway to have reasonably accurate timing information for each route. For this reason, the HELLO protocol depends on clock synchronization messages. HELLO was used in some university environments but is not widely used in corporate networks.

The Open Shortest Path First protocol was developed by the Internet Engineering Task Force to provide a more efficient IGP protocol. The name "shortest path" is inaccurate in describing this protocol's routing process. A better name would be "optimum path," in which a number of criteria are evaluated to determine the best route to a destination.

Summary

This chapter took a brief look at gateway protocols. Routers are a critical component for forwarding information from one network to another. There are several important gateway protocols, all of which have been mentioned. The details of how some of these protocols work, such as RIP and OSPF, are covered in later chapters.

14

GATEWAY PROTOCOLS

Routing Information Protocol (RIP)

by Mark A. Sportack

In This Chapter

The Routing Information Protocol, or RIP, as it is commonly called, is one of the most enduring of all routing protocols. RIP is one of a class of protocols based on distance-vector routing algorithms that predate ARPANET. These algorithms were academically described between 1957 and 1962. Throughout the 1960s, these algorithms were widely implemented by different companies and marketed under different names. The resulting products were highly related but, due to proprietary enhancements, couldn't offer complete interoperability.

This chapter delves into the details, mechanics, and uses of today's open standard RIP. RIP version 2 (RIPv2) is the latest version and adds subnet support to RIP. In addition RIPv2 uses multicasting instead of broadcasting that is used in original RIP. The original RIP is also called RIP version 1 (RIPv1).

Understanding RFC 1058

The implementation of RIP predates the standard RIP described in RFC 1038. TCP/IP's implementation of RIP is based on the Xerox Networking System's (XNS) version of RIP. XNS was a suite of protocols developed by Xerox, and widely adopted in various forms by different organizations in the early days of the network industry. TCP/IP's RIP was first implemented in BSD Unix before there was a standard describing its operation. For a number of years, the BSD Unix source code was considered to be the "standard" RIP.

In June 1988, Request for Comments (RFC) 1058 was released that described RIP. Pre-RFC 1058 versions of RIP may, therefore, not be compatible.

RFC 1058 described a new, and truly open, form of distance-vector routing protocol: an open standard RIP. This RIP, like its proprietary ancestors, was a simple distance-vector routing protocol that was specifically designed for use as an Interior Gateway Protocol (IGP) in small, simple networks.

Each device that uses RIP is assumed to have at least one network interface. Assuming that this network is one of the LAN architectures (such as Ethernet, Token Ring, and FDDI), RIP would only need to calculate routes to devices that are not directly connected to the same LAN. Depending on the application being used, devices that reside on the same LAN may communicate using just that LAN's mechanisms.

RIP Packet Format

RIP uses a special packet to collect and share information about distances to known internetworked destinations. Figure 15.1 illustrates a RIP packet with routing information fields for just a single destination.

FIGURE **15.1**

The structure of a RIP packet.

One Octet Command	One Octet Version #	Two Octet Zero Field	Two Octet AFI	Two Octet Zero Field	Four Octet Network Address	Four Octet Zero Field	Four Octet Zero Field	Four Octet Metric

RIP packets can support up to 25 occurrences of the AFI, Internetwork Address, and Metric fields within a single packet. This enables one RIP packet to be used to update multiple entries in other routers' routing tables. RIP packets that contain multiple routing entries simply repeat the packet structure from the AFI through the Metric field, including all Zero fields. The repeated structures are appended to the end of the structure depicted in Figure 15.1. A RIP packet with two table entries is illustrated in Figure 15.2.

FIGURE **15.2**

The RIP packet format with two table entries.

One Octet Command	One Octet Version #	Two Octet Zero Field	Two Octet AFI	Two Octet Zero Field	Four Octet Network Address	Four Octet Zero Field	Four Octet Zero Field	Four Octet Metric
					Four Octet Network Address	Four Octet Zero Field	Four Octet Zero Field	Four Octet Metric

The Address field can contain either the address of its originator or a series of IP addresses that the originator has in its routing table. Request packets contain a single entry and include the originator's address. Response packets can include up to 25 entries of a RIP router's routing table.

The overall size limitation of a RIP packet is 512 octets. Thus, in larger RIP networks, a request for a full routing table update may require the transmission of several RIP packets. No provisions were made for the resequencing of the packets upon arrival at their destination; individual routing table entries are not split between RIP packets. Thus, the contents of any given RIP packet are complete unto themselves, even though they may only be a subset of a complete routing table. The recipient node is free to process the updates as the packets are received, without having to resequence them.

For example, a RIP router may contain 100 entries in its routing table. Sharing its routing information with other RIP nodes would require four RIP packets, each one containing 25 entries. If a receiving node received packet number four first (containing entries numbered 76 through 100), it could simply update that portion of its routing table first. There are no sequential dependencies. This allows RIP packets to be forwarded without the overheads of a fully featured transport protocol, such as TCP.

> **Note**
>
> RIP uses UDP as its transport protocol. RIP messages are encapsulated in UDP/IP packets. The RIP processes on routers use UDP port 520.

The Command Field

The Command field indicates whether the RIP packet was generated as a request or as a response to a request. The same frame structure is used for both occurrences:

- A request packet asks a router to send all, or part, of its routing table.
- A response packet contains routing table entries that are to be shared with other RIP nodes in the network. A response packet can be generated either in response to a request or as an unsolicited update.

The Version Number Field

The Version Number field contains the version of RIP that was used to generate the RIP packet. Although RIP is an open standard routing protocol, it is not frozen in time. RIP has been treated to updates over the years, and these updates are reflected in a version number. Despite the many RIP-like routing protocols that have emerged, there are only two versions of RIP: version 1 and version 2. RIP version 1 uses broadcast to send RIP messages, whereas RIP version 2 uses multicast. Multicast is more efficient than broadcasts and in the case of RIP version 2, only RIPv2 routers process the multicast messages. RIPv2 uses the class D multicast address 224.0.0.9.

The Zero Fields

The numerous Zero fields embedded in each RIP packet are silent testimony to the proliferation of RIP-like protocols before RFC 1058. Most of the Zero fields were contrived as a means of providing backward compatibility with older RIP-like protocols, without supporting all of their proprietary features.

For example, two such obsolete mechanisms are *traceon* and *traceoff*. These mechanisms were abandoned by RFC 1058, yet the open standard RIP needed to be backward compatible with the proprietary RIP-like protocols that did support them. Thus, RFC 1058 preserved their space in the packet, but requires this space to always be set to zeroes. Packets received with these fields set to something other than zeroes are simply discarded.

Not all the Zero fields originated in this manner. At least one of the Zero fields was reserved for an unspecified future use.

In RIPv2, the first zero field is the routing tag, and the second zero field is the routing domain. The zero routing entries in RIPv1 packet format are replaced with subnet mask and next hop router information in RIPv2. RIPv1 does not support subnet mask information in routing table entries. When RIPv1 was created, the subnet mask mechanism did not exist.

The AFI Field

The Address Family Identifier (AFI) field specifies the address family that is represented by the Internetwork Address field. Although the RFC 1058 RIP was created by the IETF, which would imply the use of the Internet Protocol (IP), it was explicitly designed to provide backward compatibility with previous versions of RIP. This meant it had to provide for the transport of routing information of a wide variety of internetworking address architectures or families. Consequently, the open standard RIP needed a mechanism for determining which type of address was being carried in its packets. In the case of RIP, an AFI field value of 2 is used.

The Internetwork Address Field

The four-octet Internetwork Address field contains an internetwork address. This address can be a host, a network, or even a default gateway address code. Two examples of how this field's contents can vary are:

- In a single-entry request packet, this field would contain the address of the packet's originator.
- In a multiple-entry response packet, these fields would contain the IP addresses stored in the originator's routing table.

The Metric Field

The last field in the RIP packet, the Metric field, contains the packet's metric counter. This value is incremented as it passes through a router. The valid range of metrics for this field is between 1 and 15. The metric can actually be incremented to 16, but this value is associated with invalid routes. Consequently, 16 is an error value for the Metric field, and not part of the valid range. Thus, a metric value of 16 means that the destination is unreachable.

The RIP Routing Table

RIP hosts communicate described in the previous section. This information is stored in a routing table. The routing table contains one entry for each known, reachable destination. The one entry per destination is the lowest cost route to that destination.

> **Note**
>
> The number of entries stored per destination may vary by router vendor. Vendors may elect to follow the published specifications, or "enhance" those specifications as they see fit. Consequently, it is quite likely you will find particular brands of routers that store up to four routes of equal cost for any given destination in the network.

Each routing table entry contains the following fields:

- The Destination IP Address field
- The distance-vector Metric field
- The Next Hop IP Address field
- The Route Change Flag field
- Route timers

> **Note**
>
> Although RFC 1058 RIP is an open standard that can support a variety of internetwork address architectures, it was designed by the IETF for use in autonomous systems within the Internet. As such, it was tacitly assumed that IP would be the internetworking protocol used by this form of RIP.

The Destination IP Address Field

The most important piece of information contained in any routing table is the IP address of the known destinations. Whenever a RIP router receives a data packet, it looks up its destination IP address in its routing table to determine where to forward that packet.

The Metric Field

The metric contained in the routing table represents the total cost of moving a datagram from its point of origin to its specified destination. The Metric field in the routing table contains the sum total of the costs associated with the network links that comprise the end-to-end network path between the router and the specified destination.

The Next Hop IP Address Field

The Next Hop IP Address field contains the IP address of the next router interface in the network path to the destination IP address. This field is only populated in a router's table if the destination IP address is on a network that is not directly connected to that router.

The Route Change Flag Field

The Route Change Flag field is used to indicate whether the route to the destination IP address has changed recently. This field was deemed important because RIP records only one route per destination IP address.

Route Timers

The two timers that are associated with each route are the route time-out and the route-flush timers. These timers work together to maintain the validity of each route stored in the routing table. The routing table maintenance process is described in more detail in the section "Updating the Routing Table," later in this chapter.

Operational Mechanics

As explained in Chapter 13, "Routing in IP Networks," routers that use a distance-vector routing protocol must periodically pass copies of their routing tables to their immediate network neighbors. A router's routing table contains information about the distance between itself and known destinations. These destinations can be individual host computers, printers, or other networks.

Each recipient adds a distance vector; that is, its own distance "value," to the table and forwards the modified table to its immediate neighbors. This process occurs omnidirectionally between immediately neighboring routers. Figure 15.3 uses a simple RIP internetwork to illustrate the concept of immediate neighbors.

FIGURE 15.3
Each RIP node advertises the contents of its routing table to its immediate neighbors.

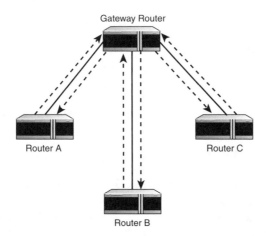

Gateway Router

Router A

Router C

Router B

Figure 15.3 shows four routers. The gateway router is interconnected with each of the other three. It must exchange its routing information with these routers. Routers A, B, and C have only one connection each: to the gateway. Consequently, they can only exchange their information with the gateway directly. They can learn about each other's hosts through the information shared with the gateway. Table 15.1 shows the abbreviated contents of each of the three routers' routing tables. This information is shared with the gateway router.

TABLE 15.1 Routing Table Contents

Router Name	Hostname	Next Hop
A	192.168.130.10	Local
	192.168.130.15	Local
B	192.168.125.2	Local
	192.168.125.9	Local
C	192.68.254.5	Local
	192.68.254.20	Local

The gateway router uses this information to build its own routing table. The abbreviated contents of this table are presented in Table 15.2.

TABLE 15.2 Gateway Router Routing Table Contents

Hostname	Next Hop	Number of Hops
192.168.130.10	A	1
192.168.130.15	A	1
192.168.125.2	B	1
192.168.125.9	B	1
192.68.254.5	C	1
192.68.254.20	C	1

The routing information in Table 15.2 is then shared via routing information update packets with each of the other routers in the network. These routers use this information to round out their own routing tables. Table 15.3 shows the abbreviated contents of Router A's routing table after it has shared routing information with the gateway router.

TABLE 15.3 Router A's Routing Table Contents

Hostname	Next Hop	Number of Hops
192.168.130.10	Local	0
192.168.130.15	Local	0
192.168.125.2	Gateway	2
192.168.125.9	Gateway	2
192.68.254.5	Gateway	2
192.68.254.20	Gateway	2

Router A knows that the gateway router is one hop away. Thus, seeing that the 192.168.125.x and 192.68.254.x hosts are also one hop away from the gateway, it adds the two numbers together, for a total of two hops to each machine.

This highly simplified step-by-step process results in each router learning about other routers and developing a cumulative perspective of the network as well as the distances between source and destination devices.

Calculating Distance Vectors

A distance-vector routing protocol uses metrics to keep track of the distance separating it from all known destinations. This distance information enables the router to identify the most efficient next hop to a destination that resides within the network.

In RFC 1058 RIP, there is a single distance-vector metric: hop count. The default hop metric in RIP is set to 1. Thus, for each router that receives and forwards a packet, the hop count in the RIP packet Metric field is incremented by one. These distance metrics are used to construct a routing table. The routing table identifies the next hop for a packet to take to get to its destination at a minimal cost.

The earlier, proprietary RIP-like routing protocols typically used 1 as the only supported cost per hop. RFC 1058 RIP preserved this convention as a default hop-count value, but provisions were made for the router's administrator to select higher cost values. Such values would be beneficial in discriminating between links of differing performance capabilities. These capabilities could be the bandwidths available on different network links (that is, 56Kbps versus T1 private lines) or even the performance difference between a new router versus an older model.

Typically, a cost of 1 is assigned to each of a router's ports that connect to other networks. This is, apparently, an artifact from RIP's pre-RFC 1058 days, when the cost per hop defaulted to 1 and was not modifiable. In a relatively small network that consisted of homogeneous transmission technologies, setting all ports to a cost of 1 would be reasonable. This is illustrated in Figure 15.4.

FIGURE 15.4

A homogeneous network with equivalent costs.

A router's administrator can change the default metric. For example, an administrator may increase the metric for slower-speed links to other routers. Although this might more accurately represent the costs or distances to a given destination, this practice is not recommended. Setting the metric to a value greater than 1 makes it correspondingly easier to reach the packet's maximum hop count of 16! Figure 15.5 demonstrates how quickly routes cane become invalid if route metrics are increased.

Figure 15.5 presents a slightly modified version of the WAN depicted in Figure 15.4. This illustration adds low-bandwidth redundant links to the topology depicted in Figure 15.4. The network administrator, to ensure that the alternate routes remained alternate routes, set the metric value of these alternate routes to 10. These higher costs preserve the bias toward the higher-bandwidth T1 transmission facilities. In the event of a failure of one of those T1 lines, the internetwork can continue to function normally, although some degraded performance levels might occur due to the lower available bandwidth on the 56 Kbps back-up facility. Figure 15.6 illustrates how the internetwork will react to a failure of a T1 line between the gateway and Router A.

FIGURE 15.5

Hop counts are modified to differentiate between primary and alternate routes.

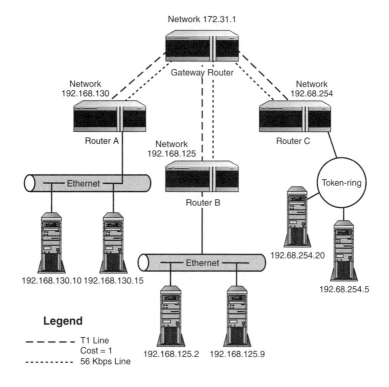

FIGURE 15.6

Hop counts add up quickly, but the network remains functional.

The alternate 56 Kbps transmission facility becomes the only way for Router A and the rest of the network to communicate. Router A's routing table, after the network converges upon a common understanding of this new topology, is summarized in Table 15.4.

TABLE 15.4 Router A's Routing Table Contents with a Link Failure

Hostname	*Next Hop*	*Number of Hops*
192.168.130.10	Local	0
192.168.130.15	Local	0
192.168.125.2	Gateway	11
192.168.125.9	Gateway	11
192.68.254.5	Gateway	11
192.68.254.20	Gateway	11

Although a higher route cost is a more accurate reflection of the lower bandwidths offered by these alternate routes, it can introduce unwanted routing problems. In Figure 15.7, two of the T1 lines have failed, thus causing two of the alternate routes to become active simultaneously.

FIGURE 15.7

Hop counts can add up to 16 too fast.

Because both alternate links had a cost metric of 10, their simultaneous activation results in a route cost of greater than 16. The valid range for RIP's hop counter is from 0 through 16, with 16 representing an unreachable route. Thus, if the metrics (or cost) of a route exceed 16, the route is declared invalid, and a notification (a triggered update) is sent to all immediately neighboring routers.

Obviously, this problem can be avoided by leaving the default cost equal to 1. If it is absolutely necessary to increment the cost metric of a given hop, the new cost value should be selected with great care. The sum total of the route between any given pair of source and destination addresses in a network should never exceed 15. Table 15.5 demonstrates the impacts of a second link failure on Router A's routing table.

TABLE 15.5   Router A's Routing Table Contents with Two Link Failures

Hostname	Next Hop	Number of Hops
192.168.130.10	Local	0
192.168.130.15	Local	0
192.168.125.2	Gateway	11
192.168.125.9	Gateway	11
192.68.254.5	Gateway	16
192.68.254.20	Gateway	16

As is evident in Table 15.5, the cost of the route between A and C exceeds 16, and all entries are declared invalid. Router A is still able to communicate with B because the total cost of that route is only 11.

Updating the Routing Table

The fact that RIP records only one route per destination requires RIP to aggressively maintain the integrity of its routing table. It does so by requiring all active RIP routers to broadcast their routing table contents to neighboring RIP routers at a fixed interval. All updates received automatically supercede previous route information that was stored in the routing table.

RIP relies on three timers to maintain the routing table:

- The update timer
- The route time-out timer
- The route-flush timer

The update timer is used to initiate routing table updates at the node level. Each RIP node only uses one update timer. Conversely, the route time-out timer and the route-flush timer are kept for each route.

As such, separate time-out and route-flush timers are integrated in each routing table entry. Together, these timers enable RIP nodes to maintain the integrity of their routes as well as to proactively recover from failures in the network by initiating activity based on the passing of time. The following sections describe the processes used to maintain the routing tables.

Initiating Table Updates

A table update is initiated every 30 seconds. The update timer is used to track this amount of time. Upon the expiration of this time, a RIP node launches a series of packets that contains its entire routing table.

These packets are broadcast to each neighboring node. Therefore, each RIP router should receive an update from each of its neighboring RIP nodes approximately every 30 seconds.

> **Note**
>
> In larger RIP-based autonomous systems, these periodic updates can create unacceptable levels of traffic. Thus, staggering the updates, from node to node is desirable. This is done automatically by RIP; each time the update timer is reset, a small, random amount of time is added to the clock.

If such an update fails to occur as expected, it indicates a failure or error somewhere in the internetwork. The failure may be something as simple as a dropped packet that contained the update. The failure could also be something as serious as a failed router, or virtually anything in-between these two extremes. Obviously, the appropriate course of action differs greatly along this spectrum of failures. It would be unwise to invalidate a series of routes just because the update packet was lost (remember, RIP update packets use an unreliable transport protocol to minimize overheads). Thus, it is reasonable to not take corrective action based upon a single missed update. To help discriminate between magnitudes of failures and errors, RIP uses timers to identify invalid routes.

Identifying Invalid Routes

Routes can become invalid in one of two ways:

- A route can expire.
- A router can learn of a route's unavailability from another router.

In either event, the RIP router needs to modify its routing table to reflect the unavailability of a given route.

A route can expire if a router doesn't receive an update for it within a specified amount of time. For example, the route time-out timer is usually set to 180 seconds. This clock is initialized when the route becomes active or is updated.

180 seconds is approximately enough time for a router to receive six routing table updates from its neighbors (assuming that they initiate table updates every 30 seconds). If 180 seconds elapse and the RIP router hasn't received an update on that route, the RIP router assumes that the destination IP address is no longer reachable. Consequently, the router marks that routing entry in its table invalid. This is done by setting its routing metric to 16, and by setting the *route change flag*. This information is then communicated to the router's neighbors via the periodic routing table updates.

> **Note**
>
> To a RIP node, 16 equals infinity. Thus, simply setting the cost metric to 16 in its routing table entry can invalidate a route.

Neighboring nodes that receive notification of the route's new invalid status use that information to update their own routing tables. This is the second of the two ways that routes can become invalid in a routing table.

An invalid entry remains in the routing table for a very brief amount of time, as the router determines whether it should be purged. Even though the entry remains in the table, datagrams cannot be sent to that entry's destination address: RIP cannot forward datagrams to invalid destinations.

Purging Invalid Routes

When a router recognizes a route as invalid, it initializes a second timer: the route-flush timer. Thus, 180 seconds after the last time the time-out timer was initialized, the route-flush timer is initialized. This timer is usually set for 90 seconds.

If the route update is still not received after 270 seconds (180 second time-out timer plus the 90-second route-flush timer), the route is removed (that is, flushed) from the routing table. The timer responsible for counting down the time to route flush is known as the route-flush timer. These timers are absolutely essential to RIP's ability to recover from network failures.

15

ROUTING
INFORMATION
PROTOCOL (RIP)

> ### Active Versus Passive Nodes
>
> It is important to note that for a RIP internetwork to function properly, every gateway within the network must participate. Participation can be active or passive, but all gateways must participate. Active nodes are those that actively engage in the sharing of routing information. They receive updates from their neighbors, and they forward copies of their routing table entries to those neighboring nodes.
>
> Passive nodes receive updates from their neighbors, and use those updates to maintain their routing table. Passive nodes, however, do not actively distribute copies of their own routing table entries.
>
> The ability to passively maintain a routing table was a particularly useful feature in the days before hardware routers, when routed was a daemon that ran on Unix processors. This kept routing overheads on the Unix host to a minimum.

Addressing Considerations

The IETF ensured that RIP was fully backward compatible with all known RIP and routed variants. Given that these were highly proprietary, it was necessary that the open standard RIP not dictate an address type. Thus, the field labeled Address in a RIP packet may contain

- The host address
- The subnet number
- The network number
- A 0, which indicates a default route

Implicit in this flexibility is the fact that RIP permits calculating routes to either individual hosts, or to networks that contain numerous hosts. To accommodate this address flexibility in operation, RIP nodes use the most specific information available when they forward datagrams. For example, when a RIP router receives an IP packet, it must examine the destination address. It attempts to match this address with a destination IP address in its routing table. If it cannot find an entry for that destination host address, it then checks whether that destination address matches a known subnet or network number. If it cannot make a match at this level, the RIP router uses its default route to forward the datagram.

Routing to a Gateway

Up to this point in the chapter, entries in the RIP routing table have been assumed to be routes to individual hosts. This was a simplifying assumption that better describes the way that routing originally worked. Today, networks may be too large and well populated with hosts for host routing to be practical. Host-based routing unnecessarily inflates the size of routing tables, and slows down routing across the internetwork.

In real-world networks, routes are calculated to network addresses rather than host addresses. For example, if each host on any given network (or subnet) is accessible through the same gateway(s), the routing table can simply define that gateway as a destination IP address. All datagrams addressed to hosts within that network or subnetwork will be forwarded to that gateway. That gateway, then, will assume responsibility for forwarding them on to their ultimate destinations. Figure 15.8 illustrates this point; it preserves the topology of the previous few illustrations, but uses more conventional IP addresses.

FIGURE 15.8

RIP nodes can deliver datagrams to gateways.

In Figure 15.8, host 172.31.254.5 needs to transmit an IP packet to host number 192.168.125.10. This address is unknown to Router C. The router checks to see the subnet mask, which is set to 255.255.255.0. From this, it is easy to deduce that 192.168.125 is a subnet number. More importantly, Router C knows a route to that subnet. Router B

15

ROUTING
INFORMATION
PROTOCOL (RIP)

assumes that the gateway router at that subnet knows how to reach that host. Consequently, Router C forwards the packet to that gateway. This approach requires hosts to be known only to the router that is closest, and not known throughout a network. The finely dotted lines in Figure 15.8 illustrate the two parts of the IP datagram's journey: its trip from Router B to the Router A, and from A to host 192.168.125.10.

> **Note**
>
> RIPv1 does not support variable length subnet masks (VLSM). Consequently, there can be only one subnet mask for each network. It is quite likely that a network may contain multiple subnets, each with its own subnet address that uses the same mask length. RIP is also known as a "classful" routing protocol because it supports only the class-based IPv4 addresses. RIPv2 can support VLSM as well as CIDR (Classless Internet Domain Routing). CIDR was discussed in earlier chapters and is a mechanism for aggregating route table entries to a block of addresses by a single routing entry.

Routing Between Gateways

In the case presented in the previous section, a potential routing problem exists. If Router C did not know the subnet mask of the destination IP address, and the host part of the address was not zero, it wouldn't be able to determine whether the address was a subnet number or a host address. Thus, the packet would be discarded as undeliverable.

To help avoid the ambiguity, routes to a subnet are not advertised outside the network that contains the subnet. The router at the border of this subnet functions as a gateway; it treats each subnet as an individual network. RIP updates are performed between immediate neighbors within each subnet, but the network gateway advertises a single network number only to its neighboring gateways in other networks.

The practical implication of this is that a border gateway will send different information to its neighbors. Immediate neighbors within the subnetted network will receive updates containing lists of all subnets directly connected to that gateway. The routing entries will list the number of each subnet.

Immediate neighbors outside the network will receive a single routing entry update that encompasses all the hosts on all the subnets contained within that network. The metric passed would be that associated with reaching the network, rather than including the costs of hops within the network. In this fashion, distant RIP routers assume that datagrams addressed to any host number within that subnet are known to, and reachable through, the network's border gateway router.

Default Routes

The IP address 0.0.0.0 is used to describe a default route. Much like the way subnets can be summarized by routing to a network gateway, a default route can be used to route to multiple networks without explicitly defining and describing them. The only requirement is that there be at least one gateway between these networks that is prepared to handle the traffic generated.

To create a default route, a RIP entry needs to be created for the address 0.0.0.0. This special address is treated just like any other destination IP address. The next hop should be the destination IP address of the neighboring gateway router. This routing entry is used just like every other entry, with one important exception: The default route is used to route any datagram whose destination address doesn't match any other entries in the routing table.

Table 15.6 demonstrates the abbreviated contents of Router A's routing table with a default route. In this table, the two local hosts are the only ones explicitly identified. Any other locally generated transmission requests are automatically forwarded to the gateway router.

TABLE 15.6   Router A's Routing Table Contents with a Default Route

Hostname	Next Hop
192.168.125.10	Local
192.168.125.15	Local
0.0.0.0	Gateway

Topology Changes

Up to this point, RIP's fundamental mechanisms and specifications have been examined in a rather static fashion. A deeper appreciation for RIP's mechanics, however, can be gained by looking at how these mechanisms interact to accommodate changes in network topology.

Convergence

The most significant implication of a topology change in a RIP internetwork is that it changes the solution set of neighboring nodes. This change may also result in different results the next time the distance vectors are calculated. Thus, the new sets of neighboring nodes must then converge, from different starting points, on a consensus of what the new topology looks like. This process of developing a consensual perspective of the topology is known as *convergence*. In simple terms, the routers develop an agreement of what the network looks like *separately,* together.

Figure 15.9 illustrates convergence; it demonstrates two possible routes to Router D from Router A and Network 192.168.125. Router D is a gateway router. The primary route to Router D's network is via Router C. If this route were to fail, it would take some time for all the routers to converge upon a new topology that didn't include the link between Routers C and D.

FIGURE 15.9

*Two possible
paths to Router D
from Router A.*

As soon as the C–D link fails, it is no longer usable, but it may take quite a while for this fact to become known throughout the network. The first step in convergence is for D to realize that the link to C has failed. This assumes that Router D's update timer elapses before Router C's timer. Because this link was the one that should have carried updates from Router D to Router C, no updates can be received. Consequently, C (as well as A and B) is still unaware that the C–D link has failed. All routers in the internetwork will continue to forward datagrams addressed to Router D's network number through that link. This first stage in convergence is illustrated in Figure 15.10.

FIGURE 15.10

Only Router D is aware of the link failure.

Upon expiration of its update timer, Router D will attempt to notify its neighbors of its perception of the change in the network's topology. The only immediate neighbor that it will be able to contact is B. Upon receiving this update, B will update its routing table to set the route from B to D (via C) to infinity. This will allow it to resume communications with D, albeit via the B–D link. After B has updated its table, it can advertise its new-found perception of the topology to its other neighbors—A and C.

Note

Remember, a RIP node invalidates a route by setting its metric to 16—the RIP equivalent of infinity.

As soon as A and C have received updates, and have recalculated network costs, they can replace their obsolete entries that used the C–D link with the B–D link. The B–D route was previously rejected by all nodes, including B, as being more expensive than the C–D link. Its cost metric of 10 compared unfavorably with the C–D cost of 1 for each node. Now, with the failure of the C–D link, the B–D link features the lowest cost. Thus, this new route replaces the timed-out route in the neighbors' routing tables.

15

ROUTING INFORMATION PROTOCOL (RIP)

When all routers agree that the most efficient route to D is via B, they have converged. This is illustrated in Figure 15.11.

FIGURE 15.11

The routers converge on B–D as the new route.

The amount of time that will elapse before convergence completes is not easy to determine. It will vary greatly from network to network, based upon a wide variety of factors that include the robustness of the routers and transmission facilities, amount of traffic, and so on.

The "Count-to-Infinity" Problem

In the example presented in the preceding section, the only failure was transmission facility connecting C and D. The routers were able to converge on a new topology that restored access to gateway Router D's network via an alternate path. A much more disastrous failure would have been if D itself had failed. The convergence process in the previous example started when D was able to notify B of the link failure. If D, rather than its link to C, had failed, neither B nor C would receive an update informing them of the change in topology.

Converging on a new topology given this type of failure can result in a phenomenon known as *counting to infinity* or the *count to infinity problem*. When a network becomes completely inaccessible, updates between remaining routers can steadily increment routing metrics to the inaccessible destination based on the mistaken belief that another router can access the lost destination. Left unchecked, the routers in that scenario will literally count to RIP's interpretation of infinity.

To illustrate the dangers from a routing perspective, inherent in this type of catastrophic failure, reconsider the topology presented in the convergence illustrations. In Figure 15.12, Router D has failed.

FIGURE 15.12

Router D has failed.

With the failure of Router D, all the hosts within its network are no longer accessible from the outside. Router C, after missing six consecutive updates from D, will invalidate its C–D route and advertise its unavailability. This is illustrated in Figure 15.13. Routers A and B will remain ignorant of the route's failure until notified by C.

At this point, both A and C believe that they can get to D via B. They recalculate their routes to include the higher costs of this detour. This is illustrated in Figure 15.14.

FIGURE **15.13**

*Router C invali-
dates its C–D
route.*

FIGURE **15.14**

*A and C believe
that they can
access D
through B.*

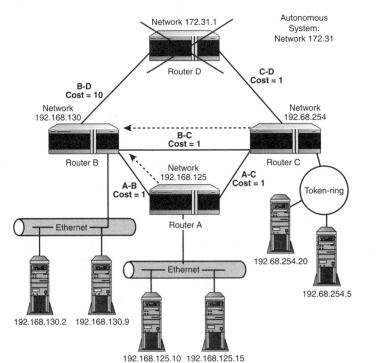

These routers send their next updates to B, an immediate neighbor of both routers. Router B, having timed-out its own route to D, believes it can still access D through either A or C. Obviously, it cannot because those routers are relying on the link that B just invalidated. In essence, a loop is formed between A, B, and C that is fed by the mistaken belief that both A and C can still reach the unreachable Router D through each other. This is because both have a connection to B, which has the connection to D.

With each iteration of updates, the cost metrics are incremented to account for the next extra hop that is added to the loop already calculated. This form of looping is induced by the time delay that characterizes independent convergence through neighbor-transmitted updates.

In theory, the nodes will eventually realize that D is unreachable. However, it is virtually impossible to tell how much time would be required to achieve this convergence. This example illustrates precisely why RIP's interpretation of infinity is set so low. Whenever a network becomes inaccessible, the incrementing of metrics through routine updates must be halted as soon as practical. Unfortunately, this means placing an upper limit on how high the nodes will count before declaring a destination unreachable. Any upper limit directly translates into a limitation on the maximum size of the routed network's diameter. In the case of RIP, its original designers felt that 15 hops were more than adequate for an autonomous system. Systems larger than this could utilize a more sophisticated routing protocol.

RIP supports three means of avoiding the count-to-infinity loop problem:

- Split horizon
- Split horizon with poisoned reverse
- Triggered updates

Split Horizon

It should be fairly obvious that the looping problem described in the preceding section could be prevented with the application of logic. The term used to describe this logic is *split horizon*. Although RIP does not support pure split horizon, understanding it will facilitate understanding its somewhat more complicated variant, *split horizon with poisoned reverse*.

The essence of split horizon is the assumption that a RIP node won't advertise an update to a particular route to a particular neighbor, if that route was originally learned from that neighbor. Figure 15.15 illustrates this point.

Figure 15.15

A split horizon.

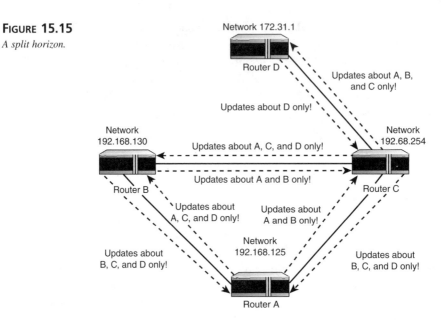

In Figure 15.15, the routers support the split horizon logic. Thus, Router C (which supports the only path to Router D) cannot receive updates from Router A about Network D. This is because A relies on C (and even B) for this route information. Router A must omit from its routing table information about routes learned from C. This simple approach to splitting loops can be relatively effective, but it does have a serious functional limitation: By omitting reverse routes from advertising, each node must wait for the route to the unreachable destination to time-out.

In RIP, a time-out occurs only after six update messages fail to update a route. Thus, five opportunities exist for a misinformed node to misinform other nodes about an unreachable destination. It is this time delay that creates the opportunity for invalid routing information to start the loop. Due to this limitation, RIP supports a slightly modified version known as split horizon with poisoned reverse.

Split Horizon with Poisoned Reverse

The simple split horizon scheme attempts to control loops by ceasing to propagate information back to its originator. Although this can be effective, there are more effective ways to stop a loop. Split horizon with poisoned reverse takes a much more proactive approach to stopping loops: This technique actually poisons the looped route by setting its metric to infinity. This is illustrated in Figure 15.16.

FIGURE 15.16

A split horizon with poisoned reverse.

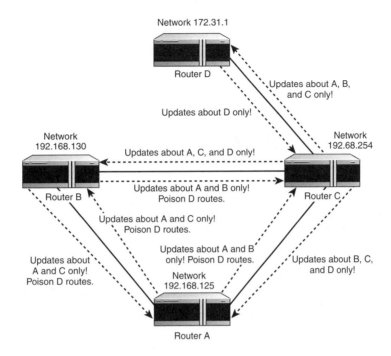

As illustrated in Figure 15.16, Router A can provide information to Router B about how to reach Router D, but this route carries a metric of 16. Thus, Router B cannot update its routing table with information about a better way to reach the destination. In fact, A is advertising that it cannot reach D, which is a true statement. This form of route advertising effectively breaks loops immediately.

Generally speaking, split horizon with poisoned reverse is much safer in distance-vector networks than just split horizon. However, neither is perfect. Split horizon with poisoned reverse will effectively prevent routing loops in topologies with just two gateways. In larger internetworks, however, RIP is still subject to the counting-to-infinity problem. To ensure that such infinite loops are caught as early as possible, RIP supports a triggered update.

Triggered Updates

Networks that feature three gateways to a common network are still susceptible to loops caused by mutual deception of the gateways. Figure 15.17 illustrates this point. This diagram features three gateways to Router D: A, B, and C.

Figure 15.17

Three gateways to D.

In the event that Router D fails, Router A may believe that B can still access D. Router B may believe that C can still access D, and C may believe that A can still access D. The net effect is a continuous loop to infinity. This is illustrated in Figure 15.18.

Figure 15.18

Counting to infinity with three gateways.

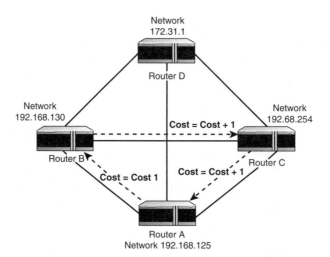

Split horizon logic would be ineffective in this scenario due to the time delay before routes can be invalidated. RIP uses a different technique, known as a *triggered update*, to accelerate convergence. A triggered update is a rule in the protocol that requires gateways to immediately broadcast an update message whenever it changes a route metric, regardless of how much time remains in the 30-second update timer.

The previous sections demonstrate how time is the Achilles' heel of split horizons, with or without reverse poisoning. Triggered updates are designed to overcome this vulnerability by reducing time delay to an absolute minimum.

Hold-Down Timers

Triggered updates are not a panacea! Updates are not propagated instantaneously throughout a network. Thus, it is possible (however unlikely) that another gateway could have just transmitted a periodic update before receiving a triggered update from another gateway. In this scenario, vestiges of an invalid route could re-propagate throughout the network. Although the likelihood of this occurring is extremely low, it is still possible for counting-to-infinity loops to occur within a RIP network despite the use of triggered updates.

The solution to this potential problem is the use of a hold-down timer. A hold-down timer works in conjunction with the triggered update logic. In essence, as soon as a triggered update has been made, a clock starts counting down to zero. Until it decrements to zero, the router will not accept any updates from any neighbors for that route or destination.

This prevents a RIP router from accepting updates for a route that has been invalidated for a configurable amount of time. This prevents a router from being misled into believing that another router may have a viable route to an otherwise invalid destination.

Limitations of RIP

Despite its lengthy heritage, RIP is not without its limitations. It was marvelously suited to calculating routes during the early days of internetworking; however, technological advance has radically changed the way that internetworks are built and used. Consequently, RIP is rapidly approaching obsolescence in today's internetwork.

Some of RIP's greatest limitations include the following:

- Inability to support paths longer than 15 hops
- Reliance upon fixed metrics to calculate routes
- Network intensity of table updates
- Relatively slow convergence
- Lack of support for dynamic load balancing

Hop Count Limit

RIP was designed for use in relatively small autonomous systems. As such, it enforces a strict hop count limit of 15 hops. As packets are forwarded by a routing device, their hop counters are incremented by the cost of the link that it is being transmitted over. If the hop counter hits 15, and the packet isn't at its addressed destination, that destination is considered unreachable, and the packet is discarded.

This effectively fixes maximum network diameter at 15 hops. This is sufficiently high to build a fairly large network, depending on how cleverly it was designed, but is still severely limited in comparison to the scalability of other, more modern, routing protocols. Thus, if you have anything but a very small network, RIP probably isn't the right routing protocol to use.

Fixed Metrics

The discussion about hop counts nicely sets the stage for an examination of RIP's next fundamental limitation: its fixed-cost metrics. Although cost metrics can be configured by the administrator, they are static in nature. RIP cannot update them in real-time to accommodate changes it encounters in the network. The cost metrics defined by the administrator remain fixed, until updated manually.

This means that RIP is particularly unsuited for highly dynamic networks, where route calculations must be made in real-time in response to changes in the network's condition. For example, if a network supports time-sensitive applications, it is reasonable to use a routing protocol that can calculate routes based on the measured delay of its transmission facilities or even the existing load on a given facility. RIP uses fixed metrics. Thus, it is not capable of supporting real-time route calculation.

Network Intensity of Table Updates

A RIP node broadcasts its routing tables omnidirectionally every 30 seconds. In large networks with many nodes, this can consume a fair amount of bandwidth.

Slow Convergence

In human terms, waiting 30 seconds for an update is hardly inconvenient. Routers and computers, however, operate at much higher speeds than humans do. Thus, having to wait 30 seconds for an update can have demonstrably adverse effects. This point is demonstrated in the section "Topology Changes" earlier in this chapter.

Much more damaging than merely waiting 30 seconds for an update, however, is having to wait up to 180 seconds to invalidate a route. And this is just the amount of time needed for just one router to begin convergence. Depending on how many routers are internetworked, and their topology, it may take repeated updates to completely converge on a new topology. The slowness with which RIP routers converge creates a wealth of opportunities for vestiges of invalid routes to be falsely advertised as still available. Obviously, this compromises the performance of the network, both in the aggregate and in the perception of individual users.

This chapter should have amply demonstrated the dangers inherent in RIP's slow convergence.

Lack of Load Balancing

Another of RIP's significant limitations is its inability to dynamically load balance. Figure 15.19 illustrates a router with two serial connections to another router in its inter-network. Ideally, the router in this illustration would split the traffic as evenly as possible between the two serial connections. This would keep congestion to a minimum on both links and optimize performance.

FIGURE 15.19

A router with redundant serial connections.

Unfortunately, RIP is unable to perform such dynamic load balancing. It would use whichever of the two physical connections that it knew about first. RIP would forward all of its traffic over that connection even though the second connection was available for use. The only way that this scenario would change would be if the router in Figure 15.19 received a routing update informing it of a change in the metrics to any given destination. If this update meant that the second link was the lowest-cost path to a destination, it would begin using that link and cease using the first link.

RIP's inherent lack of load-balancing capability reinforces its intended use in simple net-works. Simple networks, by their very nature, tend to have few (if any) redundant routes. Consequently, load balancing was not perceived as a design requirement, and support for it was not developed.

15

ROUTING
INFORMATION
PROTOCOL (RIP)

Summary

RIP's ease of configuration, flexibility, and ease-of-use have made it a highly successful routing protocol. Since its development, there have been tremendous advances in computing, networking, and internetworking technologies. The cumulative effects of these advances have taken their toll on RIP's popularity. In fact, many other routing protocols in use today are technically superior to RIP. Despite the success of these protocols, RIP remains a highly useful routing protocol, provided you understand the practical implications of its limitations, and use it accordingly. The improvements in the newer version of RIP, called RIPv2, was also discussed.

Open Shortest Path First (OSPF)

by Mark A. Sportack

IN THIS CHAPTER

As the 1980s drew to a close, the fundamental limitations of distance-vector routing were becoming increasingly apparent. One attempt to improve the scalability of networks was to base routing decisions on link states, rather than hop count or other distance vectors. A *link* is the connection between two routers in a network. The status of that link can include such attributes as its transmission speed and delay levels.

This chapter provides an in-depth look at the Internet Engineering Task Force's (IETF's) version of a link-state, interior gateway routing protocol: Open Shortest Path First (OSPF). OSPF was first specified in RFC 1131. This short-lived specification was quickly made obsolete by RFC 1247. The differences between these two OSPFs were substantial enough that the RFC 1247 OSPF was called OSPF Version 2. OSPF Version 2 continued to mature and evolve. Subsequent modifications were outlined in RFCs 1583, 2178, and 2328 (which is the current version). The current version of OSPF is version 2. Because the Internet and IP are both highly dynamic, it is likely that OSPF will continue to evolve over time to keep pace.

The Origins of OSPF

The IETF, in response to the increased need for building larger and larger IP-based networks, formed a working group specifically to develop an open, link-state routing protocol for use in large, heterogeneous IP networks. This new routing protocol was based on the moderately successful series of proprietary, vendor-specific, Shortest Path First (SPF) routing protocols that had proliferated in the market. All SPF routing protocols, including the IETF's OSPF, were directly based on a mathematical algorithm known as the *Dijkstra Algorithm*. This algorithm enables the selection of routes based upon link states, as opposed to just distance vectors.

The OSPF routing protocol was developed by the IETF during the late 1980s. OSPF was, quite literally, an open version of the SPF class of routing protocols. The original OSPF was specified in RFC 1131. This first version (OSPF Version 1) was quickly superseded by a greatly improved version that was documented in RFC 1247. The RFC 1247 OSPF was dubbed OSPF Version 2 to explicitly denote its substantial improvements in stability and functionality. Numerous updates have been made to this version of OSPF. Each has been crafted as an open standard using the IETF as a forum. Subsequent specifications were published in RFCs 1583, 2178, and 2328.

Rather than examine the iterative development of the current, open-standard OSPF, this chapter will focus on the capabilities, features, and uses of the latest OSPF version.

Understanding OSPF

OSPF was designed specifically as an IP routing protocol for use within autonomous systems. As such, it is incapable of transporting datagrams of other routable network protocols, such as IPX or AppleTalk. If your network must accommodate multiple routable protocols, you might want to consider a different routing protocol than OSPF.

OSPF calculates routes based on the destination IP address found in IP datagram headers, and no provisions are made for calculating routes to non-IP destinations. Additionally, the various OSPF messages are encapsulated directly in IP: No other protocols (TCP, UDP, and so on) are needed for delivery.

OSPF was also designed to quickly detect topological changes in the autonomous system, and to converge on a new topology after detecting a change. Routing decisions are based on the state of the links interconnecting the routers in the autonomous system. Each of these routers maintains an identical database that tracks link states in the network. Included in this database is the state of the router. This includes its usable interfaces, known-reachable neighbors, and link-state information.

Routing table updates, known as *link-state advertisements* (LSAs) are transmitted directly to all other neighbors within a router's area. The technical term for this update process is *flooding*, a rather unflattering term with a negative connotation that belies the actual performance characteristics of OSPF.

In practice, OSPF networks converge very quickly. All routers within the network run the same routing algorithm and transmit routing table updates directly to each other. This information is used to construct an image of the network and its links. Each router's image of the network uses a *tree* structure, with itself as the *root*. This tree, known as the *shortest-path tree*, tracks the shortest path to each destination within the autonomous system. Destinations outside the autonomous system may be acquired via border gateways to those external networks, and appear as *leaves* on the shortest-path tree structure. Link-state data cannot be maintained on such destinations and/or networks simply because they are outside the OSPF network. Thus, they cannot appear as branches in the shortest-path tree.

OSPF Areas

One of the key reasons for the rapidity of OSPF's convergence is its use of areas. Remember, the two main goals that the IETF sought to achieve with OSPF were

- Improved network scalability
- Rapid convergence times

The key to both goals lies in compartmentalizing a network into smaller regions. These regions are known as *areas*. An area is a collection of networked end systems, routers, and transmission facilities. Each area is defined with a unique area number that is configured into each router. Router interfaces that are defined with the same area number become part of the same area. Ideally, these areas are not arbitrarily defined. Instead, the boundaries of an area should be selected to minimize the amount of traffic between different areas. Each area should reflect actual traffic patterns rather than geographic or political boundaries. Of course, this ideal is theoretical and might prove impractical in your particular environment.

The number of areas an OSPF network can support is limited by the size of its Area ID field. This field is a 32-bit binary number. Thus, the theoretical maximum number of networks is a 32-bit binary number with all of its bits equal to 1. The decimal equivalent of this number is 4,294,967,295. Obviously, the practical maximum number of areas you can support is much less than this theoretical maximum. In practice, how well the network is designed will determine the practical maximum number of areas you can support within it. Figure 16.1 illustrates a fairly simple OSPF network with just three areas, numbered 0, 1, and 2.

FIGURE 16.1
A small OSPF network with three areas.

Router Types

It is important to remember that OSPF is a link-state routing protocol. Therefore, the links and the router interfaces that they attach to are defined as members of an area. Based upon area membership, three different types of routers can exist within an OSPF network:

- Internal routers
- Area border routers
- Backbone routers

Figure 16.2 uses the network depicted in Figure 16.1 to identify the three different types of routers in the network.

FIGURE 16.2
*Area border
routers, internal
routers, and back-
bone routers in an
OSPF network.*

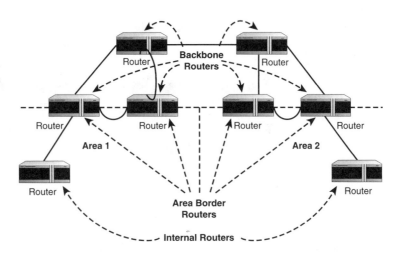

As shown in Figure 16.2, a router with multiple interfaces may belong to two or more areas. Such routers become *area border routers*. A *backbone* router is one that has at least one interface defined as belonging to Area 0. It is possible for an area border router to also be a backbone router. Any area border router that interconnects a numbered area with Area 0 is both an area border router and a backbone router.

An *internal router* features interfaces that are all defined as the same area, but not Area 0. Using these three basic types of routers, constructing highly efficient and scalable OSPF networks is possible.

Routing Types

Given the three different types of OSPF routers illustrated in Figure 16.2, it is important to note that OSPF supports two different types of routing:

- Intra-area routing
- Inter-area routing

These names are fairly self-evident. *Intra-area routing* is self-contained, and limited to just the routers internal to a single area. Using the sample network first illustrated in Figure 16.1, Figure 16.3 demonstrates intra-area communications in an OSPF network.

FIGURE 16.3

Intra-area communications in an OSPF network.

Inter-area routing requires the exchange of data between different areas. All inter-area routing must be conducted through Area 0. Nonzero area numbers are not permitted to directly communicate with each other. This hierarchical restriction ensures that OSPF networks scale gracefully, without becoming confusing morasses of links and routers. This type of hierarchical architecture is sometimes called *hierarchical routing*.

Figure 16.4 demonstrates the proper use of Area 0 to facilitate inter-area communications in an OSPF network.

FIGURE 16.4

Inter-area communications in an OSPF network.

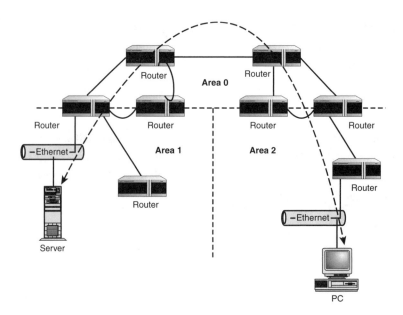

Open Shortest Path First (OSPF)

CHAPTER **16**

415

16

OPEN SHORTEST
PATH FIRST
(OSPF)

The preceding examples demonstrate, at a high level, how communications work within an OSPF network. However, OSPF can also be used to communicate routing information between OSPF networks, rather than just areas within a single network. This use of OSPF is examined in the following section.

Routing Between Networks

OSPF can be used to internetwork separate networks. Such networks could be another, complete OSPF network, or utilize a completely different routing protocol. Internetworking an OSPF network with a different routing protocol is a complicated task, and uses a technique known as *route redistribution*. This term describes the summarizing and redistributing of routing information from one network into another network. Routing information from the non-OSPF network is summarized and redistributed into the OSPF network.

The OSPF network tags all routes learned in this manner as *external*. Internetworking two different OSPF networks is easier, because there is no need to convert one routing protocol's route cost information into a format that the other protocol can understand. Additionally, OSPF enables the creation of autonomous systems. An *autonomous system* (AS) is a self-contained network. Ostensibly, an AS would feature a single network administrator or group of administrators, and use a single routing protocol.

The actual definition of an AS is somewhat fluid. In truth, it almost doesn't matter. What does matter is that OSPF permits the assignment of an AS number to a network. One very large OSPF network could be segmented into two or more autonomous systems. These systems would be interconnected via a fourth type of OSPF router, *autonomous system border router* (ASBR). The ASBR summarizes all the routing information for its AS, and forwards that summarization to its counterpart ASBR in the neighboring AS. In this regard, the ASBR functions much like an area border router. The difference, obviously, is that they comprise the border between separate autonomous systems instead of areas within a single autonomous system or network.

Figure 16.5 demonstrates internetworking autonomous systems using ASBRs.

FIGURE 16.5

Internetworked OSPF autonomous systems.

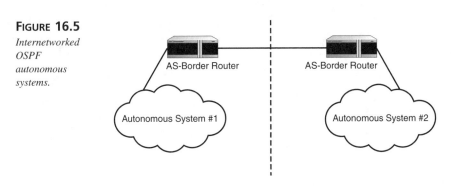

Routing Updates

One of the reasons OSPF is so scalable is its routing update mechanism. OSPF uses an LSA to share routing information among OSPF nodes. These advertisements are propagated completely throughout an area, but not beyond an area.

Thus, each router within a given area knows the topology of its area. However, the topology of any given area is not known outside of that area. Given that there are actually four different types of OSPF routers—internal area, area border, autonomous system border, and backbone—it is clear that each router type has a different set of peers that LSAs must be exchanged with.

Internal Area Routers

Internal area routers must exchange LSAs directly with each other router in its area. This includes every internal area router as well as any area border routers that may also be a member in its area. Figure 16.6 demonstrates the forwarding, or *flooding*, of LSAs throughout Area 1 of the sample OSPF network presented in this chapter's previous illustrations. It is important to note that same-area OSPF routers needn't be directly connected to each other to share LSA information. An OSPF router directly addresses LSA packets to every known router in its area, and forwards those packets using any available links.

The actual mechanism used to flood LSAs is multicasting, which is more efficient than broadcasting. Only OSPF routing processes that join the multicast group 224.0.0.5 receive LSAs. Also OSPF multicasts are efficient because they are carried directly inside an IP datagram using a protocol type 89. OSPF does not use any transport protocol such as TCP or UDP. Contrast this with RIP that uses UDP port 520.

FIGURE 16.6

LSA flooding within Area 1.

A subtle implication of Figure 16.6 is that convergence can occur quite rapidly. There are two reasons for this. The first is that an OSPF router directly addresses and transmits LSAs to all routers in its area simultaneously (known as flooding). This is in stark contrast to the neighbor-by-neighbor approach used by RIP to drive convergence. The result is an almost instantaneous convergence on a new topology within that area.

Convergence is also expedited through the definition and use of areas. Topological data are not propagated beyond an area's borders. Thus, convergence needn't occur among all routers in the autonomous system, just among the routers in the impacted area. This feature both expedites convergence and enhances the stability of the network because only a subset of the routers in the autonomous system experiences the instability that is innate in convergence.

Area Border Routers

Area border routers are responsible for maintaining topology information in their databases for each of the areas that they contain interfaces to. Thus, if an area border router interconnects two different areas, it must exchange LSAs with peers in both networks. As with internal area routers, these LSAs are addressed and transmitted directly to their peers in each area. This is illustrated in Figure 16.7.

FIGURE 16.7

Intra-area LSA flooding in an OSPF network by area border routers.

Another of the performance-enhancing features of OSPF is *route summarization*. Topological information about an area is not shared with other routers that are outside that area. Instead, the area border router summarizes all the addresses contained in all the areas it is connected to. This summarized routing data is then shared, via a link-state advertisement (LSA) packet with peer routers in each of the areas it interconnects. OSPF uses several different types of LSAs; each one has a different function. The LSA used to share summarized routing data is known as a *Type 3 LSA*. All the OSPF LSA types are described throughout the remainder of this chapter.

In Figure 16.7, the area border router advertises this summarized data directly to all routers in Area 0. OSPF prevents areas numbered greater than or equal to 1 from directly connecting to each other. All such interconnections must occur via Area 0. Thus, it is implied that area border routers interconnect Area 0 with at least one, nonzero numbered area.

Backbone Routers

Backbone routers are responsible for maintaining topology information for the backbone, as well as propagating summarized topology information for each of the other areas within the autonomous system.

Figure 16.8 illustrates the exchange of LSAs by backbone routers.

FIGURE 16.8
Intra-area LSA flooding in an OSPF network by backbone routers.

Although the distinctions between backbone, area border, and internal area routers might seem clear and distinct, there is room for confusion because of the capability of the router to support multiple I/O port connections to other routers. Each port, in theory, could be connected to a different area. Consequently, the router forms a border between the various areas that its interface ports connect to.

Exploring OSPF Data Structures

OSPF is a fairly complex routing protocol, with many performance- and stability-enhancing features. Thus, it shouldn't be a surprise to find that it uses an extensive array of data structures. Each structure, or message type, is intended to perform a specific task. All of them share a common header, known as the *OSPF header*. The OSPF header is 24 octets long and has the following fields:

- *Version Number*—The first octet of an OSPF header is allocated to the identification of the version number.

- *Type*—The second octet identifies which of the five OSPF packet types is appended to this header structure. The five types (HELLO, database description, link-state request, link-state update, and link-state acknowledgment) are identified numerically.

- *Packet Length*—The next two octets of the OSPF header are used to inform the node receiving the packet of its total length. The total length includes the packet's payload as well as its header.

- *Router ID*—Each router in an area is assigned a unique, four-octet identification number. An OSPF router populates this field with its ID number before transmitting any OSPF messages to other routers.

- *Area ID*—Four octets of the header are used to identify the area identification number.

- *Checksum*—Each OSPF header contains a two-octet checksum field that can be used to detect damage done to the message in transit. The originator runs a mathematical algorithm against each message and stores the results in this field. The recipient node runs an identical algorithm against the received message and compares its result with the result stored in the checksum field. If the message arrives undamaged, the two results will be identical. A mismatch indicates that the OSPF packet was damaged in transit. The recipient simply discards any damaged packets.

- *Authentication Type*—OSPF can guard against the types of attacks that can result in spurious routing information by authenticating the originator of each OSPF message. The Authentication Type field is a two-octet field that identifies which of the various forms of authentication is being used on this message.

- *Authentication*—The last nine octets of the header are used to carry any authentication data that may be needed by the recipient to authenticate the originator of the message. OSPF enables the network's administrator to specify various levels of authentication that range from NONE, to SIMPLE, to the strong MD5 authentication mechanism.

This basic structure contains all the information an OSPF node needs to determine whether the packet should be accepted for further processing, or discarded. Packets that have been damaged in transit (as indicated by the Checksum field) will be discarded, as will packets that cannot be authenticated.

OSPF uses five different packet types. Each is designed to support a different, highly specific function within the network. These five are

- HELLO packets (Type 1)
- Database description packets (Type 2)
- Link-state request packets (Type 3)
- Link-state update packets (Type 4)
- Link-state acknowledgment packets (Type 5)

These five packet types are sometimes referred to by their numbers, rather than by name. Thus, an OSPF Type 5 packet is really a link-state acknowledgment packet. All these packet types use the OSPF header.

> **Note**
>
> Due to the sheer number of variations on the five basic OSPF data structures, an exhaustive review of their sizes and structures is beyond the scope of this chapter. Instead, this chapter's coverage is limited to a description of the purpose and usage of each data structure.

The HELLO Packet

OSPF contains a protocol (the HELLO protocol) that is used to establish and maintain relationships between neighboring nodes. These relationships are called adjacencies. *Adjacencies* are the basis for the exchange of routing data in OSPF.

It is through the use of this protocol, and packet type, that an OSPF node discovers the other OSPF nodes in its area. Its name is intentionally significant; the HELLO protocol establishes communications between potential neighboring routers. The HELLO protocol uses a special sub-packet structure that is appended to the standard 24-octet OSPF header. Together, these structures form a *HELLO packet*.

All routers in an OSPF network must adhere to certain conventions that must be uniform throughout the network. These conventions include

- The network mask
- The interval at which HELLO packets will be broadcast (the *HELLO interval*)
- The amount of time that must elapse before a non-responding router will be declared dead (that is, the *router dead interval*) by the other routers in the network

All routers in an OSPF network must agree to use the same value for each of these parameters, or the network might not operate properly. These parameters are exchanged using HELLO packets. Together, they form the basis for neighborly communications. They ensure that neighbor relationships (known as *adjacencies*) are not formed between routers in different networks, and that all members of the network agree on how frequently to stay in contact with each other.

The HELLO packet also includes a listing of other routers (using their unique router IDs) that the source router has recently been in contact with. This field, the Neighbor field, facilitates the neighbor discovery process. The HELLO packet also contains several other fields, such as Designated Router, Backup Designated Router, and others.

These fields are useful in maintaining adjacencies, and support the operation of the OSPF network in both periods of stability and convergence. The specific roles of the Designated Router and Backup Designated Router are described in later sections of this chapter.

The Database Description Packet

The database description (DD) packet is exchanged between two OSPF routers as they initialize an adjacency. This packet type is used to describe, but not actually convey, the contents of an OSPF router's link-state database. Because this database may be quite lengthy, multiple database description packets might be needed to describe the entire contents of a database. In fact, a field is reserved for identifying the sequence of database description packets. Resequencing ensures that the recipient is able to faithfully replicate the description of the transmitted database description.

The DD exchange process also follows a poll/response method, in which one of the routers is designated as the master. The other functions as the slave. The master router sends its routing table contents to the slave. The slave's responsibilities are just to acknowledge received DD packets. Obviously, the relationship between slave and master varies with each DD exchange. All routers within the network will function, at different times, as both master and slave during this process.

The Link-State Request Packet

The third type of OSPF packet is the link-state request packet. This packet is used to request specific pieces of a neighboring router's link-state database. Ostensibly, after receiving a DD update, an OSPF router may discover that the neighbor's information is either more current, or more complete, than its own. If so, the router sends a link-state request packet, or packets, to its neighbor (the one with the more recent information) to request more specific link-state routing information.

The request for more information must be very specific. It must specify which data is being requested by using the following criteria:

- Link-state (LS) type number (1 through 5)
- LS ID
- Advertising router

Together, these criteria identify a specific subset of an OSPF database, but not its instance. An instance is the same subset of information, with a temporal boundary (that is, a time stamp). Remember, OSPF is a dynamic routing protocol: It can be expected to automatically update network perspectives in reaction to changes in the state of links in the network. Thus, the recipient of an LS request packet interprets it to be the most recent iteration of this particular piece of its routing database.

The Link-State Update Packet

The link-state update packet is used to actually transport LSAs to neighboring nodes. These updates are generated in response to an LSA request. There are five different LSA packet types. These packet types are identified by their type number, which ranges from 1 through 5.

> **Note**
>
> Potential for confusion exists because OSPF regards link-state advertisements, generically, as LSAs. Yet, the actual mechanism that is used to update routing tables is the link-state update packet—LSU, if one were to use its acronym. If this isn't confusing enough, there is another packet structure, the link-state acknowledgment packet, whose acronym would be LSA. For unknown and unspecified reasons, this packet is known as *link-state acknowledgment*, whereas *LSA* refers generically to the family of update packets.

These packet types, and their respective LSA numbers, are described as follows:

- *Router LSA (Type 1)*—Router LSAs describe the states and costs of a router's links to the area. All such links must be described in a single LSA packet. Also, a router must originate a router LSA for each area it belongs to. Thus, an area border router would generate multiple router LSAs, whereas an interior area router need generate only one such update.

- *Network LSA (Type 2)*—A network LSA is similar to a router LSA in that it, too, describes link-state and cost information for all routers that are attached in the network. The difference between a router and network LSA is that the network LSA is an aggregation of all the link-state and cost information in the network. Only the network's *designated router* tracks this information, and can generate a network LSA.

- *Summary LSA–IP Network (Type 3)*—The Type 3 LSA is somewhat awkwardly referred to as the *summary LSA–IP*, which is probably why the architects of OSPF implemented a numbering scheme for LSAs! Only area border routers in an OSPF network can generate this LSA type. This LSA type is used to communicate summarized routing information about the area to neighboring areas in the OSPF network. It is usually preferable to summarize default routes rather than propagate summarized OSPF information into other networks.

- *Summary LSA–Autonomous System Boundary Router (Type 4)*—The Type 4 LSA is a close relative of the Type 3 LSA. The distinction between these two LSA types is that Type 3 describes inter-area routes, whereas Type 4 describes routes that are external to the OSPF network.

Open Shortest Path First (OSPF)

CHAPTER 16

423

16

OPEN SHORTEST
PATH FIRST
(OSPF)

- *AS–External LSA (Type 5)*—The fifth type of LSA is the autonomous system–external LSA. As its name implies, these LSAs are used to describe destinations that are outside of the OSPF network. These destinations can be either specific hosts or external network addresses. An OSPF node that functions as the ASBR to the external autonomous system is responsible for propagating this external routing information throughout all the OSPF areas to which it belongs.

These LSA types are used to describe different aspects of the OSPF routing domain. They are directly addressed to each router in the OSPF area and transmitted simultaneously. This flooding ensures that all routers in an OSPF area have all the same information about the five different aspects (LSA types) of their network. A router's complete collection of LSA data is stored in a link-state database. The contents of this database, when subjected to the Dijkstra Algorithm, result in the creation of the OSPF routing table. The difference between the table and the database is that the database contains a complete collection of raw data, whereas the routing table contains a list of shortest paths to known destinations via specific router interface ports.

Rather than examine the structure of each LSA type, it should be sufficient to merely examine their headers.

LSA Header

All the LSAs use a common header format. This header is 20 octets long and is appended to the standard 24-octet OSPF header. The LSA header is designed to uniquely identify each LSA. Thus, it contains information about the LSA type, the link-state ID, and the advertising router's ID. The following are the LSA header fields:

- *LS Age*—The first two octets of the LSA header contain the age of the LSA. This age is the number of seconds that have elapsed since the LSA was originated.

- *OSPF Options*—The next octet consists of a series of flags that identify the various optional services that an OSPF network can support.

- *LS Type*—The one-octet LS type identifies which of the five possible types the LSA contains. The format of each LSA type is different. Thus, it is imperative to identify which type of data is appended to this header.

- *Link-State ID*—The Link-State ID field is a four-octet field that identifies the specific portion of the network environment that the LSA describes. This field is closely related to the previous header field, LS type. In fact, the contents of this field directly depend on the LS type. For example, in a router LSA the link-state ID contains the OSPF router ID of the packet's originator—the *advertising router*.

- *Advertising Router*—The advertising router is the router that originated this LSA. Thus, the Advertising Router field contains the OSPF router ID of LSA's originator. Given that OSPF router IDs are four octets long, this field must be the same length.

- *LS Sequence Number*—OSPF routers increment the sequence number for each LSA generated. Thus, a router that receives two instances of the same LSA has two options for determining which of the two is the most recent. The LS Sequence Number field is four octets long, and can be checked to determine how long the LSA has been traversing the network. It is theoretically possible for a newer LSA to have a greater LSA age than an older LSA, particularly in large and complex OSPF networks. Thus, recipient routers compare the LS sequence number. The higher number was the most recently generated. This mechanism doesn't suffer from the vicissitudes of dynamic routing and should be considered a more reliable means of determining the currency of an LSA.

- *LS Checksum*—The three-octet LS checksum is used to detect damage to LSAs en route to their destination. *Checksums* are simple mathematical algorithms. Their output depends on their input, and they are highly consistent. Fed the same input, a checksum algorithm will always return the same output. The LS Checksum field uses part of the contents of the LSA packet (includes the header, except for the LS Age and Checksum fields) to derive a checksum value. The source node runs an algorithm known as the *Fletcher Algorithm* and stores the results in the LS Checksum field. The destination node performs the same mathematical exercise and compares its result to the result stored in the Checksum field. If the values are different, it is relatively safe to assume that damage has occurred in transit. Consequently, a retransmission request is generated.

- *LS Length*—Predictably, the LS Length field informs the recipient of the LSA's length, in octets. This field is one octet in length.

The remainder of an LSA packet's body contains a list of LSAs. Each LSA describes one of the five distinct aspects of an OSPF network, as identified by the LSA number. Thus, a router LSA packet would advertise information about routers known to exist within an area.

Processing LSA Updates

OSPF differs substantially from other routing tables in that its updates are not directly usable by recipient nodes. Updates received from other routers contain information about the network *from that router's perspective*. Thus, the received LSA data must be subjected to a router's Dijkstra Algorithm to convert it to its own perspective before that data can be interpreted or used.

Ostensibly, LSAs are transmitted because a router detects a change in the state of a link or links. Thus, after receiving an LSA of any type, an OSPF router must check the contents of that LSA against the appropriate portion of its own routing database. This can't be done until after the router uses the new data to form a new perspective of the network, which is done via the SPF algorithm. The result of this output is the router's new perspective of the network. These results are compared with the existing OSPF routing database to see whether any of its routes have been affected by the network's change in state.

If one or more existing routes must change as a result of the state change, the router builds a new routing database using the new information.

Duplicate LSAs

Given that LSAs are flooded throughout an OSPF area, it is possible that multiple occurrences, known as *instances*, of the same LSA type will exist simultaneously. The stability of an OSPF network, therefore, requires a router to be able to identify the most current instance of the duplicated LSA. A router that has received two or more instances of the same LSA type examines the LS Age, LS Sequence Number, and the LS Checksum fields in the LSA headers. Only the information contained in the newest LSA is accepted, and subjected to the processes described in the preceding section.

The Link-State Acknowledgment Packet

The fifth type of OSPF packet is the link-state acknowledgment packet. OSPF features a *reliable* distribution of LSA packets (remember that LSA stands for link-state advertisement, not link-state acknowledgement). Reliability means that receipt of the packet must be acknowledged. Otherwise, the source node would have no way of knowing whether the LSA actually reached its intended destination. Thus, some mechanism was needed to acknowledge receipt of LSAs. This mechanism is the link-state acknowledgment packet.

The link-state acknowledgment packet uniquely identifies the LSA packet that it is acknowledging receipt of. This identification is based on the header information contained in the LSA's header, including LS sequence number and advertising router. There needn't be a one-to-one correlation between LSAs and acknowledgement packets. Multiple LSAs can be acknowledged with a single acknowledgment packet.

Calculating Routes

OSPF, despite its complexity, calculates the costs of a route in one of two remarkably simple ways:

- A non–bandwidth-sensitive default value can be used for each OSPF interface.
- OSPF can automatically calculate the cost of using individual router interfaces.

Regardless of which method is employed, the cost of any given route is calculated by calculating the costs of all interfaces encountered along that route. A record is kept of the calculated costs to known destinations in OSPF's shortest-path tree.

Using Autocalculation

OSPF can automatically calculate the cost of an interface. This algorithm is based on the amount of bandwidth that each interface type supports. The sum of the calculated values of all interfaces in a given route forms the basis for OSPF routing decisions. These values enable OSPF to calculate routes based, at a minimum, on the bandwidth available per link in redundant routes. Figure 16.9 presents a sample network to demonstrate this point.

In Figure 16.9, the cost of the WAN route between a host in network 193.1.3.0 and an end system in network 193.1.4.0 is 138. This cost is the sum of the two T1 links between those networks, each with a cost of 64, plus the cost of the Ethernet interface to network 193.1.4.0. The cost of the Ethernet interfaces at the origination and destination points are not included in the OSPF cost calculation because the OSPF only calculates the costs of outbound router interfaces.

FIGURE 16.9

Autocalculated costs of the links.

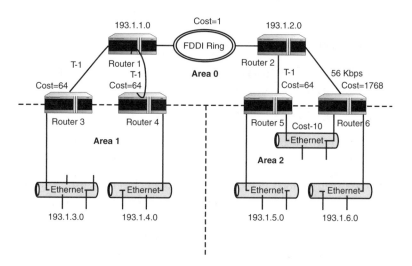

Table 16.1 summarizes the automatically calculated costs for each of the interfaces used in Figure 16.9's network diagram.

TABLE 16.1 Calculated Costs Per Interface Type

Interface Type	Calculated Cost
100Mbps FDDI	1
10Mbps Ethernet	10
1.544Mbps T1 serial link	64
56Kbps serial link	1,768

Using Default Route Costs

It is usually in your best interest to have OSPF automatically calculate route costs, although this may not be possible. For example, older routers might not support the autocalculation feature. In such cases, all interfaces will have the same OSPF cost. Thus, a T3 will have exactly the same cost as a 56Kbps leased line. Clearly, these two facilities offer very different levels of performance. This disparity should form the basis of informed routing decisions.

There are, however, circumstances that might make the use of default route costs acceptable. For example, if your network consists of relatively homogeneous transmission facilities, default values would be acceptable. Alternatively, you can manually change the cost metrics for specific interfaces. This would enable you to shape traffic patterns in your OSPF network as you see fit, while still using predominantly default routing costs.

Homogeneous Networks

In a homogeneous network, all the transmission facilities are the same. For example, all the LAN interfaces would be 10Mbps Ethernet and all the serial WAN interfaces would be T1s. In such a scenario, using the default values would not likely cause routing problems. This would be particularly true if there were little, if any, route redundancy.

To illustrate this point, consider the network diagram in Figure 16.10.

FIGURE 16.10

Acceptable use of OSPF's default interface values.

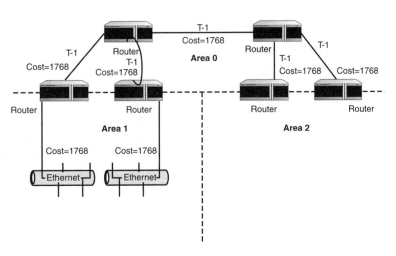

In Figure 16.10, a default value of 1,768 was assigned to each of the interfaces. All the WAN links, however, are T1s. Given that they are all the same, it doesn't matter whether the value assigned them is 1, 128, 1,768, or 1,000,000! Routing decisions, in a homogeneous network, become a simple matter of counting and comparing hops (albeit in multiples of the interface costs). This would be true regardless of how much, or how little, route redundancy existed in the network.

Obviously, in a complex network with substantial route redundancy *and* a disparity in the actual transmission technologies used, the default value would not enable selection of optimal routes to any given destination.

Manually Setting Values

In some networks, accepting OSPF's default costs, and then manually resetting those specific links that differ the most from the default might be desirable. For example, your network's default cost value might be 1,768—the calculated value for a 56Kbps serial link.

If all but one or two of the links in your network offered the same bandwidth, you could accept the default values and then reset the values for those particular links.

Whether you use automatically calculated routing costs, default costs, or manually configured costs is immaterial to OSPF nodes. They will accept all such cost values and develop a shortest-path tree perspective of the network.

The Shortest-Path Tree

The purpose of the various LSA mechanisms is to enable each router to develop a perspective of the network's topology. This topology is arranged in the shape of a tree. The OSPF router forms the tree's root. The tree gives the complete path to all known destination addresses, either network or host, even though only the next hop is actually used in forwarding datagrams. The reason for this is simple. Tracking complete paths to destinations makes comparing redundant paths, and selecting the best one to each known destination, possible. If there are multiple paths of equal cost, they are all discovered and used for load balancing by OSPF. Traffic is dynamically balanced equally across all such available links, thereby increasing the overall throughput for the route.

Router 3's Perspective

To better understand the concept of the shortest-path tree, consider the network diagram presented in Figure 16.11. The simple network depicted is a small OSPF network. The administrator has enabled autocalculation of routing costs. It is important to note that the Ethernet installed between routers 5 and 6 creates an alternate path for both networks 193.1.5.0 and 193.1.6.0. Thus, it has an OSPF autocalculated cost of 10, whereas similar costs are not assigned to the other Ethernet networks in this example.

Figure 16.11

An OSPF network with routing costs.

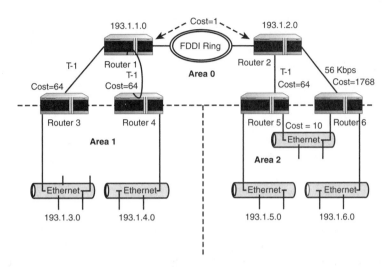

The shortest-path tree for this network (illustrated in Figure 16.10) would vary from router to router. Figure 16.12, for example, presents this tree from the perspective of Router 3.

Figure 16.12

Router 3's shortest-path tree.

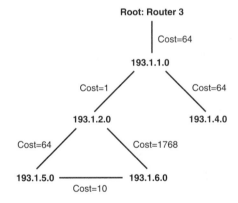

As is evident in Figure 16.12, the tree structure greatly facilitates the calculation of routing costs to any given destination. The root router (Router 3—193.1.3.0, in this case) can quickly sum the costs associated with each interface encountered along a route to a given destination. From Router 3's perspective, routing costs to each of the networks are calculated for you in Table 16.2. For destinations that are more than one hop away, the interface costs are calculated in parentheses. This will enable you to trace the path through the network in Figure 16.12.

TABLE **16.2**   Costs from Router 3 to Known Destinations

Destination	Hops Away	Cumulative Cost
193.1.3.0	—	0
193.1.1.0	1	64
193.1.2.0	2	65 (64 + 1)
193.1.4.0	2	128 (64 + 64)
193.1.5.0	3	129 (64 + 1 + 64)
193.1.6.0	3	1,833 (64 + 1 + 1768)
193.1.6.0	4	139 (64 + 1 + 64 + 10)

In this example, there are two possible routes to network 193.1.6.0. The one route contains fewer hops, but has a much higher cost due to the low-speed serial link between Routers 2 and 6. The alternate route has a higher hop count, but a much lower overall cost. In this case, OSPF would discard the higher-cost route and use the lower-cost route exclusively, even if it had more hops. If these two redundant routes had the same overall cost, OSPF would have maintained both routes as separate entries in its routing table and balanced the traffic as equally as possible between them.

Router 2's Perspective

Each router's perspective of the network is different. Although it would be somewhat monotonous to examine each router's perspective, a second example may prove useful in demonstrating the impact that perspective has on the shortest-path tree. Figure 16.13 demonstrates the shortest-path tree for Router 2.

FIGURE **16.13**

*Router 2's
shortest-path tree.*

Table 16.3 provides the summarized routing costs to all known destinations from Router 2's perspective.

TABLE 16.3   Costs from Router 2 to Known Destinations

Destination	Hops Away	Cumulative Cost
193.1.2.0	—	0
193.1.5.0	1	64
193.1.6.0	1	1,768
193.1.6.0	2	74 (64 + 10)
193.1.1.0	1	1
193.1.3.0	2	65 (1 + 64)
193.1.4.0	2	65 (1 + 64)

Comparing Tables 16.2 and 16.3 demonstrates that the cumulative distances between a source and destination in a network can vary based on the starting point. Perspective, it seems, is everything. This is why OSPF routers use data obtained from other routers via LSA updates to develop their own perspective of the network, rather than directly update their routing tables with that information.

Summary

OSPF is one of the most powerful and feature-rich open routing protocols available. Its complexity is also a source of weakness because designing, building, and operating an OSPF internetwork require more expertise and effort than a similar network using almost any other routing protocol. Accepting the default values for the routing costs will greatly simplify the design of an OSPF network. As your knowledge of both OSPF and your network's operational characteristics increase, you can slowly fine-tune its performance by manipulating the OSPF variables.

Extreme care must be used in designing the areas, and the network's topology. Done properly, your OSPF network will reward you with solid performance and quick convergence.

Network Services

PART V

Internet Printing Protocol (IPP)

by Tim Parker

The *Internet Printing Protocol* (IPP) is a new development in the TCP/IP suite of protocols. It is intended to make printing over a network or a larger internetwork much easier, based on IP addresses. Companies such as Hewlett-Packard have already introduced some devices that support the proposed IPP standards, and more are expected to arrive as IPP works toward a standard.

This chapter explains what IPP is and how it works. Although you may not have much need for IPP if you have a printer attached to your computer, it does show how network-based printing can be used.

History of IPP

IPP is the latest name attached to a series of developments, some competitive, that started in 1996 with Novell (makers of NetWare) approaching several printer companies to develop a new protocol for printing that would work over the Internet and IP. Several companies, such as Xerox, joined with Novell and developed a draft proposal and a development plan. Under Novell's stewardship, the project was called *Lightweight Document Printing Application*, or LDPA.

IBM, in the meantime, was working on a similar protocol that it called *HyperText Printing Protocol*, or HTPP. HTPP was so-named because it worked over the Web similarly to HTTP. Yet another similar effort was underway between Hewlett-Packard and Microsoft, who were developing a new print protocol for use with Windows 2000. To resolve the competing proposals and work under the Internet Engineering Task Force, the body that controls all protocols over the Internet, a *Printer Working Group* (PWG) was established. The PWG was made up of several printer and operating system companies. By pooling the best features of LDPA and HTPP together, the Internet Printing Protocol was developed.

The goal of the PWG is to form a universal standard for printing. The standard is not limited to using IP but could work under other protocols. The primary aim, though, is support for printing and print services over the Internet using IP. IPP uses HTPP as an adjunct to the next version of HTTP, called HTTP 1.1, instead of developing a completely separate protocol that sits on top of IPP. This leverages the features of HTTP 1.1 and makes implementation easier for vendors because most already are very familiar with HTTP. A new Multipurpose Internet Mail Extension (MIME) type called "application/ipp" is used for IPP.

Several targets exist for the Printer Working Group to include in the IPP specification. Tasks that IPP should support include:

- Allowing a user to determine what an IPP-based printer is capable of doing
- Allowing a user to submit a print job to an IPP printer
- Allowing a user to query the printer for the status of a print job
- Providing a facility for the user to cancel a queued print job

These four user-oriented goals cover everything a user would want to do, from determining which printers are available to sending, managing, and canceling print requests over the Internet, a LAN, or a WAN. Also part of the protocol is the ability to rapidly find accessible printers on a network or internetwork, and provide good security for the print requests and printers themselves.

Ideally, the goal of IPP is to create a client-side protocol. The server-side can be implemented in a number of ways, from a dedicated print server or from an IP-connected printer, for example. However, no change is planned to the underlying print spoolers and systems currently used, such as lpr and lpd under UNIX, or Windows' print handling system. IPP adds to these existing capabilities.

Longer-term goals for IPP are to include the ability to manage printers using IPP, provide print accounting systems, and even add commercial transaction capabilities.

Another goal of IPP is the translation of the LPR (Line PRinter) protocol onto IPP, and the translation of the IPP protocol onto LPR. However, there is no expectation to provide new IPP features to LPR clients, nor is there an explicit requirement to translate LPR extensions to IPP, beyond those features available in the 4.2BSD UNIX implementation of LPR.

> **Note**
>
> A number of RFCs are available with more details about IPP, all accessible from any RFC repository. See Appendix A, "RFCs and Standards," for more information about RFCs. In addition, the PWG has a Web site that includes current status and background information about IPP. The Web site can be found at `http://www.ietf.org/html.charters/ipp-charter.html`.

17

INTERNET PRINTING PROTOCOL (IPP)

IPP and the End User

When IPP is widely deployed, users will find a whole new world of capabilities for printing. The IPP RFC breaks down the abilities you gain into six categories:

- Finding a printer
- Creating a local instance of the printer
- Viewing the printer status and capabilities
- Submitting a print job
- Viewing print status
- Altering the print job

With IPP you can find all accessible printers using your Web browser or another application that searches for IPP-capable printers. The IPP design goal is to allow you to find a printer by a number of methods, including searching by the printer's name, by a geographic location, or by attribute.

Searching for attributes will be useful in large organizations. For example, you may want to be able to print folio-size pages (11×17 inches) and with IPP you could search for an accessible printer with this capability. You could also search for printers supporting color, legal-sized page feeds, binding abilities, and any other supported attribute. With a little search refinement, you can search for any printer that meets a number of additional criteria, such as within walking distance of your office or within a particular domain (even across the country or continent). This type of search capability is not part of IPP, but it is an inevitable spin-off.

When you find the printer you want to send a print request to, you need to be able to let your local computer know about the printer and how to access it. This is known as creating a *local instance* of the printer. To some extent, the way this is done depends on the operating system, but the overall effect is to add the printer you've chosen to the list of available printers on your machine.

In some cases, you may need to download drivers for the printer. This is currently the case when you need to access a printer across a network under Windows 95/98/ME, for example, and the process using IPP will be the same. Under some operating systems, such as UNIX, Linux, and Windows NT/2000, a little more flexibility is built-in to the creation of a local instance. You may decide that you want the queue for the printer on a different machine than your own, or you may want to have the drivers and queue reside on your machine. IPP allows enough flexibility to meet all these requirements for setting up an instance of a printer.

After you have created a local instance of a printer, it will appear as though that printer is attached to your machine. With Windows, for example, the printer (regardless of how far away it is) will appear in the Printers control panel applet, on all print dialog boxes, and any other application that accesses the printer list. You will use it exactly like you would a printer connected by a parallel cable.

Before you use an IPP-enabled printer, you may want to verify its setup or configuration and find out how busy the printer is, what kind of paper is loaded, how much memory the printer has, whether it supports a particular page descriptor language (such as PostScript or PCL), and many other status issues. IPP provides for a mechanism to relay all this status and capability information back to the user. General status messages show whether the printer is online or off, and what the default settings for the printer are.

The way the status messages are shown on the screen, and how you interact with an application to query the printer, is not defined as part of the IPP specifications. Instead, IPP handles the passing of the messages and the type of content that is possible. However, with a properly executed client application, a user should be able to determine the current status of a printer anywhere in the world that they have access to, as well as the status of the print queue.

When you have created a local instance of a printer, you are going to want to send print requests to it. The primary advantage of IPP is that you can print to any printer that has a local instance just as you would a physically connected printer. Windows applications, for example, would all recognize the IPP-capable printers in their printer dialog, whether the printer is remote or not. Some aspects of printing to a remote printer are not handled by IPP, such as selecting the proper page descriptor language interpreter (usually handled by the printer automatically) and choosing the right printer driver (usually handled by the operating system).

After a print job has been queued, IPP allows you to obtain status messages from the printer or print server that show the current queue and allow you to remove items from the queue.

Using HP's Implementation of IPP

Hewlett-Packard has already made a version of IPP available to its printer customers through its Internet Printer Connection software. Internet Printer Connection is designed to allow users to configure and print to HP (and other so-equipped) printers over the Internet or an intranet (LAN or WAN). Internet Printer Connection implements IPP as a transport for data to be printed and for printer status messages. Internet Printer Connection is an upgrade to existing software, so it is easy to add to established LANs.

In order to use HP's Internet Printer Connection, you need to have a Windows NT machine as the management host and an IPP-enabled HP JetDirect print server. A Web browser is required for users. Not all JetDirect print servers work with Internet Printer Connection; only firmware versions X.07.16 or later work. Fortunately, firmware upgrades to the JetDirect print server are available from the HP Web site. Installation of Internet Printer Connection is simple: Run a downloaded file to install the software, and reconfigure the printers that are to be used through Internet Printer Connection.

When installed, Internet Printer Connection allows any user with proper rights to print to any IPP-enabled printer by using the printer's IP address, a hostname (if DNS is enabled for hostname lookups), or the printer's URL. The beauty of Internet Printer Connection is that you can access a printer anywhere in the world, assuming you have rights to do so. If you're in a hotel room in Germany, for example, you can queue a print request to a printer in your home office in San Francisco. The same applies to east coast and west coast offices sharing print requests with each other. The Internet takes care of routing the print jobs using IPP. As far as a user is concerned, the printer looks exactly like any other printer attached to the machine or network.

Summary

IPP is not widely deployed across the Internet. However, the progress that has been made and the development of implementations such as Hewlett-Packard's Internet Printer Connection all bode well for IPP. IPP promises to become part of the standard TCP/IP services and make remote printing much easier on a TCP/IP network.

LDAP: Directory Services

by Mark Kadrich

The *Lightweight Directory Access Protocol* (LDAP) is an extremely powerful and robust protocol, and can be very complex in its implementation. A complete LDAP coverage can consume literally hundreds of pages. This chapter covers the salient points while trying to give an overview of the power and utility of LDAP.

Why Directory Services?

If you've been in the networking field for a while, you may have collected quite a wealth of information about different topics. The problem usually is not collecting this information, but rather organizing it and doing something useful with it when you need it. Like memos and other bits of paper, files tend to collect on your computer. To keep track of this information, you have probably created directories on your computer that represent bins of knowledge. You might have one for purchasing, one for manufacturing information, and another one for defects. Each bin represents a vertical line of knowledge pertaining to your discipline or career. This information is valuable to you because of what it represents: the collection of knowledge you have on a topic. However, the information you have is just part of a larger set of information.

With the proliferation of internetworking and the resulting explosion in information availability, collecting information has become a daily routine. You can collect information on whatever your discipline happens to be. New services offered by the Internet make searching for things easier than ever before. Search engines have made the chore of finding information about anything a point-and-click proposition. But now that you've found this information, how do you manage it? The answer is directory services.

What Are Directory Services?

You have used directory services before, although you might not have known it at the time. The phone book and the *TV Guide* are excellent examples of printed directories. In the case of the phone book, it's names, addresses, and phone numbers. In the case of *TV Guide*, it's times, names, descriptions, duration, subject, and content rating. You can even use the *TV Guide* to program your VCR. If you have a VCR equipped with VCR+, you can enter a directory number and the VCR will automatically program itself to record your selected program. This makes using the VCR and accessing the broadcast programming much easier to manage.

Like VCR+, LDAP offers a way to make locating things on the network significantly easier than other protocols, such as the Domain Name System (DNS). Unlike DNS, which just makes locating computers easier, LDAP allows you to keep information you find in a directory. LDAP directories contain information about users and their computers. Unlike the phone book and the *TV Guide*, LDAP directories are dynamic. The information they contain can be updated as necessary. LDAP directories are also distributed, which means they are less susceptible to failures.

Directory Services over IP

A number of other directory services run over the Internet Protocol (IP). IP is a system that uses numbers (actually, IP addresses) to identify computers and networks on the Internet. It is similar in function to identifying a room in a single apartment in an apartment complex. There is the building number, which is analogous to a network number; the apartment number, which is equivalent to the subnet number; and the room number, which can be thought of as the host number. For example, instead of saying 1234 Deep Creek Street, Apartment 128, you can use a name like John Smith to send your message.

If you've ever used a Web browser, you've used DNS. DNS functions in a manner similar to LDAP in that the client makes a request of the server and the server processes the request and returns an answer.

Figure 18.1 and Table 18.1 depict how IP addresses map to the DNS in a local lookup.

FIGURE 18.1

Local DNS lookup process.

TABLE 18.1 Sample DNS Table Relating Hostnames to IP Addresses

Hostname	IP Address
foo.com	IN A 192.0.112.1
foo	IN A 192.0.112.1

If a local server does not have the address, it will make a request of an upstream server, traversing an inverted tree very similar in structure to the one used by LDAP. This can be seen in Figure 18.2.

18

LDAP:
DIRECTORY
SERVICES

FIGURE 18.2

DNS lookup sent to upstream server.

Upstream DNS Server

3. Request sent to upstream server

4. Returns IP address of 192.0.112.1

Requesting Client

1. Request for foo.com

2. Server can't find foo.com in its internal database

5. Sends IP address of 192.0.112.1

Local DNS Server

Whois, finger, YP, NIS, NIS+, and DAP are also directory services that run over IP. You might remember the Yellow Pages, now commonly referred to as the *Network Information Service* (NIS). NIS is a service that identifies users, hosts, and in the case of NIS+, other information deemed pertinent by the system administrator. NIS is a service that enables administrators responsible for a large LAN or WAN to centralize user information. As shown in Figure 18.3, as a user logs in, a request is sent from the user's host to the YP server. This request would contain the user's information, such as UID (User Identifier, a number used to represent users internally under UNIX) and password, and host information. The YP server would send the resulting information back to the user's host, telling it to either permit or deny access to that host.

FIGURE 18.3

Yellow Pages, or Network Information Services, in a UNIX environment.

UNIX Client

YP/NIS Server
Usually UNIX

1. YP Request

2. Return Answer

Administrators like this service because it leverages the network itself. Secondary NIS servers can be set up across the network, ensuring reliability and reducing latency delays. It became a standard operating procedure to set up local NIS servers in order to reduce downtime incurred because of outages and high traffic loads.

Master NIS servers "push" tables of user information out to the secondary servers at pre-defined intervals. This usually happens during the early hours of the day along with network backups and system updates.

Occasionally, a change needs to be made immediately to a user's profile. On those special occasions when a disgruntled employee is escorted out the door, system administrators require a method of immediately removing that user's access. Sometimes new users, such as contractors, need to have access granted so they can start working. Contractors usually get paid by the hour, so getting them up and running as soon as possible was seen as a positive economic move. For these reasons, and other reasons, NIS also allows for the manual updating of secondary servers. System administrators can make a change and use a manual push to update specific network servers.

> **Note**
>
> A manual push is just as dangerous as it is useful. On more than one occasion a harried system administrator has "fat fingered" the command and inadvertently removed access for a major portion of the user community. This may be an unexpected way to test the robust nature of your PBX and voicemail system!

Whois is a text-based directory that stores information about hosts, servers, IP addresses, and networks. A whois query will reveal a considerable amount of information. Things such as the names of contacts, billing addresses, phone numbers, and domain servers are usually stored in the whois database. Our test of the Macmillan whois generated the following entry:

```
Registrant:Macmillan Magazine Limited (MACMILLAN-DOM)
4-6 Crinan Street London EnglandN1 9XW
UK Domain Name: MACMILLAN.COM
Administrative Contact, Technical Contact, Zone Contact: Humphreys,
➥    Mark (MH177)
postmaster@MACMILLAN.COM +44 71 836 6633
Billing Contact: Humphreys, Mark (MH177)
➥    postmaster@MACMILLAN.COM +44 71 836 6633
Record last updated on 05-Aug-98.
Record created on 11-Aug-94.
Database last updated on 11-Jul-99 19:39:33 EDT.
Domain servers in listed order:
NS0-M.DNS.PIPEX.NET 158.43.129.77
NS1-M.DNS.PIPEX.NET 158.43.193.77
AUTH01.NS.UU.NET 198.6.1.81
```

The OSI X.500 Directory Model

LDAP evolved from the OSI X.500 model. In this section, an overview of X.500 and the terminology used to describe Directory services is presented so you can better understand LDAP.

The OSI X.500 standard relies on code that sits on top of the Presentation Layer of the OSI stack to handle parsing and responses. Directly above the Presentation Layer, the *Association Control Service Element* (ACSE) and the *Remote Operation Service Element* (ROSE) enable the lower communication layers to exchange information via the OSI standard *Abstract Syntax Notation* (ASN.1). By standardizing on syntax as to how data is exchanged, ASN.1 provides a method for exchanging information between two disparate computer systems. This in turn enables the X.500 application to exchange information between computers on the network.

ASCE provides for the communication between two Application Layer entities. In the X.500 model, ROSE can facilitate the communication between Directory System Agents and Directory User Agents (see Figure 18.4).

The X.500 directory service model is comprised of three basic units. They are

- Directory Information Base (DIB)
- Directory System Agents (DSA)
- Directory User Agents (DUA)

FIGURE 18.4

X.500-based Directory Access Protocol components.

The information contained within the DIB is managed by DSAs so that DUAs can access and use it. DUAs use the *Directory Access Protocol* (DAP) to access DSAs. In this client/server type of arrangement, DUAs can be either people or other applications, such as an e-mail client. DSAs can communicate with other DSAs via *Directory System Protocols* (DSP) for the same reason that DNS servers communicate with each other. DSAs can be peers in a distributed environment. This provides for the extensibility that is required in today's large-scale networks.

Early X.500

In the 1980s, a group called the *International Telegraph and Telephone Consultative Committee* (CCITT) started an effort to store and retrieve information such as phone numbers and e-mail addresses.

> **Note**
>
> CCITT is now called ITU (International Telecommunications Union). The charter of ITU comes under the United Nations (UN).

At the same time, another group called *International Organization for Standardization* (ISO) started looking for a suitable service to support a name service for its OSI network. Eventually, the two groups realized that there was a duplication of effort and eventually merged their efforts into what is now the X.500 standards.

The result was a directory service that possessed some interesting qualities.

X.500's most important quality is that, as an open standard, it's not subject to the whims of individual vendors. Second, it is a general-purpose directory service capable of supporting a multitude of information. Third, it is extremely extensible and distributed. The X.500 solution was intended to support a wide and evolving network structure from the beginning, and it does that very well. Lastly, it supports a rich set of search capabilities that work within a secure framework. For a diagram of the major components, refer to Figure 18.4.

The X.500 solution was not without its problems. As was discovered early in its deployment, it was a complex solution requiring significant resources and planning. It was also intended for the OSI standard and not the TCP/IP standard used today. OSI never really took off and the speed and simplicity of TCP/IP was a hard combination to beat. It was obvious that some changes needed to be made to DAP.

> **Note**
>
> The initial specification of X.500 ran on OSI protocols and was deemed to be overly complex. As the TCP/IP protocols gradually displaced OSI communication protocols, a need was felt for a simpler version of X.500 that could run on TCP/IP protocols. This need was met by LDAP.

X.500 Today

The X.500 standards have evolved into a group of well-integrated specifications. The core of these was the *Directory Access Protocol* (DAP), which was supposed to be the center of all directory requests. The unfortunate aspect, or fortunate, depending on your perspective, of X.500 evolution was that it tried to solve all the problems at once. So a number of multiple and arcane services were provided by DAP that saw little use in a desktop environment. The full-scale implementation of DAP proved to be quite an ordeal for desktops. To relieve the complexity, an intermediary service was developed. LDAP was that bridge.

The Structure of LDAP

LDAP is intended to be simple. However, there is a strong similarity between X.500 and LDAP. LDAP uses Directory System Agents and Directory User Agents; however, in LDAP they are referred to as simply LDAP servers and clients. LDAP uses the same OSI architecture as well. The LDAP-enabled application sits atop the Presentation Layer and talks to the lower layers via the LDAP *Application Programming Interface* (API).

The basic elements of the LDAP service are

- LDAP server
- LDAP-enabled client

The main difference here is the reliance on an API instead of the stack "shim," an addition to the IP stack, that connects X.500 and the communications stack. The main similarities are the structure of the network configuration and how the data is stored. Like X.500, LDAP services are hierarchical.

LDAP Hierarchy

The LDAP information structure is similar to that of the file system described earlier. In Figure 18.5, you can see that it starts at the top with a root, usually the organization itself. The basic unit of LDAP information is the *entry*. The entry is a collection of pertinent, real-world information about the object in question, in this case, the organization itself.

FIGURE 18.5

Inverted tree structure of LDAP directories.

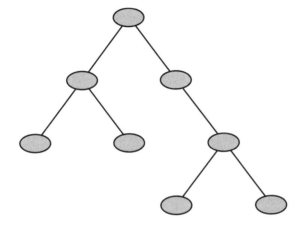

In many cases, the directory structure mirrors the structure of the organization. It starts with a description of the organization and resolves down to detailed entries such as departments, resources, and eventually people.

Naming Structures

Within the directory entry is a set of attributes that describes a single trait of the selected object. Each attribute is composed of a type and one or more values. An attribute *type* describes the information contained within the attribute. *Values* are the data entered into the attributes. For example, an attribute is Telephonenumber and a value is 1 800 555 1234.

At the top of the directory structure is the suffix. This is called the *domain component*, or dc.

Object classes provide for the naming of elements in a way that is conducive to effective searches. For example,

```
objectclass=person
```

allows for the searching of all object classes defined as persons and not as servers or buildings, thereby making the search less time-consuming.

Following this convention is the attribute cn, for common name. As shown in Figure 18.6, the common name is usually the full name of the individual or resource.

A complete directory listing would start with a distinguished name, or dn, which contains the information about the object class and the individual or resource.

Because LDAP does not support linking from the top of the directory to other directories as DAP does, aliases support this function by making your entire DIT look like a leaf to other DITs.

FIGURE **18.6**

Namespace example, Directory Information Tree.

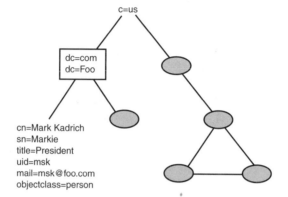

Directory System Agents and Access Protocols

Initially, DSAs were the repositories of directory information. Directory Information Bases resided on DSAs. DSAs were accessed by Directory User Agents residing on client computers. Referring again to Figure 18.4, DUAs use DAP to access DSAs, which contain DIBs. Sounds simple enough, but there is more. DSAs were designed to be distributed. As the DIB grows, it might be necessary to move portions of it to other servers or to link other DSAs together. This is accomplished via a Directory Service Protocol. Unlike DAP, which is intended to support user queries, DSP is used to enable DSAs to exchange information, pass on requests, replicate or shadow directories, and provide for management.

The Lightweight Directory Access Protocol

As previously discussed, LDAP evolved from earlier protocols. These earlier protocols, such as DAP, were developed prior to their deployment. Their complexity was the result of the architect's envisioned need for more information in a variety of formats.

The solutions proved to be too complex for the small desktop systems and too complex for administrators. The solution needed to be made simpler. The business community helped by whittling down the requirements to something that would work on a desktop, yet enable administrators to regain a large portion of configuration control that had been lost in the rush to distributed systems. The final solution was what has evolved into LDAP.

LDAP is a messaging protocol that is based on the client/server model of network computing. A server holds the information and relies on clients on the network to make requests based on their needs. The server formulates a response and sends it back to the client. Figure 18.7 shows how client requests are sent as independent messages to the server.

FIGURE 18.7
Basic LDAP messaging protocol.

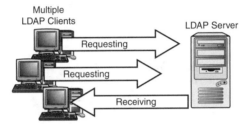

Retrieving Information

The ability of users and their applications to retrieve current information creates a powerful and robust platform from which to build.

In the LDAP model, it is assumed that the data will be read many more times than it will be written. For this reason, LDAP is optimized for read access. In a normal LAN, services such as the DNS are high transaction services. In other words, other services depend on the ability of a directory service to answer requests for information.

As mentioned earlier, the LDAP protocol is a client/server–based protocol. This enables the server to be optimized for specific processes—in this case, searching and retrieving information and sending it out on the network. The LDAP server contains the information with little regard to extraneous processes and user interfaces other than those required to manage the data and the server.

The process is started by a client binding to the server and initiating a request for information. Binding is the process that establishes a session between a host and a server. Figure 18.8 demonstrates how the basic process works. The client constructs a request asking for a single entry, for example, a user's phone number, and sends this message to the server. The server responds to the request by sending a message with the requested information and a result code message. The result code message will tell whether the request was successful and, if not, what the error is.

FIGURE 18.8

Basic LDAP protocol sequence.

LDAP Client — 1. Request Search → LDAP Server
2. Return Answer ←
3. Return Result Code ←

In the case where multiple messages must be sent to the client to respond properly, the results are sent in multiple messages with the final message being a result code message, as shown in Figure 18.9.

FIGURE 18.9

Multiple message requests via LDAP.

LDAP Client — 1. Request Search 1 → LDAP Server
2. Request Search 2 →
3. Return Answer 1 ←
4. Return Answer 2 ←
5. Return Result Code 1 ←
6. Return Result Code 2 ←

The nature of a message-based protocol is that it allows multiple messages to be sent at one time. The LDAP server will process these individual message requests and respond with individual answer messages and result code messages for each request.

LDAP allows requests to do some basic *interrogation* operations, *authentication* operations, and maintenance or *update* operations.

Under the heading of interrogation, LDAP provides *search* and *compare* operations. These operations enable the user to query the database.

Under the heading of authentication and control, LDAP provides for bind, unbind, and abandon. *Bind* is the very first thing that a client must do to initiate a session with the server. During this phase, the client will identify itself and present its credentials to the server. This works with the security protocols to prevent unauthorized access to your database.

Unbind tells the server that the client is finished with the LDAP session. The application that requested the LDAP information is satisfied with the results and the user has moved on to use the application.

When a client sends an *abandon* message, it is telling the server that it no longer needs the information. The user might have terminated the application that was requesting the information or the application might have abnormally ended, requiring the operating system to send the abandon message. Figure 18.10 shows the complete transaction from start to finish.

FIGURE 18.10

Multiple requests via one message.

Storing Information

Storing information falls under the heading of maintenance and population activities. LDAP provides for these operations by supporting the following three functions:

- **Add**—The Add function is just that, the ability to add new users and attribute values to an existing database.

- **Delete**—Delete removes attributes or entire entries from the database. This is useful when users leave the organization. However, most system administrators will simply set a user as inactive. This is done in case the "delete" operation needs to be undone.

- **Modify**—The Modify function will probably be the most used function of the system administrator. The Read function will be the second most utilized function by the user. The Modify function enables system administrators and users to modify information in the directory. Typically, users will only be able to modify a small subset of their information. Data items such as phone numbers and hair color are usually left to the users' discretion.

One thing that should be given careful consideration is to whom these capabilities are given. You might want to allow some of your users the ability to modify their own information. This means that you should pay close attention to access rights as they pertain to user directories.

18

LDAP: DIRECTORY SERVICES

Access Rights and Security

During a recent test of Internet-accessible LDAP servers, it was discovered that for the most part, all LDAP servers were easily accessible. Any information security professional will tell you that the most dangerous thing to give someone is access. If a hacker can get to your server, he can own the data.

You must have a program that ensures that your server, whether a UNIX or an NT box, is configured in a secure manner. It is also recommended that a security policy that ensures continuous checks of your server is also in place. A number of commercially available applications will check your server for a large number of security vulnerabilities in your operating system as well as the database itself.

Access rights and how they are applied to users' directories are specific to the server application you are using. Take care to understand how your application and the operating system work together to provide security.

LDAP Server-to-Server Communications

Although many users will see only the client-to-server portion of the LDAP protocol, behind-the-scenes activities ensure that users can reliably query servers.

Reliability entails supporting a robust design that is not susceptible to single point failures. It also means keeping the latency to a minimum. Latency as it applies to reliability is a perception issue, at least from the user's perspective. If it takes too long for users to access a network-based service, they will complain that the network is broken and unreliable. By setting up your LDAP server as a single point of failure, your network may be susceptible to longer down times.

The LDAP Data Interchange Format (LDIF)

LDAP uses a standard method for generating message requests and responses. The messages are exchanged using ASCII text in a predefined format called *LDAP Data Interchange Format* (LDIF). A typical LDIF file looks like the following:

```
dn: uid=msk, ou=people, dc=starwizz, dc=com
objectclass: top
objectclass: person
objectclass: managementPerson
objectclass: corpmgntPerson
cn: Mark Kadrich
cn: markie
```

```
givenname: Mark
sn: Kadrich
uid: msk
mail: msk@starwizz.com
telephonenumber: +1 408 555 1212
description: President, Starwizz Enterprises

dn: uid=ma, ou=people, dc=starwizz, dc=com
objectclass: top
objectclass: person
objectclass: managementPerson
objectclass: corpmgntPerson
cn: Mitch Anderson
cn: mitchie
givenname: Mitch
sn: Anderson
uid: ma
mail: ma@starwizz.com
telephonenumber: +1 408 555 1212
description: Vice President, Starwizz Enterprises
```

The top line forms the Relative Distinguished Name (RDN), and can be used to trace the object, in this case a person, from his name to the organization. You will note that the format is similar to how e-mail addresses work with the resolution decreasing to the right. This is referred to as *little-endian* order. In this format, the least significant element is written first, with more significant elements being added to the right. For example, msk@host.division.state.starwizz.com.

LDAP Replication

Replication is a multifaceted service that provides for increased reliability and performance. By distributing your directory information throughout your network environment, you reduce your vulnerability to server- and network-related failures. As you can see in Figure 18.11, if a replica LDAP server fails, internal requests can be sent to one of the other LDAP replicas or to the master itself. Without the LDAP replicas, the clients on the A and B networks would be without LDAP service.

This is also beneficial from a performance perspective because local queries of the LDAP server do not have to pass through the router. Local requests are handled by local resources, thereby relieving the network of unneeded traffic. Moreover the response to local requests will be faster.

The replicas do not have to contain the entire directory tree. For purposes of security or maintenance, only specific portions of the DIT may be replicated. You can choose to replicate only those services running on their associated network. In Figure 18.11,

Replica B would only contain directory entries specific to network B. Requests for information about services outside of network B would be passed on to the Master LDAP server.

FIGURE 18.11

Distributed LDAP servers on a WAN provide redundancy and reliability.

Designing Your LDAP Service

Defining requirements is a live or die proposition. Spending the time to examine how your information environment works and how it will grow is time well spent.

Defining Requirements

As you look at the requirements for setting up your directory service, you should consider a number of areas. This solution is supposed to address the user community's needs as they apply to the information environment that the users work in. This means that you must consider the users and their tools. Consider the following list:

- User needs
- User expectations
- Application needs
- Deployment constraints
- Deployment issues
- Everything else

We have all had to deal with users and their expectations. All too often designers have given users lofty expectations in order to sell a solution to the user community. The solution was not based on the perceived needs of the users, but instead on someone else's idea of what would be a great solution. When the reality of the situation becomes apparent, the users are not happy. A successful solution must meet the user's expectations because they are the ones that ultimately decide whether you are successful.

Here we are considering LDAP-enabled applications and how they are deployed within the user's environment. You will, of course, have to consider what might come down the road at a later date, but making this part of the present set of solutions is not recommended. This is not to say that you shouldn't consider what new applications are being planned for. Rather, consider what impact these planned-for applications will have on the present design without trying to design a directory for every possible contingency.

You should also take into careful consideration the user's perception of how this data will be used and protected. The idea of what is personal and what is not personal information covers a broad spectrum within the user community. Accuracy is another concern. How often will the data be updated? Users will be expecting accurate data. Having said all this, trying to predict users' needs is a little like looking into a crystal ball. It only takes one major news article about some new whiz-bang application to change their minds.

Application needs are a major design element. The type of information and the frequency with which it is needed is a major factor that must be given careful consideration. In a manner very similar to how DNS drove the way applications used the Web, user applications will drive your design of the directory service with more force than anything else.

Designing the Schema

It is easy to say that you should include as much information as possible. However, the more information there is, the more information that must be sifted through to get the correct response to a query. You also don't want a minimal solution that might not meet the needs of the users and their applications.

Where data is obtained is just as important as the data itself. You want to avoid sources that cannot be verified or are not current. This leads to the consideration of other data sources within your organization. Areas such as HR and the helpdesk keep databases that might contain the same information. In database terms, this is *redundant* data.

The basic problems that bound your efforts are

- Too much information
- Too little information
- Incorrect information

This last item is a painful one to address because it concerns the quality of the information contained within your database. Sometimes it is more than a simple query by your Web browser. In some instances decisions are being made based on the information contained in your LDAP server. The implication is that decisions may be made on stale, out-of-date information. This can be catastrophic when you consider a worst-case scenario. Take, for example, the disgruntled employee that has been dismissed because he or she continually harassed his co-workers. Assume also that this disgruntled employee is a gun collector. Taking this one step further, your LDAP server talks to the computer that authenticates employee access to the building. It does not take a rocket scientist to see the potential for severe damage.

Setting a policy that ensures that your data will be contemporary and secure is a good idea. Remember that this database will most likely contain some personal information. You data policy should cover the following areas:

- Storage
- Access
- Modification
- Maintenance
- Legal
- Exceptions

The following sections briefly discuss guidelines for each of these.

Storage Guidelines

Storage guidelines address issues pertaining to what data will be stored in your database. Constraints on size and source may also be addressed here. An example would be that no data element larger then 15K would be stored in your database.

Note

LDAP allows you to store arbitrary binary data including JPEG and IMG files. These files take up a large amount of space. You must estimate the number of LDAP objects that will have these types of attributes that will take up space. This will give you an estimate about the amount of space the LDAP database will take up. LDAP databases can get quite large, and you need to provide for appropriate and frequent backups.

Access Guidelines

Access guidelines determine who can see and use the information. Once again, choosing to store sensitive information in your database becomes an acute concern.

Modification Guidelines

Modification guidelines determine who updates information as well as how information is updated in your database. The all-important question of whether to let users update their own information is generally addressed here. Methods for authentication and encryption (privacy of the link) should also be covered here.

Maintenance Guidelines

Maintenance of the data can be an interdepartmental issue, and a policy covering it can be extremely useful. It should state how often data is reviewed as well as how redundant data is reviewed. The problem of other databases, such as HR, containing out-of-sync data is handled here.

Legal Issues

Some data is more sensitive than other data, and disclosing it to the wrong party can cost an organization more than money. It can cost the organization its good name. Have your legal department review your database. It might take some time, but in the long run it's well worth it.

Exception Guidelines

A policy without a method to petition for change or exception has a life expectancy that can be measured in days. You should include a mechanism for granting exceptions and permanent changes. These changes should be authorized at the highest level possible. A director is a good place to start.

Performance

A service that takes forever to use will very quickly fall into disservice. When you consider the construction of your LDAP service, you must also consider the environment in which it will be used. Some questions that you should consider include

- What type of LAN/WAN will the LDAP server be used in?
- How many services will be using the LDAP server?
- How much money is there to spend on hardware?

18

LDAP: DIRECTORY SERVICES

The type of LAN or WAN you will be attached to has a large bearing on how many LDAP servers you will need to support your users' requirements. In a simple LAN environment, one server might be all that is needed (see Figure 18.12). A single router connects the LAN to the Internet whereas a few network hubs connect the user's computers to the LAN. The firewall is a standard security device that controls the flow of traffic between the LAN and the Internet. See the section, "Security," later in this chapter for more information.

FIGURE 18.12

Simple LAN-based LDAP deployment.

In large organizations, having a more complex network than the one depicted in Figure 18.12 is quite common. Multiple routers connect internal WAN elements, each of which contains numerous LAN elements. Having thousands of computers distributed throughout the world using these techniques is quite possible. In a more complex environment such as this, you may consider using the inverted tree structure to deploy LDAP servers, as shown in Figure 18.13.

FIGURE 18.13

Complex WAN with distributed LDAP servers.

Network Abilities

Reliability and availability are sometimes referred to as the "abilities" of the network. Reliability directly affects availability. It stands to reason that if the server is unreliable, the service it provides may be unavailable. In the case of the network, it isn't just the server but also the devices that support the network. As discussed previously, some networks are large and distributed. To address availability, networks use redundant devices such as routers, switches, and *uninterruptible power supplies* (UPS). Not all devices are redundant. Some routers and switches, the expensive ones, can be equipped with redundant power supplies to address this most common element of failure. To address the network portion, two devices are used so that if one becomes disabled, the other will take over. This type of configuration is called *fail-over* and is referred to as high availability. As you can see in Figure 18.14, this sometimes involves multiple connections to the Internet.

FIGURE 18.14

Redundant routers and hot stand-by routers.

A more robust implementation is called *fault resilient*. Fault-resilient solutions generally use a fail-over type configuration but with care taken to ensure that redundancy within the device is as high as possible. An example of this would be two routers, each with dual power supplies, a UPS, and separate connections to the Internet.

> **Note**
>
> The basic disadvantage to these types of solutions is that you must spend twice as much money on hardware and software, and only one device is functional at a time.

18

LDAP: DIRECTORY SERVICES

The most reliable configuration is called *fault tolerant*, which means no single failure of any component will cause the total failure of the device.

A way to determine the level of reliability is by stating the permissible downtime. As you can see in Table 18.2, conventional servers can tolerate 3.5 days of downtime per year. Conversely, fault-tolerant systems are only down for *five minutes* per year.

An LDAP server should qualify for at least a designation of high availability. Fault resilient is, of course, much better.

TABLE 18.2   Reliability Designations as Measured by Time

Percent of Uptime	Maximum Downtime per Year	Availability Designation
99%	3.5 days	Conventional
99.9%	8.5 hours	High availability
99.99%	1 hour	Fault resilient
99.999%	5 minutes	Fault tolerant

Another way to mitigate single points of failure is to distribute your LDAP services throughout your network environment. A site on the West Coast would have its own server and a site on the East Coast would also have its own server. Both would report to the corporate server for updates and replication. This type of a configuration can take advantage of any network reliability factors, thereby increasing overall reliability. Refer to Figure 18.13 for an example of how this may look.

Security

Many systems have succumbed to trivial attacks, enabling some malevolent individual to steal precious information. An LDAP server is no different than any other server on the network—if it's improperly configured, anyone with a simple understanding of security exploits can access your data.

Security isn't just preventing unauthorized access to your data. It is a conscientious attitude of understanding risks, threats, mitigation, and benefit. You must make a risk versus benefit assessment each time the question of security comes up. You must also realize that many different levels of security exist. Some information is public, whereas other information is classified "burn before reading" because it is so sensitive. Other information will fall between these two extremes.

What is the issue? Simply put, LDAP enables an organization to put a huge amount of information into a service designed to provide answers in a reliable and expeditious manner. Thieves love that, especially if they can gain access to the information.

Threats

People usually associate computer security threats with hackers. This is not always the case. In reality, most security breaches are perpetrated from the inside by an organization's own people. A recent survey performed by Peter Shipley prior to the 1999 Blackhat Briefings conference indicated that a large number of corporate LDAP servers were accessible via the Internet. (The Blackhat Briefings are a yearly gathering of government, corporate, and private security professionals held in Las Vegas, Nevada.) Additionally, those that were accessible had little if no security enabled. Using a tool called nmap (available via the Internet), a scan using the command

```
nmap -P0 -p 636,639 192.168.0.0/24
```

revealed a large number of vulnerable servers. This same command, with your IP address, can be used to determine whether your servers are accessible from the Internet.

18

LDAP:
DIRECTORY
SERVICES

Note

If you download something from the Internet, especially from a hacker site, run it in a controlled environment before you turn it loose on the network. You may wind up being the recipient of a trojan horse or a virus if you don't. A *trojan horse* is a piece of software that masquerades as something that it is not. In other words, you may be downloading what you think is the greatest new tool when in reality you're downloading one tool and one piece of malicious code. For this reason, scanning all downloaded files with anti-virus software before using these files is a good idea.

Shipley also discovered that few, if any, servers were using secure methods of exchanging information. *Secure Sockets Layer* (SSL) is a standard method of encrypting information that will ensure that your data stays private.

There are a few basic types of security breaches. Because, like LDAP itself, this is an extremely complex field this section only covers the basics. Basic types of security breaches include

- Unauthorized access
- Unauthorized data modification
- Denial of Service attacks

Unauthorized access is access to your server by someone who does not have permission to do so. This is generally done for the purposes of stealing credentials, hijacking sessions, or embedding software.

Stealing credentials is very similar to password stealing except that it can be done on a much broader scale. The intruder can masquerade as the CIO or anyone else he wants to be. On more than one occasion, an individual has been terminated by someone he thought was his boss when in reality it was a fellow co-worker. By the time the error was discovered, the damage had been done. This is a sure way to create the disgruntled employee discussed earlier.

Although it requires physical access to the LAN, hijacking sessions can be accomplished after a user authenticates himself. The attacker simply inserts his packet stream to the server and sends a TCP reset to the unsuspecting user. The user thinks the network "hiccuped" and proceeds as usual. This is another reason to ensure a reliable network. A simple way to prevent session hijacking is to use encryption, such as SSL, to prevent access to the network packets. Another method is to encrypt all interactions on a network. This can be done using Virtual Private Networks (VPNs). VPNs create a tunnel or sleeve where all packet data between two endpoints are encrypted. VPNs are useful whenever the network has a security risk, such as with wireless networks. However, wireless networks are often slow, and the overhead of VPNs make them even slower.

Embedding software is generally the sign of a more sophisticated attacker. By leaving a trojan horse, attackers can do just about anything they want. Some trojans just sniff the network and send information back to the attacker, whereas others provide backdoor access to the system. Back doors will render most host security efforts useless.

Unauthorized modification of your data can be a severe hazard. By changing the "deliver to" account number, a hacker can have payroll diverted from the user's bank account to his private Swiss account.

Denial of Service, or DoS, attacks are attacks directed at stopping your LDAP server. The two types of DoS attacks that work at the application level are direct and indirect resource consumption.

In a direct resource consumption attack, a user continually makes requests for large amounts of data. By tying up the system resources, no one else can make requests. Placing limits on the number of directory resources any single client can use is a standard way to reduce the severity of this attack.

An indirect attack is harder to address because it doesn't attack the LDAP application itself. Rather, it attacks resources that the LDAP server uses. For example, assume that a trojan horse was introduced to the server and all it did was make disk requests. By denying access to the disk files, the attacker has effectively stopped the LDAP server. Preventing this type of attack requires adherence to the basic disciplines of security as stated earlier. Minimal software, a pedigreed operating system, and continued vigilance will at least make detecting these types of attacks easier.

Host Security

Host-level security is the first thing a hacker will look at, and it is probably the most overlooked aspect of a server's configuration. Depending on the environment, server software may need to be configured, compiled, and linked. This is particularly true in the UNIX environment, which uses the open source code philosophy. This means that the configuration of the operating system needs to be carefully checked. Unfortunately, all too often if the server runs, the configuration is assumed to be secure.

UNIX server security is a well-known subject. A number of good books have been written about it. Additionally, a number of commercially available software products are capable of reviewing the machine's configuration and providing you with directions to secure it.

Windows NT/2000 has similar products, although they aren't as pedigreed as their UNIX brethren. One reason is that Windows NT/2000 uses proprietary code (closed source code), and security bugs in the code remain undiscovered for a long time.

18

LDAP: DIRECTORY SERVICES

> **Note**
>
> If it doesn't need to be on the server to provide the service, remove it. Don't just disable unused software, *delete* it. Common services such as telnet and FTP should not be supported on your LDAP server.

Enable log generation and send the logs to a computer specifically set up to save and archive system logs.

Application Security

First and foremost: If it isn't needed, don't have it there.

This would seem like a simple rule to follow. However, many system administrators are pressed to use their systems to the fullest, thereby creating an insecure situation.

Other Security Issues

Physical security is another aspect that is overlooked. Because it's not a firewall or a file server, an LDAP server may not be afforded the same level of protection as other, more critical services. Remember that many of these services rely on LDAP, and it is for this very reason that LDAP servers should be monitored under lock and key.

Keep your LDAP servers in a locked room with controlled access. At a minimum, keyboard locks and password-enabled screen savers should be employed. If possible, deploy LDAP servers behind firewalls so access to them is controlled and protected.

Tools

Some tools that you can use to secure your server include

- Authentication
- Auditing
- Encryption

Authentication does not refer to just user IDs and passwords. Strong authentication systems, such as those from Secure ID and Axent Technologies, provide a token that exchanges a secure password that is only used one time. Each time the user accesses the system, he uses a new password. All the user has to remember is a simple PIN.

Auditing is the basics of security. By reviewing the audit logs of your system, you can determine whether any nefarious activity has taken place. Most security people will tell you that this task is boring and mind-numbing, but it is a necessary one.

Whit Diffie, the father of many encryption algorithms, said that "It was not encryption that was inherently weak, but how encryption was used that made it weak." This is significant when you consider that encryption is the foundation for many of our security tools. SSL uses encryption to make packets unreadable by anyone except for the designated computer. Certificates use encryption to validate, or digitally sign, documents thereby signaling to the recipient that the document is authentic.

Table 18.3 is a basic representation of how user access to information may be configured. System administrators have complete access to data, so although it isn't included in the chart, access to system administrator workstations should be protected with a strong authentication mechanism.

TABLE 18.3   LDAP Attributes and Their Associated Access Permissions and Protections

Attributes	Assessor	Access Level	Security
cn, sn, givenName, middleInitial, name	All	Read	None
cn, sn, givenName, middleInitial, name	SysAdmin	Read/Write	SSL and Certificate
mail	All authenticated	Read	Password
mail	SysAdmin	Read/Write	SSL and Certificate
mail	Self	Read/Write	Password
homeAddress, homePhone	All	User's choice	Password
homeAddress, homePhone	Self	Read/Write	Password
postalAddress, telephoneNumber	All	Read	Password
postalAddress, telephoneNumber	SysAdmin	Read/Write	SSL and Certificate
salary	Self	Read	Password
salary	Management	Read/Write	SSL and Certificate

18

LDAP: DIRECTORY SERVICES

LDAP Deployment

Deployment is the next bottleneck. You must work with the other departments that are responsible for network services and application readiness. In many instances, these departments will have windows designated specifically for deployment. Often they also have procedures for deployment of network services that must be met, such as testing and acceptance.

Consider the order in which the service will need to be deployed. If you are relying on the LDAP to support a workflow application, it is possible that some portions will not function properly without LDAP. Nothing angers a user more than a system saying that the user she is trying to reach doesn't exist when she can throw a phone book over a cubicle partition and hit him.

This can also be the area where politics must be considered. If each department has its own set of applications, you must be sure to consider the various sensitivities that drove the department to select its tools.

The Production Environment

Although many production environments are different, they do possess some similarities. First, they all contain people. Second, these people are there because they have a job to do. It's a business, so treat rolling out your LDAP service the same way. Start with a project plan that has some measurable elements and milestones. Above all else, manage to that plan. Use the plan as a blueprint to chart your course and measure your success.

Creating a Plan

The plan should have enough detail so that in the event that someone else must take over, it's not a coded mystery. A good plan will delineate a number of elements, such as

- Resources
- The project plan itself
- Success criteria
- Depending on your organization, a marketing plan

You can use a number of tools, such as Microsoft Project, to create a rollout plan that can combine the tasks and the resources in a way that makes it easy to see what is going on. Use a tool that provides the same utility, and you should be fine. Figure 18.15 is a sample of the basic steps you should follow. As you can see, resources are named in the plan. Prerequisite tasks are laid out prior to the rollout.

A good project plan can also be a great way of communicating status to management.

Establishing success criteria should happen based on the requirements. For example, is the LDAP server being added to address a new application? If so, the LDAP server cannot be used as a measure of success. Instead, the application actually being able to use the LDAP server is the ultimate measure of success.

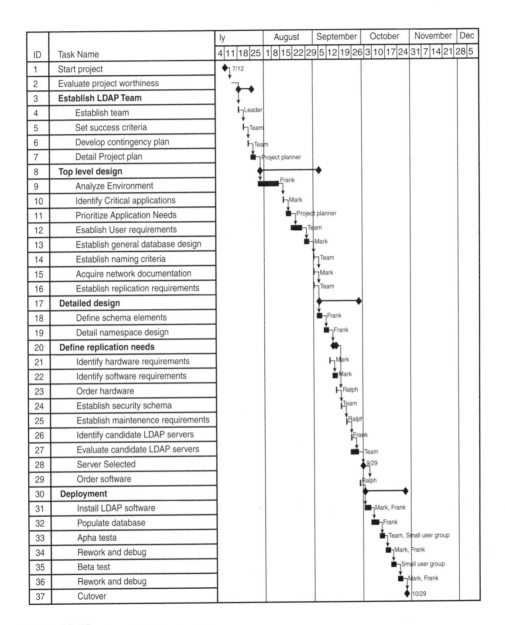

ID	Task Name	ly	August	September	October	November	Dec
		4 11 18 25	1 8 15 22 29	5 12 19 26	3 10 17 24	31 7 14 21 28	5
1	Start project	◆ 7/12					
2	Evaluate project worthiness						
3	**Establish LDAP Team**						
4	Establish team	Leader					
5	Set success criteria	Team					
6	Develop contingency plan	Team					
7	Detail Project plan	Project planner					
8	**Top level design**						
9	Analyze Environment		Frank				
10	Identify Critical applications		Mark				
11	Prioritize Application Needs		Project planner				
12	Esablish User requirements		Team				
13	Establish general database design		Mark				
14	Establish naming criteria		Team				
15	Acquire network documentation		Mark				
16	Establish replication requirements		Team				
17	**Detailed design**						
18	Define schema elements		Frank				
19	Detail namespace design		Frank				
20	**Define replication needs**						
21	Identify hardware requirements			Mark			
22	Identify software requirements			Mark			
23	Order hardware			Ralph			
24	Establish security schema			Team			
25	Establish maintenence requirements			Ralph			
26	Identify candidate LDAP servers			Frank			
27	Evaluate candidate LDAP servers			Team			
28	Server Selected			9/29			
29	Order software			Ralph			
30	**Deployment**						
31	Install LDAP software				Mark, Frank		
32	Populate database				Frank		
33	Apha testa				Team, Small user group		
34	Rework and debug				Mark, Frank		
35	Beta test				Small user group		
36	Rework and debug				Mark, Frank		
37	Cutover				◆ 10/29		

FIGURE 18.15   *Sample LDAP rollout plan.*

18

LDAP:
DIRECTORY
SERVICES

This is why a good marketing plan can help. A sponsor with the clout to make statements, publish e-mails, and send memos can be a huge advantage. The sponsor can help set expectations and fend off the naysayers, giving you the time needed to build a quality service.

Valuable Advice

Pay attention to detail! As the architect, uncovering the details specific to your organization is your responsibility.

There may be an urge to push your schedule. *Don't do that.*

During the rollout, you may discover that some things need to change. That's what the project plan is for—to help you understand the impacts of unknown situations and circumstances.

Don't hide anything. If something is broken or a mistake has been made, deal with it and move on. If they don't trust the messenger, they won't trust the message. In other words, if they don't trust you, they won't trust your service.

Manage to your plan. It is easy to get caught in the minutiae and lose focus. It's during those unfocused moments that the dreaded curse of "scope creep" begins to enter the project. A common mistake many project managers make is to get buried by details that had nothing to do with their project.

Be prepared. If possible, be prepared for the unexpected. Try to have an answer for different scenarios. A good project manager will play "what if" with the project. What if the hardware is late? What if my coder dies? What will you do? These are hard "what ifs," but a necessary process to go through.

Selecting LDAP Software

Like any other software, a selection process that addresses your internal needs is critical. Is the software a value-added proposition or just another application that adds little value. This is entirely up to you and the process you employ to select a vendor.

The basic areas of interest can be broken into the following elements:

- Core features
- Management features
- Security features
- Standards compliance

- Flexibility

- Reliability

- Interoperability

- Performance

- Extensibility

- Cost

- Other, generally political concerns

Core Features

Here you are looking to see whether the software will run on your selected hardware. The last thing you want to do is buy Windows NT/2000 software for a UNIX environment.

Does the software support the LDAP features that your applications need? If not, deselect it.

The ability to support replication features in your topology is a critical concern. If you plan on distributing LDAP servers throughout your enterprise, this item is high-priority.

How does the selected software support the introduction of data? Will you have to painstakingly enter every bit of data or are there import features?

Lastly, documentation and support need to be addressed. Will you have to install the software using inadequate or confusing installation instructions or is there adequate documentation supported by a trained helpdesk?

Management Features

Look for tools that make manipulating content easy. An additional benefit is the ability of the selected software to support scripting operations.

Difficult tasks, such as configuring security access rights, should have a tool to make the process less painful. This may even take the form of user profiles. Being able to designate a type of user and then copy it is a real time-saver.

Sometimes you aren't where you need to be to have a hands-on session with your server. This brings to mind remote management functions. Ensure that your candidate software supports *secure* remote management functionality, because you will be sending sensitive material across the network and you don't want unauthorized users stealing your information.

18

**LDAP:
DIRECTORY
SERVICES**

Security Features

Basic access controls are a must for an LDAP server. Ensure that you can accomplish the resolution or granularity required to control access. You may have to be able to grant access controls to specific users instead of to groups of users.

A robust LDAP server will support encryption capability, such as SSL or *transport layer security* (TLS). This critical feature is required if you are going to do any remote management or replication.

A broad range of authentication options is a prerequisite. Basic LDAP authentication, as well as certificates and password tokens, should be included as basic features.

Because you may want other administrators or even some users to take care of their own data, the ability to delegate is important.

Standards Compliance

Basically, the solution should comply with all relevant LDAPv2 and LDAPv3 RFCs. Check compliance to RFCs 1777 through 1779 and RFCs 2251 though 2256. Security specifications such as those called out in RFC 2222, Simple Authentication and Security Layer, should also be complied with. For the purposes of remote management function and network management, access via SNMP is a must.

You can find a good collection of LDAP information at `http://www.mozilla.org/directory/standards.html`.

A number of application programming interfaces (APIs) should be complied with, such as those for Java and C. However, a few nonstandard APIs, such as the Active Directory Services Interface (ADSI) from Microsoft, allows you to write programs in scripting languages supported by the Windows Scripting Host (WSH).

Flexibility

Few products work without some configuration. It is assumed that some aspects of your network are different from those of everyone else. The ability to address these configuration differences is important. Your selected LDAP product should be flexible enough to address your requirements. For example, can the configuration be tuned to address different hardware requirements? After all, not all machines will have 512 MB of RAM or more.

Another issue is that of adding or extending schemas. Can you manipulate the data structure without having to do a complete reinstall? New applications may bring new data elements and you may have to extend your schema to accommodate them.

Reliability

If one piece of data in the database is incorrect, the rest of the data is unreliable. If the server is unavailable, other applications that rely on it will not operate. To address this issue, you must ask some important questions. Will the server recover from a failure without losing any data? How does it process transactions?

The ability to run 24×7 is a must. Few users will tolerate your taking down the LDAP server that runs mission-critical applications so you can perform a backup.

Look for the ability to support fail-over or some other type of high-reliability solution. Although there is a hardware component to address, information must be exchanged between the primary server and the hot backup, a duplicate machine that contains a copy of the directory. Otherwise, you may have to deal with lost data and angry users after a failure.

Interoperability

Simply put, this is the LDAP server's ability to work with your applications and those that support it.

> **Note**
>
> Make your life easier and ask for proof. This may be in the form of existing customers or a demo lab. Whatever form it is in, make sure you see it work first. Many vendors claim to have high reliability solutions but they only work in specific environments. Make sure it works in your environment.

Performance

Because this service is network-based, standard questions regarding latency and throughput must be asked. You must know in advance what your users will tolerate in latency and delay. Then you must find out whether the server can meet those needs. Will it be able to handle the load of simultaneous connections without crashing? Does it have the ability to monitor its performance, and does it have the ability to change parameters to enhance performance?

Knowing the server's theoretical limit is a good idea. Much of a server's performance is linked to the hardware configuration, but at some point this changes. It may not have the internal buffers or handles that are required to go beyond a performance plateau. For the purposes of planning you need to know that limit.

Extensibility

Some applications make extending their capability beyond that of the original program easy. Some do it by supporting scripts, whereas others, like Netscape, use a software bus approach that enables the use of plug-in modules.

This ability can be very useful if you must develop your own application or address an existing homegrown application.

Cost

It would be nice if you could predict costs accurately by saying, "I'd like the blue one for $100." Unfortunately, cost is not an easy item to predict, and projects are plagued with cost overruns. Vendors seem to have made it their mission to make costing-out LDAP servers as confusing as buying a new car! Some vendors charge by the number of seats, some charge by the number of servers, some charge by the number of entries. Some inspired vendors sell unlimited licenses. Usually, it's a combination of all the above.

Don't be surprised if there is a yearly charge for maintenance. Under that same consideration, think about the day-to-day activities that must be performed, such as backups and upgrades.

Some LDAP servers are tied to a particular operating system. This is the case with Microsoft's Active Directory. You must have Windows 2000 Server to take full advantage of its features.

There is also the subject of the hardware on which the LDAP server runs. Some operating systems require a significant investment in hardware. Don't forget to add that in.

Training and support must also be added in. Some vendors supply training for free but you must still pay for the administrator's time.

Other, Generally Political Concerns

On the business side it's always nice to consider the vendor from which you're purchasing your product. Will it be around in a year? How big is this company? Will it be able to develop the product as new extensions for LDAP are published?

Consider how your vendor fits into the directory-enabled market. Although you will most likely be using products from other vendors, it's nice to see a corporate commitment from your vendors. Your vendor should be spending money on research and development to ensure that its product remains compatible with the standard. The company should also be taking part in interoperability tests to ensure its products are compatible with other vendors' products.

Summary

LDAP has the potential to be the Great Organizer of the network world. Being able to point applications at a single source of directory information relieves network administrators of a considerable burden. Not only does it make application designers' lives a lot easier, but it also makes the system administrator's life easier as well. System administrators will no longer have to manage multiple applications in order to ensure user connectivity. Users will see transparent connectivity to needed services and information.

However, LDAP is a sophisticated service that requires significant attention to detail. Planning and testing play a major role in a successful LDAP implementation.

As the network services grow, we will see a greater reliance on network-based directory services such as LDAP. Some day, it may even replace the phone book and the *TV Guide*.

18

LDAP:
DIRECTORY
SERVICES

Remote Access Protocols

by Mark Kadrich

As the Internet has grown, so has the need to access it from any location. Often, this type of access is called *remote access*. In the beginning, remote access was performed using a terminal that was connected to a mainframe or minicomputer. This method of access was satisfactory as long as you were in a fixed location such as your office. As support staffs shrank, providing system administrators with access to corporate networks from home became imperative. Thus, remote access was born. This simple type of access was via the slow modems of the time, typically at 110 baud. (Baud rate and bits per second are close enough for the purposes of this discussion that they will be used interchangeably.) System administrators were now able to monitor system activity and make system-related changes from the relative comfort of their homes. A benefit to the organization was that critical systems could now have cost-effective 24×7 monitoring by individuals who could do something in the case of an emergency. That is, as long as that emergency wasn't the terminal services going down!

The late '70s and early '80s brought advances in technology that enabled modems to increase their throughput every couple of years. Like their sister integrated circuits the memory chip, they followed Moore's law by doubling in throughput capacity every couple of years.

Today's modems typically run at around 56K with their actual throughput being governed by the antiquated copper infrastructure of the *Public Switched Telephone Network* (PSTN). This aging infrastructure, in conjunction with the introduction of more advanced reliability and security requirements, has placed special emphasis on developing protocols that effectively allow for the transmission and reception of digital data.

Remote Connectivity

As alluded to earlier, a major component of a remote access solution is a modem. MOdulator/DEModulators (mo-dem) can take the form of many different types of devices. Basically, a modem changes the digital signals generated by your computer to those that can traverse the PSTN. Each end must have a compatible modem for this operation to work properly (see Figure 19.1). On the receiving end, the analog signals are demodulated into digital signals and fed to the receiving computer.

FIGURE 19.1

A basic modem and the PSTN network.

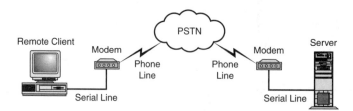

ISDN

Not all of these devices are compatible. A standard modem will not allow you to connect to an Integrated Services Digital Network (ISDN), and an NT-1 (network termination) will not allow you to connect to anything other than an ISDN line. However, ISDN offers some interesting benefits. A *Basic Rate Interface* (BRI) allows the subscriber to use analog phones as well as pure digital transmission of data. In the United States, a BRI consists of two 64K channels and one 16K channel that are *Time Division Multiplexed* (TDM) for an aggregate total of 144K bits per second (see Figure 19.2).

FIGURE 19.2
ISDN BRI configurations.

ISDN's versatility comes from the fact that at any given time all three channels can be used individually or the two 64K channels can be used together to supply a total of 128K of throughput. An interesting advantage of ISDN was that it could use the existing two-wire telephone wire that came to most businesses and homes. This was an important consideration for the businesses as well as the telephone companies that needed to provision ISDN. It meant that expensive upgrades to the existing PSTN would not be required. Although this was a wonderful solution to increasing the time that the existing PSTN would be able to provide service, the Internet revolution would apply additional stress as millions of consumers jumped online. ISDN's days were numbered.

Cable Modems

Cable modems have been in use for a couple of years now (see Figure 19.3). A cable modem takes advantage of the fact that many consumers have a broadband transmission medium, the TV cable, already in their homes.

FIGURE 19.3

Cable modem.

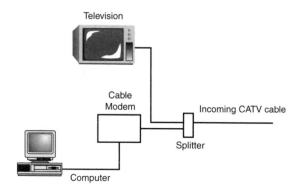

By taking advantage of the unused portion of the cable bandwidth as well as employing some interesting tricks of modulation, cable modems can supply users with access speeds at around 1Mbps. This is quite impressive in a home environment. Recent developments in software and operating systems allow multiple computers to take advantage of this single access point.

Cable modems connect the computer to the neighborhood cable line in much the same way that Ethernet used to connect computers via a coaxial cable. Everyone is on one data bus. This means that all the people in your neighborhood can potentially access your computer. Care should be taken to prevent this. One method is through *Network Address Translation* (NAT).

By using software that takes advantage of RFC 1918, "Address Allocation Techniques for Private Networks," commonly referred to as NAT, a home network can now provide each computer on the network with Internet access and security. This is convenient if you want to segregate users by age as, for example, a parent with a teenager might. As it turns out, today's computer receives just as much attention as yesterday's telephone.

Companies such as @Home have pioneered this type of access in a multitude of areas. Check with your local cable company to see whether you have this capability.

Digital Subscriber Loop (DSL)

Digital Subscriber Loop (DSL) is a relatively new service that offers a number of interesting versions of essentially the same capability. Using a price-based service-level model, DSL offers more throughput for more money. A 56K link can be acquired for about $50 per month and three times the capability can be bought for twice the cost. Table 19.1 shows a general price list of DSL connections based on throughput supplied. These are average listed prices and do not include any sales or special offers.

TABLE 19.1   General DSL Pricing List

Data Rate	High	Low
144	$124.00	$90.00
160	$149.00	$80.00
192	$169.00	$90.00
384	$199.00	$130.00
768	$359.00	$180.00
1.1	$399.00	$200.00
1.5	$359.00	$290.00

There are a number of different flavors of DSL, with *Asymmetric DSL* (ADSL) being the most popular. ADSL takes advantage of the notion that a typical user will download more than he will upload. When browsing the Web, users typically download more in graphics than they upload. Generally, most users will upload simple responses to Web queries. When you click a button on a Web page, you send a simple message back to the server telling it to do something, such as send back a picture or text. The exception to this is electronic mail. However, even with e-mail added to the mix, there is still typically a 10-to-1 ratio of downloaded versus uploaded data.

DSL was invented to address a number of unique problems that have cropped up since the Internet explosion, particularly that of capacity. The existing PSTN was built around the idea that most conversations would be about 10 minutes long, with the average household having at most two lines. This allowed the central offices (COs in telephony parlance) to be sized ratiometrically. In other words, if only 10 percent of the population was using a phone at any one time, the COs would only have to be large enough to support so many phone switches in the phone company racks.

19

REMOTE ACCESS PROTOCOLS

Note

DSL is still experiencing some teething pains. When a DSL line is part of a cable bundle that is carrying an ISDN line, a significant amount of crosstalk between the lines reduces the effectiveness of the DSL line. Talk with your vendor before you commit to a DSL line.

An interesting benefit of DSL over cable modems is a consistency of throughput. Because you share the cable segment with your neighbors, as more of your neighbors get cable modems your effective throughput will decrease. Because DSL is a point-to-point connection to your service provider, it isn't as susceptible to this problem. However, DSL is still affected by how much bandwidth is available from the CO to the Internet. Also, your DSL connection point cannot be too far from the CO. Currently, this distance limitation is around 15,000 feet but is likely to change with advances in technology.

Radio Networks

Radio networks are offered through a plethora of technologies that range from cellular networks to pure radio modems, such as those offered by Ricochet and Metricom. Communicating with transceivers located on light poles in your neighborhood, Ricochet allows an appropriately equipped computer to communicate with the Internet without wires. Along with a cell phone and a pager, your office can be at any location. Although very convenient, the disadvantage is that this communication method is not secure.

Remote Authentication Dial-In User Service (RADIUS)

The *Remote Authentication Dial-In User Service* (RADIUS), RFC 2138, provides a number of important services to remote users. RADIUS is a client/server protocol originally developed by Livingston Enterprises in 1992. It was developed in response to the need to provide an enhanced method of authenticating users to their security devices.

RADIUS has grown to be a significant component in the system administrator's effort to provide enhanced confidence in the authentication process.

A RADIUS configuration will usually consist of a central database server and one or more dial-in servers (see Figure 19.4).

The database contains the three A's of information—Authentication, Authorization, and Accounting. *Authentication* information enables the network to identify users to the system. Although this information is generally stored in ASCII text files, RADIUS servers can communicate with password files and NIS+. *Authorization* information gives users access to servers and data, such as the corporate intranet server or the phone lists. *Accounting* information is used to keep track of user accesses, failed accesses, connect time, and so on.

FIGURE 19.4

The RADIUS client-server model.

RADIUS Clients

Internet

Internal Router

Firewall

Internet Routers

Internal Clients

RADIUS SERVER

RADIUS Authentication

The RADIUS exchange is fairly straightforward. After the user has connected to the remote access server, the RAS server will prompt the user for a name and a password using the *Password Authentication Protocol* (PAP), or the *Challenge Handshake Authentication Protocol* (CHAP).

Password Authentication Protocol (PAP)

PAP is an older protocol that relies on passwords and user IDs and is documented in RFC 1334. After the user establishes the remote link, a user ID and password pair is sent to the RADIUS server. As shown in Figure 19.5, the access server continually sends the password and UID to the authentication server until a timeout occurs. If you are interested in security, this is not the protocol of choice. Passwords are sent "in the clear." In other words, there is no encryption of the user account and password information. This means that someone can record the transaction, discover the user account and password, or replay it later in order to gain access to your critical services. PAP is generally a fallback protocol that is used after protocols such as CHAP are attempted and failed.

FIGURE **19.5**

*PAP protocol
exchange.*

RADIUS Clients using PAP

Internet

Internal Router

Firewall

Where's my answer?

RADIUS SERVER using PAP

Challenge Handshake Authentication Protocol (CHAP)

CHAP is special in that it provides a stronger method of authenticating the user. CHAP is described in detail in RFC 1994. CHAP is a three-way handshake that sends a challenge code to the user and the user is expected to give the proper "handshake" response. After the user establishes the link, the server sends a "challenge" packet to the client. The client responds by calculating a response using a one-way hash function, such as MD5. The client sends the response to the server that has calculated the expected response. If the response from the client matches the response calculated by the server, the client is permitted access to the network. If the response doesn't match that calculated by the server, access is denied. To ensure that the session hasn't been hijacked, the CHAP protocol can be configured through the server to periodically re-authenticate the client. Unlike PAP, the authenticator controls the entire CHAP sequence and retries are rarely permitted.

This type of authentication prevents replay attacks such as the one discussed in the preceding section. Because each challenge is different, each calculated response is different. It should be noted that this protocol does rely on a shared secret. The secret is used as the key in the hashing function (see Figure 19.6) so it should be protected. The challenge value should follow two criteria: It should be unique and it should be unpredictable.

FIGURE **19.6**
*Diagram of
hashing method.*

The CHAP authentication method should be used if your intent is to access sensitive network resources or if you are concerned about security in general. As a matter of fact, according to the CHAP RFC 1994, PAP is actually obsolete as a password protocol when using PPP.

Account Information

Account information can take many forms, including user ID, password, temporal access restrictions, service authorizations, and auditing information.

We're all used to the usual UID and password information. RADIUS allows for the addition of auditing information. This information can be used to determine whether someone has tried to access systems that he shouldn't be accessing. You can also use the information to control when someone is permitted to access the network. If you have a receptionist who only requires access from 9 a.m. to 5 p.m., you can set the account information to reflect this. Any access outside of these limits isn't permitted. In effect, you reduce the available time of exposure of your network, thereby increasing security.

A similar effect can be obtained by using the database to limit access to various services. By entering a list of approved services, you can prevent access to unauthorized services. When users attempt to access a service they are not authorized for, they will be denied by the RADIUS server. This basic policy management provides for a centralized user database that can easily be updated.

Transporting IP Datagrams with SLIP, CSLIP, and PPP

A number of different protocols have been developed to move information from one point to another. The selection of a protocol depends on how much capability you require. The following sections discuss the history of remote access protocols and where we are today.

Serial Line Internet Protocol (SLIP)

SLIP was an early protocol used to connect remote users to a local host. RFC 1055 is an informational specification only because SLIP was already a de facto standard when RFC 1055 was written. SLIP was one of the first useful remote access protocols in that it provided for IP connectivity to the remote networks that were appearing in the early 1980s. Figure 19.7 shows how the Berkeley and Sun Microsystems operating systems used SLIP.

FIGURE **19.7**

The SLIP protocol.

SLIP is a very simple-minded protocol because it was designed when networking was simpler, and the problem that was being solved was just to send IP datagrams across serial links. The entire RFC, including code, is only five pages long. All the SLIP protocol does is define how data is framed on a serial line. There is no error correction or detection, addressing, packet identification, or compression. Its sole purpose was to push packets across a serial line.

> **Note**
>
> It is important to realize that serial line protocols such as SLIP and PPP are Data-Link Layer protocols (OSI Layer 2). There is a need for these protocols because serial lines do not have an inherent Data-Link Layer protocol. This is in contrast to LAN protocols such as Ethernet and Token Ring that have a defined packet frame at the Data-Link Layer. Many serial lines use asynchronous communications at the Physical Layer where a character is framed in a start, stop, and an optional parity bit. You may be familiar with the Physical Layer framing of asynchronous communications where the modem is set to "N,8,2", which means No parity, 8 data bits, and 2 stop bits. Descriptions such as "N,8,2" describe the Physical Layer for serial lines. Consider this question: At the Data-Link Layer what protocol should be used for serial lines? In other words, how should the characters be grouped together in a frame of information, and what should be

> the format of this Data-Link packet? As you try to answer this question, you
> begin to realize that serial lines do not have any inherent Data-Link Layer pro-
> tocol, and it is up to the protocol designer to design a format for serial lines.
> The earliest definition of Data-Link Layer protocol for serial lines is SLIP, which is
> discussed in this section. A later section describes PPP, which is in use today and
> replaces SLIP.

Due to SLIP's simple nature, a number of deficiencies make it less than desirable in a
large-scale network implementation. The most onerous is that in a SLIP session, both
ends of the session must know the other's IP address. Without it, there is no way to handle
the routing issues. In modern networks this can be an issue, especially in a DHCP-based
environment. However, this same simple nature makes SLIP easy to implement.

Datagrams are usually kept to less than 1006 bytes, well below the MTU size limit of
many links. An additional concern is maximum modem speed. It is recommended that
SLIP connections not exceed 19.2Kbps. In practice this limit is good to stay with.
Higher speed connections benefit from the additional error checking provided by PPP.

Compressed SLIP (CSLIP)

CSLIP is a protocol that reduces transport overhead by using VanJacobsen TCP header
compression to reduce the size of the combined TCP and IP header size from a 40 to
3–7-byte signature. Header compression is made possible because most of the packets
have very little that changes in the TCP and IP header. Data compression, such as run-
length encoding, can be used. This technique replaces strings of repeated characters with
a single character and a count. This can be a big difference when you're sending lots of
little packets, as can be the case with protocols like Telnet.

Point to Point Protocol (PPP)

Because of the issues and limitations of the SLIP protocols, it became apparent that a
new protocol was needed. Thus PPP was born to replace SLIP.

The original RFC 1134 describing PPP was written in 1989 by Drew Perkins of Carnegie
Mellon University. PPP is extremely versatile in that it will support the transmission of
datagrams over point-to-point serial connections and the Internet. A *datagram* is a block
of data similar in nature to a packet. By encapsulating datagrams, PPP remains independent of the medium and will support multiple non-IP protocols. Protocols such as
UDP/IP, IPX/SPX, and even AppleTalk have taken advantage of PPP.

19

**REMOTE ACCESS
PROTOCOLS**

PPP Modes of Operation

To ensure that PPP could support virtually any type of user session, a number of capabilities were built in to provide different modes of operation. PPP has three basic modes of responding to a connection request:

- An immediate PPP link
- Autodetection
- Interactive

Immediate Link

As can be summarized from its description, immediate PPP provides PPP communication after answering the request. Any authentication must take place within the PPP protocol itself. This can be a dangerous connection method because authentication can be turned off. This would allow anyone to connect to your network.

Autodetection

In autodetection, the server will select among PPP, SLIP, interactive, or other protocols as configured by the system. The key benefit to this is once again versatility. By being able to support a wide selection of protocols, the network is now able to effectively deal with upgrade and migration issues. Instead of having to do a forcible cutover to PPP, a gradual migration of users and services can take place. Immediate conversion is sometimes called *slash cutover* because all the systems are configured to migrate to the same service at the same time. This is similar to flipping a switch at midnight, and has been the bane of many system administrators' lives because immediate conversion is not always smooth and something invariably goes wrong.

Interactive

Another benefit is the support for dumb terminals and terminal emulation users who must still access the network. Some database access programs still require access to legacy systems, so be aware of this ability.

At the beginning of the session, PPP will look to see whether it's dealing with an active or passive session. An active node will begin to transmit frames in an attempt to start handshaking with its peer. A passive node will wait for the other node to start the handshaking process. It is standard procedure to configure outbound nodes to be active, whereas inbound nodes can be either active or passive. An autodetecting dial-in server should be set to passive in order to determine the line protocol of the remote node.

For PPP to successfully begin the handshaking process, one of the nodes must assume the active mode. Be aware that not all software offers the choice of modes. NT RAS is a passive server, whereas Sun's Solaris PPP is an active server. If you are running PPP 2.3, you have the choice of active or passive modes.

PPP does support a form of encryption through the use of the Encrypting Control Protocol described in RFC 1962 and RFC 1968. PPP supports a number of encryption algorithms including DES. Both endpoints must support encryption and both must agree on the encryption algorithm. Care should be exercised; not all products support encryption because it is a PPP extension.

In contrast to SLIP, PPP also supports a fully developed list of services. They are

- Simultaneous support of multiple protocols
- Link configuration
- Error detection
- Compression
- Encryption
- Network information
- Authentication

As illustrated in Figure 19.8, PPP fits in the stack at the Data Link Layer interfacing the Physical and Network Layers.

FIGURE 19.8

A TCP/IP stack with PPP connection services.

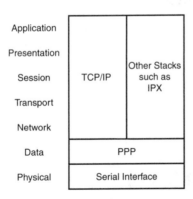

Application		
Presentation		
Session	TCP/IP	Other Stacks such as IPX
Transport		
Network		
Data	PPP	
Physical	Serial Interface	

19

REMOTE ACCESS PROTOCOLS

Using the stack in this way enables PPP to support multiple protocols. For example, an IP datagram would be encapsulated in a PPP frame, as shown in Figure 19.9.

FIGURE 19.9

Stack showing IP datagram being encapsulated and fed to wire.

IPX would function in exactly the same way. Instead of an IP datagram, an IPX datagram would be handed to the PPP-enabled Data Link Layer. This schema maintains the integrity of the stack while providing the versatility required in today's multiprotocol network environments.

PPP's flexibility is also demonstrated by the support provided to modify its operating parameters. In order to tune the link to its maximum capability, PPP can set a number of link configuration parameters such as the following:

- Maximum Receive Unit (MRU)
- Async Control Character Map (ACCM)
- Authentication Protocol
- Extensible Authentication Protocol (EAP)
- Quality Protocol
- Magic Number
- Protocol Field Compression
- Address & Control Field Compression
- FCS Alternative

Maximum Receive Unit (MRU)

The MRU tells the other node that the receiving end is capable of dealing with MTUs of a size different from the default of 1500 bytes. It should be noted that all implementations are required to accept a PPP information field of 1500 octets at all times. This is regardless of the values negotiated at connect time. As it turns out, calculating an MRU is a complicated process due to compression protocols that may inflate some types of data due to their substitution algorithms. Some implementations of PPP calculate MRUs based on the connection speed.

Async Control Character Map (ACCM)

Described in RFC 1662, the ACCM tells the peer what characters in the data stream should be "escaped" in order not to corrupt data. This is done to enable or disable the 32 ASCII control characters that live between 18 and 1F. Control sequences such as CONTROL-S and CONTROL-A (XON and XOFF) that normally act to stop and start flow sequences can corrupt data in strange and surprising ways.

Authentication Protocol

The authentication protocol in RFC, described in RFC 1661, is a way to tell the peer that it needs to identify itself before any further communication is permitted. The default for this option is no authentication. The sender can initiate a Configure-Request indicating to the peer that it needs the peer to identify itself using the indicated protocol. The receiver can issue a Configure-Nak to request another protocol, as depicted in Figure 19.10.

FIGURE 19.10

Authentication sequence.

At this point the sender can terminate the session or resend with a different protocol. Permitted authentication protocols are RFC 1334 PAP, RFC 1994 MD5 CHAP, MS CHAP, EAP, or SPAP. After the peer has responded with a Configure-Ack, it must respond using one of the listed protocols.

CHAP and PAP were described earlier, so the following sections provide a brief description of other authentication protocols and the remaining PPP fields.

Extensible Authentication Protocol (EAP)

Extensible Authentication Protocol (EAP), RFCs 2284 and 2484, is the proposed PPP authentication protocol as of 1999.

Postponing the algorithm selection until after the *Link Control Phase* (LCP), PPP builds a connection. Then, during the authentication phase, EAP interrogates the client for more information regarding specific authentication protocols. A major benefit of EAP is its ability to support back-end systems for authentication and encryption. This makes integrating PPP with RADIUS servers as well as other hardware- and software-based security tokens significantly easier.

Shiva PAP

Shiva PAP also has the ability to use hardware tokens but it seems that instead of releasing it to the public domain, Shiva will license it to select vendors. There is little documentation in the public domain.

MS CHAP

MS CHAP is basically regular CHAP using a different hashing algorithm. Instead of the usual MD5, MS CHAP uses either DES or MD4 depending on whether it is using the LAN form (DES) or the NT form (MD4). In either case, the response is generated using DES. This is similar to the standard form of CHAP except that standard CHAP uses MD5.

Quality Protocol

An interesting capability of PPP is its ability to measure *Quality of Service* (QoS) parameters. By telling the peer that you want to receive QoS information, you can monitor data loss and error rates. The default for this setting is "no protocol." The information provided is simple statistics regarding the link and its status.

Magic Number

The magic number is used in QoS requests as well as discard-requests and link quality packets. This number is chosen at random to identify the nodes to each other and to assist with error detection and loopback conditions. The default for this setting is "no number."

Protocol Field Compression

Protocol field compression performs a simple compression from a 16-bit protocol field to an 8-bit protocol field. The most significant bytes of the octet must be 0 in order for this to work. Only the least significant octet is transmitted. This is disabled by default.

Address & Control Field Compression

Another compression field, Address & Control Field, tells the peer that the fixed HDLC values of 0xff and 0x03 associated with this field can be omitted. As with the other values, the default is "off." In a latency-critical application, such as a real-time application, you can omit the unused portions of the address field this way. The end result is you save a few bytes in the transmission of packets.

FCS Alternative

The last option discussed here, FCS alternative, tells the peer that you want to receive a nonstandard default frame check sequence field. This is a Link Control Protocol configuration option that is usually absent because it isn't consistently addressed in all PPP implementations. It allows the peers to negotiate a 32-bit cyclic redundancy check (CRC) instead of the usual 16-bit CRC.

There are extensions that PPP supports but they are considered either flawed or obsolete. Use of these options should be examined carefully and other solutions should be explored if possible. These options are described in RFC 1570, RCF 1663, RFC 1976, and RFC 1990. They are

- Numbered Mode
- Multi-link Procedure
- Call-back
- Connect Time
- Compound Frames
- Nominal-Data-Encapsulation
- Multilink-MRRU
- Multilink-Short-Sequence-Number-Header-Format
- Multilink-Endpoint-Discriminator
- Proprietary
- DCE-Identifier
- Multi-Link-Plus Procedure
- Link Discriminator
- LCP Authentication Option

Tunneled Remote Access

In many cases, special techniques must be used in order to move data from one network to another. In some instances it's a simple matter of encasing one protocol inside of another, as in the case of IPX over IP (see Figure 19.11).

19

REMOTE ACCESS
PROTOCOLS

FIGURE 19.11

IPX over IP.

DLL Trailer	IPX Packet	UDP Header	IP Header	DLL Header

The native protocol, in this case IPX, does not have the ability to move data between IP internetworks. To solve this problem, IPX has an IP header appended to it in order to give it the information needed by the routers that will direct the packet to its ultimate destination. This common practice has been used since the early days of AppleTalk, and it has proven to be quite effective.

This type of solution is not without its drawbacks, however. Some applications are designed to deal directly with their native application. In our example, this would be Novell NetWare. Various implementations of IP have displayed idiosyncratic features that make the implementation less than straightforward. An example of this is once again portrayed with IPX running on Microsoft-enabled networks. In some instances of IPX on MS networks, unusual issues associated with timeouts and ghosting occurred. *Ghosting* is the effect of network resources appearing and disappearing at random intervals. This most commonly occurred with printers and was due to the incorrect distribution of network and printer drivers.

Herein lies the problem. Special attention to detail must be maintained because you are essentially using two or more network protocols to support your user community. One incorrectly installed or obsolete driver can be very difficult to diagnose and repair. More importantly, it can make the network seem unreliable—something to be avoided.

A few solutions to this problem have proven to be very effective in the past. First, use a remote management product that enables system administrators to install and manage remote nodes. Products from companies such as Vector Networks (www.vector-networks. com) and Traveling Software (www.travelingsoftware.com) provide additional capabilities that are not native to the desktop environment. These products feature remote control, remote management, remote software, and hardware inventory capabilities that can be leveraged to provide a reliable networking environment. One caveat though: These types of products bring with them their own risks. Misconfigured, they can allow unauthorized access to potentially sensitive information. Passwords must be strong, and administrative access should be given only to those who need it. If you are using ZENWorks for Desktop on a Novell network, it has built-in secure remote control management features.

In some instances, you will need an elevated level of security. In these special circumstances you can take advantage of encrypting protocols such as PPTP and L2TP.

Point-to-Point Tunneling (PPTP)

PPTP is the result of cooperation between Ascend Communications, ECI Telematics, Microsoft, 3Com, and US Robotics. The group came to be known as the *PPTP Forum*. It was reasoned that PPTP would enable users and vendors to take advantage of the pervasive nature of the Internet. By supporting a standard, users would be able to dial in through their local ISP and securely tunnel through the Internet to their corporate network. This would reduce the requirement corporations had on generating and supporting their own remote access hardware.

It was hoped that PPTP would enable corporations to leverage the structure of the Internet by letting the ISPs do what they do well: connect individual users to the Internet. Corporations were then free to buy equipment that connected to the Metropolitan Area Networks, or MANs, and local loops to demultiplex incoming remote access connections. To them it looked like a link to another Internet site instead of a remote call. Figure 19.12 depicts the difference in architecture.

FIGURE 19.12

A network using a remote access box and one using a remote ISP and multiplexers and demultiplexers.

PPP Session Aggregation

PPTP is a client/server-based protocol that is specifically designed to tunnel through IP networks using PPP and Layer 2. PPTP has the interesting ability to support multiple PPP connections through a single PPTP tunnel. This works well in the ISP model where multiple remote users must be directed to a specific corporate entity (see Figure 19.13). These tunnels are generally referred to as *Virtual Private Networks* (VPNs).

FIGURE 19.13

PPTP supporting multiple users.

This would seem like a boon to most ISPs because PPTP requires out-of-band control on TCP port 1723 using the *General Routing Encapsulation* (GRE) protocol. However, GRE is not as pervasive as TCP or its cousin UDP, so many ISPs don't support it. Without this connection, PPTP will not operate.

The most popular implementation is to provide service between a dial-up *Point of Presence* (POP). In this way the ISP merely provides the IP service while the clients negotiate their own PPTP link with the private router. It should be noted that not all PPP software supports PPTP because it is a non-standard protocol. Microsoft's version in the Windows 98 and NT operating system is an example of a client and server that do support this service.

After the LCP functions have been dispatched, the physical connection is established, and the user is authenticated, PPTP relies on PPP to create the datagrams. PPTP then encapsulates the PPP packets for transmission through the IP tunnel.

Separate Control Channel

As mentioned earlier, PPTP uses two channels to support the connection: a data channel and a control channel. The control channel runs over the TCP link using port 1723. This channel contains information related to link status and management messages. These management messages are responsible for establishing, managing, and terminating the PPTP tunnel. This management channel supports the ability of PPTP to control the rate at which data is transported. This is useful if there is significant line noise or in case of a busy network creating lots of congestion that results in dropped packets.

Data is transmitted between the nodes via a data stream that is encapsulated in an IP envelope using GRE to control routing. Once again, not all ISPs support GRE so it may be up to the client and server to establish their own tunnels.

Multiprotocol Support

Another interesting feature of PPTP is its ability to support protocols such as NetBEUI, IPX, and for those that still use it, AppleTalk. Because PPTP is a Layer 2 protocol, it also includes a media header that enables it to operate over Ethernet or PPP connections.

Authentication and Privacy

As it turns out, encryption and key management are not part of the PPTP specification. PPTP relies on the authentication provided by PPP and relies on PPP to encrypt data as well. To enhance the privacy aspect of the PPP/PPTP duo, Microsoft has incorporated a new encryption method called the Microsoft Point-to-Point Encryption algorithm, which is based on the RSA RC4 encryption standard.

For authentication, PPTP uses CHAP, PAP, EAP, and MS-CHAP as supported by PPP.

PPTP Tunnel Types

PPTP can support some basic tunnel connection configurations as discussed earlier. The type of tunnel is based on a few things. First and foremost is the ISP's ability to support the GRE requirements of PPTP. The next is the client's ability to support a PPTP connection. The user's computer will determine the end point of the tunnel: either an ISP's *Remote Access Server* (RAS) or his own computer. These two types of connections have come to be known as voluntary and compulsory tunnels.

Voluntary Tunnel

In a *voluntary* tunnel, the user initiates the PPTP connection to a corporate computer. However, this implies that the user must have a functional PPTP client such as those provided on the Windows 9X or the NT operating systems. There is no requirement for the ISP to provide anything other than basic IP services in this case (see Figure 19.14).

FIGURE 19.14

User to server PPTP over the Internet.

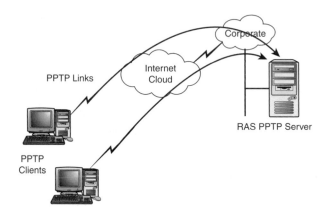

In the case where the ISP is providing a RAS server, the client need not have a PPTP client; only a PPP client is required. In a *compulsory* tunnel, the user connects to the ISP's RAS server and has no control over the tunnel (see Figure 19.15). In most cases the user doesn't even have knowledge of the PPTP tunnel's existence.

FIGURE 19.15

A compulsory tunnel.

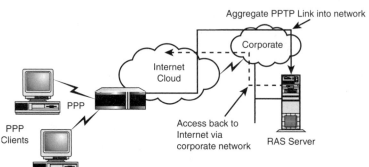

Compulsory Tunnels

Compulsory tunnels have two subclasses: static and dynamic. Static tunnels use dedicated equipment and are also referred to as realm-based, or manual tunneling. A *realm* is part of a user's name and can be associated with a user's domain. The RAS server will use this information to determine where the termination point of the PPTP connection is. RAS servers must be manually configured to support this type of connection. The advantage to this is that corporations can control how users utilize the Internet. This method allows a user to connect to the corporate intranet in order to use corporate services. Connection to the Internet is at the discretion of the "powers that be." Access to the Internet is allowed through the corporate network (refer to Figure 19.15).

Dynamic tunnels are more efficient because the tunnel is only there when the need is there. The RAS server is linked to a RADIUS server in order to obtain user information. The tunnel is built based on the user's stored information. Information regarding usage and access controls is stored in the RADIUS server and is requested by the RAS server on demand.

Another advantage of compulsory tunnels is their ability to aggregate traffic. Multiple PPP clients can be combined into one PPTP connection back to the company intranet, thereby reducing bandwidth and its associated costs.

There is a disadvantage to compulsory tunnels that relates to security. The link from the client to the RAS server is not secure. However, the same could be said for a user utilizing a voluntary tunnel because there is nothing to stop him from connecting to the Internet, downloading a malicious bit of code, and *then* connecting to the corporate network.

The Layer 2 Tunneling Protocol (L2TP)

L2TP is very similar to PPTP in many respects. It combines PPTP with Cisco's *Layer 2 Forwarding* (L2F) protocol. L2F has an advantage over PPTP in that it isn't reliant on GRE. This means that it can be compatible with other media such as ATM and other packet-based networks such as X.25 and frame relay. However, it means that the specification must delineate how L2F packets are processed. The initial work leveraged UDP, placing L2F as a possible follow-up to PPTP.

L2F

In a similar manner to PPTP, L2F used PPP as the enabler supplying the initial connection and services such as authentication. Unlike PPTP, L2F used the *Terminal Access Controller Access-Control System* (TACACS) from the beginning. TACACS is another service born from necessity. A proprietary protocol from Cisco Systems, TACACS provides authentication, authorization, and accounting to support Cisco's router products. TACACS has some limitations, which are discussed later in the chapter.

L2F also makes use of tunnel connection definitions enabling it to support multiple tunnels within the L2F connection. In an effort to enhance the level of security, L2F supports an additional level of authentication. Instead of just the authentication at the PPP level, L2F adds authentication at the corporate gateway or firewall.

The benefits of L2F were carried over into the L2TP specification. L2TP uses the same method of connecting via PPP to support remote users. Leveraging the L2F work, L2TP uses its tunneling protocol. This feature becomes extremely significant when you consider the migration to ATM and frame relay networks that has been occurring over the past few years.

Authentication

Like PPTP, L2TP provides authentication through PPP. Using PAP, CHAP, and EAP to link to RADIUS servers, L2TP can be just as effective as PPTP. Adding to this level of effectiveness, L2TP adds TACACS, TACACS+, and IPSec-based services.

IPSec Support

IPSec is different from the other services in that it is an open specification that supports not only authentication, but privacy as well. IPSec is a considerably stronger security implementation than the simple PPP model. As you can see in Figure 19.16, L2TP has the ability to support a Public Key Infrastructure (PKI) by taking advantage of LDAP and strong authentication services. In short, a PKI is a way of managing public keys and the certificates they support. IPSec provides for the use of a number of different authentication and encryption tools such as the asymmetric encryption algorithms on which PKIs are based. However, although we will discuss these security mechanisms, PKI is well beyond the scope of this chapter and as such is not discussed here.

FIGURE 19.16

L2TP and PKI.

Like PPTP, L2TP relies on PPP to set up the connection. L2TP expects PPP to establish the physical connection, perform the initial authentication, create PPP datagrams, and upon termination, close the connection. This is where the similarity ends. L2TP will talk with the other node to determine whether the calling node is authorized and whether the endpoint is willing to support the L2TP connection. If not, the session is terminated.

Like PPTP, L2TP defines two different types of messages: control and data. Control messages are used to set up and maintain the tunnel and to control the transmission and reception of data. Unlike PPTP, which requires two channels, L2TP combines the data and control channels into one data stream. On an IP network this would have the appearance of packing both data and control into one UDP datagram, as shown in Figure 19.17.

FIGURE 19.17

Example datagram of a UDP packet.

UDP Header	L2TP Header	PPP Header	IP Payload

The payload is essentially the PPP packet minus framing elements that are specific to the media. Because L2TP is a Layer 2 protocol, it must include a media header to indicate to the next layer how the packet is to be transmitted. Once again, this could be over Ethernet, frame relay, X.25, ATM, or the original PPP link. As you can see, this is quite versatile.

To alleviate network congestion, L2TP supports flow control. Flow control is implemented between an *L2TP Access Concentrator* (LAC), which functions as the network access server, and an *L2TP Network Access Server* (LNS), which has the role of providing corporate network access. Control messages contain information regarding transmission rates and buffering parameters. By exchanging this information, LACs and LNSs can regulate the flow of data and thereby control congestion (see Figure 19.18).

FIGURE 19.18

LACs and LNSs.

19

REMOTE ACCESS
PROTOCOLS

Another method of reducing network overhead employed by L2TP is by the compression of packet headers. You may recall the PPTP has a similar capability.

L2TP also supports two types of connection classes in a similar fashion to PPTP. L2TP supports voluntary and compulsory tunnels.

In a voluntary tunnel, the user initiates the L2TP connection from the user's computer. However, this implies that the user must have a functional L2TP client. There is no requirement for the ISP to provide anything other than basic connection services in this case (see Figure 19.19).

FIGURE 19.19

A user to server L2TP voluntary tunnel over the Internet.

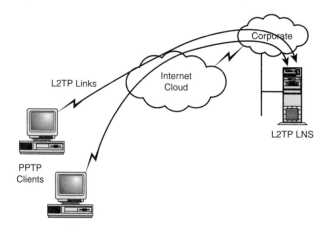

In the case where the ISP is providing a LAC, the client need not have a L2TP client; only a PPP client is required. In a compulsory tunnel, the user connects to the ISP's LAC and has no control over the tunnel (see Figure 19.20). In most cases the user doesn't even have knowledge of the L2TP tunnel's existence.

FIGURE 19.20

Compulsory tunnel via ISP LAC.

Compulsory tunnels have two subclasses: static and dynamic. Static tunnels use dedicated equipment. This is a poor use of resources because it ties up equipment even when the tunnel is not being used. Additionally, LACs must be manually configured to support this type of connection.

Dynamic tunnels are more effective because they only build the tunnel when the user needs it. User information is obtained by the LAC from an authentication server such as a RADIUS or TACACS server. There is a large advantage to using a compulsory dynamic tunnel in conjunction with an authentication server. Tunnels can be defined based on user information such as telephone numbers and authentication method. Authentication methods can include tokens and smart cards, a device we're seeing more of. Additionally, auditing and accounting can be performed in an effort to manage security and possibly finances. Auditing information could be the basis for departmental chargebacks for service or to help negotiate attractive rates from ISPs.

The advantage to this is the same as described in the preceding section. Users connect to the corporate intranet in order to use corporate services, and access to the Internet, if allowed, is through the corporate network (see Figure 19.21).

FIGURE 19.21

Compulsory L2TP connection to the Internet.

Once again, the advantage of using compulsory tunnels is traffic aggregation. Multiple connections can be combined into one L2TP tunnel back to the company intranet— bandwidth utilization is better and costs are lower.

We must remember that the disadvantage to compulsory tunnels is that the link from the client to the LAC server is not secure because it is a simple PPP link. As stated earlier, the same could be said for a user utilizing a voluntary tunnel. There is nothing to stop him from connecting to the Internet, downloading a malicious bit of code, and *then* connecting to the corporate network.

As was the case in the PPTP implementation, security must be addressed as a systems-level set of solutions. You cannot rely on technology as a sure way to provide security. Ignoring the cultural issues and processes will set you up for a security breach.

L2TP authentication via an ISP is somewhat more involved than that used by PPTP. In the initial contact with the ISP, the ISP can use one of three elements to identify the user:

- Phone number called from
- Phone number called
- Username or ID

After this has occurred, the ISP LAC will generate a new Call ID to identify the session within the tunnel and forward this information to the corporate network's LNS (see Figure 19.22).

FIGURE 19.22

The L2TP authentication sequence.

Then it's up to the corporate network to examine the information provided and decide whether to accept or reject the connection request. If the call is accepted, the next phase is PPP authentication. Although the endpoints have been identified and authenticated, it's important to note that messages are still passed in the clear. Anyone with a protocol analyzer can capture your data. Also, packets can be injected into the packet stream in an attempt to confuse or mislead the recipients. This is where IPSec can be used to prevent piracy.

Recall that PPP does provide encryption but it uses a shared secret to encrypt the data. Both parties must know this key for the process to work. This implies that some out-of-band method for key distribution must be employed. This is the case for L2TP tunnel authentication as well. Additionally, even using PPP encryption, L2TP does not protect the control information. Once again, IPSec can help.

IPSec

Because the TCP/IP protocol does not really offer any protection, a number of methods have sprung up over the years to fill this gap. However, these solutions did not offer cross-platform capability nor did they function reliably. To address this problem, the IETF has worked on a set of protocols that have come to be known as IPSec. Although this is not a section on Virtual Private Networks (VPN), a number of IPSec functions can be utilized by L2TP quite effectively, so this section will provide a brief overview of IPSec's features.

Originally designed to address the emerging IPv6 standard, RFCs 1825 through 1829 were published in 1995 and addressed how authentication and encryption would be performed on IP datagrams. Shortly thereafter, they were modified to address the Internet address scheme, IPv4, as it is today. These specifications divided the solution concept into two classes:

- Authentication
- Encryption

The authentication portion is addressed by an *Authentication Header* (AH) and the encryption element is addressed by the *Encapsulating Security Payload* (ESP). Each of these capabilities is represented by a different header that is applied to the IP packet, as shown in Figure 19.23.

Figure 19.23

IPSec packet header information.

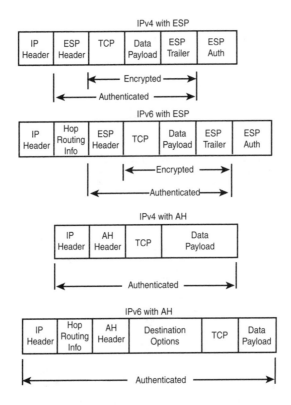

Standards-Based Encryption

When used together, both of these capabilities can provide authentication and privacy. In addition to authentication and privacy, unlike the other authentication services discussed thus far, IPSec can also provide data integrity. *Data integrity* is the ability to determine whether the data has been modified in transit. This is very important if the data happens to be a corporate contract or your payroll deposit!

To ensure compatibility, the IPSec standard is built around a number of cryptographic standards:

- D-H, or Diffie-Hellmann, for key exchanges
- Public-key cryptographic algorithm for signing D-H key exchanges

- DES encryption
- MD5, SHA, and HMAC (Hash-based Message Authentication Code) for keyed hash algorithms
- Digital certificates

The main strength of this approach is versatility. As new algorithms are developed, they can plug into the IPSec architecture, as depicted in Figure 19.24.

FIGURE 19.24

IPSec architecture.

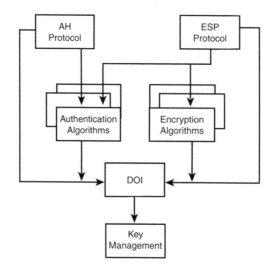

Establishing a Security Association

To start the process, both parties must establish a *Security Association* (SA). Although there are default settings for establishing a secure communications channel, IPSec provides for the negotiation of different key values, algorithms, and timing settings. To assist with the interpretation of the myriad values that are out there, IPSec uses a concept called the *Domain of Interpretation* (DOI) to assist with the standardization of these elements. This makes establishing the SA much easier. The SA determines the following:

- Authentication algorithm mode and keys used in the AH
- Encryption algorithm mode and keys used in the ESP
- Cryptographic synchronization parameters
- The protocol, algorithm, and key used for communications authentication
- The protocol, algorithm, and key used for communications privacy
- How often authentication and privacy keys are exchanged

- Authentication algorithm, mode, transform, and keys to be used by ESP
- Key lifecycles
- The lifetime of the SA
- The SA source address

Authentication

The AH offers a way to strongly authenticate the sender of the packet and the information contained within it. Using cryptographic hash functions to generate a checksum, this information is inserted with other control information between the IP header and any other packet headers (refer to Figure 19.23).

ESP

Because all the AH does is prove that the packet came from the sender and that the contents haven't been modified, it does little to protect the viewing of the packet content. This is the purpose of the ESP. The ESP will insert its information between the IP header and the rest of the packet, which is encrypted by the method specified in the *Security Parameter Index* (SPI). It should be noted that a number of different modes of operation yield some interesting capabilities. One mode of operation is *tunneling* (see Figure 19.25).

FIGURE 19.25

Tunneling IPSec.

Tunneling

In the tunneling mode, the entire packet is encrypted and authenticated and prefixed by the address of an intermediate gateway, such as a firewall. This prevents the disclosure of the ultimate destination to any would-be voyeurs. Because the entire packet including its headers is encrypted, the packet appears as data to another IP header. This IP header contains source and destination IP addresses of the tunnel endpoints and can be used to route the packet to its ultimate destination.

As you can see, IPSec offers a significant improvement over standard PPTP or L2TP security and is being widely used in products to build VPNs.

Summary

There are a number of ways to connect a remote user to a local LAN. SLIP, PPP, PPTP, and L2TP offer varying degrees of capability and protection.

PPP offers the basic services required to connect to a server and is significantly more capable than the earlier SLIP ever tried to be. With the ability to control the link and to support multiple protocols, PPP became the remote connection choice over SLIP in short order. SLIP, with its simple capabilities, may be suitable for dedicated terminal connections but it lacks the robust and versatile nature of PPP.

Adding to the capabilities of PPP, PPTP enables ISPs and corporate entities to more effectively leverage the Internet. By supporting more protocols, PPTP allows intranet services to extend to the homes and laptops of remote users. Taking advantage of remote authentication mechanisms such as PAP, CHAP, and RADIUS, PPTP offers the organization and increased control over who uses its network resources.

Adding yet again to the list of capabilities, L2TP combines the best of many protocols while leveraging the capabilities of the Internet and its related and varied media. Incorporating a strong security model as represented by IPSec, L2TP pushes the bar upward for remote access clients. As more capability is added to the network infrastructure, new methods must accompany them to ensure that they are not misused or misappropriated. L2TP promises to support that especially when used in conjunction with IPv6.

Firewalls

by Tim Parker

IN THIS CHAPTER

CHAPTER 20

It is almost impossible to talk about networks, internetworks, and the Internet without hearing terms like firewall, gateway, or proxy server at some point. You've already seen what a gateway is and what it does, but we haven't touched on the subject of firewalls and proxy servers yet. Although firewalls and proxy servers don't really have much to do with TCP/IP specifically, they are used on TCP/IP-based networks as well as the Internet.

Therefore, it's worth taking a little time to explain what firewalls and proxy servers do, and how they work within a TCP/IP network. This chapter, along with Chapter 21, "Network and System Security," deals with the issues of protecting your network, hiding your information, and preventing damage to any data.

Securing Your Network

Firewalls and proxy servers, as well as encryption and authentication
(covered in the next chapter), are all designed to provide security for your data. But why bother with security if you have nothing of value in your e-mails or on your gateway machine? The reason is simple: If you have a connection to the Internet, the Internet has a connection to you. This means that anyone on the Internet can potentially access your network if such access is not prevented. If there was no security set up on your gateway machine, anyone anywhere in the world with an Internet connection could use TCP/IP to travel through your gateway and onto any machine on your network. You probably have data that you don't want others to see stored somewhere on your network, so you need to consider security issues to prevent Internet users from accessing your network's interior.

When you set up security on a network you are actually trying to protect two things (and a third thing indirectly). The two things you are trying to protect are your data (stored throughout your network) and your equipment (anything connected to your network). If a hacker accesses your equipment, damage could result. The same applies to your data. You don't want to see your sensitive files flying all around the Internet as e-mail attachments, do you? Indirectly, you are also protecting your reputation, either individually or as a company. It wouldn't look very good for large companies like IBM or Hewlett-Packard if all their internal documents were freely available.

The most common type of security problem has already been mentioned—someone accessing your network over the Internet. Such unauthorized intrusions are the primary reason for good security. Intruders or hackers can get into your network and search your data, modify anything you have, and also cause physical damage to your systems. There are many ways intruders can access a network, ranging from exploiting known security holes in operating systems and applications to espionage. The primary role of security on a network, and the role specifically of a firewall, is to prevent unauthorized intrusion.

Another security problem is called *denial of service*. This is when hackers prevent you from using your own machines properly. Denial of service (DoS) has many forms. A typical example found on the Internet is flooding of a service such as e-mail, an FTP site, or a Web server. Flooding means that so much data is sent to the service that it is overwhelmed and either crashes or wastes time processing it so that legitimate users are denied access. Hackers routinely use e-mail flooding, in which thousands and thousands of e-mail messages are sent every hour to a target's e-mail server. The server flounders and the e-mail system is rendered unusable. The same technique works for most TCP/IP utilities such as FTP, Telnet, and Web servers. Another aspect of denial of service has to do with rerouting—instead of accessing a particular service on one machine, you are rerouted to another site. This can happen if DNS servers are compromised and where legitimate DNS names have incorrect (or illegitimate) IP addresses.

There are several ways to protect your network, its data, and its services. The one many people rely on is anonymity or obscurity. The reasoning is that if no one knows about your network and its contents, then the network is safe. This is "security through obscurity," and is false security, of course, because there are too many ways to discover what's on the Internet to keep yourself hidden for very long. It is naive to assume that hackers won't bother with your site because you think they'll find nothing of interest. The challenge of finding your data is all that most hackers need to get going.

The most widely used form of security is called host security, and has to do with securing each machine on the network separately. You rely on host security when you set up Windows access permissions, as well as UNIX file system permissions. Although host security can be used to secure individual machines, it is incorrect to assume that a whole network with individually secure machines is also secure. All it takes is one hole somewhere and the entire network may be open to hackers. Also, because host security is not equally applied across all machines, services can be exploited on a weak machine to access a strongly secure machine without any problem.

The Role of Firewalls

The level of security most of us should be looking at is network security. This means securing all points of access to the network first, then relying on host security inside as well. The key component of network security is the firewall—a machine that acts as the interface between the network and the Internet, with security its primary concern. A firewall has several roles to play:

- It restricts access to the network to a few locations.
- It prevents unauthorized users from gaining access to the network.
- It forces network traffic to leave for the Internet at particular, secure locations.

- It prevents denial-of-service attacks.
- It restricts what an Internet user can do on the network.

Firewalls are not restricted to network-to-Internet connections. They are also used for remote access servers (dial-in access) and network-to-network connections. The whole concept of the firewall is to channel all traffic in and out of your network through one or more particular locations that are set up to control access and services.

Using Firewalls

Many people think of a firewall as a single machine, and this can be the case for some networks. Dedicated single-box firewalls are available that do nothing more than act as a security gateway for your network. Alternatively, a single machine can run dedicated firewall software and nothing else. However, the term *firewall* has more to do with the functions performed than a physical device. A firewall may comprise several machines working together to control the network-Internet connection. Many different programs may be used to provide these firewall services. Firewalls may also do many tasks other than simply monitoring network access.

Firewalls are not foolproof. They are often vulnerable due to holes in their design that hackers can exploit. In addition, firewalls are often expensive to implement and require quite a bit of time to install and configure. However, the benefits most networks gain from the firewall far outweigh the problems.

Firewalls can do a lot for you. They provide a single point of security implementation for a network, so you can make changes in one location instead of on every machine (you can forbid anonymous FTP, for example). Firewalls can enforce security policies network-wide, preventing access to some Internet services for everyone inside the network, for example. Firewalls can't do some things for you, though, and you do need to understand the limitations. Firewalls are only good for the network-to-Internet connection. The firewall does nothing to stop people inside the network from doing anything they want to other machines on the network. Firewalls can't protect your network from intrusion if you have other connections, such as a Windows PC with a modem connecting to the Internet through an ISP (if it doesn't go through the firewall, you've circumvented the security a firewall offers). And a firewall can't prevent many common Internet-distributed problems, such as viruses and trojan horses.

The two basic ways to implement a firewall on a network are

- Build the firewall yourself from basic network services
- Buy a commercial product

The latter is by far the easiest, but also the most expensive. A typical firewall software package for a UNIX machine, for example, can cost upwards of $10,000 for a small network. As the network size grows, firewall software can cost 10 times that. The advantage to a commercial firewall package is simple: Most of the work has been done for you. You simply use menus to select the services you want to allow and deny, and the firewall software does it all for you. Building your own firewall means using the settings on the machine between the network and the Internet to perform these same tasks. Each service has to be tweaked manually to either allow or prevent access. For a UNIX machine, for example, this means working with the network configuration files and files such as /etc/services to prevent access to the network for some requests. Building your own firewall takes a lot of time, expertise, and quite a bit of experimentation. On the other hand, you don't have to spend lots of money for firewall software.

When setting up a firewall, either manually or from a commercial product, you will have several facets of security protection available to you. Whether you choose to implement them all is up to you. However, you should know what some of these facets, such as proxy servers and packet filters, mean. The next few sections look at these techniques in more detail.

Proxy Servers

A proxy server sits between the network and the Internet and accepts requests for a service, analyzes them, and forwards them on as allowed. The proxy service provides a replacement connection for the service, and as such acts as a proxy. For example, if you are inside a network and want to telnet to a host on the Internet, the proxy server accepts your request, decides whether to grant it, and then establishes the telnet session between itself and the target, as well as between itself and you. It gets in the middle, hides some information about you, and yet still allows the service to proceed through it. Proxy servers deal with services and applications, and as such are often called application-level gateways.

Why use a proxy server? Suppose you are on a highly secure project and want to hide information about the network you are on—its IP addresses, user logins, and so on—from the Internet in general. If you established a telnet session with a remote host through the Internet, your IP address would be transmitted in the packets. From the IP address, hackers can determine the size of your network, especially when they see a lot of different IP addresses going by. A proxy server changes your IP address to its own, and uses an internal table to resolve incoming and outgoing traffic to the proper destination. To someone on the outside, only a single IP address (the proxy server's) is visible. In other words, a proxy server, because of the way it works, also does Network Address Translation (NAT) functions.

Proxy servers are always implemented in software and need not be part of a firewall package, but usually are. Most commercial firewalls include proxy service capabilities. Most proxy server software does more than just act as a user's proxy; they can also control which applications are used and can block some incoming and outgoing data.

If you are building your own firewall, a number of packages are designed to allow you to do so. The most well known is SOCKS, which allows applications to work with a proxy conversion software package. Another popular package is TIS FWTK (Trusted Information Systems Internet Firewall Toolkit), which provides proxy servers pre-written for many TCP applications such as FTP and Telnet.

Packet Filters

A packet filtering system allows packets to go from the network to the Internet, and vice-versa, selectively. In other words, it allows some packets to be filtered out and not sent, whereas others are allowed through without hindrance. Packets are identified by the type of application that constructed them (some of the information is in the headers, as you saw in earlier chapters). The header of a TCP/IP packet contains the source and destination IP addresses, source and destination ports (which help identify the application), the protocol (TCP, UDP, or ICMP), and other information. If you have decided to block all FTP traffic in and out of your network, for example, the packet filtering software would detect anything with a port number of 20 or 21 and not allow it through. Packet filtering can be performed by the firewall software or by a router. In the latter case, the router is called a *screening* router.

The difference between a standard router and a screening router is in the way they examine packets. A normal router simply looks at the IP addresses and sends packets on the correct path to their destination. A screen router examines the header and not only figures out how to route to the destination but also whether it should, based on a set of rules. In other words, a screening router provides more than a Layer 3 functionality.

You might think you can get around a packet screening system by changing the port number, and to some extent this is possible. However, because the packet filter software is resident on your network, it can also figure out which interface the packet is going to and where it came from. So, even if the TCP port numbers are different, the packet filtering software can sometimes block the traffic properly.

You can use packet filtering software in a number of ways. The most common is to simply block a service such as FTP or Telnet. You can also specify machines that are to be blocked or let through. For example, if you find that a particular network has been the source of a lot of problems for you, you could instruct the packet filtering software to discard any packets from that network based on the IP address. In extreme cases, you can block all services, or permit only a few services, such as e-mail through the filter.

Securing Services

One of the key aspects of setting up a firewall is to decide which services are to be allowed to pass through the network-to-Internet connection, and which are to be restricted. For example: Are you going to allow FTP from outside the network to a machine inside? What about Web requests?

This section takes a very quick look at the primary services used over a firewall and the major security problems with each. You can decide whether you should allow or deny the service based on your own network's requirements.

Most network firewalls are set by default to allow six services to pass through:

- E-mail (SMTP)
- HTTP (World Wide Web access)
- FTP
- Telnet (remote access)
- Usenet (NNTP)
- DNS (hostname lookups)

These six are not without their security problems, as you will see in the following sections.

E-mail (SMTP)

E-mail is the most widely used service on the Internet, and it is very unlikely you will want to restrict access to e-mail through a firewall. There have been a number of security-related problems with mailers such as sendmail that are popularly used on the Internet, but because of the large amount of attention these problems have received, they have been fixed. So the mailers themselves are not very vulnerable to hacking, but the e-mail content is subject to the problem of viruses.

Most e-mail systems are implemented using Simple Mail Transfer Protocol (SMTP). Whenever an SMTP server handles mail, it is often done so either as a superuser account or as the account to which the e-mail is addressed. A clever hacker can exploit this change in permissions. Further, the most common SMTP server is sendmail, which runs under UNIX. You must implement the latest patches to sendmail to prevent exploitation by a hacker.

Also, another related problem is that the SMTP protocol does not provide for any authentication of the message header, and so it is easy for hackers and bulk-mail programs to forge message headers. Sendmail must be configured to check for valid e-mail or DNS names used in message headers. You can find the most recent updates to sendmail at `http://www.sendmail.org`.

20

FIREWALLS

> **Note**
>
> Recently, Microsoft's mail clients such as Outlook and Outlook Express have come under attack. Most of these attacks exploit the easy access to Outlook through scripting languages such as VBScript to do their damage. Typically, the mail client is "fooled" into executing some script to do its damage. The script can read the address book and send itself to the people listed in the address book.

HTTP: World Wide Web

Practically every network in the world has access to the Internet these days, and it is very likely you will not want to restrict access through a firewall from your internal network. Allowing access to the Web from machines inside your network doesn't pose much of a security risk other than downloads or Java applets with malicious designs, all of which should be taken care of with virus detectors on the receiving machines.

Of more importance is allowing Internet users into your network to access Web servers. This can prove to be a real security problem, and one of the best ways around the security issue is to use separate hosts outside the firewall to provide the Web services. Most of the Web servers currently available are reasonably secure, although a few holes are known that can be exploited by hackers. IIS from Microsoft has had a history of security holes that have to be fixed by applying service packs. An important security consideration is any extensions you load on your server for things such as Common Gateway Interface (CGI), which must be carefully secured with appropriate access permissions.

FTP

The File Transfer Protocol (FTP) is widely used on the Internet. However, the ability to transfer any file into the network from the Internet means that the incoming files could be laden with all kinds of programs, such as viruses and spoofs, that send information about the network back to a hacker. The FTP service itself is quite secure, but again, a few well-known holes must be patched by system administrators, depending on the version of FTP.

The more important problem with FTP is anonymous FTP, which allows anyone access to your FTP server with a guest login. Permissions for an anonymous FTP server have to be very tightly controlled; otherwise, a knowledgeable hacker can easily exploit the server.

> **Note**
>
> UNIX systems such as Linux are by default configured with the anonymous account "ftp," whose home directory is set to /home/ftp. Anonymous access is confined to this home directory using the system chroot call so that guest users cannot access files outside this area. As a safety precaution, you should prevent system administrators from using their regular accounts for logging onto an FTP server. This is because FTP sends the user password information as clear text, which can be discovered by capturing packets. To prevent certain users such as root and sysadmin from logging on using their accounts, include their account names under the /etc/ftpusers file. You might also consider using ssh (secure shell) for doing all of your telnet and ftp sessions. Ssh sets up a VPN between the client and the service. On UNIX systems, sshd (secure shell daemon must be enabled and running). To get free implementations of ssh, visit the Web site www.ssh.com.

Finally, you should not allow Trivial FTP (TFTP) to be used across a network-to-Internet interface. Only a few applications use TFTP, and these are not likely to be used across the network. The reason for this is that TFTP does not require any user authentication. You must also ensure that TFTP access is confined to a specific area. On UNIX systems, TFTP by default is restricted to the directory /tftpboot.

> **Note**
>
> On UNIX systems, TFTP can be disabled by commenting out the TFTP service entries in /etc/inetd.conf or the /etc/xinetd.conf files and restarting the inetd or xinetd daemons.

Telnet

Telnet is widely used to allow a user to connect to another machine in a remote location and behave as if it is directly connected. The Telnet utility has one major drawback: All information is sent unencrypted. If Telnet sends a login and password, they are sent in the clear, allowing a hacker to intercept and exploit the information. Authentication protocols can be used to combat this problem, but Telnet is often exploited anyway because all kinds of information flies back and forth between the client and server.

20

FIREWALLS

The Berkeley utilities (rlogin, rsh, exec, and so on) are often used in place of Telnet. The Berkeley utilities rely on trusted hosts, which are not valid over the Internet. The Berkeley r-utilities are easily hacked and are very insecure, and should not be allowed to pass through a firewall.

> **Note**
>
> Instead of using Telnet, consider using ssh (secure shell), which enables encrypted sessions between clients and servers.

Usenet: NNTP

Network News Transfer Protocol (NNTP) is the most commonly used way to send and receive Usenet newsgroups and postings. If you plan to accept a newsfeed into your network, you will have to plan carefully in order to allow NNTP to be accepted with security in mind. NNTP is quite easily exploited by hackers to allow access to an internal network. Fortunately, securing NNTP is easy because the communications between NNTP hosts is almost always the same in each session.

A more important issue for Usenet users, especially in larger organizations, is keeping internal private newsgroups from being transferred out into the Internet. You may also want to restrict incoming newsgroups to a specific type. NNTP can be configured to allow any newsgroups to be accepted or rejected.

DNS

DNS is an integral part of larger networks, and ties in to Internet hosts for lookups. DNS by itself is not usually a security issue, although it can become one because of the protocols it piggybacks onto. Authentication methods can be installed to verify that requests are genuine and that there is no misdirection. For the most part, though, DNS is quite secure.

Building Your Own Firewall

You can construct your own Internet firewall, although you really need a very good knowledge of the operating system and TCP/IP. Windows 95 and Windows 98 make poor firewalls because of the design of the operating system itself. UNIX and Windows NT/2000 are better, although Windows NT/2000 is harder to properly configure than UNIX.

The steps you must follow to construct your own firewall under Windows NT/2000 or UNIX are far beyond the scope of this book. There are several books devoted solely to the subject, depending on the operating system you choose to use. For the most part, the process involves blocking all the services you don't want to allow into your network and configuring the firewall to prevent hackers from gaining access to the firewall itself. The process of building your own firewall takes a while to complete properly even when you know what is necessary.

Note

The following Web sites can help you in setting up your own firewall:

`http://www.linux-mag.com/1999-08/guru_01.html`

`http://www.linuxgazette.com/issue26/kunz.html#fire`

`http://hotwired.lycos.com/webmonkey/01/31/index2a_page4.html`

`http://tech.irt.org/articles/js149/`

`http://www.practicallynetworked.com/serving/firewall_config.htm`

`http://www.linuxworld.com.au/article.php3?tid=8&aid=160`

`http://www.isaac.cs.berkeley.edu/simple-firewall.html`

`http://www.ncmag.com/2001_05/ifolder51/settingup..html`

Using Commercial Firewall Software

Many firewall packages are available on the market, and they are usually quite expensive. An example of a firewall solution is Cyberguard from Cyberguard Corporation. Others include BorderManager from Novell, Checkpoint from Check Point Software Technologies, and Eagle firewall from Raptor Systems. Consult the Web site `http://www.thegild.com/firewall/` for other names of commercial firewall solutions.

Cyberguard is available for Windows NT/2000 and UNIX platforms (it started on UNIX and moved to NT/2000 recently). Cyberguard is popular because it is not only one of the most secure firewalls that have been tested, but it is also extremely easy to install, configure, and manage.

20

FIREWALLS

> ### Note
>
> For more information about Cyberguard, check out the company's Web site at
> `http://www.cyberguard.com`. You'll find a description of the package as .well as
> several white papers. For more information on firewalls and security problems
> with them, check the CERT (Computer Emergency Response Team) site at
> `http://www.cert.org`.

Cyberguard is particularly easy to install and configure on a Windows NT/2000 server, taking less than 15 minutes for simple network configurations. Cyberguard is designed to work with dual-homed hosts with one connection to the internal network and the other to the Internet (either directly or though an ISP). When installing the package, Cyberguard lets you choose one of three default security configurations, as shown in Figure 20.1.

FIGURE 20.1

Three Cyberguard default settings cover most Windows NT/2000 configurations where the interface is called SecureGuard.

After choosing one of these default settings, you can check all the settings it affects by stepping through the different screens and verifying the choices. Figure 20.2 shows you one of the settings screens showing how the choice affects Windows NT/2000 accounts and passwords.

After choosing a default, Cyberguard reboots your Windows NT/2000 server and the protection is in effect from that point on. As an administrator you can modify the behavior of any aspect of the firewall. Figure 20.3 shows the Packet-Filtering Rules screen that lets you specify which packets are to be passed and which are to be stopped. As you can see, Cyberguard makes good use of Windows dialogs to simplify what is normally a complicated process.

FIGURE 20.2

Choosing a Cyberguard default affects particular items, which you can see in a series of screens like this.

FIGURE 20.3

Cyberguard's packet filtering dialog lets you choose how to filter incoming and outgoing packets.

Proxy server behavior is just as easy to set up. Figure 20.4 shows Cyberguard's proxy server dialog. Selecting proxies to be used is as simple as choosing items from a list. In this figure, we are setting up the FTP proxy service.

FIGURE 20.4

Cyberguard's proxy service window is easy to use and understand.

One other aspect of firewalls that Cyberguard excels at is DNS usage. As Figure 20.5 shows, you can set up DNS easily and even specify zones within a network.

FIGURE 20.5

Setting up DNS through the Cyberguard GUI.

Many other commercial packages are available to act as firewalls. Many magazines that deal with networking conduct head-to-head tests on a regular basis. If you are looking for a commercial firewall, conduct a fair bit of research first because the quality of available firewall software varies enormously, as does the price.

Summary

This chapter explained what a firewall is, what it does, and has shown you the basic functions that a firewall performs. You have seen how proxy servers and packet filters work, as well. The theme of IP security is continued in the next chapter, which looks at related subjects including cryptography and authentication.

Network and System Security

by Tim Parker

In the last chapter you saw how firewalls, proxy servers, and packet filters work. Firewalls are an important part of providing security to a network, preventing intrusion and access to sensitive data. However, blocking intruders into your network is only part of the security issue. You must consider many other things, including making sure any data you do send over the Internet cannot be read by unwanted parties, making sure that the person you are sending mail to (or receiving mail from) is the person you think he or she is, and providing extra levels of security inside your network in case someone does manage to get through your firewalls.

Gauging the amount of security you need is difficult in absolute terms. Although most operating systems offer basic file and directory protection, you may need encryption or other methods of locking up your system. There is no overall assessment of security levels, although the U.S. Department of Defense did try to assign different levels of security for its minicomputers and mainframes (most running versions of Unix or proprietary operating systems). The DoD defense levels and their description, in order of least to most security, are as follows:

- **D (minimal protection):** No provision for security or protection of data
- **C1 (discretionary security):** Users are identified by a login and access to files or directories can be controlled
- **C2 (controlled access):** C1 plus audit capabilities (record system activity) and assignment of administrator privileges to logins
- **B1 (labeled security):** C2 plus access controls that cannot be overridden
- **B2 (structured protection):** B1 plus security for all devices, support for trusted hosts, access controls for applications
- **B3 (security domains):** B2 plus ability to bundle system objects into discrete groups with access controls within that group
- **A1 (verified design):** B3 plus verified trusted system design of hardware and software

The A1 security level is generally regarded as unattainable, and no operating system currently is available that supports this level (at least to public knowledge). Most Unix systems and Windows NT can attain C2 security levels, and a few operating systems are certified for B1, but beyond that the constraints security imposes on the system become unmanageable.

So what can you do with your existing Windows, Macintosh, Unix, or Linux systems on a LAN? You need to take many steps to secure your systems as well as your applications from intrusions. If you are connected to the Internet through TCP/IP, you need to be aware of the security problems associated with that protocol and its applications.

This chapter starts by looking at the subject of encryption, one of the few ways of protecting your data from being read even if it is intercepted. After that, it looks at network security and TCP/IP application security.

Using Encryption

It is rare to find corporations and businesses that are not becoming more concerned about their data's security, especially with daily reports of hackers making their way into corporate networks, industrial espionage, and ex-employee sabotage. The need for tighter data security is especially important with the rapid rise of remote access work, where employees access corporate networks from home, hotels, or on the road through cellular services. You have to consider protecting the data that is being sent back and forth over the Internet and telephone lines, so that anyone who intercepts the data cannot read it. The only effective and relatively easy way to protect this data is with encryption.

Encryption has become a huge and lucrative business. Companies dedicated to encryption products are sprouting up all over the place, joining the few core companies that have pushed this technology for decades. Just a couple of years ago, getting really good encryption was difficult because intelligence agencies tried to prevent encryption algorithms from being too strong (hence preventing them from snooping themselves). Until a couple of years ago, it was illegal in the U.S. to export any encryption product that had anything better than 40-bit encryption because encryption systems are considered a weapon. With the ease of access to free or shareware encryption products through the Internet, though, as well as pressure from application and operating system vendors, 128-bit encryption products can now be distributed to all but a few countries. Even stronger encryption methods are available for selected countries, as well.

Without going into excessive detail at this point, encryption uses a key to scramble data, making it unreadable to someone who doesn't have the key to decode it. The longer the key, the more time necessary to crack the encryption code. Simple password encryption works well because the password must be known explicitly. When you scramble a message or data with the password, only that same password can decrypt the message.

If you are curious about how easy password-based encryption tools are to use, check out the CodedDrag software at `http://www.fim.uni-linz.ac.at/codeddrag/codedrag.htm`. An evaluation copy of CodedDrag is free, and registering the copy for unlimited use is a matter of making a small donation to the site's server fund. CodedDrag was developed at the University of Linz, Austria, and provides a very fast implementation of the *Data Encryption Standard* (DES) encryption tool. (In fact, CodedDrag offers DES, Triple-DES, and Blowfish encryption methods; the latter two are much more difficult to break than DES.) CodedDrag can be embedded as part of the Windows 95/98 or Windows NT desktop, adding encrypt and decrypt options to pop-up menus. After supplying a password to the system once, files are encrypted and decrypted so quickly you don't notice the process. In Windows 2000, the use of the NTFS version 5 filesystem enables you to use encryption to encrypt any file or folder contents by marking the file or folder for encryption. Only the user or recovery agent (Administrator accounts) can decrypt the files. The files are automatically decrypted when used and encrypted when they are closed.

Public-Private Key Encryption

Public-private key encryption is much more popular with Internet users because it allows for decoding of messages without knowing a different password for each. The way a public-private key system works is simple: You have two keys or password strings, one of which is freely available to anyone; the other string, your private key, is known only by you. For someone to send an encrypted message to you, they need your public key. The encryption software then scrambles the message based on your public key. After you receive the message, only the private key can unscramble it again, making you the only person who can read it. The public key cannot unscramble the message. When you want to send a message to someone else, you need his or her public key. To help spread this type of encryption, many users append their public keys to their email.

RSA Data Security

One of the earliest commercial products offering public-private key encryption tools was RSA Data Security (http://www.rsa.com), founded in 1977 by three MIT scientists. RSA is still in wide use, and is relatively inexpensive, very secure, and easy to use. The RSA software is available in several forms for different operating systems, but in its simplest form adds a few menu items to browsing tools like Windows Explorer. Selecting a file and using the Encrypt menu option automatically encrypts the document file after you enter a password. To decrypt, a menu option brings up a window asking for the password, and if correct, the restored file is available. Passwords can be stored to simplify the process.

Phil Zimmermann's PGP

One of the most famous encryption tools is Phil Zimmermann's Pretty Good Privacy (PGP). The U.S. government criminally charged Zimmermann because he made PGP freely available over the Internet. The case was eventually dropped, but it practically assured the widespread use of PGP, especially in other countries. PGP is available from many Web sites and it's not unusual to see PGP keys appended to email messages.

Symmetric Private Key Encryption

The most basic form of encryption is called *symmetric private key*. This is much like the decoder rings that were popular years ago. With a simple symmetric key a substitution code is used where some other letter replaces each letter. For example, all a's are replaced by x's, all b's are replaced by d's, and so on. The simplest form of a symmetric key chooses a new starting point for the alphabet and moves along in order (a becomes d, b becomes e, c becomes f, and so on).

More flexible symmetric keys randomize the substitution, and sometimes a password is used to figure out how the scrambling is achieved. Symmetric keys are easy to develop and they work quickly. Unfortunately, simple symmetric keys are the easiest to break. The reason is simple: Given a reasonable amount of text, you can figure out from letter frequency which letter mappings are used. The letter *e* is the most common in the language; if the scrambled text has mostly x's, you can assume x and e are mapped together. After you get a few of these mappings, other mappings start to become clear by looking at word fragments, much like a crossword puzzle. The same key is used for both encryption and decryption. To make symmetric keys more secure, more ways of scrambling the choice of each substitution have been developed.

DES, IDEA, and Others

IBM developed the Data Encryption Standard in 1976 for the U.S. government. The DES algorithm uses a 56-bit encryption key, which means that 72,057,594,037,927,936 keys are possible. The same key is used to encrypt and decrypt messages. DES is not a simple symmetric private key in that the substitution or mapping of letters changes with each letter. In theory, breaking DES has always been possible. There are 72 quadrillion possible combinations that need to be tested, but a group did rise to the challenge (and won $10,000 for its efforts) and proved that DES is not totally secure. More information about the DES challenge is available from http://www.cryptography.com/des.

> **Note**
>
> A machine built by Cryptography Research, Advanced Wireless Technologies, and EFF was used to demonstrate fast key searches for the DES. The DES Key Search Project developed specially designed hardware and software to search 90 billion keys per second, determining the key and winning the $10,000 RSA DES Challenge after searching for 56 hours.
>
> In the Proceedings of DIMACS workshop on DNA computing, 1995, a paper was published that showed the use of molecular computing to recover the DES key

> in about 4 months of work given one arbitrary (plain-text, cipher-text) pair. Furthermore this paper showed that under a chosen plain-text attack, it is possible to recover the DES key in one day using some preprocessing. This method can be generalized to break any cryptosystem that uses keys of length less than 64 bits.

Triple DES encryption (3DES) that is a modification of the basic algorithm that uses more bits, effectively making it much more difficult to break.

The *International Data Encryption Algorithm* (IDEA) is probably the most secure algorithm in use today. Developed at the Swiss Federal Institute of Technology, IDEA uses a 64-bit block in a 128-bit key with a feedback operation to strengthen the algorithm. An enhanced version of IDEA called Triple IDEA is now available. The full IDEA algorithm takes a while to work, so several simplified versions have been developed. One popular system is Tiny IDEA. IDEA is believed to be stronger than both DES (56-bit keys) and triple-DES (112-bit keys). IDEA also has the distinction of being the conventional cipher used in PGP in conjunction with the RSA public key algorithm. Some characteristics of Tiny IDEA are

- Files are processed in place (effectively wiping the original).
- It uses 8 round IDEA in ciphertext feedback mode.
- The initialization vector is set to zeros.
- The feedback is done on 8-byte blocks.
- The IDEA key is the user key followed by '\r' and filled with zeros.
- It is optimized for size, not speed, but runs fast anyway.

For more information about Tiny IDEA and to download a free copy, go to `http://www.cypherspace.org/~adam/rsa/idea.html`.

CAST (named after the developers Carlisle Adams and Stafford Tavares) uses a 64-bit key and 64-bit block for encryption. There's a lot of stuff going on in the background with CAST, called S-boxes, which use 8- and 32-bit inputs. The details are not important here, especially because they take a whole book to explain. CAST has not been deciphered to date, but like IDEA it can be slower to encrypt and decrypt. For more details on CAST, go to `http://www.cs.wm.edu/~hallyn/des/sbox.html`.

An encryption system called Skipjack was developed by the National Security Agency specifically for the Clipper chip, which the U.S. government wanted to have included in all online devices (hence allowing monitoring). The Clipper chip was never implemented, but Skipjack systems are available. The details of Skipjack are classified, but it is known to be an 80-bit key with 32 rounds of processing. Skipjack uses two keys: one private and one master held by the government. In theory, it would take 400 billion years to break Skipjack using the best available hardware today. AT&T provides the Clipper chip (and hence Skipjack) to several manufacturers, including themselves.

RC2 and RC4 were secret algorithms developed by RSA Data Security. Unfortunately for them, the source code was posted on the Internet, making the secret not very well kept! RC4 was considered quite secure and was used by Netscape for its exported versions of Navigator. The encryption was broken by two different groups at about the same time, taking about eight days to accomplish the task.

Which is the fastest and most secure of the encryption algorithms mentioned? The most secure is a toss-up, with Triple DES, IDEA, Triple IDEA, and Skipjack all secure enough to make unauthorized decryption almost impossible. However, the overhead required to encrypt and decrypt is noticeable. If we consider DES to take one second to encrypt or decrypt a document, Triple DES requires 3 seconds, IDA 2.5 seconds, and Triple IDEA 4 seconds. This may seem short, but with large documents and many files, the delays that the more secure algorithms impose become noticeable. In theory, Skipjack is as fast as DES, but who wants to trust the government with the keys?

The primary public-private key encryption system in use today is RSA, named after the inventors (Rivest, Shamir, and Adleman, for those wanting to impress others with trivia). A close competitor is Phil Zimmermann's PGP. Both RSA and PGP can use very long keys, often 100 bits or more. The longer the key, the more time required to encrypt and decrypt, and the tougher the message is to decrypt without a key. Having 1024-bit keys is not unusual. The RSA Web site (`http://www.rsa.com/rsalabs/`) discusses the strength of the encryption based on key length. A 512-bit key can be broken with a fair bit of computing power, but it can be done. Longer keys (768-bit or 1024-bit) require more horsepower than most hackers (except governments) will have access to. In theory, any key system can be broken either through brute-force analysis or some lucky guesses based on the encrypted text, but for all intents and purposes both RSA and PGP are secure as long as long keys are used.

The Diffie-Hellman system is a *Key Exchange Algorithm* (KEA), which is used to control and generate keys for public key distribution. Diffie-Hellman doesn't encrypt or decrypt messages: Its only use is to generate secure keys. The process is easy, but does require both ends of a communication (sender and receiver) to work together to generate the keys based on prime numbers.

Authenticating with Digital Signatures

Besides encrypting data, another important security issue needs to be addressed—being able to confirm the identity of the person who sent (or who receives) a message. After all, encrypted misinformation is just as secure as encrypted valuable information. To help authenticate both senders and receivers, a system known as *digital signatures* is used. Digital signatures use public-private encryption, relying on the public key to allow anyone to verify the sender's identity because the message is coded with their private key.

The U.S. government developed and adopted a system called *Digital Signature Standard* (DSS), which, as the name suggests, offers digital signature authentication. DSS has a major flaw, though, in that it is easy to accidentally reveal your keys if the same random encryption number is chosen twice and a hacker has both messages using that random number. Even worse, the contents of the message are sometimes easy to decrypt.

The *Secure Hash Algorithm* (SHA) and *Secure Hash Standard* (SHS) were developed by the U.S. government also, but are more secure than DSS. SHS uses a hashing algorithm that involves 160-bit keys. Unfortunately, SHS is somewhat slow. Given the speed with which RSA and PGP work, it's hard to understand why anyone would adopt SHS.

Another approach to digital signatures is message digest algorithms, of which at least three are in general circulation (called MD2, MD4, and MD5). The MD series of algorithms generate a digital fingerprint based on the input. The fingerprint is a 128-bit code, called a message digest. No two messages will ever have the same message digest (in theory). MD5 is the most secure of the set, developed by RSA to use a special hashing algorithm. Microsoft uses MD4 in its Windows NT user files to encrypt password entries.

> **Note**
>
> MD4 has been cracked many times. Several utilities are available on the Web for doing just this to Windows NT's password file (such as `http://is-it-true.org/nt/atips/atips92.shtml` and `http://www.atstake.com/research/lc3/index.html`). To crack passwords under Windows 2000 consult article 9186 at `http://www.windowsitsecurity.com/Articles`. A savvy administrator can use these tools to test how secure the Windows networks are. The reason for inclusion of this note is that hackers are already aware of this weakness and revealing this information here does not make Windows systems more insecure.

Certificate servers manage public-private keys for companies or organizations and usually are readily accessible through the Internet. Several commercial certificate servers are available for Windows and UNIX platforms. One of the best is Netscape's. Netscape also makes a FAQ available that describes why you would want to use a certificate server and the features of its own product. Access the FAQ at `http://home.netscape.com/certificate`.

Finally, we end up with Kerberos. If you've been on the Web or installed servers before, you've run into the Kerberos name several times. Kerberos is a way of providing network security by controlling access to network services on a user level. A Kerberos server is located somewhere on the network (usually on a secure machine). Kerberos servers are sometimes called *Key Distribution Centers* (KDCs). Whenever a user makes a request for some network service, the Kerberos server authenticates that the user is who he claims to be and that the service is on the proper machine. The security of the Kerberos system is based on the use of a private key encryption system based on DES. Every client and server on the network has a private key that is checked with every Kerberos-controlled action. Kerberos requires a dedicated server and so usually appears on larger networks and those that need tight security controls.

Cracking Encrypted Data

The science (some would call it an art) of breaking cryptography systems is called *cryptanalysis*. The process is to try to read an encrypted message without knowing the keys that were used to generate the message in the first place. There are a number of ways to get a head start on the process of breaking codes, the most common being knowledge of either the message contents or some part of the key. If you know that a message deals with shares in ABC Company, for example, you can make much better educated guesses about what certain words in the encrypted message mean. This leads to a key to the encryption faster. This type of crypto-cracking is known as *plaintext* because you know part of the message and use that to leverage the key from the rest of the message.

Sometimes private keys are made known either accidentally or on purpose. Knowing some part of a key, or having a good idea of what the key may be composed of, helps shorten the cracking time, too. For example, if you know someone has the habit of using his children's names as keys, and you know the kids' names, you are very close to being able to decipher a message. Getting the keys is usually not too difficult, especially if the messages are going over the Internet. There are many ways to intercept IP packets, and eventually an idea of a user's keys may be intercepted. If a cracker can get partial keys or the public keys of both ends of a message route, the odds of breaking the entire message are much higher.

Failing these helpful tips, cryptanalysis proceeds in a brute-force method. A number of different methods are used to break messages, depending on the cracker's techniques, guesses about the message or key, and both the brainpower and horsepower at his disposal. The ciphertext method can be used when you have only the encrypted message to work with. Computers then try different keys to decipher the message, sometimes with help from the cracker who can guess at words in the message. Because most messages follow standard formats (how many different ways can you structure a business letter?), you may be able to use part of the encrypted message to help choose a key to break the entire contents.

If the encryption algorithm is known, a modified plaintext method can be used. With this method, the cracker encrypts a message with the same technique (but not the same key) as the target message. By repeating the process with different messages and keys, an idea of the key used to encrypt the target message can be developed. This technique works surprisingly well.

There are some mathematically complex methods of cracking messages that rely on the intricacies of public-private keys. There will be a relationship between the keys and the encrypted message, and this can be deduced given enough number-crunching ability. Mathematicians have written entire books about the science of breaking encryptions in a theoretical manner, many of which have been employed by scientists and engineers working for national security agencies.

Protecting Your Network

Most LANs are not thought of as a security problem, but they tend to be one of the easiest methods of getting into a system. If any of the machines on the network has a weak access point, all the machines on the network can be accessed through that machine's network services.

PCs and Macintoshes usually have little security, especially over call-in modems, so they can be used in a similar manner to access the network services. A basic rule about LANs is that it's impossible to have a secure machine on the same network as nonsecure machines. Therefore, any solution for one machine must be implemented for all machines on the network.

Logins and Passwords

The most common access method of breaking into a system through a network, over a modem connection, or while sitting in front of a terminal is through weak passwords. Weak (which means easily guessable) passwords are very common. When system users use these, even the best security systems can't protect against intrusion.

If you're managing a system that has several users, you should implement a policy requiring users to set their passwords at regular intervals (usually six to eight weeks is a good idea), and to use non-English words. The best passwords are combinations of letters and numbers that are not in the dictionary.

Sometimes, though, having a policy against weak passwords isn't enough. You might want to consider forcing stronger password usage by using public domain or commercial software that checks potential passwords for susceptibility. Third-party commercial and shareware tools for password enforcement are available for most operating systems.

If you are running a Unix or Linux operating system, you need to pay particular attention to the /etc/passwd and /etc/group files. These need to be set up with unused accounts locked out, and with passwords protecting all accounts, used or not.

Note

On Unix systems, you should run the pwconv utility, which makes use of shadow files to store the password information. Unlike the password file, the shadow files are not world readable.

Windows NT/2000 users need to properly implement user accounts through the User Manager for Domains or the Active Directory for Users and Computers, which allows you to set up both workgroup and domain accounts. Windows 95 and 98 users are in a bit of a bind because no real account security exists on those operating systems. Anyone can create a new account by sitting in front of the screen. Unless the Windows 95 or 98 machines are part of a domain controlled by a Windows NT system, the network's weak point will always be the Windows 95/98 clients.

File and Directory Permissions

Security begins at the file permission level and should be carried out carefully. Whether you want to protect a file from snooping by an unauthorized invader or another user, you should carefully set your file permissions for maximum security.

The way you set file and directory permissions varies depending on the operating system. On Unix and Linux systems you can use the chmod (change mode) command, whereas on Windows 95, 98, and NT/2000 systems you need to use the Access Control Lists (ACLs).

Modems are the most commonly used interface into every system (unless you're running completely standalone, or on a closed network). Modems are used for remote user access, as well as for network and Internet access. Securing your system's modem lines from intrusion is simple and effective enough to stop casual browsers.

The safest technique to prevent unauthorized access through modems is to employ a callback modem. A callback modem lets users connect to the system as usual; it then hangs up and consults a list of valid users and their telephone numbers before calling the user back to establish the call. Callback modems are quite expensive, so this is not a practical solution for many systems.

Callback modems have some problems, too, especially if users change locations frequently. Also, callback modems are vulnerable to abuse because of call-forwarding features of modern telephone switches.

The typical telephone modem can be a source of problems if it doesn't hang up the line properly after a user session has finished. Most often, this is a problem with the wiring of the modem or the configuration setup.

Wiring problems might sound trivial, but there are many systems with hand-wired modem cables that don't properly control all the pins, so the system can be left with a modem session not properly closed and a logout not completed. Anyone calling that modem continues where the last user ended. To prevent this kind of problem, make sure the cables connecting the modem to the machine are complete. Replace hand-wired cables that you are unsure of with properly constructed commercial ones. Also, watch the modem when a few sessions are completed to make sure the line hangs up properly.

Trust Relationships

In a trust relationship, one machine decides to allow users of another machine to access resources without having to log in again. The assumption is that valid users of one machine can be trusted by another machine. Trust relationships were developed years ago to simplify a user's access to network resources. Suppose you were logged on to one machine and needed a file or application from another. It would be inconvenient to have to enter a login and password each time you did this, and hence trust relationships permit you to access resources without having to log in to each machine. Trust relationships are not the same as running *Network Information Service* (NIS) or *Yellow Pages* (YP), which use a central user and password file.

Most operating systems allow trust relationships to be set up, with specific routines available for trusts included with Windows NT, Unix, and Linux. The problem with trust relationships is easy to see: If someone breaks into one machine, he can access any other machine that has a trust relationship with that machine.

Trust relationships can be two-way (both machines trust each other) or one-way (one machine trusts the other but not vice-versa). Entire networks can have trust relationships. For example, suppose you have three subnetworks in your company, one of which holds very secure information; the other two are regular, nonsecure users. To prevent having to log in to each network when accessing resources, trust relationships can be set up among the three, but you will probably want to prohibit a trust relationship from the nonsecure to the secure network (but allow the secure to access anything on the nonsecure networks). Your two nonsecure networks can have two-way trusts, and only one-way trusts from the secure to nonsecure. Windows NT and Unix permit setting up trusts quite easily.

From a security point of view, you have to make sure your trusts are set up to limit damage from intrusion from a trusted machine or network. A machine with sensitive information on it should never trust machines that are widely accessible.

UUCP on Unix and Linux Systems

The Unix UUCP program was designed with good security in mind. However, it was designed many years ago, and security requirements have changed considerably since then. A number of security problems have been found over the years with UUCP, many of which have been addressed with changes and patches to the system. Still, UUCP requires some system administration attention to ensure it is working properly and securely.

If you don't plan to use UUCP, remove the uucp user entirely from the /etc/password file or provide a strong password that can't be guessed (putting an asterisk as the first character of the password field in /etc/passwd effectively disables the login). Removing uucp from the /etc/passwd file won't affect anything else on the Linux system.

You should set permissions to be as restrictive as possible in all UUCP directories (usually /usr/lib/uucp, /usr/spool/uucp, and /usr/spool/uucppublic). Permissions for these directories tend to be lax with most systems, so use chown, chmod, and chgrp to restrict access only to the uucp login. The group and username for all files should be set to uucp. Check the file permissions regularly.

UUCP uses several files to control who is allowed in. These files (/usr/lib/uucp/Systems and /usr/lib/uucp/Permissions, for example) should be owned and accessible only by the uucp login. This prevents modification by an intruder with another login name.

The /usr/spool/uucppublic directory can be a common target for break-ins because it requires read and write access by all systems accessing it. To safeguard this directory, create two subdirectories: one for receiving files and another for sending. Further subdirectories can be created for each system that is on the valid user list, if you want to go that far.

Preparing for the Worst

Assuming someone does break into your network and causes damage on your machines, what can you do? Obviously, backups of the system are helpful because they let you recover any damaged or deleted files. But beyond that, what should you do?

First, find out how the invader got in, and secure that method of access so it can't be used again. If you're not sure of the access method, close down all modems and terminals and carefully check all the configuration and setup files for holes. There has to be one, or the invader couldn't have gotten in. Also check passwords and user lists for weak or outdated material.

If you are the victim of repeated attacks, consider enabling an audit system to keep track of how intruders get in and what they do. As soon as you see an intruder log in, force him off.

Finally, if the break-ins continue, call the local authorities. Breaking into computer systems (whether in a large corporation or a home) is illegal in most countries, and the authorities usually know how to trace the users back to their calling point. They're breaking into your system and shouldn't get away with it!

Summary

This chapter has discussed encryption and authentication, as well as some basic security precautions you need to consider. An awful lot falls under the TCP security banner, and this chapter only scratched the surface. If you want to know more about computer and network security, there are many books dedicated to the subject.

Implementing TCP/IP

PART
VI

CHAPTER 22

General Configuration Issues

by Kurt Hudson

TCP/IP is the most widely used protocol, but it is also one of the more difficult to configure compared to other protocols. Consequently, the potential for configuration errors is great. This chapter explains the basic installation and configuration of the network card and networking services. Required and basic IP configuration parameters are described along with typical IP configuration errors. In addition, using IP connections to tunnel other protocols is explained. This chapter uses Windows 98 as an example operating system. Later chapters cover the individual operating systems in more detail. Windows 98 is used because of the reader's probable familiarity with the operating system. Not every one has upgraded to Windows ME, which was not very popular. And upgrading to Windows NT/2000 or Windows XP is not always possible because of the increased hardware requirements of these operating systems.

Installing a Network Card

In order for your computer to connect to and properly communicate on any network, you must configure the network card. There are several different types of network cards and the configuration of each varies slightly. However, all network cards must be installed physically (as hardware components), and logically configured with their software drivers.

> **Note**
>
> It is important to realize that if a computer has two or more network cards and you expect to communicate through both cards using TCP/IP, then both cards must be set up with separate IP addresses and other TCP/IP parameters.

The physical configuration typically involves turning off the PC, removing the CPU cover, and physically inserting the network card. On a laptop system, the physical installation may be as simple as inserting the PC Card into the appropriate slot. No matter what type of system you are configuring, the physical connection must be made.

After the physical connection is made, the resources for that network card must be assigned. Some network cards can be configured to obtain their resources automatically and others must be manually configured.

Network Cards

When you want to install a network card into your PC, you must first obtain the correct type of card. This means that you must know what type of hardware slots you have inside the PC. For a desktop PC, you will typically use an *Industry Standard Architecture*

(ISA) or *Peripheral Component Interconnect* (PCI) network card. The manufacturer's documentation for the motherboard or the PC will indicate which type of slots you have on board. You must then identify which slots are available (open) to receive a new card. You can place the network card in any open slot.

> **Note**
>
> Proper safety precautions must be taken when installing any device in a PC. You must turn off the power to the device before adding or removing components, and you should wear an electrostatic discharge wrist wrap. For more information on installing hardware, obtain a book that specifically discusses upgrading and repairing PCs.

After you know what type of slot you have available, you must also determine the type of network to which the card will be connected. The physical connection from the card to the network is typically referred to as the *transceiver type*. The standard connections to a network are *RJ-45*, *British Naval Connector* (BNC), and *Attachment Unit Interface* (AUI). The RJ-45 interface allows your network card to be connected to a twisted-pair network. The BNC connector allows your network card to be part of a thin-net coaxial network (a.k.a. 10Base-2 network). The AUI interface allows you to connect your card to a thick-net coaxial network (a.k.a. 10Base-5). You must know the type of network to which you will connect the network card in order to select a card with the appropriate interface.

Many network cards support multiple transceiver types. Some network cards require you to configure the appropriate transceiver type before you install the card. This is typically done via vendor-supplied configuration software or occasionally hardware jumpers (connectors) on the actual card. Be sure to check the network card documentation before installing the device. However, most network cards that have multiple transceiver types will automatically configure themselves by sensing the connection during the startup process.

After the card has been inserted into the appropriate slot and the transceiver is set (if required), the physical connection to the PC is complete. The next step is to configure the resources. However, you should know about a couple of other types of network cards before learning to configure resources; these are PC Cards, modems (a.k.a. dial-up adapters), and parallel port adapters.

PC Cards (PCMCIA Cards)

PC Cards were originally called PCMCIA (Personal Computer Memory Card International Association) cards. However, most people found the acronym too lengthy to remember, so the name was shortened to PC Card. PC Cards are most often used in laptop computers and are used for network cards, modems, and external hard drive support. The PC Card network interfaces typically have a media access unit that attaches to the PC Card and then to the actual network cable.

PC Card NICs utilize typical resources, such as a single IRQ and I/O range. However, PC Cards also require socket services and card services. Systems that support PC Cards will provide such services for these devices.

Modems

Modems can also function as network cards and are often referred to as dial-up adapters. When a modem connects to a remote network or the Internet, it functions as a network card. Modem configuration is a little different from that of other network cards because modems are typically configured to use serial communication ports such as COM1, COM2, COM3, or COM4. Many modems provide their own COM port so you must disable the COM port on the motherboard via the CMOS/BIOS settings. Modems also use whatever IRQ is assigned for the given COM port. Typically, COM1 and COM3 are configured for IRQ4. COM2 and COM4 use IRQ3 by default.

After the modem is installed, the dial-up networking components must be installed to configure the modem to transfer network traffic. Chapter 24, "Dial-Up Networking with Windows 98," covers the installation and configuration of dial-up networking components.

Parallel Port Adapters

Some modems and other network devices such as routers can be connected to parallel ports (instead of the serial COM ports). Typically, these devices include a cable or transceiver for the parallel port to which the device connects. The configuration is similar to that of a COM port because the parallel ports also have default IRQ and I/O settings. The networking devices that utilize the parallel port often accept the default IRQ and I/O range used for that port.

Resource Configuration

Any network card that is installed in a PC must be configured with an IRQ line and I/O range. Typically, the manufacturer's documentation explains the default IRQ and I/O range settings for the card. In order to get the card working with the operating system, you must determine whether that IRQ and I/O range is available. If the IRQ and I/O range are available, you should have no problem configuring the card. However, if the IRQ or the I/O range is not available, you must find settings that are open.

Newer network cards and other devices support *Plug and Play* (PnP), which means that resources (IRQ and I/O range) are configured automatically during the boot process. PnP must be supported by the operating system; Windows 95, Windows 98, and Windows 2000 do support PnP adapters. During the boot process, the operating system and the PnP device work together to configure a set of open resources for the device. If you do not have a PnP adapter, you will have to locate open resources and configure your device to support those resources.

> **Note**
>
> If you are configuring an Integrated Services Digital Network (ISDN), or other connection that can utilize a Universal Serial Bus (USB), you need only to locate a free I/O range for your device.

In Windows 98, it is quite simple to determine which resources are available by looking in the Device Manager. The Computer Properties dialog box in the Device Manager allows you to view the used IRQ and I/O ranges (see Figure 22.1).

FIGURE 22.1

Use Device Manager to locate open resources.

To access the Computer Properties dialog box in Windows 98, follow these steps:

1. Right-click the My Computer icon on the desktop.

2. Choose Properties from the resulting menu.

3. Click the Device Manager tab.

4. Click the Properties button.

You can see which IRQs and I/O ranges are not in use by selecting the IRQ and Input/Output (I/O) options. When you have determined which resources are open, consult the documentation for your network card to determine which resources it can be configured to accept. You may need to set jumpers, dip switches, or use the manufacturer's software to configure the correct resources for the network card.

Installing the Adapter Software

After you have properly set the network card to use open resources on the operating system, you must install the network card drivers. Some operating systems ship with drivers for various network cards built-in, but most network cards come with their own drivers anyway. You can use the network drivers from the operating system (if available) from the manufacturer-provided media, or the manufacturer's Internet Web site.

If you were installing network card software inside Windows 98, you would follow these steps:

1. Right-click the Network Neighborhood icon.

2. Choose Properties from the resulting context menu.

3. From the Configuration tab of the Network dialog box, click Add.

4. In the Select Network Component Type dialog box, choose Adapter from the options listed and then click Add (see Figure 22.2).

5. The next dialog box presents you with a list of Manufacturers and Network Adapter types. Choose the appropriate combination or insert the manufacturer-provided disk into the CD-ROM or floppy drive and click Have Disk.

6. After you have the correct combination, or you have inserted the manufacturer-provided drivers, click OK to continue. During this operation, you may be required to configure the resources (IRQ and I/O range) for your network adapter.

7. After the software is installed, click OK on the Network dialog box and reboot the system, if necessary.

FIGURE 22.2

You must add a software adapter for your NIC.

After the network card driver is installed, you can begin to install and configure the software networking components, such as the appropriate redirector, server services (if any), and TCP/IP protocol suite.

Redirectors and APIs

A *redirector*, as its name implies, is a software component in the protocol stack that redirects local queries for resources over the network. That is to say, the redirector is an operating system component that allows the computer to obtain resources and services on the network. Sometimes the redirector is called the client or workstation service because it provides this functionality.

The redirector must be compatible with the type of network it is expected to utilize. Redirectors from different networking vendors are rarely interchangeable. On a heterogeneous network, this often means that client systems must be configured with multiple redirectors.

In order to facilitate the inclusion of multiple redirectors and to separate the protocol stack from application development, networking vendors have created interfaces inside the protocol stack. For example, Microsoft uses the NetBIOS interface to separate the protocol stack from the operating system code. Many different protocols and redirectors can be integrated through this interface. NetBIOS is called an *Application Programming Interface* (API) because it segregates the applications from the network components. This allows application developers to focus on the application they are writing instead of worrying about the underlying network on which the application may be used.

To install the appropriate redirector from the Windows 98 operating system, follow these steps:

1. Right-click the Network Neighborhood icon.
2. Choose Properties from the resulting context menu.
3. From the Configuration tab of the Network dialog box, click Add.
4. In the Select Network Component Type dialog box, choose Client from the options listed and then click Add.
5. The next dialog box presents you with a list of Manufacturers and Network Clients. This is essentially a list of network vendors and their respective network redirectors. Choose the appropriate pair and click OK.
6. You may have to map the correct location to the installation files. After you do, click OK. Click OK again, if necessary.
7. After the software is installed, click OK on the Network dialog box and reboot the system, if necessary.

22

GENERAL CONFIGURATION ISSUES

Services

Services, like redirectors, are typically implemented at the top of the protocol stack in the TCP/IP Application Layer. Services such as *File Transfer Protocol* (FTP), *Hypertext Transfer Protocol* (HTTP), and Telnet all operate at the TCP/IP Application Layer. Services also benefit from APIs in the protocol stack because they can be developed independently of the underlying network.

File and printer sharing services are usually dependent upon the type of network that is supported. For example, NetWare networks require a different type of file and printer sharing services than do Microsoft networks. In the Windows 98 operating system, both Microsoft and NetWare file and printer sharing services are available and their installation process is very similar to that of the installation of a redirector. The only difference is that the component selected in the Select Network Component Type dialog box should be Service instead of Client.

NIC Interfaces

In the early days of networking, protocol stacks did not display modularity. Instead of utilizing separate redirectors, services, and protocols, the protocol stack was a single monolithic software component that provided a far more limited set of functionality. Each vendor only produced software that worked with one type of network.

One of the first and most obvious limitations of this type of networking was the inability to utilize multiple transport protocols. In order to work around such limitations, networking vendors and standards organizations, such as the International Organization of Standardization (ISO), worked to provide modularity in the protocol stack.

The early solutions produced two interfaces that are still in use today—Open Datalink Interface (ODI) and *Network Driver Interface Specification* (NDIS). ODI was developed by Novell to allow its networking components to utilize multiple protocols with one or more network cards. NDIS is part of the Microsoft protocol stack that allows multiple protocols and multiple network cards to be bound on the same computer system.

Network and Transport Protocols

In addition to the correct adapter software, redirector, and service, you must have a protocol in order to communicate with the other systems on the network. The protocol you install will depend on the type of network to which you are connecting and the other systems with which your system must communicate. You must ensure that the network supports the protocol you install. In order for two systems to communicate with each other, they must have common protocols.

Because the focus of this book is the TCP/IP protocol suite, this section deals with configuration issues for TCP/IP.

IP Configuration Requirements

The most basic configuration requirements for TCP/IP include the IP address and subnet mask. These two items may be all that you need to configure to communicate on a local network with TCP/IP.

The IP address must be set correctly for the local segment in order for your computer to be able to communicate properly. Your system must be configured with a unique IP address and have the appropriate subnet mask. The subnet mask for any individual system should be identical to the mask of other systems on the same subnet in order for those machines to communicate. In addition, the IP address should be unique for the subnet, but it must contain the correct network identifier and subnet identifier (if used). It is the subnet mask that determines the correct network identifier. For example, the subnet mask 255.255.0.0 specifies that the first two octets of the IP address identify the network segment (a.k.a. subnet address). If the first two octets identify the network, the last two octets should uniquely identify a host on that network segment. Consider the combinations shown in Table 22.1.

TABLE 22.1   IP Address and Subnet Mask Configuration

Hostname/IP Address	*Subnet Mask*
HostA/192.168.1.12	255.255.0.0
HostB/192.168.2.17	255.255.255.240
HostC/192.168.1.250	255.255.0.0
HostD/192.168.2.30	255.255.255.240
HostE/192.168.2.33	255.255.255.240

In the example in Table 22.1, HostA and HostC are on the same logical network (network ID 192.168.0.0). HostB and HostD are on the same logical subnet (subnet ID 192.168.1.16). HostE is on a different logical network than the other hosts (subnet ID 192.168.1.32). If all of these hosts were on the same physical cable, HostA and HostC would be able to communicate with each other, and HostB and HostD would be able to communicate with each other. No other combinations of communication could occur because of the difference in logical subnets.

An Example of Subnetting

The reason that HostE is not on the same subnet as HostD and HostB may not be readily apparent. However, if you review Chapter 4, "Names and Addresses in an IP Network," you will see that the network identifier when using the mask 255.255.255.240 is at every 16th number starting with 16 and ending with 224. The valid network identifiers and ranges for 192.168.1.0 subnetted with 255.255.255.240 are as follows:

```
192.168.1.16 with host range 192.168.1.17 - 192.168.1.30

192.168.1.32 with host range 192.168.1.33 - 192.168.1.46

192.168.1.48 with host range 192.168.1.49 - 192.168.1.62

192.168.1.64 with host range 192.168.1.65 - 192.168.1.78

192.168.1.80 with host range 192.168.1.81 - 192.168.1.94

192.168.1.96 with host range 192.168.1.97 - 192.168.1.110

192.168.1.112 with host range 192.168.113 - 192.168.1.126

192.168.1.128 with host range 192.168.1.129 - 192.168.1.142

192.168.1.144 with host range 192.168.1.145 - 192.168.1.158

192.168.1.160 with host range 192.168.1.161 - 192.168.1.174

192.168.1.176 with host range 192.168.1.177 - 192.168.1.190

192.168.1.192 with host range 192.168.1.193 - 192.168.1.206

192.168.1.208 with host range 192.168.1.209 - 192.168.1.222

192.168.1.224 with host range 192.168.1.225 - 192.168.1.238
```

Notice that this creates 14 logical subnets with 14 hosts on each subnet. If you look at 192.168.1.33 and 192.168.1.30, you will see they are on different logical subnets.

In order for hosts on the same local network to communicate, they must have unique host identifiers and identical network/subnet identifiers. In order for hosts to communicate with other hosts on remote segments (across a router), they must both be configured with default gateway addresses.

Configuring a Default Gateway Address

If you want your system to be able to communicate with remote networks, or with network segments on a LAN separated by a router, you must configure a default gateway address. The default gateway address is typically the IP address of the local router. However, in instances where more than one router is configured for a local segment, the default gateway is the preferred path for communications bound for remote networks.

A host on the network uses its subnet mask to determine whether a communication is bound for a local or remote segment. If the subnet identifier for the destination is the same as the local network identifier, the communication is transmitted on the local segment. However, if the subnet identifier is different, the communication is sent to the default gateway. The default gateway is typically a router that forwards the packet to the appropriate destination or next hop along the path to the ultimate destination.

In order to communicate with the default gateway appropriately, the local host must be configured with a valid and unique IP address, the correct subnet mask, and the address of the default gateway. If any of these items are incorrect, the host will have problems communicating on the network. The default gateway address must be an address on the local segment. In other words, you cannot configure a remote host as your system's default gateway.

If your system can communicate with local hosts, but is unable to communicate with remote hosts, there is usually a problem with the default gateway or its configuration. Potential problems with the default gateway include the following:

- The default gateway is offline.
- The cable or interface connecting the default gateway and local segment is not functioning properly.
- The default gateway address is incorrect on the client.
- The default gateway address is not configured on the client.
- The *Address Resolution Protocol* (ARP) cache entry for the router is incorrect. This is usually solved by rebooting the client, unless the client uses a static entry in the ARP cache.

Most of those configuration issues are easy to understand and correct. However, the incorrect ARP cache entry might be overlooked. You must remember that all communications on the local segment are eventually conducted between two *Media Access Control* (MAC) hardware addresses. If the network interface for the default gateway was changed and clients continued to use the hardware address of the old interface, they would fail to communicate with the default gateway. Typically, rebooting the client system would refresh the ARP cache and cause the client to resolve the MAC address again. However, if the operating system were configured to insert a static ARP entry for the default gateway, a simple reboot would not correct the problem. In such a case, the file that was entering the static entry into the ARP cache would have to be updated.

22

GENERAL CONFIGURATION ISSUES

Configuring the Name Server Address

Another important item to configure on a TCP/IP host is the IP address of the name server. The two basic types of name servers are *Domain Name System* (DNS) servers and *Windows Internet Name Service* (WINS) servers. DNS servers convert Internet-style hostnames into IP addresses so that communications take place between TCP/IP hosts. WINS servers convert NetBIOS names (used with Microsoft networks) to IP addresses. DNS services and servers are detailed in Chapter 6, "DNS: Name Services"; WINS servers and services are covered in Chapter 7, "WINS."

For the individual IP host, it is important that you configure the correct IP address of the appropriate name server. Microsoft clients may require both the IP address of a DNS server and the IP address of a WINS server in order to properly resolve computer names to IP addresses. If you can communicate with a host using its IP address but not its computer name, there is a name resolution problem. This problem could be caused by any of the following issues:

- The name server address is incorrect on the client.
- The name server is down.
- A router between the name server and your system is down (not allowing communications to pass through), but the host to which you are connecting is not on the other side of that router.
- A physical connection problem exists between your system and the name server, but not between your system and the system to which you are connecting.
- The name for the system to which you are trying to connect is not correctly configured in the name server or is not listed with the name server.

Configuring the Mail Server Address

If you want to send and receive mail from the local host, you must configure the address of the mail server with your mail application. Messages transmitted on TCP/IP networks typically run through the *Simple Mail Transfer Protocol* (SMTP). Clients typically receive mail using the *Post Office Protocol* (POP) or *Internet Message Access Protocol* (IMAP). Typically, the configuration for incoming mail is either POP or IMAP, not both.

Most Internet mail applications allow you to decide whether you will use the hostname of the mail server or the IP address. For example, you can either enter mail.server.com or 192.168.1.50 to access the mail server. Many *Internet Service Providers* (ISPs) use the same mail server for both incoming and outgoing mail, but some utilize different servers for each function. In order to ensure that your system can both send and receive mail, you must configure the address(es) of the mail server(s) correctly.

Registering Your Domain Name

If you plan to communicate on the Internet using a specific domain name, such as domain.com, you must register with the InterNIC. Typically, you arrange the registration of your domain name through an ISP. It usually handles the necessary paperwork to set up your domain name. However, the information necessary to register a domain name is available on the Web via the InterNIC at http://www.internic.net.

IP Configuration Variations

Some devices and operating systems natively support TCP/IP and expect it to be configured as the device or operating system is configured. The configuration concepts previously described are essentially the same; however, their implementation is often different. One type of device that anticipates IP configuration during a typical setup routine is a router, such as a Cisco router. Because routers have multiple interfaces, the configuration is done on a per-interface basis. During the Cisco automated setup routine, called the System Configuration Dialog, you have the option to configure IP on each interface. Alternatively, you can bypass this screen and enter Cisco IOS commands directly at the command line to configure an interface.

There are also variations on configuring IP addresses and subnet masks on different systems. For example, when configuring the IP subnet mask for an address on a Cisco router, you do not enter the entire 32-bit mask (on the menu interface) because the default mask is assumed. For example, if you are configuring the IP address 192.168.1.1 for an interface on a Cisco router, you need not enter 255.255.255.0 as a subnet mask. Because the address is a known Class C address, the default subnet mask 255.255.255.0 is assumed. You will be given the opportunity to enter only the number of additional bits that you would like to subnet. For example, for a subnet mask of 255.255.255.240 you would enter the number 4 because that is 4 bits beyond the default subnet mask.

In addition, when you are reviewing the IP settings on some devices, you may not always see dotted-decimal subnet masks. You can either see the binary format of the subnet mask or *Classless InterDomain Routing* (CIDR) format. The binary format is simply the numbers represented as binary digits. For example, 255.255.240.0 becomes 11111111.11111111.11110000.00000000. CIDR format shows the IP address followed by the number of bits that are masked. For example, 192.168.1.1 with the subnet mask 255.255.255.240 would be represented as 192.168.1.1/28 because 28 masked binary digits are in the subnet mask.

Configuring the Routing Table

Routing table problems can also cause communication trouble on IP networks. Many routers are automatically configured by dynamic routing protocols such as *Routing Information Protocol* (RIP) and *Open Shortest Path First* (OSPF). However, when routes are statically entered by an administrator, the potential for typos increases the chance that there could be errors in the routing table. Other than typos in the routing table, configuring the wrong interface for the next hop is a common problem. Consider the network configuration shown in Figure 22.3.

FIGURE 22.3

Use Route Print to locate routing table configuration problems.

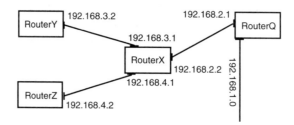

RouterX Routing Table

Network	Mask	Interface
192.168.4.0	255.255.255.0	192.168.4.1
192.168.3.0	255.255.255.0	192.168.3.1
192.168.2.0	255.255.255.0	192.168.2.2
192.168.1.0	255.255.255.0	192.168.2.2

The problem with the routing table of RouterX is subtle but will cause problems on the network. Notice that the last line shown in the RouterX routing table example shows that communications bound for network 192.168.1.0 go through interface 192.168.2.2, but this is incorrect. The router is supposed to route communication to the correct next hop. From the perspective of RouterX, the next hop to 192.168.1.0 is the interface on RouterQ, which has an IP address of 192.168.2.1. If this configuration problem is not corrected, packets destined for network 192.168.1.0 going through RouterX will fail.

Notice that because RouterX is connected to all other segments shown in its routing table, it uses its own interfaces to connect to those segments. Only when the router is not directly connected to the segment will it use the interface of another router to pass communications to the remote segment.

In order to correct the configuration problem illustrated in Figure 22.3, you would correct the interface to which RouterX sends communications destined for network 192.168.1.0. The corrected line for the routing table would be

```
192.168.1.0  255.255.255.0  192.168.2.1
```

IP Encapsulation of Foreign Protocols

IP can be used to encapsulate other Network Layer protocols in order for them to be sent over the network. One example of this is the IPX over IP tunnel. Novell NetWare networks natively use the IPX/SPX protocol. If you want to connect two Novell NetWare LANs over the Internet, you can use an IPX over IP tunnel.

The word *tunnel* actually describes the concept of what happens in such a configuration. After the higher layer protocols are encapsulated in the IPX packet, the entire set is then encapsulated into an IP packet for routing over the network to a remote IPX network. Figure 22.4 illustrates this concept.

22

GENERAL
CONFIGURATION
ISSUES

FIGURE 22.4
You can use the IPX over IP tunnel to effectively create an IPX WAN.

A server on each side of the TCP/IP network must be configured to package/unpackage the IPX over IP packets. When NetWare servers are used to do this, they use an IP Tunnel driver. The following lines are typically added to the NET.CFG file on the NetWare server to enable this:

```
Link Driver IPTUNNEL
        Gateway 192.168.1.50
Protocol IPXODI
        Bind #2
```

The first part indicates the gateway machine that will be used to unwrap the packets at the remote site. The second part binds IPXODI to the second defined driver, which is the IP Tunnel driver. In addition to those changes to the NET.CFG, the TCP/IP protocol suite (tcpip) must be installed and loaded on the server as well as the IP Tunnel driver (iptunnel).

> **Note**
>
> Unix and Linux servers can also support the IPX over IP tunnel. This is often done when the systems are running IPX applications over the Internet, rather than routing between LANs. The application that provides this support is called `ipxtunnel` and is available from `sunsite.unc.edu` and elsewhere on the Internet.

In addition to sending IPX over TCP/IP networks, other protocols besides the normal TCP/IP protocol suite can be encapsulated in IP packets. Microsoft uses the *Point-to-Point Tunneling Protocol* (PPTP) to encrypt communications between hosts connected on the Internet. Other choices are to use L2TP in combination with IPSec to build a secure tunnel. This type of tunneling secures communications going over the Internet. Many firewalls employ similar encryption techniques by encapsulating proprietary protocols between two remote points on the Internet. This allows companies to have a secure connection, or *Virtual LAN* (VLAN), over the Internet. The encapsulation makes it more difficult (some say virtually impossible) for hackers to spy on communications transferred over these VLAN connections.

Summary

When you set up a host on an IP network, there are many items to configure. If you haven't already installed and configured the network card, you must consider the configuration of the hardware resources. In addition, you may need to check your system's open resources IRQ and I/O range in order to determine which resources are available. Software drivers from the manufacturer are often required in order to properly configure network cards; however, the Windows operating systems contain the necessary drivers for many different network cards.

When you have the network card and driver configured, you may need to install a redirector and additional services. The actual redirector and services that you install depend on the type of network to which you are connecting and the services you want to provide on that network.

If you intend to communicate on an IP network, you must either have a device that natively supports IP or you must install the TCP/IP protocol suite. If the device natively supports IP, the configuration of the protocol is typically part of the setup routine. The absolute requirements to get an IP host to operate on an IP network are the IP address and subnet mask. If you intend for your system to communicate with IP hosts on remote networks, you must also configure a default gateway. The default gateway is the destination for packets that are to be routed to remote segments. The default gateway is the IP address of a router on the local segment that has the capability to forward packets to remote networks and/or other routers. For your host to communicate via the computer or hostname of a remote system, you must have some type of name resolution. The address of the name server must be entered into the client configuration in order to obtain name resolution services.

22

GENERAL CONFIGURATION ISSUES

Configuring TCP/IP for Windows 95 and Windows 98

by Kurt Hudson

IN THIS CHAPTER

This chapter covers the Windows 98 networking component configuration. Emphasis is placed on two main areas: network software driver configuration and TCP/IP settings. In addition, the Windows 98 network architecture is addressed. Specific configuration information such as TCP/IP static files and some Windows 98 Registry locations is also covered.

> **Note**
>
> Windows 95 and Windows 98 are virtually identical when it comes to configuring networking components. The information contained in this chapter can be easily applied to either operating system.

Windows 98 Network Architecture

The Windows 98 network architecture is based around two main interfaces: NetBIOS (Network Basic Input/Output System) and NDIS (Network Device Interface Specification). Additionally, the main protocol used by the highest layers of Microsoft networking (which, of course, applies to Windows 98) is *Server Message Blocks* (SMBs). A basic picture of the Windows 98 protocol stack is compared to the OSI Network Model in Figure 23.1.

FIGURE 23.1

Above the Transport Layer and at the Data Link Layer, Microsoft's implementation of TCP/IP is unique.

OSI Layer	Windows 98
Application	Server Message Blocks
Presentation	Server Message Blocks
Session	NetBIOS WinSocks
Transport	TCP UDP
Network	IP
Data Link	LAN Drivers / NDIS
Physical	Network Card

The figure illustrates how those components fit into the TCP/IP protocol stack. Several other transport and network protocols could have been inserted where TCP, UDP, and IP were placed in the graphic because the NDIS Layer allows multiple protocols to be bound to one or more network adapters. The purpose of the NetBIOS Layer is to provide protocol independence for NetBIOS applications. Microsoft network designers wanted to make the building of network applications as independent as possible from the protocol in use. This enables application developers to focus on the application they are building and not worry about which network protocol stack is to be used.

Notice that WinSocks (Windows Sockets) has also been added to the Session Layer of the model in the graphic. Microsoft developed the Windows Sockets interface to allow the use of existing applications and utilities for TCP/IP with Microsoft clients. For example, utilities such as ping and tracert use the Windows Sockets interface to access the protocol stack.

The items in the Windows 98 protocol stack that the user or administrator can configure and control are limited to the LAN drivers, Network and Transport protocols, and type of network card. SMB, NetBIOS, and NDIS are permanent fixtures of Windows 98 networking. In addition, when Microsoft TCP/IP is installed, the Windows Sockets interface is automatically added.

Therefore, the main components that the user can add are network card (software drivers), protocol, and type of networking services (client and server components). The software components listed in the Network dialog box of Windows 98, as shown in Figure 23.2, illustrate this point. As this chapter progresses, you will learn more about each of these software components.

23

CONFIGURING
TCP/IP FOR
WINDOWS

FIGURE 23.2

The Windows 98 Network dialog box is the central configuration point for most network settings in Windows 98.

Installing the Network Card

In Chapter 22, "General Configuration Issues," the installation of the physical network card was described. In addition, the software configuration of the network card resources and drivers through Windows 98 were also described. In this section, the various methods for adding and configuring network card software are briefly revisited and expanded upon.

> **Note**
>
> In this section, it is assumed that you have already inserted the physical network card into the computer. In addition, you should know the card manufacturer name, Web site address, and the model number of the card.

As explained in the preceding chapter, before you install the software for the network card, ensure that you have determined which interrupt request lines (IRQ) and I/O ranges are available. You can use the Device Manager to make this determination (see Chapter 22 for the exact steps). You may have to configure the network card via a software utility provided by the manufacturer to set the proper IRQ and I/O range before you begin.

Using the Add New Hardware Wizard

The Add New Hardware Wizard can be used to install the proper software for your network card. To access the Add New Hardware Wizard, open the Control Panel by clicking Start, selecting Settings, then choosing Control Panel.

1. Double-click the Add New Hardware icon to begin.

2. The Add New Hardware Wizard first asks you to close all other open applications. After you have done so, click Next to continue.

   The subsequent screen indicates that Windows will search for Plug and Play devices on your system. If you have installed a Plug and Play network adapter, the system should find it and automatically configure the IRQ and I/O address range for the adapter. If you do not have a Plug and Play adapter, you will have to manually configure the resources for the card.

3. Click Next to continue.

4. If you see your network card listed, select it by clicking the icon representing the device in the Devices window.

   Choose the Yes, the Device Is In the List radio button and click Next. This should automatically install and configure your Plug and Play network adapter.

If you don't see your network card listed, choose the No, the Device Isn't In the List radio button and click Next. If you had to choose "No..." you do not have a Plug and Play network adapter.

For non–Plug and Play adapters the subsequent screen will ask whether you want Windows to run detection routines to locate your network adapter. The only problem here is that the detection routines might cause your computer to freeze and you will have to reboot. Still, if Windows 98 can successfully detect the adapter, you won't have to select it from a list of devices.

5. If you would like Windows 98 to attempt to detect your adapter, be sure that Yes (Recommended) is selected, and click the Next button. If your network card is detected, it can then be confirmed and configured.

   If, however, you know exactly which network card you need to install or you have a driver from the NIC manufacturer that you would like to install, choose No, I Want to Select the Hardware from a List option; then, click the Next button.

   Assuming your device wasn't in the list (or you skipped detection), you will be presented with a dialog box that will allow you to choose your device from a list of possible devices.

6. In this dialog box, scroll down to the Network Adapters icon, select it by clicking the icon, and then click Next to continue.

   The next screen presents a list of manufacturers on one side and models on the other.

7. Select the correct network card manufacturer and model from each list. For example, if the network card you installed is a 3COM 3C509 ISA adapter, you would select "3COM" from the list of manufacturers and then scroll down in the second window to locate "3COM Etherlink III ISA (3C509/3C509b) in ISA mode" from the list of models.

8. To continue, click OK.

Your other option is to click the Have Disk button to install a driver that was provided by the hardware vendor.

You will then be asked to insert a floppy disk, CD-ROM, or map the path to the software drivers. When you do, you can continue the installation process. You may also be asked to select and confirm the appropriate driver files from the software disk. Refer to the network card manufacturer documentation to determine the correct driver file.

23

CONFIGURING
TCP/IP FOR
WINDOWS

> **Note**
>
> You may be asked to set or confirm the adapter resource settings before you proceed. After you have confirmed these settings, click the Next button to continue.

After the driver has been located and installed by the Windows 98 Add New Hardware Wizard, a confirmation dialog box will appear. The dialog box informs you that installation was completed successfully and you can click the Finish button in order to conclude the installation process. You should be able to reboot your system immediately, or you can choose to wait. The installation of the network card driver won't take effect until your system is rebooted.

Manually Adding the Network Card

The process for installing a network adapter manually in Windows 98 was detailed in Chapter 22. (The detailed steps to install network driver software manually are not repeated here.) Briefly stated, instead of using the Add New Hardware Wizard, you use the Network icon in the Control Panel. This opens the Network dialog box. You can then click Add, select the adapter, and install the appropriate driver. After you click the Add button on the Network dialog box, the process is nearly identical to adding a non–Plug and Play adapter via the Add New Hardware Wizard.

Using 16-Bit Network Drivers

If you have an old network adapter that you must use in your Windows 98 system, you may have to use the old 16-bit drivers. This solution is not optimal and should be avoided whenever possible. However, Windows 98 does provide the old configuration files, such as AUTOEXEC.BAT, CONFIG.SYS, and SYSTEM.INI, so that legacy (pre–Windows 95) software and hardware can be used.

The configuration of a legacy network adapter is quite simple. First, run the setup or installation program that was provided by the network card manufacturer. This should install the appropriate driver and update the old configuration files. If you have to update those configuration files manually, an easy way to access all of them at once is to use the SYSEDIT program. To access SYSEDIT, type **SYSEDIT** in the Run dialog box (Start, Run). SYSEDIT automatically opens all the legacy configuration files in the SYSEDIT window via Notepad. You can then make the necessary modifications.

Altering the Network Card Configuration Settings

You can modify the network card resources via the Device Manager in Windows 98. After the network card is installed, you should see an icon for the device in the Device Manager.

1. To access the Device Manager, click the System icon in the Control Panel or right-click the My Computer icon and choose Properties.

2. Click the Device Manager tab.

3. Click the plus sign by the Network Adapters icon in the Device Manager. You should then see the installed network adapters.

4. Double-click the adapter you want to modify.

The actual number of configuration tabs you see for the card depends on the card and configuration options. However, most devices have three tabs:

- *General*—This tab gives you information about the current operational status of the device (for example, working properly or resource conflict).

- *Driver*—This tab allows you to change or update the network card driver.

- *Resources*—This tab allows you to change the resource configuration of the network card.

When Windows 98 Fails to Boot

If the network card is causing a configuration conflict, you may have difficulty when you reboot the system. Some hardware drivers can cause the Windows 98 system to fail during the boot process. At that point, your option is to try Windows 98 Safe Mode. Typically, this option is activated by default if Windows 98 discovers that a boot failure occurred. However, if you must activate this option manually, you can press the F8 key during the boot process.

23

CONFIGURING
TCP/IP FOR
WINDOWS

> **Note**
>
> Your window of opportunity to press the F8 key is limited, so you should probably press it repeatedly after the system boots. If you see the Windows 98 splash screen that says Starting Windows 98, you missed it.

Pressing F8 during the boot process should take you to the Windows 98 Startup menu where you can select from several options. Safe Mode is probably the best first option to reset your network adapter.

Safe Mode gives you the same familiar Windows 98 interface that you were working in when you first configured the network adapter. Use this mode to locate any network resource problem. If the problem concerns a 16-bit driver, use SYSEDIT to access the configuration files. If the problem concerns 32-bit network drivers, use the Device Manager to reconfigure the resources.

If you cannot fix or determine the error via Safe Mode, you may have to create a bootlog.txt file to determine why Windows 98 is failing to boot. It could be that you installed the wrong driver file. To generate a bootlog:

1. Choose Logged... from the Windows 98 Startup menu.

2. Reboot the system and let it fail.

3. Boot into Safe Mode or Command Prompt Only and locate the bootlog.txt file that should be in the root directory (C:\).

4. Read the file with a text editor such as DOS Edit or Windows Notepad. You should be able to determine where the failure occurred by going to the bottom of the file to see the last driver that Windows 98 attempted to load before failing.

If you determine that the network card driver is failing to load, obtain the appropriate driver. Ensure the driver was not corrupted. You may want to run Windows 98 ScanDisk to ensure disk surface errors are not causing corruption on your drivers. Be sure the driver you have installed is good. Check the network card vendor Web site for known configuration errors or call its support line.

If you determine that there is a hardware resource conflict, you must reset the resources of the network card or the conflicting device. If both devices require the same hardware resources, you may have to choose between one device and another to resolve the conflict. When you have rectified the situation, you can reboot the system and expect it to operate correctly.

Configuring Windows 98 for TCP/IP

The basic configuration of TCP/IP for Windows 98 is quite simple and can be done via easy-to-use graphical interfaces. However, some of the configuration parameters can only be modified by editing the Windows 98 Registry and/or configuration files. In this section, both the easy graphical configuration and the more complex Registry editing are explored and explained.

Before You Start

Prior to installing TCP/IP on your Windows 98 system, you should know the basics about your network segment. You must use an IP address and subnet mask that is available for the given segment unless you plan to use a Dynamic Host Configuration Protocol (DHCP) server. If DHCP is implemented, you must determine which options will be automatically configured by the DHCP server.

In addition to the correct IP address and subnet mask, you will require an address for the default gateway (also known as the local router) if you plan on contacting hosts on remote segments. Again, if DHCP is being used, you must find out whether the IP address of the router will be automatically configured. If not, you will have to add this manually to your local TCP/IP configuration.

If you need to connect to hostnames on the network, you must also have the address for a DNS server that will provide name resolution services. Otherwise, you will have to configure a HOSTS file to list all the IP addresses and hostnames to which you would like to connect. You will also require some form of NetBIOS name resolution, such as a WINS server or LMHOSTS file. Both the DNS server and WINS server addresses can be released by the DHCP server, if that service is in use on the local network.

After you have all this information, you are ready to install the TCP/IP protocol suite. Be sure that you know where your Windows 98 CD or installation files are located because you will need those to install the protocol.

Installing TCP/IP

In Windows 98, the TCP/IP protocol suite can be installed from the Network dialog box. You can access this dialog box from the Windows 98 Desktop Network Neighborhood icon or from the Control Panel. To access the dialog box from the Desktop, right-click the Network Neighborhood icon and choose Properties. To access the Network dialog box from the Control Panel (Start, Settings, Control Panel), double-click the Network icon. Then, follow these steps:

1. From the Network dialog box, click the Add button.
2. Select Protocol from the Select Network Component Type dialog box and click the Add button on that dialog box. You are presented with a list of protocol options.
3. Choose Microsoft from the list of manufacturers and TCP/IP from the list of network protocols. Click OK to proceed.
4. You may have to enter the path to the Windows 98 source files. Enter this path or use the Browse button to locate the files. Click OK and the protocol will be added.
5. Click OK on the Network dialog box and you will be asked to reboot your system. Confirm the reboot to complete the installation process.

23

CONFIGURING
TCP/IP FOR
WINDOWS

The installation for the TCP/IP protocol suite for Windows 98 doesn't ask whether you want to configure DHCP; it defaults to it. Therefore, if you are not using DHCP on your IP segment, you will have to reboot and reconfigure your TCP/IP settings.

Configuring Microsoft TCP/IP

To configure the Microsoft TCP/IP settings, such as IP address, subnet mask, and default gateway, you must again access the Network dialog box. After the TCP/IP protocol is installed, you should see it appear under the Configuration tab. If you have more than one network adapter or even a dial-up adapter, TCP/IP will automatically bind to all available cards. If you want to unbind the protocol from any adapter, locate the icon that shows the protocol with an arrow pointing to the specific adapter. Highlight the icon that represents the TCP/IP bound to the adapter and click the Remove button. After you close the Network dialog box by clicking OK, the binding modification is implemented. However, if you click Cancel on the Network dialog box, the changes you have made won't be implemented.

To configure the TCP/IP protocol manually for your network card, double-click the icon from the list that shows TCP/IP bound to your network card. (Alternatively, you can select the icon and click the Properties button.) This action opens the TCP/IP Properties dialog box (see Figure 23.3).

FIGURE 23.3

You can use the TCP/IP Properties dialog box to configure your TCP/IP settings.

The IP Address tab is the default tab of the TCP/IP Properties dialog box. On this property sheet you can either set your system to use DHCP or manually configure the IP address and subnet mask. This is because the absolute minimum configuration information that the DHCP server provides is an IP address and subnet mask. Of course, the DHCP server can provide additional options such as the address of the default gateway if configured to do so.

Gateway Configuration

If you want to configure the default gateway manually, click the Gateway tab. On the Gateway property sheet you can configure one or more default gateway addresses for your computer. The address at the top of the list will be the default gateway, and the other gateway addresses will only be used if the default gateway is unavailable. The order in which the gateway addresses appear is the order in which they will be contacted (top to bottom).

WINS Configuration

You should also configure a WINS server, if one is available, for your Windows 98 machine. The WINS server will allow you to resolve NetBIOS computer names to IP addresses. NetBIOS is the required network interface for Microsoft operating systems prior to Windows 2000. You will need some type of NetBIOS name resolution if you are using Windows 98 with the TCP/IP protocol suite. NetBIOS name resolution, along with WINS and the LMHOSTS file, is described in Chapter 7, "WINS."

The WINS Configuration tab on the TCP/IP Properties dialog box allows you to enable WINS resolution and enter the IP address(es) for your WINS server(s) (see Figure 23.4). When you have configured WINS resolution, the Windows 98 computer will use the first available WINS server to resolve the NetBIOS name. If the first WINS server on the list is not available, the next name server will be contacted. Other WINS servers are only contacted in the event that the previous WINS server cannot be contacted. If any WINS server provides an answer, even if the answer is that the name doesn't exist in the database, no other WINS servers will be contacted.

23

CONFIGURING
TCP/IP FOR
WINDOWS

FIGURE 23.4

The WINS Configuration tab allows you to set WINS Server addresses or use the DHCP Server for WINS services.

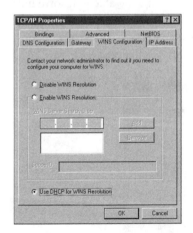

On the WINS Configuration tab you will also see a text box labeled Scope ID, which you should leave blank in most cases. This setting refers to the NetBIOS scope identifier, which can be any combination of alphanumeric characters that is appended to the NetBIOS computer name. For example, if you entered 123ABC as the scope ID, and your system's NetBIOS computer name was Server2, the full name of your system would be Server2.123ABC. The interesting point to note about the NetBIOS scope identifier is that Microsoft systems using TCP/IP will only be able to communicate with other Microsoft systems that have the same scope identifier. Furthermore, because the scope identifier changes the computer name, you could actually configure another computer on the network using the same name, Server2, with a different scope identifier. Due to the name and connectivity confusion that it can create, the NetBIOS scope ID is rarely used.

By default, the Use DHCP for WINS Resolution radio button is checked. This means that the DHCP server is considered to be the WINS server and is expected to provide both services. If this is not the case, you should configure the correct IP address of the WINS server in the text boxes provided.

WINS Resolution can also be disabled. Disabling WINS is appropriate when WINS is not being used on the network for name resolution. By disabling WINS, you will prevent the system attempting to find a WINS server on the network. If you have WINS enabled, and no WINS servers are present on the network, the WINS client will waste time checking for a WINS server.

DNS Configuration

In addition to NetBIOS names, you may need to be able to resolve hostnames (for example, www.InformIT.com). This is especially important if you are connecting to the Internet or have non-Microsoft systems on your network. To configure your system for hostname resolution, click the DNS Configuration tab (see Figure 23.5).

FIGURE 23.5

You can enable, disable, or configure DNS settings via the DNS tab.

If you click the Enable DNS radio button, you will be able to enter a host and domain name for your Windows 98 computer. Typically, you will want to use the same hostname for your computer as the NetBIOS computer name. If you decide to use a different NetBIOS name, you will make connectivity troubleshooting more complex because some utilities attempt to contact the computer via its hostname and others use its NetBIOS name.

You can enter the address(es) of Domain Name System (DNS) servers that can be used to resolve hostnames to IP addresses. The address entry works the same way as the WINS server entry on the WINS Configuration tab. Enter the IP addresses for the DNS servers you want to use for name resolution. If the first DNS server answers, no other DNS servers will be contacted even if the first DNS server doesn't have a mapping for the IP address. The other DNS servers will only be contacted in the event that the first DNS server is not available (that is, offline).

When DNS services are not provided on the network, you may decide to disable (or leave disabled) DNS Name Resolution. If the network is connected to the Internet, the client will require a DNS server in order to resolve Web addresses like http://www.microsoft.com. However, if connections to domain names or hostnames is not required or desired, then DNS could be disabled. On an internal Microsoft-only network, DNS would not be needed unless internal Web servers with hostnames or domain names were being utilized.

Bindings Configuration

The Bindings tab of the TCP/IP Properties dialog box allows you to control which services the protocol can communicate with. For example, if you want to use TCP/IP to obtain network services, but do not want to share files over TCP/IP, you would configure your bindings as shown in Figure 23.6.

FIGURE 23.6

If you don't want to share files over TCP/IP, unbind the File and Printer Sharing service from TCP/IP.

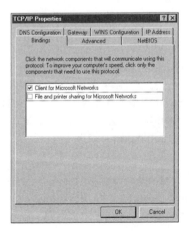

Notice that the box for File and Printer Sharing for Microsoft Networks is unchecked and the Client for Microsoft Networks box is checked. This means that you can use TCP/IP to connect to other Microsoft systems sharing files or printers, but they cannot use TCP/IP to connect to your local files or printers.

Installing File and Printer Sharing for Microsoft Networks

If you do not have File and Printer Sharing for Microsoft Networks installed, you will not see it in the Binding tab, and other Microsoft clients will not be able to connect to your system for file or printer sharing. To install File and Printer Sharing for Microsoft networks, follow these steps:

1. Open the Network dialog box (right-click Network Neighborhood and choose Properties from the resulting context menu).
2. Click the Add button.
3. Click the Service icon and then click the Add button.
4. Choose Microsoft from the list of Manufacturers and ensure that File and Printer Sharing for Microsoft Networks is added under Network Services.
5. Click OK and enter the path to the installation files, if requested.
6. Click OK to confirm the path and again to confirm installation.
7. Reboot the system as requested.

Advanced Configuration

The Advanced tab has only one useful configuration option—the Set This Protocol to Be the Default Protocol check box. If you select this option, your client system will attempt to use TCP/IP before using any other configured protocols. If you have only TCP/IP installed, it will automatically be the default protocol.

NetBIOS

The NetBIOS tab is not really a configuration tab at all. For Microsoft clients prior to Windows 2000, NetBIOS is an essential part of the Microsoft Networking components using the TCP/IP protocol suite. The option to uncheck NetBIOS over TCP/IP is grayed out (not available) and the box is permanently checked. It is possible to enable or disable NetBIOS support for the IPX/SPX- compatible protocol, but not for TCP/IP.

Static Configuration Files

As described in Chapter 7, the HOSTS and LMHOSTS.SAM files are located in the Windows root directory.

> **Note**
>
> If you cannot find the Windows directory, keep in mind that sometimes it is not named "Windows." If you want to locate the Windows directory, you can type `%windir%` inside the Run dialog box. Click the Start button, then click Run to open the Run dialog box.

Another static configuration file that is located in the Windows root directory is the SERVICES file (notice that it does not have a file extension). The services file corresponds to RFC 1700 listing the Well Known Port Numbers for TCP and UDP services. The file itself says that it relates to RFC 1060, but that RFC was revised by RFC 1700 (`http://www.ietf.org/rfc/rfc1700.txt`). The SERVICES file lists various services, port numbers, and protocols established in the RFCs for Well Known services. For example, the FTP and FTP-data ports (21/TCP and 20/TCP, respectively) are listed in this file. The built-in Microsoft FTP client will use this file in order to determine which port to use for FTP communications. A change to this file will create a change in the default port accessed via the command-line FTP utility. However, this SERVICES file is not used by all TCP/IP-related utilities. As a matter of fact, the specific utility must be configured to access this file. Most third-party utilities and even the Microsoft Internet Explorer Web browser do not access the SERVICES file.

Registry Settings

Most of the important TCP/IP configuration options that are not available through the TCP/IP Properties dialog box are available only through the Windows 98 Registry. In this section, you learn about some of the more common TCP/IP configuration settings that can be configured via the Windows 98 Registry.

> **Note**
>
> If you want to reference a Microsoft document that describes even more configuration parameters for TCP/IP in the Windows 98 Registry, search for Knowledge Base Article Q158474 on the Microsoft support Web site at `www.microsoft.com/support` or obtain a copy of Microsoft TechNet.

23

CONFIGURING TCP/IP FOR WINDOWS

All the parameters discussed in this section can be configured at HKEY_LOCAL_MACHINE\ System\CurrentControlSet\Services\VxD\MSTCP in the Windows 98 Registry (shown in Figure 23.7). To edit the Windows 98 Registry:

1. Click Start and choose Run.

2. Type **REGEDIT** in the Run dialog box and click OK.

   Note: REGEDIT can be typed in upper- or lowercase and will still work. For the vast majority of commands, Windows 98 is not case sensitive and any executable, such as REGEDIT, can be run without regard to case.

Note

Changes made to the Registry could cause the system to fail and may even prevent the system from restarting properly. Therefore, only modify Registry settings that you understand or practice on a system that is not of critical importance. Before editing your Registry, you can save it by exporting it. To export your Registry, follow these steps:

1. Click Start, then choose Run.

2. In the Run dialog box, type **REGEDIT**.

3. After the Registry Editor is open, click the Registry menu item and select Export Registry File.

4. Enter a name for your file, for example **SaveReg**.

5. Set the location where you would like to save the file via the Save In selection box. Probably the easiest location is the desktop.

6. Click the Save button.

7. Close the Registry Editor. You should be able to see your file (RegSave.reg) on the desktop or the directory in which you saved it.

If after editing the Registry you find that the system doesn't operate properly, you can double-click your saved Registry file to revert to your old configuration.

If you want to back up the actual files that form the Registry, you can locate the system.dat and user.dat files in the Windows directory and copy them to an alternate location. If the system won't boot after you make the changes, you can copy the system.dat and user.dat file back to the Windows directory.

FIGURE 23.7

Use Regedit.exe *to modify TCP/IP Configuration Parameters in the Registry.*

Enable Routing

If you want to use Windows 98 as a static router, you can configure the setting in the Windows 98 Registry. To do so, you must go to the MSTCP key in the Registry and add a string value named EnableRouting and set that value to 1. Here's how you do this:

1. Click Start and choose Run.

2. Type **REGEDIT** in the Run dialog box.

3. Click the plus signs to expand the Registry keys to access and select the MSTCP key (refer to Figure 23.7).

4. Go to the Edit menu and choose New, String Value.

5. A new value should appear on the right-hand side of the Registry Editor. Rename this value **EnableRouting**, then press Enter.

6. Double-click the EnableRouting icon.

7. In the Value Data text box, type **1**.

8. Click OK and close the Registry Editor.

To confirm that your Registry change to enable routing actually worked, use WINIPCFG. Launch WINIPCFG from the Run dialog box; click the More Info button. You should see that the IP Routing Enabled check box is checked (see Figure 23.8).

23

CONFIGURING TCP/IP FOR WINDOWS

FIGURE 23.8

After you have enabled IP routing in the Registry, you can confirm the change via WINIPCFG.

Windows 98 and Microsoft TCP/IP do not come with any routing protocols such as Routing Information Protocol (RIP) or Open Shortest Path First (OSPF). Therefore, if you want to update your Windows 98 routing table, you will have to do it manually. To add static routes to your new router, you must use the route command:

1. Open a command prompt.
2. Type **route /?**.
3. Press Enter to learn more.

If you enable routing, you can also configure the routing buffer size, which defaults to 73,216. If you want to modify the routing buffer, add the string value RoutingBufSize to the MSTCP location and set the value. You can also set the RoutingPackets number, which is the number of packets that can be routed simultaneously (default is 50).

Random Adapter

Another Registry parameter that can be used for a Windows 98 computer configured with multiple network adapters is the RandomAdapter setting. This allows your Windows 98 system to report back a random address from its set of IP addresses no matter which network card received the request. This setting can be useful when you are attempting to load-balance services among multiple network adapters. To configure this setting, add the string value RandomAdapter to the MSTCP key and set the value to 1. By default, the Windows 98 network cards will report the address that received the resolution request.

Name Resolution Timeouts

When a Windows 98 WINS client system attempts to resolve a NetBIOS computer name to an IP address, it will call the WINS server up to three times, waiting 750 milliseconds between each try before it attempts another name resolution method. You can add the `NameSrvQueryCount` and `NameSrvQueryTimeout` string values to the MSTCP location in the Registry to modify the default name resolution behavior for Windows 98. `NameSrvQueryCount` is the value that controls the number of times the Windows 98 client will contact the WINS server before timing out. The Registry value `NameSrvQueryTimeout` controls how long the Windows 98 client will wait before it either gives up or tries again to contact the WINS server.

If the Windows 98 client is not configured to use a WINS server or receives no response from the WINS server, it will attempt to resolve a NetBIOS computer name to an IP address by broadcasting. By default, the system will attempt up to three broadcasts, waiting 750 milliseconds between each before giving up. You can add and modify the MSTCP `BcastNameQueryCount` and `BcastNameQueryTimeout` values to control these default settings.

Default TTL

By default, the IP packets from the Windows 98 system will have a Time to Live (TTL) of 32. In order to modify the TTL of the Windows 98 IP packets, you must add the `DefaultTTL` string value to the MSTCP location of the Registry. Configure the value equal to the number of hops that you would like the IP packets to live.

TCP Window Size

The default receive TCP window size is 8192 for Windows 98. In order to modify this default you must add the `DefaultRcvWindow` string value to the MSTCP key in the Windows 98 Registry. Set the receive window value to the number of bytes you would like your system to advertise.

Testing TCP/IP

Windows 98 ships with several utilities that allow you to test your TCP/IP configuration after it has been installed. Ping, tracert, and WINIPCFG are the main utilities that will allow you to check your configuration immediately.

After installing the TCP/IP protocol suite, use WINIPCFG to verify your configuration. If your system is configured via DHCP, WINIPCFG will show you the settings as configured by the DHCP server. If you manually configured IP, you can use WINIPCFG to verify that the settings you entered are correct.

Ping will verify your basic connectivity. To ensure that your protocol is operating correctly, first ping your loopback address.

1. Open a command prompt by typing **command** in the Run dialog box and pressing Enter. A command prompt window will be displayed.
2. Type **Ping 127.0.0.1** and press Enter.

You should receive a response from your system. If you do not, you should reinstall the TCP/IP protocol suite. If you do receive a response, then ping your own IP address. Again, WINIPCFG can be used to obtain your IP address.

If both your loopback and your local system address work, you should try to ping your local default gateway. If the gateway responds, then ping a host on a remote network. After you have done this, you will have verified your TCP/IP installation and connectivity. If you have configured name resolution, such as DNS and WINS, you can also ping those servers to ensure they are operational.

If you have trouble using ping to get a response from a remote host, the tracert utility can be quite useful. Tracert can be used from the command line to trace the route to a remote host from your local system. Tracert will issue successive ICMP messages with progressively larger TTL values. This enables the request to work its way from your local system to the remote system, reporting its progress as it goes. If the request stops anywhere along the way, you will have a good idea of where in the network the problem is located.

In order to test your name resolution configuration, you can use ping or tracert with computer hostnames to verify your DNS name resolution. You can attempt to map a drive to a Microsoft server name to ensure that NetBIOS name resolution is working properly. If there is a problem with either operation, check the respective server and your configuration.

NBTSTAT

The NBTSTAT utility stands for NetBIOS over TCP/IP Status. This utility can be used to check several items concerning your TCP/IP configuration. To access the utility, open a command prompt and type **NBTSTAT /?**. You will receive a list of options that can be used with the NBTSTAT command.

You can check your NetBIOS name cache with the NBTSTAT -c command. By default, the resolved NetBIOS names to IP addresses will be maintained in the name cache for 360,000 milliseconds (6 minutes). You can modify this by adding the CacheTimeout value to the MSTCP Registry key and configuring a different number. You can purge and preload the NetBIOS name cache via the NBTSTAT -R command. If you have an LMHOSTS file configured with #PRE entries, they will be added to the name cache after you issue the NBTSTAT -R command.

> **Note**
>
> LMHOSTS entries are described in the LMHOSTS.SAM file in the Windows root directory. Open the LMHOSTS.SAM file with Notepad or another text editor to learn more.

Another useful option available through the NBTSTAT command is the ability to list the name table of a remote or local host. Type **NBTSTAT -A** followed by the IP address of the computer for which you would like to list the name table. If you prefer to use the remote computer name, type **NBTSTAT -a** followed by the remote system's computer name. You can also type your own system's computer name or IP address to check the name table. This command will also list the remote system's MAC address.

NETSTAT

NETSTAT is a useful utility to check TCP, UDP, and IP connections. For example, you can use the command NETSTAT -p TCP to check the status of your TCP protocol; you will receive a list of TCP ports in use. You can issue the command NETSTAT -s to get a full status list of all protocols.

ARP

All local IP addresses must be resolved to MAC addresses. You can use ARP to see the MAC addresses of local systems that exist in your local ARP cache. ARP cache entries remain for two minutes when an IP address is resolved once, but not used again. If the IP address is used again within the two minutes, the ARP entry gets a life of ten minutes. You can also add static entries to the ARP cache, which will remain until the system is rebooted. Static entries allow you to reduce the number of ARP broadcasts for MAC addresses that occur on the local segment. You can see the syntax for adding a static ARP entry by typing **ARP /?** at the Windows 98 command prompt.

Summary

Microsoft produces its own version of the TCP/IP protocol suite for the Windows 98 operating system. Microsoft's TCP/IP protocol uses include support for NetBIOS and the Windows Sockets interfaces to support both NetBIOS- and UNIX-style utilities (such as ping and tracert). Also, the Microsoft IP protocol stack includes NDIS, which allows multiple protocols to be bound to one or more adapter cards.

To install and configure the TCP/IP protocol suite, you must access the Network dialog box. You can use the Add button to install the protocol suite. If you need to configure the protocol suite after installation, use the Network dialog box to access the icon for the protocol. Double-click to access the TCP/IP Properties dialog box and configure the options via the configuration tabs.

If the settings you want to configure are not available via the TCP/IP Properties sheet, then you will probably have to configure them via the Windows Registry Editor. The Microsoft Knowledge Base article Q158474 (available at `http://support.microsoft.com/support/kb/articles/q158/4/74.asp`) describes the Windows 98 TCP/IP Registry configuration options.

In the next chapter, you will learn how to configure Windows 98 to connect to the Internet via Dial-Up Networking. Many of the concepts you learned in this chapter will apply to the next one, but you will see that configuring the dial-up adapter is a little different than configuring a LAN network adapter.

Dial-Up Networking with Windows 98

by Kurt Hudson

IN THIS CHAPTER

In the previous chapter you saw how to install and configure the TCP/IP Protocol Suite settings for Windows 98 hosts. In this chapter, the discussion of Windows 98 and TCP/IP continues with the focus on remote access. In Windows 98 the remote access service (RAS) is called *Dial-Up Networking* (DUN). You will learn about DUN, how to configure TCP/IP to work with DUN, and the line protocols that are part of DUN.

This chapter focuses on Windows 98 because of its large installed base. Even though Microsoft has announced successors to Windows 98 such as Windows ME/2000/XP, people have been slow to adopt these newer OSs. This chapter therefore focuses on Windows 98 in spite of the fact that Microsoft does not support the older operating systems.

Dial-Up Adapter Configuration

Before you configure the Dial-Up Adapter components, you must install your Dial-Up Adapter or modem. Although you could use the Add New Hardware icon in the Control Panel to install your modem, using the Modems icon, which is also in the Control Panel, is easier. Double-click the Modems icon to open the Modems Properties dialog box (see Figure 24.1).

FIGURE 24.1

Configuring the Dial-Up Adapter starts with installing the modem.

If you click the Add button, you can allow Windows to detect your modem. If you already know the type of modem you have, or you plan to install the driver from a file provided by the manufacturer, you should select the Don't Detect My Modem; I Will Select It From a List check box. Click Next to continue. If Windows is not able to detect your modem, or if you didn't let Windows try to detect your modem, the Install New Modem dialog box will list Manufacturers and Models (see Figure 24.2). Notice that you can also use a serial or parallel cable between two PCs with DUN, if you like. Choose the manufacturer and modem that match your hardware configuration or click the Have Disk button and install the driver from the hardware vendor. Click Next to continue.

FIGURE 24.2

Select the correct modem from the choices presented.

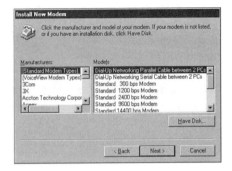

Next, you are asked to select the appropriate port for your modem configuration. Choose the correct port and click Next to continue. When you have successfully installed the modem, click the Finish button to continue.

If you need to configure your modem further, you can click the Modems icon in the Control Panel and double-click the modem that appears in your list. This will open a modem properties dialog box and you can verify and/or set the connection speed, dialing features, type of ring, and call forwarding features (see Figure 24.3). When you have your modem installed and properly configured, you can continue with DUN configuration.

FIGURE 24.3

Ensure that you set the modem configuration to match your needs.

Dial-Up Networking Installation

To begin the installation and configuration process for DUN, double-click the My Computer icon on the desktop. Then, follow these steps:

1. Double-click the icon labeled Dial-Up Networking to access the Dial-Up Networking folder, which contains the Make New Connection icon.

24

DIAL-UP NETWORKING WITH WINDOWS 98

2. To configure a DUN connection, double-click the Make New Connection icon. This action initializes the Make New Connection dialog box (see Figure 24.4).

   If you don't see the DUN folder, you may have to add Dial-Up Networking to your configuration. To do so, click Start, Settings, Control Panel and then double-click the Add/Remove Programs folder. Click the Windows Setup. In the Components window, double-click the icon labeled Communications. Ensure that the Dial-Up Networking check box is selected. Click OK twice to confirm that you would like to add DUN to your configuration. You may also be asked to enter the path to your Windows 98 source files.

Note

If you don't have a modem installed and you attempt to configure a Dial-Up Networking connection, DUN will automatically launch the Install New Modem wizard.

FIGURE 24.4

You must enter your dialing and location informa-tion in the Make New Connection dialog box.

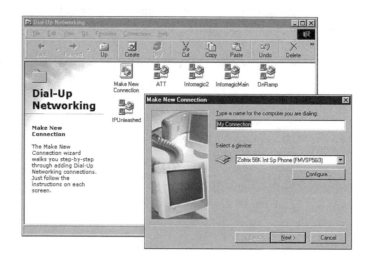

The first item you can enter is a friendly name for this Dial-Up Connection.

3. Type something that clearly identifies the connection because this will become the name of the connection icon. For example, notice the various connection icons shown in Figure 24.4 (InfomagicMain, ATT, OnRamp, and so on).

4. Select the modem you would like to use for the Dial-Up Networking connection.

5. Click Next to continue.

   The next dialog box asks you to input a phone number you would like to dial.

6. Enter the area code and phone number, or change the country and enter the correct dialing information. This should be the phone number of your Internet service provider (ISP) or the remote access services (RAS) server to which you intend to connect.

7. Click Next to continue.

8. Click the Finished button to confirm your new connection.

You should see your new connection icon appear in the Dial-Up Networking folder. To further configure or modify the Dial-Up Networking connection, select the representative icon and choose File, Properties from the menu bar. You should see the following four tabs on your connection dialog box:

- General
- Server Types
- Scripting
- Multilink

Each of these is described in the following sections.

General Tab

If you want to change the phone number, modify the modem settings, or change the modem you are using for the connection, use the General tab. You can even click the Configure button to edit the configuration of your modem from the General tab, if necessary.

Server Types

After the Dial-Up Networking connection has been created, Windows 98 DUN connections usually require additional configuration via the Server Types dialog box. The Server Types dialog box allows you to configure the type of server to which you will be connecting, as well as the TCP/IP and protocol options that will be used.

You can access the Server Types dialog box through the Properties of your Dial-Up connection icon, as noted in the following steps:

1. Open the Dial-Up Networking dialog box.

2. Right-click the connection you would like to configure.

3. Choose Properties from the resulting context menu.

4. In the resulting dialog box, choose the Server Types tab (see Figure 24.5).

FIGURE 24.5

Although it isn't shown in the wizard, configuring the DUN Server is an important item for most dial-up connections.

Here you can configure the type of server that you intend to contact. The options in the Type of Dial-Up Server drop-down menu are

- PPP: Internet, Windows NT Server, Windows 98
- SLIP: Unix Connection
- CSLIP: Unix Connection with IP Header Compression
- NRN: NetWare Connection version 1.0 and 1.1

The NRN: NetWare Connection version 1.0 and 1.1 option supports only IPX/SPX-compatible protocol connections. The Windows for Workgroups and Windows NT 3.1 options support only NetBEUI connections. Because these two options do not support TCP/IP connections, they are not discussed further. SLIP, CSLIP, and PPP are detailed in the following sections.

SLIP and CSLIP

The *Serial Line Internet Protocol* (SLIP) and the *Compressed SLIP* (CSLIP) are typically associated with Unix RAS servers. If your ISP or Unix RAS server supports either SLIP or CSLIP, you can choose these connection options for your Windows 98 client. However, Microsoft RAS servers, such as Windows 98 and Windows NT, do not support inbound SLIP connections. Essentially, Microsoft has included a SLIP client, but not SLIP services. If you want to connect to a Microsoft RAS server, you will have to use a PPP connection.

> **Note**
>
> SLIP and CSLIP are not part of the default Windows 95 installation. If you want CSLIP and/or SLIP support in Windows 95, you will have to install Dial-Up Scripting Tool, which is on the Windows 95 CD-ROM. To add this support, go to the Add/Remove Programs icon in the Control Panel, click the Windows Setup tab, and then click the Have Disk option. Set the installation path to your Windows 95 CD-ROM drive letter under the `\admin\apptools\dscript` directory and click OK. Choose the SLIP and Scripting for Dial-Up Networking option and click the Install button.

The main difference between SLIP and CSLIP is that CSLIP supports IP header compression and SLIP does not. This makes CSLIP faster than SLIP over dial-up connections. Other than this difference, through Windows 98, SLIP and CSLIP provide the same functionality and configuration options. When you select SLIP or CSLIP from the Type of Dial-Up Server drop-down menu, you will notice that the Enable Software Compression and both encryption selections are not available. This is because SLIP and CSLIP do not provide the capability to perform additional data compression or encryption.

SLIP and CSLIP can only transmit one network protocol at a time. Therefore, the options to transport IPX/SPX and NetBEUI are unavailable if either CSLIP or SLIP is chosen from the Type of Dial-Up Server drop-down menu. Only TCP/IP can be used with SLIP and CSLIP in Windows 98.

SLIP does not provide a mechanism for error correction. SLIP relies on the physical hardware and the error correction capabilities of TCP/IP to maintain data integrity. Furthermore, there are no built-in compression algorithms for SLIP. CSLIP does provide limited compression of the IP header only, but not of the data contained within the packet.

PPP

Point-to-Point Protocol (PPP) is the default connection method for Windows 98 DUN clients. PPP is a line protocol that encapsulates, and is used for the transmission of, other protocol datagrams via a point-to-point connection. PPP can support one or more protocols. It can even host multiple network protocols simultaneously. By default, the Windows 98 RAS client is configured to use all three protocols (NetBEUI, IPX/SPX, and TCP/IP). However, for the sake of network efficiency, you should select as few protocols as possible for your connection. For this book, the assumption is that you will choose TCP/IP.

24

DIAL-UP
NETWORKING
WITH WINDOWS 98

In addition to supporting multiple network protocols, PPP provides a Data Link Layer protocol, the *Link Control Protocol* (LCP), which is responsible for configuring and monitoring the line connection. This means that PPP is more reliable than its predecessor, SLIP. PPP does contain more information and overhead than SLIP, but due to more advanced compression techniques, PPP connections are faster and more efficient than SLIP connections.

> **Note**
>
> The option to enable software compression is selected by default on Windows 98 PPP connections, but is not available on SLIP or CSLIP connections.

PPP connections also allow you to configure additional security for your passwords and data. The Require Encrypted Password and Require Data Encryption check boxes are available for PPP connections, but they are not an option for SLIP or CSLIP connections (refer to Figure 24.5).

If your ISP or remote RAS server allows you to use SLIP, CSLIP, or PPP, your best choice would be to use PPP. PPP is more efficient, more flexible, and more secure than the other two line protocols.

Advanced Options

The Advanced Options section on the Server Types tab allows you to configure certain dial-up options and security features based on the type of dial-up server you configured. As previously mentioned, choosing PPP: Internet, Windows NT Server, Windows 98 offers the highest number of configuration options. The Advanced Options are described in the following list:

- *Log on to Network*—This option is mainly used when you are connecting to a Windows NT RAS server, Windows for Workgroups RAS server, or NetWare network. If you must log on to the remote network, you should ensure that this option is selected. However, the Log on to Network option is not typically required for Internet connections. Although the default option is to log on to the network, if you are making a connection to an ISP, deselect the Log on to Network check box to speed connection time.

- *Enable Software Compression*—This option is available for PPP, but not SLIP or CSLIP connections. Software compression increases the speed of your dial-up connection. Compression should only be disabled if the RAS server doesn't support it.

- *Require Encrypted Password*—PPP connections support password encryption. If this option is selected the client attempts to use the *Challenge Handshake Authentication Protocol* (CHAP) encryption to transmit its password. This will only work if both the client and server are configured to support encrypted authentication. If this option is cleared, the client can still use the *Password Authentication Protocol* (PAP), which is less secure than CHAP. The client will only use PAP if the RAS server requests it.

- *Require Data Encryption*—This option is available for PPP connections and forces data encryption. If selected, the client will only connect with servers that support data encryption. This typically does not work for Internet dial-up connections. However, if a Windows 98 server is directly dialing into a Windows NT RAS server that supports data encryption, this option can be enabled to encrypt data transferred over the PPP connection. SLIP and CSLIP do not support this option.

- *Record a Log File for This Connection*—If you are connecting to the Internet, you will probably want to configure additional TCP/IP settings for your dial-up connection. You can configure a static IP address for your system, and the IP addresses of name servers and WINS servers. These options can be established for any line protocols that utilize TCP/IP (PPP, SLIP, and CSLIP). Click the TCP/IP Settings button to open the TCP/IP Settings dialog box and configure these options for your dial-up connection (see Figure 24.6).

FIGURE 24.6

Typically, you will have to configure the TCP/IP Settings sheet, especially the DNS server IP addresses.

24

DIAL-UP NETWORKING WITH WINDOWS 98

If your ISP, or the RAS server to which you are connecting, allows you to configure your own static IP address, click the Specify an IP Address radio button. Configure the static IP address you have been assigned in the IP Address box below that radio button.

One of the most important additional configuration items for Internet connections via DUN is to configure a name server. The name server allows your system to resolve hostnames (www.microsoft.com) to IP addresses. This is important if you want to establish connections to host or domain names. Your ISP should provide you with the IP addresses of its name servers.

If you are not connecting to the Internet, you may still need to configure a name server IP address to obtain hostname resolution. You may also need to configure WINS server address(es) to obtain NetBIOS name resolution. Check with the administrator of the RAS server to which you are connecting to get the appropriate connection settings information (that is, the address of the WINS or DNS servers on the remote network).

Scripting

Most ISPs today support the Microsoft Dial-Up Networking method of passing the username and password directly from the DUN connection dialog box. However, some providers may still expect their clients to use a terminal window or script in order to connect to their servers. Each DUN connection (that doesn't use the VPN adapter) has a Scripting tab as part of its property sheets. The Scripting tab allows you to map the path for the script to be used for connecting to the ISP (see Figure 24.7). ISPs that require terminal login usually provide a dial-up script for their clients.

On the Scripting tab you can also enable a terminal window pop-up during the dial-up connection negotiation process. This allows you to enter your username and password, which should log you in to your ISP RAS server.

FIGURE 24.7

You can use or modify one of the available scripts in the Program Files\Accessories directory.

> **Note**
>
> You can learn more about writing scripts for DUN connections via the `script.doc` file in the Windows directory.

Multilink

PPP Multilink allows you to combine the bandwidth capabilities of multiple dial-up devices to increase your effective connection throughput. With Multilink, you can combine two or more modems, ISDN lines, or any combination thereof to increase your connection speed.

> **Note**
>
> The PPP Multilink support in Windows 98 conforms to the Internet Engineering Task Force (IETF) standard defined in RFC 1717.

Although you can use different types of dial-up connections with Multilink, you will achieve the best performance by using identical dial-up adapters. This is because Multilink only makes use of the highest common connection speed. For example, if you connect at 48,000 bps with one modem and 28,000 bps with the other, the connection of 28,000 bps will be used on both modems. If you choose to combine two ISDN B-channels to form a single Multilink connection, you will not be able to use the other channel for fax or voice communications.

One of the most important issues with Multilink is that your ISP or remote RAS server must be configured to support Multilink; otherwise, the Multilink connection will fail. If you are connecting to an ISP, you should contact your provider to determine whether its servers support PPP Multilink connections.

To configure Multilink, you must have multiple dial-up adapters configured in your system. Each dial-up adapter must be connected to its own telephone line or ISDN line. The steps to configure an additional device for a Multilink connection are as follows:

1. Open the Dial-Up Networking folder.
2. Right-click the dial-up connection for which you would like to enable Multilink. Choose Properties from the resulting context menu.
3. Click the Multilink tab.

4. Click the Add button. If the Add button is disabled, Windows 98 does not recognize that you have more than one dial-up adapter configured. Ensure that you have more than one dial-up adapter (modem) configured for your system.

5. In the Edit Extra Device dialog box, select the device that you would like to add to this connection. The device you select will work with the device you have already configured for this connection. If you are planning to use two ISDN lines, choose the new ISDN line number in this dialog box.

6. When you have correctly configured the additional device(s), see Figure 24.8. Click OK to close the Multilink dialog box.

FIGURE 24.8

If you want to configure multiple dial-out lines you must configure Multilink.

After you have properly configured the Multilink and your dial-up adapters, you can make your Multilink DUN connection. Double-click the icon representing the Multilink DUN connection that you configured, and then click the Connect button. DUN will connect using the primary device and follow with the secondary device.

To determine whether your Multilink connection is operational, double-click the Dial-Up Networking Connection icon displayed in the taskbar. In the Connected To dialog box, click the Details button to view your connection information. This should display the type of connection, the adapters, and network protocol in use.

PPTP

The purpose of implementing the *Point-to-Point Tunneling Protocol* (PPTP) is to provide a secure connection between two hosts on a network connection. The typical example for this provides a virtual private network (VPN) connection between two hosts over the Internet. The connection between the two hosts is "private" because they are the only devices involved in the encryption and decryption of the packets transferred over the connection. The encryption algorithm is negotiated between the two PPTP hosts and known only to those hosts. Even though the data is transferred over the public Internet, the connection is considered secure and private between those two points. This doesn't mean that the usefulness of PPTP is limited to the Internet, because PPTP could also be employed between two hosts on an internal private network.

> **Note**
>
> PPTP is not completely immune to security breaches. However, in order for a hacker to decode PPTP packets, the hacker must know or predict some of the data that is transmitted over the PPTP connection. Then, the hacker would use that "known" packet to decode the encrypted data that flows between the PPTP hosts. This is certainly more difficult and time consuming than simply collecting data packets and reading the data inside with a protocol analyzer.

Like PPP, PPTP can support multiple network protocols such as IP, IPX, and NetBEUI. However, the PPTP connection is limited to two computers, one at each end of the connection. Additionally, even if you are using a private LAN connection to host your VPN, you will require a Dial-Up Networking connection using your virtual private network adapter (software component) in Windows 98. Both ends of the PPTP connection must be configured to use DUN or RAS with PPTP.

Although PPTP can be used in a variety of scenarios, the three main configuration scenarios for PPTP connections are

- PPTP Client to ISP to PPTP Server. You establish this type of connection by connecting your PPTP dial-up client to an ISP. Then, establish a virtual private networking connection over the Internet to a PPTP server. The PPTP server should be attached to the Internet and remote target network. When the dial-up client has established the PPTP connection with the server, it can access the remote network securely over the Internet.

- Creating a VPN Within a Permanent LAN or WAN Connection. If your client system is on the same network, (using a permanent connection), you can use Dial-Up Networking to connect directly to that server over your existing permanent connection. This gives you the ability to encrypt your data within this permanent connection.

- ISP to PPTP Server. Some ISPs support PPTP connections to remote networks. Therefore, by simply dialing in to the ISP with a typical DUN connection, your data may actually be encrypted over the Internet. This is, of course, something that the ISP must configure and it doesn't affect the DUN client configuration. In this scenario, the DUN client does not need to configure PPTP or the virtual private networking adapter locally.

The most common of these three scenarios is the first scenario. Typically, the desire to encrypt data from one remote dial-up client to a RAS server is the most critical need. If you are connecting to an ISP using PPTP, the remote PPTP server to which you are connecting must have an established valid IP address. Otherwise, you will be unable to connect to the PPTP server over the Internet.

In the following sections, the basic installation, configuration, and connection steps for establishing a VPN over PPTP are described.

Installing and Configuring PPTP

There are a few items to consider before you begin to configure a PPTP connection. Probably the most significant item is that a VPN over PPTP is only possible if both hosts support PPTP. If the RAS server to which you are attempting to connect does not provide PPTP support, your VPN will not work.

PPTP connections can be made over dial-up connections, Ethernet networks, or Token Ring networks. However, all PPTP connections make use of the Dial-Up Networking (or RAS in the case of Windows NT) components. Therefore, DUN or RAS and PPTP support must be installed and configured in order to establish a PPTP connection. PPTP also requires the use of PPP, so you must configure and have available a dial-up connection and server that supports PPP.

PPTP clients must still be authenticated as remote clients in order to connect over PPTP. This is true even if the client is on the same LAN as the PPTP server.

To install PPTP support, you must add a virtual private networking adapter. This adapter is installed as if it were a physical device, similar to a modem. It is also configured through DUN as if it were a physical device. The steps to install VPN support on a Windows 98 client system are as follows:

1. Right-click the Network Neighborhood icon on the desktop and choose Properties from the resulting context menu.
2. Click Add in the Network dialog box.
3. Choose Adapter and click Add in the Select Network Component Type dialog box.

4. On the left-hand side of the Select Network Adapters dialog box, locate Microsoft in the list of Manufacturers.

5. On the right-hand side of the dialog box, select Microsoft Virtual Private Networking Adapter.

6. Click OK. The adapter should now be added to your Network dialog box configuration (see Figure 24.9).

7. Confirm and/or close all remaining dialog boxes.

FIGURE 24.9

You must install the VPN adapter as a separate component.

After you have installed the Microsoft VPN adapter, you must configure a separate dial-up connection to utilize that adapter. The steps to configure a Dial-Up Networking connection for the VPN adapter are as follows:

1. Open the Dial-Up Networking folder (My Computer, Dial-Up Networking).

2. Click the Make New Connection icon.

3. Type the name for your connection. This name is for your reference only, so choose something that makes sense to you.

4. In the Select a Device selection box, choose Microsoft VPN Adapter. Click Next to continue.

5. Enter the hostname or IP address of the PPTP server to which you plan to connect. Click Next to continue.

6. Click Finish to finalize your configuration.

After both your VPN adapter is installed and the Dial-Up Networking connection using VPN is configured, you can establish your VPN with a PPTP server.

24

DIAL-UP
NETWORKING
WITH WINDOWS 98

Making the PPTP Connection

If you are connecting through a Dial-Up Networking connection, you must first connect using your Dial-Up Networking connection, and then connect using your VPN connection (see Figure 24.10).

1. After you've connected to your ISP, click the PPTP connection icon you created with the name of your PPTP server.

2. Type the User Name and Password for the remote network.

3. Click the Connect button and your secure PPTP connection should be established over your existing connection to the ISP.

FIGURE 24.10

You must make a VPN connection after you establish the network connection.

After you are connected to the PPTP server on the remote network, the traffic from your workstation is routed via the Internet directly to the PPTP server. Within the remote network, the PPTP server routes traffic to the correct location. Because the connection is made directly to the remote network via the Internet, you may no longer be able to access the Internet. You will only be able to access the Internet if your remote network will allow it.

ISP Provided PPTP Connection

If your ISP provides a PPTP connection to the remote server, you do not need to configure a PPTP connection on your workstation. Your ISP will be able to tell you whether they provide this service.

The data you send to the ISP will not be PPTP encrypted in this case. However, the ISP's PPTP connection to the remote server will encrypt the data before passing it over the Internet.

To make this type of PPTP connection, you need only configure the Dial-Up Networking connection to your ISP. There is no need to configure a VPN connection on the workstation. The ISP must handle the configuration of the PPTP connection to your remote PPTP server.

PPTP Over LAN Connections

If you are connected via a LAN or permanent WAN connection to your PPTP server, you can still use PPTP to encrypt your data as previously mentioned. The data transferred between your workstation and the PPTP server will be encrypted over the permanent network connection. The PPTP connection allows you access to any system to which the PPTP server is connected. Therefore, you could create a separate virtual private network within your network. This type of additional security is usually desirable for the personnel departments of larger companies to ensure employee privacy.

In order to create your connection to the PPTP server, you must still configure Dial-Up Networking and add a VPN adapter. The PPTP server must also have configured dial-up (or RAS) services over a VPN adapter. Then, you must configure a dial-up connection to the PPTP server, as previously described. Finally, launch the dial-up connection in order to connect to the PPTP server.

PPTP Over Firewalls and Routers

If you must connect to your PPTP server via a firewall, router, or proxy server, you may need to enable the appropriate TCP port and IP protocol ID. As specified by the Internet Assigned Numbers Authority (IANA), PPTP traffic is sent over TCP port 1723 and the IP protocol ID for PPTP traffic is 47. If you enable the correct TCP port and IP protocol ID, you should be able to send VPN traffic through your router, proxy server, or firewall.

Windows 98 Dial-Up Server

Windows 98 also has a Dial-Up Server that you can use to host a dial-up connection. You can install the DUN server from the Windows 98 Add/Remove Programs icon. To install the DUN server in Windows 98, follow these steps:

1. Open the Control Panel (Start, Settings, Control Panel).
2. Double-click the Add/Remove Programs icon.
3. Click the Windows Setup tab.
4. Double-click Communications.

5. Select the Dial-Up Server check box.

6. Click OK twice to install the components.

7. Enter the path to the Windows 98 installation files and click OK to begin installation.

After you have added the DUN Server to your configuration, you can access it through the Dial-Up Networking folder. Click the Connections drop-down menu from that folder and select Dial-Up Server. You will see a dialog box similar to the one shown in Figure 24.11.

FIGURE 24.11

Windows 98 has a Dial-Up Networking Server that can be added to the DUN configuration.

The configuration options for the DUN server are fairly limited. As you can see in the figure, you can enable or disable the service by clicking either the Allow Caller Access or No Caller Access radio button. If you allow caller access, you can configure a password for the dial-up connection. This would be a share-level protection, meaning that all users would enter the same password to establish a connection with the DUN server. The server can host only one connection at a time.

If you click the Server Type button on the Dial-Up Server dialog box, you will see two additional options. You can Enable Software Compression and Require Encrypted Password for the connection. You can also choose the type of dial-up server that you would like your system to support. You can configure the DUN server as a PPP: Internet, Windows NT Server, Windows 98 DUN server. The default option is the former and is the only option that supports TCP/IP over the dial-up connection. No other configuration options are available via the Windows 98 DUN server. Even though you may have multiple dial-up adapters configured on your Windows 98 DUN server, the server will not support Multilink connections.

Note

The DUN server for Windows 95 is part of the Windows 95 Plus! Pack CD-ROM.

For more advanced RAS features and support, consider using the Windows NT RAS server, which does support Multilink, multiple dial-in connections, and data encryption.

Troubleshooting Dial-Up Connections

There are a few items to keep in mind when you are troubleshooting problems with dial-up connections. Some of these issues are obvious but often overlooked. For example, if the hardware is not functioning correctly, a DUN connection cannot occur. If the modem is disconnected, or improperly configured, DUN connections will certainly fail.

When troubleshooting a DUN problem, first confirm the modem configuration and operation. If possible, have the modem connect to another location. If you establish that the modem is working correctly, you can move to troubleshooting the DUN components. To verify modem operation, you can use the More Info button on the Diagnostics tab of the Modem control panel applet.

Confirming the DUN Configuration

If the modem is working and properly configured, the next item to check is the DUN settings. Right-click the connection that is not working in the Dial-Up Networking folder and choose Properties. Confirm that the correct phone number and area code are entered on the General tab. Remember that Windows 98 DUN will dial long distance if this phone number shows an area code other than the one configured for DUN. If the area code is giving you trouble, you can uncheck the Use Area Code and Dialing Properties check box on the General tab.

Ensure that the correct modem is selected in the DUN configuration box. You should also click the Configure button to ensure that the settings you see are correct for the modem. It is possible to install the modem driver twice and configure it different ways. Ensure that the configuration for the modem is correct.

Click the Server Types tab to confirm that the appropriate settings are configured here. Ensure that you are attempting to connect to the right type of server. Check with your ISP or the RAS server administrator to determine the correct settings.

If data encryption is not supported by the RAS server, your connection will fail if Require Data Encryption is selected. If your password is not being accepted by the remote server, try changing the Require Encrypted Password check box setting. Another troubleshooting step is to try clearing the Enable Software Compression check box. Some RAS servers do not support this feature and clearing this box might solve the problem.

24

DIAL-UP
NETWORKING
WITH WINDOWS 98

The Log on to Network check box is not required for most ISP connections, but shouldn't cause a problem if it is checked. However, you should clear this check box if your ISP or RAS server does not require you to log on.

PPP Logging

If you are using a PPP connection, you can click the Record a Log File for This Connection check box to troubleshoot the PPP connection. When this check box is selected, a PPPLOG.TXT file will be created in your Windows root directory. The PPPLOG.TXT documents the connection process and helps you to identify where the connection is failing. Microsoft has produced a Knowledge Base article (Q156435) titled "How to Interpret the PPPLOG.TXT file." You can locate this article on the Microsoft TechNet CD or online at www.microsoft.com/support. Search for the article identifier Q156435.

Summary

Windows 98 Dial-Up Networking allows you to connect to remote systems over dial-up connections. The DUN client software can be used to connect to a wide variety of RAS servers, including SLIP, CSLIP, and PPP. PPP is the default and most efficient of the DUN connections you can make with Windows 98. Most ISPs now support PPP connections; however, Windows 98 does support CSLIP and SLIP client connections as well.

To configure DUN, you must first install a dial-up networking device. Because DUN is considered networking, you add the DUN adapter through the Network dialog box. If you don't have a modem installed, the DUN setup routine will launch the modem wizard. After you have configured both the modem and the dial-up adapter software, you can create the DUN connection.

To create a DUN connection, you must go to the Dial-Up Networking folder and use the Make New Connection wizard. After creating the connection, you will most likely have to modify the properties of your DUN connection. For example, you may need to configure a static IP address for your client system or add the IP addresses of DNS or WINS servers for name resolution. You can also configure encryption, compression, and the type of server to which you will be connecting in the DUN connection properties dialog box. If you have more than one DUN-capable device installed on your system, you can also enable Multilink via the DUN connection properties.

Windows 98 supports PPTP, which can provide a secure connection between two points on a public or private network. To use PPTP, both the client system and the server must support and configure PPTP and a VPN adapter. The PPTP connection can be made over a permanent LAN or WAN connection or a dial-up connection. Either way, the network or dial-up network connection is established before the PPTP connection. A separate VPN adapter and Dial-Up Networking connection is required to implement the VPN.

When troubleshooting your dial-up connection, do not neglect modem verification. If the modem is not configured or functioning correctly, the dial-up connection will consistently fail. After you have verified the modem settings and driver, check the DUN configuration. Ensure that you have the appropriate server type configured. Also, ensure that your client is not attempting to use encryption or compression that is not supported by the RAS server. If you cannot see the configuration problem for a PPP configuration, enable logging on the Server Types tab of your DUN connection properties. Attempt your connection, and then review the PPPLOG.TXT file in your Windows root directory. You should then be able to determine the point at which your connection is failing.

24

DIAL-UP
NETWORKING
WITH WINDOWS 98

Configuring TCP/IP for Windows NT

by Kurt Hudson

In This Chapter

This chapter covers how Microsoft TCP/IP is applied and used on Windows NT systems. The troubleshooting tools and Microsoft TCP/IP architecture that apply to Windows 98 are also true for Windows NT; therefore, you are encouraged to read Chapter 23, "Configuring TCP/IP for Windows 95 and Windows 98," and Chapter 24, "Dial-Up Networking with Windows 98," before proceeding with this chapter. In this chapter you learn how to configure and implement TCP/IP on a Windows NT server. You also learn how to install and configure the DHCP server, TCP/IP printing, and other TCP/IP-related services on the Windows NT server.

Windows NT Versions

Several different versions of Windows NT as well as different product types exist within the Windows NT category. For example, Windows NT Server, Windows NT Workstation, and Windows NT Enterprise are all different products. Divisions also exist within the product line, such as Windows NT 4, Windows NT 3.51, and so on.

> **Note**
>
> The discussion in this chapter assumes the use of Windows NT Server 4 unless otherwise specified. Other versions and/or products in the Windows NT category are mentioned only when noteworthy differences exist between them and Windows NT 4. For the majority of the discussion presented in this chapter, the Microsoft TCP/IP protocol suite is implemented identically in all version 4 releases of Windows NT.

Architecture

The Microsoft TCP/IP architecture for Windows NT is the same as it is for Windows 98. Therefore, the architecture of the Microsoft TCP/IP protocol suite presented in Chapter 23 applies here. One important point meriting another mention is that NetBIOS is part of the Microsoft TCP/IP protocol suite in Windows NT systems prior to Windows 2000.

Installation

The default protocol for Windows NT 4 is TCP/IP, so it is typically added during the installation process. However, skipping the installation of networking components during setup, or installing a different protocol during the installation process is possible. The configuration of the protocol during installation and after installation is nearly identical.

The only noticeable difference is that the configuration process is automated during the setup routine and doesn't allow you to configure as many options as you could after the process is complete. Given that you have more control over your TCP/IP installation after you have installed the product, this chapter focuses on installing and configuring the protocol as if it were not added during the installation process.

> **Note**
>
> If you did not install any networking components during the Windows NT installation process, you will be prompted to run the Network Configuration wizard, which is identical to the process skipped during installation.

Before you install the TCP/IP protocol you should be ready with configuration information, unless you are using DHCP to configure your protocol. Even if DHCP is employed on the network, you may still have to configure a few additional options such as a DNS and/or WINS server address. However, the DHCP server could also set these options.

Installing the TCP/IP Protocol Suite

To install the TCP/IP protocol suite, you can use the Network icon in the Control Panel or the Network Neighborhood icon on the Windows NT Desktop. Follow these steps:

1. To use the Network icon in the Control Panel, open the Control Panel by clicking Start, Settings, Control Panel.

2. Inside the Control Panel, double-click the Network icon. The Network dialog box opens (see Figure 25.1). (Another way to open the Network dialog box is to right-click the Network Neighborhood icon, then choose Properties from the resulting context menu.)

You can configure several network settings via the Network dialog box. The following sections describe the configurable setting in each tab of the Network dialog box.

Identification Tab

The first tab you see on the Network dialog box is the Identification tab. This is similar to the Identification tab in Windows 98 (as described in the previous chapter). The Identification tab shows the NetBIOS name of the computer and either the workgroup or domain name of which the computer is a member. Do not confuse the domain name shown here with the DNS domain name. The domain name shown on the Identification tab is specific to Microsoft networking and is part of the user and computer account administration system.

FIGURE 25.1

Use the Network dialog box to configure your Windows 98 network settings.

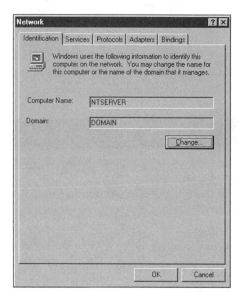

Services Tab

The Services tab is used for installation and in some cases configuration of services related to the network. For example, this is where you would install the DNS server service, WINS server service, and even some additional TCP/IP services. These services are discussed in greater detail as this chapter progresses.

Bindings Tab

The Bindings tab illustrates the services, adapters, and protocols that have been linked (bound) together in the system. Essentially, the binding programmatically associates components so that they may be used together. You can use the Bindings tab to bind or unbind protocols from adapters or services. You can even unbind services from adapters.

Note

When placing a Windows NT system on the Internet via a dial-up adapter, unbinding the server service from the WAN adapter is wise. Doing so keeps your Windows NT system more secure because it will not advertise its shared directories on the Internet, nor will it allow connectivity over NetBIOS via the Internet.

Adapters Tab

The Adapters tab illustrates the devices you have configured in the Windows NT system. You will see both network adapters and dial-up networking (DUN) equipment listed under this tab. If you must install a network adapter or update a network driver, you can do so from this tab. Some adapters also allow you to manage physical resource settings through this tab. Other cards may need to be manually set or configured via a vendor-specific installation program. You can also use the Adapters tab to remove a network device.

Protocols Tab

The Protocols tab of the Network dialog box is where you install and configure the Microsoft TCP/IP protocol suite. To install the TCP/IP protocol from the Network dialog box, follow these steps:

1. Click the Protocols tab.
2. Click the Add button.
3. Choose TCP/IP Protocol from the list of network protocols (select by clicking).
4. Click the OK button.
5. Confirm or enter the path to the Windows NT installation files and click the Continue button.
6. Click Close on the Network dialog box and reboot as requested.

After you have finished installing the protocol, you will be asked to configure your TCP/IP settings. In the next section, TCP/IP configuration is explained.

Configuring TCP/IP

After you have installed the TCP/IP protocol suite, you will be asked whether you want to configure the protocol. Whether or not you decide to at that time, you can return to the Network dialog box to configure the protocol at any time. On the Protocols tab, double-click the TCP/IP Protocol icon. The Microsoft TCP/IP Properties dialog box appears, as shown in Figure 25.2.

25

CONFIGURING TCP/IP FOR WINDOWS NT

FIGURE 25.2

The Microsoft TCP/IP Properties dialog box gives you several configuration options.

The five tabs on the Microsoft TCP/IP Properties dialog box are

- IP Address
- DNS
- WINS Address
- DHCP Relay
- Routing

The following sections describe each of these tabs.

IP Address

This tab allows you to configure your system's IP address, subnet mask, and default gateway settings. You can also choose to utilize DHCP to obtain your IP configuration, in which case the IP address and subnet mask fields are made unavailable. However, the default gateway can be configured whether you have decided to use DHCP or to manually configure your settings. You can also enter a default gateway address, whether or not you are using DHCP. If you manually enter a default gateway, it will override any default gateway setting if it has been configured on the DHCP server.

Advanced IP Addressing

If you click the Advanced button on the IP Address tab, you will open the Advanced IP Addressing dialog box (see Figure 25.3). This dialog box allows you to configure multiple IP addresses for any one of your installed network adapters. You can also set different default gateways for each card.

FIGURE 25.3

The Advanced IP Addressing dialog box allows you to configure multiple IP addresses and separate default gateways.

Notice that you can select the network card you are configuring in the Adapter selection box. This enables you to configure different settings for each card you have installed in your Windows NT Server.

Enable PPTP Filtering

The Enable PPTP Filtering check box allows you to force the given network card to accept only PPTP packets and discard all others. Essentially, this option turns the network adapter into a PPTP-only link, which means that only PPTP clients will be able to communicate with the given adapter.

To make this feature work correctly, you would still have to install the Point to Point Tunneling Protocol from the Protocols tab on the Network dialog box. If RAS has not been installed before you install PPTP, the RAS installation routine will be launched automatically. Unlike Windows 98, it is the installation of the protocol that allows you to create a PPTP connection. (In Windows 98, it is the installation of a Virtual Private Network adapter.) After the protocol is added, you will have a VPN adapter installed (see Figure 25.4).

FIGURE 25.4

When a VPN adapter is installed, you can see it graphically.

After you have installed PPTP and RAS, you can modify settings via the Network dialog box. For example, if you want to increase the number of Virtual Private Networks you will allow, click the Protocols tab and double-click the Point to Point Tunneling Protocol icon. This action opens the PPTP Configuration dialog box, in which you can change the number of VPNs you are allowing. If you want to configure your RAS settings, click the Services tab and then double-click the Remove Access Service icon. This opens the Remote Access Setup dialog box, where you can configure protocols, network settings, and adapters.

> **Note**
>
> RAS server installation and configuration is covered in greater detail later in this chapter. Refer to Chapter 24 for a more in-depth discussion of PPTP and VPN.

Enable Security

Another setting on the Advanced IP Addressing dialog box (refer to Figure 25.3) is the Enable Security check box. Selecting this allows you to click the Configure button, which opens the TCP/IP Security dialog box (see Figure 25.5).

FIGURE 25.5

You can restrict access to specific ports and protocols via the TCP/IP Security dialog box.

You can select which adapter you would like to configure your TCP/IP security options via the Adapter selection box. There are also three different columns where you can configure additional restrictions. The default setting is to permit all TCP and UDP ports and all IP protocol identifiers. However, if you want to secure the network card so only specific ports and protocol identifiers are allowed to pass through the network card, you can select the appropriate Permit Only button and enter the number of the port to permit. Notice that after you configure a restriction you can only enable ports; all others in that category will be denied. Essentially, this means that you cannot selectively deny ports, you can only selectively enable ports after globally denying all ports.

As an example, if you wanted to allow anyone to access a Web server attached to your Windows NT Server, you would click Permit Only on the first column and add 80 into the list. Then, you would select Permit Only in the UDP column and not enter any numbers. This would effectively limit your Windows NT server to receiving only TCP Port 80 traffic on that network card. All other traffic would be denied.

> **Note**
>
> TCP Port 80 is the well-known port for HTTP (Web) services. To review the other well-known port settings, see RFC 1700.

DNS

To configure your IP client's DNS settings, click the DNS tab on the Microsoft TCP/IP Properties dialog box (see Figure 25.6). This tab allows you to configure the hostname and DNS domain name for your computer.

FIGURE 25.6

The DNS tab allows you to configure the computer's hostname, domain name, and the name services it will use to resolve names.

The default hostname is the same as the NetBIOS computer name (on the Network dialog box Identification tab). You should leave the NetBIOS and hostnames the same because the computer will be easier to identify on the network. For example, if you tried to troubleshoot a connectivity problem for a system that had a hostname that was different than the NetBIOS name, you would see the NetBIOS name when looking in Network Neighborhood. However, if you tried to use `ping` on the computer name, the hostname of the system would be assumed by the `ping` utility.

25

CONFIGURING
TCP/IP FOR
WINDOWS NT

DNS Service Search Order

In the DNS Service Search Order window you can configure the IP addresses of the DNS servers you would like to provide hostname resolution services. If your local Windows NT Server installation is providing DNS services, you can configure the local host address here. You can also add additional addresses of DNS servers in case one fails. The DNS client only queries additional DNS servers if the previous DNS server is unavailable. If the client receives a response from its DNS server, even a negative response, the DNS client will not attempt to contact additional DNS servers by default.

Domain Suffix Search Order

The Domain Suffix Order configuration box allows you to set the order in which you would like your client to search the DNS structure when seeking name resolution. Setting this feature is usually not required. For example, if most of the Internet sites you access by name are United States Air Force (military) sites, you may want to place AF.MIL at the top of your search order list. This tells the DNS server to search the AF.MIL structure first.

> **Note**
>
> You can modify the order of IP addresses or domain suffixes via the Up and Down arrows to the right of each of the DNS Service Search Order and/or the Domain Suffix Search Order windows. You should modify the order so that DNS suffixes that are more frequently used should be at the top of the list.

WINS Address

You can configure the WINS servers, by IP address, that your client will use for name resolution. In Windows NT 4 systems, you can only type a primary and/or secondary WINS address into the dialog box. The secondary WINS server is another WINS server on the network queried for name resolution if the primary WINS server is down. The terms *primary* and *secondary* are relative to the order in which the WINS client will access them, but there is no difference in the WINS server installations.

Enable DNS for Windows Resolution

If the Enable DNS for Windows Resolution check box is selected, your WINS client will attempt to resolve NetBIOS computer names via the hosts file. After the hosts file, your system will check the DNS server. Use this option if your primary name resolution method on the network is DNS. An example of this would be a network that has mostly

Unix machines with some Windows machines. Some DNS servers can be configured with a $WINS directive that can forward unresolved name queries to a specific WINS server.

Enable LMHOSTS Lookup

If you want your client to search an LMHOSTS file for NetBIOS name resolution, you can select the Enable LMHOSTS Lookup check box. You can also click the Import LMHOSTS file button to browse your network and copy an LMHOSTS file to your local system.

> **Note**
>
> For more information on NetBIOS and hostname resolution via Microsoft clients, see Chapter 7, "WINS."

Scope ID

You should leave the Scope ID text box blank unless you want to limit communications for your Windows NT system. The scope ID allows you to segregate communications at the NetBIOS level on your network. Only systems with the same NetBIOS scope ID can communicate on your network. By default, all systems can communicate because they have the same scope ID (nothing). However, you can enter any alphanumeric combination here to set a scope ID for your computer. If you do, you will only be able to communicate with computers that have an identical scope ID.

The scope ID is actually appended to the computer name for the system. Therefore, setting multiple systems to the same computer name, but with different NetBIOS scope ID fields, is possible. However, realize that those computers will be unable to communicate with one another.

DHCP Relay

The Dynamic Host Configuration Protocol (DHCP), as described in Chapter 8, "Automatic Configuration," provides dynamic IP address and subnet mask configuration for clients. However, because DHCP relies on broadcasts, sometimes routers can prevent DHCP requests from correctly traversing network segments. RFC 1542 defines the service that a router should provide in order to allow DHCP packets to be appropriately handled. However, not all routers support this RFC. Therefore, when these RFC 1542 non-compliant routers separate a DHCP client and DHCP server, the client cannot get an address without some type of workaround.

As a workaround for networks that use routers that do not support RFC 1542, Windows NT computers can be used as DHCP Relays. The function of a DHCP Relay is to forward a DHCP request to a DHCP server. The DHCP Relay modifies the 'giaddr field of the DHCP Request packet, which indicates the subnet identifier of the requesting client. Then, the DHCP Relay forwards that packet directly to the DHCP server. The DHCP server uses the 'giaddr field to assign an appropriate address and sends the request back to the DHCP Relay, which forwards it to the requesting client system.

Enabling DHCP Relay

If you want to enable your system as a DHCP Relay, enter the IP address(es) of the DHCP server(s) on your network in the DHCP Servers window via the Add button (see Figure 25.7). You can also configure the maximum number of hops your DHCP request packet should travel before being discarded and the number of seconds your system will wait for a response.

FIGURE 25.7

The DHCP Relay tab allows you to enable DHCP Relay services on your NT system for your subnet.

Installing the DHCP Relay Agent Service

In addition to entering a DHCP server address, you must also install the DHCP Relay Agent service. This can be done through the Network dialog box Services tab. The specific steps to install the DHCP Relay Agent are as follows:

1. Right-click the Network Neighborhood icon on the desktop.

2. Choose Properties from the resulting context menu.

3. Click the Services tab on the Network dialog box.

4. Click the Add button.

5. Select DHCP Relay Agent from the list of network services.

6. Click the OK button to confirm your selection.

7. Confirm or enter the path to the Windows NT installation files and click the Continue button.

8. Click Close on the Network dialog box and reboot the system as requested.

Routing

The Routing tab is the last configuration tab on the Microsoft TCP/IP Properties dialog box. There is only one check box on the entire configuration tab labeled Enable IP Forwarding, which can either be checked or cleared. When checked, the Windows NT system is enabled as an IP router. If the system has multiple network cards, packets can be routed from one segment to another via the Windows NT system.

Windows NT Server 4 supports static routing and dynamic routing via the *Routing Information Protocol* (RIP). If you want to utilize RIP, you must install it via the Services tab on the Network dialog box (click the Add button and choose RIP for Internet Protocol). The Enterprise version of Windows NT 4 includes the routing protocol *Open Shortest Path First* (OSPF). RIP and OSPF allow your system to dynamically build its routing table via an information exchange with other RIP or OSPF routers. If you do not use RIP or OSPF, you will have to build and maintain the routes to remote networks manually.

You can obtain OSPF in a downloadable product called Routing and Remote Access Service (RRAS) for Windows NT 4. This product is a free update to Windows NT RAS and offers additional capabilities as well as the OSPF support. See `http://www.microsoft.com/ntserver/nts/downloads/winfeatures/rras/rrasdown.asp?RLD=188` for more information.

> **Note**
>
> You can find Registry settings for Microsoft TCP/IP on Windows NT via Knowledge Base article Q120642 on the Microsoft support site at `www.microsoft.com/support` or on the Microsoft TechNet CD-ROM.

Simple TCP/IP Services

You can install the Simple TCP/IP Services from the Services tab of the Network dialog box. This is actually a separate component of services that can be added to your system after the installation of the TCP/IP Protocol.

Adding Simple TCP/IP Services

To add the Simple TCP/IP Services, follow these steps:

1. Click the Services tab on the Network dialog box and then click Add.

2. Choose Simple TCP/IP Services from the list of components and then click OK.

3. Enter or confirm the path to your Windows NT installation files and click Continue.

4. Click Close on the Network dialog box and reboot as requested.

You should then see Simple TCP/IP Services listed in the Network Services window. The Simple TCP/IP Services include Character Generator (RFC 864), Daytime (RFC 867), Echo (RFC 862), Discard (RFC 863), and Quote of the Day (RFC 863).

Remote Access Services (RAS)

Windows NT can be a RAS server and client. The RAS software is built into the product. The Windows NT RAS server software can host up to 256 connections on Windows NT Server 4, but is limited to hosting only one connection when running on Windows NT Workstation 4.

You can use the following steps to install RAS on your Windows NT 4 system:

1. To install RAS you must open the Network dialog box (right-click the Network Neighborhood icon, and then choose Properties).

2. RAS is a network service, so click the Services tab of the Network dialog box.

3. Click the Add button and choose Remote Access Service from the list of installable network services.

4. Click OK. Confirm or enter the path to your Windows NT installation files and click the Continue button.

5. Click Close on the Network dialog box and reboot as requested.

When you are installing RAS you must select, or add and select, a RAS-capable device. If you do not have a RAS-capable device when you install RAS, the Modem Wizard program will guide you through adding a modem to your Windows NT System. This process is nearly identical to the process for installing a modem via Windows 98, described in the previous chapter.

Configuring Your RAS Server

After the modem and RAS are installed, you can configure your RAS server via the Network dialog box Services tab. Double-click the Remote Access Service icon to open the Remote Access Setup dialog box (see Figure 25.8).

FIGURE 25.8

You can configure, add, or remove RAS devices from the Remote Access Setup dialog box.

From the Remote Access Setup dialog box you can Add, Remove, or Configure your RAS-capable devices. You can also configure whether to allow inbound, outbound, or both direction RAS capabilities. You can also configure the Network protocols that will be allowed and how they will be implemented on the RAS server.

If you click the Add button on the Remote Access Setup dialog box, you can choose to install a modem or X-25 device for RAS access. If you choose to install a modem, the Modem Wizard will be launched. The X-25 option allows you to configure an X-25 packet-switching connection. ISDN devices are considered modems, so use the Install Modem icon to add your ISDN device.

If you click the Configure button, you can configure the capabilities for your RAS device's port. The Configure Port Usage dialog box allows you to configure your device to dial out, receive calls, or both. The default setting for Windows NT Server is to allow inbound calls only. The default setting for Windows NT Workstation is to allow outbound calls only. If you do enable outbound calling, you will enable RAS from the logon dialog box. This option allows remote users to establish a dial-up connection and log in to their remote network at the same time they are logging in to their local system.

If you click the Network button on the Remote Access Setup dialog box, you will be able to configure the network protocols allowed for your system (see Figure 25.9). For your RAS client, you enable the use of NetBEUI, TCP/IP, and/or IPX. The Server Settings section allows you to enable and configure NetBEUI, TCP/IP, and IPX for your dial-up connections.

FIGURE 25.9

The TCP/IP Network Configuration dialog box allows you to configure IP settings that will be unique to your RAS connection.

> **Note**
>
> The options you can configure in the Network Configuration dialog box depend on the type of access you allowed via the Configure Port Usage dialog box. For example, if you are set to Receive Calls Only, then your options on the Network Configuration dialog box will be limited to the Server Settings section. Likewise, the protocols that are enabled by default on the Network Configuration dialog box are the protocols that you have installed on your system.

Each of the protocols you configure can limit the access of the remote client to the local server or allow them access to the entire network. The TCP/IP options allow you to use DHCP to assign IP addresses to RAS clients, or you can configure a range of addresses to be released to RAS clients. There is also an option to allow remote clients to request a predetermined (static) IP address (see Figure 25.10).

Also, on the Network Configuration dialog box you can set different authentication types for your system. For example, you can allow any authentication type (including clear text), require encrypted authentication, or require Microsoft encryption. If you decide to enable Microsoft encryption, only Microsoft operating systems will be able to participate in the RAS connections. Also, with Microsoft encryption, you can configure data encryption. For the widest range of compatibility for dial-in users, you should allow any authentication.

FIGURE 25.10

When allowing dial-in access on your Windows NT Server, you must configure the RAS Server TCP/IP Configuration dialog box.

If some of your clients will be using Multilink connections, you can enable inbound Multilink connections by checking the Multilink check box on the Network Configuration dialog box.

When you are finished making changes, click OK to confirm and click the Continue button on the Remote Access Setup dialog box to commit all changes.

DHCP Server

The Windows NT Server product can be used as a DHCP server. The DHCP server service is part of the installable network services for the Windows NT server. One condition for installing the DHCP server service is that the DHCP server must have a statically configured IP address. In other words, a DHCP server cannot obtain its IP address from another DHCP server.

> **Note**
>
> DHCP was explained in Chapter 8. This chapter focuses on installing and configuring DHCP on the Windows NT server, not on the benefits or potential pitfalls of using DHCP.

Installing the DHCP Server Service

In Windows NT, the DHCP server service is installed as a networking service. To install a networking service, you must access the Services tab of the Network dialog box. The steps to install the DHCP server service are as follows:

1. Right-click the Network Neighborhood icon on the desktop, and then click Properties.

2. Click the Services tab on the Network dialog box.

3. Click the Add button on the Services tab.

4. Choose the Microsoft DHCP Server from the list of network services.

5. Click OK.

6. Enter or confirm the path to the Windows NT Server installation files and click the Continue button. Reboot as requested.

Controlling the DHCP Server Service

After the DHCP server service is installed, you can see the service listed in the Services dialog box. You can access the Services dialog box by double-clicking the Services icon in the Control Panel. The DHCP server service is listed as Microsoft DHCP Server. If you highlight the service in the list you can stop, start, and pause the service. You can also review its current operational status and configure how the service will be started.

To stop a running service, highlight that service and click the Stop button on the Services dialog box. You can also pause the running service by using the Pause button. Pause means that the service cannot make any new connections, but existing connections will be maintained. Stop means that all existing connections will be dropped and all new connections will be refused. You can also choose to continue the service, but that is only available when the service has been paused.

If you highlight a service and click the Startup button, you can configure how that service will be run. You can choose between automatic, manual, and disabled. Automatic services start automatically during the boot process. Manual services must be started by the administrator, and disabled means that the service will not start until the Service Type designator is changed.

There is also an option for the service to log on with the credentials of a user account. This is only necessary when the service must perform functions that require certain privileges to accomplish its tasks. For example, if a service is used to automatically back up files and folders, it most likely requires the rights to access those files. If the service is able to log on to the system with the correct user permission(s), (that is, backup files and folders), the service can perform its job.

You can also stop, start, pause, and continue the service from the Services interface via the Stop, Start, Pause, and Continue buttons. If you pause the service, you can use the Continue button to enable that service again. When a service is paused, existing connections will continue to work, but no new connections to the service can be made. When you stop a service, all existing connections are dropped and no new connections are allowed.

Command-Line Functions

You can also stop, start, pause, and continue the DHCP service from the command line.

> **Note**
>
> The discussion of command-line functions in this section applies to Windows NT and Windows 2000 alike.

Use the following commands from the Windows NT Server command prompt to initiate these activities:

- `net start DHCP`   This starts the DHCP server service.
- `net stop DHCP`   This stops the DHCP server service.
- `net pause DHCP`   This pauses the DHCP server service.
- `net continue DHCP`   This resumes the DHCP service.

Compressing the DHCP Database

The DHCP database is similar to the WINS Database, as described in Chapter 7. Both DHCP and WINS use `.mdb` file extensions on their databases; therefore, the filename for the DHCP database is `DHCP.MDB`. Whenever either database becomes larger than 30MB, it is time to compress the database to keep it performing effectively. You can use the JetPack command to reduce the size of the DHCP or WINS database. To compress the DHCP database, you must first stop the DHCP service. When the service is stopped, use the `Jetpack dhcp.mdb temp.mdb` command to compress the database. You should issue that command from the `%systemroot%\system32\DHCP` directory.

25

> **Note**
>
> Typically, the `%systemroot%` directory in Windows NT is named WINNT. However, it is possible that the directory can go by another name. To determine the name of the `systemroot` directory, you can type `%systemroot%` in the Run dialog box to open the proper directory. You can also use that command from the command prompt. You can literally type `CD %systemroot%\system32\DHCP` to select the appropriate directory.

Administering DHCP

You can administer DHCP via the DHCP Manager in the Administrative Tools list of the Start menu (Start, Program Files, Administrative Tools). After DHCP has been installed and the system has been restarted, the DHCP Manager will appear in the Start menu. Click the DHCP Manager selection to open the DHCP Manager application, shown in Figure 25.11.

FIGURE 25.11

The main configuration utility for DHCP in Windows NT 4 is the DHCP Manager.

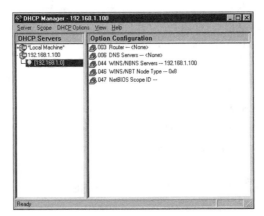

Adding Servers

After installing DHCP, the first thing you must do is add a DHCP server to the DHCP Manager. The DHCP Manager can be used to manage multiple DHCP servers, but you must add them to the list, including your local DHCP server. To add your server, click the Server menu, then choose Add. Enter the IP address for your DHCP server, then click the OK button.

Before you will be able to provide any addresses to DHCP clients, you will have to add a scope with a range of available addresses.

Configuring Scopes

To add a scope to your DHCP server, follow these steps:

1. Click the Scope selection on the toolbar, then choose Create. The Scope Properties dialog box opens (see Figure 25.12).

2. Enter the first address (Start Address) you would like to make available to clients on that network location.

3. Next, enter the last address (End Address) in that range you would like to make available to network clients. You must also enter a subnet mask, so that the DHCP server can determine the subnetwork identifier for the address range.

4. You can also enter a range of IP addresses within the scope range you want to exclude from the scope. Use the Exclusion Range Start Address and End Address to configure this, if desired.

You can configure a Lease Duration for this range of addresses. The duration is the length of time you would like the clients to be able to use the address before they have to renew it. Clients will actually attempt to renew their addresses after half the lease is expired. If they don't get an answer by the expiration of 7/8ths of the lease period, the client will contact any available DHCP server for a new address. When the lease does expire, if the client could not obtain a new address or renewal prior to that, the client will release the address and consequently be unable to communicate via TCP/IP on the network. You can also decide to give clients unlimited leases, which means they will keep their address after it is assigned.

FIGURE 25.12

A DHCP scope defines the range of addresses you would like to release on a per-segment basis.

The Name and Comment text boxes at the bottom of the DHCP Options: Scope dialog box can be left blank. These items are only used for administrative reference and have no bearing on the operation of the scope.

> **Note**
>
> When you configure a scope, you will be prompted to activate that scope. You can choose Yes to activate the scope. Otherwise, you can use the Scope menu to activate or deactivate your scopes.

Global and Scope Options

By default, the DHCP server will only provide an IP address and a subnet mask. However, the DHCP server can provide many more configuration options. If you would like to configure options for every scope on your DHCP server, follow these steps:

1. Click the DHCP Options menu on the DHCP Manager toolbar and choose Global.

2. If you want to add options to certain ranges of addresses, choose Scope from the DHCP Options menu.

Depending on the Windows NT Service Pack you have installed, you can configure over 65 different options for your DHCP scopes. The most common options to release for Microsoft clients are Router (003), DNS Servers (006), WINS/NBNS Servers (044), and WINS/NBT Node Type (046). After you have chosen your options, select each in the Active Options window and click the Value button to configure the addresses and required settings, if any. For example, if you want to release the address of the default gateway for a particular scope of addresses, follow these steps:

1. Click DHCP Options and select Scope.

2. Choose 003 Router from the list of Unused Options.

3. Click the Add button to move the 003 Router option to the list of Active Options.

4. Select 003 Router in the list of Active Options and click the Value button.

5. Click the Edit Array button and enter the IP address of the default gateway in the new IP Address text box.

6. Click Add to add it to the list of default gateways.

7. Alternately, you can enter the Server Name of the default gateway, instead of the IP address. Then, click the Resolve button, which will return the IP address of the default gateway, if name resolution is available for that server and IP address.

You can configure other options to be released by your Windows NT Server using a similar method.

Static Addresses

If you want to configure a permanent address for one or more clients on your network, you can use the Add Reservations selection under the Scope menu in the DHCP Manager. The following shows the steps to reserve IP addresses:

1. After you click Add Reservations, you will see the Add Reserved Clients dialog box.

2. Complete the IP address in the IP Address text box, ensuring that it's the address you want to reserve for the client.

3. In the Unique Identifier text box, you must enter the MAC address of the network card you would like to release the IP address to.

4. You can also enter the name of the DHCP client to which you are releasing this address and a comment, if desired.

After you have reserved an address for a DHCP client in your scope, the address will be released only to the DHCP client with a network card using that MAC address. If you want to review the reservations you have made for clients, click the Scope menu on the DHCP Manager, then choose Active Leases. You will first see all the active leases your DHCP server has provided. However, you can click the Show Reservations Only check box to view only the addresses you have reserved. You can also use this dialog box to sort, refresh, and reconcile addresses.

Using Microsoft DNS

The Windows NT Server product also includes an installable Domain Name System (DNS) service. This service provides RFC 974, 1034, and 1035 standard DNS support and provides hostname resolution over TCP port 53. In addition, the DNS server files can be configured through a graphical interface.

> **Note**
>
> Chapter 6, "DNS: Name Services," describes the concepts and structure of DNS. This chapter does not focus on the concepts of DNS, but rather the installation and operation of the Microsoft DNS server.

25

CONFIGURING
TCP/IP FOR
WINDOWS NT

Installing DNS

Because the Microsoft DNS server service is considered a networking service, it can be added through the Network dialog box. To add Microsoft DNS to your Windows NT Server version 4, follow these steps:

1. Right-click the Network Neighborhood icon on the desktop and select Properties from the resulting context menu.

2. Click the Services tab on the Network dialog box.

3. Click the Add button on the Services tab.

4. Choose Microsoft DNS Server from the list of network services and click OK.

5. Confirm or enter the path to your Windows NT installation files and click Continue.

6. After the service is added to the list of installed network services, click the Close button on the Network dialog box.

7. Click Yes to reboot your system and complete the installation process.

After the service is installed, you will find the DNS Manager in the Start Menu, Programs, Administrative Tools section. Click the DNS Manager to begin configuring the DNS server. Before you can set up your DNS files, you must add your server to the list of DNS servers. To add your server, click the DNS menu, then choose New Server. You can enter the hostname of the server or the IP address.

Creating a Zone

After your server appears in the list, you can create a zone for your server so that you can begin entering records. To create a zone on your server, follow these steps:

1. Right-click the icon representing your server in the Server List of the DNS Manager.

2. Choose New Zone from the resulting menu.

3. Select the appropriate type of zone you would like to create. If you choose secondary, you will have to enter the appropriate zone and server for which you would like this system to be secondary. Click Next to continue.

4. Enter the name of your zone in the following dialog box, and then press the Tab key and the Zone File name will be automatically filled in. Click Next to continue.

5. Click Finish to complete the process. You will immediately see that the Start of Authority (SOA) and Name Server (NS) records for your server have been entered in the list (see Figure 25.13).

FIGURE 25.13

To configure your Windows NT 4 DNS server, use the Domain Name Service Manager.

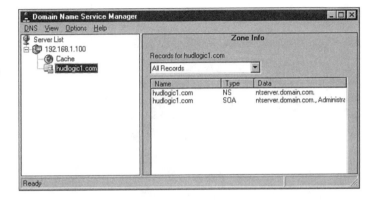

Everything you enter through the DNS Manager creates properly formatted DNS config-uration files in the %windir%\system32\DNS directory. You can take a look at your zone text file by accessing this directory. Your zone file will have the name of your zone followed by the file extension .dns. For example, if your domain name is domain2.com, then your zone file would be named domain2.com.dns.

To ensure that your DNS text configuration files and the DNS Manager interface are synchronized, you can right-click your DNS server icon in the Server List of the DNS Manager, then choose Update Server Data Files. This action synchronizes the interface with the data files.

> **Note**
>
> If your DNS server disappears from the DNS Manager, you can typically recover it by adding the name or IP address of the server as a New Server. This usually brings back all the old data files from the %windir%\system32\DNS directory. Conversely, if you ever need to remove your DNS server, remove the service from the Network dialog box, and then delete the %windir%\system32\DNS directory.

Creating Zone Records

To create records for your zone:

1. Right-click the icon that shows your zone name.
2. Choose New Record. The New Resource Record window opens (see Figure 25.14).
3. You can add the record type of your choice. For example, to add a new host address record, select A Record from the list and enter the IP address and hostname.

25

CONFIGURING
TCP/IP FOR
WINDOWS NT

FIGURE 25.14
*Use the New
Record option
to add a new
resource record
(a.k.a. address
and hostname to
your DNS data-
base).*

You may notice a check box to add a PTR record for the new A Record. This allows you to automatically create an `in-addr.arpa` entry for new hosts. Doing this saves you the time of creating a PTR manually. However, to have this done for you automatically, you must first create the `in-addr.arpa` domain for your server.

Configuring Inverse Domain Name Resolution

To configure inverse name resolution for your server, you must create an `in-addr.arpa` domain. This is done by inverting the network portion of your IP address and appending `in-addr.arpa`. After you do, Microsoft DNS will identify this as an inverse name resolution domain and configure your name resolution text files accordingly. To create an `in-addr.arpa` domain, follow these steps:

1. Right-click the icon that represents your server and choose New Zone.
2. Select the Primary radio button and click the Next button.
3. Enter your network identifier in reverse and the suffix `.in-addr.arpa`. Figure 25.15 shows how this would look for the network 192.168.1.0.
4. Press the Tab key to get the correct Zone File name, then click the Next button to continue.
5. Click Finish and notice that your Inverse Name resolution domain has been created.

After you have created the inverse name resolution domain, PTR records can be automatically added to your `in-addr.arpa` domain during hostname creation.

FIGURE 25.15

To configure name lookup from the IP address, you must implement an inverse name resolution domain.

Configuring DNS to Contact a WINS Server

Microsoft DNS can also be used with the Microsoft WINS server to enhance name resolution capabilities. You can configure the DNS server to call the WINS server to resolve the hostname of the *fully qualified domain name* (FQDN). For example, in the name server1.domain.com, DNS would have to resolve the domain.com portion, but could call the WINS server to ascertain the IP address for server1.

To configure your Microsoft DNS to contact a WINS server, follow these steps:

1. Right-click the name of your zone, and then choose Properties.
2. Click the WINS Lookup or WINS Reverse Lookup tab to configure the address(es) of your WINS server(s). If you click a normal zone, the WINS Lookup tab appears. If you click an in-addr.arpa zone, the WINS Reverse Lookup tab appears.
3. Choose WINS Resolution and enter the IP address of your WINS server. You can enter multiple WINS servers here. Click the Add button after each entry. For WINS Reverse Lookup (WINS-R), you need only check Use WINS Reverse Lookup and configure the domain name for which this will be used.

After you have configured these options, your DNS server will be able to get supplemental name resolution services from the WINS server.

Adding Secondary Name Servers

If you add a secondary server to your domain, you can configure the primary server to send it updates. To do so, you must add the IP address of the secondary name server to the property sheet of the primary name server. To do this, perform the following steps:

25

CONFIGURING
TCP/IP FOR
WINDOWS NT

1. Right-click your zone and choose Properties.

2. Next, click the Notify tab and enter the secondary server's IP address(es) to the Notify List.

3. After this is complete, the primary server will automatically update the secondary server.

FTP and HTTP Services

In Windows NT Server versions prior to Windows NT 4, Microsoft shipped an individually installable FTP server. In Windows NT 4, the FTP server is part of the *Internet Information Server* (IIS) product. The IIS version that ships with Windows NT 4 is called IIS 2.0, but the latest independent version of IIS is version 4. With IIS 4, you can install an HTTP and FTP server. The HTTP server provides support for Web clients over the HTTP 1.1 protocol. Microsoft calls its HTTP support the WWW Publishing Service because it is used to publish Web pages and sites on the Internet. The FTP server is also part of the IIS 4 and later products, and you can use it to share files to FTP clients on the Internet.

IIS is tightly integrated in the Windows NT environment and the FTP and WWW services appear in the Control Panel Services applet when they are installed. You can also manage the services via the *Microsoft Management Console* (MMC), which can be launched from the Start Menu, Programs, Administrative Tools section.

TCP/IP Printing Services

Windows NT can provide TCP/IP Printing services to Microsoft and Unix clients on the network. Installation of a TCP/IP Printing device has several steps. First, you must install the TCP/IP Printing Service from the Network dialog box Services tab. Then, you must configure an LPR port via the Printers folders.

Installing TCP/IP Printing Services

To install the TCP/IP Printing service from Microsoft, follow these steps:

1. Right-click the Network Neighborhood icon, and then choose Properties.

2. Click the Services tab on the Network dialog box.

3. Click the Add button on the Services tab.

4. Select Microsoft TCP/IP Printing from the list of network services.

5. Click the OK button to install the service.

6. Confirm or enter the path to the Windows NT Server installation files and click Continue.

7. Click Close on the Network dialog box and reboot as requested.

Installing LPR Services

After you have installed the Microsoft TCP/IP Printing service, you must still configure your printer to provide LPR services on the printer port. Follow these steps to install LPR printing services:

1. Choose Printers from the Start Menu (Start, Settings, Printers).

2. Double-click the Add Printer icon, unless you already have a printer installed. (If you already have a printer installed, right-click the icon for your printer, choose Properties, and then select Ports. Skip to step 4.)

3. Ensure that the My Computer radio button is selected, and then click the Next button. (By doing this you are indicating that your system will be the printer server.)

4. Click the Add Port button.

5. Select LPR Port from the list of available ports, and then click the New Port button.

6. Enter the IP address of your server in the top text box.

7. Enter a name for your LPR printer. This can be any name, but making it the same name as the printer would be wise.

8. Click OK to confirm the installation. If you see an error message that the printer cannot be contacted, click OK. (If you already have a printer installed, click the OK button, and the process is complete.)

9. Choose the correct manufacturer and printer from the list and click OK.

10. Click the Shared radio button to make this printer available to other clients on the network. Then enter the name under which it will be shared. It is wise to use the same name for the printer, the share, and the LPR queue, which is the default.

11. Click the Next button to continue.

12. Decide whether or not you would like to print a test page by choosing the corresponding radio button. Then, click the Finish button.

13. You may need to map the path to your Windows NT installation files and click the OK button. You should then see your printer appear in the Printers folder.

You can print to the TCP/IP Printing device using an LPR printing client. This is common on Unix operating systems. Microsoft also provides an LPR client for Windows NT. To learn the syntax of the LPR command, open a command prompt and type **LPR** /?.

25

CONFIGURING
TCP/IP FOR
WINDOWS NT

If you wanted to print your BOOT.INI file on an LPR printer named LPRPRINT, which resided on an NT Server named NTSERV, you would issue the following command:

```
lpr -S NTSERV -P LPRPRINT -d BOOT.INI
```

Be careful when issuing the command because the names are not case sensitive, but the switches (-S, -P, and -d) are.

Summary

Windows NT uses NetBIOS over Microsoft TCP/IP to provide compatibility with other IP networks. The Microsoft TCP/IP Architecture is consistent between Windows 98 and Windows NT version 4. Microsoft TCP/IP clients use both NetBIOS computer names and hostnames to provide compatibility with the Internet and other TCP/IP networks, as well as Microsoft networks.

Network computer names, services, adapters, bindings, and protocols are configured and managed via the Network dialog box. You can install the TCP/IP protocol suite via the Protocols tab on the Network dialog box. After you have added the protocol, you can double-click its icon on the Protocols tab to configure the TCP/IP options.

On the Identification tab of the TCP/IP Properties dialog box, you can configure the IP address, subnet mask, and default gateway. On the DNS tab you can set the hostname, which should be the same as your NetBIOS computer name (located on the Identification tab of the Network dialog box). You can also configure your DNS domain name, the DNS servers to be used for name resolution, and the order in which names should be resolved. The WINS tab allows you to configure the address of a Primary and Secondary WINS server to provide NetBIOS name resolution. You can also decide whether your system will use an LMHOSTS file and/or DNS to resolve NetBIOS names. The DHCP Relay tab allows your system to relay DHCP requests to remote segments passing through RFC 1542 non-compliant routers. You must install the DHCP Relay Agent before this feature will be operational. You can also enable IP routing via the Enable IP Routing check box on the Microsoft TCP/IP Properties dialog box Routing tab.

Windows NT Server can also provide DHCP and Microsoft TCP/IP printing services. These items can be installed via the Network dialog box Services tab. To configure DHCP services, you must use the DHCP Manager after the service is installed. To configure the TCP/IP printer, you must enable an LPR port via the Printers folder after installing the Microsoft TCP/IP Printing service.

Windows 2000 promises the end of NetBIOS over TCP/IP. The sole naming convention required for Windows 2000 will be Internet-style hostnames. The administrative structure will also be changed and Dynamic DNS will be added.

Configuring TCP/IP
for Windows 2000

by Karanjit S. Siyan, Ph.D.

IN THIS CHAPTER

This chapter addresses how the network components and TCP/IP protocols are installed and configured on Windows. Windows 2000 workstations are also covered. Normally TCP/IP should be installed during the installation of network services when installing the operating system. However, in some situations a standalone computer must connect with a network after the addition of suitable networking hardware. In this case you must explicitly install TCP/IP software.

This chapter also teaches you how to configure the TCP/IP stack to make use of name services such as Windows Internet Naming Service (WINS) and Domain Name System (DNS).

Installing TCP/IP

A Windows 2000 installation automatically includes the TCP/IP protocol stack if you choose to install any network services. This section discusses the procedures for installing and configuring the Windows 2000 TCP/IP protocol stack. You must install the TCP/IP protocol stack manually only if you have previously removed it but now need to add support for TCP/IP services. Follow these steps:

1. Log on to the Windows 2000 computer as an Administrator user.
2. Select Start, Settings, Network and Dial-Up connections. Right-click on Local Area Network and choose Properties. The Local Area Connection Properties dialog box appears (see Figure 26.1). Alternatively, you can right-click on My Network Neighborhood and choose Properties. Then right-click on Local Area Connection and choose Properties.
3. If you are reinstalling the TCP/IP protocol stack, click the Install button. The Select Network Component Type dialog box appears (see Figure 26.2). Select Protocol and click the Add button. You should see a list of protocols you can add from the Select Network Protocol screen.
4. Select TCP/IP Protocol and choose OK.
5. Complete the remaining procedure as instructed onscreen.

The TCP/IP protocol is now installed. Your next step is to configure at least the basic TCP/IP settings.

Configuring TCP/IP for Windows 2000

CHAPTER 26

635

26

CONFIGURING
TCP/IP FOR
WINDOWS 2000

FIGURE 26.1

The Local Area Connection Properties dialog box.

FIGURE 26.2

The Select Network Component Type dialog box.

Configuring the IP Address

Every network interface the TCP/IP protocol stack communicates with is described by a set of IP parameters. These parameters include the IP address, subnet mask, default gateway, and IP address of name servers—the domain name settings. You must specify, at minimum, the IP address and subnet mask settings for each network interface.

You can set IP parameters in two ways: manually or automatically. Setting IP parameters manually (also called *statically*) requires that you keep a proper log of the IP address parameter settings for each computer and that each network interface is assigned a unique IP address. Making mistakes in setting IP parameters is easy if you are not careful, and these mistakes can be costly in terms of the time required to troubleshoot the settings. For this reason, many networks prefer the automatic way of setting IP parameters from a central server, such as a DHCP server.

If you're not using DHCP to assign a TCP/IP address to the Windows 2000 Server dynamically, the Internet Protocol (TCP/IP) Properties dialog box appears (see Figure 26.3).

FIGURE 26.3

The Internet Protocol (TCP/IP) Properties dialog box.

You can also display this dialog box by highlighting the Internet Protocol (TCP/IP) in the Local Area Connection Properties dialog box. In this dialog box, you specify the IP address, subnet mask, and default gateway address of the network interface. The IP address, subnet mask, and default gateway parameter settings should be consistent with the network on which the Windows 2000 computer is connected. For example, if the network to which the Windows 2000 computer is connected is described by a network address of 192.120.12.0/255.255.255.255, the IP address setting for the computer on such a network is restricted to these IP addresses:

- 192.120.12.1 to 192.120.12.254
- With a subnet mask of 255.255.255.0

The default gateway should also have an IP address that is in this range, because it needs to be on the same network that the Windows 2000 computers connect to.

The IP address range described previously is the legal range of addresses for the network 192.120.12.0/255.255.255.0.

Follow these steps for configuring the IP address:

1. If a DHCP server is already on the network and you want to use it to configure the Windows 2000 computer, you should choose the Obtain an IP Address automatically option. A DHCP server contains TCP/IP configuration information for other TCP/IP hosts. When a TCP/IP host starts, it requests its configuration information from the DHCP server.

If you choose Obtain an IP Address automatically, the Windows 2000 computer obtains the IP address and subnet mask values from the DHCP server. If you enter values for the IP address and subnet mask, you effectively disable the DHCP client and will not download any information from the DHCP server.

If no DHCP server is yet on the network, or if you are installing the Windows 2000 server for use as a DHCP server, you must set the IP address and subnet mask manually. Enter the IP address and subnet mask for the Windows 2000 server's network interface as shown in Figure 26.3.

2. If your network is connected to other TCP/IP networks or subnetworks, you must specify a value for the Default Gateway field so that you can reach the other networks. TCP/IP recognizes whether the destination address is on another network and forwards the packet to the default gateway (or default router, correctly speaking). (The term *default gateway* is still used because historically the devices now known as routers were called gateways.)

3. If you have multiple network adapters, each must be configured individually. Specify the IP address configuration (IP address, subnet mask, default gateway, use of DHCP server) for each adapter bound to the TCP/IP protocol by selecting the network cards in the Adapter field one at a time.

4. Click the Advanced button if you want to configure multiple IP addresses for a single network adapter, multiple default gateways for a network adapter, or security options. Select the network adapter to configure from the Adapter field in the Advanced TCP/IP Settings dialog box (see Figure 26.4). Note that the IP configuration settings in this dialog box apply to only the selected network adapter. You can enter the WINS/DNS information in the advanced dialog box. The procedure for doing this task is discussed later in this chapter.

5. You can enter multiple IP addresses and subnet masks for the selected adapter by entering the IP address and subnet mask values in the IP Address and Subnet Mask boxes in the Advanced TCP/IP Settings dialog box (refer to Figure 26.4) and clicking the Add button.

Multiple IP addresses and subnet masks are particularly useful when you want a single physical system to look like several systems. The mail server might be 199.245.180.1, for example; the DNS server, 200.1.180.2; and the FTP server, 203.24.10.3. Also, multiple IP addresses and subnet masks can help during the transition to a different IP network number assignment for the network. You also can use multiple IP addresses if your network consists of multiple logical IP networks. During the transition phase, having both IP network numbers be applicable is useful.

FIGURE 26.4

The Advanced TCP/IP Settings dialog box.

6. If you must specify alternative default gateways, you can enter the IP addresses of the default gateways in the Default Gateways field in the Advanced TCP/IP Settings dialog box (refer to Figure 26.4) and choose the corresponding Add button.

The default gateway field is the IP address of a router on the local network. When a packet is sent to an IP address that is not on the local network and not specified in the local routing table at the Windows 2000 computer, the default gateway is used. If you have specified multiple default gateways, they are tried in the order in which they are listed if an attempt to use a particular gateway is unsuccessful. You can change the order in which the default gateways are tried by selecting a gateway's address and moving it using the Up and Down buttons.

Note

To remove an IP address and subnet mask combination, highlight it and click the Remove button.

Note

To remove a gateway, highlight it and choose the Remove button.

Configuring TCP/IP for Windows 2000

CHAPTER **26**

639

26

CONFIGURING
TCP/IP FOR
WINDOWS 2000

IP Address Assignment When DHCP Server Fails

The Windows 2000 DHCP client handles IP address assignment differently if a DHCP server cannot be found. If the Windows 2000 computer is installed to obtain an IP address automatically, the following steps occur:

1. When the client is installed, it attempts to locate a DHCP server. Many TCP/IP networks use DHCP servers that are administratively configured to lease IP addresses and set other information.

2. If the attempt to locate a DHCP server fails, the Windows 2000 DHCP client autoconfigures with a selected IP address from the IANA-reserved class B network of 169.254.0.0 with the subnet mask 255.255.0.0. This unregistered private address is registered to Microsoft. The DHCP client uses Address Resolution Protocol (ARP) to perform a Duplicate Address Test (DAT) to ensure that the IP address it has chosen is not already in use. If the address is in use, the client selects another IP address and tries again, as many as ten times. When the DHCP client has selected an address that is not in use, it configures the interface with this address. Meanwhile, it continues to check for a DHCP server in the background every five minutes. If a DHCP server is found, the autoconfiguration information is released, and the configuration offered by the DHCP server is used instead.

If the DHCP client has previously obtained a lease from a DHCP server, the following modified sequence of events occurs:

1. If the client's lease has not expired at boot time, the client tries to renew its lease with the DHCP server. If the client fails to locate a DHCP server during the renewal attempt, it tries to ping the default gateway, which is listed in the lease. If pinging the default gateway succeeds, the DHCP client assumes that it is still located on the same network where it obtained its current lease and continues to use the lease; but for some reason the DHCP server is unavailable. The client attempts to renew its lease in the background when half its assigned lease time has expired. The renewal attempt at half the lease interval is part of the standard DHCP operation.

2. If the attempt to ping the default gateway fails, the client assumes that it has been moved to a network that has no DHCP services available. It then autoconfigures itself as described previously using the 169.254.0.0/24 network. After the client is autoconfigured, it continues to try to locate a DHCP server every 5 minutes in the background.

Configuring the DNS Settings

Users can specify DNS names for computers that the Windows 2000 computers can resolve to their corresponding IP addresses. The Windows 2000 computers have a DNS client, also called the *name resolver*, that issues a request to the DNS server for resolving the DNS names. The Windows 2000 computers need to be configured with at least the IP address of one DNS server. Because name resolution is critical to the operation of Windows 2000 computers, you should have a secondary DNS server on the network in case the first DNS server is down.

If you want to configure Windows 2000 computers with addresses of DNS servers, select the DNS tab from the Microsoft TCP/IP Properties dialog box. DNS is the most commonly used name-resolution method on the Internet and other Unix-based networks. If you enable DNS name resolution, you must have a DNS server that the Windows 2000 computer can contact or have the Windows 2000 computer configured as a DNS server. The Windows 2000 computer needs to know the IP address of the DNS server. The IP address of the DNS server is specified on the TCP/IP DNS tab. This section discusses the DNS client software.

If you are using DHCP servers for setting the IP parameters, you can also use DHCP to configure DNS settings for the Windows clients.

When accessing other TCP/IP hosts on the network, you can use their IP addresses. Users typically find it easier to remember and use symbolic names for computers rather than IP addresses. This is why the computer names usually are used for Windows 2000 computers rather than just IP addresses. The DNS is used for naming TCP/IP nodes, such as Windows 2000 computers and Unix hosts. The naming scheme is hierarchical and consists of names such as wks1.kinetics.com or wks2.cello.org. DNS is the most widely used name service for Unix hosts and on the Internet. If you plan to use your Windows 2000 computer on a Unix network or the Internet, you should configure your Windows 2000 computer to use DNS. TCP/IP applications written to use the Windows Sockets API (such as Internet Explorer, File Transfer Protocol [FTP], and Telnet) use DNS or the local HOSTS file to resolve symbolic names.

When TCP/IP is installed on a Windows 2000 computer, the DNS client software for resolving DNS names is also installed. The DNS client software is, in addition to dynamic name resolution, used for resolving NetBIOS computer names through WINS servers and NetBIOS over TCP/IP. When you configure DNS on a Windows 2000 computer, it applies to all network adapters installed on the computer.

The following steps outline the procedure to follow in configuring your Windows 2000 computer to use DNS client software:

1. Select the DNS tab from the Advanced TCP/IP Settings dialog box (refer to Figure 26.4). The DNS tab is displayed (see Figure 26.5).

FIGURE 26.5

The DNS tab in the Advanced TCP/IP Settings dialog box.

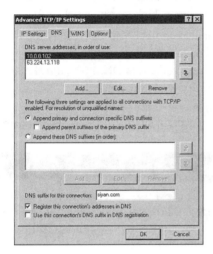

2. Click the Add button to add the DNS server IP addresses. To change an IP address, click Edit; to remove an IP address from the DNS server list, click Remove. The purpose of this dialog box is to manually set one or more DNS servers. The DNS servers are identified by their IP addresses. The DNS client attempts to resolve DNS names by contacting the first DNS server on the list. If the DNS name cannot be resolved, it tries to contact the second client, and so on, until all the DNS servers have been tried. You can change the order of the DNS servers by clicking the up and down buttons.

The next three settings apply to all TCP/IP connections and deal with the resolution of unqualified domain names.

The Append primary and connection specific DNS suffixes option is used to specify that unqualified domain names will have the parent DNS domain name appended. If the name of the computer is NTWS1 and the parent domain name is KINETICS.COM, the host name that is searched for is NTWS1.KINETICS.COM. With this option the name is searched for in only the parent domain. If the host name cannot be resolved, no further searches for the name are performed.

The purpose of the Append these DNS suffixes (in order) option is used to specify a list of DNS suffixes that can be appended to the unqualified domain name in order to resolve it. If you need to change the search order of the domain suffixes, highlight the domain name and use the up and down buttons to move the domain name. To remove a domain name, highlight it on the list and click the Remove button. To edit a domain name suffix, highlight it and click Edit.

In the DNS suffix for this connection field, you can specify the DNS suffix to be used for this connection. You have the additional options of setting the option labeled Register this connection's address in DNS, which makes a host entry for this IP address and the connection's DNS name with the DNS server. When you register this DNS name, you can use the DNS suffix with the host name by enabling the option labeled Use this connection's DNS suffix in DNS registration.

Optional Domain Name

The domain name is optional because a small organization not connected to the Internet doesn't need to use hierarchical domain names. As shown here, the domain name is combined with the host name to create a fully qualified domain name (FQDN) for the computer:

FQDN = host name + domain name

The FQDN for host NTWS1 is the following in the domain name KINETICS.COM:

FQDN = NTWS1 + KINETICS.COM = NTWS1.KINETICS.COM

When the Windows 2000 computer uses a DNS query to resolve a name that is a simple host name without the domain extension, the domain name specified in the Domain Name field is appended to the host name.

The domain name can be any combination of A to Z letters, 0 to 9 digits, and the hyphen (-), using the period (.) character as a separator.

Note

Host name to IP address mappings are stored on DNS servers. The Berkeley r-utilities, such as rcp, rsh, and rexec, use the host names for authentication. In host names, you cannot use some characters that you can use in Windows 2000 computer names, particularly the underscore. If you are connected to the Internet, you should use registered DNS names.

Configuring TCP/IP for Windows 2000

CHAPTER 26

643

26

CONFIGURING
TCP/IP FOR
WINDOWS 2000

Figure 26.6 shows a sample DNS configuration for the host NTS. The local domain name is SIYAN.COM. The DNS servers are 10.0.0.102 and 63.224.13.118. First, the DNS server with IP address 10.0.0.102 is used to resolve a name. If this server can't resolve the name to its IP address, the DNS server at 63.224.13.118 is used. The domain suffix search order is SIYAN.COM, KINETICS.COM, and SCS.COM. In some earlier Windows clients (Windows 95 without Winsock2 and Windows NT earlier than SP5), the DNS resolver contacts the second DNS server only if the first DNS server does not respond. On these clients, if the first DNS server cannot resolve a name, the client does not try to resolve the name using the second DNS server.

FIGURE 26.6

Sample DNS settings in the Advanced TCP/IP Settings dialog box.

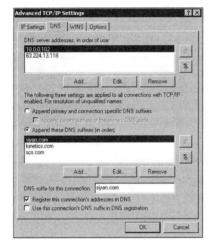

3. Click OK after you set the DNS configuration options.

Windows 2000 DNS implements negative caching. If a DNS server cannot resolve the query, succeeding queries for that name are answered negatively for a duration specified by the Registry parameter NegativeCacheTime (a default of 300 seconds).

Configuring the WINS Address

If you have Windows Internet Name Services (WINS) servers installed on the network, you can use WINS servers in combination with name query broadcasts to resolve computer names. The WINS server is an example of a NetBIOS Name Server (NBNS) type of server used for resolving NetBIOS names, as per the rules specified in RFC 1001 and RFC 1002.

Windows 2000 clients and Windows NT, Windows 95, and Windows 98 clients with the Active Directory upgrade installed no longer need to use the NETBIOS namespace. WINS is still required for down-level clients to find servers and vice-versa. When no more down-level clients are in the enterprise, the WINS servers can be turned off. Down-level clients are Windows 95, Windows 98, and Windows NT clients.

If you are not using the WINS server, the Windows 2000 computer uses name query broadcasts and the local LMHOSTS file to resolve computer names to IP addresses. Broadcast resolution is confined to the local network. The name query broadcasts use the b-node for NetBIOS over TCP/IP.

To configure the WINS address, follow these steps:

1. To specify that you are using WINS servers, enter the IP addresses of the primary and other backup secondary WINS servers on the WINS tab of the Advanced TCP/IP Settings dialog box (see Figure 26.7). The secondary WINS server is used as a backup in case the primary WINS server cannot respond. Select Add to add the WINS IP addresses. Use the up and down arrow keys to change the order the WINS servers are searched.

Figure 26.7

The WINS tab in the Advanced TCP/IP Settings dialog box.

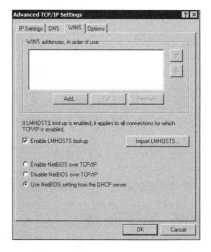

2. You can use the local file LMHOSTS for resolving NetBIOS computer names on Windows networks. If you want to use the LMHOSTS file, enable the Enable LMHOSTS Lookup check box. You can import computer names and IP addresses from an existing LMHOSTS file by clicking the Import LMHOSTS button and specifying the directory path for the LMHOSTS file. You can use the Import LMHOSTS option when you have already created an LMHOSTS file for the computer names on your network and want to use the information in this file for all computers on the network.

Configuring TCP/IP for Windows 2000

CHAPTER 26

645

26

CONFIGURING
TCP/IP FOR
WINDOWS 2000

3. If a computer is configured to use DHCP, you can specify whether NetBIOS settings will be taken from the DHCP server by setting the option Use NetBIOS setting from the DHCP server.

4. You can set the options Enable NetBIOS over TCP/IP or Disable NetBIOS over TCP/IP. These options do just what they sound like. The operation of NetBIOS over TCP/IP is described in RFCs 1001 and 1002. Applications that use the Winsock interface do not need NetBIOS, and you can safely disable this option. Newer applications are directly hosted on TCP/IP, which means that they are written to use the TCP/IP stack directly without involving NetBIOS. The Windows 2000 services use DNS to resolve names and do not need NetBIOS name resolution. On a pure Windows 2000 network that does not use any NetBIOS-specific applications, you can disable NetBIOS over TCP/IP. Disabling it has the advantage of less network traffic caused by NetBIOS. Also, the Windows 2000 computer does not have to expend resources supporting the NetBIOS protocol.

> **Note**
>
> By default the LMHOSTS file is in the \%SystemRoot%\SYSTEM32\DRIVERS\ETC directory. If you are using a WINS server, the LMHOSTS file is consulted last after trying the WINS server. Using LMHOSTS files works well for Windows networks that have a small number of computers and for networks that do not experience many changes, although using LMHOSTS files is problematic for larger, more dynamic networks. Keeping all the different computers' LMHOSTS files in sync becomes difficult on a larger network, and creating situations in which two computers (even ones sitting next to each other) might have different views of the network becomes all too easy. Also if you are using DHCP to assign IP addresses, the IP address specified in the LMHOSTS file might not be valid for a specified host that might be on a different subnet.

Configuring the DHCP Relay in Windows NT

> **Note**
>
> Although most of the tabs in the Windows 2000 Advanced TCP/IP Settings dialog box are similar to those for Windows NT, they have some differences. Notably, Windows NT has the DHCP Relay tab and the Routing tab. In Windows 2000, the DHCP relay and routing functions are configured using the Routing and Remote Access tool. If you have down-level computers in a mixed-mode domain (Windows 2000 and Windows NT 4 computers in a domain) environment, this section and the next one are useful.

IP Security and Filtering

Windows 2000 provides IP security and filtering for the TCP/IP protocol. To access these capabilities, access the Options tab in the Advanced TCP/IP Settings dialog box (see Figure 26.8) by clicking the Advanced button in the Internet Protocol (TCP/IP) properties. You get to the Internet Protocol (TCP/IP) Properties dialog box by highlighting the Internet Protocol (TCP/IP) in the Local Area Network properties and clicking Properties.

FIGURE 26.8

The Options tab in the Advanced TCP/IP Settings dialog box.

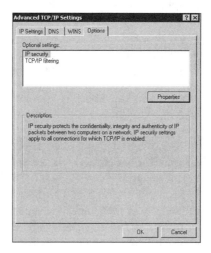

The IP Security option protects the confidentiality, integrity, and authenticity of IP packets between two computers on a network. These security settings apply to all connections for which TCP/IP has been enabled. Highlight the IP Security option, click the Properties button, and on the IP Security screen (see Figure 26.9), select the Use this IP security policy button. Your choices are Client (Respond Only), Secure Server (Request Security), and Server (Request Security).

Note

You might want to disable routing when connected to multiple networks if the Windows NT and Windows 2000 server is performing an important function (such as being a Web server), and you do not want it to use CPU cycles to deal with other tasks that you already have other systems dedicated to performing.

You should also disable routing on firewalls and proxy servers. You do not want the packets to bypass the firewall or proxy software that subjects the packet to the network security policy. If routing is enabled, the packets could be forwarded by the router regardless of any restrictions on the packet placed by the firewall/proxy software.

FIGURE 26.9

The IP Security screen.

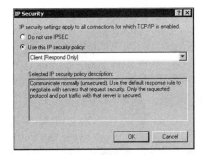

The Client (Respond Only) option communicates normally in an unsecured session. If the server requests IP security, then the requested protocol and port traffic with that server will be secured.

The Secure Server (Request Security) option requires that security on IP traffic be enabled using Kerberos trust. Untrusted communication with unsecured clients is not permitted. Because many hosts on the Internet are not enabled for Kerberos trust, using the Secure Server (Request Security) option effectively disables communication with the majority of hosts on the Internet.

The Server (Request Security) option requests that security on IP traffic be enabled using Kerberos trust. Untrusted communications with unsecured clients is permitted with clients that do not respond to the request.

To configure TCP/IP filtering, highlight it on the Options tab in the Advanced TCP/IP Settings dialog box and click Properties. The TCP/IP Filtering screen appears (see Figure 26.10). Set the Enable TCP/IP Filtering (All adapters) option. The default is to permit all TCP ports, User Datagram Protocol (UDP) ports, and IP protocols. To permit connections on only specific TCP ports, UDP ports, or IP protocols, check the appropriate Permit only option. Click the Add button and add the TCP port, UDP port, or IP protocol to the permitted list.

FIGURE 26.10

The TCP/IP Filtering screen.

Setting up filtering is appropriate if you want to accept traffic for only some well-defined services with specific port numbers. You can find the official port and protocol numbers in the RFC 1700, "Assigned Numbers." By default, all TCP ports, UDP ports, and the IP protocol are enabled, which means that the Windows 2000 computer accepts packets destined to any TCP or UDP port in an IP packet. To change the default values, select the option Permit Only and use the Add and Remove buttons to edit the criteria for filtering IP packets.

Configuring Name Resolution Services in Windows 2000

In the previous section you learned how to specify the Windows Internet Name Service (WINS) server and Domain Name System (DNS) server in the Internet Protocol (IP) configuration parameters for Windows 2000 computers. WINS and DNS servers are used for resolving names on a Windows network. Two additional files, LMHOSTS and HOSTS, are useful in configuring name resolution. For small networks that do not have a WINS or DNS server, you can use the LMHOSTS and HOSTS files for name resolution because they can be edited using a text editor to provide name-to-IP-address mappings.

Another point to note is that network basic input output system (NetBIOS) name resolution using WINS is not needed in pure Windows 2000 networks (native mode) that use DNS for name resolution instead. However, in mixed-mode networks consisting of Windows 2000 and Windows NT computers, you might need to provide NetBIOS name resolution for older clients, which is the primary reason for discussing NetBIOS name resolution in this chapter.

NetBIOS Services

NetBIOS provides name services, datagram services, and session services (see Table 26.1). When NetBIOS is run over Transmission Control Protocol (TCP), the name and datagram services use ports 137 and 138 of the User Datagram Protocol (UDP) Transport Layer protocol. The session services use port 139 of the TCP Transport Layer protocol. Name and datagram services use UDP because the nature of the traffic generated by these services tends to be request-reply oriented. Also, name services make frequent use of broadcasts to resolve names, and UDP is better suited than TCP for handling broadcasts. On large networks, broadcasts can be a problem because they can lead to broadcast storms. For this reason, many routers are configured by default to block broadcasts. The procedure for configuring a router to block broadcasts is router specific.

Configuring TCP/IP for Windows 2000

CHAPTER 26

649

26

CONFIGURING
TCP/IP FOR
WINDOWS 2000

TABLE 26.1 NetBIOS Services

Service Name	Port	Protocol	Short Name
NetBIOS Name Service	137	UDP	nbname
NetBIOS Datagram Service	138	UDP	Nbdatagram
NetBIOS Session Service	139	TCP	Nbsession

The session services in NetBIOS use TCP; TCP guarantees data delivery, whereas UDP does not. Also, the model of a TCP session more accurately reflects the behavior of a NetBIOS session. Both TCP and NetBIOS issue open primitives to open a connection and the close primitive to close a connection.

A given computer can have several processes. Processes that provide services are *application services*. Some of these application services are registered as NetBIOS names. Windows 2000 allows as many as 250 NetBIOS names to be registered on a computer. Some examples of application services on a Windows computer are

- Server Service—Identifies the application service that is running; typically refers to the service that allows the sharing of files and printers on the computer.

- Workstation Service—Enables a workstation to act as a client and use services provided by the server service on another computer.

- Messenger Service—Receives and displays messages for names registered on the computer.

The maximum length of NetBIOS names is 16 characters. The first 15 characters specify the NetBIOS name, and the last character is a byte that specifies the type of the NetBIOS name. This 1-byte identifier can have a value from 0 to 255. The following list shows the names of some services that can be registered (the numbers in brackets are the hexadecimal values of the 1-byte identifiers):

- Computername[0x00]—The Workstation service registered for the computer
- Computername[0x03]—The Messenger service registered for the computer
- Computername[0x06]—The remote access service (RAS) Server Service registered for the computer
- Computername[0x1F]—The NetDDE Service registered for the computer
- Computername[0x20]—The Server service registered for the computer
- Computername[0x21]—The RAS Client service registered for the computer
- Computername[0xBE]—The Network Monitor Agent service registered for the computer

- Computername[0xBF]—The Network Monitor Application service registered for the computer
- Domainname[0x00]—Registers the computer as a member of the domain name or workgroup
- Domainname[0x1E]—Used to facilitate browser elections
- Domainname[0x1B]—Registers the computer as the domain master browser

> **Note**
>
> Initially NetBIOS referred to computer names only. There was only a single user for a computer. A message sent to the computer was received by the sole user on the computer.
>
> As networks grew large with many users, NetBIOS names were added for the user and the workgroup or domain. The NetBIOS username allowed a user to receive a message. If more than one instance of the username existed (if the user logged in several times), only the first username that was registered received the message.
>
> The workgroup or domain name was added in order to group different systems under a common name to provide easier browsing, manageability, and domain security in the Windows NT domain model. These group names are registered as NetBIOS names on the network.
>
> In Windows 2000, NetBIOS is still used when you are using mixed-mode domains that include Windows NT domains and computers. This is the reason NetBIOS is discussed in this section.
>
> In a native Windows 2000 domain, there is no need to configure or use NetBIOS because name resolution is performed using DNS.

Because Active Directory in Windows 2000 is self-configuring, no additional configuration needs to be done. However, Active Directory does depend on DNS, which must be configured separately.

- Domainname[0x1C]—Registers the computer as a domain controller
- Domainname[0x1D]—Registers the computer as the local subnetwork's master browser
- Username[0x03]—The username registered by the messenger for the logged-on username
- Group—The group name
- \\-__MSBROWSE__[01h]—The master browser

Configuring TCP/IP for Windows 2000

CHAPTER 26

651

26

CONFIGURING
TCP/IP FOR
WINDOWS 2000

For example, consider that user Phylos on Windows 2000 Professional workstation WS1 in domain KINETD wants to retrieve files from a Windows 2000 server named ADS, using the universal naming convention (UNC) name of the file, \\ADS\sharename. The username "Phylos [0x03]" uses the workstation service with NetBIOS name "WS1 [0x00]" to be first authenticated by the domain controller with the NetBIOS name "KINETD [0x1C]." After the authentication, the workstation service "WS1 [0x00]" communicates with the server service "ADS [0x20]" to retrieve files.

Types of Name Resolution Methods

Windows 2000 name resolution methods can be grouped into these categories:

- Standard resolution, sometimes called host name resolution
- Specific resolution, sometimes called NBT NetBIOS name resolution

These methods are discussed in the following sections.

Standard Resolution

The standard resolution method is used by Unix systems and software ported from Unix to the Windows environment. The standard resolution method is performed in this order:

1. Local hostname
2. Using the HOSTS file
3. Using DNS
4. NetBIOS name resolution, if DNS fails

The local host is the name of the locally configured machine. The name to be resolved is first checked to determine whether it is the name of the local machine.

> **Note**
>
> In Windows 2000, DNS name resolution is performed by the DNS Client service. This service implements the DNS resolver, which issues the Windows socket calls `gethostbyname()` and `getnamebyhost()`.

If the name to be resolved is not that of the local machine, the HOSTS file is consulted. The HOSTS file is a table of mappings of IP addresses and hostnames. The format of the HOSTS file is taken from the 4.3 Berkeley Software Distribution (BSD) Unix HOSTS file. The HOSTS file is consulted by applications such as Telnet, FTP, and ping.

The HOSTS file is not kept at a central location. Instead, each computer is required to maintain its own HOSTS file. If it is to be changed for the network, it must be changed on all computers on the network.

If the name to be resolved is not found in the HOSTS file, a name query is sent to the DNS server. The DNS servers hold, among other things, the name-to-IP-address mappings in a distributed database on the network. Most DNS servers on the Internet are Unix based, although DNS implementations are available on platforms, such as Windows 2000.

Specific Resolution

The specific resolution method is unique to Windows networks. It consists of a combination of these methods:

- Local broadcast
- WINS
- LMHOSTS file

The local broadcast is a broadcast request sent on the local network requesting the IP address of the name that is to be resolved. The computer that recognizes its name in the broadcast request responds with its IP address. If no such computer exists, no response to the broadcast is received and the local broadcast is unable to resolve the name to its IP address. The local broadcast is also called the broadcast node (b-node) name resolution method.

The WINS is an example of a NetBIOS Name Server (NBNS). The most common example of NBNS is the WINS implementation on Windows NT and Windows 2000 servers. NBNS name resolution is specified by Request for Comments (RFCs) 1001 and 1002.

> **Note**
>
> Hosts files are not commonly used on most networks, but are used on very small networks. DNS is more commonly used for name resolution for TCP/IP applications.

> **Note**
>
> Before doing name resolution, a check is made if the NetBIOS name being resolved is a local name, in which case no name resolution needs to be done.
>
> The results of previous name queries are stored in the name cache. Before performing a name resolution, a check is also made to see whether the answer is already in the name cache—if it is, the name resolution is not attempted.

Configuring TCP/IP for Windows 2000

CHAPTER 26

653

26
CONFIGURING
TCP/IP FOR
WINDOWS 2000

The LMHOSTS file is a table of mappings between IP addresses and NetBIOS names. The structure of the LMHOSTS file is similar to the HOSTS file, with the added distinction that it contains a number of additional directives to make name resolution configuration easier. Windows 2000 checks the LMHOSTS file only when other name resolution methods fail.

The exact order in which the specific name resolution method is implemented depends on the name resolution configuration for the Windows 2000 computer. These name resolution methods include b-node, peer node (p-node), mixed node (m-node), and hybrid node (h-node). The following list describes each method:

- In the b-node name resolution, only broadcast packets are used for name registration and resolution. Because broadcasts can quickly flood the network, this name resolution mode is best for small local networks that do not have a WINS server. To configure your network to use this mode, ensure that no WINS servers are on the network and that the Windows computers are configured to not use WINS. That is, for the Windows client computers, ensure that you do not specify the IP address of a WINS server.

- The p-node name resolution uses WINS servers exclusively to resolve names. If the name cannot be resolved using WINS, other name resolution methods are not attempted.

- The m-node name resolution is a combination of b-node and p-node methods. First, the b-node name resolution method is attempted. If the b-node fails, the client resorts to using p-node name resolution. This method tends to generate broadcast traffic first and then attempt WINS resolution. It is suitable for small networks that have a WINS server and where it is known that the WINS server's database has not been updated for some time with new hostname entries.

Note

LMHOSTS files are not commonly used on most networks, but are used on very small networks. DNS is more commonly used for name resolution for TCP/IP applications.

Note

B-node broadcasts work only on local subnets unless the connecting routers to other subnets are enabled to forward broadcasts.

Note

Note that in the p-node and b-node methods, either the p-node or b-node method is attempted. If these methods fail, the other methods, such as LMHOSTS, are still attempted.

Note

You could use this node type for small regional offices on the far side of a WAN link, if they have local resources or servers.

- The h-node name resolution is also a combination of b-node and p-node methods. However, this method first tries the p-node name resolution. If the p-node method fails, the client resorts to using b-node name resolution. This method tends to generate broadcast traffic as a last resort because the first attempt is to contact a WINS server. This method, the most efficient, is suitable for larger networks that have a reliable WINS server and in which it is known that the WINS server's database has been updated with new hostname entries.

Configuring the NetBIOS Name Cache

A Windows 2000 computer requesting name resolution first consults a special area in memory, the NetBIOS name cache. This data area contains a list of computer names and their IP addresses. Because this information is cached in memory, found information is quickly retrieved. The name cache entries come from two sources:

- Answers to resolved name queries
- Preloading of the name cache from the LMHOSTS file using the #PRE directive

With the exception of the preloaded name cache entries, all other entries are timed out and flushed from the cache. The default timeout period is ten minutes. Readers familiar with the Address Resolution Protocol (ARP) will recognize that the NetBIOS name cache acts in a similar manner.

To purge and reload the name cache, you can use this command:

```
Nbtstat -R
```

The -R option is case sensitive. Another option, -r, is used for displaying name resolution statistics.

Configuring TCP/IP for Windows 2000

CHAPTER 26

655

26

CONFIGURING
TCP/IP FOR
WINDOWS 2000

The two Registry entries that can be used to configure the name cache parameters are under this Registry key:

```
HKEY_LOCAL_MACHINE\SYSTEM\CurrentControlSet\Services\NetBT\Parameters
```

> **Note**
>
> For small networks with low network traffic and a lack of qualified administrators, using the b-node method for name resolution is adequate.
>
> For larger networks, the h-node method is the most efficient because it tries direct name resolution using WINS first (p-node). Only when WINS fails to resolve the name is the b-node method attempted. For a properly configured WINS server, the h-node method generates the least amount of network traffic.

The name cache entries are

- Size/Small/Medium/Large. This entry is used to specify the number of names kept in the name cache. The settings are for small, medium, and large. Small corresponds to a value of 1 and sets the name size cache to 16 names. Medium corresponds to a value of 2 and sets the name size cache to 64 names. Large corresponds to a value of 3 and sets the name size cache to 128 names. The default value is 1, which is adequate for many networks. The parameter type is REG_DWORD.

- CacheTimeout. This entry is used to specify the number of seconds an entry will remain in the name cache. The default value is 0x927c0 (600,000 seconds, or ten minutes), which is adequate for many networks. The parameter type is REG_DWORD.

These parameter entries and others for NetBT are shown in Figure 26.11. Note that if a Registry parameter value is not listed, its default value is taken.

Configuring the Name Broadcasts

If the name resolution process does not find the name to be resolved in the name cache, it might send a broadcast if it is configured as b-node, m-node, or h-node. NetBIOS broadcasts a Name Query packet to the local network on UDP port 137 (refer to Table 26.1). Every computer on the local subnet processes the broadcast packet. If a computer on the network is configured for the NetBIOS over TCP/IP (NetBT) protocol, the NetBIOS module in the computer receives the broadcast. The NetBIOS module compares the name request with the name of the registered NetBIOS names. If there is a match, the NetBIOS module sends a Positive Name Query Response packet.

FIGURE 26.11

NetBT Parameters entry keys.

Receiving more than one response indicates a duplicate NetBIOS name, which is reported on the computer console of the computer that receives the response. It is interesting to note that the Name Query broadcast is processed by every computer up to the Session Layer, whether or not the computer has the answer. Therefore, the broadcast not only generates network traffic but also results in wasted central processing unit (CPU) cycles on many computers.

The two Registry entries that can be used to configure the name query broadcast parameters are under this Registry key:

```
HKEY_LOCAL_MACHINE\SYSTEM\CurrentControlSet\Services\NetBT\Parameters
```

The broadcast entries are

- BcastNameQueryCount. This entry is used to specify the number of times the system tries to send a Name Query broadcast. The default value is 3, which is adequate for networks with small to moderate network traffic loads. The parameter type is REG_DWORD.

- BcastQueryTimeout. This entry is used to specify the number of seconds to wait before retrying the Name Query broadcast. The default value is 7.5 seconds and is listed in 1/100-second intervals. The parameter type is REG_DWORD.

Configuring the LMHOSTS File

On small Windows 2000 networks (with as many as 30 computers) that use NetBIOS over TCP/IP, the name resolution for computer names typically is provided by the b-node method or the LMHOSTS file. If you have WINS servers on the networks, it is not necessary to use the LMHOSTS file, except as a backup. The use of LMHOSTS is adequate for small networks, where maintaining the LMHOSTS file is a simple task. On larger networks, however, keeping the LMHOSTS files updated can become a laborious task, and you should consider other name resolution techniques, such as DNS or WINS.

> **Note**
>
> If network traffic loads are consistently high and you see repetitions of the same unresolved NetBIOS name query, you should consider increasing the BcastNameQueryCount and BcastQueryTimeout parameters. For the BcastQueryTimeout parameter, increase the value by 0.5 to 1 second; for the BcastNameQueryCount parameter, increase the value by 1. You can monitor network traffic by using a protocol analyzer tool, such as Network Monitor, which comes with Windows 2000 Server and System Management Server (SMS).

Understanding the Syntax of the LMHOSTS File

The LMHOSTS file contains mappings between Windows 2000 NetBIOS names and their IP addresses. The file is located in the %SystemRoot%\SYSTEM32\DRIVERS\ ETC directory and is compatible with the LMHOSTS file syntax used in Microsoft local area network (LAN) Manager 2.x.

The following is an example of the Windows 2000 LMHOSTS file that is installed on Windows 2000 computers:

```
# Copyright (c) 1993-1999 Microsoft Corp.
#
# This is a sample LMHOSTS file used by the Microsoft TCP/IP for Windows.
#
# This file contains the mappings of IP addresses to computernames
# (NetBIOS) names.  Each entry should be kept on an individual line.
# The IP address should be placed in the first column followed by the
# corresponding computername. The address and the computername
# should be separated by at least one space or tab. The "#" character
# is generally used to denote the start of a comment (see the exceptions
# below).
#
# This file is compatible with Microsoft LAN Manager 2.x TCP/IP lmhosts
# files and offers the following extensions:
#
```

```
#       #PRE
#       #DOM:<domain>
#       #INCLUDE <filename>
#       #BEGIN_ALTERNATE
#       #END_ALTERNATE
#       \0xnn (non-printing character support)
#
# Following any entry in the file with the characters "#PRE" will cause
# the entry to be preloaded into the name cache. By default, entries are
# not preloaded, but are parsed only after DNS fails.
#
# Following an entry with the "#DOM:<domain>" tag will associate the
# entry with the domain specified by <domain>. This affects how the
# browser and logon services behave in TCP/IP environments. To preload
# the host name associated with #DOM entry, it is necessary to also add a
# #PRE to the line. The <domain> is always preloaded although it will not
# be shown when the name cache is viewed.
#
# Specifying "#INCLUDE <filename>" will force the RFC NetBIOS (NBT)
# software to seek the specified <filename> and parse it as if it were
# local. <filename> is generally a UNC-based name, allowing a
# centralized lmhosts file to be maintained on a server.
# It is ALWAYS necessary to provide a mapping for the IP address of the
# server prior to the #INCLUDE. This mapping must use the #PRE directive.
# In addition the share "public" in the example below must be in the
# LanManServer list of "NullSessionShares" in order for client machines to
# be able to read the lmhosts file successfully. This key is under
# -\machine\system\currentcontrolset\services\lanmanserver\parameters\
Â nullsessionshares
# in the registry. Simply add "public" to the list found there.
#
# The #BEGIN_ and #END_ALTERNATE keywords allow multiple #INCLUDE
# statements to be grouped together. Any single successful include
# will cause the group to succeed.
#
# Finally, non-printing characters can be embedded in mappings by
# first surrounding the NetBIOS name in quotations, then using the
# \0xnn notation to specify a hex value for a non-printing character.
#
# The following example illustrates all of these extensions:
#
# 102.54.94.97    rhino          #PRE #DOM:networking  #net group's DC
# 102.54.94.102   "appname         \0x14"             #special app server
# 102.54.94.123   popular          #PRE               #source server
# 102.54.94.117   localsrv         #PRE               #needed for the include
#
# #BEGIN_ALTERNATE
# #INCLUDE \\localsrv\public\lmhosts
# #INCLUDE \\rhino\public\lmhosts
# #END_ALTERNATE
#
```

```
# In the above example, the "appname" server contains a special
# character in its name, the "popular" and "localsrv" server names are
# preloaded, and the "rhino" server name is specified so it can be used
# to later #INCLUDE a centrally maintained lmhosts file if the "localsrv"
# system is unavailable.
#
# Note that the whole file is parsed including comments on each lookup,
# so keeping the number of comments to a minimum will improve performance.
# Therefore it is not advisable to simply add lmhosts file entries onto the
# end of this file.
```

Comments are preceded with the # character. If the first several characters following # match any of the keywords explained in Table 26.2, the characters are treated as commands to perform special processing. Because the keywords are preceded with the comment character, the contents of the files are compatible with the syntax used by the HOSTS file. The HOSTS file is used by Windows Socket applications and Unix applications.

TABLE 26.2 LMHOSTS Keywords

Keyword	Description
#PRE	This keyword is added after an entry in LMHOSTS to preload the entry into the name cache. Entries that do not have a #PRE keyword are not preloaded into the name cache and are parsed only after WINS and Name Query broadcasts fail to resolve a name. You must preload entries that are added using the #INCLUDE statement. #PRE, therefore, must be appended for entries in the files referenced in #INCLUDE statements; otherwise, the entry is ignored.
#DOM: domain_name	This keyword is used to identify that the computer name is that of a domain controller. domain_name is the name of the Windows 2000 domain of which the computer is a domain controller. #DOM affects the behavior of the Browser and Logon services on a network consisting of network segments joined by routers.
#INCLUDE filename	The specified filename is processed for computer name mappings. The filename can use UNC names, which enables the mappings file to be on remote computers. If the computer referenced in the UNC name is outside the local broadcast region, you must include a mapping for the computer name in the LMHOSTS file so that the name can be found. You can add #PRE for the UNC computer name mapping to ensure that it is preloaded. Entries that appear in the INCLUDE file must be preloaded using the #PRE keyword, or else the entries are ignored.

TABLE 26.2 Continued

Keyword	Description
#BEGIN_ALTERNATE	This keyword is used to mark the beginning of a group of #INCLUDE statements. The name resolver attempts to use the #INCLUDE statements in the order in which they are listed. Any single successful attempt to use one of the #INCLUDE statements causes the group to succeed, in which case none of the other #INCLUDE statements in the group are processed. If none of the files in the #INCLUDE statement can be accessed, an event is added to the event log indicating that the inclusion failed. You can examine this event log by using the Event Viewer program.
#END_ALTERNATE	This keyword marks the end of the #INCLUDE block. Every #BEGIN_ALTERNATE must have a corresponding #END_ALTERNATE.
\0xnn	This keyword is the escape code for including nonprintable characters in NetBIOS names. The NetBIOS names that use this code must have quotes around the names. Use this code only for special device names and custom applications. When using this notation, remember that the NetBIOS name in quotes is padded with spaces if it is fewer than 16 characters.

Notice that the previous sample LMHOSTS file has this entry:

```
102.54.94.102    "appname    \0x14"   #special app server
```

Eight spaces of padding are between the name and the special character; the total length of the name is 16 characters.

The code 0x14 is the 1-byte identifier identifying the application service.

Understanding How the LMHOSTS File Is Processed

The LMHOSTS file is particularly useful if the network segment on which the Windows 2000 client resides does not have a WINS server. In this case, broadcast name resolution is used. Broadcast name resolution makes use of IP-level broadcast packets that are usually blocked by IP routers. The broadcast name resolution, therefore, never is transmitted beyond a router boundary. To solve this problem, Windows 2000 name resolution operates in the following manner when a WINS server is not specified:

1. Windows 2000 maintains a local cache of names that is initialized during system startup. The name cache is consulted first to see whether the name can be resolved. You can use the #PRE directive to load the name cache, as explained later in this chapter.

Configuring TCP/IP for Windows 2000
CHAPTER 26

661

26

CONFIGURING
TCP/IP FOR
WINDOWS 2000

2. If no matching entry is in the name cache, Windows 2000 uses network broadcasts to resolve names. The broadcast name resolution is called the b-node broadcast protocol and is documented in RFCs 1001 and 1002.

3. If broadcast name resolution fails, the LMHOSTS file is parsed and any matching entry is used.

4. If no matching entry is in the LMHOSTS file, name resolution fails and an error message is generated.

Figure 26.12 illustrates the name resolution for the LMHOSTS file.

FIGURE 26.12

LMHOSTS name resolution.

The name cache is initialized with entries that are marked with the #PRE keyword in the LMHOSTS file. For example, the LMHOSTS file could contain the following entries, with only some entries marked with the #PRE keyword:

144.19.74.1	uziel	
144.19.74.2	zadkiel	#PRE
144.19.74.3	gabriel	
144.19.74.4	uriel	
144.19.74.5	michael	#PRE
144.19.74.6	chamuel	

You might want to preload entries for hosts such as servers that are always expected to be up. By preloading these entries, the names are in the name cache, and it avoids rereading the file to perform name resolution.

In this LMHOSTS file, the mappings for host zadkiel and michael are preloaded into the name cache on system startup. If the Windows 2000 computer needs to resolve the names zadkiel and michael, no broadcast packets are generated because the name cache provides the name resolution. If the Windows 2000 computer needs to resolve the names uziel, gabriel, uriel, and chamuel, broadcast name resolution is used. If broadcast name resolution is unsuccessful, the LMHOSTS file is parsed for these names. When a non-preloaded name is resolved by parsing the LMHOSTS file, it is cached for a period of time so that it can be reused. Names resolved through broadcasts are also saved in the cache until the timeout period expires.

The preloaded cache has a limit of 100 entries. If more than 100 entries in the LMHOSTS file are marked with #PRE, only the first 100 entries are preloaded. Additional entries are not loaded in the name cache, but are resolved if the LMHOSTS file is parsed.

If you have made changes to the LMHOSTS file in terms of the entries marked with the #PRE keyword, you can purge and reload the name cache by using this command:

```
nbtstat -R
```

The advantage of using `nbtstat` is that you can preload the cache without restarting the Windows 2000 computer.

If you use the -RR option, the NetBIOS names registered by the computer are refreshed:

```
nbtstat -RR
```

Strategy for Using Common LMHOSTS Files

The LMHOSTS file is kept on the local Windows 2000 computer in the %SystemRoot%\SYSTEM32\DRIVERS\ETC directory. The maintenance of this local LMHOSTS file on every computer can become a problem when frequent changes are made.

The use of the #INCLUDE statement can simplify the maintenance of the LMHOSTS file. You could keep the LMHOSTS file on a Windows 2000 server named AKS and include the following reference to this file on other Windows 2000 computers:

```
#INCLUDE \\AKS\ETC\LMHOSTS
```

In this example, ETC is the shared name of the %SystemRoot%\SYSTEM32\DRIVERS\ETC directory on the AKS computer. The advantage of this approach is that all common names that need to be preloaded are kept in a common file. If the AKS computer is not in the broadcast region, you must include a specific mapping for it. If the NTKS has an IP address of 134.21.22.13, for example, you could use these entries in the LMHOSTS file:

```
134.21.22.13    AKS            #PRE
#INCLUDE        \\AKS\ETC\LMHOSTS
```

To ensure that the common LMHOSTS file is always available, you can replicate this file to other Windows 2000 computers using the Windows 2000 replicator service. The common LMHOSTS file must be on a Windows 2000 server (either Windows 2000 Server or Windows 2000 Advanced Server) because only the Windows 2000 server can act as an export server for replication.

If you have redundant servers, you need to specify that the LMHOSTS file can be found on any of the redundant servers. In this situation, using the #BEGIN_ALTERNATIVE and #END_ALTERNATIVE commands comes in handy. Recall from Table 26.1 that these statements mark a block of #INCLUDE statements so that any one of the #INCLUDE statements can be used.

Consider the following example, in which an alternative list of LMHOSTS files is specified on Windows 2000 computers on a network segment:

```
134.21.22.13    AKS        #PRE
134.21.22.14    AC1        #PRE
134.21.22.15    AC2        #PRE

#BEGIN_ALTERNATIVE
#INCLUDE \\AKS\ETC\LMHOSTS    # Main source of LMHOSTS file
#INCLUDE \\AC1\ETC\LMHOSTS    # Backup 1
#INCLUDE \\AC2\ETC\LMHOSTS    # Backup 2
#END_ALTERNATIVE
```

In this example, the LMHOSTS file on AKS is assumed to be replicated to backup Windows 2000 computers AC1 and AC2. The shared name for the %SystemRoot%\ SYSTEM32\DRIVERS\ETC directory is ETC on all the Windows 2000 computers. The block inclusion is successful if any of the files on the three Windows 2000 computers is available. If the file is not available because the Windows 2000 computers are down or an incorrect path is specified, an event is added to the Windows 2000 computer's event log.

Configuring the HOSTS File

The HOSTS file is used by Unix TCP/IP-derived tools, such as PING and NETSTAT, to resolve hostnames to their IP addresses.

The HOSTS file syntax is similar to the syntax of the LMHOSTS file. The HOSTS file is also in the same directory (%SystemRoot%\SYSTEM32\DRIVERS\ETC) as the LMHOSTS file. The HOSTS file syntax differs from the LMHOSTS file in the following ways:

- No special tags (such as #PRE and #DOM) are in the HOSTS file.
- You can define several alias names for an IP address by listing the names on the same line separated by spaces.

The general syntax of each line in the HOSTS file can be either of the following:

```
IPAddress    Name1 [Name2 ... NameN] # Comment
# Comment
```

Name2 and NameN are optional aliases for the name Name1. As with the LMHOSTS configuration file, anything after the symbol # is treated as a comment.

The following is an example of a HOSTS file:

```
# Copyright (c) 1993-1999 Microsoft Corp.
#
# This is a sample HOSTS file used by Microsoft TCP/IP for Windows.
#
# This file contains the mappings of IP addresses to host names. Each
# entry should be kept on an individual line. The IP address should
# be placed in the first column followed by the corresponding host name.
# The IP address and the host name should be separated by at least one
# space.
#
# Additionally, comments (such as these) may be inserted on individual
# lines or following the machine name denoted by a '#' symbol.
#
# For example:
#
#      102.54.94.97      rhino.acme.com          # source server
#      38.25.63.10       x.acme.com              # x client host

127.0.0.1        localhost
199.245.180.1    ntws1
199.245.180.2    ntws2
199.245.180.3    ntws3
199.245.180.4    ntws4
199.245.180.5    ntws5
199.245.180.6    ntws6 phylos anzimee
ntsmain ntc ntcontroller
```

Other Support Files for TCP/IP Services

As mentioned earlier in this chapter, the HOSTS file must be configured for many Unix-based services ported to Windows 2000. In addition to the HOSTS file, three other files can be used by the Windows 2000 port of Unix-based services: the NETWORKS, PRO-TOCOL, and SERVICES files that are in the %SystemRoot%\SYSTEM32\DRIVERS\ETC directory. For the most part, you do not need to configure these files unless you want to add symbolic names for networks, or you are a software developer porting new services and protocols to the Windows environment.

The NETWORKS File

The NETWORKS file is used to identify the networks that exist on the internetwork (a network consisting of several networks, usually connected through routers). The NETWORKS file is similar in concept to the HOSTS file. Whereas the HOSTS file contains the association between host addresses and hostnames, the NETWORKS file contains the association between network addresses and network names.

Each line in the NETWORK text file contains information in this format:

```
network_name        network_number[/subnet_mask]        alias #comment
```

network_name is an identifier representing the name of the network, and network_number is the netid part of the IP address for the network. The network name cannot contain a tab, space, or number (#) character and must be unique in the NETWORKS file.

subnet_mask is the subnet mask for the network. It can be expressed in dotted decimal or dotted hexadecimal notation. The square brackets ([]) in the previously stated syntax for the NETWORKS file entry indicate that the subnet mask is optional. If the subnet mask is left out, a default mask indicates that no subnet mask is being used.

The optional alias identifies other names by which this network is known. Usually the network_name is in lowercase characters and an alias is included that lists the service in uppercase characters.

#comment is used to place comments. All characters between the # and the end of the line are ignored and treated as comments. The #comment can occur on a line by itself.

The network names specified in the NETWORKS file can be used in configuration utilities and commands that deal with the network address. For example, the network name can be used as an alternative to using the network addresses. This file can be modified by network administrators to enable the use of network names in configuration commands and utilities rather than use the network addresses, which are more difficult to remember.

> **Note**
>
> The NETWORKS file is useful when you want a symbolic display of network values, such as when you are using tools like the route command to display routing tables.

The following is an example of a NETWORKS file:

```
# Copyright (c) 1993-1999 Microsoft Corp.
#
# This file contains network name/network number mappings for
# local networks. Network numbers are recognized in dotted decimal form.
#
# Format:
#
# <network name>  <network number>    [aliases...]  [#<comment>]
#
# For example:
#
#     loopback    127
#     campus      284.122.107
#     london      284.122.108

loopback                127
Kinet                   199.245.180
SCSnet                  200.24.4.0
MyNet                   144.19
```

The PROTOCOL File

The PROTOCOL file is used to identify the names of protocols and the corresponding protocol number. The protocol number for the Internet suite of protocols is the value protocol identifier (protocol ID) field of the IP header. The protocol ID field is used to identify the upper-layer protocol that uses the Internet Protocol.

The PROTOCOL file accompanies the TCP/IP protocol module and contains common protocols; you should not have to modify the file.

Each line in the PROTOCOL text file contains information in this format:

```
protocol_name      protocol_number     [alias]    #comment
```

protocol_name is an identifier representing the name of the protocol, and protocol_number is the number used in the IP header to identify the protocol. The protocol name cannot contain a tab, space, or number (#) character and must be unique in the PROTOCOL file.

The optional alias identifies other names by which this protocol is known. Usually the protocol_name is in lowercase characters and an alias is included that lists the service in uppercase characters.

Configuring TCP/IP for Windows 2000

CHAPTER 26

667

26

CONFIGURING
TCP/IP FOR
WINDOWS 2000

> **Note**
>
> The symbolic names of networks in the NETWORKS file are aliases for the net-works. The symbolic names, rather than the IP addresses, are displayed when TCP/IP commands for displaying routing tables are executed.

#comment is used to place comments. All characters between the # and the end of the line are ignored and treated as comments. #comment can occur on a line by itself.

A sample PROTOCOL file for Windows 2000 is listed next:

```
# Copyright (c) 1993-1999 Microsoft Corp.
#
# This file contains the Internet protocols as defined by RFC 1700
# (Assigned Numbers).
#
# Format:
#
# <protocol name>  <assigned number>  [aliases...]   [#<comment>]

ip       0    IP       # Internet protocol
icmp     1    ICMP     # Internet control message protocol
ggp      3    GGP      # Gateway-gateway protocol
tcp      6    TCP      # Transmission control protocol
egp      8    EGP      # Exterior gateway protocol
pup      12   PUP      # PARC universal packet protocol
udp      17   UDP      # User datagram protocol
hmp      20   HMP      # Host monitoring protocol
xns-idp  22   XNS-IDP  # Xerox NS IDP
rdp      27   RDP      # "reliable datagram" protocol
rvd      66   RVD      # MIT remote virtual disk
```

The SERVICES File

The SERVICES file is used to identify the following:

- Names of services
- The transport protocol
- The port number used by the service

The names of services are programs that run in the Process/Application Layer of the TCP/IP model (sometimes called the DoD model). Examples of these services are Telnet, FTP, Simple Mail Transport Protocol (SMTP), and SNMP. These services can use a Transport protocol, such as TCP or UDP. The SERVICES configuration file identifies the Transport protocol that is used. Some services are available through both the TCP and UDP transport protocols. In this case, the service is listed twice: once for the TCP protocol and once for the UDP protocol. The port number identifies the application service that uses the Transport protocol.

> **Note**
>
> The PROTOCOL file is useful for TCP/IP application code ported from the Unix environment. Some of the BSD Sockets code uses the PROTOCOL file to get the protocol number for the TCP and UDP transports, whereas other TCP/IP code directly hard-codes these protocol number values.

This SERVICES file accompanies the TCP/IP protocol module and contains common TCP/IP services; you should not have to modify the file.

Each line in the SERVICES text file contains information in this format:

```
service                port/transport          [alias]    #comment
```

service is an identifier representing the name of the service. Examples of service values are Telnet, FTP, FTP-DATA, SMTP, and SNMP. The service name cannot contain a tab, space, or number (#) character and must be unique in the SERVICES file.

The optional alias identifies other names by which this service is known.

#comment is used to place comments. All characters between the # and the end of the line are ignored and treated as comments. #comment can occur on a line by itself.

A sample SERVICES file for a Windows 2000 computer is shown next:

```
# Copyright (c) 1993-1999 Microsoft Corp.
#
# This file contains port numbers for well-known services defined by IANA
#
# Format:
#
# <service name>  <port number>/<protocol>  [aliases...]   [#<comment>]#
```

```
echo            7/tcp
echo            7/udp
discard         9/tcp    sink null
discard         9/udp    sink null
systat         11/tcp    users                #Active users
systat         11/tcp    users                #Active users
daytime        13/tcp
daytime        13/udp
qotd           17/tcp    quote                #Quote of the day
qotd           17/udp    quote                #Quote of the day
chargen        19/tcp    ttytst source        #Character generator
chargen        19/udp    ttytst source        #Character generator
ftp-data       20/tcp                         #FTP, data
ftp            21/tcp                         #FTP, control
telnet         23/tcp
smtp           25/tcp    mail                 #Simple Mail Transfer
                                              ➥ Protocol

time           37/tcp    timserver
time           37/udp    timserver
rlp            39/udp    resource             #Resource Location
                                              ➥Protocol

nameserver     42/tcp    name                 #Host Name Server
nameserver     42/udp    name                 #Host Name Server
nicname        43/tcp    whois

domain         53/tcp                         #Domain Name Server
domain         53/udp                         #Domain Name Server
bootps         67/udp    dhcps                #Bootstrap Protocol Server
bootpc         68/udp    dhcpc                #Bootstrap Protocol Client
tftp           69/udp                         #Trivial File Transfer
gopher         70/tcp
finger         79/tcp
http           80/tcp    www www-http         #World Wide Web
kerberos       88/tcp    krb5 kerberos-sec    #Kerberos
kerberos       88/udp    krb5 kerberos-sec    #Kerberos
hostname      101/tcp    hostnames            #NIC Host Name Server
iso-tsap      102/tcp                         #ISO-TSAP Class 0
rtelnet       107/tcp                         #Remote Telnet Service
pop2          109/tcp    postoffice           -#Post Office Protocol -
                                              ➥Version 2

pop3          110/tcp                         -#Post Office Protocol -
                                              ➥Version 3

sunrpc        111/tcp    rpcbind portmap      #SUN Remote Procedure Call
sunrpc        111/udp    rpcbind portmap      #SUN Remote Procedure Call
auth          113/tcp    ident tap            #Identification Protocol
uucp-path     117/tcp
nntp          119/tcp    usenet               #Network News Transfer
                                              ➥Protocol
ntp           123/udp                         #Network Time Protocol
epmap         135/tcp    loc-srv              #DCE endpoint resolution
epmap         135/udp    loc-srv              #DCE endpoint resolution
netbios-ns    137/tcp    nbname               #NETBIOS Name Service
netbios-ns    137/udp    nbname               #NETBIOS Name Service
```

```
netbios-dgm      138/udp    nbdatagram       #NETBIOS Datagram Service
netbios-ssn      139/tcp    nbsession        #NETBIOS Session Service
imap             143/tcp    imap4            #Internet Message Access
                                             ➥Protocol
pcmail-srv       158/tcp                     #PCMail Server
snmp             161/udp                     #SNMP
snmptrap         162/udp    snmp-trap        #SNMP trap
print-srv        170/tcp                     #Network PostScript
bgp              179/tcp                     #Border Gateway Protocol
irc              194/tcp                     #Internet Relay Chat
                                             ➥Protocol
ipx              213/udp                     #IPX over IP
ldap             389/tcp                     -#Lightweight Directory
                                             ➥Access Protocol
https            443/tcp    MCom
https            443/udp    MCom
microsoft-ds     445/tcp
microsoft-ds     445/udp
kpasswd          464/tcp                     # Kerberos (v5)
kpasswd          464/udp                     # Kerberos (v5)
isakmp           500/udp    ike              #Internet Key Exchange
exec             512/tcp                     #Remote Process Execution
biff             512/udp    comsat
login            513/tcp                     #Remote Login
who              513/udp    whod
cmd              514/tcp    shell
syslog           514/udp
printer          515/tcp    spooler
talk             517/udp
ntalk            518/udp
efs              520/tcp                     #Extended File Name Server
router           520/udp    route routed
timed            525/udp    timeserver
tempo            526/tcp    newdate
courier          530/tcp    rpc
conference       531/tcp    chat
netnews          532/tcp    readnews
netwall          533/udp                     #For emergency broadcasts
uucp             540/tcp    uucpd
klogin           543/tcp                     #Kerberos login
kshell           544/tcp    krcmd            #Kerberos remote shell
new-rwho         550/udp    new-who
remotefs         556/tcp    rfs rfs_server
rmonitor         560/udp    rmonitord
monitor          561/udp
ldaps            636/tcp    sldap            #LDAP over TLS/SSL
doom             666/tcp                     #Doom Id Software
doom             666/udp                     #Doom Id Software
kerberos-adm     749/tcp                     #Kerberos administration
kerberos-adm     749/udp                     #Kerberos administration
kerberos-iv      750/udp                     #Kerberos version IV
```

```
kpop          1109/tcp              #Kerberos POP
phone         1167/udp              #Conference calling
ms-sql-s      1433/tcp              #Microsoft-SQL-Server
ms-sql-s      1433/udp              #Microsoft-SQL-Server
ms-sql-m      1434/tcp              #Microsoft-SQL-Monitor
ms-sql-m      1434/udp              #Microsoft-SQL-Monitor
wins          1512/tcp              -#Microsoft Windows
                                    ➥Internet Name Service
wins          1512/udp              -#Microsoft Windows
                                    ➥Internet Name Service
ingreslock    1524/tcp    ingres
l2tp          1701/udp              #Layer Two Tunneling
                                    ➥Protocol
pptp          1723/tcp              -#Point-to-point
                                    ➥tunnelling protocol
radius        1812/udp              -#RADIUS authentication
                                    ➥protocol
radacct       1813/udp              #RADIUS accounting protocol
nfsd          2049/udp    nfs       #NFS server
knetd         2053/tcp              #Kerberos de-multiplexor
man           9535/tcp              #Remote Man Server
```

> **Note**
>
> If you are installing a new TCP service that is a direct port of a Unix application on Windows 2000, the new service might expect to see its port and transport protocol definition in the SERVICES file. You might have to add a line in the SERVICES file describing the new service, if the installed service does not automatically add its description to the SERVICES file.

Installing and Configuring the FTP Server Service

Windows 2000 servers (both Windows 2000 Server and Windows 2000 Advanced Server) and Windows 2000 Professional workstations can be set up as FTP servers to enable files in the Windows 2000 computer to be accessed by FTP clients. The FTP clients can be other Windows 2000 computers, Unix computers, disk operating system (DOS) or Windows computers, Macintosh computers, and VMS computers.

The Windows 2000 FTP Server service supports all FTP client commands, is implemented as a multithreaded Win32 application, and complies with RFCs 959, "File Transfer Protocol (FTP)," and 1123, "Requirements for Internet Hosts," which describe the FTP protocols and services.

FTP servers use the user accounts of the host operating system. In the case of Windows 2000, the FTP user accounts are the domain accounts created on the FTP computer and the FTP anonymous user account.

The FTP Server is a part of the Microsoft Internet Information Server (IIS). The following section includes some general installation and utilization information.

Installing and Configuring the FTP Server Service on Windows 2000 Server

You can choose to install the FTP Service and other Internet services when you do your original Windows 2000 installation. Select the Internet Information Server box during installation when you are selecting the Windows components to install. The FTP Server automatically is installed as a part of IIS.

If you have already installed Windows 2000 Server without the Internet Information Server, you can add IIS now. Because the FTP Server service relies on the TCP/IP protocol, you must install and configure the TCP/IP protocol before you can install FTP Server services.

> **Note**
>
> In Windows 2000 most FTP service parameters can be configured using the IIS console in the Computer Management tool and the Internet Services Manager tool. In Windows NT some of the more advanced parameters had to be configured using the Registry. You do not have to resort to using the Registry in Windows 2000.
>
> All FTP Service parameters are under the Registry key HKEY_LOCAL_MACHINE\ SYSTEM\CurrentControlSet\ Services\MSFTPSRV\Parameters.

If the FTP Server is not installed, install IIS and follow these steps to configure the default FTP site:

1. Log in as an Administrator user.
2. Select Start, Settings, Control Panel.
3. Double-click Add/Remove Programs, and then click Add/Remove Windows Components. You should see the Windows Components Wizard.
4. Enable IIS and select Details. Make sure that the FTP Server is checked.
5. Click OK. Click Next on succeeding screens (ensure that a Windows 2000 distribution CD is in your drive), and then click Finish to complete the installation.

Configuring TCP/IP for Windows 2000

CHAPTER 26

673

26

CONFIGURING
TCP/IP FOR
WINDOWS 2000

6. Reboot the Windows 2000 computer. View the list of services on the Windows 2000 computer to verify that the FTP Server service has started. You can view a list of services that are running by selecting Computer Management from the Administrative Tools applet in the Control Panel. Open the Services and Applications folder.

7. Double-click on the Services icon in the right pane, and verify that the FTP Publishing Service has started.

8. From the Computer Management screen, open the Services and Applications\IIS folder.

9. Right-click on Default FTP Site (it might also be labeled FTP Site #1) and select Properties. The Default FTP Site Properties screen appears.

10. You can specify a description in the Description field or change an existing description. In the IP Address field, select the IP address of the Windows 2000 computer. Leave the TCP port number set to 21; it is the default port number for accepting TCP control connections at the FTP server.

11. In the Connection box, specify the number of simultaneous FTP sessions to the FTP server. The number of connections can be limited to a specified number, or it can be unlimited. Use this field to perform appropriate load balancing. Restricting the number of FTP connections to between 50 and 250 connections is common practice to avoid overwhelming a server.

12. Use the Connection Timeout field to specify how long an FTP user can remain connected without generating any activity before being disconnected. The default value is 900 seconds (15 minutes). A value of 0 disables the idle timeout feature. The value is used primarily for security reasons to reduce the threat of unattended FTP sessions.

13. Select Enable Logging to control the FTP session log and the format of the log messages (Microsoft IIS Log File, Open Database Connectivity (ODBC) Logging, or W3C Extended Log File).

14. Select the Security Accounts tab to set who can access the FTP server.

15. Enable the option Allow Anonymous Connections to allow users with the user account named anonymous or FTP to log on to the FTP server. A user is not required to enter a password while logging on as an anonymous user, even though the user is prompted for an e-mail address as a password.

16. Use the Password field to specify the password for the user account specified in the Username field.

17. Enable the Allow Only Anonymous Connections check box option if you want only anonymous user logons to ensure that Windows 2000 users do not log on with their Windows 2000 username and password. Remember that FTP passwords are not encrypted and that if they are used on the network, security can be compromised. By default, this option is disabled. You can set the Allow IIS to control password option.

18. In the FTP Site Operators box, you can grant operator privileges to Windows user accounts for this FTP site by clicking the Add button. By default the operators are members of the local Administrators group.

19. Select the Messages tab to specify messages the user sees at logon (Welcome field) and logout (Exit field) and the number of maximum connections allowed if the limit is exceeded (Maximum Connections field).

20. Select the Home Directory tab to specify the folder to which the user connects when she logs in. You can specify that the home directory be on the local computer or a share on another computer. You can specify Read, Write, or Log visits permissions on the home directory and whether the user sees an MS-DOS–style or Unix-style directory listing.

21. Select the Directory Security tab to specify TCP/IP access restrictions of granted or denied from the specified IP address and subnet mask. First check the option Granted access or Denied access, and then click the Add button. In the Deny Access On dialog box, enable the Single computer or Group computer option, and then specify the IP address and (optionally) subnet mask for a group of computers. Click OK to close the boxes.

> **Note**
>
> The username *anonymous* is reserved on the Windows 2000 computer for anonymous logon. You cannot, therefore, use a Windows 2000 user account named anonymous. In the Username field, specify the name of the Windows 2000 user account to be used for the user who logs on as anonymous. Access permissions for the anonymous FTP user are the same as that for the specified user. By default, the IUSR_computername account is used for the anonymous user.

Configuring TCP/IP to Print from Windows 2000 to Unix Printers

Windows 2000 supports printing to Unix printers on the network. The print jobs are sent using the TCP/IP protocol. Windows 2000 printing support for Unix printers conforms to RFC 1179, "Line Printer Daemon Protocol."

To print to a Unix computer, only one Windows 2000 computer (workstation or server) needs to have the TCP/IP protocol installed and configured in addition to the Microsoft TCP/IP Printing Service. This Windows 2000 computer then acts as the print gateway for other Microsoft clients (see Figure 26.13). The other Microsoft clients do not need TCP/IP installed on them to use the print gateway. Figure 26.13 shows that the computer named AKS has TCP/IP print support and has defined the shared printers \\AKS\Unix_PR1 and \\AKS\Unix_PR2. These printers correspond to a directly connected Unix printer and to a printer attached to a Unix computer. Other Microsoft clients connect to the shared printers as though they were Microsoft print devices. A print job sent to the shared printer names \\AKS\Unix_PR1 and \\AKS\Unix_PR2 is redirected by AKS to the corresponding Unix printer.

FIGURE 26.13

TCP/IP printing under Windows 2000.

Installing and Configuring TCP/IP Printing

TCP/IP printing is installed at the time of Windows 2000 installation as part of the Other Network File and Print Services Windows components. If it has not been installed, follow these steps to install this component:

1. Log in as an Administrator user.

2. Select Start, Settings, Control Panel.

3. Double-click Add/Remove Programs and then click Add/Remove Windows Components. You should see the Windows Components Wizard.

4. Enable Other Network File and Print Services and select Details. Make sure that the Print Services for Unix option is checked.

5. Select OK. Ensure that the Windows 2000 distribution CD is in the CD-ROM drive. Keep clicking Next and then click Finish. This step installs the selected components.

The following steps outline the process for configuring TCP/IP printing on a Windows 2000 computer to use the Print Services for Unix service running on another Windows 2000 computer or the equivalent line printer daemon (LPD) service running on a Unix machine:

1. Log in as an Administrator user on the Windows 2000 computer (Windows 2000 Server or Workstation).

2. Select Start, Settings, Printers.

3. Double-click the Add Printer icon. When the Add Printer Wizard appears, click Next.

4. The Local or Network Printer screen appears. Select either local or network management of the printer, and then click the Next button. If you select the Local option, the Wizard tries to detect plug-and-play printers. If it does find any, you have to make the selection manually.

5. The Printer Wizard finally displays a list of available printer ports. Enable the Create a new port option. From the Type drop-down list, select LPR port and then click Next.

   You should see the Add LPR compatible printer dialog box.

6. In the Name or address of server providing LPD field, enter the DNS name or IP address of the Unix device (host or directly attached printer) on which the LPD service is running. The LPD service is the line printer daemon service, which acts as a Unix print server.

Note

If you are printing to a networked printer that supports LPR, you do not need to install this service. It is required only if the printer queue is hosted on a generic Unix host.

7. In the Name of printer or print queue on that server field, enter the Unix printer name on that computer system.

8. Choose OK after filling in the Add LPR compatible printer dialog box. If the LPD service is not enabled, a message lets you know. Select OK.

9. Select the manufacturer from the Manufacturers list and the printer from the Printers list by highlighting the appropriate choices on the Add Printer Wizard screen. Click the Next button after you finish.

10. The Add Printer Wizard displays the printer name and asks whether you want it to be the default printer. Select Yes or No, and then click the Next button.

11. The Add Printer Wizard now enables you to choose whether this printer will be shared on the network. Select Share as or Do not share this printer. Type the share name in the Share Name field. By default, the share name is the same as the printer name you entered earlier. Click Next.

12. The Location and Comment screen appears. This printer name is seen by other Microsoft clients. Complete the Location and Comment fields to describe the location and printer capabilities. Click Next.

13. Optionally, you can print a test page. This step is recommended in order to verify that your configuration is accurate. Select Yes or No, click Next, and then click the Finish button.

14. Choose OK if your test page printed, or troubleshoot the printing process. The new printer icon should appear. To examine the printer settings, right-click on the printer icon and select Properties.

15. On the Device Settings tab, you can make changes such as selecting the form type, form source, and printer memory that are specific to the printer you are using. Choose OK to save your changes. Make any other changes.

The TCP/IP printer is configured. You can close the Printers window.

Printing to a Windows 2000 Computer from a Unix Computer

The preceding section outlined the configuration procedure for printing to a Unix printer from Microsoft clients. On a network consisting of a mix of Unix computers and Microsoft clients, you might need to print from a Unix client to a Windows 2000 printer.

To print from a Unix client to a Windows 2000 computer, you must have TCP/IP Print Server Services running on the Windows 2000 computer. Unix print clients expect to communicate with a Unix LPD. You can start the Windows 2000 LPDSVC service, which emulates a Unix line-printer daemon. Figure 26.14 shows how Unix clients can print to a Windows 2000 computer.

FIGURE 26.14

Printing from Unix to a Windows 2000 computer.

You can start, pause, continue, or stop the Windows 2000 LPDSVC by using these NET commands:

- NET START LPDSVC
- NET PAUSE LPDSVC
- NET CONTINUE LPDSVC
- NET STOP LPDSVC

Configuring TCP/IP for Windows 2000

CHAPTER 26

679

26

CONFIGURING
TCP/IP FOR
WINDOWS 2000

Alternatively, you can use the Services icon in the Control Panel to start, pause, continue, or stop the lpdsvc. The LPDSVC is called TCP/IP Print Server in the Server Properties dialog box (see Figure 26.15). By default, this service is started automatically. You can use the Startup type field in the Server Properties dialog box to change the startup conditions of this service when the Windows 2000 computer is started.

FIGURE 26.15
The TCP/IP Print Server services properties.

On the Unix printer, you must use the appropriate Unix command, usually lpr, to submit print jobs to the Windows 2000 computer. Consult your Unix documentation for the details of this command. The general syntax of the lpr command is

```
lpr -s NTHost -P NTPrinter filename
```

NTHost is the DNS name of the Windows 2000 computer running the LPDSVC; NTPrinter is the name of the Windows 2000 printer created on NTHost; and filename is the name of the Unix file to be printed.

Using TCP/IP Command-Line Tools

Windows 2000 comes with a number of TCP/IP command-line tools. They are, for the most part, based on their Unix counterparts. If you have used these tools on Unix computers, you are already familiar with their function.

In addition to command-line tools, Windows 2000 supports simple TCP/IP services, such as ECHO, DAYTIME, CHARGEN, and DISCARD. These services are available on most Unix computers. You must, however, install them in Windows 2000 using the Simple TCP/IP Services option.

Windows 2000 supports these command-line tools:

- arp
- hostname
- ipconfig
- lpq
- lpr
- nbtstat
- netstat
- ping
- route

- tracert
- finger
- rcp
- rexec
- rsh
- ftp
- tftp
- telnet
- pathping

Although the ftp, rexec, and telnet utilities require authentication, the passwords are not encrypted before they are sent. Using these utilities, therefore, is a potential security risk. You should try to use different user accounts for these utilities so that the Windows 2000 user account passwords are not compromised. In Windows 2000, Telnet supports encrypted authentication. You should use encrypted authentication if there is a significant risk that the Telnet user account password will be compromised.

This section describes the installation of the Simple TCP/IP services and then the basic command-line tools.

Simple TCP/IP Services is part of the Network Services Windows component installed during the Windows 2000 installation. The following steps outline the process for installing Simple TCP/IP Services, if you have not already done so:

1. Log in as an Administrator user.

2. Select Start, Settings, Control Panel.

3. Double-click Add/Remove Programs, and then click Add/Remove Windows Components. You should see the Windows Components Wizard.

4. Enable Network Services and select Details. Make sure that the Simple TCP/IP Services option is checked (see Figure 26.16).

FIGURE 26.16

Simple TCP/IP Services option.

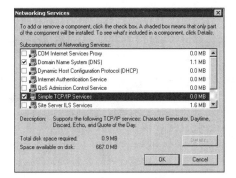

5. Click OK. Ensure that the Windows 2000 distribution CD is in the CD-ROM drive. Keep clicking Next, and then click Finish. This step installs the selected components.

Note

The Simple TCP/IP Services are CHARGEN, DAYTIME, DISCARD, ECHO, and QUOTE. You can use these services as diagnostics tools.

The CHARGEN service uses TCP port number 19. If you make a connection to this port using Telnet, you see a display of 95 printable American Standard Code for Information Interchange (ASCII) characters cycle on your screen. The following Telnet command makes a connection to the CHARGEN service running on the remote computer:

> telnet remote 19

You can use CHARGEN as a debugging tool for testing to ensure that the remote computer is operational up to the TCP layer.

The DAYTIME service uses TCP port number 13. If you make a connection to this port using Telnet, you see an ASCII representation of the current time on the remote machine. The following Telnet command makes a connection to the DAYTIME service running on the remote computer:

> telnet remote 13

You can use this command to see the time on the remote computer and to verify that you have connectivity up to the TCP layer on the remote machine.

The DISCARD service uses TCP port number 9. If you make a connection to this port using Telnet, any data you send is discarded. The DISCARD service acts as a data "sink," or "black hole." The following Telnet command makes a connection to the DISCARD service running on the remote computer:

> telnet remote 9

TCP port 9 can be used as a null port for testing programs. For example, you can use the DISCARD service to receive TCP test messages that are not important to store or display and can be safely discarded.

The ECHO service uses TCP port number 7. If you make a connection to this port using Telnet, any data you send is echoed back. You can use this tool as a debugging tool to see whether messages sent to the remote computer can be returned intact. The following Telnet command makes a connection to the ECHO service running on the remote computer:

telnet remote 7

After you make this connection, you should type a few characters and see whether they are echoed back.

The QUOTE service uses TCP port number 17. If you make a connection to this port using Telnet, it sends you a Quote of the Day message taken randomly from the file %SystemRoot%\System32\Drivers\Etc\Quotes. You can use this tool as a debugging tool to see whether messages can be sent from the remote computer. The following Telnet command makes a connection to the QUOTE service running on the remote computer:

telnet remote 17

After you make this connection, you should see a Quote of the Day message.

Summary

Configuring TCP/IP for Windows 2000 involves the configuration of basic TCP/IP parameters, such as the IP address, subnet mask, default gateways, and name servers. Windows 2000 computers need to know about at least one default gateway to go beyond the current network. In a native-mode network consisting only of Windows 2000 computers, the only name server the Windows 2000 computer needs to know about is the DNS server. However, if you need connectivity to older Windows clients and servers, the Windows 2000 computers need to be configured with WINS. In Windows 2000 networks, knowledge of NetBIOS name resolution is still important for backward compatibility.

Although the Windows 2000 Active Directory depends on TCP/IP, no configuration needs to be done to the TCP/IP protocol stack other than to specify the DNS server that will be used for name resolution.

## CHAPTER 27

IP Support in Novell NetWare

by Joe Devlin and Emily Berk

IN THIS CHAPTER

Arguably the father of all modern network operating systems, Novell's NetWare is a reliable product that has been evolving for almost 18 years. Today, NetWare is installed on almost five million servers and 81 million workstations worldwide.

Novell and TCP/IP

Novell's adoption of TCP/IP has come slowly and in stages. In 1987, Novell shipped release 3.11 of NetWare with built-in support for IP tunneling and the availability of the TCP/IP stack and TCP/IP application services such as FTP and NFS. Since that time, Novell has added a wide variety of TCP/IP solutions to its network operating systems. Many of these older solutions remain useful. Novell builds reliable operating systems, and it is common practice in the NetWare world to leave old servers running as departmental solutions while assigning new servers the more demanding jobs of wide area or Internet management.

IP and NetWare 4

NetWare 4 represented Novell's first serious attempt to produce an operating system that fully embraced the Internet. NetWare 4 introduced Novell Directory Services (NDS), a facility that simplifies management of a wide variety of network resources running on a wide area network full of NetWare, NT, and Unix servers. NDS caught the attention of network managers everywhere and added luster to Novell's image as a company that delivers useful solutions that seemed beyond the technical ability of Microsoft.

NetWare 4 less successfully incorporated mainstream Internet development tools into NetWare. NetWare 4.11 (dubbed IntranetWare), which began shipping in October 1996, bundled a grab bag of Internet-related utilities including the NetWare Web Server, NetWare FTP server, and NetWare Internet Access Services (NIAS). Novell also threw in tools for connecting NetWare servers and clients to Internet devices running under TCP/IP.

NDS was a huge success. But a single Novell 4.x server running NDS is quite capable of managing an impressive conglomeration of Novell 3.x, NT, and Unix servers. Corporations wanted to enable their Novell servers to talk TCP/IP, but that could be accomplished in any number of ways using either NetWare 3.x or 4.x servers. There was just no compelling reason to migrate all the way to NetWare 4.x. That incentive came with the introduction of NetWare 5 and Pure IP.

NetWare 6, released in 2001, builds on the capabilities of NetWare 5 and adds iFolder, iPrinter, Storage Area Network (SAN), Remote Management, built-in clustering and a host of other services. However, the basic TCP/IP protocol support is the same as in NetWare 5. Therefore, in this chapter the discussion on TCP/IP services for NetWare 5 also apply to NetWare 6.

NetWare 5/NetWare 6 and the Pure IP Initiative

NetWare 5 represented a major change in Novell's relationship with IP. IPX, Novell's old native communications protocol, is elegant, bulletproof, and easy to use. But IP has taken the world by storm. Novell read the writing on the wall and redesigned NetWare from the ground up making IP (not IPX) its core communications protocol.

NetWare 5 was shipped in September 1998 as a "Pure IP" solution, and NetWare 6, shipped in 2001, also uses pure IP. The term "Pure" indicates that IPX encapsulation is no longer required. Novell's application service protocol NCP (NetWare Core Protocol) is carried directly over TCP/IP.

NetWare 5 uses IP services for discovery, addressing, and data transfer. Compared to the Windows NT NetBIOS routing or the IPX encapsulation used by earlier versions of NetWare, NetWare's Pure IP offers direct, unimpeded access to other IP-based networks, including Unix platforms and the Internet. The result is better performance, lower costs, and simpler management for companies that rely on IP for communications.

Novell has done a good job of extending familiar management tools such as NDS so that they work better in this new TCP/IP-centered world. NetWare also embraces other standards-based technologies such as SLP, DHCP, and DNS and has extended them to support IP and IPX networks and hybrids. Nor has Novell abandoned the huge installed base of IPX-based NetWare 3.x and 4.x servers. Although IP is now the default communications protocol, NetWare 5 remains fully compatible with older versions of NetWare built around IPX.

Legacy Solutions: IP for NetWare 3.x through 4.x

IPX/SPX (often shortened to IPX) is Novell's historical counterpart to TCP/IP. It serves as the core communications protocol for all NetWare 3.x and 4.x servers. IPX is reliable and stable, but has become much less popular than TCP/IP. Novell began bundling support for IPX to TCP/IP connectivity into NetWare in 1987. Since that time, Novell has introduced quite a few IPX to TCP/IP bridge products, each with its own capabilities. Table 27.1 summarizes the strengths and appropriate uses for each of the major IPX to TCP/IP bridges.

TABLE 27.1   Major IPX to TCP/IP Bridge Products

Tool	Definition	When Indicated	When Inappropriate
IP Tunneling	Server wraps TCP/IP header around each outgoing IPX packet and de-encapsulates incoming packets.	Good for establishing communications between two IPX-based Novell Networks linked by a TCP/IP backbone or via an Internet connection. Well-suited for connecting a small number of servers.	Does not provide workstation to workstation TCP/IP connectivity. Not appropriate for connecting large numbers of servers.
IP Relay	Encapsulates IPX communications within TCP/IP packets, which can be transmitted across an IP backbone.	Optimized to support permanently enabled connections such as leased lines; IP relays are commonly used to create virtual private networks.	IP relays offer the same advantages and disadvantages as IP tunneling, but are better suited for use with larger networks.
LAN Workplace	Provides concurrent access to TCP/IP and NetWare IPX resources by giving client TCP/IP applications the ability to read and write to TCP/IP as well as IPX stacks.	Client installation provides access to TCP/IP resources by non-networked PCs. Server installation supports centralized installation, configuration, and maintenance of IP resources.	Network managers must be comfortable with both IPX and TCP/IP to use this product.
IPX-IP Gateway	The gateway converts IPX communications into TCP/IP communications and routes them to their proper destination.	Because the only IP address that needs to be assigned is that of the gateway itself, standard IPX users connecting through the gateway are free to use standard Web browsers or other WinSock compliant TCP programs as if TCP/IP were configured on their desktops.	Requires the installation of both server and client software. Workstations are forced to communicate with IP hosts through the gateway, which adds overhead to all communications sessions.

TABLE 27.1 Continued

Tool	Definition	When Indicated	When Inappropriate
NetWare/ IP	Encapsulates all IPX communications within IP.	Because the IPX stack is still available on each workstation, old IPX-based applications can still communicate directly with that stack.	Requires the installation of several independent cooperating client and server components.

IP Tunneling

To establish communication between two IPX-based Novell Networks linked by TCP/IP backbones or via an Internet connection, *IP tunneling* is the way to go. Every version of NetWare, starting with 3.11, supports IP tunneling. With this solution, IPX-based work-stations address their normal IPX packets to either a local or remote tunnel server. The server running the IPX-Tunnel software listens for IPX packets. When it finds one, it wraps a TCP/IP header around that packet and routes it off across the TCP/IP network to the specified address. Typically, a NetWare Loadable Module, IPTUNNEL.NLM, is used to implement Novell Tunneling. The IPTUNNEL driver on the server encapsulates IPX/NCP packets inside an IP frame, then adds a User Datagram Protocol (UDP) header, an IP header, and an IP checksum field for a cyclic redundancy check (CRC).

Each tunnel server uses a standard IP address so that packets can be routed back and forth between those servers, via the Internet or through a TCP/IP-based backbone. When the packet arrives at the other end, the receiving IPX tunnel partner strips off the TCP/IP header and forwards the clean IPX packet to its final destination.

The primary advantage of IP tunneling is that it provides IP/IPX interconnectivity with minimal impact on network administrators and users. For example, you need not install any special client software at the workstation level to implement tunneling. In fact, work-stations never need to know their IPX data packets were ever encapsulated. As a result, all existing IPX applications should operate just as they did in a pure IPX world.

The primary disadvantage of IP tunneling is that it does not provide workstation-to-workstation TCP/IP connectivity. Still, it is a reliable, low-cost solution that works well, especially when used for connecting a small number of servers. The encapsulation process used to create a tunnel does add overhead and additional management and troubleshooting duties to the job of maintaining the network. Thus, tunneling is not appropriate for connecting large numbers of servers.

27

IP SUPPORT IN
NOVELL
NETWARE

IP Relay

Novell's IP Relay solution builds upon the core features provided by IP tunneling. Like tunneling, it utilizes server-level encapsulation of IPX communications within TCP/IP packets, which are then transmitted across an IP backbone. The difference is that IP relays are optimized to support connections between permanently enabled paths of communications such as the leased lines commonly used to connect branch and main offices or suppliers to a manufacturer. IP relays are commonly used to create virtual private networks that work without any need to install and maintain expensive client-side software. In all other respects, IP relays offer the same advantages and disadvantages as IP tunneling. Novell's IP Relay product is included as part of the NetWare MultiProtocol Router (MPR) version 2.0 and higher and is integrated with the WAN version of NetWareLink Services Protocol.

IP Relay uses encapsulation, but its point-to-point WAN design makes it much easier to deploy and administer than IP tunneling. An IP Relay network is best implemented in a star or hub design with IP Relay loaded on the hub server and on the destination (remote) servers. The hub server is provided with a table of all the IP address for each destination server. The destination servers do not need to be provided with the IP address for the hub server. Remote servers can be run in listen mode waiting for the moment when the hub opens the communication line.

Designed for point-to-point LAN architectures, IP Relay generates substantially less traffic than a tunneling solution and simplifies the installation and administration process. As a result, IP Relay scales up better than tunneling does.

LAN WorkPlace

Novell's LAN WorkPlace products provide Windows, NT/2000, and DOS users with concurrent access to both TCP/IP and NetWare IPX resources. LAN WorkPlace products do not encapsulate IPX datagrams within a TCP/IP header. Instead, it uses client-side software capable of reading and writing both TCP/IP and IPX stacks. Thus, LAN WorkPlace can be used to allow DOS, Windows, and NT workstations to use TCP/IP to access both Unix hosts and to examine NetWare drives.

LAN WorkPlace can be installed either at the workstation or the server level. Installed on a PC, LAN WorkPlace provides even non-networked PCs with access to TCP/IP resources. When installed on a server, LAN WorkPlace enables all network users to access TCP/IP resources. The server installation also enables NetWare network supervisors to perform centralized installation, configuration (including workstation IP address assignment), and maintenance.

The downside of LAN WorkPlace is that it does not actually transform IPX networks into TCP/IP networks. Instead, it adds TCP/IP connectivity separately and independently from any support provided for IPX connectivity. This means that managing a LAN WorkPlace network requires all the skills it would take to manage separate IPX and TCP/IP networks.

IPX-IP Gateway

Novell began bundling its IPX-IP Gateway product into NetWare 4.0 in 1996. This solution requires the installation of components on the server (the gateway) and on the client (redirector). However, only the gateways require IP addresses. The gateway then handles all TCP/IP and IPX addressing and routing to and from clients.

The beauty of the IPX-IP Gateway is that it saves network administrators from having to deal with the headache of IP addressing (because only the gateways need IP addresses). Routing by the gateway is thorough enough that any connected IPX workstation is free to use a standard Web browser or other WinSock-compliant TCP programs just as if TCP/IP were configured natively at the desktop.

Routing all IP communications though a gateway does add a layer of overhead to all communications sessions. It also creates a situation in which the gateway can serve as a simple firewall. By tying into Novell's NDS directory utility, the IPX-IP Gateway provides the network administrator with a single console from which all user-, group-, and organizational-access rights can be defined and monitored.

NetWare/IP

First introduced as an add-on for NetWare 3.1x and NetWare 4.x in 1993, NetWare/IP was designed specifically to integrate NetWare services into a TCP/IP environment. It is also shipped as a component of Novell's MultiProtocol Router.

NetWare/IP more thoroughly integrates NetWare 3.x or 4.x services into a TCP/IP environment than any of the previously described approaches. It does so by using both encapsulation and transmission of standard IP packets. It is also a solution that requires more effort than the previously described solutions. For example, NetWare/IP requires the installation of several independent cooperating client and server components.

The NetWare/IP client software consists of a TCP/IP stack (`TCPIP.EXE`), a module called `NWIP.EXE`, and either the NetWare shell (`NETX.EXE`) or the NetWare DOS Requester (VLMs). The NetWare/IP client architecture remains the same as traditional NetWare client architecture at the Hardware, ODI, and Application Layers. The Transport Layer, however, is altered, using the UDP-TCP/IP protocol stack (`TCPIP.EXE`) (also used in Novell's LAN WorkPlace products), in place of the traditional IPX addressing scheme.

This solution also bundles and builds upon Novell versions of standard IP management utilities. For example, Domain Name System (DNS), a distributed look-up service, is used to centralize hostname-to-IP address information. Domain SAP Server (DSS) maintains a database used to store and disseminate IPX SAP information to NetWare/IP clients and servers.

NetWare 3.x and 4.x services, such as file, print, and directory services, advertise themselves via Novell's *Service Advertising Protocol* (SAP). Every 60 seconds, these services broadcast a packet that lists name, service type, and address information. When a NetWare/IP server boots, it advertises itself to the rest of the network by sending the SAP record directly to its nearest DSS using UDP.

With NetWare/IP, all IPX communications are encapsulated within IP. Because the IPX stack is still available on each workstation, old IPX-based applications can still communicate directly with that stack. Because it operates under an IP encapsulation, those same IPX applications can also be accessed by users logging in using TCP/IP. There are, of course, limitations to what the TCP/IP emulation can do. For example, applications that depend on IPX broadcast mechanisms will not work properly when they are sent through an IP router.

NetWare 5/NetWare 6—IP and All the Comforts of Novell

NetWare 5 and NetWare 6's native support for pure TCP/IP is a neat trick. Novell has completely redesigned the operating system and the management tools shipped as part of that operating system so that it can be configured as a pure IP network, as a pure IPX network, or as a hybrid that supports both protocols simultaneously. All the old IPX dependencies have been removed from the operating system's core. Close hooks between NetWare's Core Protocols (NCP) and TCP/IP have been added wherever they are appropriate. As a result, all the NetWare services available in previous versions are now available over TCP/IP.

Pure IP

The NetWare 5 and NetWare 6 operating system and associated management tools such as NDS now feature full native support for TCP/IP. The operating system, clients logged in to the operating system, and applications running on that operating system can communicate with each other using TCP/IP as the only communication protocol stack. There is no longer a need to resort to IPX encapsulation, routing, tunneling, or gateways. These tricks got the job done for earlier versions of NetWare and are still used by most other (non-Unix) operating systems, but they also consumed network bandwidth and impacted hardware resources. Using only IP traffic on the wire reduces software and hardware routing requirements, expands network bandwidth, frees you from the need to support multiple protocols, and provides greater opportunities for remotely connecting to the Internet and your own corporate intranets.

Multiple Protocols

Although IP is now the default communications protocol, Novell has not cut its ties to the millions of users of NetWare 3.x, 4.x, and older IPX-based tools. Hooks to IPX remain in NetWare 5 and NetWare 6 so they can be turned back on by those who need them. With NetWare 5 and NetWare 6, you can move to an IP-only environment without having to convert every IPX-based application or needlessly disrupt enterprise operations. Or, you can choose to install IPX as the default and completely avoid issues that must be dealt with when migrating to IP. You can also operate in a hybrid environment and slowly move away from IPX and into IP as needs require or as new skills are developed.

Installation Options

When you install NetWare 5 or NetWare 6, you choose one of three modes:

- IP
- IP/IPX
- IPX

The choice you make determines how NetWare binds itself to protocol stacks and to network adapters but does not determine which protocol stacks are loaded in the system. For example, systems that are installed using the IP-only install option have both the TCP/IP and the IPX stacks loaded but only the TCP/IP stack is bound to the network adapter. In this case, IP is the native protocol. The IPX stack is loaded here to give the system the ability to execute IPX applications and to connect with IPX systems through use of the Novell Migration Agent.

Systems installed with the IP and IPX option are configured to establish NCP connections over either the TCP/IP stack or over the IPX stack.

By providing for simultaneous access to both IPX and TCP/IP, NetWare 5 and NetWare 6 maintain support for existing IPX-bound applications and all IP and IPX routing investments as necessary. NetWare 5 and NetWare 6 also bundle Compatibility Mode routines (described in detail later), which can be used to manage IPX-based applications on a network installed using the Pure IP installation. Another bundled facility, the NetWare Migration Agent, provides a mechanism for supporting communication between two networks, one installed as a pure IP network and one based upon the IPX protocol.

Figure 27.1 illustrates the IP/IPX installation options.

FIGURE 27.1

NetWare 5 IP/IPX installation options.

IP-Only Installation of NetWare 5 and NetWare 6

Customers awash in IP-based communications may find that NetWare 5 and NetWare 6's IP-only installation simplifies their lives immensely, eliminating multiple protocols and freeing up valuable network bandwidth. The IP-only configuration allows the server to communicate directly with any client or server that uses TCP/IP stacks. The IPX stack is loaded but not bound to the network card. You can use Novell's bundled Compatibility Mode utility to execute IPX-based applications, but first you'll need to install the Migration Agent (a Novell gateway) to connect to IPX-bound servers or clients. Benefits include the fact that managing a single protocol requires less hardware and software, lessens management overhead, makes more efficient use of bandwidth, increases performance, and lowers cost. Pure IP also tends to be more efficient when networks get very large.

What You Need to Know Before Installing

When you enable TCP/IP as part of the NetWare 5 and NetWare 6 installation, you are asked to enter a standard IP address for the server. Both TCP/IP and the IPX stacks are loaded but only the TCP/IP stack is bound to the network adapter. The IPX stack is used to allow applications written with IPX in mind to run and to provide Novell's Migration Agent to facilitate connections to users logging in from an IPX-only network.

IPX-Only Installation

For small networks, and even some medium-sized ones, IPX remains an attractive solution. The administrative costs of setting up and maintaining a small IPX network are much lower than doing the same for a similarly scaled TCP/IP network. NetWare uses dynamic updates to eliminate much of the burden of administering IPX. For example, adding new devices and interconnecting network segments is easy. Add the name of the new device to the local AUTOEXEC.NCF file and the server takes over the job from there. IPX broadcasts updates every 60 seconds providing each server and router on the network with the information it needs to update its internal tables, letting them know how to reach that new device.

All this automation does add a certain amount of overhead. As the number of connections increases, so, too, does the overhead of all those updates. Thus, TCP/IP is undoubtedly a more appropriate solution for very large networks. But users of more moderate needs should consider staying in the IPX camp.

Obviously, a NetWare 5 or NetWare 6 server installed in IPX-Only mode can communicate with other IPX servers and clients efficiently and without translation. It can also, albeit less efficiently, communicate with servers and clients running pure TCP/IP by using the intermediation of the bundled Novell Migration Agent (described in detail later).

What You Need to Know Before Installing

If you choose to make an IPX-only install, you are asked to select an internal IPX address for the server, just as was required in a NetWare 3.x or 4.x installation.

Hybrid IPX/IP Installations

Novell has a long history of providing solutions that allow transmission of both TCP and IPX communications across a single network. Anyone faced with the daunting task of managing such a hybrid network will find a lot to like in NetWare 5 and NetWare 6.

Servers and clients installed using the NetWare 5 and NetWare 6 hybrid IP/IPX installation can communicate using either protocol. This approach allows the NetWare 5 or NetWare 6 server to freely exchange messages with any well-behaved IP or IPX server or client. Such a server can also execute applications written with IPX in mind.

Hybrid installations are complicated by the fact that users are given a great deal of freedom to choose which IP and IPX addressing schemes they want their new network to support. As might be expected, the more options installed, the greater the overhead. Thus, most network administrators install only those features their networks are most likely to use on a regular basis.

Some breakdowns are inevitable if you try to establish communications between two hybrid NetWare 5 or NetWare 6 servers configured by different people at different times. For example, complications may arise when routing messages sent out by a Pure IP NetWare client configured to use a pure IP addressing scheme are sent to another server connected to NetWare clients that were configured to recognize only IPX addressing schemes. These kinds of mismatches can be easily rectified by the Migration Agent utility, which Novell bundles into NetWare 5 and NetWare 6. The Migration Agent automatically translates cross-protocol communications as needed. Use of the Migration Agent does impose overhead. The key to an efficient installation is to configure the network so that it includes all facilities needed on a regular basis and to pass all infrequently encountered IP/IPX translations off to utilities such as the Migration Agent.

What You Need to Know Before Installing

If you choose to install both the IP and IPX option, the system is configured to establish NetWare Core Protocol connections over either the TCP/IP stack or over an IPX stack. You will need to provide both an internal IPX address and a standard IP address for the server.

Tools That Aid in IP Migration

Novell realizes that the jump from IPX to TCP/IP will be a big one for much of its user base. It is trying to make the transformation as easy as possible by bundling a host of transformation tools along with NetWare 5 and NetWare 6. Some of these are updates of old familiar tools. For example, NDS has been reworked so that it can track and support TCP/IP resources as well as IPX resources. Novell has extended NDS's reach by creating links between NDS and other standard IP utilities bundled with NetWare. These utilities include Novell's versions of DNS, DDNS, and DHCP. SLP is another standard IP utility that has been revised to work in a NetWare IP/IPX environment. Novell's Compatibility Mode and Migration Agent provide collections of routines that can perform on-the-fly translations between IPX and TCP/IP.

NDS

Novell's NetWare Directory Services is a global and extensible directory service that provides a central console from which network administrators can view and manage all sorts of network resources distributed across a single network or across a mixed array of NT/2000, NetWare, and Unix networks organized as a WAN. First introduced as part of NetWare 4, the NDS database contains complete information about every user, object, and other resource within its reach. NetWare 5 has extended NDS's reach so that it is now capable of managing a mixture of IP and IPX devices and sessions.

DNS

The Domain Name System is commonly used to match user-defined system names with their unique IP network or Internet addresses. The NetWare DNS server can be coupled with a non-NetWare DNS server as either a primary or a slave. Facilities are provided to allow bi-directional transfer of data between primary and secondary servers. Allowing this sort of transfer of information can significantly reduce the cost of incorporating a NetWare 5 network into a larger enterprise-wide network.

DHCP

Dynamic Host Configuration Protocol is a protocol that automatically assigns and tracks IP addresses and other configuration data in network devices. DHCP options can be set at the enterprise, subnet, or client level. For example, you can allocate a specific amount of time that DHCP clients will be allowed to use a particular IP address. Frequent reallocation of IP resources can be used to purge inactive resources, and thus allow a large number of clients to share a limited number of IP addresses.

DDNS

NetWare 5 and NetWare 6's Dynamic DNS (DDNS)) helps coordinate the functions of the Novell DNS and DHCP facilities. For example, DDNS updates DNS information on-the-fly, matching address changes made via DHCP. The DHCP services in NetWare also provide NDS configuration information to clients, such as their initial context, NDS server name, and tree name.

SLP

On mixed IP/IPX servers, NetWare 5 and NetWare 6 use a standard Internet protocol called *Service Location Protocol* (SLP) to provide naming and discovery services. SLP does not provide name resolution services like DNS or NDS. Its purpose is to discover infrastructure services such as NDS servers, DNS servers, DHCP servers, NDPS registration servers, and various protocol gateways.

SLP provides backward compatibility with the services and applications of SAP (Novell's old IPX-specific discovery agent). Pure IP networks that don't require backward compatibility don't need to run SLP. IPX-only installations can continue to use SAP and may have no need for SLP.

Compatibility Mode

Compatibility Mode provides on-demand IPX support to Pure IP NetWare 5 and NetWare 6 networks. It does so by encapsulating IPX datagrams inside a UDP stack so they can be carried across networks wired for TCP/IP, and by resolving RIP and SAP requests through the use of the Service Location Protocol.

Both client and server compatibility drivers are installed automatically as part of any Pure IP NetWare 5 or NetWare 6 install. When not in use, Compatibility Mode drivers (the SCMD.NLM module) lie dormant, with no appreciable effect on network communications. Encapsulation is performed only when IPX-specific support is required. All traffic that does not require IPX-specific support is automatically routed through IP without encapsulation.

The beauty of Compatibility Mode is that it makes phased migrations feasible. You can make the move to pure IP at your own pace, secure in the knowledge that Compatibility Mode will bridge occasional protocol mismatches whenever they occur.

Compatibility Mode drivers are brought into play as soon as any linked client or server is asked to pass an IPX protocol stack across wiring set up to handle TCP/IP-only communications. This happens, for example, when a message formatted for IPX arrives at the firewall door and asks to be routed to a user inside the IP network. Compatibility Mode can also be used to provide backbone support. For example, it can allow two disconnected IPX networks to pass information back and forth through an IP-only network. Compatibility Mode also provides facilities to ensure backward compatibility with NetWare 3.x bindery services.

Migration Agent

The Migration Agent performs two essential services. First, it translates between IP and IPX. Second, it provides a bridge between the old and new naming and discovery services (NetWare's SLP and NetWare 4's SAP).

The Migration Agent is only needed when you want to link the two logical worlds of IP and IPX. It provides emulation that prevents IPX protocol families from populating the IP world, and it replaces SAP and RIP packets on behalf of IPX clients. The Migration Agent uses IP and IPX addresses and the routing information contained in IPX packets to send each packet to the appropriate destination.

NetWare 5 and NetWare 6 servers installed with the Migration Agent enabled can communicate directly with other systems without regard to the install option used during installation. They are also capable of routing network traffic between IP and IPX systems.

Migration Strategies

Gradual migration is probably the best choice for most users and is possible because Novell vows to continue support for existing IPX installations. However, the arrival of NetWare 5 and then NetWare 6 built around a Pure IP infrastructure provides just one more acknowledgement that IPX's days are numbered and that TCP/IP will quickly become dominant even in the world of NetWare networks. The question that NetWare users now face is how fast to move into the TCP/IP camp. Fortunately, Novell is providing users with lots of options. You can make the transition slowly or in one fell swoop. What's important is that you think before you migrate.

Using a Test Platform

Do not conduct migration experiments on your mission-critical network. Most Novell networks have evolved slowly and tend to be a mixture of old and new software and hardware that no one person fully understands. Working out all your migration issues on a working network is not a good idea. The use of a test migration platform can save you from a lot of grief. Better to isolate and cure your IPX withdrawal symptoms on a lab guinea pig rather than with some user working on a mission-critical problem. It is worthwhile to start with a test platform installed using NetWare's Pure IP mode (no IPX stacks installed). Test to see which of your legacy applications can run as-is or with aid of a free or low-cost upgrade. Try running the applications that fail on the test platform installed in the hybrid IPX/IP mode.

Suggested Migration Scenarios

If everything runs just fine on your Pure IP test platform, you may decide to upgrade your whole network to Pure IP in one fell swoop. Chances are, the only networks that fit into this category will be small ones—networks that provide little more than simple file and print sharing capabilities.

Larger networks, on the other hand, are best migrated slowly and incrementally. The trick is to select small network segments that can operate autonomously. For example, one good approach is to start the migration by removing IPX from the network backbone and replacing it with IP. The advantage to this approach is that backbones are not likely to be running messy IPX-bound applications and the migration should be fairly straight-forward.

A Pure IP backbone can be used to connect one or more IPX-based servers as long as a Novell Migration Agent is installed wherever IP segments touch IPX. The Migration Agent performs encapsulation and any other conversions required to send IPX messages across an IP pipe. With luck, a backbone migration will result in a drastic cut in the administrative costs associated with maintaining IPX over the backbone and set you up nicely for your next attempted segment migration.

Another approach is to start by migrating a few network segments that would most benefit from the move to IP, say, for example, your company's Internet server. The idea here is to provide management with a good, clean success story to validate the move toward IP. The downside of this approach is that because the backbone remains untouched, administrative costs may not be offset as quickly.

The most difficult part of the migration will come when you try to set up your IP network so that it can run legacy applications. Although NetWare 5 and NetWare 6 are designed so that all core protocols can be addressed using IP, many legacy applications write directly to the IPX stack or make use of older IPX utilities such as SAP and the Novell Bindery. Whenever possible, it makes sense to replace such older applications with newer versions written with IP in mind.

The sad fact is that many useful legacy applications are sure to be IPX-bound and that IP-friendly versions of many of those applications will not be available. Such programs can be accommodated by using NetWare's IPX Compatibility Mode. Be aware, however, that Compatibility Mode incurs a certain amount of overhead. For example, the compatibility drivers are dependent upon the proper installation of SLP. Setting up a SLP infrastructure will take time. On the other hand, SLP is an Internet standard of increasing importance and the likelihood is that its usefulness will increase as more and more applications take advantage of the services it provides.

Summary

This chapter began with a discussion of the various ways that IPX-based NetWare servers (NetWare 3.x and 4.x) can operate in a world that is rapidly moving to IP. The second part of the chapter focused on NetWare 5 and NetWare 6. It discussed how to migrate from an IPX-based NetWare 3.x or 4.x network to a Pure IP–based NetWare 5 and NetWare 6 networks. It also described the facilities Novell provides to allow IP and IPX to interoperate. We described some of the components and tools Novell bundles along with NetWare 5 and NetWare 6 to help users make the move toward IP. The chapter ended with a discussion of migration strategies that can be used to move from IPX to IP.

Configuring TCP/IP for Linux

by Tim Parker

In This Chapter

Linux is a popular public domain Unix version for Intel-based systems. It has also been ported to other processors such as SPARC, Alpha, Motorola 6800, Power PC, ARM, Hitachi SuperH, IBM S/390, MIPS, HPPA-RISC, Intel IA-64, DEC-VAX, AMD x86-64, and other processor architectures.

A Linux system consists of a kernel component, called the Linux kernel, and system tools and applications. The Linux kernel is controlled by Linus Torvalds and a close group of kernel programmers. However, many distributions of Linux exist. Each of these distributions uses the standard Linux kernel but differs in the bundling of system utilities and application software. The Linux kernel aims at POSIX and Single Unix Specification (SUS) compliance.

The Linux kernel is popularly available as a key component of distributions such as RedHat, Debian, Mandrake, Susie, Slackware, and so on. These distributions bundle the Linux kernel along with system utilities and application software. Most of the system utilities come from the GNU project, which produces some of the highest quality software ever written and is based on an open source license. To learn more about the open source license consult `http://www.eff.org` and related sites.

Because Linux is a Unix-like operating system, it is capable of acting as both client and server on a TCP/IP system.

Without going into excessive detail about the Linux operating system, this chapter looks at how you can configure your Linux machine to act as both client and server for a TCP/IP-based network, as well as provide both PPP and SLIP support.

The version of Linux distribution used as an example in this chapter is the SlackWare CD-ROM distribution, although the procedure is the same for RedHat and many other Linux distributions. For the purposes of this chapter, it is assumed you have properly installed Linux and its networking components.

> **Note**
>
> Linux is an "infinitely" configurable system, and some of the distributions also differ in the manner in which Linux system services are bundled and started. Linux kernels have version numbers such as 2.0, 2.2, and 2.4. The "2" in the version number represents a major release from the previous version. The number after the "." represents a minor release with even numbers, such as 2.0, 2.2, 2.4, implying a stable release of the Linux kernel.
>
> Odd numbers for the minor version are used for kernel versions with experimental features that have not been completely tested. Therefore, kernel versions 2.1 and 2.3 are "experimental" kernels. Deploying experimental kernels in a production environment is not generally considered a good idea.

> You can get the latest Linux kernel from http://www.kernel.org and its mirror sites.
>
> Distributions such as RedHat, Debian, Mandrake, and Slackware take a Linux kernel and add system utilities, and start up scripts and applications around it. They differ in the manner in which these services are added and configured. These distributions have their own version numbers. For example, RedHat 7.0 used a Linux 2.2 kernel whereas RedHat 7.2 uses the 2.4 kernel.

Preparing Your System for TCP/IP

Before configuring TCP/IP on your Linux system, you need to perform a few small steps to ensure that your filesystem is ready. The first step is to make sure the networking software has been installed. You can install the network package through the setup program, as shown in Figure 28.1. Selecting the networking option installs the applications you need to use TCP/IP under Linux.

Note

Other distributions, notably RedHat, now have a GUI installation that makes installing the Linux system easier for the novice.

After the network software has been installed, you might have to reboot your system.

FIGURE 28.1

The Linux setup program lets you install the networking software easily.

Some versions of Linux (notably those that use the 2.0 kernel and many of the latest releases) require a /proc filesystem for networking to function properly. Most Linux kernels that inherently support networking automatically create the /proc filesystem when the operating system is installed, so you shouldn't have to do anything more than make sure it is properly mounted by the kernel. (The /proc filesystem is a quick interface point for the kernel to obtain network information, as well as to help the kernel maintain tables usually kept in the subdirectory /proc/net.) You can verify that your Linux version uses the /proc filesystem by trying to do a "cd /proc" command to change to the /proc directory, as shown in Figure 28.2.

FIGURE 28.2

If you can change into the /proc filesystem and obtain a directory listing, the filesystem exists and TCP/IP can be configured properly.

```
merlin:~# cd /proc
merlin:/proc# ls
1/            46/       73/       80/         kcore      pci
174/          49/       74/       cpuinfo     kmsg       self/
24/           51/       75/       devices     ksyms      stat
38/           55/       76/       dma         loadavg    uptime
40/           6/        77/       filesystems meminfo    version
42/           7/        78/       interrupts  modules
44/           72/       79/       ioports     net/
merlin:/proc#
```

If you can't change into /proc, it probably doesn't exist (assuming you have access permissions, of course). If the /proc filesystem was not created for you by the Linux installation routine, you have to rebuild the kernel and select the /proc option. Change to the Linux source directory (such as /usr/src/Linux) and run the kernel configuration routine with this command:

```
make config
```

If you have X-Windows running and properly configured, you can run the following GUI-based configuration process:

```
make xconfig
```

When you are asked whether you want procfs support (or a similarly worded question), answer yes. If you do not get asked about the /proc filesystem support, and the /proc directory is not created on your filesystem, you need to upgrade your kernel to support networking.

The /proc filesystem should be mounted automatically when your Linux system boots. To force the /proc filesystem to be mounted automatically, edit the /etc/fstab file and add a line similar to this (if it isn't already there):

```
none           /proc          proc           defaults
```

Another step you should take before configuring TCP/IP is to set the system's hostname. To set the hostname, use this command:

```
hostname name
```

name is the system name you want for your local machine. If you have a full domain name assigned to your network and your machine, you can use that name for your system. For example, if your Linux machine is attached to the domain yacht.com and your machine's name is spinnaker, you can set the full domain name using this command:

```
hostname spinnaker.yacht.com
```

If you don't have a fully qualified domain name, you can make up your own domain name as long as you are not connected to the Internet. (A made-up domain name does not have any meaning outside your local area network.) Alternatively, you do not have to assign a domain at all for your machine, but can simply enter this short name:

```
hostname spinnaker
```

An entry is made in the /etc/hosts file to reflect your machine's name. You should verify that your machine's name appears in that file. You also need to know the IP address assigned to your machine. You should have a unique IP address ready for your Linux machine for use in the configuration process.

One file that you might need to work with if you plan to direct information across many networks is /etc/networks. The /etc/networks file contains a list of all the network names your machine should know about, along with their IP addresses. Applications use this file to determine target networks based on the network name. The /etc/networks file consists of two columns for the symbolic name of the remote network and its IP address. Most /etc/networks files have at least one entry for the loopback driver that should be on every Linux system (the loopback driver is used as a default IP address by some Linux applications and is discussed in more detail later in this chapter). A sample /etc/networks file looks like this:

```
loopback        127.0.0.0
merlin-net      147.154.12.0
BNR             47.0.0.0
```

This sample file has two networks entered in it with their network IP addresses. Only the network portion of the IP address is specified, leaving the host component of the IP addresses set to zeros.

Network Interface Access

You need to make the network interface accessible to the operating system and its utilities. This is done with the `ifconfig` command. When run, `ifconfig` makes the Network Layer of the kernel work with the network interface by giving it an IP address, and then issuing the command to make the interface active. When the interface is active, the kernel can send and receive data through the interface.

You need to set up several interfaces for your machine, including the loopback driver and the Ethernet interface (I assume you are using Ethernet throughout this chapter, but you can use other interfaces). The `ifconfig` command is used for each interface in order. The syntax of the `ifconfig` command is

```
ifconfig interface_type IP_Address
```

where *interface_type* is the interface's device driver name (such as `lo` for loopback, `ppp` for PPP, and `eth` for Ethernet). *IP_Address* is the IP address used by that interface.

After the `ifconfig` command has been run and the interface is active, you use the `route` command to add or remove routes to the kernel's routing table. This is necessary to enable the local machine to find other machines. The syntax of the `route` command is

```
route add|del IP_Address
```

where either `add` or `del` is used to add or remove a route from the kernel's routing table, and *IP_Address* is the remote route being affected.

You can display the current contents of the kernel's routing table by entering the `route` command with no arguments. For example, if your system is set up only with a loopback driver, you will see this:

```
$ route
Kernel Routing Table
Destination    Gateway    Genmask     Flags  MSS  Window  Use Iface
loopback       *          255.0.0.0   U      1936 0        16  lo
```

Note

You can also display the routing table using the following command:

```
netstat -rn
```

The `-r` option displays the routing table and the `-n` option displays IP addresses instead of symbolic names.

The columns with which you should be concerned are the destination name, which shows the name of the configured target (in this case `loopback`), the mask to be used (`Genmask`), and the interface (`Iface`, in this case `/dev/lo`). You can force `route` to display the IP addresses instead of symbolic names by using the `-n` option:

```
$ route -n
Kernel Routing Table
Destination     Gateway    Genmask     Flags  MSS  Window  Use Iface
127.0.0.1          *       255.0.0.0     U    1936   0       16 lo
```

As mentioned earlier in this section, a typical Linux network configuration includes a loopback interface (which should exist on every machine) and a network interface such as Ethernet. You can set these interfaces up in order.

Setting Up the Loopback Interface

A loopback interface should exist on every machine. It is used by some applications that require an IP address in order to function properly, which may not exist if the Linux system is not configured for networking. The loopback driver is also used as a diagnostic utility by some TCP/IP applications. The loopback interface has the IP address 127.0.0.1, so the `/etc/hosts` file should have an entry for this interface.

> **Note**
>
> A loop back address is any address of the form 127.*x.x.x* where *x* is a number from 0 to 255. The address of 127.0.0.1 is commonly used as a loopback address for historical reasons. This was the format in which the loopback address was specified in the `/etc/hosts` file on Unix systems.

A loopback driver might have been created by the kernel during software installation, so check the `/etc/hosts` file for a line similar to this:

```
localhost         127.0.0.1
```

If such a line exists, the loopback driver is already in place and you can continue to the Ethernet interface. If you are not sure about the `/etc/hosts` file, you can use the `ifconfig` utility to display all the information it knows about the loopback driver. Use this command:

```
ifconfig lo
```

28

CONFIGURING
TCP/IP FOR
LINUX

You should see several lines of information. If you get an error message, the loopback driver does not exist.

If the loopback interface is not in the /etc/hosts file, you need to create it with the ifconfig command. The following command creates the necessary line in /etc/hosts:

ifconfig lo 127.0.0.1

You can view the specifics of the newly created loopback driver with ifconfig. For example, the following command shows the loopback driver's typical configuration:

```
$ ifconfig lo
lo              Link encap: Local Loopback
inet addr 127.0.0.1 Bcast {NONE SET] Mask 255.0.0.0
UP BROADCAST LOOPBACK RUNNING   MTU 2000 Metric 1
RX packets:0 errors:0 dropped:0 overruns:0
TX packets:0 errors:0 dropped:0 overruns:0
```

As long as the loopback driver's details are shown as output from the ifconfig command, all is well with that interface. After checking the ifconfig routine, you should add the loopback driver to the kernel routing tables with one of these two commands:

```
route add 127.0.0.1
route add localhost
```

It doesn't matter which command you use. As a quick check that all is correct with the loopback driver, you can use the ping command to check the routing. If you issue this command:

ping localhost

you should see output like this:

```
PING localhost: 56 data bytes
64 bytes from 127.0.0.1: icmp_seq=0.  ttl=255 time=1 ms
64 bytes from 127.0.0.1: icmp_seq=1.  ttl=255 time=1 ms
64 bytes from 127.0.0.1: icmp_seq=2.  ttl=255 time=1 ms
64 bytes from 127.0.0.1: icmp_seq=3.  ttl=255 time=1 ms
64 bytes from 127.0.0.1: icmp_seq=4.  ttl=255 time=1 ms
64 bytes from 127.0.0.1: icmp_seq=5.  ttl=255 time=1 ms
64 bytes from 127.0.0.1: icmp_seq=6.  ttl=255 time=1 ms
64 bytes from 127.0.0.1: icmp_seq=7.  ttl=255 time=1 ms
^C
 localhost PING Statistics
7 packets transmitted, 7 packets received, 0% packet loss
round-trip (ms) min/avg/max = 1/1/1
```

The ping command's progress was interrupted by issuing a Ctrl+C. If you get no output from the ping command, the localhost name wasn't recognized. Check the configuration files and route entry again and repeat the ping to the loopback address.

Setting Up the Ethernet Interface

You can follow the same procedure to set up the Ethernet driver. You use `ifconfig` to tell the kernel about the interface, and then add the routes to the remote machines on the network. If the network is attached to your machine, you can test the connections immediately with the `ping` command.

Set up the Ethernet interface using `ifconfig`. To make the interface active, use the `ifconfig` command with the Ethernet device name (usually `eth0`) and your IP address. For example, use the following command to set up your system with the IP address 147.123.20.1:

```
ifconfig eth0 147.123.20.1
```

You don't have to specify the network mask with the `ifconfig` command because it can deduce the proper value from the IP address. If you want to provide the network mask value explicitly, append it to the command line with the keyword `netmask`:

```
ifconfig eth0 147.123.20.1 netmask 255.255.255.0
```

You can check the interface with the `ifconfig` command using this Ethernet interface name:

```
$ ifconfig eth0
eth0                    Link encap 10Mps: Ethernet Hwaddr
inet addr 147.123.20.1 Bcast 147.123.1.255 Mask 255.255.255.0
UP BROADCAST RUNNING  MTU 1500 Metric 1
RX packets:0 errors:0 dropped:0 overruns:0
TX packets:0 errors:0 dropped:0 overruns:0
```

You might notice in the output that the broadcast address is set based on the local machine's IP address. This is used by TCP/IP to access all machines on the local area network at once. The *Maximum Transfer Unit* (MTU) size is usually set to the maximum value of 1500 (for Ethernet networks).

Next, you need to add an entry to the kernel routing tables to let the kernel know the local machine's network address. The IP address that is used with the `route` command to do this is that of the network as a whole, without the local identifier. To set the entire local area network at once, the `-net` option of the `route` command is used. In the case of the IP addresses shown earlier, the command is

```
route add -net 147.123.20.0
```

This command adds all the machines on the local area network identified by the network address 147.123.20 to the kernel's list of accessible machines. If you didn't do it this way, you would have to manually enter the IP address of each machine on the network.

An alternative is to use the /etc/networks file to specify only the network portions of the IP addresses. The /etc/networks file might contain a list of network names and their IP addresses. If you have an entry in the /etc/networks file for a network called foobar_net, you could add the entire network to the routing table with this command:

```
route add foobar_net
```

Using the /etc/networks file approach has the security problem that any machine on that network is granted access. This may not be what you want.

After the route has been added to the kernel routing tables, you can try the Ethernet interface. To ping another machine (assuming you are connected to the Ethernet cable, of course), you need either its IP address or its name (which is resolved either by the /etc/hosts file or a service like DNS). The command and output looks like this:

```
tpci_sco1-45> ping 142.12.130.12
PING 142.12.130.12: 64 data bytes
64 bytes from 142.12.130.12: icmp_seq=0.  time=20.  ms
64 bytes from 142.12.130.12: icmp_seq=1.  time=10.  ms
64 bytes from 142.12.130.12: icmp_seq=2.  time=10.  ms
64 bytes from 142.12.130.12: icmp_seq=3.  time=20.  ms
64 bytes from 142.12.130.12: icmp_seq=4.  time=10.  ms
64 bytes from 142.12.130.12: icmp_seq=5.  time=10.  ms
64 bytes from 142.12.130.12: icmp_seq=6.  time=10.  ms
^C
 142.12.130.12 PING Statistics
7 packets transmitted, 7 packets received, 0% packet loss
round-trip (ms) min/avg/max = 10/12/20
```

If you don't get anything back from the remote machine, verify that the remote is connected and you are using the proper IP address. If all is well there, check the configuration and route commands. If that checks out, try pinging another machine.

After these steps are completed, your Linux system should be able to access any machine on the local area network through TCP/IP. If you are on a small network, that's all you really have to do. On larger networks, or those that implement special protocols or employ gateways, you need to take a few more configuration steps. These steps are covered in the following sections.

If you want to allow a few other machines on the TCP/IP network to access your Linux machine, you can put their names and IP addresses in the /etc/hosts file. Figure 28.3 shows a sample /etc/hosts file with a name and possible variations (such as godzilla and godzilla.tpci), and its IP address. That machine (which can be any operating system running TCP/IP) can now connect to your Linux system using telnet, ftp, or a similar utility. Of course, a user on the remote machine can't log in unless you set up an account for him. If the name of a remote machine is in the /etc/hosts file, you can also telnet or ftp to that machine using either its name or IP address.

FIGURE 28.3

This /etc/hosts file lets remote machines connect to the Linux server.

```
merlin:/etc# cat hosts
#
# hosts          This file describes a number of hostname-to-address
#                mappings for the TCP/IP subsystem. It is mostly
#                used at boot time, when no name servers are running.
#                On small systems, this file can be used instead of a
#                "named" name server. Just add the names, addresses,
#                and any aliases to this file...
# By the way, Arnt Gulbrandsen <agulbra@nvg.unit.no> says that 127.0.0.1
# should NEVER be named with the name of the machine. It causes problems
# for some (stupid) programs, irc and reputedly talk. :^)
#

# For loopbacking.
127.0.0.1       localhost
147.120.0.1                  merlin.tpci.com merlin
147.120.0.2     pepper pepper.tcpi.com
147.120.0.3     megan megan.tcpi.com
147.120.0.4     godzilla godzilla.tcpi.com
# End of hosts.
merlin:/etc#
```

Name Service and Name Resolver

TCP/IP uses the /etc/hosts file to resolve symbolic names into IP addresses. For example, when you give the name darkstar for a target machine, TCP/IP examines the /etc/hosts file for a machine of that name, and then reads its IP address. If the name isn't in the file, you can't send data to it.

Suppose you connect to several different machines. Adding all those entries to the /etc/hosts file can be tiresome and difficult, and maintaining the files as changes occur in the networks can be even more bothersome. On those rare instances where you need to connect to only about a dozen machines, maintaining the /etc/hosts file is all that you need. To solve the general name resolution problem, BIND was developed. BIND (Berkeley Internet Name Domain service) was developed to help resolve the IP addresses of remote machines. BIND was later developed into DNS (Domain Name System). Most Linux distributions implement the BIND version, although a few DNS-specific versions of software are appearing. Both BIND and DNS are complex subjects and involve many details that simply are not of interest to most Linux users. If you already have a DNS server on your network, or if you intend on using an ISP's DNS server, you do not need to configure your machine to run BIND. However, you should at least configure your machine to use a DNS server, because entering host names of all sites that are of interest to you in the /etc/hosts file is a tedious process. The name resolver is the DNS client, and in the case of Linux, is a set of library routines that are called whenever an application needs to resolve a name using DNS. The name resolver is configured using the /etc/resolv.conf file.

28

CONFIGURING TCP/IP FOR LINUX

Typical contents of this file include a search directive and name server directives. The search directive takes the following form:

```
search domain1 domain2 domainN
```

The *domain1*, *domain2*, and *domainN* are replaced by a list of the domain name suffixes the name resolver will append to a hostname that is not in its Fully Qualified Domain Name (FQDN) form. As an example, consider the following search directive:

```
search xyz.com us.xyz.com europe.xyz.com
```

If a name such as www.abc.com is used, it is in the FQDN form and has a full domain name abc.com suffixed to the host name, www. In this case, the search directive is not used. However, if a TCP/IP service uses the name www, it is not in the FQDN form. In this case, the search directive will try to resolve this as first www.xyz.com, then www.us.xyz.com, and finally www.europe.xyz.com. If any of these names is properly resolved, there is no need to search for other names.

The DNS server the name resolver uses is specified by the nameserver directive:

```
nameserver IPaddress
```

The *IPaddress* is the IP address of the DNS server. For example, if the first DNS server has an IP address of 199.231.13.10, then this directive will appear as the following:

```
nameserver 199.231.13.10
```

Up to three DNS servers can be specified, each with its own nameserver directive on a line by itself. For example, if the second and third DNS servers are 199.231.13.20 and 199.231.13.15, the full set of name server directives would appear as

```
nameserver 199.231.13.10

nameserver 199.231.13.20

nameserver 199.231.13.15
```

Combining the full set of search and nameserver directives, the example /etc/resolv.conf will have the following contents:

```
search xyz.com us.xyz.com europe.xyz.com

nameserver 199.231.13.10

nameserver 199.231.13.20

nameserver 199.231.13.15
```

You can also configure whether the name resolution process will consult the /etc/hosts file first and then DNS, or first DNS and then the /etc/hosts file. This order can be controlled by configuring the /etc/nsswitch.conf file.

For larger systems, or if you want to run the full Internet services available to your Linux machine, you need to configure BIND properly. Luckily, BIND usually needs to be configured only once, and then it can be ignored. You need the BIND software, which is usually included in the distribution software. The BIND package includes all the files and executables, as well as a copy of the BIND Operator's Guide (BOG) that you can consult for information on how to configure BIND database files.

Gateways

When two or more local area networks are connected, they use a gateway. A *gateway* is a machine that acts as the connection between the two networks, routing data between the two based on the IP address of the destination machine. You have to make some changes to the network configuration files whenever your local machine is going to use a gateway, as well as if your machine is going to act as a gateway.

To use the services of another machine as a gateway, you have to tell the routing tables about the gateway and the networks that it connects to. The simplest use of a gateway is one used to connect to the rest of the world, such as the Internet. This is configured with the route command like this:

```
route add default gw net_gate
```

net_gate is the name of the machine on your local area network that acts as the gateway. The gateway machine follows the keyword gw in the route command. The use of the word default in the command indicates that the kernel's routing table should assume that all networks can be reached through that gateway.

If you want to configure a gateway to another local area network, the name of that network should be in the /etc/networks file. For example, if you have a gateway machine called gate_serv that leads from your own local area network to a neighboring network called big_corp (and an entry exists in the /etc/networks file for big_corp with its network IP address), you could configure the routing tables on your local machine to use gate_serv to access big_corp machines with this command:

```
route add big_corp gw gate_serv
```

An entry should be made on the remote network's routing table to reflect your network's address; otherwise, you would only be able to send data and not receive it.

If you want to set up your local machine to act as a gateway itself, you need to configure the two network connections your machine is joining. This usually requires two network boards, PPP connections, or SLIP connections in some combination. Assume your machine is going to act as a simple gateway between two networks called small_net and big_net, and you have two Ethernet cards installed in your machine. You configure both Ethernet interfaces separately with their respective network IP addresses (for example, your machine might have an IP address on big_net of 163.12.34.36, whereas on small_net it might have the IP address 147.123.12.1).

You should add the two network addresses to your /etc/hosts file to simplify network name resolution. For the networks and IP addresses mentioned, you will have the following two entries in the /etc/hosts file:

```
163.12.34.36            merlin.big_net.com merlin-iface1
147.123.12.1            merlin.small_net.com merlin-iface2
```

This example shows the fully qualified domain names in the /etc/hosts file (this example assumes the machine has the name merlin on both networks, which is perfectly legal). You can also add shorter forms of the name, as well (such as merlin, merlin.big_net, and so on). Finally, the interface names have been included for convenience (so merlin-iface1 is the first interface on merlin, and merlin-iface2 is the second).

You then use the ifconfig commands to set up the connections between the interface and the names used in the /etc/hosts file:

```
ifconfig eth0 merlin-iface1
ifconfig eth1 merlin-iface2
```

These commands assume that the Ethernet device /dev/eth0 is for the interface to big_net and /dev/eth1 is for small_net.

Finally, the kernel routing table must be updated to reflect the two network names. The commands for this example are shown here:

```
route add big_net
route add small_net
```

When these steps are completed, you can use your machine as a gateway between the two networks. Other machines on either network can also use your machine as a gateway between the two networks.

Using Graphical Tools to Configure Network Interfaces

The procedures described so far show how network interfaces are configured from scratch from the command line. When a Linux system starts, you seldom have to issue these commands, because the startup scripts for the Linux system distribution will execute them in the startup scripts. These startup scripts are shell (bash, actually which is the Born Again Shell) scripts, and differ from distribution to distribution. Some distributions use the BSD Unix-style startup scripts (such as Slackware) whereas others use the System VR4 Unix-style startup scripts (such as RedHat). The details of the startup script change from distribution to distribution. Even within the same distribution, different versions of the distribution sometimes make radical changes in their startup scripts.

However, many distributions come with a graphical tool to simplify network configuration. These tools will automatically make changes so that your Linux system startup scripts will find the appropriate TCP/IP parameters.

The following sections discuss the use of netcfg and linuxconf in configuring TCP/IP for Linux.

Using netcfg

One of the first graphical tools for configuring Linux is netcfg. Simply run netcfg from the command line to start it, and explore its structure. Figure 28.4 shows the netcfg starting menu. The netcfg tool can be used to configure names, hosts, interfaces, and routing.

FIGURE 28.4

The GUI tool netcfg.

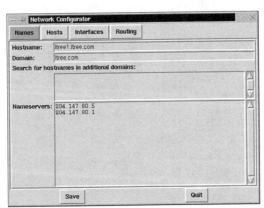

Using linuxconf

Another very powerful tool is linuxconf, which can be used to configure networking and perform most system administration tasks. This is a worthwhile tool to master because it can quickly perform both routine and complex tasks. Simply run linuxconf from the command line. Your X-Windows Desktop Manager such as KDE or GNOME may already have linuxconf in one of the program groups, in which case you can select it with a mouse and run the program. Figure 28.5 shows the starting screen of linuxconf.

FIGURE 28.5

The GUI tool linuxconf.

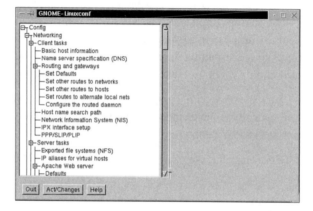

To change host names, expand the directory tree by making the selections Config, Networking, Client tasks, Basic host information (see Figure 28.6).

FIGURE 28.6

Linuxconf—Basic Host Configuration.

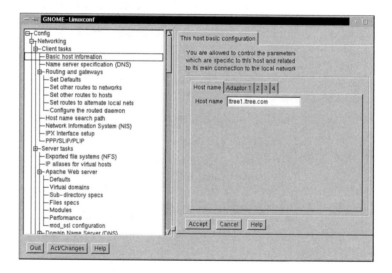

To configure the name resolver, expand the directory tree by making the selections
Config, Networking, Client tasks, Name server specification (DNS) (see Figure 28.7).

FIGURE 28.7

Linuxconf—
Configuring name
resolver.

To configure host routing, expand the directory tree by making the selections Config,
Networking, Client tasks, Routing and gateways, Set Defaults (see Figure 28.8).

FIGURE 28.8

Linuxconf—
Configuring
default router.

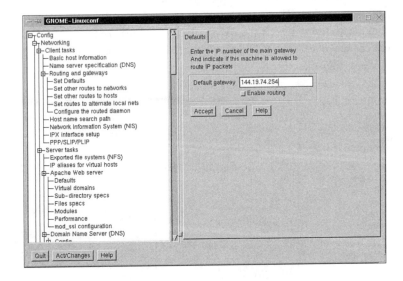

28

CONFIGURING
TCP/IP FOR
LINUX

To configure the order of name resolution, expand the directory tree by making the selections Config, Networking, Client tasks, Host name search path (see Figure 28.9).

FIGURE 28.9

*Linuxconf—
Host name search
path.*

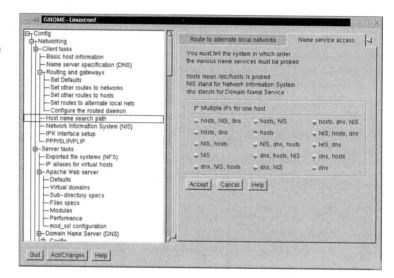

You can even configure BIND if you expand the directory tree by selecting Config, Networking, Server tasks, Domain Name Server (DNS), Config (see Figure 28.10). You can configure domains, IP reverse mappings, secondaries, forward zones, features, and IP allocation space. However, if you are serious about learning to configure BIND, you should learn the syntax of the BIND startup file (`/etc/named.boot` for BIND 4 and `/etc/named.conf` for BIND 8 and 9), and the syntax of the zone data files, and learn to edit these files directly.

FIGURE 28.10

*Linuxconf—
Configuring
BIND.*

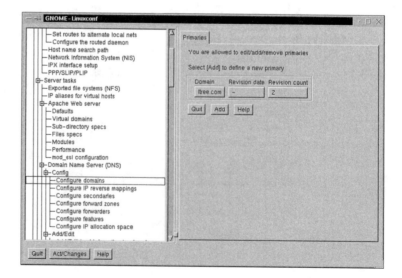

Configuring SLIP and PPP

The configuration and setup for either Serial Line Internet Protocol (SLIP) or Point-to-Point Protocol (PPP) follows the general TCP/IP configuration you have just completed. Both SLIP and PPP work over a modem, establishing a modem link with a remote system, and then invoking either the SLIP or PPP protocols. You can configure SLIP and PPP when you are configuring the general TCP/IP files, or you can wait until you need to set them up for SLIP or PPP access. Not all installations require SLIP or PPP, although many Internet service providers prefer SLIP or PPP access from small systems.

Setting Up the Dummy Interface

A dummy interface is a trick used to give your machine an IP address to work with when it uses only SLIP and PPP interfaces. A dummy interface solves the problem of a standalone machine whose only valid IP address is the loopback driver (127.0.0.1). Although SLIP and PPP can be used for connecting your machine to the outside world, when the interface is not active you have no internal IP address that applications can use.

Creating a dummy interface is simple. If your machine has an IP address already assigned for it in the /etc/hosts file, all you need to do is set up the interface and create a route. The two commands are shown here:

```
ifconfig dummy machine_name
route add machine_name
```

where *machine_name* is your local machine's name. This creates a link to your own IP address. If you do not have an IP address for your machine in the /etc/hosts file, you should add one before you create the dummy interface. Add a line with your machine name and its aliases along with the IP address, such as this line:

```
147.120.0.34    merlin    merlin.tpci.com
```

Setting Up SLIP

SLIP can be used with many dial-up Internet service providers, as well as for networking with other machines. When a modem connection is established, SLIP takes over and maintains the session for you. The SLIP driver is usually configured as part of the Linux kernel. The Linux SLIP driver also handles CSLIP, a compressed SLIP version that is available with some implementations. The SLIP driver is usually installed into the Linux kernel by default, but some versions of Linux require you to rebuild the kernel and answer Yes to a question about SLIP and CSLIP usage. You can use CSLIP only when both ends of a connection employ it; many Internet service providers offer both CSLIP and SLIP support, but you should check with them first. CSLIP packs more information into packets than SLIP, resulting in a higher throughput.

For Linux systems that use SLIP, a serial port has to be dedicated to the device. That serial port cannot be used for any other purpose. The kernel uses a program called SLIPDISC (SLIP discipline) to control the SLIP serial port and block other non-SLIP applications from using it.

The easiest way to dedicate a serial port for SLIP is the slattach program. This takes the device name of the serial port as an argument. For example, to dedicate the second serial port (/dev/cua1) to SLIP, you would issue this command:

```
slattach /dev/cua1 &
```

The command is sent into background by the ampersand. Failure to send to background means the terminal or console the command was issued from is not usable until the process is terminated. You can embed the slattach command in a startup file.

When the attachment has own succeeded, the port is set to the first SLIP device /dev/sl0. By default, most Linux systems set the SLIP port to use CSLIP. If you want to override this default, use the -p option and the SLIP name:

```
slattach -p slip /dev/cua1 &
```

You must make sure that both ends of the connection use the same form of SLIP. For example, you cannot set your device for CSLIP and communicate with another machine running SLIP. If the versions of SLIP don't match, commands like ping fail.

After the serial port has been set for SLIP usage, you can configure the network interface using the same procedure as normal network connections. For example, if your machine is named merlin and you are calling a system named arthur, you issue these commands:

```
ifconfig sl0 merlin-slip pointopoint arthur
route add arthur
```

The preceding ifconfig command configures the interface merlin-slip (the local address of the SLIP interface) to be a point-to-point connection to arthur. The route command adds the remote machine called arthur to the routing tables. You can also issue a route command to set the default route to arthur as a gateway:

```
route add default gw arthur
```

If you want to use the SLIP port for access to the Internet, it has to have an IP address and an entry in the /etc/hosts file. That gives the SLIP system a valid entry on the Internet.

When the `ifconfig` and `route` commands have been executed, you can test and use your SLIP network. If you decide to remove the SLIP interface in the future, you must remove the routing entry, use `ifconfig` to take down the SLIP interface, and then kill the `slattach` process. The first two steps are done with these commands:

```
route del arthur
ifconfig sl0 down
```

The termination of the `slattach` process must be done by finding the process ID (PID) of `slattach` (with the `ps` command), and then issuing a `kill` command.

Some Linux versions own include a utility called `dip` (dial-up IP) that helps automate the steps shown earlier, as well as provide an interpretive language for the SLIP line. Many versions of `dip` are currently available.

Setting Up PPP

PPP is a more talented own protocol than SLIP and is preferable unless your connection cannot support PPP. Linux divides the PPP functions into two parts: one for the *High-Level Data Link Control* (HDLC) protocol that helps define the rules for sending PPP datagrams between the two machines, and one for the PPP daemon, called `pppd`, which handles the protocol once the HDLC system has established communications parameters. In addition, Linux uses a program called `chat` that calls the remote system. As with SLIP, PPP establishes a modem link between the two machines, and then hands over the control of the line to PPP.

It is best to use PPP with a special user account for optimum protection and behavior. This is not necessary, and you can easily use PPP from any account, but for more secure operation you should consider creating a PPP user. First, you need to add a new user to the `/etc/passwd` file. A sample `/etc/passwd` entry for the PPP account (with UID set to 201 and GID set to 51) looks like this:

```
ppp:*:201:51:PPP account:/tmp:/etc/ppp/pppscript
```

In this case, the account is set with no password and a home directory of `/tmp` (because no files are created). The startup program is set to `/etc/ppp/pppscript`, a file you create with the contents like this:

```
#!/bin/sh
mesg n
stty -echo
exec pppd -detach silent modem crtscts
```

The first line forces execution of the script into the Bourne shell. The second command turns off all attempts to write to the PPP account's `tty`. The `stty` command is necessary to stop everything the remote sends from being echoed again. Finally, the `exec` command runs the `pppd` daemon (which handles all PPP traffic). You will see the `pppd` daemon and the options later in this section.

PPP requires you to establish a modem connection to the remote machine before it can take over and handle the communications. Several utilities are available to do this, the most commonly used of which is `chat`.

To use `chat`, you have to assemble a command line that tells `chat` how to talk to a modem and connect to the remote system. For example, to call a remote machine with a Hayes-compatible modem (using the AT command set) at the number 555-1234, you use the following command:

```
chat "" ATZ OK ATDT5551234 CONNECT "" ogin: ppp word: secret1
```

All the entries are in a `send-expect` format, with what you send to the remote specified after what you receive from it. The `chat` script always starts with an expect string, which you must set to be empty because the modem won't talk to you without any signal to it. After the empty string, you send the `ATZ` (reset) command, wait for an OK back from the modem, then send the `dial` command. When a CONNECT message is received back from the modem, the login script for the remote machine is executed. You send a blank character, wait for the `ogin:` (login) prompt, send the login name `ppp`, wait for the `word:` (password) prompt, then send your password. After the login is complete, `chat` terminates but leaves the line open.

> **Note**
>
> Why use "ogin" and "word" instead of "login" and "password" in the script? The best reason is so that case differences on the remote system are not important, so that both "login" and "Login" are treated the same way. The shortening of "password" lets some characters get lost without causing a lock-up or failure of the session.

If the other end of the connection doesn't answer with a login script as soon as its modem answers, you might have to force a `break` command down the line to jog the remote end:

```
chat -v "" ATZ OK ATDT5551234 CONNECT ""
ogin:-BREAK-ogin: ppp word: secret1
```

To set up a PPP connection, you need to invoke the `pppd`. If you have a PPP connection already established and your machine is logged in to a remote using the PPP account, you can start the `pppd`. If you assume your local machine is using the device `/dev/cua1` for its PPP connection at 38,400 baud, you would start up the `pppd` with this command:

```
pppd /dev/cua1 38400 crtscts defaultroute
```

This command tells the Linux kernel to switch the interface on `/dev/cua1` to PPP and establish an IP link to the remote machine. The `crtscts` option, which is usually used on any PPP connection above 9,600 baud, switches on hardware handshaking.

Because you need `chat` to establish the connection in the first place, you can embed the `chat` command as part of the `pppd` command if you want. This is best done when reading the contents of the `chat` script from a file (using the `-f` option). For example, you could issue the following `pppd` command:

```
pppd connect "chat -f chat_file" /dev/cua1 38400
-detach crtscts modem defaultroute
```

The `chat_file` contains this string:

```
"" ATZ OK ATDT5551234 CONNECT "" ogin: ppp word: secret1
```

You will notice a few modifications to the `pppd` command other than the addition of the `chat` command in quotation marks. The `connect` command specifies the dial-up script that `pppd` should start with, and the `-detach` command tells `pppd` not to detach from the console and move to background. The `modem` keyword tells `pppd` to monitor the modem port (in case the line drops prematurely) and hang up the line when the call is finished.

The `pppd` begins setting up the connection parameters with the remote by exchanging IP addresses, and then setting communications values. After that is done, `pppd` sets the Network Layer on your Linux kernel to use the PPP link by setting the interface to `/dev/ppp0` (if it's the first PPP link active on the machine). Finally, `pppd` establishes a kernel routing table entry to point to the machine on the other end of the PPP link.

PPP has quite a few options, as well as some files and authentication processes that might be required for you to connect to some remote systems. This subject involves far too much detail to cover here, so you should consult a book such as *Linux System Administrator's Survival Guide* for more information.

Summary

When you have followed the steps shown in this chapter, your TCP/IP connection is properly configured. You can now use your Linux system as a client onto other TCP/IP machines or allow others to connect to your Linux server. This chapter also has looked briefly at PPP and SLIP, both modem-based protocols you can use to connect to the Internet.

28

CONFIGURING TCP/IP FOR LINUX

Using TCP/IP
Applications

IN THIS PART

Whois and Finger

by Neal S. Jamison

IN THIS CHAPTER

CHAPTER 29

Finding information on the Internet is getting easier thanks to the multitude of search engines, meta-search engines, intelligent agents, and more. However, with the ever-growing number of users, hosts, and domains, locating information about people, host computers, and domains can be difficult. Two TCP/IP application-level protocols can help: Whois and Finger. Whois can be used to gather information about specific hosts and domains. Finger, on the other hand, can be used to find out specific information about people on Internet hosts. Both are discussed in this chapter.

Understanding the Whois Protocol

Whois is the TCP/IP protocol and service used to gather information about Internet hosts and domains. Originally designed to be the "white pages" of the Internet, Whois was once (and still is in some cases) used in conjunction with large personnel databases. However, the growth of the Internet made maintaining such personnel databases impossible, so Whois information was limited to hosts and domains. Today, popular Whois databases contain information such as host and domain points-of-contact, organizations, and addresses. Whois is also used when registering a domain to determine whether the domain is already in use.

The Whois protocol runs on well-known TCP port 43, and is defined in RFC 954. Additional information on whois and the related finger command can be found in the following RFCs:

2167—Referral Whois (RWhois) Protocol V1.5. S. Williamson, M. Kosters, D. Blacka, J. Singh, K. Zeilstra. June 1997.

1834—Whois and Network Information Lookup Service, Whois++. J. Gargano, K. Weiss. 1995.

1835—Architecture of the WHOIS++ service. P. Deutsch, R. Schoultz, P. Faltstrom, C. Weider. 1995.

1913—Architecture of the Whois++ Index Service. C. Weider, J. Fullton & S. Spero. 1996.

1914—How to Interact with a Whois++ Mesh. P. Faltstrom, R. Schoultz & C. Weider. 1996.

1288—The Finger User Information Protocol. D. Zimmerman. 1991.

Internet Registration

Internet Registration can be a somewhat confusing topic with no one party in complete control of the Internet. (For more information on the major players of the Internet, refer to Chapter 2, "TCP/IP and the Internet.") This confusion has an impact on the traditional Whois service because each major registrar party maintains its own database.

Understanding Domain Names

Internet domain names are composed of levels. The most common U.S. top-level domains are .com, .edu, .gov, .mil, .net, and .org. There are also country-code top-level domains, such as us (United States), ca (Canada), nl (The Netherlands), de (Germany), and int (International; see RFC 1591). Second-level domains further define the top level, as in ibm.com, mit.edu, nasa.gov, and army.mil. Third-level domains go one step further, as in whois.nic.mil and www.internic.net.

An organization called the *Council of Registrars* (CORE) has introduced other top-level domains known as *generic top-level domains* (gTLD). They are

.firm—For businesses, or firms

.shop—For businesses offering goods for sale

.web—For entities emphasizing activities related to the World Wide Web

.arts—For cultural- and entertainment-related organizations

.rec—For recreation/entertainment-related organizations

.info—For entities providing information services

.name—For those wanting individual or personal nomenclature; that is, a personal nom de plume

.biz—For registering businesses

.tv—For TV related businesses

.coop—For cooperatives

.museum—For museums

.pro—For professionals (accountants, lawyers, physicians)

.aero—For air transport industry

For more information on this initiative, refer to http://www.icann.org/.

29

WHOIS AND
FINGER

The InterNIC (operated by Network Solutions, Inc.) has been the primary registrar for the top-level domains since 1993. The InterNIC is overseen by the *National Telecommunications & Information Administration* (NTIA), part of the Department of Commerce. The InterNIC has delegated some of its responsibility to other official registrars (such as the Department of Defense NIC, and the Asia-Pacific NIC). More recently, there have been other initiatives that could break up the InterNIC even further. One such initiative, known as the *Shared Registry System* (SRS), strives to introduce fair and open competition to the domain registration process. One of the leading competitors is Register.com. Visit its Web site (http://www.register.com/) for more information.

All of this fair competition and delegation is great for the registration process, but it tends to complicate the Whois service. As previously mentioned, each registrar maintains its own database of registrants. For example, the InterNIC Whois database doesn't contain any military domains, and vice versa. The end result of this is that you have to know which database is most likely to have the information you are looking for, and target your query to that database.

Using NIC Handles

The InterNIC assigns a nickname, or handle, to everyone who is registered as a domain point-of-contact.

My NIC handle is NJ1181. Querying the InterNIC Whois database for my handle returns the following:

```
Jamison, Neal (NJ1181)   jamisonn@ANVI.COM
AnviCom, Inc.
7921 Jones Branch Dr.
Suite G-10
McLean, VA 22102
```

The Whois Databases

Several databases exist in which you can find Whois information. As discussed earlier, most of the major Whois databases only list information as it pertains to registered Internet hosts and domains. However, some databases out there contain more detailed "white pages" information.

The InterNIC

The primary source of host and domain registration information for the United States is the InterNIC, currently maintained by Network Solutions, Inc. As previously mentioned, the InterNIC has the authority to register all top-level domains in the United States. As such, its database contains information on a large majority of domains.

For more information on the InterNIC, refer to Chapter 2 or `http://www.internic.net/`.

The InterNIC Whois server is at `whois.internic.net`.

The U.S. Department of Defense

The Department of Defense *Network Information Center* (NIC) maintains registry information for all `.mil` hosts. The DoD NIC is currently maintained by the Boeing Corporation. For more information on the DoD NIC, refer to `http://whois.nic.mil/`.

The U.S. DoD Whois server is `whois.nic.mil`.

The U.S. Federal Government

The U.S. Federal Government NIC maintains registry information for all `.gov` and `.fed` hosts. This NIC is currently maintained by the *General Services Administration* (GSA). For more information, refer to `http://whois.nic.gov/`.

The U.S. Government Whois server is `whois.nic.gov`.

RIPE (Réseaux IP Européens)

RIPE is the European Network Coordination Center. For more information on RIPE, refer to `http://www.ripe.net/`.

RIPE's Whois server is `whois.ripe.net`.

The Asia Pacific Network Information Center (APNIC)

The APNIC is the registrar for the Asia-Pacific region. For more information on APNIC, go to `http://www.apnic.net/`.

APNIC's Whois server is `whois.apnic.net`.

Other Whois Servers

Many other Whois databases contain white-page information for corporations, universities, and other organizations. A complete list of Whois servers is compiled by Matt Power of M.I.T. and can be located at `ftp://sipb.mit.edu/pub/whois/whois-servers.list`.

Web-Based Whois

Although the Whois protocol and service has been around much longer than the Web, several Web-based interfaces exist to help you query Whois databases and find the information you need.

Table 29.1 lists several Web-based Whois clients.

29

WHOIS AND FINGER

TABLE 29.1 Major Web-Based Whois Client Sites

Site	URL
InterNIC	`http://www.networksolutions.com/cgi-bin/whois/whois/`
IANA	`http://www.isi.edu:80/in-notes/usdnr/rwhois.html`
RIPE (European)	`http://www.ripe.net/db/whois.html`
APNIC (Asia-Pacific)	`http://www.apnic.net/apnic-bin/whois.pl`
U.S. Military	`http://www.nic.mil/cgi-bin/whois`
U.S. Government	`http://www.nic.gov/cgi-bin/whois`

Allwhois.com

With all the databases out there, deciding which one to use can sometimes be difficult. But maybe it doesn't matter. There is a site on the Web called Allwhois.com (`http://www.allwhois.com`) that allows you to search all the major Whois databases at once. Figure 29.1 shows the Allwhois.com homepage.

FIGURE 29.1

The Allwhois.com homepage.

As you will see later, an enhancement to the Whois service, known as *referral Whois* (RWhois) can help as well.

Command-Line Whois

Although the command-line version of the Whois client has found competition on the Web, it is still included in many modern operating systems and TCP/IP suites. The following sections describe the whois command and its variants.

The Unix `whois` Command

The standard Unix Whois client is `whois`. The following describes the syntax of the whois command:

Usage: `whois [ -h host ] identifier`

Options: `-h`—Specifies the whois server.

Prefixing the identifier with certain characters will limit your search. For example, to search for names only, prefix the identifier with a period (.). Table 29.2 lists allowed characters and how their use will limit your search. These characters can be combined as well.

TABLE 29.2   Characters Used to Limit `whois` Searches

Character	Definition
.	Search for names only.
!	Search for handles only.
*	Search for groups or organizations only.

The upcoming "Examples" section will allow you to see these defining characters in action.

`fwhois`

`fwhois` (Finger Whois) is an open source Whois client for BSD Unix systems written by Chris Cappuccio. It is freely available over the Internet, and can easily be added to your Unix system. The following describes the syntax of the `fwhois` command.

Usage: `fwhois user[@<whois.server>]`

Examples

In this first example you can use the Unix `whois` command to query for people, for example, with the last name "jamison" and first name "neal." By not specifying a particular server (using the –h option), `whois` will search the InterNIC by default. The following shows the output of the `whois` command:

```
% whois jamison,n
[rs.internic.net]
```

29

WHOIS AND
FINGER

```
The Data in Network Solutions' WHOIS database is provided by Network
Solutions for information purposes, and to assist persons in obtaining
information about or related to a domain name registration record.
Network Solutions does not guarantee its accuracy.  By submitting a
WHOIS query, you agree that you will use this Data only for lawful
purposes and that, under no circumstances will you use this Data to:
(1) allow, enable, or otherwise support the transmission of mass
unsolicited, commercial advertising or solicitations via e-mail
(spam); or  (2) enable high volume, automated, electronic processes
that apply to Network Solutions (or its systems).  Network Solutions
reserves the right to modify these terms at any time.  By submitting
this query, you agree to abide by this policy.

Jamison, Neal (NJ795)          jamisonns@PATRIOT.NET
Jamison, Neal (NJ1181)         jamisonn@ANVI.COM


To single out one record, look it up with "!xxx", where xxx is the
handle, shown in parenthesis following the name, which comes first.
```

Then (still using Unix whois) you can pick the record that you want to learn more about. Notice the use of the defining character "!", escaped with the "\" character to prevent it from being processed by the Unix shell:

```
% whois \!NJ1181
[rs.internic.net]
The Data in Network Solutions' WHOIS database is provided by Network
Solutions for information purposes, and to assist persons in obtaining
information about or related to a domain name registration record.
Network Solutions does not guarantee its accuracy.  By submitting a
WHOIS query, you agree that you will use this Data only for lawful
purposes and that, under no circumstances will you use this Data to:
(1) allow, enable, or otherwise support the transmission of mass
unsolicited, commercial advertising or solicitations via e-mail
(spam); or  (2) enable high volume, automated, electronic processes
that apply to Network Solutions (or its systems).  Network Solutions
reserves the right to modify these terms at any time.  By submitting
this query, you agree to abide by this policy.
Jamison, Neal (NJ1181)         jamisonn@ANVI.COM
    AnviCom, Inc.
    7921 Jones Branch Dr.
    Suite G-10
    McLean, VA 22102
    Record last updated on 20-Feb-99.
    Database last updated on 20-Aug-99 04:31:00 EDT.
```

This is my InterNIC record.

fwhois can be used to achieve the same results. In this example, I will query for information about a popular space agency:

```
% fwhois nasa.gov
```

```
[rs.internic.net]
The Data in Network Solutions' WHOIS database is provided by Network
Solutions for information purposes, and to assist persons in obtaining
information about or related to a domain name registration record.
Network Solutions does not guarantee its accuracy.  By submitting a
WHOIS query, you agree that you will use this Data only for lawful
purposes and that, under no circumstances will you use this Data to:
(1) allow, enable, or otherwise support the transmission of mass
unsolicited, commercial advertising or solicitations via e-mail
(spam); or  (2) enable high volume, automated, electronic processes
that apply to Network Solutions (or its systems).  Network Solutions
reserves the right to modify these terms at any time.  By submitting
this query, you agree to abide by this policy.
No match for "NASA.GOV".
```

Note that I forgot to specify the U.S. Federal Government server. Trying again, I do use the following:

```
% fwhois nasa.gov@whois.nic.gov
[nic.gov]
National Aeronautics and Space Administration (NASA-DOM)
   NASA Marshall Space Flight Center
   MSFC, AL 35812

   Domain Name: NASA.GOV
   Status: Active
   Administrative Contact:
      Pirani, Joseph L.   (JLP1)
      JOSEPH.PIRANI@MSFC.NASA.GOV

   Domain servers in listed order:

   E.ROOT-SERVERS.NET          192.203.230.10
   NS1.JPL.NASA.GOV            137.78.160.9
   NS.GSFC.NASA.GOV            128.183.10.134
   MX.NSI.NASA.GOV             128.102.18.31
%
```

Telnet-Based whois

Many Whois servers used to have a Telnet interface. Using Telnet to connect to the Department of Defense Network Information Center Whois server (whois.nic.mil) now results in the following:

```
% telnet whois.nic.mil
Trying 207.132.116.6...
Connected to is-1.nic.mil.
Escape character is '^]'.
The telnet service to nic.mil has been discontinued.
For WHOIS usage, please use the online web form at
```

```
http://nic.mil
On Unix platforms, you can also use the WHOIS client service,
included with most operating systems.
$ whois -h nic.mil 'keyword'
Connection closed by foreign host.
```

However, some Telnet-accessible Whois services are still out there. One such service is found at `whois.ripe.net`. The following shows the use of the Telnet version of `whois`.

```
% telnet whois.ripe.net
Trying 193.0.0.200...
Connected to joshua.ripe.net.
Escape character is '^]'.
*************************************************************************
* RIPE NCC
*
* Telnet-Whois Interface to the RIPE Database
*
* Most frequently used keys are: IP address or prefix (classless),
* network name, persons last, first or complete name, NIC handle,
* and AS<number>.
*
* Use 'help' as key to get general help on the RIPE database.
* Contact <ripe-dbm@ripe.net> for further help or to report problems.
*************************************************************************

Enter search key [q to quit]:
```

Expanding Whois

Whois provides a rich protocol and service that allows us to query specific Whois databases for information pertaining to registered hosts, domains, and in some cases, people. However, Whois has some weaknesses. For instance, determining the right database to use for your query can sometimes be difficult. This problem can make finding the information you are looking for difficult. Two protocols expand on Whois:

- Referral Whois (RWhois)
- WHOIS++

They are briefly explained in this section.

Referral Whois (RWhois)

Due to the size of the Internet, maintaining one single database of all the host, domain, and user information is impossible. In order to keep the size and maintenance of the Whois databases to manageable proportions, a decentralized approach is necessary.

RWhois is a Directory Services protocol and service that extends the Whois concept to allow single queries to any number of decentralized Whois databases. RWhois accomplishes this in much the same manner as the Domain Name Service (DNS). If one RWhois database does not contain the information needed to satisfy the query, it can refer the query to another database. This process repeats until the proper database is found and the query is answered.

For more information on RWhois, see RFC 2167 or `http://www.rwhois.net/`.

WHOIS++

WHOIS++ is an extension to the traditional Whois protocol and service whose goal is to permit Whois-like servers to make available more detailed and structured information.

WHOIS++ is specified by RFCs 1834, 1835, 1913, and 1914.

Using Finger

Finger is the name for both a protocol and a program that allow us to find out the status of hosts or users on the Internet. It is typically used to find out whether an Internet user is logged on or to locate his e-mail address or username. Finger runs on TCP port 79.

One of the simpler TCP/IP services, a Finger client/server session resembles the following:

- The Finger client sends a request to the Finger server.
- The server opens a connection to the client.
- The client sends a one-line query.
- The server searches local "user account" files for information, and returns the results.
- The server closes the connection.

Telnet can be used to demonstrate the simplicity, as in the following example:

```
% telnet host.mydomain.com 79
Trying...
Connected to host.mydomain.com.
Escape character is '^]'.
jamisonn
Login: jamisonn              Name: Neal Jamison
Directory: /users/home/jamisons     Shell: /bin/tcsh
On since Mon Aug 16 19:20 (EDT) on ttyp4 from pool180-128
No mail.
No Plan.
Connection closed by foreign host.
%
```

Finger is specified in RFC 1288.

29

WHOIS AND FINGER

CSO Eases Burden of Researching Information

CSO is an electronic phonebook database concept developed at the University of Illinois Computing and Communications Services Office. A CSO server maintains the phonebook data and runs a program called qi (query interpreter) that receives query requests and sends back information. The client runs a program called ph that sends requests to the server. ph has been ported to many major platforms, and several client products (for example, Eudora and Mosaic) incorporate the ph client. Look for CSO qi/ph to catch on and make finding information about people even easier.

For more information, refer to the ph FAQ at http://www.landfield.com/faqs/ph-faq/.

The `finger` Command

The Unix command `finger` is used to find information about local and remote users. This section concentrates on using `finger` to look up remote users.

Solaris `finger`

In the Solaris operating system, the client command of the finger protocol is appropriately named `finger`. The `finger` command requests a connection with the server, and after the connection is opened, `finger` passes along a one-line query. The following shows the syntax of the Solaris `finger` command:

Usage:

```
finger [ -bfhilmpqsw ] [ username...  ]

finger [-l ] [ username@hostname1[@hostname2...@hostnamen]

finger [-l ] [ @hostname1[@hostname2...@hostnamen] ...  ]
```

Note

When using finger to look up remote users, only the -l option is allowed.

Options:

-b—Suppresses long format printout.

-f—Suppresses the header.

-h—Does not print the .project file.

-i—Similar to short format except that only the login name, terminal, login time, and idle time are printed.

-l—Forces long output format.

-m—Matches arguments only on username (not first or last name).

-p—Does not print the .plan file.

-q—Forces quick output format (similar to short format except that only the login name, terminal, and login time are printed).

-s—Forces short output format.

-w—Does not print the full name.

Example:

```
$finger jamisonn@mydomain.com
Login name: jamisonn    In real life: Neal Jamison
Directory: /www/home/jamisonn    Shell: /bin/csh
On since Aug  3 13:21:37 on pts/1 from hostname1
No unread mail
Project:  AlphaBeta Project
Plan: To finish this AlphaBeta project.
$
```

Linux finger

The Linux version of finger is similar to the Solaris implementation. The following shows the syntax of the Linux finger command:

Usage:

```
finger [-lmsp] [user ...] [user@host ...]
```

Options:

-s—Displays the user's login name, real name, terminal name and write status (as an * after the terminal name if write permission is denied), idle time, login time, office location, and office phone number.

-l—Displays the information described for the -s option plus the user's home directory, home phone number, login shell, mail status, and the contents of the files .plan, .project, and .forward from the user's home directory.

-p—Prevents the `-1` option of `finger` from displaying the contents of the `.plan` and `.project` files.

-m—Prevents matching of usernames. User is usually a login name; however, matching will also be done on the users' real names, unless the `-m` option is supplied. All name matching performed by `finger` is non–case sensitive.

If no options are specified, `finger` defaults to the `-1` style output if operands are provided; otherwise it defaults to the `-s` style. Note that some fields might be missing in either format if information is not available for them.

If no arguments are specified, `finger` will print an entry for each user currently logged in to the system.

Example:

```
$finger jamisonn@mydomain.com
Login name: jamisonn    In real life: Neal Jamison
Directory: /www/home/jamisonn    Shell: /bin/csh
On since Aug  3 13:21:37 on pts/1 from hostname1
No unread mail
Project:  AlphaBeta Project
Plan: To finish this AlphaBeta project.
$
```

The Finger Daemon

`fingerd` and `in.fingerd` are the daemons that listen for `finger` requests. These daemons are invoked by `inetd`. Sometimes Finger (the Finger daemon) is disabled by site administrators for "privacy" reasons. Fingering a site with Finger disabled will produce results similar to the following:

```
$ finger jamisonn@host.mydomain.com
[host.mydomain.com]
Connection refused.
$
```

Solaris `in.fingerd`

`in.fingerd` is the Solaris finger daemon. It is controlled by `inetd`, where it waits for a connection request. When a request is made, `in.fingerd` passes the query along to `finger`, which locates the requested information among the system files. `in.fingerd` responds to the client and then closes the connection. The following shows how to start the `in.fingerd` daemon.

Usage: `/usr/sbin/in.fingerd`

Options: None

Table 29.3 lists the `in.fingerd`-related files/commands.

TABLE 29.3 Commands and Files Related to `in.fingerd`

File/Command	Description
`.plan`	User-defined file
`.project`	User-defined file that can contain information about projects
`/var/adm/utmp`	User and accounting information
`/etc/passwd`	System password file that contains user information
`/var/adm/lastlog`	Last login time

Linux `fingerd`

The Linux `fingerd` is similar to the Solaris `in.fingerd`. The following shows how to start the `in.fingerd` daemon.

Usage: `fingerd [-wul] [-pL path]`

Options:

-w—Provides welcome banner to include system status (that is, `uptime`).

-u—Rejects requests of the form `finger @hostname`.

-l—Logs `finger` requests.

-p—Provides an alternate location for `fingerd` to find the local `finger` command.

Finger in a Non-Unix Environment

As with most TCP/IP commands and utilities, Finger was born in a Unix environment. However, several non-Unix parties have made Finger available within other operating systems. Table 29.4 lists two applications that provide Finger and URLs to help you find more information.

TABLE 29.4 Non-Unix Finger Software

Manufacturer	URL
Hummingbird Communications LTD	`http://arctic.www.hummingbird.com/products/nc/nfs/index.html`
Trumpet Winsock	`http://www.trumpet.com.au/`

29

WHOIS AND FINGER

There are also several Web interfaces to Finger or Finger gateways. Some that I've come across include the following:

- http://www.cs.indiana.edu/finger/

- http://webrunner2.webabc.com/cgi-bin/finger

Figure 29.2 shows a Web-to-Finger gateway in action.

FIGURE 29.2

NASA News via the Indiana University Finger gateway.

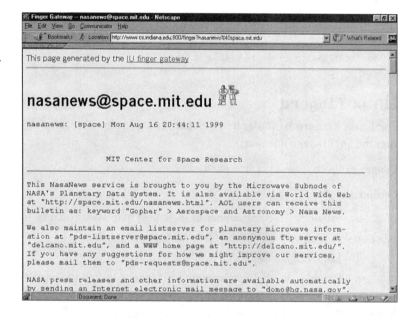

Finger Fun

Occasionally, you will stumble upon someone who uses a TCP/IP tool to accomplish a job it wasn't really designed for. The following example shows how some smart (and caffeinated) college students put Finger to use. The output has been slightly truncated for space:

```
% finger coke@cs.wisc.edu
[cs.wisc.edu]
[coke@lime.cs.wisc.edu]
Login name: coke                        In real life: Coke

Directory: /var/home/coke              Shell: /var/home/cokead/bin/coke

On since Aug 10 11:47:46 on term/a       3 hours 6 minutes Idle Time
```

```
Plan:
This Coke (tm) machine is computer operated.  It is available to SACM
members, Computer Sciences personnel, and CS&S building support staff.
(Plus anyone else who asks really nice. :-)


If you do not have an account set up or your account is below $.40,
then you can leave a check made out to SACM in a sealed envelope in
the SACM mailbox (fifth floor) with your email address and an initial
password.  The Coke machine will email you when your account has been
created/updated.

Contents of the Coke machine:
  Coke, Diet Coke, Mendota Springs Lemon (sparkling mineral water),
  Sprite, Barq's Root Beer, Cherry Coke, Nestea Cool
%
```

Another, perhaps more useful use of Finger can be found at Pacific Northwest
Seismograph Network. Again, the output here has been truncated:

```
% finger quake@geophys.washington.edu
[geophys.washington.edu]

Earthquake Information (quake)
Plan:
The following catalog is for earthquakes (M>2) in Washington and Oregon
produced by the Pacific Northwest Seismograph Network, a member of the
Council of the National Seismic System.  PNSN support comes from the
US Geological Survey, Department of Energy, and Washington State.
Additional catalogs and information for the PNSN (as well as other networks)
are available on the World-Wide-Web at URL:`http://www.geophys.washington.edu/'
For specific questions regarding our network send E-mail to:
              seis_info@geophys.washington.edu
DATE-TIME is in Universal Time (UTC) which is PST + 8 hours. Magnitudes are
reported as duration magnitude (Md).  QUAL is location quality A-excellent,
B-good, C-fair, D-poor, *-from automatic system and may be in error.
Updated as of Tue Sep 18 09:00:12 PDT 2001
  DATE-(UTC)-TIME   LAT(N) LON(W)   DEP  MAG QUAL COMMENTS
 yy/mm/dd hh:mm:ss  deg.   deg.     km   Ml
01/07/31 05:07:32  47.73N 117.44W   0.6 2.2   AC  FELT   7.4 km NNW of Spokane,
01/08/01 14:29:48  47.71N 117.44W   0.6 2.2   AD  FELT   5.9 km NNW of Spokane,
01/08/02 15:35:23  47.72N 122.38W  27.0 2.2   BA     14.3 km WNW of Kirkland, Wa
01/08/13 11:47:28  48.25N 120.02W   7.2 2.3   CD     35.3 km WSW of Okanogan, WA
01/08/15 00:37:29  47.66N 122.41W  26.1 2.2   BA      9.6 km  NW of Seattle, WA
01/08/19 06:17:32  48.25N 121.61W   1.7 3.0   CC  FELT   1.0 km WSW of Darringt
01/08/20 06:14:09  45.29N 120.14W   8.8 2.1   BD      6.8 km NNE of Condon, OR
01/08/25 17:52:34  48.23N 121.60W   2.7 2.1   CC  FELT   2.1 km   S of Darringt
01/08/30 03:47:31  48.23N 121.62W   4.8 2.7   CC  FELT   2.9 km  SW of Darringt
01/08/31 14:39:17  47.02N 121.86W  17.9 2.1   BA     20.9 km NNW of Mt Rainier, WA
01/09/06 21:40:44  45.78N 124.54W  35.1 2.9   CD     65.7 km  NW of Tillamook, OR
01/09/08 17:30:41  48.85N 125.15W  10.0 2.5   CD     64.4 km ESE of Tofino, BC
```

```
01/09/09 04:06:29  48.19N 122.68W  56.4 2.3  BA  35.5 km  SW of Mount Vernon,
01/09/10 21:46:58  47.34N 123.05W  46.2 2.3  BA  35.3 km NNW of Olympia, WA
01/09/12 20:38:21  45.30N 121.72W   2.7 2.0  BB   8.1 km SSW of Mt Hood, OR
01/09/12 21:26:43  45.30N 121.72W   4.5 2.3  BB   8.2 km SSW of Mt Hood, OR
01/09/14 10:52:14  45.30N 121.72W   5.1 2.1  BB   8.4 km SSW of Mt Hood, OR
01/09/14 11:22:57  45.30N 121.73W   5.2 2.9  BA   8.0 km SSW of Mt Hood, OR
01/09/15 12:21:09  45.30N 121.72W   4.2 2.5  BB   8.1 km SSW of Mt Hood, OR
01/09/15 19:51:03  47.71N 120.07W   4.0 2.5  BB  12.7 km ENE of Entiat, WA
```

Summary

This chapter explained two of the major protocols and command sets used to locate information about hosts, domains, and users. Whois is the service/protocol primarily used to gather information about registered hosts and domains. This information usually is limited to registering organizations, points-of-contact, and mailing addresses. Whois was originally designed to be a white-pages information service for all Internet users. However, the growth of the Internet has complicated that. Referral Whois (RWhois) and WHOIS++ expand traditional Whois in an attempt to make Whois a more complete white-pages service. Many organizations, such as corporations and universities, effectively use Whois to provide directory services within their organization.

Finger is the service/protocol used to gather information about Internet hosts and their users. As shown, Finger can be used to determine whether a user is logged on, as well as to gather information about that user such as his last login time, phone number, or his "plan." Finger can also be used to represent other types of information. As shown, Finger can be used to get weather forecasts, current news, or even to check the status of a drink vending machine.

File Transfer Protocols

by Anne Carasik

Sending files from one system to another is a very important part of networking. You could use e-mail attachments to do this, but this is an indirect way, and not as efficient as direct file transfer. If you want more immediate results, you'll want to use a file transfer protocol. This includes the Internet *File Transfer Protocol* (FTP) and *Trivial File Transfer Protocol* (TFTP). Remote copying is covered in Chapter 32, "Using the R-Utilities."

The Role of FTP and TFTP in Today's World

Because many users use the HTTP protocol to transfer files between servers, file transfer applications such as FTP and TFTP are not as popular as they once were. However, not all systems are running Web servers, so FTP and TFTP are still needed to transfer files back and forth, with or without a Web server. Also, it should be noted that HTTP is not as efficient as FTP for file transfer operations. If the URL (Uniform Resource Locator) embedded in the HTML tags is specified using the ftp protocol (for example, `ftp://ftp.xyz.com`), then the FTP client on the system will be invoked to do file transfers.

Even with the Web, transferring files to a server is still difficult. Many of the Web commands are not as robust as FTP and do not enable as many options and functions.

The file transfer command-line applications allow you to transfer files without having to install a Web server on your system. And for most Unix and Linux systems, FTP comes installed.

Because most of these commands are not graphically based (some programs exist that do the same thing but with a graphical interface), FTP is best illustrated by using the command-line–based client that comes with Unix. One such popular tool is Cute-FTP. However, regardless of whether the FTP client is graphical or command-line oriented, they all use FTP commands for their underlying operation.

Even though TFTP is not used nearly as much as FTP, both are discussed in this chapter.

Transferring Files with FTP

FTP is the standard method of transferring files on the Internet and on IP networks. Back in the early days of the Internet before the World Wide Web became popular, people used command-line applications to run file transfers. One of the most common applications besides mail (SMTP) was FTP.

FTP is a TCP/IP application, which means it works on Layer 7 of the OSI model and Layer 4 of the TCP model. FTP is defined by RFC 959, and it uses TCP for transport instead of UDP. FTP is located on the Application Layer of both the OSI and TCP models (see Figure 30.1).

FIGURE 30.1
Where FTP sits on the OSI and TCP models.

Originally, FTP was the file transfer protocol between computers on the ARPANET, the predecessor to the Internet. The ARPANET was an older network that the United States Department of Defense ran from the 1960s through the 1980s. Back then, the primary function of FTP was to transfer files efficiently and reliably among hosts. FTP still provides this reliability today, and it also allows remote storage for files. This enables you to work on one system and store the files somewhere else. For example, if you have a Web server and you want to retrieve the HTML files and CGI programs to work with on your local computer, you just need to get those files from the storage site (which is the remote Web server).

When you're done, you can send the files back to the Web server via FTP. This way you don't have to be logged in and working on the remote computer, as you would with Telnet.

FTP Connections

When you open an FTP connection, you are connecting to two ports: ports 20 and 21. These two ports have two different functions—port 20 is the data port and port 21 is the control port.

Figure 30.2 illustrates how the FTP client connects to the FTP daemon on the remote server.

30

FILE TRANSFER PROTOCOLS

FIGURE 30.2

How FTP client and server connect.

The Control Port
=================

The control port for FTP is used for exchanging commands and replies to those commands. It is analogous to a drill sergeant and his or her recruits: The drill sergeant barks out the commands, and the recruits reply to those commands.

In FTP, if you send a command such as get thisfile, the response you get will be

```
200 PORT command successful.
150 Opening ASCII mode data connection for .message (127 bytes).
226 Transfer complete.
local: .message remote: .message
135 bytes received in 1.4 seconds (0.09 Kbytes/s)
```

Notice that the control port uses commands that are appended at the beginning with PORT. This signifies that the commands go through port 21 instead of the data port. In some FTP implementations, commands are allowed through the data port through passive (PASV) commands, not through the control commands (PORT).

This communication is used to show you the status of the data, what mode it's in, the transfer status, and the amount of data received. This connection uses the Telnet Protocol, defined in RFC 495.

The PASV commands for some FTP implementations allow a "raw" FTP connection, which does not use the commands that the user is familiar with. This enables someone to do file transfers using only one port, port 20, instead of both 20 and 21.

> **Note**
>
> The real use of the PASV command is to make FTP firewall-friendly. In normal FTP operation, the FTP client sends a PORT command to the FTP server that identifies the endpoint to which the FTP server must create a data connection. This is often called a *back connection*. Because the data endpoint on the client side is a temporary port that can be anywhere in the range of 1024 to 65535, the firewall does not know of this and cannot allow access to a specific port if it does not know the port number. The problem is solved by the FTP server issuing

the PASV command, which puts the FTP server in a "passive mode." The PASV command identifies the server endpoint for the data connection to the FTP client. The FTP client then makes an active FTP connection to the server data endpoint. Because firewalls typically allow outgoing connections to any port number, FTP operation proceeds smoothly.

A user can use the same commands with the PASV connection; however, the "csooked" connection of using the control commands is a lot more secure and manageable because an administrator can set which commands are accessible to the user.

The Data Port

The data port is where the FTP data (files) is sent to the FTP server (ftpd).

Note

The FTP server, ftpd (or in.ftpd), is a Unix server daemon. This may be different with other operating systems.

This differs from the control port, which is where a user interface sends commands. When you're transferring files via FTP, the files themselves, not the commands, are being sent through port 20, the data port.

Connections to the data port are known as *passive* connections, which have their own set of commands. All the data connection knows is the mode of the file, the type of the file, and the number of files transferred. You can also send only a portion of a file, even though there aren't very many practical uses for doing so.

When waiting for a connection, the passive data process listens on the data port (port 20) for a connection from the control process to open a data connection. The passive connection is opened at the same time as the control connection.

In this case, commands are sent through the control port. But, you can control the data port directly with the passive FTP commands.

30

FILE TRANSFER PROTOCOLS

Passive FTP Commands

The PASV command is not used by the user; the PORT command is the user interface. FTP servers are required to support passive commands (RFC 1123), although not all of them do.

You can call these commands by telnetting to port 21 like this:

```
tigerlair:/home/stripes- telnet localhost 21
```

Next, you'll see

```
Trying 1.2.3.4...
Connected to localhost.
Escape character is ë^]í
220 mysystem.tigerlair.com FTP server (SunOS 5.6) ready.
```

Next, all the commands you type will have to be passive commands.

Now, PWD will display your current directory:

```
PWD
257 "/home/stripes" is current directory.
```

If you use the CDUP passive FTP command, it will change you to the parent directory:

```
CDUP
250 CWD command successful.
```

Now, PWD will display your current directory:

```
PWD
257 "/home" is current directory.
```

You can now see the other users' home directories.

You won't see the commands appended at the beginning with PORT because you are not using the control port—instead, you are accessing the data port directly.

Connecting with FTP Clients

To open a connection with FTP, run the ftp command followed by the hostname. The syntax for FTP is

```
ftp [options] [hostname]
```

For example, if I want to FTP to ftp.tigerlair.com, I would run the following command:

```
tigerlair:/home/stripes- ftp ftp.example.org
```

If you want the FTP client to do something that it usually doesn't do, you would use one of the options. Table 30.1 lists the available options for FTP clients.

TABLE 30.1   FTP Command-Line Options

Option	What It Does
-d	Enables debugging
-i	Turns off prompting
-n	Disables auto-login
-v	Shows responses from remote server
-g	Disables wildcards (globbing)

If you wanted to use your FTP client to disable an auto-login (where the FTP client automatically prompts you for a username and login) that does not prompt during multiple file transfers, your command would be

```
ftp -i -n ftp.example.org
```

So, let's go back to the original example of using the FTP client without any options:

```
tigerlair:/home/stripes- ftp ftp.example.org
```

The next message you get should be this:

```
Connected to ftp.example.org.
220 ftp.example.org FTP Server (Version wu-2.4.2-VR16(1)
Wed Apr 7 15:59:03 PDT 1999) ready.
Name (ftp.example.org:stripes):
```

When you see this, you'll see that the default login FTP uses for the remote site is your local account name (in this case, `stripes`). If it is something different, you'll want to type it in here:

```
Connected to ftp.example.org.
220 ftp.example.org FTP Server (Version wu-2.4.2-VR16(1)
Wed Apr 7 15:59:03 PDT 1999) ready.
Name (ftp.example.org:stripes): ahc
Password:
```

Note

Do not use example.org as an FTP site. It is used for illustration purposes only. If you want to play with FTP without being destructive on a remote system, you can use your own by running an FTP client that connects to a local host. This assumes that the FTP server is running on the same machine as the client.

30

FILE TRANSFER PROTOCOLS

You'll be prompted for your password; make sure you type it correctly. It won't appear onscreen, and it won't even be masked with asterisks as you type.

Next, you should have an FTP prompt that looks like this:

`ftp>`

This will enable you to input commands to transfer files. This is known as the *command interpreter*.

FTP Command Interpreter

The FTP command interpreter enables you to be in an interactive mode with the FTP client. This enables you to send the client commands to open and close certain connections, transfer files, change the transfer file type, and so on without leaving FTP.

Table 30.2 lists commands available to you when you use FTP in interactive mode.

TABLE 30.2   FTP Commands

Option	What It Does
`!<local command>`	Executes a shell on the local system
`$<macro>`	Executes a macro
`account [password]`	Applies an extra user/password to get additional access to the remote system
`ascii`	Sets file transfer mode to ASCII
`append localfile [remotefile]`	Appends the localfile to the remotefile (file on the remote computer)
`bell`	Rings bell after file transfer
`binary`	Sets file transfer mode to binary
`bye, exit`	Exits, ending remote connection
`case`	Toggles case sensitivity
`close, disconnect`	Closes a remote connection
`cd <directory>`	Changes directory on remote system
`cdup`	Changes to the parent directory
`debug <level>`	Sets the debugging level
`dir`	Prints the directory
`delete <filename>`	Removes file from remote computer
`get <filename>`	Retrieves a file from the remote system to the local system
`glob`	Toggles wildcards for file transfer

TABLE 30.2 Continued

Option	What It Does
`hash`	Prints "#" for each 1,024 bytes transferred
`help`	Prints a help file
`lcd <directory>`	Changes directory on local system
`ls`	Prints directory of remote computer
`lpwd`	Prints working directory of local computer
`macdef <macroname>`	Defines a macro
`mdel <filename(s)>`	Deletes multiple files
`mdir <filename(s)>`	Prints directory listing of multiple files
`mget <filename(s)>`	Retrieves multiple files from the remote system to the local system
`mkdir <directory>`	Creates directory on remote computer
`mput <filename(s)>`	Transfers multiple files to remote computer
`open <site>`	Opens a connection to `<site>`
`prompt`	Interactive prompting control
`put <filename>`	Transfers file to remote computer
`pwd`	Displays present working directory
`user [user] [password]`	Logs in to the remote system
`verbose`	Toggles verbose mode

With all of these commands at your disposal, you'll find you can do a lot with FTP. To give you an idea of how all this information is used, the next section shows you an example of an FTP session.

An Example of an FTP Session

Not all of your FTP sessions will be this involved—this example is designed to show you some of the things you can do when you're using FTP. The first thing you'll want to do is open up access to a remote FTP site, as shown here:

```
tigerlair:/home/stripes- ftp ftp.example.org
Connected to ftp.example.org.
220 ftp.example.org FTP Server (Version wu-2.4.2-VR16(1)
Wed Apr 7 15:59:03 PDT 1999) ready.
Name (ftp.example.org:stripes): ahc
Password:
230 User ahc logged in.
ftp>
```

30

FILE TRANSFER PROTOCOLS

Now that you have access, you'll want to see what files are on the remote site. The two ways to list files are `ls` and `dir`. Note that we are making an FTP connection to a Unix system. Here's what an `ls` output looks like:

```
ftp> ls
200 PORT command successful.
150 ASCII data connection for /bin/ls (1.2.3.4,52262) (0 bytes).
ISS-SOLARIS.TAR
Mail
ar302sol.tar.Z
c-files.tar.gz
debug.ssh
deshadow.c
e205-pdf.pdf

226 ASCII Transfer complete.
468 bytes received in 0.0077 seconds (59.35 Kbytes/s)
ftp>
```

The `dir` command creates the following output:

```
ftp> dir
200 PORT command successful.
150 ASCII data connection for /bin/ls (1.2.3.4,52263)    (0 bytes).
total 56220
drwxr-xr-x  16 ahc    users     1536 May 25    09:22 .
drwxr-xr-x   6 root   other      512 Oct 27    1998 ..
-rw-------   1 ahc    users      168 May  7    11:26 .Xauthority
-rw-r--r--   1 ahc    users      424 Dec  2    14:43 .alias
-rw-r--r--   1 ahc    users      313 Jun  2    1998 .cshrc
drwxr-xr-x  11 ahc    users      512 May  7    11:27 .dt
-rwxr-xr-x   1 ahc    users     5111 Nov  2    1998 .dtprofile
drwx------   2 ahc    users      512 Jan 27    15:04 .elm
-rw-r--r--   1 ahc    users      174 Dec  2    14:45 .login
-rw-r--r--   1 ahc    users      556 Dec  2    15:32 .tcshrc
-rw-------   1 ahc    users3655680 Jan  4    08:27 ISS-SOLARIS.TAR
drwx------   2 ahc    users      512 Dec  8    16:01 Mail
-rw-r--r--   1 ahc    users5919933 Nov  3    1998 ar302sol.tar.Z
-rw-------   1 ahc    users    14605 May 13    10:43 c-files.tar.gz
-rw-------   1 ahc    users     1818 Mar  8    12:09 debug.ssh
-rw-r--r--   1 ahc    users     2531 Jan  7    10:07 deshadow.c
-rw-r--r--   1 ahc    users    54532 Nov 19    1998 e205-pdf.pdf
-rw-r--r--   1 ahc    users 898279 Jan  6    09:50 neotr122.zip
226 ASCII Transfer complete.
3830 bytes received in 0.047 seconds (79.06 Kbytes/s)
ftp>
```

Not only did this give you more information about the files listed in `ls`, but `dir` listed the Unix hidden files, or dot files, as well.

> **Note**
>
> On Unix, `ls` and `dir` will list your files, but `dir` will give you more information about the files, including last modification date, owner, permissions, and size. If you're making an FTP connection to a Windows NT/2000 or Windows 9x system, `ls` will work a little differently. You may want to use `dir` to list the files.

Now that you've seen a list of files, you want to get one from the remote system and place it in your local computer. You'll want to check your local directory to make sure you're putting the file in the right directory.

```
ftp> !pwd
/home/stripes
ftp>
```

You want to put these files in your home directory, which is where you are. Now, get the file:

```
ftp> get notes
200 PORT command successful.
150 ASCII data connection for notes (1.2.3.4,52264) (210 bytes).
226 ASCII Transfer complete.
local: notes remote: notes
226 bytes received in 0.019 seconds (11.81 Kbytes/s)
ftp>
```

The filename for the remote file does not change on the local system unless you specify the filename to change. To do that, use the following syntax:

```
get remotefilename localfilenameyouwant
```

So, if you want to get another file called `notes`, you'll want to rename one of the files. Now that you have a file called `notes` on your local system, you either want to rename it or rename the remote file when it hits your local system. In this case, call the second file you're getting `notes2`. You can see from the output that FTP will tell you what the local file is called and what the remote file is called.

```
ftp> get notes notes2
200 PORT command successful.
150 ASCII data connection for notes (1.2.3.4,52264) (210 bytes).
226 ASCII Transfer complete.
local: notes2 remote: notes
226 bytes received in 0.019 seconds (11.81 Kbytes/s)
ftp>
```

30

FILE TRANSFER PROTOCOLS

Those notes files are text files. You can see that FTP uses ASCII to transfer by default. This ensures that the files transferred are text files. What if you want to transfer a binary file? You can change the file type by telling FTP.

```
ftp> bin
200 Type set to I.
```

Type I is binary, and type A is ASCII. Binary files include executables, compressed files, and library files. Basically, a binary file is not readable by humans.

Now that you have your file type set to binary, you can transfer binary files.

```
ftp> get vr40a.exe windowsfile.exe
200 PORT command successful.
150 Binary data connection for vr40a.exe (1.2.3.4,52265) (2338635 bytes).
226 Binary Transfer complete.
local: windowsfile.exe remote: vr40a.exe
2338635    bytes received in 1.4 seconds (1593.23 Kbytes/s)
ftp>
```

Note that FTP will tell you whether your transfer is ASCII or binary. If you want to set the file type back to ASCII, just type, **ascii**.

```
ftp> ascii
200 Type set to A.
```

Insert code

Note

You should transfer text files in the ASCII mode because this takes account of the end-of-line conventions in different operating systems and does the end-of-line conversions automatically. For example, Unix systems use a single <LF>(line feed) as an end-of-line character. On the other hand, Windows systems use a <CR><LF> combination character sequence where <CR> is the Carriage Return and <lf> is the Line Feed character. When you transfer a file from a Unix system to a Windows system in the ASCII mode, the extra carriage return will automatically be added for the end of the line. Similarly, when you transfer a file in the ASCII mode from a Windows to a Unix system, the extra carriage return for the end of line will be removed.

Because main frames do use the EBCDIC code instead of the ASCII code for characters, you must use the ebcdic command instead of the ascii command for mainframes.

Transferring a binary file in the ascii mode is a mistake, because this will perform end-of-line conversions which can add or remove carriage return characters in the transferred file. Altering a binary file will corrupt it.

This works well if you want to get one file. What do you do if you want to get multiple files? If you want to get every file that begins with "s", for example, you use `get s*`. Unfortunately, your result is the following:

```
ftp> get s*
550 s*: No such file or directory.
```

The response shows that this does not work. For FTP to recognize "globbing" or wildcards, you need to use `mget` to get multiple files, as shown in the following:

```
ftp> mget s*
mget s3-Solaris.tar?
```

Notice that prompting is enabled by default, and occurs any time you ask to `get` or `put` multiple files. Now to get every file that follows, you need to type **y** after being prompted to get the file:

```
mget s3-Solaris.tar? y
200 PORT command successful.
150 ASCII data connection for s3-Solaris.tar
(127.0.0.1,52452) (0 bytes).
226 ASCII Transfer complete.
mget sendmail.8.9.2.tar.gz? y
200 PORT command successful.
150 ASCII data connection for sendmail.8.9.2.tar.gz
(127.0.0.1,52453) (0 bytes).
226 ASCII Transfer complete.
mget solsniffer.c? y
200 PORT command successful.
150 ASCII data connection for solsniffer.c
(127.0.0.1,52454) (0    bytes).
226 ASCII Transfer complete.
mget spade110.exe? y
200 PORT command successful.
150 ASCII data connection for spade110.exe
(127.0.0.1,52455) (8192 bytes).
226 ASCII Transfer complete.
mget sun-sniff.c? y
200 PORT command successful.
150 ASCII data connection for sun-sniff.c
(127.0.0.1,52456) (8192 bytes).
226 ASCII Transfer complete.
ftp>
```

Responding with a 'y' is tedious, especially if you're trying to get a large number of files. To get rid of the prompting, type **prompt**.

```
ftp> prompt
Interactive mode off.
```

30

FILE TRANSFER PROTOCOLS

Now, if you do the same command again, you won't get prompted—thus, the file transfer moves a lot faster:

```
ftp> mget s*
200 PORT command successful.
150 ASCII data connection for s3-Solaris.tar
(127.0.0.1,52458) (0 bytes).
226 ASCII Transfer complete.
200 PORT command successful.
150 ASCII data connection for sendmail.8.9.2.tar.gz
(127.0.0.1,52459) (0 bytes).
226 ASCII Transfer complete.
200 PORT command successful.
150 ASCII data connection for solsniffer.c
(127.0.0.1,52460) (0 bytes).
226 ASCII Transfer complete.
200 PORT command successful.
150 ASCII data connection for spade110.exe
(127.0.0.1,52461) (0 bytes).
226 ASCII Transfer complete.
200 PORT command successful.
150 ASCII data connection for sun-sniff.c
(127.0.0.1,52462) (0 bytes).
226 ASCII Transfer complete.
ftp>
```

This is much quicker and less tedious than using the prompting mode.

> **Note**
>
> If you are going to overwrite a file (in the preceding example, you did, but with the same file), FTP will not warn you ahead of time that you're going to overwrite a file.

Now that you've learned how to download files, you should learn to upload files to a remote FTP server. To do this, use the command put:

```
ftp> mput h2obj.jpg
200 PORT command successful.
150 Binary data connection for h2obg.jpg (1.2.3.4,52270).
226 Transfer complete.
local: h2obj.jpg remote: h2obg.jpg
1194 bytes sent in 0.019 seconds (60.82 Kbytes/s)
ftp>
```

This will send a local file to a remote system. If you want to send more than one file, use mput:

```
ftp> mput dd*
mput debug.ssh? y
200 PORT command successful.
150 ASCII data connection for debug.ssh    (1.2.3.4,52266).
226 Transfer complete.
mput deshadow.c? y
200 PORT command successful.
150 ASCII data connection for deshadow.c (1.2.3.4,52267).
226 Transfer complete.
ftp>
```

Just like mget, you need to turn off prompting so you do not have to type "y" or "n" for each file you want to transfer:

```
ftp> prompt
Interactive mode off.
ftp> bin
200 Type set to I.
ftp> mput k*
200 PORT command successful.
150 Binary data connection for kayaking.jpg (1.2.3.4,52268).
226 Transfer complete.
200 PORT command successful.
150 Binary data connection for key.tar (1.2.3.4,52269).
226 Transfer complete.
ftp>
```

> **Note**
>
> If a command involves transferring files (get, put, or delete), just put an "m" in front of it to transfer multiple files.

> **Note**
>
> Before uploading files using FTP, you must have permissions to copy files to the remote FTP server. FTP uses the remote FTP server's authentication system when you log on as an FTP user. This means that if you are logging on as user linda, the user account linda must exist on the remote FTP server. If linda wants to upload files, she must have the "write" permission to the directory where she wants to upload files.

On TFTP servers, you need to additionally ensure that a filename already exists that will be overwritten by the uploaded file. You need to have access to the remote system with sufficient permission to create an empty file. On Unix systems, you can create an empty file by issuing the touch command:

```
touch nameoffile
```

Some development tools (such as the Borland C++ compiler for Windows) also contain the Windows version of the 'touch' utility.

If you want to get rid of a file on the remote system (and you have the permissions to do so), you can delete it very easily. You can use the `delete` command, which can be abbreviated `del`:

```
ftp> del h2obg.jpg
250 DELE command successful.
ftp>
```

If you want to delete multiple files, use `mdel`. Again, the prompt command has the same effect on `mdel` as it does on `mget` or `mput`.

```
ftp> mdel s*
250 DELE command successful.
250 DELE command successful.
250 DELE command successful.
ftp>
```

Note

As with overwriting a file, you are not warned that you are about to delete a file on the remote system.

Not only can you move files back and forth between the remote and local systems, but you can also create and remove directories. To create a directory, use the `mkdir` command:

```
ftp> mkdir morestuff
257 MKD    command    successful.
```

You can also move around in different directories. Similar to Unix and Windows command line (the command interpreter formerly known as DOS), you use `cd` to change between directories.

```
ftp> cd    morestuff
250 CWD    command    successful.
```

If you're lost and you want to see which directory you're in, use the pwd command for the remote system:

```
ftp> pwd
257 "/home/ahc/morestuff" is current directory.
```

If you are doing file transfers for a big file, you may want to enable hashing. This will show you that FTP is still awake even though it may be sitting there idle for minutes or even hours on end. To do this, just type **hash**:

```
ftp> hash
Hash mark printing on (8192 bytes/hash mark).
```

If you put or get a file with hashing, you can see its progress through the file transfer:

```
ftp> put sendmail.8.9.2.tar.gz
200 PORT command successful.
150 Binary data connection for sendmail.8.9.2.tar.gz (1.2.3.4,52271).
################################################################
226 Transfer complete.
local: sendmail.8.9.2.tar.gz remote: sendmail.8.9.2.tar.gz
1063534    bytes sent in 0.56 seconds (1870.03 Kbytes/s)
ftp> pwd
```

If you're done using this site, but you don't want to exit FTP—you just want to close the connection. Type **close**, and you will disconnect from the remote system but stay at the FTP command interpreter:

```
ftp> close
221 Goodbye.
ftp>
```

Note that you still have your ftp> prompt. So, to open a connection to another host, use the open command:

```
ftp> open another-example.org
Connected to another-example.org.
220 another-example.org FTP server (SunOS 5.6) ready.
Name (localhost:ahc):
331 Password required for ahc.
Password:
230 User ahc logged in.
ftp>
```

Now you're on a totally different system. You can do the same commands, but what you find should be different than the first system you were on.

When you're completely done with FTP, just type **quit** or **bye**, as shown here:

```
ftp> quit
221 Goodbye.
```

FTP Security

Even though FTP is about being able to access files, you don't want to enable someone to make a mess of your system. FTP comes with some basic access control, but it does not solve the fundamental security problems with FTP.

FTP always uses clear-text authentication, meaning that your passwords are sent non-encrypted through the network. This is a very big security problem. Improperly configured anonymous FTP environments that allow users to snoop around areas that they shouldn't be able to access, and having two ports open for the FTP server instead of just one like most TCP/IP network services, are also security problems.

Another important aspect of FTP security is the fact that FTP uses the local operating system user account and password information for authentication unless you are logging on as an anonymous user. Because FTP sends password information as plain text, the regular user account password can be compromised.

The /etc/ftpusers File

If you want to control who has access to a specific account on your FTP server, you'll want to use the /etc/ftpusers file. This file contains a list of users who cannot use FTP. It does not restrict the users from other applications including rsh, telnet, and Secure Shell (ssh).

A good /etc/ftpusers file should look something like this:

```
tigerlair:/home/stripes- cat /etc/ftpusers
root
uucp
bin
```

This should keep the administrative accounts and accounts you don't want from trying to exploit FTP.

Using .netrc

The .netrc file is used for automating logging into a remote host for FTP. This file sits in the user's home directory and is used to get to different systems without typing in a username or password. The file should have the permissions 700 (with no one able to read or write to it except for the owner).

The file format for the .netrc file looks like this:

```
machine <machinename> login <username> password <mypassword>
```

So, if I wanted to set one up for example.org, it would look something like this:

```
tigerlair:/home/stripes- cat .netrc
machine example.org login ahc password stuff
```

Because .netrc is popular for logging into accounts, it can be used safely for anonymous FTP sites, which do not require a password other than your e-mail address. Also, anonymous FTP sites only provide you with public information—nothing you should be privy to without a password.

> **Caution**
>
> In the world we live in today, having a .netrc file is a bad idea. It contains passwords readable by anyone, and therefore, an account can be compromised quite easily.

Using Different FTP Clients

The preceding example is the standard FTP client that comes with operating systems such as Unix, Windows, and VMS. Additionally, it should function in a similar fashion with few differences depending on what operating system you're using. The following sections cover some of these differences.

Unix

On Unix, two different FTP clients can provide more functionality than a vanilla FTP client can: Ncftp and xftp.

Ncftp automates anonymous FTP logins, so you don't have to type a password (being your e-mail address) or have to worry about keeping a .netrc file. It also provides some text-based graphics that include a status bar on file transfers and has additional benefits including command-line editing. Ncftp is available at http://www.ncftp.com.

The xftp program provides a graphical user interface (GUI) to the FTP client. This enables you to use an FTP client without dealing directly with the command interpreter. See Figure 30.3 for a screen shot of xftp. The xftp program is available from http://www.llnl.gov/ia/xdir_xftp/xftp.html.

FIGURE 30.3

*A screenshot of
an active* xftp
session.

Windows and Macintosh Clients

There are a few Windows and Macintosh FTP clients. Many of them have GUIs similar to xftp, which allows you to drag and drop files to and from the remote and local systems.

There is also a command-line feature FTP for some implementations of Windows. Others will pop up an Internet Explorer window, which does not give you full FTP functionality.

Table 30.3 is a partial list of the FTP clients for Windows and Macintosh.

TABLE 30.3   FTP Clients for Windows and Macintosh

FTP Client	*Web Site*
WS-FTP Pro	`http://www.ipswitch.com`
fetch	`http://www.dartmouth.edu/pages/softdev/fetch.html`
CuteFTP	`http://www.cuteftp.com`
FTPPro2000	`http://www.ftppro.com`

E-mail

Believe it or not, you can use an FTP client through e-mail. FTPmail makes FTP available to users with only e-mail access to the Internet. This way someone with only e-mail access can obtain files from an FTP site without having to use FTP directly.

Some servers on the Internet offer an FTPmail service to Internet users. These servers have an FTPmail account, and users can include FTP requests in e-mail messages addressed to this account (they would use commands similar to the command interpreter for FTP).

FTP sessions are carried out in response to the mailed FTP requests, and the results are sent back to users via their e-mail address. If FTPmail fails to connect to the FTP server, an e-mail message is sent to the user explaining why it failed.

Several sites offer the FTPmail service, and anyone with access to e-mail can use them. Please use the service in your country.

Table 30.4 lists some of the FTPmail servers and where they are located.

TABLE 30.4 FTPmail Servers

FTPmail Server	*Country*
ftpmail@grasp.insalyon.fr	France
ftpmail@doc.ic.ac.uk	United Kingdom
ftpmail@decwrl.dec.com	United States

FTP Servers and Daemons

After you have an understanding of the FTP client, you can get a better understanding of the FTP server and how it functions. Because FTP has to be controlled by a server, you should keep in mind some basic things about running an FTP server.

Unix and Linux

On Unix and Linux, the FTP daemon, `in.ftpd`, is usually run by the Internet Super-daemon, `inetd`. Because `inetd` listens for the connection instead of the `in.ftpd`, it's able to manage connections more securely. For more information on `inetd`, see Chapter 39, "Protocol Configuration and Tuning."

So, in `/etc/inetd.conf`, you will have a line that looks like this:

```
ftp     stream tcp      nowait root    /usr/sbin/in.ftpd.    in.ftpd
```

This is the line that starts `in.ftpd`. You can pass `in.ftpd` some options, including `-d` for debugging, `-l` for logging to syslogd, and `-t` to change the inactivity timeout period.

Windows NT/2000

There are FTP servers for NT/2000 and Windows 95 and 98 as well. This includes FTP Serv-U (available at `http://www.ftpserv-u.com`) and War FTP daemon (available at `http://www.jgaa.com/tftpd.htm`).

30

FILE TRANSFER PROTOCOLS

Anonymous FTP Access

Anonymous FTP sites are an important part of the Internet, even today with the popularity of the Web. An infinite number of anonymous FTP sites are available to retrieve various information, files, and software. One of the most popular anonymous FTP sites is `wuarchive.wustl.edu`.

Many anonymous FTP sites have files publicly available because they are trying to distribute files without the inconvenience of issuing passwords and usernames to the growing number of people on the Internet.

Anonymous FTP Servers

Anonymous FTP servers provide a public site for files. Back before the Web became the driving force of the Internet, gopher (a menu-driven Internet application) and FTP were the main ways people obtained files and information from the Internet.

As a result, anonymous FTP became very popular, and it is still used today. Anonymous FTP servers need to have a separate environment and disk space that is completely separate from the system files. This is known as a `chrooted` environment.

For example, a Unix system will have `/usr` and `/etc` directories. So will the anonymous FTP server on the Unix system. But the files stored in the `/etc` directory of the Unix system are *not* the same as the `/etc` directory in the anonymous FTP server. This is because ftp clients access is limited to the home directory of the ftp user account, which is typically `/home/ftp`. The `/etc` and `/public` files of the FTP server are under `/home/ftp`, and appear as `/home/ftp/etc` and `/home/ftp/public`.

Keep in mind that this means that system files are not stored in the anonymous FTP directory. This environment is set aside specifically for FTP to create an environment that is completely separate from the vital parts of the operating system.

Anonymous FTP Clients

For convenience, anonymous FTP allows people to enter "anonymous" or "ftp" as a username, and an e-mail address for the password (`stripes@tigerlair.com`, for example).

There are also access restrictions for anonymous FTP. Usually the users are only allowed to access public files, not system or configuration files for security reasons.

The following illustrates an anonymous FTP session and an example of a banner for an anonymous FTP site:

```
tigerlair:/home/stripes- ftp wuarchive.wustl.edu
Connected to wuarchive.wustl.edu.
220 wuarchive.wustl.edu FTP server (Version wu-2.4.2-academ[BETA-16]
```

```
(1) Wed Apr 1 08:28:10 CST 1998) ready.
Name (wuarchive.wustl.edu:stripes): anonymous
331 Guest login ok, send your complete e-mail address as password.
Password:
230- If your FTP client crashes or hangs shortly after login please try
230- using a dash (-) as the first character of your password.  This
230- will turn off the informational messages that may be confusing your
230- FTP client.
230-
230- This system may be used 24 hours a day, 7 days a week.  The local
230- time is Wed May 26 12:02:37 1999.  You are user number 23 out of a
230- possible 500.  All transfers to and from wuarchive are logged.  If
230- you don't like this then please disconnect.
230-
230- Wuarchive is currently a Sun Ultra Enterprise 2 Server.
230-
230- Wuarchive is connected to the Internet over a T3 (45Mb/s) line from
230- STARnet and MCI. Thanks to both of these groups for their support.
230-
230- Welcome to wuarchive.wustl.edu, a public service of Washington
230- University in St. Louis, Missouri USA.
230-
230-
230-
230 Guest login ok, access restrictions apply.
Remote system type is Unix.
Using binary mode to transfer files.
ftp>
```

Because of the popularity of the Web, many anonymous FTP sites are used through a Web browser instead of the FTP client itself.

Tip

You don't have to type your entire e-mail address as a password. You only need to type

```
yourusername@
```

For example, you could enter

```
stripes@
```

instead of

```
stripes@tigerlair.com
```

30

Using TFTP

TFTP can be used to transfer files within a Local Area Network. TFTP is Trivial FTP, which is used for transferring files as well. TFTP uses UDP as its transport protocol and transmits data on UDP port 69.

Because TFTP does not use any form of login validation by usernames, TFTP has its share of security problems. Today the most common usage is to send router access lists from the workstation to the router itself or configure the router. It is also used to boot diskless systems by downloading the operating system for the diskless system from a TFTP server. One advantage of TFTP over FTP is that it is simpler and less complex (also has less features) than FTP, and is easy to embed in the ROM of network cards for a diskless workstation.

> **Caution**
>
> Do not turn on TFTP unless you absolutely need it. It has some security issues, including accessibility to your password files, if you're not careful. By default, TFTP is restricted to the /tftpboot directory as a rudimentary form of security. If you disable this restriction, a TFTP client can have access to other parts of the filesystem without going through authentication. A dangerous situation!

TFTP is currently in version 2, and is specified in RFC1350. Unlike FTP, which uses TCP, TFTP uses UDP. As a result, TFTP is simple and compact. Like FTP, TFTP is run through `inetd`.

Each packet exchange between the client and the server begins with a client request to the server to read or write a file. Those are the only choices.

Files are transferred in either *octet* or *netascii* mode. In netascii mode, data lines consist of ASCII text terminated by a carriage return and line feed (CR/LF).

How TFTP Differs from FTP

TFTP does not have the functionality that FTP does. For example, TFTP does not give you the ability to use wildcards, create or remove directories, or even remove files. It also does not prompt you for a username or password; thus, access is restricted by other means (TCP Wrappers, for example).

Because of its simplicity, routers use TFTP to transfer access lists and router configurations through this protocol. Because routers do not have logins (unless you're running TACACS+ or RADIUS for access control), it's easier to work on an editor than to manually type in each line on a router.

TFTP Commands

If you understand FTP, TFTP will not be difficult to pick up. TFTP has very few commands, which are listed in Table 30.5. Many of them are similar to FTP.

TABLE 30.5 TFTP Commands

Command	Description
ascii	Sets mode to netascii (text)
binary	Sets mode to octet (non-text)
connect	Connects to remote TFTP
mode	Sets file transfer mode
put	Sends file to the remote site
get	Gets a file from the remote site
quit	Exits TFTP
rexmt <value>	Sets per-packet value for timeout
status	Shows the status of the server
timeout <seconds>	Sets transmission timeout (seconds)
trace	Turns on packet tracing
verbose	Toggles verbosity

Summary

File transfers are important for sending files to different systems on a TCP/IP network. TCP/IP uses the File Transfer Protocol (FTP) and the Trivial File Transfer Protocol (TFTP) as the main ways to send files through a TCP/IP network.

FTP, which uses TCP to transfer files, requires that two ports be open: port 20 for the data port and port 21 for the control port. The data port is used only for transferring files, whereas the control port is used to send commands and messages.

30

FILE TRANSFER PROTOCOLS

TFTP, which uses UDP to transfer files, requires that only port 69 be open for TFTP. TFTP is a much simpler protocol than FTP, and does not have as much functionality. However, TFTP is commonly used with routers to manage access lists and configurations. It is also used to boot diskless systems.

In the next chapter, Telnet is discussed. This will give you more of an understanding of another type of interactive TCP/IP network service.

Using Telnet

by Neal S. Jamison

Although terminal emulation isn't used as widely today as it once was, it is still a necessary tool for accessing shell accounts and other multiuser systems. Telnet is also used as the basis of other protocols such as X-Windows that establish a session with an X-client. Telnet is the ultimate thin client because all execution takes place on the Telnet server. Telnet is often used as a troubleshooting tool as well. This chapter discusses the terminal emulation service of the Internet: the TCP/IP Telnet protocol and its associated programs.

Understanding the Telnet Protocol

Telnet is one of the original TCP/IP protocols. In fact, RFC 15 (written in 1969!) provides some interesting reading on the subject. Telnet is currently specified in RFC 854.

The Telnet protocol was created to simplify the connection to remote hosts. If you had an IBM mainframe, you needed IBM terminals to connect to that mainframe. If you had a DEC, you needed DEC terminals. The result was similar to the diagram in Figure 31.1.

FIGURE 31.1

An unwieldy network prior to the creation of Telnet.

What was needed was a terminal emulation service that could speak all the proprietary language sets. This would allow a user to sit at one terminal and work on many disparate host systems. Enter Telnet.

Telnet is the standard Internet application protocol for logging in to remote hosts. It provides the encoding rules and other services necessary to link a user's system with a remote host.

Telnet uses the reliable TCP transport mechanism because it must maintain a reliable, stable connection. The Telnet server listens, by default on well-known TCP port 23. The Telnet client can be configured to connect to any other port on which another service is running. This enables you to use the Telnet client to send commands to a specific application service. This technique enables Telnet to be used for troubleshooting the application services.

Telnet can operate in any of the following modes:

- Half Duplex
- Character-at-a-time
- Line-at-a-time (a.k.a. Kludge Line Mode)
- Linemode

Half Duplex mode is obsolete.

In Character-at-a-time mode, each character typed is immediately sent to the remote host for processing and then echoed back to the client. This can be painfully cumbersome over slow networks, but is a common default with many implementations.

In Line-at-a-time mode, text is echoed locally, and completed lines are sent to the remote host for processing.

In Linemode, character processing is done on the local system, under the control of the remote system.

Additional details on Telnet can be found in the following RFCs:

15   Network subsystem for time sharing hosts. C.S. Carr. 1969.

854   Telnet Protocol Specification. J. Postel, J.K. Reynolds. 1983.

855   Telnet Option Specifications. J. Postel, J.K. Reynolds. 1983.

856   Telnet Binary Transmission. J. Postel, J.K. Reynolds. 1983.

857   Telnet Echo Option. J. Postel, J.K. Reynolds. 1983.

858   Telnet Suppress Go Ahead Option. J. Postel, J.K. Reynolds. 1983.

859   Telnet Status Option. J. Postel, J.K. Reynolds. 1983.

860   Telnet Timing Mark Option. J. Postel, J.K. Reynolds. 1983.

861   Telnet Extended Options: List Option. J. Postel, J.K. Reynolds. 1983.

1123   Requirements for Internet hosts—application and support. R.T. Braden. 1989.

1184   Telnet Linemode Option. D.A. Borman. 1990.

1205, 5250   Telnet interface. P. Chmielewski. 1991.

1372   Telnet Remote Flow Control Option. C. Hedrick, D. Borman. 1992.

1408   Telnet Environment Option. D. Borman, Editor. 1993.

1411   Telnet Authentication: Kerberos Version 4. D. Borman, Editor. 1993.

1412   Telnet Authentication: SPX. K. Alagappan. 1993.

1416   Telnet Authentication Option. D. Borman, Editor. 1993.

1571   Telnet Environment Option Interoperability Issues. D. Borman. 1994.

1572   Telnet Environment Option. S. Alexander. 1994.

2066   TELNET CHARSET Option. R. Gellens. 1997.

2217   Telnet Com Port Control Option. G. Clark. 1997.

For some slightly less-serious Telnet information, refer to the following RFCs:

748   Telnet randomly-lose option. M.R. Crispin. 1978.

1097   Telnet subliminal-message option. B. Miller. 1989.

The Network Virtual Terminal

Because we use many different types of computers with many different keyboards as well as other input devices, Telnet's task is non-trivial. Our input devices and computers speak a variety of languages, from different dialects of ASCII to EBCDIC. This makes interoperability very difficult. The *Network Virtual Terminal* (NVT) was created to simplify this problem. Clients, servers, and their respective network virtual terminals work as depicted in Figure 31.2.

FIGURE 31.2

Terminal-to-host connections simplified by Telnet and the NVT.

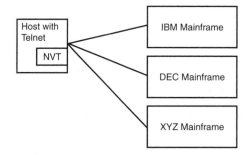

The NVT takes the input from the client system and converts it into a universal language. The NVT on the host end takes the universal language and converts it into the proprietary language understood by the host.

The NVT allows any proprietary client to talk with any proprietary host, and vice versa.

The Telnet Daemon

As with other TCP/IP client/server services, Telnet depends on the presence of a daemon to respond to client requests. In the Unix world, that daemon is `telnetd` (or `in.telnetd`). The Telnet daemon is the Telnet server that responds to requests from the Telnet client. By default, the Telnet daemon runs on port 23.

The following usage and option information for `in.telnetd` was taken from the Linux operating system man page. Please consult your operating system documentation or man pages for more information specific to your implementation.

Usage: `/usr/sbin/in.telnetd [-hns] [-a authmode] [-D debugmode]`
`[-L loginprg] [-S tos] [-X authtype] [-edebug] [-debug port]`

Options:

> `-a authmode`—Specifies the mode to use for authentication. Note that this option is only useful if `telnetd` has been compiled with support for authentication. The following are valid values for `authmode`:
>
> - `debug`—Enables authentication debugging.
> - `user`—Only allows connections when the remote user can provide valid authentication information to identify the remote user, and is allowed access to the specified account without providing a password.
> - `valid`—Only allows connections when the remote user can provide valid authentication information to identify the remote user.
> - `other`—Only allows connections that supply some authentication information.
> - `none`—This is the default state. Authentication information is not required.
> - `off`—Disables the authentication code.
>
> `-D debugmode`—This option may be used for debugging purposes. This allows `telnetd` to print out debugging information to the connection, allowing the user to see what `telnetd` is doing. There are several possible values for `debugmode`:
>
> - `options`—Prints information about the negotiation of telnet options.
> - `report`—Prints the options information, plus some additional information about what is going on.
> - `netdata`—Displays the data stream received by telnetd.
> - `ptydata`—Displays data written to the pseudo-terminal.
>
> `-e debug`—Enables encryption debugging.
>
> `-h`—Disables the printing of host-specific information before login has been completed.

-L loginprg—This option may be used to specify a different login program. By default, /bin/login is used.

-n—Disables TCP keep-alives. Normally, telnetd enables the TCP keep-alive mechanism to probe connections that have been idle for some period of time to determine whether the client is still there, so that idle connections from machines that have crashed or can no longer be reached can be cleaned up.

-s—This option is only enabled if telnetd is compiled with support for SecurID cards. It causes the -s option to be passed on to login, and thus is only useful if login supports the -s flag to indicate that only SecurID validated logins are allowed. This is usually useful for controlling remote logins from outside a firewall.

-S tos—Sets the IP type-of-service (TOS) option for the Telnet connection to the value tos.

-X authtype—This option is only valid if telnetd has been built with support for the authentication option. It disables the use of authtype authentication, and can be used to temporarily disable a specific authentication type without having to recompile telnetd.

Using Telnet

Telnet is very simple to use. In fact, its use typically consists of three very simple tasks:

- Run a Telnet client command to initiate the session.
- Enter a login ID and password.
- When you are done, terminate the session.

Telnet has two modes: input and command. However, in most situations, the only user interaction with Telnet is in starting and stopping the session and working within the remote operating system or program through input mode.

The Unix telnet Command

This section discusses the usage and options associated with a Linux implementation of telnet. You will find that most implementations are very similar; however, you should check your documentation or man page for information specific to your telnet command. The following shows the syntax of the telnet command:

Usage: telnet [-8ELadr] [-S tos] [-e escapechar] [-l user] [-n tracefile] [host [port]]

Options:

-8—Requests 8-bit operation.

-E—Disables the escape character functionality.

-L—Specifies an 8-bit output data path.

-a—Attempts automatic login. Passes the username via the USER variable if supported by the remote host.

-d—Sets the initial value of the debug toggle to TRUE.

-r—Emulates rlogin.

-S tos—Sets the IP type-of-service (TOS) option for the Telnet connection to the value specified by tos.

-e escapechar—Sets the escape character to the value specified by escapechar.

-l user—Specifies user as the user to log in as on the remote system. Similar to the -a option.

-n tracefile—Opens tracefile for recording trace information.

Host—Specifies a host to contact over the network.

Port—Specifies a port number or service name to contact. If not specified, the well-known port 23 is used.

Telnet GUI Applications

Several popular GUI Telnet applications can provide non-Unix users with the client program and make using Telnet even easier. Two popular versions are Microsoft Telnet and CRT. Microsoft Telnet comes with the Microsoft Windows operating system (Windows NT/2000, Windows 98, and so on). CRT is a shareware application from VanDyke Technologies that is easily downloaded from common Windows shareware Web sites.

Figures 31.3 and 31.4 show these two applications in action.

FIGURE 31.3

The very common Microsoft Telnet application.

FIGURE 31.4

Another popular terminal emulation application. (CRT by Van Dyke Technologies, Inc.)

Telnet Commands

Due to Telnet's simple user interface, there is really no reason for the general user to issue any of the following commands. As mentioned earlier, most (if not all) of your Telnet session will be spent in input mode, talking to the remote operating system or program. Advanced users or systems administrators may find some of the commands (such as TOGGLE) helpful when troubleshooting problems.

You can retrieve the Telnet commands by executing the HELP command while in command-line mode. For example:

```
$ telnet
telnet> help
Commands may be abbreviated.  Commands are:

close        close current connection
logout       forcibly logout remote user and close the connection
display      display operating parameters
mode         try to enter line or character mode ('mode ?' for more)
open         connect to a site
quit         exit telnet
send         transmit special characters ('send ?' for more)
set          set operating parameters ('set ?' for more)
unset        unset operating parameters ('unset ?' for more)
status       print status information
toggle       toggle operating parameters ('toggle ?' for more)
slc          set treatment of special characters

z            suspend telnet
environ      change environment variables ('environ ?' for more)
telnet>
```

You can get help on any specific command by issuing the command followed by a ?, as in the following example:

```
telnet> mode ?
format is:  'mode Mode', where 'Mode' is one of:

character      Disable LINEMODE option
               (or disable obsolete line-by-line mode)
line           Enable LINEMODE option
               (or enable obsolete line-by-line mode)

               These require the LINEMODE option to be enabled
isig           Enable signal trapping
-isig          Disable signal trapping
edit           Enable character editing
-edit          Disable character editing
softtabs       Enable tab expansion
-softtabs      Disable character editing
litecho        Enable literal character echo
-litecho       Disable literal character echo

?              Print help information
telnet>
```

Table 31.1 describes the complete Telnet command set.

Note

The Telnet command and option information found in Tables 31.1, 31.2, and 31.3 was gathered from the Linux operating system man page for `telnet`. Please consult your operating system documentation or man pages for more information specific to your implementation.

TABLE 31.1   Telnet Commands

Command	Description
CLOSE	Closes the connection to the remote host.
DISPLAY	Displays specified operating parameters.
ENVIRON	Changes or propagates environment variables.
HELP (or ?)	Shows helpful information (also, COMMAND ? can be issued to get help on a specific command).
LOGOUT	Forcibly logs out the remote user and closes the connection. Similar to CLOSE.
MODE	Asks the server to enter line or character mode.

TABLE 31.1   Continued

Command	Description
OPEN	Opens a connection to the specified host.
QUIT	Closes the session and exits Telnet.
SEND	Transmits special protocol character sequences. See Table 31.3 for SEND sequences.
SET	Sets operating parameters. See also UNSET.
SLC	(Set Local Characters) Sets definition and/or treatment of special characters.
STATUS	Shows current status information such as hostname, mode, and so on.
TOGGLE	Toggles operating parameters. See Table 31.2 for some common parameters.
UNSET	Unsets operating parameters. See also SET.
Z	Suspends Telnet (the suspended command can be resumed with fg).
! [command]	Executes the specified shell command. If no command is specified, a sub-shell is opened.

Some of the Telnet commands, such as TOGGLE and SEND, require further options. Table 31.2 lists some of the common Telnet TOGGLE command options, and Table 31.3 lists the Telnet SEND command option set.

The TOGGLE command toggles (TRUE or FALSE) specified options.

TABLE 31.2   A Few Common Telnet TOGGLE Options

Command	Description
debug	Toggles socket level debugging. The initial value for this toggle is FALSE.
skiprc	When the skiprc toggle is TRUE, Telnet does not read the .telnetrc file. The initial value is FALSE.
?	Displays the legal toggle commands.

The SEND command is used to transmit commands and options to the remote host. Table 31.3 lists the SEND command options.

TABLE 31.3   Telnet SEND Command Options

Command	Description
EOF	End-of-file
SUSP	Suspend current process (job control)
ABORT	Abort process

TABLE 31.3 Continued

Command	Description
EOR	End of record
SE	Suboption end
NOP	No operation
DM	Data mark
BRK	Break
IP	Interrupt process
AO	Abort output
AYT	Are you there?
EC	Escape character
EL	Erase line
GA	Go ahead
SB	Suboption begin
WILL	Option negotiation
WONT	Option negotiation
DO	Option negotiation
DON'T	Option negotiation
IAC	Data byte 255

Examples of Using Telnet

The following example demonstrates the negotiation that goes on behind the scenes. This verbose output is achieved by using the TOGGLE OPTIONS command:

```
% telnet
telnet> toggle options
Will show option processing.
telnet> open host1.mydomain.com
Trying...
Connected to host1.mydomain.com.
Escape character is '^]'.
SENT DO SUPPRESS GO AHEAD
SENT WILL TERMINAL TYPE
SENT WILL NAWS
SENT WILL TSPEED
SENT WILL LFLOW
SENT WILL LINEMODE
SENT WILL NEW-ENVIRON
```

```
SENT DO STATUS
RCVD DO TERMINAL TYPE
RCVD DO TSPEED
RCVD DO XDISPLOC
SENT WONT XDISPLOC
RCVD DO NEW-ENVIRON
RCVD WILL SUPPRESS GO AHEAD
RCVD DO NAWS
SENT IAC SB (terminated by -1 -16, not IAC SE!) NAWS 0 95 (95) 0 29 (29)
RCVD DO LFLOW
RCVD DONT LINEMODE
RCVD WILL STATUS
RCVD IAC SB (terminated by -1 -16, not IAC SE!) TERMINAL-SPEED SEND
RCVD IAC SB (terminated by -1 -16, not IAC SE!) ENVIRON SEND
SENT IAC SB (terminated by -1 -16, not IAC SE!) ENVIRON IS
RCVD IAC SB (terminated by -1 -16, not IAC SE!) TERMINAL-TYPE SEND
RCVD DO ECHO
SENT WONT ECHO
RCVD WILL ECHO
SENT DO ECHO

Access to this system is restricted to authorized users only.
login:
```

Advanced Topics

This section discusses several Telnet-related topics of interest. These topics include security, Telnet applications, and using Telnet to access other popular TCP/IP services.

Security

As with all TCP programs and applications, Telnet comes with security issues. However, tools are available to help better secure Telnet, or to replace it altogether.

TCP Wrappers

TCP Wrappers (known sometimes as `tcpd`) are a collection of tools that wrap around the TCP daemons (such as `in.telnetd`) and provide monitoring and filtering for TCP programs. Using TCP Wrappers, you can configure your system to respond only to Telnet requests coming from specific network computers or domains. TCP Wrappers were created by Wietse Venema.

Wrapper functionality comes preinstalled on some systems. Depending on your operating system, you may need to download and install TCP Wrappers yourself. The following sections describe how to configure the `/etc/hosts.allow` and `/etc/hosts.deny` files for TCP wrappers.

Configuring the `/etc/hosts.allow` and `/etc/hosts.deny` Files

The `/etc/hosts.allow` and `/etc/hosts.deny` files are used by the host access or TCP Wrapper program to determine who can and cannot run certain commands on your computer. For example, your `hosts.deny` file might contain:

```
In.telnetd:    All
```

and your `hosts.allow` file would contain

```
in.telnetd:    *.mydomain.com
```

In the preceding example, the entry in the `hosts.deny` file denies Telnet access to everyone. The `hosts.allow` entry overrides the `hosts.deny` entry for hosts coming from `mydomain.com`.

For more information on TCP Wrappers, refer to `ftp://ftp.porcupine.org/pub/security/index.html`.

Secure Shell

Secure Shell (SSH) is a secure alternative to Telnet. Due to its use of encryption mechanisms, such as the Data Encryption Standard (DES) and RSA host authentication, SSH can protect hosts from several common attacks, such as IP spoofing and password interception. SSH creates a Virtual Private Network (VPN) between the client and server.

SSH is free for non-commercial use. For more information on SSH, refer to `http://www.ssh.fi/sshprotocols2/` and `www.openssh.org`.

Telnet Applications

Telnet is often used to access remote applications. Hytelnet is an index of Telnet-accessible libraries and other resources around the world. Although somewhat displaced by the popularity and ease of access of the Web, many of these sites are still available.

Figures 31.5 and 31.6 show Hytelnet 6.9 for Windows in action.

Hytelnet can also be accessed via the Web at `http://www.lights.com/hytelnet/`.

Other Telnet applications include interfaces for Whois and Finger. For more information, refer to Chapter 29, "Whois and Finger."

FIGURE 31.5

A little bit about Hytelnet for Windows.

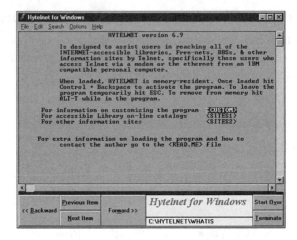

FIGURE 31.6

Using Hytelnet for Windows and CRT to access an online library.

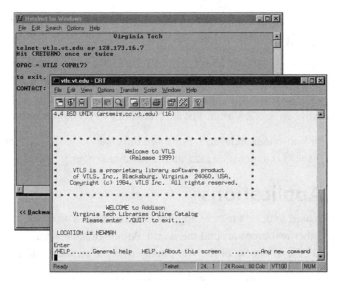

Using Telnet to Access Other TCP/IP Services

While Telnet uses TCP port 23 to achieve its primary function, the Telnet daemon listens and responds to other well-known TCP ports as well. This allows Telnet to be used in conjunction with the other TCP/IP services. Table 31.4 shows the TCP port numbers of some of the common TCP/IP services that work with Telnet.

TABLE 31.4 Ports of Common, Telnet-Enabled TCP Services

Service	Port
FTP	21
SMTP	25
Whois	43
Finger	79
HTTP	80

Telnet can be used to connect to these services by issuing Telnet commands of the following form:

```
telnet hostname port
```

or

```
telnet hostname service
```

In the latter usage example, the service (for example, SMTP) is used instead of the port number (for example, 25). The Telnet server on the host looks up the service number in a system file (/etc/services on most Unix systems) and opens a connection to the port mapped to the requested service. The following sections discuss this further and show some examples.

Sending Mail with Telnet

You can use Telnet to connect to the well-known SMTP port 25. Postmasters and administrators often do this to troubleshoot mail problems. The following example demonstrates using Telnet to connect to the SMTP port and run a VRFY (verify) command. For more information on SMTP, refer to Chapter 35, "Internet Mail Protocols."

```
$ telnet host.mydomain.com SMTP
Trying...
Connected to host.mydomain.com.
Escape character is '^]'.
220 host.mydomain.com ESMTP Sendmail 8.8.8+Sun/8.8.8; 8 Aug 1999 17:14
vrfy jamisonn
250 Neal Jamison <jamisonn@host.mydomain.com>
quit
221 host.mydomain.com closing connection
Connection closed by foreign host.
```

By executing the necessary SMTP commands, you can even use this method to send messages.

Finger

Telnet can also be used to connect to the finger port (79) of a remote host, as shown in the following example:

```
$ telnet host1.mydomain.com 79
Trying ...
Connected to host1.mydomain.com.
Escape character is '^]'.
jamisonn
Login: jamisonn                        Name: Neal Jamison
Directory: /users/home/jamisonn        Shell: /bin/tcsh
On since Sun Aug  8 17:16 (EDT) on ttyp7 from pool180-68
No mail.
No Plan.
Connection closed by foreign host.
```

After the connection was established, the one-line query (jamisonn) was entered. The Finger server responded with the answer to the query. This could come in handy if you find yourself in an environment without a Finger client. For more information on Finger, refer to Chapter 29.

Surfing the Web with Telnet

Telnet can also be used to connect to the HTTP port (80) of a Web server, as shown in the following example:

```
$ telnet mywebserver.com 80
Trying...
Connected to mywebserver.com.
Escape character is '^]'.
GET /
<HTML>
<HEAD>
<TITLE>Makoa Corporation</TITLE>
</HEAD>
<BODY>
<H1>Welcome to Makoa Corporation</H1>
<p>
This is the homepage of Makoa Corporation.
<br><br>
</BODY>
</HTML>

Connection closed by foreign host.
```

After the connection was established, the HTTP command GET / was entered. This requested the root document of the Web server. Unless you can translate HTML as well as your Web browser can, this will be of no use to you. It is shown here for demonstration purposes only and for checking whether the HTTP server is alive on TCP port 80. For more information on HTTP, refer to Chapter 36, "The HTTP (World Wide Web) Service."

Summary

This chapter described in detail the TCP/IP terminal emulation protocol, Telnet. As discussed, Telnet solved the ever-growing problem of terminal incompatibilities that was common at the time the Internet was born. Thanks to Telnet and the Network Virtual Terminal, scientists and researchers went from having several computer terminals on their desk to having just one.

This chapter presented the syntax and options associated with the common Unix Telnet client and server commands, and although they are rarely used by the end user, presented descriptions of the Telnet commands.

Security was touched upon, as was the subject of Telnet applications. It was demonstrated how you can use Telnet to connect to and use several other TCP/IP services, such as SMTP mail, Finger, and HTTP.

The chapter also included a complete listing of Telnet-related RFCs, including the original: RFC 15 from 1969.

Using the R-Utilities

by Neal S. Jamison

IN THIS CHAPTER

As you know by now, TCP/IP is the suite of protocols that allows computers to communicate with each other. But it takes more than just communication protocols to build an internet. There must be Application Layer programs that utilize the TCP/IP protocols and services, and it's these programs that perform the high-level communication. This chapter discusses a particular set of programs that allow remote computers to communicate in different ways.

Understanding R-Commands

The r-commands were born from the Berkeley BSD Unix community, where they were created to allow computer programmers and users to run sessions and commands on remote (hence the "r" in r-commands) computers. These commands are prevalent today in and around the Unix and TCP/IP community, and still perform their duties as originally designed. The r-commands allow us to copy files from one system to another, execute commands on remote computers, and even create login sessions on remote computers. Unlike telnet and ftp, however, these commands can be configured to run without requiring user interaction (that is, typing username and password).

The commonly used r-commands are listed in Table 32.1.

TABLE 32.1 The Unix R-Commands

Command	Description
rsh	Remote Shell: Executes a program on a remote computer. Sometimes referred to as rshell, remsh, or rcmd on some non-BSD Unix distributions, where rsh refers to the restricted shell.
rcp	Remote Copy: Copies files from one computer to another. Provides functionality similar to ftp.
rlogin	Remote Login: Logs in to a remote computer. rlogin provides functionality similar to telnet.
rup	Remote Uptime: Shows the status of a remote computer.
ruptime	Remote Uptime: Shows the status of a remote computer. (Similar to rup.)
rwho	Remote Who: Displays the current users on a remote computer.
rexec	Remote Execution: Same as rsh, but requires a password.

Security Implications

The theory behind the r-commands is that of "host equivalency." Computers are configured to allow specific "trusted" hosts and users to transparently log in and run commands. This approach has several problems: Your system becomes as weak as the weakest trusted host, and in the event of improper configuration, you might inadvertently give access to others. Another problem with the r-commands is that in many cases, when a user is not trusted and is asked to enter a password, that password is sent over the network as clear, unencrypted text. This clear text transmission could be intercepted by someone snooping your network and used to gain unauthorized access.

Because of the security implications of the r-commands, most experts recommend that they be disabled. However, because they are still commonly used, this chapter focuses on their proper configuration and use. It will also offer an alternative in the event that you choose to disable the commands as recommended (see "Alternatives to Using R-Commands" later in this chapter).

For more information on proper configuration, see the "R-Command Reference" section later in this chapter.

32

USING THE
R-UTILITIES

> **Note**
>
> Because of the many unique "flavors" of operating systems available, this chapter discusses the r-commands as they are implemented in Linux. The concept and use of the commands is very similar, regardless of your chosen operating system. Consult your OS documentation for specific commands and/or options.

Disabling the R-Commands

If you choose to disable the r-commands, you must comment-out the related lines in the /etc/inetd.conf file. The lines are commented by placing a "#" at the beginning of the line. Here is a sample /etc/inetd.conf file with the proper lines commented (note that the file has been slightly abbreviated to save space):

```
#
# inetd.conf   This file describes the services that will be available
#    through the INETD TCP/IP super server.  To reconfigure
#    the running INETD process, edit this file, then send the
#    INETD process a SIGHUP signal.
# Version:   @(#)/etc/inetd.conf   3.10   05/27/93
# Authors:   Original taken from BSD Unix 4.3/TAHOE.
#   Fred N. van Kempen, <waltje@uwalt.nl.mugnet.org>
# Modified for Debian Linux by Ian A. Murdock <imurdock@shell.portal.com>
# Modified for RHS Linux by Marc Ewing <marc@redhat.com>
#
```

```
# <service_name> <sock_type> <proto> <flags> <user> <server_path> <args>
# Echo, discard, daytime, and chargen are used primarily for testing.
#
# These are standard services.
#
ftp     stream tcp   nowait root   /usr/sbin/tcpd   in.ftpd -l -a
telnet  stream tcp   nowait root   /usr/sbin/tcpd   in.telnetd
#
# Shell, login, exec, comsat and talk are BSD protocols.
#
#shell  stream tcp   nowait  root   /usr/sbin/tcpd  in.rshd
#login  stream tcp   nowait  root   /usr/sbin/tcpd  in.rlogind
#exec   stream tcp   nowait  root   /usr/sbin/tcpd  in.rexecd
#
...
```

As you can see, a "#" comment character has been placed at the beginning of the lines that start in.rshd, in.rlogind, and in.rexecd, respectively.

Note

You must be the superuser to modify the files and run the commands discussed in this chapter.

After commenting out the r-command daemons, you will need to restart the inetd daemon. This is accomplished by running the following command:

```
killall -HUP inetd
```

The Role of Daemons in Unix

In Unix, a daemon is a program that runs in the background and waits for some event to take place. By definition, a daemon is an intermediary between man and a divine being. In the Unix world, it is an intermediary between two events or processes. An example daemon is in.rlogind, which waits for an rlogin request. Upon receiving a request, in.rlogind attempts to authenticate the user. If the user is trusted, he or she is allowed access. Otherwise in.rlogind denies the request.

Securing the R-Commands

If you decide that you can't live without the functionality of the r-commands, you can take some extra steps to make them as secure as possible. Here are some methods you can use:

- TCP wrappers
- Kerberos authentication
- Data Encryption Standard (DES)

TCP Wrappers

TCP wrappers (known sometimes as `tcpd`) are a host access control mechanism that "wraps" around the TCP daemon and provides monitoring and filtering for TCP programs. Using TCP wrappers, you can configure your system to respond only to r-command requests coming from specific network computers or domains.

Wrapper functionality typically comes preinstalled on most Linux distributions (see `http://howto.tucows.com/LDP/LDP/LG/issue46/pollman/tcpwrappers.html` or the man page for `host_access(5)` for more details). Depending on your operating system, you might need to download and install them yourself.

Configuring the `/etc/hosts.allow` and `/etc/hosts.deny` *Files*

The `/etc/hosts.allow` and `/etc/hosts.deny` files are used by the host access or TCP Wrapper program to determine who can and cannot run certain commands on your computer. The basic syntax of an entry to these files is

```
daemon : client
```

For example, your `hosts.deny` file might contain

```
All:   All
```

and your `hosts.allow` file would contain

```
in.telnetd:   All
in.ftpd:   All
in.rshd:   *.mydomain.com
in.rlogind   *.mydomain.com
in.rexecd   *.mydomain.com
```

In this example, the `hosts.deny` entry of `All: All` specifies that everyone is denied access to everything. This might seem extreme at first, but then we examine the `hosts.allow` file, which overrides the severity of the `deny` file. It states that everyone should be allowed to enter the system using the interactive telnet and ftp programs, but only hosts in the trusted domain, `mydomain.com`, should be allowed to attempt the trusted r-commands.

This section has presented just an overview of the options and functionality supported by host access and TCP Wrappers. Consult your operating system documentation for more information.

Exploiting Systems with IP Spoofing

IP spoofing is a technique used to "spoof" or fool a computer system into thinking that incoming requests or data are coming from a trusted computer, when actually they are not. It is commonly used to exploit trusted systems like those utilized by the r-commands and TCP Wrappers.

The methods involved in IP spoofing are beyond the scope of this chapter, but in general, the impostor must somehow modify the network packet headers to make them appear as if they are coming from a trusted network.

Kerberos Authentication

In an attempt to better secure the r-commands, many distributions of `rsh`, `rcp`, and `rlogin` are now using *Kerberos authentication.*

Kerberos is an authentication system that allows two parties to exchange secure information across an unsecured network. Each communicating party is assigned a ticket, which is embedded in messages and used in place of a password to identify the sender.

For more information about Kerberos, refer to `http://web.mit.edu/kerberos/www/`.

Data Encryption Standard (DES)

Certain distributions of `rsh` can be configured to use a powerful encryption standard known as DES. Created in the 1970s, DES provides a strong level of encryption.

For more information on DES, refer to `http://www.itl.nist.gov/fipspubs/fip46-3.htm`.

Alternatives to Using R-Commands

With all the security ramifications of using the r-commands, you are probably thinking that there must be an alternative. Well, there is: Secure Shell (SSH).

Secure Shell is a secure way to log in to remote computers, execute remote commands, and copy remote files. You can achieve the same functionality with SSH as you can using the less secure `rlogin`, `rsh`, and `rcp`.

What makes SSH secure is its use of encryption mechanisms such as the Data Encryption Standard (DES) and RSA host authentication. These mechanisms allow SSH to protect your system against several common attacks, such as

- IP spoofing
- Interception of clear text passwords
- Manipulation of data

RSA Public Key/Private Key Authentication

Short for Rivest, Shamir, and Adelman, the inventors of the algorithm, RSA provides public key/private key encryption. The basic idea is that data encrypted with the public key can only be decrypted with a private key. In the case of host authentication, the sending host encrypts a random string of data using the public key of the receiving (remote) host. If the remote host can successfully decrypt it using its private key, the two hosts know without a doubt that they are legitimate.

For more information on RSA, refer to `http://www.rsa.com/`. For a good introduction to public key/private key encryption, refer to `http://www.rsa.com/rsalabs/pkcs/`.

SSH versions 1 and 2 are free for non-commercial use. For more information on SSH, refer to `http://www.ssh.fi/sshprotocols2/`.

R-Command Reference

This section presents the syntax and usage of the r-commands. As mentioned earlier, this information is gleaned from the Linux operating system. Refer to your own man pages or documentation for usage and options specific to your operating system of choice.

R-Command Daemons

Table 32.2 lists several daemons that must be running (or enabled to be run by `inetd`) on the server in order for the r-commands to function properly. See your server documentation or man pages for more information.

TABLE 32.2   R-Command Daemons

Daemon	Description
rshd	Remote shell server. Provides remote execution without authentication.
rlogind	Remote login server. Provides remote login without authentication.
rwhod	System status server.
rstatd (or rcp.rstatd)	Remote status server.

rsh

The remote shell command (rsh) allows the execution of commands on a remote system. The following shows the syntax for using the rsh command:

> **Note**
>
> rsh is sometimes referred to as rshell, remsh, or rcmd on some Unix distributions, where rsh refers to the unrelated restricted shell.

Usage: rsh [-Kdnx] [-k realm] [-l username] host [command]

Options:

- -K—Disables Kerberos authentication.
- -d—Enables socket debugging.
- -n—Redirects input from /dev/null.
- -k—Causes the remote Kerberos ticket to be obtained in the specified realm instead of the remote host's realm.
- -l—Allows the remote username to be specified, instead of using the current username.
- -x—Enables DES encryption if available.

If no command is specified, the user is given an rlogin session. The following example shows how to use a rsh command:

Example:

```
%rsh hostname1 who
jamisonn    pts/1    Jul 26 09:13    (hostname2)
evanm       pts/13   Jul 25 12:30    (hostname3)
```

This example executes the who command on the remote host hostname1. The output shows two users currently using hostname1.

rcp

Remote copy (rcp) copies files from one machine to another. It can be thought of as a non-interactive ftp. The following shows the syntax for using the rcp command:

Usage: `rcp [-px] [-k realm] file1 file2`

`rcp [-px] [-r] [-k realm] file ... directory`

The format for a file or directory is *username@hostname:filepath*.

Options:

- -r—Performs a recursive copy (the destination must be a directory).

- -p—Attempts to preserve the modification times and modes of the source files.

- -k—Causes the remote Kerberos ticket to be obtained in the specified realm instead of the remote host's realm.

- -x—Enables DES encryption if available.

The following shows an example of using the rcp command:

Example:

`%rcp /home/jamisonn/report jamison@hostname2:report`

This example would copy the file report from my local home directory to my home directory on the remote hostname2.

rlogin

rlogin starts a terminal session on a remote host. The following shows the syntax for using the rlogin command:

Usage: `rlogin [-8EKLdx] [-e char] [-k realm] [-l username] host`

Options:

- -8—Allows an eight-bit input data path.

- -E—Prevents the use of an escape character.

- -K—Disables Kerberos authentication.

- -L—Allows the rlogin session to be run in "litout" mode.

- -d—Enables socket debugging.

- -e—Allows the user to specify an escape character, which is "~" by default.

- -k—Causes the remote Kerberos ticket to be obtained in the specified realm instead of the remote host's realm.

- -x—Enables DES encryption if available.

The following shows an example of using the `rlogin` command:

Example:

```
%rlogin -l jamisonn hostname1
```

This example would create a login session for the user `jamisonn` on the remote host `hostname1`.

The `rlogind` daemon must be enabled on the remote host.

rup

`rup` displays the status of the specified remote system. If no host is specified, `rup` returns the status of all hosts on the network. The following shows the syntax for using the `rup` command:

Usage: `rup [-dhlt] [host ...]`

Options:

> `-d`—Displays the local time for the host.

> `-h`—Sorts output alphabetically by hostname.

> `-l`—Sorts output by load average.

> `-t`—Sorts output by uptime.

Example output:

```
% rup hostname1
hostname1    up 15 days, 11:13,   load average: 0.21, 0.26, 0.19

%rup -d hostname1
hostname1    4.08pm  up 15 days, 11:13,   load average: 0.21, 0.26, 0.19
```

The `rstatd` (or `rpc.rstatd`) daemon must be enabled on the remote host in order for `rup` to work properly.

ruptime

`ruptime` is similar in function to `rup`. The following shows the syntax for using the `ruptime` command:

Usage: `ruptime [ -alrtu ]`

Options:

> `-a`—Displays hosts that have been idle for an hour or more.

> `-l`—Sorts output by load average.

-r—Reverses sort order.

-t—Sorts output by uptime.

-u—Sorts output by number of users.

The rwhod daemon must be enabled on the remote host in order for ruptime to work properly.

rwho

rwho displays users logged in to remote systems. Its output is similar to the Unix who command. By default, rwho only displays users who have actively used the system in the last hour. The following shows the syntax for using the rwho command:

Usage: rwho [-a]

Options:

-a—Displays all users, including those who have been idle for more than an hour.

The rwhod daemon must be enabled on the remote host in order for rwho to work properly.

rexec

rexec is similar in functionality to rsh, but it requires the entry of a password. The following shows the syntax of the rexec command:

Usage:

rexec [username@hostname] [**-DNn**] [**-l** username] [**-p** password] command

rexec [**-DNn**] [**-l** username] [**-p** password] [username@hostname] command

Options:

-D—Enables socket debugging on the TCP sockets used for communication with the remote host. This option also displays the user name sent to the **rexecd** service (or daemon).

-l username—Specifies the remote username to be used when executing the command. This can also be specified by including username@hostname on the command line.

-N—Does not generate a separate standard error stream. All output is sent to standard output. This is useful when you are running an interactive command. For example,

```
rexec -N localhost cmd
rexec -N localhost sh -i
```

-**n**—Redirects input from the special device `/dev/nul`.

-**p** `password`—Specifies the password of the specified user on the remote host.

If no password is specified, the `~/.netrc` file is checked for "machine hostname login username password string" combination. If a password is not found, the user is prompted to enter a password.

Related Files

Several files must be configured properly in order for the r-commands to run, including the following:

- `/etc/hosts`
- `/etc/hosts.equiv`
- `.rhosts`
- `/etc/hosts.allow` and `/etc/hosts.deny`

These files are discussed in the following sections.

/etc/hosts

It is vital that the communicating computers each know about the other. This is accomplished via entries in the `/etc/hosts` file. If `hostname1` wants to allow `hostname2` to run the r-commands, `hostname1` must have an entry for `hostname2` in its `/etc/hosts` file, and vice versa.

/etc/hosts.equiv

The `hosts.equiv` file specifies the hosts and users that are allowed (or denied) transparent r-command privileges. An improperly configured `hosts.equiv` file could open your system to everyone.

The basic format for the `/etc/hosts.equiv` file is

`[+ | -][hostname][username]`

Preceding *hostname* or *username* with a + allows trusted access from that host or user. Similarly, preceding *username* with a – denies trusted access from that host or user. Table 32.3 shows several sample entries with brief explanations of the result.

TABLE 32.3 `hosts.equiv` Entries and Their Results

Entry	Result
`Hostname1`	Allows all users from `Hostname1` trusted access
`-Hostname1`	Denies trusted access to all users from `Hostname1`
`Hostname2 -root`	Denies trusted access to the user `root` coming from `Hostname2`
`Hostname2 +admin`	Gives trusted access to the user `admin` coming from `Hostname2`
`-root`	Denies access to the user `root` from any system
`+admin`	Allows access by the user `admin` coming from any system
`+`	Grants trusted access to everyone (Dangerous!)
`-`	Denies trusted access to everyone

Note

Some distributions may come with the + entry in the `hosts.equiv` file. This tells your system that any system is a trusted host, and can be very dangerous. If you have a + entry in your `hosts.equiv` file, remove it.

.rhosts

The `.rhosts` file is identical to the `hosts.equiv` file. However, `.rhosts` files are used to allow or deny trusted access to a specific user account, whereas the `hosts.equiv` file specifies the entire system.

A common use of the `.rhosts` file is to allow a user trusted access to multiple systems upon which the user has accounts. For example, the user has an account on `hostname1` with the username of `jamison`. On another system, `hostname2`, he might have an account under the username `jamisonn`. Creating `.rhosts` files in each of the accounts could allow you to grant yourself trusted access to the other system.

A sample `.rhosts` file in `jamison`'s home directory on `hostname1` would look like

`hostname2 +jamisonn`

On `hostname2` the file in the `jamisonn` home directory would contain the entry

`hostname1 +jamison`

These two files would allow you trusted privileges on each system.

One of the weaknesses of the r-command's use of trusted hosts and users is that it is not too difficult to spoof the system into thinking you are someone or are coming from somewhere you are not. In the preceding example, if an intruder were to gain access to the first system, hostname1, as either jamison or the superuser, that intruder would have free access to hostname2. This is an example of user spoofing. IP or hostname spoofing, or making it seem as if you are coming from a trusted host, is not quite as straightforward, but unfortunately it's often used to exploit these types of trusted systems.

The `/etc/hosts.allow` and `/etc/hosts.deny` Files

These files are used by the host access or TCP Wrapper program to determine who can and cannot run certain commands on your computer. For a more complete description of these files and their syntax, refer to the "TCP Wrappers" section earlier in this chapter. The following shows several examples of using the hosts.allow and hosts.deny files:

Example `/etc/hosts.deny`:

```
All:All
```

Example `/etc/hosts.allow`:

```
in.telnetd: All
in.ftpd: All
in.rshd: *.mydomain.com
in.rlogind: *.mydomain.com
```

In these examples, the `hosts.deny` file sets the stage by disallowing everyone for everything. This is a good security practice. The `hosts.allow` file then opens telnet and ftp to anyone, and allows hosts coming from the trusted domain `mydomain.com` to run the r-commands.

Achieving R-Command Functionality in Non-Unix Environments

The r-commands are inherently found in Unix environments. However, they are starting to appear in other TCP/IP products, such as the Microsoft TCP/IP component of Windows NT/2000. Several third-party products are available that will allow other systems to achieve r-command functionality.

Table 32.4 shows several vendors and manufacturers, and a URL for more information. In some cases these programs are shareware, so the author is listed in place of a manufacturer.

TABLE 32.4   Third-Party R-Command Products

Manufacturer	*URL*
Hummingbird Communications LTD	`http://www.hummingbird.com/products/nc/inetd/`
Denicomp Systems	`http://www.denicomp.com/products.htm`
Didier CASSEREAU	`http://www.loa.espci.fr/winnt/rshd/rshd.htm`
Markus Fischer	`http://www.uni-paderborn.de/StaffWeb/getin`

Summary

This chapter introduced you to the Unix r-commands that you can use to log in to remote computers, copy remote files, and execute other remote commands. There are some large security implications of running these commands and services that must not be ignored. As such, this chapter offered alternatives such as the secure shell (SSH). It discussed using r-commands in non-Unix environments, and numerous URLs were provided throughout the chapter to enable you to seek out more information on your own.

The command summaries provided throughout the chapter are unique to the Linux environment. Be sure to check your own documentation and Unix man pages for information specific to your environment.

32

**USING THE
R-UTILITIES**

Filesystem-Sharing Protocols: NFS and SMB/CIFS

by Neal S. Jamison

IN THIS CHAPTER

TCP/IP provides the services and protocols that allow computers to share data with one another. It was this capability that sparked the Internet revolution that we are enjoying today. One of the most useful applications of TCP/IP is the *Network File System*, more commonly known as NFS.

What Is NFS?

NFS is a distributed filesystem that allows computers to share resources over a TCP/IP network: It allows NFS client applications to transparently read and write files that reside on NFS servers. Prior to its implementation, the only way for computers to share data was either to duplicate or centralize the data, or to distribute the data via a network of homogeneous computers. There were clearly downsides to all of these options— duplication of data wasted space and could cause real consistency problems, centralization of data meant costly mainframes and dumb terminals, and who wanted to be limited by a homogeneous network?

Along came NFS, which allowed us to share data independent of platform, and all of our problems were solved.

> **Note**
>
> For the purpose of this text, a "filesystem" is a set of organized data files grouped together in a directory structure. For example, in Unix, /usr is a file-system.

NFS servers share resources, making them available for use by clients on the network. As discussed later, NFS can be used on both LANs and WANs. NFS was designed to be operating system- and hardware-independent, allowing a wide range of computers to share resources. The basic NFS service is actually made up of two protocols: Mount and NFS.

A Brief History of NFS

NFS was introduced by Sun Microsystems in 1984. It was first implemented under Sun's 4.2BSD (more commonly known as SunOS). Due to its popularity and a need in the industry for such a protocol, it was soon ported to a wide variety of operating environments. By 1986, NFS allowed shared resources over 16 different hardware platforms using five different operating systems. Today, NFS runs on many different hardware and OS platforms, and it has even been enhanced to run over the Web.

Why NFS?

NFS was created to allow computers to share resources. At the time of its development (the early 1980s) the computer industry was rapidly changing. Cheap CPUs and client/server technology were allowing the industry to decentralize their computing environments. However, while processors were getting cheaper, large capacity storage systems were still relatively expensive. Something was needed that would allow the computers to share storage and data while still maximizing their individual processing power. NFS was the answer.

Implementation—How NFS Works

NFS uses the protocols and services provided by TCP/IP. NFS runs on the Application Layer of the OSI model, as shown in Table 33.1.

TABLE 33.1   NFS on the OSI Layer Model

Layer	Name	Function
1	Application	NFS
2	Presentation	XDR
3	Session	RPC
4	Transport	UDP, TCP
5	Network	IP
6	Data Link	Many choices
7	Physical	Many choices

33

FILESYSTEM-
SHARING
PROTOCOLS

Due to the greater performance of the utilitarian UDP transport protocol, NFS was originally designed to use UDP instead of the TCP transport protocol. However, although UDP works well on reliable local area networks, it does have drawbacks when running over less reliable WANs such as the Internet. Recent advances in TCP now enable NFS to run efficiently using the more reliable transport protocol. Starting with Solaris 2.6, Sun Microsystems now uses NFS over TCP. TCP support was added to NFS, in NFS version 2, but was not optimized. NFS version 3 optimized TCP support and removed the arbitrary block size limitation of 8KB. The latest version of NFS is version 4.

> **Note**
>
> For more information about UDP and TCP, please refer to Chapter 9, "Overview of the IP Family of Protocols."

Remote Procedure Calls (RPC) and External Data Representation (XDR)

To be wholly platform-independent, NFS relies on the workhorses of the lower OSI layers. The Session Layer *Remote Procedure Call* (RPC) and Presentation Layer *External Data Representation* (XDR) provide the network connections for NFS and the format of the data sent over these connections. In short, they are used to allow NFS to work over a wide range of different platforms. This chapter examines each of these from the bottom up.

Understanding RPC

RPC operates at the Session Layer of the OSI stack, and provides computer systems with a set of procedures that can be called as if they were local. Using RPC, a local computer or application can call and use a service running on a remote computer. RPC provides an entire library of procedures that allow higher-level applications to run without needing to know the lower-level details of the remote system. It is this level of abstraction that allows the application-level NFS to be platform-independent.

Understanding XDR

The External Data Representation library is responsible for translating the RPC data between heterogeneous computer systems. XDR designates a standard data representation that all computers understand.

Together, RPC and XDR provide the client/server relationship required by NFS.

Hard Mounts Versus Software Mounts

As explained in a previous section, the stateless nature of NFS allows clients and client applications to recover from periods of server unavailability. The type of the mount determines how your client or client applications will respond when the server becomes unavailable. Mount types will be discussed again in the "Common NFS Problems and Solutions" section later in this chapter.

Hard Mounts

In the event that the NFS server or resource becomes unavailable, a hard-mounted resource will result in RPC calls being tried and retried indefinitely. When the server responds, the RPC will succeed and the next procedure will be executed. If there are persistent server or network problems, the hard mount can result in a constant wait state, which will cause the NFS client application to appear to be hung. Also the mount retries will contribute to network traffic. There is an option that can be specified to make a hard mount interruptible.

Soft Mounts

With a soft-mounted resource, repeated RPC failures will result in the NFS client application failing as well, which can result in unreliable data. They should not be used with filesystems that are writeable, or from which mission-critical data or executable programs will be read.

> **Note**
>
> The following section contains data similar to Unix man page information. For more complete information, see the man pages for the specific files and programs.

NFS Files and Commands

This section introduces you to the daemons, programs, and files that are used by NFS. Due to the fact that NFS is so closely tied to Unix, the following sections will demonstrate the steps to share and use NFS resources with two popular Unix operating systems: Sun Solaris 2.x and Linux. A discussion about other implementations, including PC-based clients, appears in the later section "Related Protocols and Products."

> **How Daemons Work**
>
> In Unix, a *daemon* is a program that runs in the background and waits for some event to take place. By definition, a daemon is an intermediary between man and a divine being. In the Unix world, it is an intermediary between two processes. An example of a daemon is a print process that waits for a print job to enter the queue or, in the case of NFS, waits for a client to request a filesystem.

NFS Daemons

There are several server daemons that work together to make NFS work. They are described in the following sections for the Solaris and Linux operating systems.

Solaris 2.x

The following Solaris daemons are used to listen for, handle, and maintain NFS requests. The Solaris server daemons are started with the script /etc/init.d/nfs.server.

nfsd

nfsd is the server daemon that listens for NFS client requests. The following shows the syntax of running the nfsd daemon:

Usage: /usr/lib/nfs/nfsd [-a] [-c #_conn] [-l listen_backlog] [-p protocol] [-t device] [nservers]

Options:

-a—Starts an NFS daemon over all available connectionless and connection-oriented transports, including UDP and TCP.

-c #_conn—Sets the maximum number of connections allowed to the NFS server over connection-oriented transports. By default, the number of connections is unlimited.

-l—Sets connection queue length for the NFS TCP over a connection-oriented transport. The default value is 32 entries.

-p protocol—Starts an NFS daemon over the specified protocol.

-t device—Starts an NFS daemon for the transport specified by the given device.

Nservers—Specifies the maximum number of requests that can be handled concurrently.

Related files: /etc/init.d/nfs.server; the shell script that starts nfsd.

mountd

mountd answers requests for NFS access information and filesystem mounts. It reads /etc/dfs/sharetab to determine the availability of filesystems. The following shows the syntax of running the mountd daemon:

Usage: /usr/lib/nfs/mountd [-v] [-r]

Options:

-v—Runs in verbose mode, logging to the console.

-r—Rejects client requests.

Related files: /etc/dfs/sharetab (see the "NFS-Related Files" section later in this chapter).

statd

statd works with lockd to provide crash and recovery for the file locking service. statd is a client daemon. The following shows the syntax of running the statd daemon:

Usage: /usr/lib/nfs/statd

Related files: lockd

lockd

lockd is part of the NFS lock manager, which helps support locking of NFS files. lockd is a client daemon. The following shows the syntax of running the lockd daemon:

Usage: /usr/lib/nfs/lockd [-g graceperiod] [-t timeout] [nthreads]

Options:

> -g graceperiod—The number of seconds a client has to reclaim a lock after the server reboots. (Default 45)
>
> -t timeout—The number of seconds a client should wait before retransmitting a lock request. (Default 15)
>
> nthreads—The number of threads available to respond to lock requests. (Default 20)

Related files: statd

Linux

The following Linux daemons are used to listen for, handle, and maintain NFS requests. Their use and syntax are very similar to the daemons found in Solaris.

rpc.nfsd

rpc.nfsd is the server daemon that handles NFS requests. The following shows the syntax of running the rpc.nfsd daemon:

Usage: /usr/sbin/rpc.nfsd [-f exports-file] [-d facility] [-P port]
[-R dirname] [-Fhlnprstv] [--debug facility] [--exports-file=file]
[--foreground] [--help] [--allow-non-root] [--re-export]
[--public-root dirname] [--no-spoof-trace] [--port port]
[--log-transfers] [--version] [numservers]

Options:

-f exports-file—Specifies the exports file. By default, this is /etc/exports.

-h or –help—Provides a help summary.

-l or --log-transfers—Logs all file transfer information.

-n or --allow-non-root—Allows incoming NFS requests to be honored even if they do not originate from reserved IP ports.

-P portnum or --port portnum—Makes nfsd listen on port portnum instead of the default port 2049 or the one listed in /etc/services.

-p or –promiscuous—Instructs the server to serve any host on the network.

-v or –version—Reports the current version number of the program.

numservers—Allows you to run several instances of nfsd in parallel.

Related files: exports, mountd

rpc.mountd

rpc.mountd receives mount requests and checks for the availability of the NFS filesystem in /etc/exports. If the requested resource is available, rpc.mountd creates a file handle and adds the entry to /etc/rmtab. Upon receipt of a UMOUNT request, rpc.mountd removes the entry from /etc/rmtab. The following shows the syntax of running the rpc.mountd daemon:

Usage: /usr/sbin/rpc.mountd [-f exports-file] [-d facility] [-P port] [-Dhnprv] [--debug facility] [--exports-file=file] [--help] [--allow-non-root] [--re-export] [--no-spoof-trace] [--version]

Options:

Please refer to the previous command, rcp.nfsd, for rcp.mountd command options.

Related files: /etc/exports, /etc/rmtab

rpc.statd

Refer to the Solaris implementation of statd for more information on this daemon.

rpc.lockd

Refer to the Solaris implementation of lockd for more information on this daemon.

biod

biod starts a specified number of asynchronous block I/O daemons on an NFS client. These daemons perform read-ahead and write-behind operations on the NFS filesystem.

These operations help improve NFS performance. The following shows the syntax of running the `biod` daemon:

Usage: `/usr/etc/biod [numdaemons]`

NFS-Related Files

Several server and client files must be modified in order to successfully share or mount NFS filesystems.

Solaris 2.x Files

The following sections describe the files used in Solaris to define and track NFS resources.

/etc/dfs/dfstab

The `dfstab` file contains a list of `share` commands that control the export of NFS filesystems. For more information on `share`, see the "Solaris 2.x Server Commands" section later in this chapter.

Example:

```
share   -F nfs   -o rw=engineering   -d "home dirs"   /export/home2
```

/etc/dfs/sharetab

`sharetab` contains an entry for every filesystem shared by the `share` command. It is automatically generated by the system. Each entry in the `sharetab` file contains the following fields:

- `pathname`—The pathname of the shared resource.
- `resource`—The name by which remote systems can access the resource.
- `fstype`—The type of the shared resource.
- `specific_options`—Specific options that were used when the resource was shared.
- `description`—A description of the shared resource, provided when the resource was shared.

Example:

```
/export/home2      -        nfs     rw=engineering   "Engineering Home"
```

/etc/rmtab

`rmtab` contains a listing of NFS filesystems that are currently mounted by clients. It, too, is generated by the system. It contains lines in the form of

```
hostname:fsname
```

Example:

```
engineering5:/export/home2
```

/etc/vfs/vfstab

vfstab is the file used to describe the local and remote systems to be mounted. This is an NFS client file. Entries in the vfstab file contain the following fields:

- device to mount
- device to fsck
- mount point
- filesystem type
- fsck pass
- mount at boot
- mount options (see the section "NFS-Client Commands" for mount options)

Example:

```
servername:/export/home2   -   /export/home   NFS   -   y   -
```

Linux Files

The following files are used in Linux to define and track NFS resources.

/etc/exports

exports is the access control list of files that can be exported to NFS clients. Each line in the exports file contains an NFS resource and the hosts that are allowed to mount it. A list of access options can be specified in parentheses, but is not required. There is an extensive list of options and parameters that can be used to manage access to the resource. Please refer to your specific documentation for details.

Example:

```
/users/home host.mydomain.com(ro)
```

This example indicates that the host host.mydomain.com is allowed to mount the /users/home file system in read-only mode.

/etc/rmtab

rmtab contains a list of NFS filesystems that are currently mounted by clients. It is maintained by the system. The format of the file is

```
hostname:resource
```

Example:

```
datahouse.anvi.com:/users/home
```

/etc/fstab

/etc/fstab contains an entry for every filesystem to be utilized by the system. It is the Linux equivalent of vfstab. Each entry in the fstab file contains the following fields:

- remote filesystem—The path name of the remote resource.
- mountpoint—The local mount point for the remote resource.
- fstype—The type of the remote resource (for example, nfs).
- mount_options—Specific options to be associated with the filesystem.
- dump option—Indicates whether the filesystem should be dumped (backed up). A default value of 0 indicates that it should not.
- fsck pass—Indicates at which pass fsck should check the filesystem. A default value of 0 indicates that the filesystem should not be checked by fsck.

Consult your man pages or documentation for a complete list of options and other fstab information.

Example:

```
solaris:/www    /mnt   nfs    rsize=1024,wsize=1024,hard,intr   0   0
```

NFS Server Commands

After the required daemons are running and necessary files modified, sharing and mounting NFS resources is easy.

Creating Shared Resources

Before NFS resources can be used by the clients on your network, they must be shared by the NFS server. The following sections explain the commands for Solaris and Linux that are used to share (that is, export) these resources.

Solaris 2.x Server Commands

The following Solaris commands are used to share and monitor NFS resources.

share

The share command makes a specified filesystem available to client systems. The following shows the syntax for the share command:

Usage: `share [ -F FSType ] [ -o specific_options ] [ -d description ]`
`[ pathname ]`

Options:

`-F FSType`—Specifies the filesystem type.

`-o specific_options`—Used to control access of the shared resource. They can be any of the following:

`rw`   Pathname is shared read/write.

`rw=client[:client]`   Pathname is shared read/write only to the specified clients.

`Ro`   Pathname is shared read-only.

`ro=client[:client]`   Pathname is shared read-only only to the listed clients.

`-d description`—Used to provide a description of the resource being shared.

Example:

`share  -F nfs  -o rw=engineering  -d "home dirs"  /export/home2`

shareall

`shareall` shares the resources from the specified file, the standard input, or the default `dfstab` file. The following shows the syntax for `shareall` command:

Usage: `shareall [-F FSType[,FSType...]] [- | file]`

Options:

`-F FSType`—The filesystem type.

`[- | file]`—If the `-` is used, `shareall` takes its input from standard input. If a file is specified, `shareall` takes its input from there. If none is specified, `shareall` uses the default `dfstab` file (`/etc/dfs/dfstab`).

showmount

`showmount` lists all clients that have mounted a filesystem from the server upon which the command is run. The following shows the syntax for the `showmount` command:

Usage: `/usr/sbin/showmount [ -ade ] [ hostname ]`

Options:

`-a`—Prints all remote mounts.

`-d`—Lists directories that have been remotely mounted.

`-e`—Prints the list of shared filesystems.

Linux Server Commands

The following Linux commands are used to share and monitor NFS resources.

exportfs

exportfs causes the /etc/exports file to be reread by the system. Some Linux distributions don't have exportfs. If this is your case, you can create a short shell script that achieves the same functionality.

```
#!/bin/sh
killall -HUP /usr/sbin/rpc.mountd
killall -HUP /usr/sbin/rpc.nfsd
```

> **Note**
>
> In RedHat 7 (and higher distributions), you can restart the nfs services, which causes the /etc/exports file to be read again, by running the following script:
>
> ```
> /etc/rc.d/init.d/nfs restart
> ```
>
> Besides restart the script accepts arguments such as start and stop, which have the obvious meanings.

33

FILESYSTEM-
SHARING
PROTOCOLS

showmount

showmount checks the mount daemon on an NFS server for information about the currently mounted filesystems. The following shows the syntax for the showmount command:

Usage: /usr/sbin/showmount [-adehv] [--all] [--directories]
[--exports] [--help] [--version] [host]

Options:

-a or –all—Lists the client hostname and mounted directory in host:dir format.

-d or –directories—Lists only the directories mounted by a client.

-e or –exports—Shows the list of exported filesystems.

-h or –help—Provides helpful information.

-v or –version—Reports the current program version.

--no-headers—Suppresses the descriptive headings from the output.

Unsharing Resources

There will come a time when you will want to prevent a filesystem from being mounted. You can use the reject (-r) option with the `mount` command, as discussed previously, or you can simply unshare the resource.

Solaris 2.x

The following sections describe the Solaris commands used to unshare NFS resources.

unshare

unshare makes a shared filesystem unavailable. The following shows the syntax for the unshare command:

Usage: `unshare [ -F FSType ] [ -o specific_options ] [ pathname | resourcename ]`

If `-F FSType` is unspecified, `unshare` will use as a default the `FSType` of the first entry in the `/etc/dfs/dfstab` file. The `-o specific options` depend on the `FSType` used. See your specific documentation for more information.

unshareall

unshareall unshares shared resources of type `FSType`. The following shows the syntax for the `unshareall` command:

Usage: `unshareall [-F FSType[,FSType...]]`

If called without a specific `FSType`, `unshareall` unshares all shared resources.

Using showmount *to Verify*

showmount can be used to verify that the filesystem is no longer mounted by any clients. Refer to the syntax in the previous section.

Unsharing with Linux exportfs

Linux lacks any official command to unshare a shared resource. The best way to achieve this functionality is to edit the share file (`/etc/exports`), removing the filesystem that you no longer want to be shared. Then run `exportfs` to have the system reread the share file. If your Linux system lacks the `exportfs` command, you can create an equivalent shell script:

```
#!/bin/sh
killall -HUP /usr/sbin/rpc.mountd
killall -HUP /usr/sbin/rpc.nfsd
```

NFS Client Commands

The following sections show the client commands used to mount or unmount an NFS resource.

> **Note**
>
> It is important that the mount point (empty directory) upon which you will be mounting your resources is created beforehand.

Mounting NFS Resources

The following commands can be used to mount a shared resource.

mount (Solaris/Linux)

mount is used to mount remote NFS filesystems. The following shows the syntax for the mount command:

Usage (Solaris):

```
mount [ -p | -v ]

mount [ -F FSType ] [ generic_options ] [ -o specific_options ] [ -O ]
special | mount_point

mount [ -F FSType ] [ generic_options ] [ -o specific_options ] [ -O ]
special mount_point

mount -a [ -F FSType ] [ -V ] [ current_options ] [ -o specific_options ]
[ mount_point. . . ]
```

Usage (Linux):

```
mount [-hV]   (print help and version)

mount -a [-fFnrsvw] [-t vfstype]

mount [-fnrsvw] [-o options [,...]] device | dir

mount [-fnrsvw] [-t vfstype] [-o options] device dir
```

The Solaris and Linux versions of mount are similar in function but have some extensive and unique options. Please refer to your specific documentation or man page for more information.

The easiest way to mount a resource is to specify its mount point or device as specified in the `vfstab` or `fstab` files.

For example, assume the following entry in a Solaris `vfstab` file:

```
remotehost:/export/home2   -   /export/myhome   NFS   -   y   -
```

This filesystem could be easily mounted by executing one of the following commands:

```
# mount /export/myhome
```

```
# mount remotehost:/export/home2
```

`mountall` (Solaris)

`mountall` will `mount` all the resources specified in your `vfstab` file. The following shows the syntax for the `mountall` command:

Usage: `mountall [ -F FSType ] [ -l|-r ] [ file_system_table ]`

Options:

> `-F FSType`—In this case, NFS.
>
> `-l`—Mounts all local filesystems.
>
> `-r`—Mounts all remote filesystems.
>
> `file-system-table`—By default, `/etc/vfstab`.

How Automounting Works

It is possible to set up a special NFS daemon and have it monitor the need for a remote NFS filesystem. This process is called *automounting*. When an unmounted remote filesystem is required by an application or user, the automounter automatically mounts it from the NFS server. When the remote filesystem is not being used, the automounter unmounts it. There are many benefits to automounting, including better network utilization and easier administration.

Automounting is available in both Solaris and Linux, and with most other Unix platforms as well. Refer to your operating system documentation or Unix man pages for more information.

Unmounting NFS Resources

The following sections describe the commands used to unmount a shared resource.

umount (Solaris/Linux)

umount unmounts a mounted resource. The following shows the syntax for the umount command:

Usage (Solaris):

```
umount [ -V ] [ -o specific_options ] special | mount_point

umount -a [ -V ] [ -o specific_options ] [mount_point. . . ]
```

Usage (Linux):

```
umount [-hV]   (print help and version)

umount -a [-nrv] [-t vfstype]

umount [-nrv] device | dir [...]
```

Like mount, umount in Linux and Solaris are very similar but have some unique options. Please refer to your specific documentation or man page for information.

Also like mount, umount can be run using only the mount point or device as specified in the vfstab or fstab files.

For example, assume the following entry in a Linux fstab file:

```
remotehost:/export/home2   /export/myhome   nfs
rsize=1024,wsize=1024,hard,intr   0   0
```

This filesystem could be easily unmounted by executing one of the following commands:

```
# umount /export/myhome
```

```
# umount remotehost:/export/home2
```

umountall (Solaris)

umountall will unmount all of your mounted file systems. Useful options allow you to specify only to unmount remote file systems, or even just those that are mounted from the specified host. The following shows the syntax for the umountall command:

Usage:

```
umountall [ -k ] [ -s ] [ -F FSType ] [ -l|-r ]

umountall [ -k ] [ -s ] [ -h host ]
```

33

FILESYSTEM-
SHARING
PROTOCOLS

Options:

-k—Attempts to kill any processes that are using the filesystem.

-s—Does not unmount filesystems in parallel.

-F FSType—Only unmounts filesystems of type FSType (NFS in this case).

-l—Only unmounts local filesystems.

-r—Only unmounts remote filesystems.

-h host—Only unmounts remote filesystems from host.

A Practical Example: Sharing and Mounting an NFS Filesystem

This section puts what you've just learned into practice. You will share a filesystem from a Solaris 2.6 system and mount it on a Linux (RedHat 6.0) system.

First you need to edit the /etc/dfs/dfstab file to add an entry for your filesystem. The entry you will add is

```
share  -F nfs   -d "WWW Directory"  /www
```

This entry will share the filesystem /www.

After adding the line to your dfstab, a quick execution of the shareall command will make the /www filesystem ready for remote mounting.

```
#shareall
```

Running share will verify that it is, in fact, exported.

```
#share

-                  /www   "WWW Directory"
```

Now you need to ensure that the proper daemons are running. On the Solaris server, you need to have nfsd and mountd running. The Unix ps command will allow you to see their status.

```
#ps -ef
```

The ps command shows a listing of all active processes, in which you can find your NFS daemons, as shown in the following output:

```
root 27282    1  0 08:10:59 ?       0:00 /usr/lib/nfs/nfsd -a 16
root 27280    1  1 08:10:59 ?       0:00 /usr/lib/nfs/mountd
```

If they are not running (indicated by their absence from the output of the ps command), they can be started using the NFS init procedure:

```
#/etc/init.d/nfs.server start
```

Now you are ready to move over to your Linux client and mount the shared resource.

On the Linux machine, a properly executed mount command will do the trick.

```
mount -o rsize=1024,wsize=1024 solaris:/www /mnt
```

And to unmount the filesystem:

```
umount /mnt
```

To make the mount more permanent, you can add an entry to the /etc/fstab file.

```
solaris:/www   /mnt   nfs   rsize=1024,wsize=1024,hard,intr   0   0
```

This entry specifies that we want to mount the NFS /www filesystem from the server Solaris on the mount point /mnt. The hard,intr options specify that the mount must be a hard, interruptible mount (more reliable in the event of a server problem).

That's how easy it is. Now, as we all know, in the real world there are problems. NFS is no different. The next section describes some of the common problems you might encounter, and the solutions for these problems.

Common NFS Problems and Solutions

This section introduces you to some of the trials and tribulations of setting up NFS in a Unix environment. Several common problems and solutions are offered. Because of the number of daemons and files that must be running and/or configured properly, NFS can sometimes be challenging to perfect. Most of the problems you experience at first will involve trying to get the resource mounted.

Unable to mount

Mounting problems are most likely caused by either improper configuration or a network problem.

When troubleshooting mount problems, unless you have some suspicion as to where the problem may lie (like you tried to configure the vfstab file without looking at the instructions), starting at the top is sometimes best.

Verify that you can contact the NFS server. The `ping` command is useful to ensure that connectivity exists but only tests connectivity at the IP Layer.

If you have access to the server, verify that the proper daemons are running. See the "NFS Daemons" section earlier in this chapter for more details. Ensure that the resource is shared properly by using the `share` command or its equivalent. If it is not shared, examine the server configuration files (`dfstab` or `exports`). Refer to the "NFS-Related Files" section earlier in this chapter for more details. Make sure that the client is known to the server. The client hostname should reside in the `/etc/hosts` file in the same form as it is in the configuration file. For example, if the server specifies that the system named *loco* is allowed to mount a resource, ensure that *loco* is in the `hosts` file. NFS can be picky—even if *loco.mydomain.com* is in the file, so, too, must be *loco*.

If you don't have access to the server, you may need to call upon your friendly Systems Administrator for help.

Assuming that you can get to the NFS server and all is well there, it's time to examine the client configuration. Again, ensure that the necessary daemons are running and that the files (`fstab` or `vfstab`) are properly configured. Check for name consistency between the `hosts` file and the NFS configuration files.

Unable to unmount

If you ever find yourself unable to unmount a resource, the first thing you will need to do is make sure that you are not using that resource. The most logical use of a resource is sometimes the easiest to overlook. In this case you will receive an ambiguous message that says that the filesystem is busy. Check all open shells and terminals, and make sure there are no open "file manager" programs viewing the filesystem. Also make sure there are no editors using files resident on the filesystem. As you find these, terminate them and try again. Don't forget to check the shell you are working in—the System Administrator's equivalent of losing your glasses on your head.

Hard Mounts Versus Soft Mounts

NFS filesystems can be mounted using either the *hard* or *soft* method. As was stated earlier, the hard mount is the most reliable, and is preferred if you are mounting resources for writing or accessing mission-critical files or programs. However, if a resource is mounted hard and the server crashes or the network connection is otherwise dropped, any programs (or users) accessing that resource will hang. This can be undesirable. By default, NFS resources are mounted hard.

The opposite of a hard mount is a soft mount. With soft mounts, broken communication between the client and server will cause the programs using the NFS resource to abort. However, soft mounts on unreliable networks can result in undesirable results as well.

A solution to this problem is to mount your NFS resources using the hard and intr options. These mount command options will result in a hard mount that will respond to an interrupt and terminate.

Related Protocols and Products

Due to the popularity of NFS and the need for shared resources among different computer platforms, many tools based upon and similar to NFS have been created. This section goes over a few of the highlights.

WebNFS

Sun Microsystems has recently introduced WebNFS, an enhanced version of the NFS protocol. WebNFS provides greater scalability, reliability, and performance over the Internet than its predecessor, NFS. WebNFS also works through firewalls—a challenge for the RPC-based NFS. WebNFS requires NFS version 3 or higher. WebNFS is supported by the major independent Internet vendors including Netscape, Novell, Apple, IBM, and other NFS vendors. WebNFS 1.2 includes a JavaBean component, dependent on Java 2 SDK.

For more information, visit http://www.sun.com/webnfs/.

PC-NFS and Other Client Software

PC-NFS by Sun Microsystems is an NFS client product for non-Unix computers. It allows your non-Unix systems to take advantage of your organization's shared resources. It relies on the daemon pcnfsd, which is shipped with several Sun products.

33

FILESYSTEM-
SHARING
PROTOCOLS

> **Note**
>
> If pcnfsd is not available for your NFS server, you might need to find the source code for pcnfsd on the Internet, and compile and install it. On Linux systems, the pcnfsd is called rpc.pcnfsd.

Many other NFS client products are available. Table 33.2 lists some of these and provides a Web address for more information.

TABLE 33.2 A Sampling of NFS Client Products

Product	Vendor	URL
Solstice NFS Client	Sun Microsystems	`http://www.sun.com/netclient/nfs-client/`
Reflection NFS Connection	WRQ	`http://www.wrq.com/`
NFS Maestro	Hummingbird Communications, Ltd.	`http://www.hcl.com/products/nc/nfs/`
Omni-NFS	Xlink Technology	`http://www.xlink.com/`

SMB and CIFS

SMB, or Service Message Block, is a public standard developed by IBM, Microsoft, and others that allows computers to share filesystems, printers, and other resources. SMB is natively supported by Windows NT, OS/2, and Linux, and is supported by many other systems through the use of third-party software.

For more information on SMB, refer to `http://www.samba.org/cifs/docs/what-is-smb.html`.

The Common Internet File System (CIFS) is being developed by a team of vendors (Microsoft, SCO, and more) as a public version of the SMB protocol. The initial implementation is expected to be very similar to NT LM (the LAN Manager component in Microsoft NT), with improved support for sharing resources over the Internet.

For more information on CIFS, visit `http://msdn.microsoft.com/library` and search for CIFS./.

Some products that implement SMB are

- Samba
- Windows for Windows NT, 95/98/ME/2000/XP
- LAN Manager

Samba Supports SMB and CIFS Protocols

Samba is an "open source" client/server product that supports the SMB and CIFS protocols. It is available under the GNU General Public License.

Samba allows you to easily share server resources, such as filesystems and printers, with clients on your network.

For more information, visit `http://www.samba.org`.

Other Products

Several other products are out there that allow computers to share resources. Other than NFS and SMB, most of these do not readily support disparate computer platforms. Examples of these other protocols are AppleTalk, Decnet, NetWare, and more.

Summary

This chapter has discussed NFS, its history, and its implementation. The NFS-related daemons, files, and other programs were introduced, and you walked through a practical example of sharing and mounting an NFS filesystem. Several related programs and protocols were discussed, such as client NFS programs and the SMB protocol.

Due to the number of daemons, files, and options associated with NFS and its suite of commands, this chapter touched briefly on troubleshooting NFS problems and left you with some references to allow you to learn more about NFS.

33

FILESYSTEM-SHARING PROTOCOLS

Using IP Based Applications

PART
VIII

IN THIS PART

## CHAPTER 34

Integrating TCP/IP with Application Services

by Bernard McCargo

IN THIS CHAPTER

TCP/IP is a layered set of protocols. In order to understand what this means, it is useful to look at an example. A typical situation is sending mail. First, there is a protocol for mail. This defines a set of commands that one machine sends to another—for example, commands to specify who the sender of the message is, who it is being sent to, and the text of the message. However, this protocol assumes that there is a way to communicate reliably between the two computers. Mail, like other application protocols, simply defines a set of commands and messages to be sent. It is designed to be used with TCP and IP.

TCP is responsible for making sure that the commands get through to the other end. It keeps track of what is sent, and retransmits anything that did not get through. If any message is too large for one datagram, such as the text of the mail, IP will split it up into several datagrams.

IP takes care of fragmentation and reassembly of the datagram if the MTU size of an intermediate network is smaller than the datagram size. However, it is the function of TCP to ensure that the datagrams making up the message are assembled correctly at the destination.

Because reliability is needed for many applications, the applications are put together into a separate protocol, rather than being part of the specifications for sending mail. You can think of TCP as forming a library of routines that applications can use when they need reliable network communications with another computer. Similarly, TCP calls on the services of IP. Although the services that TCP supplies are needed by many applications, there are still some kinds of applications that don't need the full reliability of TCP such as those applications that depend on UDP. However, there are some services that every application needs, so these services are put together into IP. As with TCP, you can think of IP as a library of routines that TCP calls on, but which is also available to applications that don't use TCP. This strategy of building several levels of protocol is called *layering*. Think of the application programs such as mail, TCP, and IP as being separate layers, each of which calls on the services of the layer below it. Generally, TCP/IP applications use four layers:

- An application protocol such as mail.
- A protocol such as TCP that provides services needed by many applications.
- IP, which provides the basic service of getting datagrams to their destination.
- The protocols needed to manage a specific physical medium, such as Ethernet or a point-to-point line.

The following sections describe the function of these layers.

Using a Browser As the Presentation Layer

The Presentation Layer performs certain functions that are requested sufficiently often to warrant finding a general solution for these functions, rather than letting each user solve the problems. In particular, unlike all the lower layers, which are just interested in moving bits reliably from here to there, the Presentation Layer is concerned with the syntax and semantics of the information transmitted.

A typical example of a presentation service is encoding data in a standard, agreed-upon way. Most user programs do not exchange random binary bit strings. They exchange things such as names, dates, amounts of money, and invoices. These items are represented as character strings, integers, floating-point numbers, and data structures composed of several simpler items. Different computers have different codes for representing character strings, integers, and so on. In order to make it possible for computers with different representations to communicate, the data structures to be exchanged can be defined in an abstract way, along with a standard encoding to be used "on the wire." The Presentation Layer handles the job of managing these abstract data structures and converting from the representation used inside the computer to the network standard representation.

The Presentation Layer is also concerned with other aspects of information representation. For example, data compression can be used to reduce the number of bits that have to be transmitted and cryptography is frequently required for privacy and authentication.

> **Note**
>
> Although encryption can be considered a Presentation Layer function, it is not exclusively a Presentation Layer function. Many of the standards, such as IPSec, implement encryption as part of the Network Layer (IPv6) or a sublayer between the Network Layer and Transport Layer (IPv4).

34

INTEGRATING TCP/IP WITH APPLICATION

In questioning how the browser is used as the Presentation Layer, some browser-specific issues need to be examined. Frames are an artifact of browser presentation. To the server (HTTP server included) they don't come into play. The server is just getting content for a URL and placing it where the browser says to place it. If you knew what pages you had dumped into the frames the user is viewing, you could write an action handler to create an instance of the page in the other frame and have it do something for you.

Integrating TCP/IP with Legacy Applications

Integrating TCP/IP with legacy applications is becoming the norm. Vendors such as Novell are integrating TCP/IP as a standard protocol as seen in products such as NetWare 5 and NetWare 6. Some companies have protocol converters (also sometimes called gateways) to integrate TCP/IP with other protocols.

Integrated TCP/IP support for applications offers users the following benefits:

- Eases TCP/IP protocol selection by fully integrating protocol selection into the application installation process.
- Simplifies IP address management through DHCP/BootP server software by continually providing a pool of IP addresses that are automatically allocated to users as needed.
- Allows mobile users with a SLIP or PPP connection to use the Internet to access application servers anywhere in the world.
- Improves wide-area network performance by eliminating unnecessary broadcast traffic, freeing bandwidth on wide-area connections and improving throughput.
- Enables users to connect to heterogeneous IP-based network devices such as servers and printers attached to Unix hosts.
- Leverages existing client stacks to provide full access to network resources for a wide variety of desktop clients, including DOS, Windows 3.1, Windows for Workgroups, Windows 9x, and Windows NT/2000 Server and Workstation.

Using TCP/IP with Other Networks

TCP/IP is sometimes only one of a number of protocols used in any given network. The interactions between TCP/IP (and its associated protocols) and the other protocols that may be working are important. The layers of a TCP/IP protocol are designed to be independent of each other, allowing mixing of protocols. When a message is to be sent over the network to a remote machine, each protocol layer builds on the packet of information sent from the layer above, adding its own header and then passing the packet to the next lower layer. After being received over the network (packaged in whatever network format is required), the receiving machine passes the packet back up the layers, removing the header information one layer at a time.

As the packet travels up the layers, protocol information in the lower layers is used to identify which upper layer protocol should process the packet.

Replacing any layer in the protocol stack requires that the new protocols work with all the other layers, as well as perform all the required functions of that layer (for example, duplicating the services of the replaced protocol). The process begins with a message of some form from an *Upper Layer Protocol* (ULP) that itself is passing a message from an application higher up. As the message is passed to TCP, it adds its own header information and passes to the IP Layer, which does the same. When the IP message is passed to the Ethernet Layer, Ethernet adds its own information at the front and back of the message and sends the message out over the network. When working with other operating systems or network architectures, replacing one or more layers in the TCP/IP structure with layers from another system is often necessary.

The following are examples of services that use different layers of the network.

NetBIOS and TCP/IP

NetBIOS resides above the TCP or UDP protocol, although it usually has solid links into that layer (so the two layers cannot be cleanly separated). NetBIOS acts to connect applications together in the upper layers, providing messaging and resource allocation.

Three Internet port numbers are allocated for NetBIOS. These are for the NetBIOS name service (port 137), datagram service (port 138), and session service (port 139). There is also the provision for a mapping between Internet's *Domain Name Service* (DNS) and the *NetBIOS Name Server* (NBNS). The NetBIOS Name Server is used to identify PCs that operate in a NetBIOS area. In the interface between NetBIOS and TCP, a mapping between the names is used to produce the DNS name.

On Windows machines, IP can be configured to run above NetBIOS, eliminating TCP or UDP entirely and running NetBIOS as a connectionless service. In this case, NetBIOS takes over the functions of the TCP/UDP Layer, and the upper-layer protocols must have the data integrity, packet sequencing, and flow control functions. In this architecture, NetBIOS encapsulates IP datagrams. Strong mappings between IP and NetBIOS are necessary so that NetBIOS packets reflect IP addresses. (To do this, NetBIOS codes the names as IP.*nnn*.*nnn*.*nnn*.*nnn*.)

This type of network requires that the upper-layer protocols handle all the necessary features of the TCP protocol, but the advantage is the network architecture is simple and efficient. For some networks, this type of approach is well suited, although the development of suitable ULPs can be problematic at times.

34

INTEGRATING
TCP/IP WITH
APPLICATION

> **Note**
>
> However, the reliance on NetBIOS creates its own sets of problems. NetBIOS is often implemented at the protocol level in terms of the NetBEUI protocol. NetBEUI is a non-routable protocol, which means that it does not scale very well for building large networks. Another problem with NetBIOS is its excessive use of broadcasts. Broadcasts can consume network bandwidth, and many routers by default block broadcasts. In the case of Windows NT domains, the fact that broadcasts do not propagate across routers led to the rule of each subnet having its own master browser—an unnecessary complication. Starting with Windows 2000, Microsoft has eliminated the use of NetBIOS. You can configure SMB (Server Message Block) and MS-RPC (Microsoft Remote Procedure Call) to run purely on an IP network without using NetBIOS over TCP/IP (NBT). In Windows 2000 networks, NetBIOS is only required for supporting down-level clients such as Windows NT and Windows 9x.

IPX and UDP

Novell's NetWare networking product has a protocol similar to IP called the *Internet Packet Exchange* (IPX), which is based on Xerox's XNS. IPX usually uses UDP for a connectionless protocol, although TCP can be used when combined with LLC Type 1.

The stacking of the layers (with IPX above UDP) ensures that the UDP and IP headers are not affected, with the IPX information encapsulated as part of the usual message process. As with other network protocols, a mapping is necessary between the IP address and the IPX addresses. IPX uses a network and host number of four and six bytes, respectively. These are converted as they are passed to UDP.

It is possible to reconfigure the network to use IPX networks by using TCP instead of UDP, and substituting the connectionless LLC Type 1 protocol. When using this layer architecture, IP addresses are mapped using ARP.

Summary

Many applications need a mechanism to open a connection to a specified computer, log into it, and tell it what file you want, and control the transmission of the file. This is done by application protocols. The application protocols run on top of TCP/IP. That is, when they want to send a message, they give the message to TCP. TCP makes sure it gets delivered to the other end reliably. Because TCP and IP take care of all the networking details, the application protocols can treat a network connection as if it were a simple byte stream, like a terminal or phone line.

CHAPTER 35

Internet Mail Protocols

by Neal S. Jamison

IN THIS CHAPTER

Electronic mail is by far the most prevalent use of the Internet today. Whether it's a message to your boss, your insurance agent, your bank teller, or your long-distance relatives and friends, there is no doubt that e-mail has changed the way we communicate.

Electronic Mail

Person-to-person communication is a fact of life. We must communicate with our family members, friends, and peers. Without a doubt, one of the most important technologies to emerge from the information age is electronic mail or, more familiarly, e-mail. E-mail messages are flying around the world as I write this, delivering business and personal communication to the desktops of millions.

This section briefly introduces the concept of e-mail, and looks at its evolution into what it is today. It introduces the standards that make e-mail work and the standard-making groups who bring it all together.

History of E-mail

The Internet was developed to improve communication between the scientists and government technologists who were in charge of its creation. And although e-mail wasn't the first way that they communicated, it can be argued that e-mail is the most widely used application on the Internet. The Internet has blossomed into much more than an e-mail–transport mechanism.

The earliest e-mail systems were little more than programs designed to copy a message into a user's mailbox. At that time, users were all local to one machine. One user on a multiuser computer could send a message to another user on that same computer. That was it. This functionality was carried to LANs through the development of products such as cc:Mail and other similar proprietary e-mail systems. A short time later, a component known as a gateway was introduced to allow users of one e-mail server to send and receive messages to and from other servers. Gateways were built to allow different types of e-mail systems to communicate. cc:Mail users could utilize the gateway to send messages to Microsoft Mail users in other organizations. But these gateways were still sending and receiving proprietary–formatted messages. What the world needed was a standard.

The Standards and the Groups Who Make Them

There are really two standards in electronic mail. X.400, developed by the International Telecommunications Union–Telecommunications Standards Sector (ITU-TSS) and the International Organization for Standardization (ISO), and the Simple Mail Transfer

Protocol (SMTP), developed through the early research and development efforts of the Internet and made standard by the Internet Engineering Task Force (IETF). The following sections discuss both of these standards.

X.400

First specified by the ITU in 1984 and later updated in 1988, X.400 is a complex, robust protocol for electronic messaging. However, due to its complexity and a current lack of vendor support, it has not enjoyed the popularity and widespread adoption that SMTP has. For that reason, this chapter only briefly introduces X.400 and will go into far greater detail on the Internet standard SMTP.

E-mail Terminology 101

The e-mail world uses a few special terms to describe the components of an e-mail system:

User Agent (UA)—The e-mail client program that runs on the user's computer and is used to create and read e-mail messages.

Message Transfer Agent (MTA)—The e-mail server. The MTA stores and forwards messages.

Message Store (MS)—Stores messages until read or otherwise processed by the recipient.

X.400 messages can contain highly structured information and attachments. X.400 messages carry attributes that specify terms of delivery and add value to the message. Example attributes are

- Sensitivity and importance level
- Priority
- Expiration date
- Delivery and receipt notification
- Reply-by date

Like the structure of the message, X.400 addressing is somewhat complex. Table 35.1 shows the common attributes that make up an X.400 address.

35

INTERNET MAIL
PROTOCOLS

TABLE 35.1 Common X.400 Attributes

Attribute	Description
G	Given name
I	Initial
S	Surname
Q	Generation (Jr., Sr.)
CN	Common name
O	Organization
OU	Organizational unit
P	Private management domain
A	Administrative management domain
C	Country

Consider this example:

```
C=US;A=XXX;P=Acme;O=Acme;OU=IT;S=Jamison;G=Neal;
```

In this sample address, my country is the United States (C=US); my administrative domain, or the company that offers the X.400 service I am using, is XXX (A=XXX); my private domain is Acme (P=Acme); my organization or employer is Acme (O=Acme); and the organizational unit is the IT department (OU=IT). My name needs no explanation. Compare this to my SMTP address of `jamisonn@mycompany.com`.

The Role of Directory Services

One of the complications of the X.400 standard is the address scheme. Unlike an SMTP address (`username@domain.com`), X.400 addresses can be quite complex. Enter the directory services: X.500 and the Lightweight Directory Access Protocol (LDAP). These protocols specify a standard format for the structure of global directories. X.400 mail systems can use these directories to look up correspondents.

For more information on X.500 and LDAP, see Chapter 18, "LDAP: Directory Services," refer to RFC 2256, or visit the International Telecommunication Union at `http://www.itu.int/`.

X.400's complex structure gives it several distinct advantages and disadvantages.

The advantages are as follows:

- Great for supporting applications where data must be complex and/or secure (such as e-commerce)
- Strong security
- Reliable non-delivery notification
- International standardization

The disadvantages are as follows:

- Often expensive to implement
- High administration and configuration overhead
- Lack of vendor support
- Many of X.400's great features (such as security) are not yet incorporated into products

For more information on X.400, refer to the International Telecommunication Union at `http://www.itu.int/`.

The Simple Mail Transport Protocol (SMTP)

The Internet standard for e-mail is the Simple Mail Transport Protocol (SMTP). SMTP is the application-level protocol that handles message services over TCP/IP networks. SMTP was defined in 1982 by the Internet Engineering Task Force (IETF) and is currently specified in RFCs 821 and 822.

SMTP uses TCP port 25.

> **Note**
>
> Although SMTP is the most prevalent of the e-mail protocols, it lacks some of the rich features of X.400. A primary weakness of standard SMTP is the lack of support for non-text messages.

35

INTERNET MAIL PROTOCOLS

MIME and SMTP

MIME (Multipurpose Internet Mail Extensions) supplements SMTP and allows the encapsulation of multimedia (non-text) messages inside a standard SMTP message. MIME uses Base64 encoding to convert complex files into ASCII.

MIME is a relatively new standard, and although it is supported by almost all UA applications at this time, there is the chance that your e-mail application does not support MIME. If that is the case, you will likely use one of the other encoding methods (BinHex or uuencode) described later in this chapter.

MIME is described in RFCs 2045–2049.

S/MIME

A new specification for MIME exists that allows it to support encrypted messages. S/MIME is based on RSA's public key encryption technology and helps prevent messages from being intercepted and forged.

RSA Public Key/Private Key Authentication

Short for Rivest, Shamir, and Adelman, the inventors of the algorithm, RSA provides public key/private key encryption. The basic idea is that data encrypted with the public key can only be decrypted with a private key. With S/MIME, the sending UA encrypts a random string of data using the public key of the receiving (remote) user or UA. The recipient UA then decrypts the message using the private key.

For more information on RSA, refer to `http://www.rsa.com/`.

S/MIME is currently specified in RFCs 2311 and 2312.

Other Encoding Standards

Several other standards exist for encoding non-ASCII messages. The more popular of these are BinHex and uuencode.

BinHex stands for Binary Hexadecimal and is considered by some to be a Macintosh version of MIME. Uuencode stands for Unix-to-Unix Encoding because of its Unix origin, although it is now supported by many non-Unix platforms. Although MIME, uuencode, and BinHex do have several fundamental differences, they accomplish the same primary goal—allowing non-text files to be sent in text messages. The method you use will depend upon your mail UA and the UAs used by your target recipients. Fortunately, most modern UAs take care of the encoding and decoding for us.

SMTP Commands

Part of the simplicity of SMTP is that it uses a small number of commands. Table 35.2 lists these commands.

TABLE 35.2 SMTP Commands as Specified in RFC 821

Command	Description
HELO	Hello. Used to identify the sender to the receiver. This command must accompany the hostname of the sending host. In the extended protocol (ESTMP), the command EHLO is used instead. See the "Extended SMTP" section later in the chapter for more information.
MAIL	Initiates a mail transaction. Arguments include the "from" field or the sender of the mail.
RCPT	Identifies the recipient of the message.
DATA	Announces the beginning of the actual mail data (the body of the message). The data can contain any 128-bit ASCII code and is terminated with a single line containing a period (.).
RSET	Aborts (resets) the current transaction.
VRFY	Used to confirm a recipient user.
NOOP	This "no operation" command specifies no action.
QUIT	Closes the connection.
SEND	Lets the receiving host know that the message must be sent to another terminal.
The following commands are specified, but not required, by RFC 821:	
SOML	Send or mail. Tells the receiving host that the message must be sent to other terminals or mailboxes.
SAML	Send and mail. Tells the receiving host that the message must be sent to other terminals and mailboxes.
EXPN	Used to expand a mailing list.
HELP	Requests helpful information from the receiving host.
TURN	Requests that the receiving host take on the role of the sending host.

SMTP command syntax is simple as well, as you can see in the following SMTP example:

```
220 receivingdomain.com ñ
    Server ESMTP Sendmail 8.8.8+Sun/8.8.8; Fri, 30 Jul 1999 09:23:01
HELO host.sendingdomain.com
250 receivingdomain.com Hello host, pleased to meet you.
```

```
MAIL FROM:<username@sendingdomain.com>
250 <username@sendingdomain.com>Ö Sender ok.
RCPT TO:<username@receivingdomain.com>
250 <username@receivingdomain.com>Ö Recipient ok.
DATA
354 Enter mail, end with a ì.î on a line by itself
Here goes the message.
.
250 Message accepted for delivery
QUIT
221 Goodbye host.sendingdomain.com
```

The resulting mail message would look something like:

```
From username@sendingdomain.com Fri Jul 30 09:23:39 1999
Date: Fri, 30 Jul 1999 09:23:15 -0400 (EDT)
From: username@sendingdomain.com
Message-Id: <199907301326.JAA13734@mail.receivingdomain.com>
Content-Length: 23

Here goes the message.
```

SMTP Status Codes

When a sending MTA issues SMTP commands to the receiving MTA, the receiving MTA responds with special status codes to let the sender know what is happening. Table 35.3 lists the SMTP reply codes as specified in RFC 821. These codes are grouped by status, as defined by the first digit in the code (5xx for failure, 4xx for temporary problem, 1xx–3xx for success).

TABLE 35.3 SMTP Reply Codes

Code	Description
211	Help reply, system status
214	Help message
220	Service ready
221	Closing connection
250	Requested action okay
251	User not local, forwarding to <path>
354	Start mail input
421	Service not available
450	Action not taken, mailbox busy
451	Action aborted, local error

TABLE 35.3   Continued

Code	Description
452	Action not taken, insufficient storage
500	Command unrecognized or syntax error
501	Syntax error in parameters or arguments
502	Command not supported
503	Bad sequence of commands (given out of order)
504	Command parameter not supported
550	Action not taken, mailbox unavailable
551	Not a local user
552	Aborted: Exceeded storage allocation
553	Action not taken, mailbox name not allowed
554	Transaction failed

The numeric codes are defined in the RFC. However, the accompanying text, while suggested in the RFC, is left up to the postmasters and MTA administrators to define. Sometimes they get a little creative.

Extended SMTP

SMTP has proven itself to be a strong, useful e-mail protocol. However, there is a recognized need for extensions to standard SMTP. RFC 1869 spells out a means by which extensions can be added to SMTP. It does not list specific extensions, but rather provides a framework for the addition of necessary commands. An example is the SIZE command. This extension allows a receiving host to limit the size of incoming messages. Without ESMTP this would not be possible.

When a system connects to an MTA, it can provide the extended version of the HELO command, EHLO. If the MTA supports extended SMTP (ESMTP), it will respond with a list of commands it will support. If it does not support ESMTP, it provides an error (500 Command not recognized) and the sending host reverts back to SMTP. The following is a sample ESMTP transaction:

```
220 esmtpdomain.com ñ
    Server ESMTP Sendmail 8.8.8+Sun/8.8.8; Thu, 22 Jul 1999 09:43:01
EHLO host.sendingdomain.com
250-mail.esmtpdomain.com Hello host, pleased to meet you
250-EXPN
250-VERB
250-8BITMIME
```

35

```
250-SIZE
250-DSN
250-ONEX
250-ETRN
250-XUSR
250 HELP
QUIT
221 Goodbye host.sendingdomain.com
```

Table 35.4 describes the common ESMTP commands.

TABLE 35.4   Common ESMTP Commands

Command	Description
EHLO	Extended version of HELO
8BITMIME	Indicates 8-bit MIME transport
SIZE	Used to specify the size limit of the message

Examining SMTP Headers

You can learn a wealth of information by closely examining the headers of your SMTP messages. Not only can you see whom the message is from, the subject, the date sent, and the intended recipient, you can see every stopping point made by the message en route to your mailbox. RFC 822 specifies that the header contain, at a minimum, the sender (From), the date, and a recipient (TO, CC, or BCC).

> **Note**
>
> Technically, TO and CC are identical. CC (Carbon Copy) is a historical term that dates back to a time when everything was typed on typewriters and carbon paper was used to produce duplicates.
>
> BCC (Blind Carbon Copy) Received header allows you to see everywhere a message has been prior to arriving at your inbox. It can be a great troubleshooting tool. Consider the following example:
>
> ```
> From someone@mydomain.COM Sat Jul 31 11:33:00 1999
> Received: from host1.mydomain.com by host2.mydomain.com (8.8.8+Sun/8.8.8)
>     with ESMTP id LAA21968 for <jamisonn@host2.mydomain.com>;
>     Sat, 31 Jul 1999 11:33:00 -0400 (EDT)
> Received: by host1.mydomain.com with Internet Mail Service (5.0.1460.8)
>     id <KNJ6NT2Q>; Sat, 31 Jul 1999 11:34:39 -0400
> Message-ID: <C547FF20D6E3D111B4BF0020AFF588113101AF@host1.mydomain.com>
> ```

```
From: "Your Friend" <someone@mydomain.COM>
To: "'jamisonn@host2.mydomain.com'" <jamisonn@host2.mydomain.com>
Subject: Hello There
Date: Sat, 31 Jul 1999 11:34:36 -0400
```

In this example, you can see that a message was sent from someone@mydomain.com. From mydomain.com, the message was delivered to host1. That message was then received by host2 from host1, where it was delivered to me. At each stop along the way, the receiving host is required to add its header, which must include a date/time stamp. It is interesting to note that in the preceding example, there is a discrepancy in timestamps. Host2 (my computer) reports that it received the message at 11:33:00. Host1 reports that it received the message at 11:34:36, over a minute after I received the message. This is due to a lack of clock synchronization between the two hosts.

Advantages and Disadvantages of SMTP

Like X.400, SMTP has several primary advantages and disadvantages.

The advantages are as follows:

- SMTP is very popular.
- It is supported on many platforms by many vendors.
- SMTP has low implementation and administration costs.
- SMTP has a simple addressing scheme.

The disadvantages are as follows:

- SMTP lacks certain types of functions.
- SMTP lacks the security specified in X.400.
- Its simplicity limits its usefulness.

Client Mail Retrieval with POP and IMAP

In the early days of Internet e-mail, users were required to log in to their e-mail server and read their messages there. Mail programs were usually text-based, and lacked the user-friendliness that many users were used to. To solve this problem, some protocols were developed that enable you to have your mail messages delivered directly to your computer desktop. These UA retrieval protocols also come in very handy when a user "roams," or works at several different computers.

Two widely used methods are Post Office Protocol (POP) and Internet Mail Access Protocol (IMAP).

The Post Office Protocol (POP)

POP allows local mail UAs to connect to the MTA and pull mail down to your local computer, where you can read and respond to the messages. POP was first defined in 1984, then updated by POP2 in 1988. The current standard is POP3.

POP3 UAs connect via TCP/IP to the server (typically port 110). The UA enters a username and password (either stored internally for convenience or entered each time by the user for stronger security). After authorized, the UA can issue POP3 commands to retrieve and delete mail.

POP3 is a receive-only protocol. POP3 UAs use SMTP to send mail to the server.

POP3 is defined by RFC 1939.

Table 35.5 lists the POP3 commands.

TABLE 35.5   POP3 Commands

Command	*Description*
USER	Specifies the username
PASS	Specifies the password
STAT	Requests the mailbox status (number of messages, size of messages)
LIST	Lists an index of the messages
RETR	Retrieves the specified messages
DELE	Deletes the specified messages
NOOP	Does nothing
RSET	Undeletes messages (rollback)
QUIT	Commits changes and disconnects

The Internet Mail Access Protocol (IMAP)

POP3 is a very good and simple protocol for retrieving messages to your UA. However, its simplicity results in a lack of several desired features. For instance, POP3 only works in offline mode, meaning that the messages are downloaded to the UA and deleted from the server.

> **Note**
>
> Some implementations of POP3 support a "pseudo-online" mode that allows the messages to be left on the server.

The Internet Mail Access Protocol (IMAP) picks up where POP3 leaves off. IMAP was first conceived in 1986 at Stanford University. IMAP2 was first implemented in 1987. IMAP4, the current specification, was accepted as an Internet standard in 1994. IMAP4 is currently specified in RFC 2060. IMAP4 is found at TCP port 143.

Table 35.6 lists the IMAP4 commands as specified in RFC 2060.

TABLE 35.6 IMAP4 Commands

Command	Description
CAPABILITY	Requests a list of supported functionality
AUTHENTICATE	Specifies an authentication mechanism
LOGIN	Provides username and password
SELECT	Specifies the mailbox
EXAMINE	Specifies mailbox in read-only mode
CREATE	Creates a mailbox
DELETE	Deletes a mailbox
RENAME	Renames a mailbox
SUBSCRIBE	Adds mailbox to active list
UNSUBSCRIBE	Removes mailbox from active list
LIST	Lists mailboxes
LSUB	Lists subscribed mailboxes
STATUS	Requests mailbox status (number of messages, and so on)
APPEND	Adds a message to the mailbox
CHECK	Requests a mailbox checkpoint
CLOSE	Commits deletions and closes mailbox
EXPUNGE	Commits deletions
SEARCH	Searches mailbox for messages meeting specified criteria
FETCH	Fetches parts of a specified message

35

INTERNET MAIL PROTOCOLS

TABLE 35.6   Continued

Command	Description
STORE	Changes data of specified messages
COPY	Copies message to another mailbox
NOOP	Does nothing
LOGOUT	Closes the connection

POP3 Versus IMAP4

There are many fundamental differences between POP3 and IMAP4. Depending on your UA, your MTA, and your needs, you might use one or the other, or even both. The advantages of POP3 are

- It is very simple.
- It is widely supported.

Due to its simplicity, POP3 is often limited. For example, it can only support one mailbox, and the messages must be deleted from the server (although many implementations support a "pseudo-online" mode allowing messages to be left on the server).

IMAP4 has several distinct advantages:

- Stronger authentication
- Support for multiple mailboxes
- Greater support for online, offline, or disconnected modes of operation

IMAP4's online mode support allows UAs to download only a subset of the messages from the server, search for and download only messages matching a certain criteria, and so on. IMAP4 also allows a user or UA to move messages between server folders and delete certain messages. IMAP4 is much better suited for the mobile user who needs to work at several different computers, or the user who needs to access and maintain several different mailboxes.

The major drawback to IMAP4 today is that it is not widely deployed by ISPs, not withstanding the fact that many IMAP4 clients and servers exist today.

Advanced E-mail Topics

As e-mail use becomes more prevalent, so do its related topics. This section introduces several topics that concern e-mail users. These topics include security, junk mail, and other types of e-mail services.

Security

As in every other aspect of computer networking, e-mail security has become an important subject. It is vital that we have mechanisms to ensure the safe and reliable delivery of e-mail.

Encryption

As discussed earlier, S/MIME provides a means of encrypting e-mail data. This encryption protects the data and ensures that it arrives as intended.

Another method of encrypting messages is Pretty Good Privacy (PGP). PGP uses public key/private key pairs to encrypt and decrypt messages. A sender encrypts a message with the recipient's public key. The recipient uses her private key to decrypt the message. For more information or to obtain PGP, see `http://www.pgp.com/`.

Digital signatures (also known as digital IDs) can be used to certify that a message is really from its apparent author. Digital signatures also utilize key pair encryption. For more information on digital signatures, refer to
`http://www.verisign.com/client/index.html`.

Refer to RFCs 1421–1424 for more information on e-mail privacy and encryption.

Content Filters

There are also e-mail content filters that work much like firewalls. They scan incoming and outgoing messages to ensure that they meet the criteria set up by e-mail policy administrators and postmasters. An example use of this type of tool is a high-tech corporation that is concerned about data getting out and into a competitor's hands. This corporation could use the e-mail filter to make sure that certain types of attachments (for example, blueprints or design documents) are not sent out. Other uses are to block out offensive messages (based on keywords) or spam, and to scan for virus-infected or otherwise inappropriate attachments.

Viruses

E-mail viruses have become a very hot subject with the outbreak of many computer and e-mail–specific viruses. Although transmitting a virus through e-mail ASCII text is impossible, embedding a virus in an e-mail attachment is possible. Many of these viruses exploit the macro programming capabilities of e-mail clients such as the e-mail clients from Microsoft (Outlook and Outlook Express).

> **Note**
>
> The Melissa virus demonstrated to many e-mail users the importance of scanning all e-mail attachments for viruses.

For more information on viruses in general, refer to the Internet Society's site at `http://www.isoc.org/internet/issues/viruses/`.

Forgeries

Due to the weak security of SMTP, forging e-mail messages or giving them the appearance that they are coming from someone other than you is easy. Using the `telnet` command to connect to the SMTP port is possible. After connected, the counterfeiter can issue the commands in the same manner that your MTA would. Consider the following SMTP transaction:

```
$ telnet mail.mydomain.com 25
Trying...
Connected to mail.mydomain.com.
Escape character is '^]'.
220 mail.mydomain.com ñ Server ESMTP Sendmail 8.8.8+Sun/8.8.8;
    Fri, 30 Jul 1999 09:23:01
help
214-This is Sendmail version 8.8.8+Sun
214-Topics:
214-    HELO    EHLO    MAIL    RCPT    DATA
214-    RSET    NOOP    QUIT    HELP    VRFY
214-    EXPN    VERB    ETRN    DSN
214-For more info use "HELP <topic>".
help mail
214-MAIL FROM: <sender> [ <parameters> ]
214-    Specifies the sender.  Parameters are ESMTP extensions.
214-    See "HELP DSN" for details.
214 End of HELP info
helo fakedomain.com
250 mail.mydomain.com Hello realhost.mydomain.com, pleased to meet you
mail from:<charlatan@fakedomain.com>
```

```
250 <charlatan@fakedomain.com>... Sender ok
rcpt to:jamisonn
250 jamisonn... Recipient ok
data
354 Enter mail, end with "." on a line by itself
This is not really from charlatan@fakedomain.com.
.
250 MAA07012 Message accepted for delivery
quit
221 mail.mydomain.com closing connection
Connection closed by foreign host.
$
```

Notice that the real hostname was known and disclosed in the 250 response to the HELO
command. The resulting e-mail sent to user jamisonn appears as follows:

```
From charlatan@fakedomain.com Sun Aug  1 12:18:08 1999
Date: Sun, 1 Aug 1999 12:17:43 -0400 (EDT)
From: charlatan@fakedomain.com
Message-Id: <199908011617.MAA07012@realhost.mydomain.com>
Content-Length: 50

This is not really from charlatan@fakedomain.com.
```

Although at first glance it appears as if the message is from charlatan@fakedomain.com,
closer inspection of the header reveals the real hostname in the Message-Id line.

A warning to those who may think this is worth trying: Savvy postmasters and administrators have sophisticated wrapping and logging mechanisms that can reveal the true
sender or even make forgery impossible. Forging e-mail is not a good idea and the
preceding example is provided to show only that it is possible.

Spam and Other Junk

You might have noticed lately that your electronic mailbox is starting to resemble your
non-electronic mailbox in one annoying way: It is starting to fill up with junk mail.

Junk mail, or spam as it is referred to in netspeak, is a real problem. Our mailboxes are
bombarded with sales pitches, get-rich-quick schemes, and other unwanted and unsolicited
annoyances. Our e-mail addresses are being sold or otherwise shared without our consent
in the same manner that our physical addresses are shared. The result is an inbox full
of junk.

An interesting method of blocking those annoying messages is through the use of "bozo
filters" and "kill files." These cute-sounding mechanisms are actually tools included with
some mail UAs that will allow you to block messages that meet certain criteria. The most

common variety works by reading the SMTP header of the incoming message and looking up the sender's address or subject keywords in your bozo file. If the message is not an offender, it is allowed through. However, if the message is from a bozo or contains a bozo subject, it is either deleted or stored in a bozo mailbox in case you want to do anything about it later.

Outside of these mechanisms, you can do some other things to fight spam. However, they are beyond the scope of this chapter. Refer to `http://spam.abuse.net/` or see the Internet Society's spam page at `http://www.isoc.org/internet/issues/spamming/` for more information.

Anonymous E-mail Services or Remailers

Anonymity on the Internet is a topic that raises some ethical questions. There are those who insist that anonymity should be provided, and those who insist that all actions must be traceable. Of course, the subject gets even more heated when it comes to person-to-person communication like e-mail.

Programs and services are available on the Internet that allow you to send e-mail anonymously. The most basic of these services utilize programs that strip the SMTP headers from your message and send it along to your intended recipient. This provides an untraceable message path, but it also provides no way for the recipient to reply, which could be good or bad depending on your objective.

More advanced services actually store a database of their anonymous users. Each user is assigned an ID, which allows him to send messages anonymously (as long as the database is properly safeguarded). The mapping of an anonymous ID back to the user's actual e-mail address allows recipients to respond.

Another form of anonymous e-mail can be accomplished through the use of online service and e-mail providers. There is a recent outcropping of "free" e-mail services (for example: Hotmail, Yahoo!, Usanet, and so on) that allow you to pick your own handle, or e-mail username. There is nothing to say that you have to use your real name or even any portion of it. By using a handle other than your true name, you can send e-mail almost anonymously.

Summary

This chapter explained in detail the Internet e-mail protocol: SMTP. It briefly explained the history of e-mail to demonstrate how far we have come. Some attention was given to X.400, a powerful but underutilized e-mail specification. SMTP was explained through a look at its command set, response codes, and methods of encoding non-text data. We looked at two methods of retrieving mail from the message transfer agent (MTA) or message store (MS): the utilitarian POP3 and the more powerful IMAP4.

Several e-mail–related issues were discussed. E-mail security issues were explored with special attention paid to encryption, content filtering, and viruses. We looked into spam and provided some pointers to help you deal with this nuisance. Finally, a section was included to point you to the Internet e-mail–related RFC documents, as well as the Web sites of groups responsible for the protocols we use today.

The HTTP (World Wide Web) Service

by Neal S. Jamison

CHAPTER

36

The World Wide Web is often referred to as the killer application of the 1990s. No other technology or tool has opened so many doors, putting as much information literally right at our fingertips. The phenomenal growth of the Web is evidence of the importance and potential of Internet technologies.

The World Wide Web

The World Wide Web. The Information Super Highway. The Net. No matter what you prefer to call it, there is no doubt that the Web is the biggest thing to hit since the dawn of the personal computing revolution. From a small physics lab in the early 1990s to an estimated 200 million users today, the Web has come a long way in its short lifetime. In 1995, we surfed blindly around a few thousand Web sites and thought we were really getting somewhere. Today, with the help of intelligent search engines we navigate and quickly find exactly what we are looking for, and in some cases, order it, and even pay for it online. And this is just the beginning.

This section discusses the World Wide Web and its short but turbulent history.

Brief History of the Web

The World Wide Web was initially developed at CERN, the European Laboratory for Particle Physics. It was created to help improve file sharing and communication among physicists. In 1993, the National Center for Supercomputing Applications (NCSA) developed the first graphic Web browser, Mosaic. The development of this Web client launched the World Wide Web as we know it today.

Who's Who—The Creators and Maintainers of the Web

Tim Berners-Lee is the CERN employee credited with the invention of the Web. He wrote the first Web server, and in doing so, defined the languages and protocols of the Web. He also wrote the first basic WWW client.

The first popular Web server (NCSA HTTPd) was created by Rob McCool at the National Center for Supercomputing Applications. That server went on to become the base for the Apache Web server, the most prevalent server on the Web today. The first graphical browser was also created at NCSA by Marc Andreessen, who later founded Netscape Communications Corporation, makers of Netscape Navigator.

Tim Berners-Lee now serves as the Director of the *World Wide Web Consortium* (W3C), an organization largely responsible for the continuing enhancement of the Web and its protocols and standards. For more information about the W3C and its important work, visit its Web site at `http://www.w3c.org/`.

Another important group is the Internet Engineering Task Force (IETF). From its charter, "the Internet Engineering Task Force is a loosely self-organized group of people who make technical and other contributions to the engineering and evolution of the Internet and its technologies" (Source: `http://www.ietf.org/tao.html`). As such, they play a role in the evolution of the Web, and more specifically, HTTP. For more information on the role that the IETF plays, refer to `http://www.ics.uci.edu/pub/ietf/http/`.

Others are responsible as well for the continued development and standardization of the Internet and Web. They include the *Internet Architecture Board* (IAB), the *Internet Society* (ISOC), and the *Internet Research Task Force* (IRTF).

The Web Explosion

In mid-1994, it was estimated that there were approximately 3 million people using the Web, which at the time consisted of about 3,000 Web sites. July 2001 estimates by Nielsen/NetRatings (`http://www.nielsen-netratings.com/`) indicate that the home use Internet population now exceeds 257 million.

> **Note**
>
> In the numbers previously quoted, "people" actually refers to hosts. Counting the number of actual people on the Web is hard; counting host computers is easier, and everyone agrees that there is at least one user per host.

The Web has grown from an immature but promising medium used by a handful of scientists and engineers to a stable, securable environment suitable for e-commerce and other vital functions. And as computer and network technology improves, we can expect to see these populations increase, and the Web used for much more.

Uniform Resource Locators

The key to finding information on the Web is knowing how Web servers and browsers refer to server and file locations. The Web uses a schema known as *Uniform Resource Locators* (URL) to identify Web pages and other resources.

Here is an example URL:

```
http://www.w3c.org/Protocols/index.html
```

This URL, which would take you to the Web site of the World Wide Web Consortium, is broken down into the following segments:

```
Protocol://  servername.domain/  directory/  file
```

In the preceding example:

- The protocol is `http`.
- The full domain name is `www.w3c.org`.
- The directory is `Protocols`.
- The file is `index.html`.

> **Note**
>
> Most Web servers are configured to automatically provide default pages. In most cases, the default page is called `index.html`. However, other defaults include `home.html`, `default.html`, `home.htm`, and `index.htm`. With this option turned on and configured, a URL for `http://www.w3c.org/Protocols/` would return the `index.html` file found in the `Protocols` directory.

Other common URLs are

```
ftp://servername/directory/file
```

```
ftp://username@servername/directory/file
```

```
telnet://servername
```

```
news://newsservername/newsgroup
```

These examples represent URLs that request a document via anonymous FTP, request a document via FTP using "username," request telnet access to a server, and request access to the Usenet newsgroup, respectively.

The HTTP (World Wide Web) Service

CHAPTER 36

859

36

THE HTTP
(WORLD WIDE
WEB) SERVICE

It is also possible to pass data within a URL to be used by the server. A typical use of this would be the passing of parameters to a server-side function; for example

```
http://servername/directory/file.html?username=Jamison&uid=300
```

This URL would send to the page `file.html` two key-value pairs: a username of Jamison and a UID of 300.

Sometimes it is necessary to include special characters such as spaces or slashes (/) in the URL. In this case, these special characters must be "encoded" to prevent problems on the server end. The process of encoding (sometimes referred to as hexadecimal encoding) involves replacing these special characters with their hexadecimal equivalents. For example, suppose we want to pass a user's full name on the URL:

```
http://servername/directory/file.html?name=Neal%20Jamison
```

In this example the space between Neal and Jamison has been replaced with its hexadecimal equivalent 20. This practice of passing information on the URL is commonly used with *Common Gateway Interface* (CGI) programs. For more information on CGI, see the section "The Languages of the Web," later in this chapter.

Web Servers and Browsers

Web servers are the content providers of the Web. In response to a request from a client, a Web server provides data in some form or another. In most cases, this data takes the form of a page of *Hypertext Markup Language* (HTML). Servers can provide other forms of documents, such as images, sound, application files, or even video. Web browsers are the clients of the Web. Browsers include the software necessary to communicate with the Web server, and to translate and display the content returned by the server. Table 36.1 shows some of the leading servers found on the Web today. Table 36.2 shows the leading browsers.

TABLE 36.1   Popular Web Servers

Server	URL for More Information
Apache	`http://www.apache.org`
Microsoft Internet Information Server (IIS)	`http://www.microsoft.com/ntserver/techresources/` `webserv/default.aspNetscape Enterprise Server` `http://home.netscape.com/enterprise/`

TABLE 36.2   Popular Web Browsers

Browsers	*URL for More Information*
Netscape Navigator	`http://home.netscape.com/browsers/`
Microsoft Internet Explorer	`http://www.microsoft.com/windows/ie/`
Opera	`http://opera.nta.no/`

Apache and the Internet Philosophy of Freedom

It's no surprise that the leading Web server on the Internet is "free." The Internet was born of hackers and scientists who embraced free thinking and free software. As of October 2001, over 57 percent of the Web servers surveyed are running Apache. The next closest Web server is Microsoft IIS with 30 percent.

The success of Apache and other free software products, such as the Perl programming language and Linux operating system, has relaunched the free software or "Open Source" movement. Software products that are now available under this movement include Netscape Navigator (`http://www.mozilla.org`) and the AOL Web server (`http://www.aolserver.com`). Other companies to join the initiative include Sun Microsystems and IBM.

For more information on the philosophy of free software, refer to `http://www.gnu.org/philosophy/`.

For more information about Apache, see `http://www.apache.org/`. Linux information can be found at `http://www.linux.com/` and `http://www.linux.org/`.

The protocol used for communication between Web servers and browsers is the *Hypertext Transfer Protocol* (HTTP).

Understanding HTTP

HTTP is the protocol that allows Web servers and browsers to exchange data over the Web. It is a request/response protocol, meaning the server waits for and responds to client requests. HTTP does not maintain a connection with the client. HTTP predominantly uses reliable TCP connections, most often on TCP port 80. These client/server transactions can be divided into four basic steps: 1) the browser connects to the server, 2) the browser requests a document from the server, 3) the server responds to the browser, and 4) the connection is dropped. HTTP is a stateless protocol in that it does not maintain any information about the connections.

The HTTP (World Wide Web) Service

CHAPTER 36

861

36

THE HTTP
(WORLD WIDE
WEB) SERVICE

This section discusses the current recognized standard version of HTTP.

HTTP/1.1

> **Note**
>
> At the time of this writing, HTTP/1.1 is the current standard, and as such will be the version discussed here. It is described in RFC 2616, which can be found at http://www.w3c.org/Protocols and at http://www.rfc-editor.org.

To make communication possible between the server and the client, the HTTP protocol establishes a language of the Web that is made up of request and response messages.

Client Request

A client request contains the following information:

- Request Method
- Request Header
- Request Data

The Request Method is the program to be applied to the specified URL or Web page. The methods available are shown in Table 36.3.

TABLE 36.3   HTTP Request Methods

Method	Description
GET	Requests the specified document.
HEAD	Requests only the document head.
POST	Requests that the server accept the specified document as an executable and pass it some information.
PUT	Replaces the contents of the specified document with data from the client.
DELETE	Requests that the server delete the specified page.
OPTIONS	Allows the client to see the capabilities or requirements of the server.
TRACE	Used for testing—allows the client to see how the message was retrieved.

The header information is optional, and is used to provide the server with additional information about the client. Request headers are shown in Table 36.4.

TABLE 36.4 HTTP Request Headers

Header	Description
Accept	The type of data the client will accept.
Authorization	Includes authentication information like username and password.
User-Agent	The type of client software being used.
Referer	The Web page from which the user is coming. (Yes, it is misspelled.)

If the method used requires data from the client (for example, POST) the client follows the header with data. Otherwise the client waits for a response from the server.

Server Response

Server responses also contain several key items:

- Status code
- Response Header
- Response Data

HTTP defines several groups of status codes to communicate back to the browser. Table 36.5 lists these codes.

TABLE 36.5 HTTP Status Codes

Informational (1xx)	
100	Continue
101	Switching Protocols
Successful (2xx)	
200	OK
201	Created
202	Accepted
203	Non-Authoritative Information

TABLE 36.5 Continued

Successful (2xx)

204	No Content
205	Reset Content
206	Partial Content

Redirection (3xx)

300	Multiple Choices
301	Moved Permanently
302	Moved Temporarily
303	See Other
304	Not Modified
305	Use Proxy

Client Error (4xx)

400	Bad Request
401	Unauthorized
402	Payment Required
403	Forbidden
404	Not Found
405	Method Not Allowed
406	Not Acceptable
407	Proxy Authentication Required
408	Request Timeout
409	Conflict
410	Gone
411	Length Required
412	Precondition Failed
413	Request Entity Too Large
414	Request URI Too Long
415	Unsupported Media Type

TABLE 36.5   Continued

Server Error (5xx)	
500	Internal Server Error
501	Not Implemented
502	Bad Gateway
503	Service Unavailable
504	Gateway Timeout
505	HTTP Version Not Supported

Response headers provide the client with information about the server and/or the requested document. Headers are shown in Table 36.6. All headers are terminated with a blank line.

TABLE 36.6   HTTP Response Headers

Method	Description
Server	Information about the Web server.
Date	The current date/time.
Last Modified	The date/time that the requested document was last modified.
Expires	The date/time that the requested document expires.
Content-type	The MIME type of the data.
Content-length	The size (in bytes) of the data.
WWW-authenticate	Used to tell the client the information that is required for authentication (for example, username, password).

If the client has requested data, that data will follow. Otherwise the server closes the connection.

MIME and the Web

Multipurpose Internet Mail Extensions (MIME) are used on the Web to specify the classification of a chunk of data (for example, a file or Web page). MIME allows you to send data in formats other than plain text. Thanks to MIME, you can send and receive Web pages that contain non-ASCII data such as sound, video, images, applications, and more.

When Web browsers and servers communicate, they discuss MIME types. The browser can send information about the MIME types it can accept in the request header. The server tells the client the MIME type of the data it is about to send.

Table 36.7 lists some of the MIME types commonly seen on the Web.

TABLE 36.7 Common MIME Types on the Web

MIME Type	Description
text/plain	Plain ASCII text
text/html	HTML text
image/gif	GIFF image
image/jpeg	JPEG image
application/msword	Microsoft Word
video/mpeg	MPEG video
audio/wave	Wave audio
application/x-tar	TAR compressed data

Sample HTTP Communication

Now that you've seen the things that a server and browser can say to one another and the types of data they can share, here's an example of the protocol in action.

The Request

In this example, the browser is requesting the document identified by the URL http://www.hostname.com/index.html. All requests end with a single blank line, as shown here:

```
GET /index.html HTTP/1.1
Accept: text/plain
Accept: text/html
User-Agent: Mozilla/4.5 (WinNT)
                (blank line)
```

The browser is using the GET method to request the document /index.html. The browser indicates that it will accept only plain text and HTML data, and that it is using the Mozilla/4.5 (Netscape) engine.

The Response

The server responds with a status code, some header information (followed by a blank line), and if applicable, the requested data. This first example assumes the data was found:

```
HTTP/1.1 200 OK
Date Sunday, 15-Jul-99 12:18:03 GMT
Server: Apache/1.3.6
MIME-version: 1.0
Content-type: text/html
Last-modified: Thursday, 02-Jun-99 20:43:56 GMT
Content-length: 1423
                (blank line)
<HTML>
<HEAD>
<title>Example Server-Browser Communication</title>
</HEAD>
<BODY>
...
```

This next example assumes the document was not found:

```
HTTP/1.1 404 NOT FOUND
Date Sunday, 15-Jul-99 12:18:03 GMT
Server: Apache/1.3.6
```

Advanced Topics

This section briefly discusses some of the advanced topics of the Web. These advanced topics include server-side functionality and mechanisms for securing information.

Server-Side Functionality

Web servers can provide a wide range of data to the browser. Typical content includes HTML pages, video, audio, and images. This data can come from static pages and files, or can be dynamically generated at the time of the request. Dynamic content allows pages to be built that are specific to the actual request for the page. For example, a request to a hypothetical telephone directory would generate a very specific page responding to that request. Several technologies are commonly used to prepare dynamic data. These include

- Common Gateway Interface (CGI)
- Application Programming Interface (API)

The HTTP (World Wide Web) Service

CHAPTER 36

867

36

THE HTTP
(WORLD WIDE
WEB) SERVICE

- Java Servlets
- Server-Side JavaScript
- Server-Side Includes

For more information about these technologies, see "The Languages of the Web," later in this chapter.

SSL and S-HTTP

Secure Socket Layer (SSL) and *Secure HTTP* (S-HTTP) are two protocols used to send sensitive data over the Web.

SSL, developed by Netscape Communications Corporation, uses private key encryption to send sensitive data securely. It is concerned with securing the connection. SSL-based servers are identified by the https protocol in the URL instead of http.

For more information on SSL, refer to `http://home.netscape.com/security/techbriefs/ssl.html`.

S-HTTP is an enhanced version of HTTP. Its concern is sending secure messages. Not all browsers and servers support S-HTTP.

The Languages of the Web

HTTP provides a specific set of rules by which Web servers and browsers communicate. However, it is the programming languages of the Web that make that communication interesting and provide us, the users of the Web, with the information we are looking for. The most common Web language is HTML. But there are others that are used either in conjunction with HTML or alone to provide us with rich content. Some of these languages are discussed in the following sections.

HTML

Hypertext Markup Language is a standard language that is understood by all Web browsers. It consists of a set of tags that specify the look of Web page content. HTML is platform independent, and therefore is highly transportable from one computer environment to another. These characteristics have allowed HTML to become the true language of the Web.

Note

HTML is an application of SGML, or *Standard Generalized Markup Language*. SGML is the international standard for the markup of electronic text. With SGML you can create *Document Type Definitions* (DTDs), such as HTML.

HTML uses tags to specify the appearance of information. Tag syntax is as follows:

```
<tag>information</tag>
```

where `<tag>` begins the type specification and `</tag>` ends it. Tags can be nested as well.

An example HTML Web page follows:

```
<html>
<head>
<title>Sample Page</title>
</head>
<body>
<h1>Hello World</h1>
<b1>Bold text</b1>
<i>Italics</i>
<u>Underlined text</u>
<li>List Item 1</li>
<li>List Item 2</li>
</body>
</html>
```

This example shows the simplicity of HTML. Tags are used around information to specify its style, font type, color, and more. For more information on HTML, refer to `http://www.builder.com/`.

XML

Extensible Markup Language (XML) is a subset of SGML that enables generic SGML to be served over the Web. XML can be thought of as SGML without some of the more complex and less used specifications. A simple XML document looks like this:

```
<?xml version="1.0" standalone="yes"?>
<conversation>
<greeting>Hello, world!</greeting>
<response>Hello to you too!</response>
</conversation>
```

Although XML is relatively new, it is gaining support. Microsoft Internet Explorer 5 supports XML, and a version of Mozilla (Netscape's Open Source browser) does as well.

There is a Mozilla-based browser called DocZilla (http://www.doczilla.com) which reads HTML, XML, and SGML. DocZilla contains extra components providing parsing and displaying SGML/XML documents on-the-fly without a precompilation step.

For more information on XML, see the W3C site at http://www.w3.org/XML/, www.xml.org, or visit Peter Flynn's XML FAQ at http://www.ucc.ie/xml/.

CGI

The Common Gateway Interface is a standard that allows the passing of data from a Web server to a CGI-based program. CGI programs can be written in almost any language, but are typically written in C or Perl. Typical uses for CGI scripts are to retrieve information from a Web page, process that information, then turn around and provide some information back to the user.

For more information on CGI, visit http://www.w3.org/CGI/.

Perl

Perl is an open-source programming language that is very commonly used on the Web. Due to its text processing capabilities, it was originally written as a language for Unix systems administrators to help simplify the mundane tasks they have to do. That text-processing power also comes in handy with CGI programs on the Web.

An example Perl CGI script that outputs information to the user follows:

```
#!/usr/local/bin/perl
#
#   helloworld.pl: CGI output sample program.
#

# Print the CGI response header, required for all HTML output
# Follow with an extra \n, to send a blank line
print "Content-type: text/html\n\n" ;

# Print simple HTML to STDOUT
print <<EOF ;
<html>
<head><title>CGI Results</title></head>
<body>
<h1>Hello, world.</h1>
</body>
</html>
EOF

exit ;
```

For more information, visit The Perl Institute at http://www.perl.org/perl.html.

Java

Java, created by Sun Microsystems, is an object-oriented language similar to C++. Java's design, which strives to be easier to code and more robust than C++, makes it a perfect tool for Web development. For more information on Java, refer to `http://java.sun.com/`.

Java can be used on the Web in two primary ways: on the client or on the server. A client-side Java program (known as an *applet*) is downloaded from the server to the client where it is executed in a special, protected area known as the sandbox. Due to the often-large size of the applet, this can be too time-consuming. For security reasons, applets are also limited in the functions they can perform on the client. For instance, an applet is never allowed write access to the client computer, and it is unable to run local programs as well.

The alternative is to run Java on the server in the form of applications called *servlets*. Although servlets may require more processing power on the part of the Web server, they drastically cut the time required to get the data to the client, and get around some of the security restrictions placed on applets. Servlets are often preferable over CGI programs due to performance. Servlets remain in memory after execution, making subsequent executions faster. CGI programs do not remain in memory.

JavaScript

JavaScript was developed by Netscape Communications Corporation to enable Web programmers to add interactive content to their pages. The common client-side variation can be used to add Web page-hit counters, rollover buttons, and other forms of interactive content. JavaScript can also perform some of the functions usually handled by a CGI program. For example, error checking on a Web form: Instead of sending the data back to the server to verify its completeness or correctness, it is more efficient to do so on the client via JavaScript. The following example shows how that would work:

```
<html>
<head>
<script language="JavaScript">
<!--Hide

function testsomething(form) {
if (form.something.value == "")
   alert("I said something!")
else
   alert("Thank you!");
```

```
}
// -->
</script>
</head>
<body>
<form name="example">
Enter something:<br>
<input type="text" name="something"><br>
<input type="button" name="button" value="Test Input"
   onClick="testsomething(this.form)">
<P>
</body>
</html>
```

There is a variation of JavaScript known as Server-Side JavaScript. This variation runs on the Web server and performs CGI-like functions. Netscape Enterprise Server has powerful built-in Server-Side JavaScript capabilities. For more information on JavaScript (as well as many other technologies) see `http://developer.netscape.com/tech/`.

Active Server Pages

Microsoft Active Server Pages are a somewhat simplified way to incorporate CGI-like functionality into your Web pages. Unlike CGI, which demands some programming prowess, ASP can be implemented using simpler scripting languages such as JScript, VBScript, and Visual Basic.

For more information on ASP and its supporting languages, please refer to `http://msdn.microsoft.com/workshop/server/asp/ASPover.asp`.

The Future of the Web

Although it is only a few years old, the Web has shown tremendous growth. Hidden just beyond that growth, however, is a tremendous potential for more growth and expansion. While the statistical numbers of the Web will continue to rise, so, too, will the capabilities. Initiatives such as HTTP-ng, IPv6, IIOP, and more will ensure that the Web advances. At this time, the possibilities are endless.

HTTP-ng

The next generation of HTTP, aptly named HTTP-ng, will be a more secure, faster replacement for HTTP. It will provide more functionality, making it better suited for commercial application. Some of the enhancements will include

- Improved modularization
- Improved network efficiency

- Improved security and authentication
- Simple structure

For more information on HTTP-ng, refer to `http://www.w3.org/Protocols/HTTP-NG/`.

IIOP

The *Internet Inter-ORB* (Object Request Broker) *Protocol* (IIOP) promises to give us a much more efficient way to access data via the Web. Unlike HTTP, which can only pass text over the Web, IIOP can pass more complex data such as arrays and other objects. IIOP is designed to implement CORBA (Common Object Request Broker Architecture) via the Web. CORBA allows programmers to develop reusable, platform-independent applications.

For more information on IIOP and CORBA, please refer to the Object Management Group at `http://www.omg.org/`.

IPv6

The next generation of the Internet is underway. Internet Protocol version 6 (IPv6), also known as IPng, will upgrade the current Internet Protocol (20-year-old IPv4) in many ways, including

- Increased address space
- Improved security/privacy
- Improved network Quality of Service (QoS)

For more information on IPv6, refer to `http://www.ipv6.org/`.

IPP

The *Internet Printing Protocol* (IPP) was conceived by Novell and Xerox, and developed by the IETF. IPP is interesting because it is based on HTTP/1.1. IPP provides a means for users to accomplish several common printing functions:

- Determine available printers
- Submit and cancel print jobs
- Get status feedback on print jobs

For more information on IPP, refer to the IETF at `http://www.ietf.org/html.charters/ipp-charter.html`.

XML

An exciting development for Web-related software is the Extended Markup Language (XML). XML is used to represent structured data. Structured data includes things like spreadsheets, address books, configuration parameters, financial transactions, and technical drawings. XML enables you to specify a set of rules for designing text formats that let you structure your data. XML is a data representational language and not a programming language. XML is Unicode compliant and makes it easy for a computer to generate data, read data, and ensure that the data structure is unambiguous.

XML is similar to HTML in its use of *tags,* which are keywords bracketed by "<" and ">" and *attributes* of the form `name="value"`. In HTML the tag specifies how the tagged text will display in a browser. In XML the tags are only used to delimit pieces of data, and the interpretation of the data is left to the application that reads it. For example, if you see "<p>" in an XML file, do not assume it is a paragraph. Depending on the context, it may be a price, a parameter, a person, and so on.

XML is too vast a topic to cover in this chapter. You can get more information on XML from `www.xml.org`.

Summary

This chapter has introduced you to the World Wide Web and the technologies that make it possible. We have discussed Uniform Resource Locators (URL) and how they are used to retrieve information from the Web. We have looked into Web servers and browsers, and the communication protocol that allows them to transfer information. HTTP/1.1 was explained in detail. We have explored some of the languages of the Web, such as HTML, Perl, and Java. We have also looked toward the future with HTTP-ng, IIOP, and other revolutionary technologies that promise to change the Web for the better. Web URLs have been cited throughout this chapter, and you, the reader, are encouraged to seek out those Web sites and learn more about the exciting technologies that have helped spark the information revolution.

The NNTP (Network News) Service

by Daniel Baker

This chapter covers a variety of topics that are major factors in how Usenet news operates. Usenet news is one of the oldest forms of Internet communication still available today. Additionally, this chapter covers how you can directly interface with a *Network News Transfer Protocol* (NNTP) server.

Although NNTP wasn't the original protocol for Usenet news traffic, it has made all the prior transportation methods such as Unix-to-Unix Copy Protocol (UUCP) quite obsolete.

Usenet News

Usenet news, created in 1979 by two Duke University graduate students, is one of the oldest and most popular Internet services today. Usenet allows Internet-wide group discussions in a text-based communication format. In this respect, it is very similar to public, group e-mails.

Usenet discussions are not real-time; there is sometimes a delay during the transfer of articles from site to site. However, this delay is typically insignificant, and does not impede the ability of Internet users to carry on a discussion.

In recent years, Usenet has experienced substantial growing pains due to its popularity and the expansion of the Internet. Many years ago, hosting a news server required only an occasional Internet connection, a single computer, and 20 to 100 megabytes of disk space. Today, most Internet service providers (ISPs) have a number of Usenet servers; they typically operate a couple of backbone news boxes that handle communication between your site and other Internet sites, and additionally have several client servers that provide Usenet article data to the end user. To provide high-quality Usenet content, a Usenet client server must now have full-time, multi-megabit Internet connections, at least half a gigabyte of memory, 50 gigabytes of disk space, and several high-end processors.

Technical limitations aren't the only source of problems with Usenet. A lack of centralized management, unsolicited commercial messages, and a typically uneducated user base make it very difficult for Usenet to scale to the size that is required.

> **Note**
>
> UsenetII, a new Usenet, attempts to solve most of Usenet's problems by setting up restrictions and controls that allow it to head in the right direction. The UsenetII Web site is www.usenet2.org.

Although better alternatives have not been proposed, it is widely agreed that Usenet uses an inefficient method of storing and transferring articles. Currently, every Usenet server gets a copy of every article posted within the hierarchies that it carries.

Articles are transferred from server to server via a method known as *peering*. News administrators can negotiate peering between sites and decide which Usenet hierarchies they want to exchange with another site. It is common for a news server to have from 1–200 peers. For every article that a server receives, it connects to each one of its peers (with the exception of the peer that sent the article to it) and offers the article to the peering site via the NNTP command, `ihave`.

> **Note**
>
> Because of this storage method, even a small Usenet article takes an astounding amount of storage space. Assuming, for example, that there are 1,500 Usenet servers on the Internet, a reasonably sized post of 2,500 bytes will take 3.75 megabytes (2500 bytes x 1500 servers) of storage space, Internet-wide. (This figure only calculates for storage on servers and doesn't include storage space used by clients that read the article.) A CD-quality song (about 3.5 megabytes) post to Usenet takes up 5.25 gigabytes. A major motion picture (about 1.2 gigabytes) post takes up 1.95 terabytes.

Newsgroups and Hierarchies

Usenet discussion groups are divided into literally tens of thousands of newsgroups, which are traditionally organized in a hierarchy format by category. However, there are a number of "root" top-level hierarchies. The main hierarchies are referred to as the "big seven."

Table 37.1 shows the "big seven" top-level hierarchies, along with a general description of what is expected within each hierarchy. Table 37.2 shows some of the other major hierarchies that are active on Usenet.

TABLE 37.1   "Big Seven" Top-Level Hierarchies

Name	Description
comp	Computing
misc	Miscellaneous
news	Usenet administration
rec	Recreation
sci	Science
soc	Society
talk	General discussion

TABLE 37.2   Other Popular Hierarchies

Name	*Description*
alt	Uncontrolled hierarchy with "alternative" newsgroups
bionet	Biology
clari	Live news information from Reuters, Associated Press, and so on
k12	Kindergarten through twelfth grade

To minimize confusion, it is both customary and convenient to separate different languages into different hierarchies. Thus, countries often have separate hierarchies, as shown in Table 37.3.

TABLE 37.3   Language and Country Hierarchies

Name	*Description*
ch	Switzerland
fr	France
de	Germany

Most of the top-level hierarchies have restrictive controls to ensure that only authorized administrators create and delete newsgroups. However, the largest hierarchy, alt, does not have any official or effective methods to do so. Regardless, a news server administrator has to decide whether he or she wants to enforce the restrictions for the hierarchy in question. The administrator then must configure his or her server accordingly. However, conflicting choices by news server administrators can often cause inconsistencies within hierarchies. For example, some servers may think a newsgroup exists, whereas others don't because there is an inconsistency in leniency between news server administrators on hierarchy rules. Such inconsistencies are extremely confusing to users and make Usenet administration difficult.

> **Note**
>
> It's a very good idea to have a firm understanding of a hierarchy's policies for newsgroup management before issuing any control messages. *Control messages* are Usenet messages that are intended to be parsed by a Usenet server's newsgroup management scripts. Control messages can request that a server create a new newsgroup (`newgroup`), delete an existing newsgroup (`rmgroup`), cancel a Usenet post (`cancel`), or other management requests.

Given the wide range of topics that the Usenet hierarchies cover, you can easily find a newsgroup to discuss most specialized interests. For example, over 350 newsgroups contain "unix" in the name. Among the most popular are `comp.unix.solaris` and `comp.unix.aix`. Such names provide a clear indication of the group's primary focus. `comp` indicates a computer-related discussion group, whereas `unix` indicates that the groups within that second-level hierarchy will be related to Unix-based operating systems. `solaris` indicates Sun Microsystems's Solaris. Accordingly, it can be stated that `comp.unix.solaris` is for the computer-related, Unix-based discussion of Solaris.

The hierarchy names can also offer a user key indications as to what type of content is allowed within a group. For example, every group within the `alt.binaries` hierarchy is for binary postings such as computer programs, audio files, pictures, and so on. Unless otherwise stated, it can be safely assumed that a group is for ASCII English text.

> **Note**
>
> It is extremely poor form to post binary content to a non-binary newsgroup. For example, posting an audio clip file to `alt.tv.seinfeld` would represent a substantial inconvenience to news administrators and defeat the purpose of a tiered hierarchy organizational system. However, posting that same file to `alt.binaries.sounds.tv` would be considered appropriate and would be the most effective way of transferring the file over Usenet.

Now that you know the basics of what Usenet is and how it is organized, we can begin to take a look at how Usenet transfers article data.

The Network News Transfer Protocol

The *Network News Transfer Protocol* (NNTP) is the most common way for news servers and news clients to transfer Usenet article data. NNTP is an ASCII protocol that typically communicates on TCP port 119. Although directly interfacing with news servers in NNTP (as is demonstrated in this section) is possible, typically a news user agent handles all NNTP services (posting, reading, and so on) for the user. Example NNTP clients for Unix users are `tin` and `trn`, whereas Windows users typically use Netscape, Forte's Free Agent, and Microsoft's Outlook Express.

This section covers a variety of NNTP-related topics, including

- Retrieving newsgroup lists
- Retrieving specific Usenet articles
- Posting messages to Usenet

This should give you a solid understanding of the base structure of NNTP functionality.

Retrieving Newsgroups

In order to retrieve a list of newsgroups from an NNTP server, you must first establish a connection with an NNTP server, enable reader mode, and then request the "active" list.

To establish a connection, type

```
unixbox% telnet news.utb.edu 119
```

You should see the following:

```
200 news.utb.edu DNEWS Version 5.5c6, S0, posting OK
```

At this point, enter

```
MODE reader
```

and the following is displayed:

```
200 DNews is in reader mode - posting ok.
```

After the preceding status line appears, type the command to list the Usenet groups:

```
LIST active
```

At this point, the NNTP server will list all Usenet groups that it carries.

```
215 list of newsgroup follows
alt.test 0000000967 0000000947 y
comp.unix 0000000343 0000000343 y
comp.unix.admin 0000094331 0000094080 y
comp.unix.advocacy 0000068422 0000068413 y
comp.unix.aix 0000162768 0000162368 y
comp.unix.amiga 0000019141 0000019132 y
comp.unix.aux 0000023507 0000023502 y
comp.unix.bsd.bsdi.announce 0000000090 0000000091 m
comp.unix.bsd.bsdi.misc 0000009195 0000009192 y
comp.unix.bsd.freebsd 0000000201 0000000197 y
comp.unix.bsd.freebsd.announce 0000000955 0000000955 m
```

When you're done, type

```
QUIT
```

The NNTP server will end the session as follows:

```
205 closing connection - goodbye!
```

> **Note**
>
> Most news servers carry a very large number of newsgroups. Having 30,000 to 60,000 newsgroups in a server's active file is not unreasonable. When you issue the LIST active command, the server may produce a large file totaling several megabytes. It would be optimal to avoid unnecessarily fetching this file for the sake of bandwidth on both sides of the connection.

The server explains that it is listing the newsgroups in form "group high low flags." High and low is the local article number range that the NNTP server currently has available for reading by NNTP clients. Flags show the control status on the newsgroup; "m" means moderated and "y" means unmoderated.

> **Note**
>
> There are many more NNTP commands than those mentioned in this chapter. You can learn about these additional commands by typing **HELP** when you are connected to an NNTP server. Most client servers will respond with a list of available commands and any arguments required for their use.

Retrieving Messages

Usenet messages can be retrieved from an NNTP server by connecting, selecting a group, and then requesting an article ID. After receiving that article, a user can either continue requesting subsequent articles by ID, or by issuing the next command.

To establish a connection, type

```
unixbox% telnet news.utb.edu 119
```

You should see the following:

```
200 news.utb.edu DNEWS Version 5.5c6, S0, posting OK
```

At this point, enter

```
MODE reader
```

and the following is displayed:

```
200 DNews is in reader mode - posting ok.
```

After the preceding status line appears, type the command to tell the news server which newsgroup you want to access:

GROUP alt.test

The server should respond with some information about the group in question:

```
211 386 603537 603922 alt.test selected
```

The second number in the response is the number of articles in this group that the server currently has. The third and fourth are the beginning and ending range of the article numbers. There is a discrepancy in the total number of articles being held and the range of article numbers because some articles get canceled after the server has received them. They have an article number, but are no longer being held on the server.

At this point, you can pick any number within the given range and request the article, as shown:

ARTICLE 603922

You should see the following:

```
220 603922 <3c0d06c5@newsreader.utb.edu> article retrieved - head and body f
ws
From: "Gary Kercheck" <gary.kercheck@aei.com>
Newsgroups: alt.test
Subject: test
Date: Tue, 4 Dec 2001 09:31:36 -0800
Lines: 3
Organization: Sekidenko
X-Priority: 3
X-MSMail-Priority: Normal
X-Newsreader: Microsoft Outlook Express 5.50.4807.1700
X-MimeOLE: Produced By Microsoft MimeOLE V5.50.4807.1700
NNTP-Posting-Host: 65.162.27.214
X-Original-NNTP-Posting-Host: 65.162.27.214
Message-ID: <3c0d06c5@newsreader.utb.edu>
X-Trace: newsreader.utb.edu 1007486661 65.162.27.214 (4 Dec 2001 11:24:21 -0
Path: newsreader.utb.edu
Xref: news.utb.edu alt.test:603922

.
```

At this point, you can either continue your NNTP session, or exit by typing **QUIT**.

As shown, you must only specify a group and the article number in order to receive article data.

The Path header shows what route that message took to reach your NNTP client server. The route begins on the right and moves left with hostnames or aliases separated by exclamation points. In the preceding example, the article was posted to news.distributed.net and took two hops to reach news.cuckoo.com, the example NNTP client server.

The NNTP-Posting headers identify which client connected to the NNTP client server. The example indicates that the host, at 65.162.27.214, posted the article on 4 Dec 2001 11:24:21.

The next command can also be used to request that the server increment the article number and output the header and body of that message.

Posting Messages

You can post messages to Usenet by connecting to the NNTP server, enabling reader mode, and issuing a POST command. Once that is done, the article can be typed as usual. Only the From, Newsgroups, and Subject headers are required for a post. However, many other headers are standard and are used by news clients.

```
unixbox% telnet news.utb.edu 119
200 news.utb.edu DNEWS Version 5.5c6, S0, posting OK
```

```
MODE reader
```

```
200 DNews is in reader mode - posting ok.
```

Now, you need to let the NNTP server know that you want to enter article post mode:

```
POST
```

The following is displayed to acknowledge your request:

```
340 Ok, recommended ID 3c0d21df@newsreader.utb.edu
```

At this point, you can begin your Usenet post. Before your article data, you will need to enter your headers, which minimally include From, Newsgroups, and Subject.

```
From: Karanjit
Newsgroups: alt.test
Subject: Updated test!

This is a generic test!
- Karanjit

.
240 article posted ok
```

You end the post by entering only a period on a blank line:

```
.
```

If all is well with your article, the NNTP server should confirm that your post was a success:

```
240 article posted ok
```

You can then exit your session:

```
QUIT
```

As shown, only minimal amounts of information are necessary for a Usenet post.

It is noteworthy that the final period in the post is the termination character. It must be on its own line and begin with the period in order for the NNTP server to realize that the period signifies the end of the file.

The next section takes a look at some of the key problems with Usenet today. Because of the inherent design of Usenet, there are no official administrators of the entire infrastructure; specific hierarchy administrators handle administration, and thus problems are tackled with a variety of different approaches.

Spamming and News Blackholing

Massive advertisements ("spamming") posted to Usenet are a serious problem. Rogue corporations are taking advantage of the free medium and posting advertisements to inappropriate groups. These inappropriate advertisements waste massive amounts of the resources of news servers, and are frustrating to end users who have to filter through a huge number of advertisements to reach the desired content.

Some news administrators are attempting to take care of this problem by *blackholing*, or ignoring, sites that allow Usenet spamming, create Usenet spam, or relay Usenet spam. Blackholing is very much what it sounds like; it means that sending traffic is sent to a "black hole" of sorts. Any site that enforces the blackholing policies ignores a site that is blackholed. This puts major pressure on the sites involved to stop the spamming; an ISP's news server is blackholed when it fails to take action against an abusive customer.

Another technique to discourage spam involves canceling inappropriate articles. Programs called *cancelbots* attempt to identify commercial posts and, upon detection, issue a control message that requests that Usenet servers delete the article in question.

As these policies and methods become more widespread and accepted, they'll eventually make it nearly impossible for spammers to post advertisements to Usenet.

> **Note**
>
> MAPS RBL (`http://mail-abuse.org/rbl/`) is one of the largest organizations organizing such blackholing.

Summary

Aside from providing a public discussion forum, over the years, Usenet has transferred an extraordinary amount of knowledge and information that is readily available to the entire Internet user-base. Web sites such as Deja (now acquired by Google, `http://groups.google.com/googlegroups/deja_announcement.html` /) archive all Usenet posts and then allow you to search through literally years of Usenet data. Given the broad topics covered by Usenet, Deja's archive contains an article on almost every topic imaginable. Recent implementations such as this reinforce the belief that Usenet can still prove useful.

Usenet is a conceptually wonderful service that has a great deal of potential. However, there are still a number of significant issues that need to be handled before Usenet can be successful, manageable, and scalable. There is no question that these issues can be tackled and handled in a way that will allow Usenet to prosper and reach its full potential.

The next chapter covers a variety of administration issues involved in running Web site services. Specifically, you will learn the fundamentals of Apache Web server, Netscape enterprise Web server, and Microsoft Internet Information server.

Installing and Configuring the Web Server

by Neal S. Jamison

IN THIS CHAPTER

The World Wide Web has become by far the most popular service available on the Internet. Many individuals are taking to the Web to gather information, search for jobs, shop, and even trade stocks. Businesses are flocking to the Web to meet increasing consumer demand. This chapter instructs you on installing, configuring, and running the most popular Web server on the Internet: the Apache HTTP Server.

A Quick Look at How Web Servers Work

The World Wide Web works largely in part due to a TCP/IP protocol called the *Hypertext Transmission Protocol* (HTTP). HTTP is a request/response service that allows clients (browsers) and Web servers to exchange information. A Web server is a software program that listens for requests from a browser, and provides data in HTML format via HTTP. A typical HTTP session is as follows:

- The browser connects to the server.
- The browser requests a file or some other information.
- The server responds and drops the connection.

For example, a browser sends an HTTP GET request for a file called index.html:

```
GET /index.html HTTP/1.1
Accept: text/plain
Accept: text/html
User-Agent: Mozilla/4.5 (WinNT)
        (blank line)
```

The server answers with an HTTP response that includes the requested file:

```
HTTP/1.1 200 OK
Date Sunday, 15-Jul-99 12:18:03 GMT
Server: Apache/1.3.6
MIME-version: 1.0
Content-type: text/html
Last-modified: Thursday, 02-Jun-99 20:43:56 GMT
Content-length: 1423
     (blank line)
<HTML>
<HEAD>
<title>Example Server-Browser Communication</title>
</HEAD>
<BODY>
    ...
```

After the file is transmitted, the connection is closed. HTTP is a stateless protocol, meaning no information about the browser or the session is maintained (beyond what the server writes to its log file).

By default, HTTP runs on TCP well-known port 80.

Web Server Nomenclature

This section explains a few Web server–related terms that you will see either later in this chapter or in other Web server documentation.

Web Server

A Web server is a computer that serves documents (Web pages) over the Internet using the HTTP protocol. The term *Web server* can be used to refer to the computer (a combination of hardware and Web server software) or to the software package itself (for example, the Apache Web server).

Browser

A browser is the client program of the Web. Common browsers include Lynx, Netscape Communicator, Opera, and Microsoft Internet Explorer.

URL

A URL is the universal address used to reference Web pages. For example, `http://www.apache.org/`. See the "What Exactly Is a URL?" sidebar later in this chapter for more information.

Server Root

A server root is the location on the computer where the Web server resides. By default all log and configuration files, as well as the daemon and other supporting documents, will fall below the root; for example, `/usr/local/apache` or `c:\netscape\suitespot\ https-myserver`.

Document Root

A document root is the top location on the Web server from where Web pages are served. This is the directory that will be explored given a URL of the form `http://www.yourserver.com/`.

Port

TCP/IP services use ports to make connections and pass information. By default HTTP uses port 80, although it can be configured to use any unused port number between 1 and 65535. Other common ports are Telnet (23), SMTP e-mail (25), and FTP (21).

Virtual Host (or Virtual Server)

Most Web servers have the ability to represent more than one domain. This is done using the concept of virtual hosts, in which one Web server can serve multiple sites. Virtual hosts are commonly used by Internet service providers (ISPs) as a low-cost alternative to having a separate Web server for every customer.

Secure Sockets Layer (SSL)

SSL is a protocol developed by Netscape to allow data to be sent over the Web securely. SSL uses public-key technology to encrypt the data passed over the connection.

MIME—Multipurpose Internet Mail Extensions

MIME allows Web servers and browsers to exchange files that are not in HTML or ASCII format, such as Microsoft Word documents and images.

For more information on HTTP and Web servers, refer to Chapter 36, "The HTTP (World Wide Web) Service."

What Exactly Is a URL?

The Web uses an addressing schema known as the *Uniform Resource Locator* (URL) to identify Web pages and other resources.

Consider a sample URL:

```
http://www.apache.org/docs/index.html
```

This URL, which would take you to the Apache Group's documentation page, is broken down into the following segments:

```
Protocol:// servername.domain/ directory/ file
```

Or, in the above example:

- Protocol: `http`
- Full domain name: `www.apache.org`
- Directory: `docs`
- File: `index.html`

The Popular Web Servers

There's a lot of talk in the press about the war to rule the Internet. On the server side, however, it's not Microsoft or Netscape server products in the front. In fact, it's not a commercial product at all. The Web server world is largely dominated by a free, open source server called Apache.

Open Source Software

In the beginning, the Internet was based upon a philosophy of freedom. Ideas were free. Help was free. Even software was free. This freedom inspired growth and advancement. Computer scientists and engineers fed off of a synergy created by great minds coming together to solve a common problem. As the Net grew, so did the opportunity to use it as a business tool. But business tools are supposed to help a business gain a competitive advantage, and that is something that not many are willing to share. Therefore, our corporate culture quickly conquered the philosophy of freedom. But a few projects live on, enjoying the synergy. One of the main ideas behind open source is that thousands of programmers on the Net can foster the growth and improvement process of a software program better than one small group of corporate programmers.

Some of the popular open source software projects today include the following:

- **Apache Web server:** The most popular Web server on the Internet
- **Linux:** An increasingly popular operating system
- **Perl:** The programming language of the Web (also enjoyed by many Unix systems administrators, and by savvy Windows system administrators as a powerful scripting language).

For more information on open source, refer to `http://www.opensource.org/`.

38

INSTALLING AND
CONFIGURING THE
WEB SERVER

An Internet consulting firm, Netcraft Ltd. (`http://www.netcraft.com/`), regularly surveys the Web to see the types of Web server software that Web sites are running. Table 38.1 shows the results of the most recent Netcraft survey for active Web sites.

Note that iPlanet is the sum of sites running iPlanet-Enterprise, Netscape-Enterprise, Netscape-FastTrack, Netscape-Commerce, Netscape-Communications, Netsite-Commerce & Netsite-Communications. And Microsoft is the sum of sites running Microsoft-Internet-Information-Server, Microsoft-IIS, Microsoft-IIS-W, Microsoft-PWS-95, & Microsoft-PWS.

Table 38.1 Web Server Market Share for August 2001 (30,775,624 Sites Surveyed)

Server	*Market Share*
Apache	60.33%
Microsoft	28.29%
iPlanet	4.29%
Zeus	1.53%

Running the Apache HTTP Web Server

The Apache Web server is an open source server based upon the once-popular NCSA httpd server. Apache is now one of the most popular, robust, and feature-rich servers available, and it's free! No wonder Apache powers more than half of the Web servers on the Internet.

Downloading, Installing, and Configuring Apache

This section walks through the download, installation, and configuration of the Apache HTTP Web server in a Linux environment.

> **Note**
>
> Because Apache was originally designed for Unix and is still predominantly a Unix-based Web server, this section deals mostly with installing and configuring Apache in a Unix environment (specifically Linux). At the time of this writing, Apache 1.3.22 is available for Win32, but is not as stable as the Unix port. There is a very brief discussion on installing Apache for Windows at the end of this section. However, if you are serious about running a Web server in a Windows environment, you should consider a more robust server, such as Microsoft's Internet Information Server, O'Reilly's WebSite, or Netscape's Enterprise Server.

If you are running the Linux operating system, there is a very good chance that your installation included the Apache Web server. If it did, great. You are on your way. However, it would be to your benefit to uninstall Apache and start over for two reasons:

1) The version that came with your installation may be outdated or improperly configured; and 2) Downloading, compiling, and installing Apache will give you great insight into how it works. So, with that in mind, let's get started. First, let's examine a few requirements:

- **Disk Space**—You will need at least 12MB of temporary disk space. After installation, Apache will require approximately 3MB of space, plus whatever space is required to store your Web pages.

- **ANSI C Compiler**—You will need to have an ANSI C compiler installed and properly configured. The GNU C compiler is recommended. See `http://www.gnu.org/` to obtain GCC. If you do not have an ANSI C compiler, see the following section.

Downloading Apache

Apache can be downloaded from the main Apache site (`http://www.apache.org/`) or any of its mirror sites.

> **Note**
>
> It will be faster to download from a mirror site that is geographically close to you. See `http://www.apache.org/mirrors/` for a list of mirror sites.

You will need to decide whether you want to download the full source code to compile yourself, or if you want to skip the compilation step and download just the binaries.

> **Note**
>
> If you are going to download a precompiled binary, make sure you do that from the official Apache site or one of its mirrors. Other binaries may be out there that are improperly compiled, and may even contain security holes.

The following example illustrates how to download the source.

Go to `http://www.apache.org/dist/httpd/`. You will see a list of available files. Select the version you want to download, and click it to begin the download. The following is a sample list of files for an Apache release.

```
Announcement.html        21-May-2001 19:11  7.2K  Apache 1.3 Release note
Announcement.txt         20-May-2001 05:07  6.4K  Apache 1.3 Release note
Announcement2.html       04-Apr-2001 13:05  4.2K  Apache 2.0 Release note
Announcement2.txt        04-Apr-2001 13:05  4.2K  Apache 2.0 Release note
```

```
Apache-1.3-docs.pdf.gz        03-Apr-2000 13:03  1.4M  Apache 1.3.12 document>
CHANGES_1.3                   20-May-2001 05:08  367K  List of changes in 1.3
CHANGES_2.0                   04-Apr-2001 13:05  415K  List of changes in 2.0
KEYS                          28-Mar-2001 11:57   43K  Developer PGP keys
apache_1.3.19.tar.Z           28-Feb-2001 06:11  2.9M  1.3.19 compressed sour>
apache_1.3.19.tar.Z.asc       28-Feb-2001 06:11  248   PGP signature
apache_1.3.19.tar.Z.md5       28-Feb-2001 06:11   61   MD5 hash
apache_1.3.19.tar.gz          28-Feb-2001 06:11  1.8M  1.3.19 gzipped source
apache_1.3.19.tar.gz.asc      28-Feb-2001 06:11  248   PGP signature
apache_1.3.19.tar.gz.md5      28-Feb-2001 06:11   62   MD5 hash
apache_1.3.19.zip             28-Feb-2001 10:34  2.4M  1.3.19 pkzipped source
apache_1.3.19.zip.asc         28-Feb-2001 10:32  477   PGP signature
apache_1.3.20.tar.Z           15-May-2001 10:12  3.0M  Current Release 1.3.20
apache_1.3.20.tar.Z.asc       15-May-2001 10:19  477   PGP signature
apache_1.3.20.tar.Z.md5       21-Sep-2001 04:47   61   MD5 hash
apache_1.3.20.tar.gz          15-May-2001 10:12  1.9M  Current Release 1.3.20
apache_1.3.20.tar.gz.asc      15-May-2001 10:19  477   PGP signature
apache_1.3.20.tar.gz.md5      21-Sep-2001 04:46   62   MD5 hash
apache_1.3.20.zip             15-May-2001 12:42  2.5M  Current Release 1.3.20
```

Note

You can use the MD5 checksum to ensure that you are getting the actual package as intended by the author. This is especially important if you are downloading a precompiled binary. Doing this will depend upon your operating environment. In Linux, you can run the following command:

```
# md5sum apache_1.3.6.gz
b4114ed78f296bfe424c4ba05dccc643  apache_1.3.6.tar.gz
```

Compare the output with the contents of the md5 file on the Apache site (in this case apache_1.3.6.gz.md5). If they are the same, everything is fine. If they differ, you should attempt the download again.

After you have the Apache package downloaded into a temporary directory, you will need to expand the archive using gzip or uncompress (whichever corresponds to the format you downloaded), and tar.

Note

gzip (GNU zip) is a free compression tool provided under GNU's General Public License. Due to its superior compression abilities, it is very popular in the Unix and Internet communities.

To obtain gzip or to learn more about this popular utility, refer to http://www.gzip.org/.

Compiling and Installing Apache

The easiest way to compile and install Apache is by using the Apache Autoconf-style Interface (APACI) available with Apache versions 1.3 and higher. The APACI provides an "out-of-the-box" type installation process.

> **Note**
>
> You can still compile and install Apache using the older method. Instructions for doing so are in the INSTALL file in the src directory.

To install Apache using the APACI, change directory to the new temporary directory that contains the Apache files. In most cases you will not need to edit the Configuration file unless you want to install any special modules beyond those that are installed by default. However, if you receive installation errors, read through the documentation in the Configuration file. Common options that may need attention are EXTRA_CFLAGS, LIBS, LDFLAGS, INCLUDES, and CC. Review the INSTALL file in this directory for more information.

To begin the installation process, run the following command:

```
# ./configure –prefix=PREFIX
```

where PREFIX is the target root directory for your Web server (for example, /usr/local/apache).

Then build the Apache package using make:

```
# make
```

> **Note**
>
> If make is not in your path (that is, you get a command not found response), you will need to add make to your path (probably /usr/bin/ or /usr/ccs/bin). The procedure for doing this will vary based on the shell you are running. For bash, run
>
> ```
> # PATH=$PATH:/usr/ccs/bin/
> # export PATH
> ```

make will take several minutes, depending on the speed of your system. After it is complete, you are ready to install Apache. Run the make command:

```
# make install
```

38

INSTALLING AND
CONFIGURING THE
WEB SERVER

This will install the Apache Web server and its related files under the `PREFIX` directory specified in the first step. When this step is complete, you are ready to configure Apache for your specific environment.

Configuring Apache

Apache uses three primary configuration files. They are

- `access.conf`—Controls access to your Web server's resources.
- `httpd.conf`—The primary configuration file. This tells Apache how to run.
- `srm.conf`—Specifies which resources you want to offer on your site.

To get your server up and running initially, these files need very little editing if any at all. Some of the configuration items, or server directives, that may need editing are detailed in the following sections. The configuration files are very well documented, and you should be able to identify the directives that need to be changed by reading through the files. Refer to `http://www.apache.org/docs/` for more information on configuring Apache. For information on performance tuning for the Apache server, refer to `http://httpd.apache.org/docs/misc/perf-tuning.html`.

> **Note**
>
> In the most recent version of Apache, all three configuration files are collapsed into one file: `httpd.conf`. The contents of `httpd.conf` are discussed in the next section.

httpd.conf

The `httpd.conf` file contains the directives that tell Apache how to run. Some of the directives that may need your attention are

- **ServerName**—The name of your Web server.

  `ServerName www.mydomain.com`

- **ServerType**—Options are standalone or inetd. A standalone server will run all the time. A ServerType of inetd will cause the server to run only when it is requested. Standalone is recommended for best performance.

  `ServerType standalone`

- **Port**—By default, HTTP servers run on port 80. However, you may prefer to run your server on a non-standard port. One reason to do so would be to "hide" your server from the public. If you were to run your server on a non-standard port, say

1234, your users would need to know the port and include it in the URL to access your pages. Valid port numbers are unused port numbers in the range 1–65535, although typically the first 1024 are reserved.

```
Port 80
```

- **User**—This specifies which user the Apache server will run as. There are security implications to this directive because Apache will take on the privileges of its controlling user. Many Unix systems have a user called "nobody" just for this purpose. If your system does not have an unprivileged user, you should create one.

```
User nobody
```

- **ServerAdmin**—This should be set to the administrative user. Apache will send mail to this user in the event of any problems.

```
ServerAdmin root
```

- **ServerRoot**—The root directory of the Apache installation. All of your configuration files and log files will be stored under this root unless you instruct Apache otherwise.

```
ServerRoot /usr/local/apache
```

- **ErrorLog**—The location and name of the error logfile.

```
ErrorLog logs/error.log
```

- **TransferLog**—The location and name of the transfer (or access) logfile.

```
TransferLog logs/access.log
```

- **Timeout**—The length of time (in seconds) that the Web server will wait for a browser to respond before assuming the connection is dead. The default value is 300 seconds.

```
Timeout 300
```

The following directives are used to control Apache's resources. Historically they were contained in the `srm.conf` file, although newer releases of Apache combine them all in the `httpd.conf` file. Some of the more interesting directives are

- **DocumentRoot**—The root directory of your Web server's document tree.

```
DocumentRoot  /usr/local/apache/htdocs/
```

- **DirectoryIndex**—If a user requests a URL from your server that ends in a path, the Web server will attempt to serve a document that matches DirectoryIndex. For example, loading `http://www.apache.org/` results in the file `index.html` being served to your browser.

```
DirectoryIndex index.html
```

- **IndexIgnore**—By default, if a user requests a URL from your server that ends in a path and there is no `index.html` file available, the Web server will present the user with a listing of files in the directory. There may be files there that you don't want displayed (such as `.htaccess`, or `README` files). The server will not display files set in the IndexIgnore directive.

```
IndexIgnore .??* *~ *# HEADER* README* RCS CVS *,v *,t
```

The `access.conf` file is historically where you would set up access rules to your entire Web server, or parts thereof. Recent releases of Apache also include these directives in the `httpd.conf` file.

Consider the following block:

```
<Directory /><Directory />
    Options FollowSymLinks
    AllowOverride None
    </Directory></Directory>
```

This block is similar to what you may find in a typical `access.conf` file. The `<Directory />` tag opens the container. Every directive in the file before a `</Directory>` tag will apply to the directory `/`. In this example, Apache is instructed to follow symbolic links for this directory and to prohibit other control files from overriding settings.

Consult the Apache documentation that came with your Web server for more information on using `access.conf` to control access to your site.

Starting and Stopping Apache

Once Apache is compiled, installed, and configured, you are ready to go. You can start Apache by running the following command:

```
# PREFIX/bin/apachectl start
```

where `PREFIX` is the ServerRoot.

A quick check of the processes should verify that it was started.

```
# ps -ax | grep http
 3514  ?  S     0:00 /usr/local/apache/bin/httpd
16201  ?  S     0:00 /usr/local/apache/bin/httpd
16635  ?  S     0:00 /usr/local/apache/bin/httpd
16661  ?  S     0:00 /usr/local/apache/bin/httpd
16662  ?  S     0:00 /usr/local/apache/bin/httpd
    ...
```

Using your Web browser, point to your newly installed Web server by loading the ServerName URL (`http://www.yourdomain.com/` or `http://localhost/`). If Apache is properly configured and running, you will see the test page in Figure 38.1.

38

INSTALLING AND
CONFIGURING THE
WEB SERVER

FIGURE 38.1

The Apache test page.

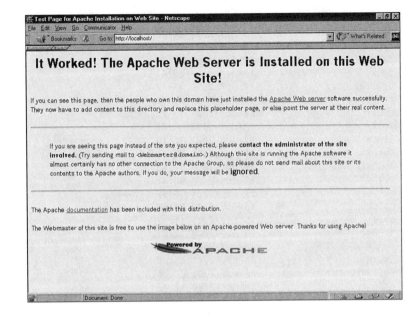

You can stop Apache by running the following command:

```
# PREFIX/bin/apachectl stop
```

/etc/rc.d

You can use the rc.d system to automatically start Apache for you. Some versions of Unix or Linux will have an httpd.init file (for example, /etc/rc.d/init.d/httpd.init in Red Hat Linux) already installed. If this is true in your case, you will need to edit the file to ensure it knows where your httpd executable file resides.

For most systems, a simple entry such as

```
/usr/local/apache/bin/apachectl start
```

in your /etc/rc.d/rc.local file will suffice.

Downloading Precompiled Apache

If you prefer to download a precompiled binary, go to http://www.apache.org/dist/ httpd/binaries/. You will see a list of available operating environments. The following is a sample directory structure of Apache binaries available for different operating environments.

```
aix/            20-Jun-2001 11:47    -
aux/            06-May-2000 12:56    -
beos/           02-Nov-2000 02:17    -
```

```
bs2000-osd/             23-Jan-2001 01:26    -
bsdi/                   18-Oct-2000 00:22    -
cygwin/                 12-Jun-2001 01:22    -
darwin/                 10-Apr-2001 21:11    -
dgux/                   12-Jun-2000 03:47    -
digitalunix/            12-Jun-2000 03:47    -
freebsd/                31-May-2001 01:47    -
hpux/                   20-Jun-2001 13:25    -
irix/                   13-Oct-2000 04:57    -
linux/                  21-Aug-2001 08:18    -
macosx/                 10-Apr-2001 21:11    -
macosxserver/           30-Oct-2000 17:42    -
netbsd/                 12-Jun-2000 03:47    -
netware/                21-May-2001 16:52    -
openbsd/                13-Oct-2000 04:59    -
os2/                    19-May-2001 11:37    -
os390/                  03-Aug-2000 12:01    -
osf1/                   12-Jun-2000 03:47    -
qnx/                    31-May-2001 01:22    -
reliantunix/            22-May-2001 01:26    -
rhapsody/               30-Oct-2000 17:42    -
sinix/                  22-May-2001 01:26    -
solaris/                20-Jun-2001 13:28    -
sunos/                  24-Feb-2000 18:27    -
unixware/               13-Oct-2000 04:58    -
    win32/                  03-Sep-2001 08:25    -
```

Enter the directory that corresponds to your operating environment. You will then see a list of available formats and versions similar to the following:

```
apache_1.3.1-sparc-whatever-linux.README        06-Apr-2000 14:05   522
apache_1.3.1-sparc-whatever-linux.tar.gz        06-Apr-2000 14:05   1.3M
➥GZIP compressed file
apache_1.3.12-i686-whatever-linux2.README       06-Apr-2000 14:05   1.8K
apache_1.3.12-i686-whatever-linux2.tar.gz       06-Apr-2000 14:05   2.6M
➥GZIP compressed file
apache_1.3.14-i686-whatever-linux2.README       13-Oct-2000 04:57   1.8K
apache_1.3.14-i686-whatever-linux2.tar.gz       13-Oct-2000 03:21   2.8M
➥GZIP compressed file
apache_1.3.14-i686-whatever-linux2.tar.gz.asc   13-Oct-2000 03:10   292
➥PGP signature
apache_1.3.20-i686-whatever-linux22.README      20-Jun-2001 11:36   1.9K
➥Current Release 1.3.20
apache_1.3.20-i686-whatever-linux22.tar.gz      20-Jun-2001 11:36   3.1M
➥Current Release 1.3.20
apache_1.3.20-i686-whatever-linux22.tar.gz.asc 20-Jun-2001 11:36    477
➥PGP signature
apache_1.3.20-ia64-whatever-linux22.README      21-Aug-2001 08:15   2.1K
➥Current Release 1.3.20
apache_1.3.20-ia64-whatever-linux22.README.asc 21-Aug-2001 08:18    293
```

```
➥PGP signature
apache_1.3.20-ia64-whatever-linux22.tar.gz      21-Aug-2001 08:16   3.4M
➥Current Release 1.3.20
apache_1.3.20-ia64-whatever-linux22.tar.gz.asc 21-Aug-2001 08:17   293
➥PGP signature
apache_1.3.20-ia64-whatever-linux22.tar.gz.md5 21-Aug-2001 08:16    84
➥MD5 hash
apache_1.3.6-armv4l-whatever-linux2.README      06-Apr-2000 14:05   1.9K
apache_1.3.6-armv4l-whatever-linux2.tar.gz      06-Apr-2000 14:05   2.2M
➥GZIP compressed file
apache_1.3.6-i586-whatever-linux2.README        06-Apr-2000 14:05   1.9K
apache_1.3.6-i586-whatever-linux2.tar.gz        06-Apr-2000 14:05   2.1M
➥GZIP compressed file
apache_1.3.6-i686-whatever-linux2.README        06-Apr-2000 14:05   1.9K
apache_1.3.6-i686-whatever-linux2.tar.gz        06-Apr-2000 14:05   2.1M
➥GZIP compressed file
apache_1.3.6-mips-whatever-linux2.README        06-Apr-2000 14:05   1.9K
apache_1.3.6-mips-whatever-linux2.tar.gz        06-Apr-2000 14:05   2.2M
➥GZIP compressed file
apache_1.3.6-sparc-whatever-linux2.README       06-Apr-2000 14:05   1.9K
apache_1.3.6-sparc-whatever-linux2.tar.gz       06-Apr-2000 14:05   2.1M
➥GZIP compressed file
apache_1.3.9-alpha-whatever-linux2.README       06-Apr-2000 14:05   1.8K
apache_1.3.9-alpha-whatever-linux2.tar.gz       06-Apr-2000 14:05   3.5M
➥GZIP compressed file
apache_1.3.9-alpha-whatever-linux2.tar_gz.asc   06-Apr-2000 14:05   286
➥PGP signature
apache_1.3.9-i586-whatever-linux2.README        06-Apr-2000 14:05   1.8K
apache_1.3.9-i586-whatever-linux2.tar.gz        06-Apr-2000 14:05   2.3M
➥GZIP compressed file
apache_1.3.9-i586-whatever-linux2.tar_gz.asc    06-Apr-2000 14:05   286
➥PGP signature
apache_1.3.9-i686-whatever-linux2.README        06-Apr-2000 14:05   1.8K
apache_1.3.9-i686-whatever-linux2.tar.gz        06-Apr-2000 14:05   2.3M
➥GZIP compressed file
apache_1.3.9-i686-whatever-linux2.tar_gz.asc    06-Apr-2000 14:05   286
➥PGP signature
apache_1.3.9-mips-whatever-linux2.README        06-Apr-2000 14:05   1.8K
apache_1.3.9-mips-whatever-linux2.tar.gz        06-Apr-2000 14:05   2.5M
➥GZIP compressed file
apache_1.3.9-sparc-whatever-linux2.README       06-Apr-2000 14:05   1.8K
apache_1.3.9-sparc-whatever-linux2.tar.gz       06-Apr-2000 14:05   2.7M
➥GZIP compressed file
apache_1.3.9-sparc-whatever-linux2.tar_gz.asc   06-Apr-2000 14:05   286
    ➥PGP signature
```

Select the version you want and download it into a temporary directory on your system.

38

INSTALLING AND
CONFIGURING THE
WEB SERVER

Installing and Configuring Precompiled Apache

After you have downloaded the package, you are ready to install and configure Apache. First, in the temporary directory, unpack (using `uncompress` or `gzip`, and `tar`) the package you have just downloaded.

To install Apache, run the shell script `install-bindist.sh`. If you prefer that Apache be installed into a directory other than the default directory (`/usr/local/apache/`), you must specify the target directory (ServerRoot) on the command line. See the INSTALL file for more information.

```
# ./install-bindist.sh [ServerRoot]
```

After the Apache Web server is installed, you can configure, start, and stop Apache using the steps outlined in the previous sections.

Using Apache for Windows

This section instructs you on downloading, installing, and configuring Apache for a Microsoft Windows platform.

> **Note**
>
> Apache for Windows is still not as stable as the Unix version. It is not optimized for performance, and may contain bugs that could leave your system vulnerable to a security attack. If you prefer to run your Web server in a Microsoft environment, it is recommended that you use Microsoft IIS or one of the other Windows-compatible servers.
>
> See "Exploring Other Web Servers" at the end of this chapter or refer to `http://webcompare.internet.com/` for a complete list of Web servers.

Downloading Apache for Windows

You can download a precompiled version of Apache for Win32 from `http://www.apache.org/dist/httpd/binaries/win32/`.

Download the file to a temporary directory or to your Windows Desktop.

Installing Apache for Windows

To begin installation, run the self-extracting executable you have just downloaded. You will be prompted for a directory into which Apache is to be installed. Either accept the default or change to your preferred directory. If the directory does not yet exist, the installer will make it for you.

Next you will be asked for the name under which Apache should be found in the Start menu. Again, either accept the default or change it to your preferred name.

Choose your preferred installation type. "Typical" installs everything except the source code. "Minimum" does not install the manuals or the source code. "Custom" will allow you to specify what is installed (the manuals, source code, and so on).

Configuring Apache for Windows

After you install Apache for Windows, you will probably want to edit the configuration files. As with the Unix version, the three configuration files are

- `access.conf`
- `httpd.conf`
- `srm.conf`

These files are self-documenting, and a read through them will enable you to see what needs to be configured. No edits are required to run the Apache Web server. Refer to the "Configuring Apache" section earlier in the chapter for more information.

Starting Apache for Windows

Apache for Windows can be started in several ways:

- From the Windows Start menu
- From a DOS console (Command Prompt)
- As an NT Service

Running Apache from the Start Menu and/or DOS Console

To start Apache from the Start menu, select the Start Apache option. This will run a DOS console window in which Apache will be started, and the window will remain active as long as Apache is running. To stop or restart Apache, open another console window and run

```
apache -k shutdown
```

or

```
apache -k restart
```

Similarly, Apache can be started from a DOS console by running the command

```
apache -k start
```

The console will remain active as long as Apache is running.

Running Apache as an NT Service

Before Apache can be run as an NT service, it must be installed as a service. From a DOS console, run

```
apache -i -n "Apache Webserver"
```

To remove Apache as a service, run

```
apache -u -n "Apache Webserver"
```

After Apache is installed as an NT service, you can configure, start, and stop the Apache service using the Services utility in the Windows Control Panel.

Exploring Other Web Servers

Although Apache holds a large market share in the Internet Web server arena, many other Web server products are out there for you to choose from. This section briefly describes a few of the most popular Web servers.

- **Netscape Enterprise Server**—Netscape's most robust Web server (see also FastTrack). Environment: HP-UX, Solaris, NT. (`http://www.iplanet.com/products`)

- **Netscape FastTrack**—Netscape's entry-level Web server (see also Enterprise). Environment: Unix, Windows 95/98, NT. (`http://www.iplanet.com/products`)

- **Microsoft Internet Information Server (IIS)**—A popular server for Windows NT. Environment: NT Server. (`http://www.microsoft.com/`)

- **Microsoft Personal Web Server (PWS)**—An entry-level Web server; however, not recommended for high-traffic sites. Environment: Windows. (bundled in NT 4.0 Option Pack). (`http://www.microsoft.com/`)

- **AOLserver**—A small, free server with support for Web application development. Environment: Unix, Linux. Open Source. (`http://www.aolserver.com`)

- **Zeus**—A full-featured Web server with support for secure virtual servers. Environment: Unix. (`http://www.zeus.co.uk/products/zws/`)

- **O'Reilly WebSitePro**—A full-featured server, great for Web application development. Environment: Windows 95/98, NT. (`http://website.ora.com/`)

- **Stronghold**—A commercial, secure version of Apache. Environment: Unix. (`https://www.c2.net/products/sh3/`)

- **WebSTAR**—WebSTAR from StarNine Technologies is a full-featured Web server for the Macintosh environment. (`http://www.webstar.com/`)

For more information on these specific Web servers and many more, please refer to the URLs included in the previous descriptions or use the following sites:

- Webserver Compare, the definitive guide to HTTP server specs:
  `http://webcompare.internet.com/`
- Server Watch, the quintessential resource for Internet servers:
  `http://serverwatch.internet.com/`

Summary

With the World Wide Web still doubling in size every year, there appears to be no end in sight. And experts agree that we've only scratched the surface of what's possible using the Internet and the Web. In a short time we have gone from a very small number of "information-only" sites on the Web to many millions of sites offering a wealth of information and services. People use the Web on a daily basis for research, shopping, banking, and much more.

Everything you do on the Web is brought to you by Web servers like those discussed in this chapter. In fact, over half of the sites on the Web use Apache, the Web server featured in this chapter. The goal of this chapter was to provide you with the information you need to download, install, configure, and run the Internet's most popular Web server. There was some discussion about Web servers in general, and a short introduction to some of the top Web servers out there at the time of this writing. Hopefully, you will take what you have learned in this book, particularly this chapter, and become part of the fastest growing, most life-changing technology yet to be seen: The World Wide Web.

38

INSTALLING AND
CONFIGURING THE
WEB SERVER

Operating and Administering a TCP/IP Network

PART
IX

IN THIS PART

PART

IX

Protocol Configuration and Tuning on Unix Systems

by Anne Carasik

IN THIS CHAPTER

With any system, you need to know how the system initializes and where the configuration files are located. This will help you fine-tune your network configuration and help with troubleshooting. Also, there are some details to consider that may not be directly related to networking, but to the system itself, when configuring and fine-tuning your network setup.

System Initialization Issues

When you're booting up a Unix or a Linux system, you have many issues to consider. Among them are network daemons—when they start up, what starts them, and which daemons are running.

Each flavor of Unix has a "grandfather" process, known as init. The init process starts all other processes on the Unix system, including the user shells and the networking processes.

The init Process and /etc/inittab

Two things make up Unix: files and processes. In Unix, all other processes fork from init—eventually, all processes link back to init through their parents. Figure 39.1 illustrates how the init process is linked to the others.

FIGURE 39.1

The init *process and the child processes.*

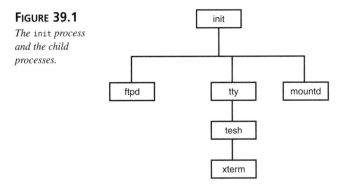

Because the init process is the last step in the boot process, after all the filesystems have been checked and the disks mounted, init determines into which user mode (single or multiuser) to go. Some Unix systems use a configuration script for init, the /etc/inittab file, which follows:

```
# inittab       This file describes how the INIT process should set up
#               the system in a certain run-level.
#
# Author:       Miquel van Smoorenburg, <miquels@drinkel.nl.mugnet.org>
#               Modified for RHS Linux by Marc Ewing and Donnie Barnes
#
```

```
# Default runlevel. The runlevels used by RHS are:
#   0 - halt (Do NOT set initdefault to this)
#   1 - Single user mode
#   2 - Multiuser, without NFS (The same as 3, if you do not
                                have networking)
#   3 - Full multiuser mode
#   4 - unused
#   5 - X11
#   6 - reboot (Do NOT set initdefault to this)
#
id:3:initdefault:

# System initialization.
si::sysinit:/etc/rc.d/rc.sysinit

l0:0:wait:/etc/rc.d/rc 0
l1:1:wait:/etc/rc.d/rc 1
l2:2:wait:/etc/rc.d/rc 2
l3:3:wait:/etc/rc.d/rc 3
l4:4:wait:/etc/rc.d/rc 4
l5:5:wait:/etc/rc.d/rc 5
l6:6:wait:/etc/rc.d/rc 6

# Things to run in every runlevel.
ud::once:/sbin/update

# Trap CTRL-ALT-DELETE
ca::ctrlaltdel:/sbin/shutdown -t3 -r now

# When our UPS tells us power has failed, assume we have a few minutes
# of power left.  Schedule a shutdown for 2 minutes from now.
# This does, of course, assume you have powerd installed and your
# UPS connected and working correctly.
pf::powerfail:/sbin/shutdown -f -h +2
"Power Failure; System Shutting Down"

# If power was restored before the shutdown kicked in, cancel it.
pr:12345:powerokwait:/sbin/shutdown -c
"Power Restored; Shutdown Cancelled"


# Run gettys in standard runlevels
1:2345:respawn:/sbin/mingetty tty1
2:2345:respawn:/sbin/mingetty tty2
3:2345:respawn:/sbin/mingetty tty3
4:2345:respawn:/sbin/mingetty tty4
5:2345:respawn:/sbin/mingetty tty5
6:2345:respawn:/sbin/mingetty tty6

# Run xdm in runlevel 5
# xdm is now a separate service
x:5:respawn:/etc/X11/prefdm -nodaemon
```

39

PROTOCOL
CONFIGURATION
AND TUNING

In this `/etc/inittab` file for Red Hat Linux, you can see that the networking starts at run-level 3. For most Unix flavors, run-level 3 starts the networking processes including the Internet daemon (`inetd`), NFS, DNS, and Sendmail.

The `rc` Scripts

In order to start running child processes, `init` will run the start-up scripts, known as the `rc` scripts. These scripts start up desired network processes so that the Unix system is no longer "standalone."

In Red Hat Linux and other System V–based systems such as HP-UX, `init` will start running any networking start-up scripts in the `/etc/rc.d/rc3.d` directory. Other systems may call networking scripts in other files like `rc.M` (for multiuser) or `rc.inet` (for Internet). This is all operating system dependent.

For this example, we'll stick with Red Hat Linux for consistency. Because this book is on networking, we'll take a look at the `/etc/rc.d/rc3.d/` directory.

```
[root@tigerlair stripes]# ls /etc/rc.d/rc3.d/
K05innd          K20rwalld    K45arpwatch
K80random    S40atd    S85sound
K08autofs        K20rwhod    K45named    K85netfs
S40crond         S90xfsK10xntpd          K25squid
K50snmpd     K88ypserv    S50inet
S99linuxconfK15postgresql  K30mcserv    K55routed
K89portmap   S55sshd        S99local
K20bootparamd  K30sendmail    K60lpd
K96pcmcia    S72amdK20nfs          K34yppasswdd    K60mars-new    S05apmd
S75keytableK20rstatd      K35dhcpd    K75gated    S10network
S85gpm
K20rusersd       K35smb        K80nscd

    S30syslog    S85httpd
```

All of these files start up a particular service. For run-level 3, many features are started in addition to networking. For the networking, you can see which daemons are started by what follows the S## or K## (K is for Kill and S is for Start). The sequence numbers are for starting and stopping in a particular order.

These scripts also specify which options the network daemon is going to use when it's first started.

Note that a start-up script or kill script does not need to have a counterpart. For example, `S50inet` does not have a `K50inet`. Here's what the `S50inet` looks like:

```
#! /bin/sh
#
# inet        Start TCP/IP networking services. This script
```

```
#                 sets the hostname, creates the routes and
#                 starts the Internet Network Daemon & RPC portmapper.
#
# Author:         Miquel van Smoorenburg, <miquels@drinkel.nl.mugnet.org>
#                 Various folks at Red Hat
#
# chkconfig: 345 50 50
# description: The internet superserver daemon (commonly called inetd) \
#                 starts a variety of other internet services as needed. \
#                 It is responsible for starting many services, including \
#                 telnet, ftp, rsh, and rlogin. Disabling inetd disables \
                  all of the services it is responsible for.
# processname: inetd
# pidfile: /var/run/inetd.pid
# config: /etc/sysconfig/network
# config: /etc/inetd.conf


# Source function library.
. /etc/rc.d/init.d/functions

# Get config.
. /etc/sysconfig/network

# Check that networking is up.
if [ ${NETWORKING} = "no" ]
then
        exit 0
fi

[ -f /usr/sbin/inetd ] || exit 0

# See how we were called.
case "$1" in
  start)
        echo -n "Starting INET services: "
        daemon inetd

        echo
        touch /var/lock/subsys/inet
        ;;
  stop)
        # bringing down NFS filesystems isn't
        # inet's problem I don't know
        # why this script used to do that -- ewt

        echo -n "Stopping INET services: "
        killproc inetd

        echo
        rm -f /var/lock/subsys/inet
```

```
            ;;
    status)
            status inetd
            ;;
    restart|reload)
            killall -HUP inetd
            ;;
      *)
            echo "Usage: inet {start|stop|status|restart|reload}"
            exit 1
esac

exit 0
```

A kill script for K45named looks like this:

```
#!/bin/sh
#
# named
# This shell script takes care of starting and stopping
#                named (BIND DNS server).
#
# chkconfig: 345 55 45
# description: named (BIND) is a Domain
# Name Server (DNS)  that is used to resolve
# host names to IP addresses.
# probe: true

# Source function library.
. /etc/rc.d/init.d/functions

# Source networking configuration.
. /etc/sysconfig/network

# Check that networking is up.
[ ${NETWORKING} = "no" ] && exit 0

[ -f /usr/sbin/named ] || exit 0

[ -f /etc/named.conf ] || exit 0

# See how we were called.
case "$1" in
  start)
        # Start daemons.
        echo -n "Starting named: "
        daemon named
        echo
        touch /var/lock/subsys/named
        ;;
  stop)
```

```
        # Stop daemons.
        echo -n "Shutting down named: "
        killproc named
        rm -f /var/lock/subsys/named
        echo
        ;;
status)
        /usr/sbin/ndc status
        exit $?
        ;;
restart)
        /usr/sbin/ndc restart
        exit $?
        ;;
reload)
        /usr/sbin/ndc reload
        exit $?
        ;;
probe)
        # named knows how to reload intelligently;
        # we don't want linuxconf
        # to offer to restart every time
        /usr/sbin/ndc reload >/dev/null 2>&1 || echo start
        exit 0
        ;;

  *)
        echo "Usage: named {start|stop|status|restart}"
        exit 1
esac

exit 0
```

> **Note**
>
> Please note that not all Unix systems have their start-up scripts in the same location. Some may have them in /etc, /etc/rc, or other system-specific locations.

Most of the scripts at different run levels in the directories such as /etc/rc.d/rc3.d are symbolic links to scripts in the directory /etc/rc.d/init.d. For example, the /etc/rc.d/rc3.d/S50inet script is a symbolic link to the following file:

    ../init.d/inet

When the S50inet is executed, the script file ../init.d/inet is called with the 'start' argument.

Similarly, `/etc/rc.d/rc3.d/S53named` is a symbolic link to the `../init.d/named` script. When the `S53named` is executed, it executes the `../init.d/named` script with the `'start'` argument. When the system is shutting down, the `/etc/rc.d/rc3.d/K45named` is executed. This file is also a symbolic link to the `../init.d/named` script. But when the `K45named` script is executed, the `../init.d/named` script is executed with a `'stop'` argument. This is why within each of these scripts there is logic to handle the `'start'`, `'stop'` and other arguments passed to the script. Knowing this, you can use the scripts in `/etc/rc.d/init.d` to stop and start different services. For example, if you want to stop BIND services, you can use the following command:

```
/etc/rc.d/init.d/named stop
```

If BIND is not running, you can start it using

```
/etc/rc.d/init.d/named start
```

After making changes to the BIND (named) database files, you can restart it using

```
/etc/rc.d/init.d/named restart
```

Configuration Files

In order to get your network working properly, you need to pay careful attention to the configuration files. On Unix, you need to pay attention to several important configuration files. These include

- `/etc/inetd.conf`
- `/etc/services`
- `/etc/protocols`
- `/etc/hosts.equiv`
- `/etc/resolv.conf`
- `/etc/exports`

Other Unix systems will have other configuration files; however, this differs from operating system to operating system.

Defining Network Protocols in `/etc/protocols`

In order to define which network protocols run on your Unix system, you need to define them in the `/etc/protocols` file. Most of these should run fine on your system; however, you should not need to define anything by hand—this should be done by the system at setup.

Note that these are IP protocols—no non-IP protocols are listed here (such as AppleTalk, NetWare, or SNA).

The following is a sample `/etc/protocols` file:

```
# /etc/protocols:

#
# Internet (IP) protocols
#
#   from: @(#)protocols    5.1 (Berkeley) 4/17/89
#
# Updated for NetBSD based on RFC 1340, Assigned Numbers (July 1992).

Ip       0      IP            # internet protocol, pseudo protocol
                                            number
icmp     1      ICMP          # internet control message protocol
igmp     2      IGMP          # Internet Group Management
ggp      3      GGP           # gateway-gateway protocol
ipencap      4      IP-ENCAP    # IP encapsulated in IP
                                            (officially ''IP'')
st           5      ST            # ST datagram mode
tcp      6      TCP           # transmission control protocol
egp      8      EGP           # exterior gateway protocol
pup      12     PUP           # PARC universal packet protocol
udp      17     UDP           # user datagram protocol
hmp      20     HMP           # host monitoring protocol
xns-idp  22     XNS-IDP        # Xerox NS IDP
rdp      27     RDP           # "reliable datagram" protocol
iso-tp4  29     ISO-TP4       # ISO Transport Protocol class 4
xtp      36     XTP           # Xpress Tranfer Protocol
ddp      37     DDP           # Datagram Delivery Protocol
idpr-cmtp    39     IDPR-CMTP   # IDPR Control Message Transport
rspf     73     RSPF          #Radio Shortest Path First.
vmtp     81     VMTP          # Versatile Message Transport
ospf     89     OSPFIGP       # Open Shortest Path First IGP
ipip     94     IPIP          # Yet Another IP encapsulation
encap    98     ENCAP         # Yet Another IP encapsulation
```

39

PROTOCOL
CONFIGURATION
AND TUNING

Recognizable Hosts in `/etc/hosts`

For some local systems, you may want to define some hosts that can be discovered by name without needing the Domain Name Service (DNS). In order to do this, you need to have an `/etc/hosts` file.

A barebones `/etc/hosts` will look like this:

`127.0.0.1   localhost   loopback`

This will define the localhost, or loopback, which is the default IP address for the host you are currently on. The IP address 127.0.0.1 is defined by default for localhost.

To add another host, use the following syntax:

```
IPaddress   hostname   alias
```

You need to have the IP address of the host, the hostname assigned to it, and any aliases you want. A sample /etc/hosts file will look something like this:

```
# a sample /etc/hosts file
127.0.0.1   localhost       loopback
1.2.3.4     wednesday.addams.com   mymachine
1.2.3.5     pugsley.addams.com   yourmachine
1.2.3.6     gomez.addams.com   hismachine
1.2.3.7     cousinit.addams.com   itsmachine
1.2.3.8     morticia.addams.com   hermachine
```

So, if a telnet session were done to yourmachine, it would connect to pugsley.addams.com. With the alias, you don't have to type in the entire domain name.

> **Note**
>
> You don't have to include the fully qualified domain name if the system in your /etc/hosts file is on the local network.

The file /etc/nsswitch.conf controls the order in which the name resolution is performed. For example, you can specify that /etc/hosts should be searched before DNS, or DNS should be searched before /etc/hosts. The simplest way to configure the name resolution order under Linux is to use the linuxconf configuration tool.

TCP/IP and /etc/services

In order to determine what type of TCP/IP services are offered on your Unix system, you need to set the appropriate services you want running on your system. You can do this two different ways: from the /etc/services file and from the inetd configuration file, inetd.conf, which is discussed later in this chapter.

The /etc/services file assigns specific ports to network services such as FTP, Telnet, time server, name server, Secure Shell, finger, and others.

Many of these services are commonly assigned to the same port and are known as well-known ports. This includes any network service that runs at port 1024 or lower.

Other network services that are not nearly as common are also included in the /etc/services file. The syntax for a listing in the /etc/services file looks like this:

```
networkservice       portnumber/tcporudp
```

First you define your network service (such as Telnet, echo, SMTP), and then you define the port number. After the port number, you need to define whether the service uses either TCP or UDP.

The following is a sample /etc/services file:

```
# /etc/services:
#
# Network services, Internet style
#
# Note that it is presently the policy of IANA to assign a
# single well-known port number for both TCP and UDP;
# hence, most entries here have two entries
# even if the protocol doesn't support UDP operations.
# Updated from RFC 1700, ''Assigned Numbers'' (October 1994).
# Not all ports
# are included, only the more common ones.


tcpmux      1/tcp            # TCP port service multiplexer
echo        7/tcp
echo        7/udp
discard     9/tcp      sink null
discard     9/udp      sink null
systat      11/tcp     users
daytime     13/tcp
daytime     13/udp
netstat     15/tcp
qotd        17/tcp     quote
msp         18/tcp           # message send protocol
msp         18/udp           # message send protocol
chargen     19/tcp     ttytst source
chargen     19/udp     ttytst source
ftp-data    20/tcp
ftp         21/tcp
fsp         21/udp     fspd
ssh         22/tcp           # SSH Remote Login Protocol
ssh         22/udp           # SSH Remote Login Protocol
telnet      23/tcp
# 24 - private
smtp        25/tcp     mail
# 26 - unassigned
time        37/tcp     timserver
nameserver  42/tcp       name      # IEN 116
whois       43/tcp     nicname
domain      53/tcp       nameserver   # name-domain server
domain      53/udp       nameserver
bootps      67/tcp         # BOOTP server
bootpc      68/tcp         # BOOTP client
tftp        69/udp
gopher      70/tcp           # Internet Gopher
```

39

PROTOCOL
CONFIGURATION
AND TUNING

```
finger      79/tcp
www         80/tcp       http        # WorldWideWeb HTTP
www         80/udp                   # HyperText Transfer Protocol
link        87/tcp       ttylink
kerberos    88/tcp       kerberos5 krb5    # Kerberos v5
kerberos    88/udp       kerberos5 krb5    # Kerberos v5
supdup      95/tcp
# 100 - reserved
pop-3       110/tcp                  # POP version 3
sunrpc      111/tcp      portmapper  # RPC 4.0 portmapper TCP
sunrpc      111/udp      portmapper  # RPC 4.0 portmapper UDP
auth        113/tcp      authentication tap ident
sftp        115/tcp
nntp        119/tcp      readnews untp  # USENET News Transfer
                                                        Protocol
ntp         123/tcp
netbios-ns   137/tcp                 # NETBIOS Name Service
netbios-dgm  138/tcp                 # NETBIOS Datagram Service
netbios-ssn  139/tcp                 # NETBIOS session service
imap2       143/tcp      imap        # Interim Mail Access Proto v2
imap2       143/udp      imap
snmp        161/udp                  # Simple Net Mgmt Proto
snmp-trap   162/udp      snmptrap    # Traps for SNMP
cmip-man    163/tcp                  # ISO mgmt over IP (CMOT)
bgp         179/tcp                  # Border Gateway Proto.
irc         194/tcp                  # Internet Relay Chat
qmtp        209/tcp                  # The Quick Mail Transfer Protocol
#
# Unix specific services
#
exec        512/tcp
biff        512/udp      comsat
login       513/tcp
who         513/udp      whod
shell       514/tcp      cmd         # no passwords used
syslog      514/udp
printer     515/tcp      spooler     # line printer spooler
talk        517/udp
ntalk       518/udp
route       520/udp      router routed   # RIP
#
# Kerberos (Project Athena/MIT) services
# Note that these are for Kerberos v4, and are unofficial.  Sites running
# v4 should uncomment these and comment out the v5 entries above.
#
kerberos4   750/udp      kerberos-iv kdc  # Kerberos (server) udp
kerberos4   750/tcp      kerberos-iv kdc  # Kerberos (server) tcp
kerberos_master   751/udp            # Kerberos authentication
kerberos_master   751/tcp            # Kerberos authentication
passwd_server   752/udp              # Kerberos passwd server
krb_prop    754/tcp                  # Kerberos slave propagation
```

```
krbupdate   760/tcp      kreg    # Kerberos registration
kpasswd     761/tcp      kpwd    # Kerberos "passwd"
#
# Services added for the Debian GNU/Linux distribution
poppassd    106/tcp         # Eudora
poppassd    106/udp         # Eudora
ssmtp       465/tcp         # SMTP over SSL
rsync       873/tcp         # rsync
rsync       873/udp         # rsync
simap       993/tcp          # IMAP over SSL
spop3       995/tcp          # POP-3 over SSL
socks      1080/tcp        # socks proxy server
socks      1080/udp        # socks proxy server
icp        3130/tcp       # Internet Cache Protocol (Squid)
icp        3130/udp       # Internet Cache Protocol (Squid)
ircd       6667/tcp        # Internet Relay Chat
ircd       6667/udp        # Internet Relay Chat
```

`inetd` and `/etc/inetd.conf`

On Unix, many network services are started by the Internet super daemon `inetd`. In order for `inetd` to know what to run, it needs to read its configuration file `inetd.conf`, which is usually located in the `/etc` directory.

> **Note**
>
> Because of `inetd`'s ability to launch other network daemons, there is a desire to use `inetd` all the time. However, there are times when this will decrease performance enough that it may not be worth it. For example, Secure Shell takes quite a large performance hit because of the cryptographic keys it has to spin off.
>
> On some Linux systems, the `inetd` daemon is replaced by an extended `inetd` daemon called `xinetd`. The configuration for this daemon is in the `/etc/xinetd.conf` file.

For most network daemons, `inetd` is fine to use to watch the other network daemons. Daemons go through `inetd` instead of using their own daemon because `inetd` can listen for all sockets, instead of the network daemons having to listen for themselves.

This prevents too many daemons sitting around and waiting for a socket to bind to, and it also prevents sockets from being let in randomly. In a way, `inetd` acts like a security guard in a corporation, letting in only the people that should go in and directing everyone else to the right area. This makes security easier, and also makes the traffic (bandwidth) much more manageable.

39

PROTOCOL
CONFIGURATION
AND TUNING

Figure 39.2 illustrates how `inetd` acts like the security guard for networking processes.

FIGURE 39.2

The `inetd` *process management.*

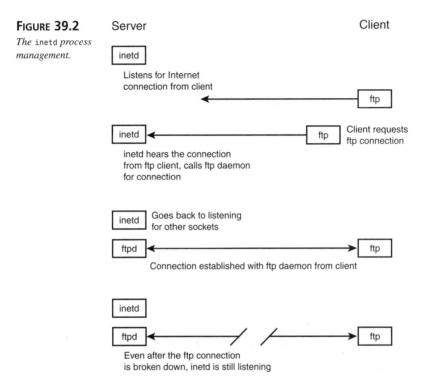

Because `inetd` doesn't know which of the network daemons you want to run, you need to define them in `/etc/inetd.conf`. The format for an entry in `/etc/inetd.conf` looks like this:

```
nameofservice sockettype protocol flags user serverpath arguments
```

So, for the ftp daemon, the syntax looks like this:

```
ftp stream tcp nowait root /usr/sbin/tcpd in.ftpd -l -a
```

This translates to the ftp protocol, which uses the socket type `stream` and runs as `root`. The server path is located at `/usr/sbin/tcpd` and the arguments it takes are `in.ftpd -l -a`. Note that there are no flags. If there are no flags, the option is skipped completely. The `/usr/sbin/tcpd` is a TCP wrapper daemon that controls access to the service specified in the argument to tcpd. Access to service is controlled by the `/etc/hosts.deny` and `/etc/hosts.allow` file. Using the TCP wrapper, you can specify a security policy, which controls who can access the specified service.

A portion of my `inetd.conf` file looks like this:

```
#
# Authors:   Original taken from BSD Unix 4.3/TAHOE.
#       Fred N. van Kempen, <waltje@uwalt.nl.mugnet.org>
#
echo    stream   tcp   nowait   root    internal
echo    dgram    udp   wait     root    internal
discard   stream   tcp   nowait   root    internal
discard   dgram    udp   wait     root    internal
daytime   stream   tcp   nowait   root    internal
daytime   dgram    udp   wait     root    internal
chargen   stream   tcp   nowait   root    internal
chargen   dgram    udp   wait     root    internal
time    stream   tcp   nowait   root    internal
time    dgram    udp   wait     root    internal


# These are standard services.
#
ftp    stream   tcp   nowait   root   /usr/sbin/tcpd   in.ftpd -l -a
telnet   stream   tcp   nowait   root      /usr/sbin/tcpd   in.telnetd
#
# Shell, login, exec, comsat and talk are BSD protocols.
#
shell   stream   tcp   nowait   root   /usr/sbin/tcpd   in.rshd
login   stream   tcp   nowait   root   /usr/sbin/tcpd   in.rlogind
#exec   stream   tcp   nowait   root   /usr/sbin/tcpd   in.rexecd
#comsat   dgram   udp   wait    root   /usr/sbin/tcpd   in.comsat
talk    dgram   udp   wait    root   /usr/sbin/tcpd   in.talkd
ntalk   dgram   udp   wait    root   /usr/sbin/tcpd   in.ntalkd
#dtalk   stream   tcp   waut    nobody  /usr/sbin/tcpd   in.dtalkd
#
# Pop and imap mail services et al
#
#pop-2   stream   tcp    nowait   root    /usr/sbin/tcpd   ipop2d
pop-3   stream   tcp    nowait   root    /usr/sbin/tcpd   ipop3d
imap    stream   tcp    nowait   root    /usr/sbin/tcpd   imapd
#
# The Internet UUCP service.
#
#uucp   stream   tcp   nowait   uucp   /usr/sbin/tcpd
    /usr/lib/uucp/uucico   -l
#
# Tftp service is provided primarily for booting.  Most sites
# run this only on machines acting as "boot servers." Do not uncomment
# this unless you *need* it.
#
#tftp   dgram   udp   wait   root   /usr/sbin/tcpd   in.tftpd
#bootps   dgram   udp   wait   root   /usr/sbin/tcpd   bootpd
#
# Finger, systat and netstat give out user information which may be
```

39

```
# valuable to potential "system crackers."  Many sites choose to disable
# some or all of these services to improve security.
#
finger   stream   tcp   nowait   root    /usr/sbin/tcpd   in.fingerd
#cfinger stream   tcp   nowait   root    /usr/sbin/tcpd   in.cfingerd
#systat  stream   tcp   nowait   guest   /usr/sbin/tcpd   /bin/ps   -auwwx
#netstat  stream   tcp   nowait   guest   /usr/sbin/tcpd
     /bin/netstat   -f inet
#
# Authentication
#
auth   stream   tcp   nowait   nobody
     /usr/sbin/in.identd in.identd -l -e -o
#
# End of inetd.conf
```

Note that by default many of these network daemons are commented out with the #. This means that you should not run these commands unless you're absolutely sure of what you're doing. They are considered a security risk either because they are easy to use to gain access to or bring down your system.

> **Note**
>
> Daemons usually run as either the nobody or root users. The nobody user is a guest user with limited privileges. Make sure that you are especially careful with running daemons that run as root, because root users have full access to the system.

If you make any changes to the /etc/inetd.conf file, such as commenting out a network daemon or adding an additional one, you will need to restart inetd by sending it the HUP signal, like this:

```
# killall -HUP inetd
```

Recognizable Networks in /etc/networks

Not many systems use this, but you can define your networks in the /etc/networks file. This will help you organize which networks your system connects to.

The DNS Client and /etc/resolv.conf

To get DNS name resolution working, you need to have your DNS client configured properly. In order to do this, you need to have an /etc/resolv.conf file.

In the /etc/resolv.conf file, you will have your domain name defined, your nameserver (either your primary or your primary and secondary), and any other directives it needs.

Basically, this allows your system to perform domain name lookups, such as converting www.example.com to its IP address, as shown here:

```
search example.com sub.example.com
nameserver 200.1.1.1
nameserver 200.1.1.2
nameserver    200.1.1.3
```

The search directive specifies the domain suffixes that will be used if an attempt is made to resolve a name that is not fully qualified. For example, if you try to access a server by its name, s100, then DNS will try to resolve it first as s100.example.com, and then as s100.sub.example.com. The nameserver directive can be used to specify up to three DNS servers. The DNS servers are queried in the order in which they are specified by the nameserver directive.

> **Note**
>
> Even though /etc/resolv.conf pertains to DNS, you need to make sure it is set properly. Test your DNS with nslookup, dig, dnsquery, or whatever other tools you can find.
>
> Otherwise, you may end up with vexing problems that do not relate to DNS.

Summary

Some of the most important issues concerning network administration include system initialization, configuration files, and making the right changes in the right places.

It is important to know where the networking functionality starts up on your system. In Unix, there are run levels that define the services the system is capable of running. This includes knowing which run level starts up your networking functionality. On some systems, it starts up on run-level 3; others start up at different run levels, including multi-user (defined as "M"). The run level configuration is defined in the /etc/inittab file on some Unix systems.

For networking, it is also critical for bandwidth and security reasons to make sure that the configuration files are set up properly. On Unix, this includes the Internet super daemon configuration in inetd.conf, the DNS client configuration in /etc/resolv.conf, the accessible networks in /etc/networks, the hosts in /etc/hosts, and the network services in /etc/services.

After you have your TCP/IP network services set up, you'll learn how to manage the name service with DNS, learn about network management and its protocol SNMP, and learn how to secure and debug a TCP/IP network.

39

PROTOCOL
CONFIGURATION
AND TUNING

Implementing DNS

by Tim Parker

IN THIS CHAPTER

Instead of tediously remembering and entering the IP address of every service-providing host on your network, you can enter hostnames using the *Domain Name System* (DNS). If assigned meaningfully, hostnames can be easily remembered and used.

The Domain Name System, as its name implies, works by dividing the Internet namespace into a set of domains, which can be further divided into subdomains. The first set of domains is called the top-level domains, and they are familiar to anyone who's browsed the Web or used the Internet. Seven top-level domains are in regular use:

- `arpa`—Internet-specific organizations
- `com`—Commercial enterprises
- `edu`—Educational organizations
- `gov`—Governmental bodies
- `mil`—Military organizations
- `net`—Service providers
- `org`—Noncommercial organizations

In addition to these top-level domains, there are dedicated top-level domains for each country. These are usually identified by a short form of the country's name, such as `.ca` for Canada and `.uk` for the United Kingdom. Beneath the top-level domains is another level for the individual organizations within each top-level domain (such as `ibm.com` and `linux.org`). The domain names are all registered with the *Network Information Center* (NIC) and are unique to the network.

The Name Server

Each DNS name server manages a distinct area of a network (or an entire domain, if the network is small). The domains over which a name server is authoritative is called a *zone*. Several zones may be managed by one name server, with each zone consisting of one or more domains. Within each zone, there is almost always a designated secondary or backup name server, with the two (primary and secondary) name servers holding duplicate information. The name servers within a zone communicate using a zone transfer protocol.

DNS operates by having a set of nested zones. A name server communicates with other name servers. Each name server also knows the address of at least one other name server. Each zone has at least one name server responsible for knowing the address information for each machine within that zone.

When a user application needs to resolve a symbolic name into a network address, a query is sent by the application to the DNS resolver, which then communicates the query to the name server. The name server checks its own tables and returns the network address corresponding to the symbolic name. If the name server doesn't have the information it requires, it can send a request to another name server. Both the name servers and the resolvers use database tables and memory caches to maintain information about the machines in the local zone, as well as recently requested information from outside the zone.

When a name server receives a query from a resolver, the name server can perform several types of operations. Name resolver operations fall into two categories: nonrecursive (or iterative) and recursive.

A *recursive* operation is one in which the name resolution request must be answered with the required information or error message. The server that receives the request can query other DNS servers for information. On obtaining the answer (or no answer) the server that received the request forwards the answer to the requestor. *Nonrecursive* (or *iterative*) operations performed by the name server include a full answer to the resolver's request, a referral to another name server (which the resolver must send a query to), or an error message.

When a recursive operation is necessary, the name server contacts another name server with the resolver's request. The remote name server will reply to the request with either a network address or a negative message indicating failure. In recursion, DNS rules prohibit a remote name server from sending a referral to yet another name server.

Resource Records

The information required to resolve symbolic names is maintained by the name server in a set of resource records, which are entries in a database.

> **Note**
>
> Resource records (often abbreviated RR) are inputted through text files called zone data files. After the text files are read by the DNS information, they are cached in the DNS server memory in the form of tables that are designed for fast retrieval. Typically, some form of the "hash" table that can be accessed via fast indexes is maintained.

40

IMPLEMENTING DNS

You saw the structure of resource records earlier, so the information isn't repeated here.

Address fields used by DNS, such as in the address resource record type, use a special format called IN-ADDR-ARPA. This allows reverse mapping from the address to the hostname as well as host-to-address mapping. To understand IN-ADDR.ARPA, it is useful to begin with a standard-format resource record. One of the simplest types of resource record is for the address (type A). The following is an extract from an address file:

```
TPCI_HPWS1     IN    A    143.12.2.50
TPCI_HPWS2     IN    A    143.12.2.51
TPCI_HPWS3     IN    A    143.12.2.52
TPCI_GATEWAY   IN    A    143.12.2.100
               IN    A    144.23.56.2
MERLIN         IN    A    145.23.24.1
SMALLWOOD      IN    A    134.2.12.75
```

Each line of the file represents one resource record. In this case, they are all simple entries that have the machine's symbolic name (alias), the class of machine (IN for Internet), A to show it is an address resource record, and the Internet address. The entry for the machine TPCI_GATEWAY has two corresponding addresses because it is a gateway between two networks. The gateway will have a different address on each of the networks, hence two resource records in the same file.

This type of file makes name-to-address mapping easy. The name server simply searches for a line that has the symbolic name requested by the application and returns the Internet address at the end of that line. The databases are indexed on the name, so these searches proceed very quickly.

Searching from the address to the name is not quite as easy. If the resource record files were small, time delays for a manual search would not be appreciable, but with large zones there can be thousands or tens of thousands of entries. The index is on the name, so searching for an address would be a slow process. To solve this reverse-mapping problem, IN-ADDR.ARPA was developed. IN-ADDR.ARPA uses the host address as an index to the host's resource record information. When the proper resource record is located, the symbolic name can be extracted.

IN-ADDR.ARPA uses the PTR resource record type to point from the address to the name. There may be one of these pointer indexes maintained on each name server. An example of a number-to-name file follows:

```
23.1.45.143.IN-ADDR.ARPA.    PTR    TPCI_HPWS_4.TPCI.COM
1.23.64.147.IN-ADDR.ARPA.    PTR    TPCI_SERVER.MERLIN.COM
3.12.6.123.IN-ADDR.ARPA.     PTR    BEAST.BEAST.COM
143.23.IN-ADDR.ARPA          PTR    MERLINGATEWAY.MERLIN.COM
```

The Internet addresses are reversed in the IN-ADDR.ARPA file for ease of use. As shown in the sample file, specifying the complete address for a gateway is not necessary because the domain name will provide enough routing information.

Name Resolver

The DNS client is called the name resolver. As far as user applications are concerned, resolving the symbolic names into actual network addresses is easy. The application sends a query to a process called the name resolver, or resolver (which sometimes resides on another machine). The name resolver may be able to resolve the name directly, in which case it sends a return message to the application. If the resolver cannot determine the network address, the resolver communicates with the name server (which might contact another name server).

The resolver is intended to replace existing name resolution systems on a machine, such as the /etc/hosts file. The replacement of these common mechanisms is transparent to the user, although the administrator must know whether the native name resolution system or DNS is to be used on each machine so the correct tables can be maintained.

When the resolver acquires information from a name server, it stores the entries in its own cache to reduce the need for more network traffic if the same symbolic name is used again (as is often the case with applications that work across networks). The amount of time the name resolver stores these records is dependent on the Time-to-Live (TTL) field in the resource records sent, or on a default value set by the system.

When a name server cannot resolve a name, it may send back a message to the resolver (in case of an iterative query) with the address of another name server in the Authority field of the message. The resolver must then address a message to the other name server in the hopes of resolving the name. The resolver can ask the name server to conduct the query itself by setting the RD (recursive) bit in the message. The name server can refuse or accept the request.

The resolver uses UDP in its query process. However, transfers of large amounts of information such as in-zone transfer, may require the use of TCP because of its higher reliability.

Under the Unix and Linux operating systems where DNS originated, several different implementations of the name resolver are in use. The resolver supplied with the original BSD versions of Unix was particularly limited, offering neither a cache nor iterative query capabilities. To solve these limitations, the *Berkeley Internet Name Domain* (BIND) server was added in 4.2 BSD Unix. BIND provides both caching and iterative query capabilities in three different modes: as a primary server, as a secondary server, or as a caching-only server (which doesn't have a database of its own, only a cache). The use of BIND on BSD systems allowed another process to take over the workload of name resolution, a process that may be on another machine entirely.

> **Note**
>
> Note that current development of BIND and its evolution is managed by the Internet Software Consortium (www.isc.org). BIND is available for Unix as well as the MS Windows operating systems.

Configuring a Unix or Linux DNS Server

Configuring a DNS server requires a number of files and databases to be modified or created. The process is time-consuming, but luckily has to be done only once for each server. The files involved in most DNS setups, and their purposes, are

- named.hosts—Defines the domain with hostname-to-IP mappings
- named.rev—Uses IN-ADDR.ARPA for IP-to-hostname mappings
- named.local—Used to resolve the loopback driver
- named.ca—Lists root domain servers
- named.boot (for BIND 4) and named.conf for (BIND 8 and higher)—Used to set file and database locations

With the exception of named.boot and named.conf files, these filenames are examples, but they can be changed to suit your own personal needs. The primary file in the list is named.boot (BIND 4) or named.conf (BIND 8 and higher), which is read when the system boots up and defines the other files in the set. Therefore, any filename changes are reflected in these files. Each of the previously listed files is a database with entries in the form of a resource record.

Entering the Resource Records

For a typical server configuration, you will use standard names and network layouts. DNS allows you to get very complex, but it's easier to see what the files and resource records are doing with a simple layout.

An SOA resource record is placed in the `named.hosts` file. Semicolons in the record are used for comments. This resource record has been formatted as one field per line to make its entries clear, although this is not necessary. This resource record defines an upper boundary of the `tpci.com` domain with `server.tpci.com` as the primary name server for the domain, `root.merlin.tpci.com` as the e-mail address of the person responsible for the domain, and the rest of the entries identified by comments.

```
tpci.com.   IN   SOA     server.tpci.com.
    root.merlin.tpci.com. (
    2  ; Serial number
    7200 ; Refresh (2 hrs)
    3600 ; Retry (1 hr)
    151200 ; Expire (1 week)
    86400 ); min TTL
```

Note that the information from the serial number to the TTL field is enclosed in parentheses. This is part of the command syntax and must be included to indicate the parameter order.

In addition to the SOA RR, the `named.hosts` file contains Address (A) records. These records are used for the actual mapping of a hostname to its IP address. A few address resource records will show the format of these entries:

```
artemis    IN    A    143.23.25.7
merlin     IN    A    143.23.25.9
pepper     IN    A    143.23.25.72
```

The hostnames are typically not given as fully qualified domain names because the server can deduce the full name. If you want to use the full domain name, you must follow the name with a period. The machines shown in the preceding example would be given as follows using fully qualified domain names:

```
artemis.tpci.com.    IN    A    143.23.25.7
merlin.tpci.com.     IN    A    143.23.25.9
pepper.tpci.com.    A    143.23.25.72
```

The Pointer (PTR) resource record is used to map an IP address to a name using IN-ADDR.ARPA. A single PTR RR helps make this clear. The record indicates that the machine named `merlin` has the IP address 147.120.0.7:

```
7.0.120.147.in-addr.arpa IN PTR merlin.tpci.com.
```

The name server resource records point to the name server that has authority for a particular zone. Name server (NS) records are used when a large network has several subnetworks each with its own name server. An entry looks like this:

```
tpci.com.   IN   NS  merlin.tpci.com.
```

40

IMPLEMENTING
DNS

This record indicates that the DNS server for the `tpci.com` domain is called `merlin.tpci.com`. If there were several subnets used in `tpci.com`, there would be an NS RR for each subnet.

Completing the DNS Files

As you know, DNS uses a number of files to hold resource records describing the zones used by DNS. The first file of interest is `named.hosts`, which contains the SOA, NS, and A resource records. All entries in the `named.hosts` file must begin in the first character position of each line. Here's a sample `named.hosts` file with comments added to show the records:

```
; named.hosts files
; Start Of Authority RR
tpci.com.IN SOA merlin.tpci.com.
root.merlin.tpci.com. (
2  ; Serial number
7200 ; Refresh (2 hrs)
3600 ; Retry (1 hr)
151200 ; Expire (1 week)
86400 ); min TTL
;
; Name Service RRs
tpci.com.   IN   NS   merlin.tpci.com.
subnet1.tpci.com. IN NS goofy.subnet1.tpci.com.
;
; Address RRs
artemis     IN    A    143.23.25.7
merlin      IN    A    143.23.25.9
windsor     IN    A    143.23.25.12
reverie     IN    A    143.23.25.23
bigcat      IN    A    143.23.25.43
pepper      IN    A    143.23.25.72
```

The first section sets the SOA record that defines the parameters for time-to-live, expiry, refresh, and so on. It sets the name server for the `tpci.com` domain to be `merlin.tpci.com`. The second section uses the name service resource records to define the name server for the `tpci.com` domain as `merlin.tpci.com` (the same as the SOA) and a subdomain of tpci called `subnet1`, for which the name server is `goofy.subnet1.tpci.com`. The third section has a list of the address record name-to-IP address mapping. There will be an entry in this section for each machine on the network.

The `named.rev` file provides the reverse mapping of IP address to machine name and is composed of pointer resource records. The same format as the `named.hosts` file is followed, except for the swapping of name and IP address, and the conversion of the IP address to IN-ADDR.ARPA style. The equivalent `named.rev` file for the `named.hosts` file shown earlier looks like this:

```
; named.rev files
; Start Of Authority RR
23.143.in-addr.arpa.     IN     SOA      merlin.tpci.com.
          root.merlin.tpci.com. (
          2   ; Serial number
          7200 ; Refresh (2 hrs)
          3600 ; Retry (1 hr)
          151200 ; Expire (1 week)
          86400 ); min TTL
;
; Name Service RRs
23.143.in-addr.arpa.     IN     NS  merlin.tpci.com.
100.23.143.in-addr.arpa.    IN NS goofy.subnet1.tpci.com.
;
; Address RRs
9.25.23.143.in-addr.arpa.     IN     PTR merlin.tpci.com.
12.25.23.143.in-addr.arpa.    IN     PTR windsor.tpci.com.
23.25.23.143.in-addr.arpa.    IN     PTR reverie.tpci.com.
43.25.23.143.in-addr.arpa.    IN     PTR bigcat.tpci.com.
72.25.23.143.in-addr.arpa.    IN     PTR pepper.tpci.com.
```

There must be a separate `named.rev` file for each zone or subdomain on the network. These files can have different names or be placed in different directories. If you have only a single zone, one `named.rev` file is all that's needed.

The `named.local` file contains an entry for the loopback address (which is usually set to the IP address 127.0.0.1, even though any address of the form 127.x.x.x will do). This file must contain information about the IN-ADDR.ARPA mapping of the loopback driver, as well as a domain again (because the `named.rev` file doesn't cover the 127 network). A `named.local` file looks like this:

```
; named.local files
; Start Of Authority RR
0.0.127.in-addr.arpa. IN
SOA merlin.tpci.com.
root.merlin.tpci.com. (
2   ; Serial number
7200 ; Refresh (2 hrs)
3600 ; Retry (1 hr)
151200 ; Expire (1 week)
86400 ); min TTL
;
; Name Service RR
0.0.127.in-addr.arpa.     IN     NS     merlin.tpci.com.
;
; Address RR
1.0.0.127.in-addr.arpa.   IN     PTR localhost.
```

This file then provides the mapping from the machine named `localhost` to the IP address 127.0.0.1.

40

IMPLEMENTING
DNS

The `named.ca` file is used to specify the name of root servers that the system can resort to. The machines specified in the `named.ca` file should be stable and not subject to rapid change. A sample `named.ca` file looks like this:

```
; named.ca
; servers for the root domain
;
.  99999999  IN   NS   ns.nic.ddn.mil.
   99999999  IN   NS   ns.nasa.gov.
   99999999  IN   NS   ns.internic.net
; servers by address
;
ns.nic.ddn.mil.   99999999   IN   A   192.112.36.4
ns.nasa.gov.      99999999   IN   A   192.52.195.10
ns.internic.net.  99999999   IN   A   198.41.0.4
```

In this file, only three DNS servers have been specified. A normal `named.ca` may have a dozen or so name servers, depending on their proximity to your system.

For operational requirements of root servers, consult RFC 2870. The following is a complete list of root servers. The root servers are placed in the ROOT-SERVERS.NET domain. The root servers are A.ROOT-SERVERS.NET to M.ROOT-SERVERS.NET making up a total of 13 root servers. Their locations are as follows:

East Coast of USA:

A.ROOT-SERVERS.NET	NSF-NSI. Herndon, VA
C.ROOT-SERVERS.NET	PSI. Herndon, VA
D.ROOT-SERVERS.NET	UMD. College Park, MD
G.ROOT-SERVERS.NET	DISA. Boeing, VA
H.ROOT-SERVERS.NET	US Army. Aberdeen, MD
J.ROOT-SERVERS.NET	NSF-NSI. Herndon, VA

West Coast of USA:

E.ROOT-SERVERS.NET	NASA. Moffet Field, CA
F.ROOT-SERVERS.NET	ISC. Woodside, CA
B.ROOT-SERVERS.NET	DISA-USC. Marina Del Rey, CA
L.ROOT-SERVERS.NET	DISA-USC. Marina Del Rey, CA

Europe:

K.ROOT-SERVERS.NET	LINX/RIPE. London, UK
I.ROOT-SERVERS.NET	NORDU. Stockholm, Sweden

Asia:

M.ROOT-SERVERS.NET	WIDE. Keio, Japan

The current list of root servers can be obtained from the site
`ftp://ftp.rs.internic.net/domain/named.root`. The zone data file for the root
servers is shown here:

```
;       This file holds the information on root name servers needed to
;       initialize cache of Internet domain name servers
;       (e.g. reference this file in the "cache  .  <file>"
;       configuration file of BIND domain name servers).
;
;       This file is made available by InterNIC registration services
;       under anonymous FTP as
;           file            /domain/named.root
;           on server       FTP.RS.INTERNIC.NET
;       -OR- under Gopher at RS.INTERNIC.NET
;           under menu      InterNIC Registration Services (NSI)
;               submenu     InterNIC Registration Archives
;           file            named.root
;
;       last update:    Aug 22, 1997
;       related version of root zone:   1997082200
;
;
; formerly NS.INTERNIC.NET
;
.                       3600000  IN  NS   A.ROOT-SERVERS.NET.
A.ROOT-SERVERS.NET.     3600000      A    198.41.0.4
;
; formerly NS1.ISI.EDU
;
.                       3600000      NS   B.ROOT-SERVERS.NET.
B.ROOT-SERVERS.NET.     3600000      A    128.9.0.107
;
; formerly C.PSI.NET
;
.                       3600000      NS   C.ROOT-SERVERS.NET.
C.ROOT-SERVERS.NET.     3600000      A    192.33.4.12
;
; formerly TERP.UMD.EDU
;
.                       3600000      NS   D.ROOT-SERVERS.NET.
D.ROOT-SERVERS.NET.     3600000      A    128.8.10.90
;
; formerly NS.NASA.GOV
;
.                       3600000      NS   E.ROOT-SERVERS.NET.
E.ROOT-SERVERS.NET.     3600000      A    192.203.230.10
;
; formerly NS.ISC.ORG
;
.                       3600000      NS   F.ROOT-SERVERS.NET.
F.ROOT-SERVERS.NET.     3600000      A    192.5.5.241
;
```

40

IMPLEMENTING DNS

```
; formerly NS.NIC.DDN.MIL
;
.                          3600000        NS     G.ROOT-SERVERS.NET.
G.ROOT-SERVERS.NET.        3600000        A      192.112.36.4
;
; formerly AOS.ARL.ARMY.MIL
;
.                          3600000        NS     H.ROOT-SERVERS.NET.
H.ROOT-SERVERS.NET.        3600000        A      128.63.2.53
;
; formerly NIC.NORDU.NET
;
.                          3600000        NS     I.ROOT-SERVERS.NET.
I.ROOT-SERVERS.NET.        3600000        A      192.36.148.17
;
; temporarily housed at NSI (InterNIC)
;
.                          3600000        NS     J.ROOT-SERVERS.NET.
J.ROOT-SERVERS.NET.        3600000        A      198.41.0.10
;
; housed in LINX, operated by RIPE NCC
;
.                          3600000        NS     K.ROOT-SERVERS.NET.
K.ROOT-SERVERS.NET.        3600000        A      193.0.14.129
;
; temporarily housed at ISI (IANA)
;
.                          3600000        NS     L.ROOT-SERVERS.NET.
L.ROOT-SERVERS.NET.        3600000        A      198.32.64.12
;
; housed in Japan, operated by WIDE
;
.                          3600000        NS     M.ROOT-SERVERS.NET.
M.ROOT-SERVERS.NET.        3600000        A      202.12.27.33
; End of File
```

This file can be pasted into `named.ca`. The servers specified in the `named.ca` file are each identified by two entries, one giving the root domain (the period) followed by the name server name; the other has the name server IP address. The time-to-live is set very large because these servers are expected to be always available.

The `named.boot` (or `named.conf`) file is used to trigger the loading of the DNS daemons and to specify the primary and secondary name servers on the network. A sample `named.boot` file looks like this:

```
; named.boot
directory       /usr/lib/named
primary    tpci.com        named.hosts
primary    25.143.in-addr.arpa      named.rev
primary    0.0.127.in-addr.arpa     named.local
cache    .      named.ca
```

The first line of the `named.boot` file has the keyword directory followed by the directory of the DNS configuration files. Each following line with the keyword *primary* tells DNS the files that it should use to find configuration information. The first line, for example, sets `named.hosts` as the file for locating the primary server of `tpci.com`. The IN-ADDR.ARPA information is kept in the file `named.rev` for the 143.25 subnet. The localhost information is in `named.local`, and finally the server and name cache information is in `named.ca`.

A secondary name server is configured only slightly differently than a primary server. The difference is in the `named.boot` file, which points back to the primary server.

Starting the DNS Daemons

The final step in the DNS configuration is to ensure the DNS daemon called `named` is loaded when the system boots. This is usually done through the `rc` startup scripts. Most versions of Unix and Linux have the routines for DNS startup already entered in the startup script, usually in the form of a check for the `named.boot` (or `named.conf`) file. If the `startup` file exists, the DNS daemon `named` starts. The code for checking the `named.boot` file usually looks like this:

```
# Run DNS server if named.boot exists
if [ -f /etc/inet/named.boot -a -x /usr/sbin/in.named ]
then
    /usr/sbin/in.named
fi
```

The exact directory paths and options may be different in your `rc` script, but the command should check for the `named.boot` file and start `named` if it exists.

Configuring a Client

Configuring a Unix or Linux machine to use a primary DNS server for resolution is a quick process. First, the `/etc/resolv.conf` file is modified to include the primary server's address. For example, a `resolv.conf` file may look like this:

```
domain tpci.com
nameserver    143.25.0.1
nameserver    143.25.0.2
```

The first line establishes the domain name, which is followed by the IP addresses of available name servers. You could also replace the domain directive with the more flexible search directive that allows you to specify more than one domain suffix as noted earlier. In this example, this file points to two name servers on the 143.25 subnet.

40

IMPLEMENTING DNS

Windows and DNS

Windows NT, Windows 95, and Windows 98 can all act as clients of a DNS server by simply filling in the DNS server's IP addresses in the DNS tab of the Networking applet. Multiple DNS servers can be specified, and they are searched in the order shown in the DNS page tab. The DNS servers can be either inside your network or an ISP's DNS server leading out to the Internet. Of course, the ISP's server won't know the makeup of your internal network.

There is the ability to configure Windows to act as a DNS server using add-on applications, but in a Windows-only network, DNS is not as easy to configure and set up as WINS and DHCP. In a heterogeneous network of Windows and Unix machines, installing DNS on a Unix machine is much better, both because of performance reasons and also because of the architecture of the operating systems.

> **Note**
>
> In Windows 2000 Server, DNS is used for resolving Active Directory domain names and services. Windows 2000 uses Dynamic DNS but the manner in which it updates the service records is non-standard, leading to all kinds of "interesting" problems while you're trying to integrate Windows 2000 and Unix servers.

Summary

DNS is a little complicated to set up on a server but clients are much easier. Considering the benefits DNS bestows, it is usually well worth the time and energy required to install and configure it on a network. Unix and Linux are ideally suited to roles as DNS servers, whereas Windows machines work well as clients.

TCP/IP Network Management

by Bernard McCargo

CHAPTER 41

When a network came from a single vendor, that vendor was responsible for its support. Thus it used to be that AT&T and the local telephone company took responsibility for the telecommunication lines, IBM managed the mainframe in the accounting department, and DEC managed the minicomputers in the engineering department. The network manager simply identified the malfunctioning system, and the appropriate vendor would solve the problem.

Today's internetworks are far more difficult to manage for three reasons:

- Centralized data processing has been replaced by distributed systems.
- The divestiture of AT&T in 1984 dramatically changed the way customers manage their telecommunication circuits. Today's internetwork manager must interface with the LEC (Local Exchange Carriers), IXC (Inter-Exchange Carriers), and other providers, such as Packet Switched Public Data Networks (PSPDN).
- The economic growth of the data communications industry has dramatically increased the number of vendors in the marketplace.

All of these developments increase the likelihood of finger-pointing between vendors.

Both vendors and standards bodies have proposed solutions to these challenges. The predominant standard, ISO 7498-4, defines five functional management areas:

- **Fault management**—Deals with detection, testing, and correction of network failures.
- **Accounting management**—Allocates network costs to the responsible party.
- **Configuration management**—Maintains the current status of all elements within the network.
- **Performance management**—Collects and logs statistical information regarding system performance.
- **Security management**—Protects network resources and controls access to the network.

Various standards bodies have developed protocols to support these standards. However, the most popular network management protocol is the *Simple Network Management Protocol* (SNMP), which was developed by the Internet (TCP/IP) community. Its popularity is largely due to its simplicity: The initial version of SNMP defines only five commands/responses. Thus, it makes network management as painless as possible by minimizing the amount of management data transmitted between network elements and the management console. Later versions added a few extra commands for making it easy for SNMP Management stations to collect information from other SNMP Management stations.

Finally, vendors in the data communications industry have developed network management systems that incorporate standard protocols, such as SNMP, into proprietary architectures. Major players in this market include AT&T (Unified Network Management Architecture—UNMA), DEC now part of Compaq, which may merge with Hewlett-Packard) (Management Control Center—DECmcc), Hewlett-Packard (OpenView Network Management), Bay Networks (Optivity), Cisco Systems (Cisco Works), and IBM (NetView). Look for growth in this area as internetwork complexity increases.

Note that this chapter discusses how to develop a network management plan and the tools needed to manage a network. Although this chapter discusses network management tools, the SNMP protocol is not discussed in detail. The formal definition of SNMP and its protocols are covered in Chapter 42 "SNMP: The Network Management Protocol."

Developing a Plan for Network Monitoring

All of these factors—centralized versus distributed computing architectures, wideband transmission facilities, specialized workstations, multiple protocols, new methods for LAN/WAN connectivity, and dissimilar network management systems—can result in an interesting mixture. The internetwork may use a combination of cabling types, including twisted pair, coax, and fiber optics. The LAN hardware may include incompatible access methods, such as CSMA/CD (IEEE 802.3) and token passing (IEEE 802.5). Connectivity devices such as bridges may use different algorithms, such as spanning tree (IEEE 802.3) or source routing (IEEE 802.5). The electronic mail package from one network operating system may not communicate with one from its competitor. So how do you analyze the internetwork stew to ensure that your]network performs well?

You might start by defining what it means to have a network that "performs well." The question could be answered in a number of ways. To end users, it probably means sub-second response time. To (non-systems) managers, it may mean adequate equipment at a low price. To administrators, it most certainly means a network that doesn't require a lot of attention to keep running. To network engineers the answer lies between bandwidths, forwarding rates, latency, and the like.

In designing a well-performing network monitoring system, user expectations and organizational constraints must indeed be considered the starting point. The designer's task is to negotiate a series of trade-offs to build a system that meets reasonable expectations. The expression "A chain is only as strong as its weakest link" certainly applies to networks. All components must be balanced for optimum performance.

Some of the issues directly affecting network performance that the designer must look at are network bandwidth, hardware capacity, and applications. These areas are key in the implementation of a network baseline. The network baseline is a healthy snapshot of the network, which can be used for comparative analysis when a problem occurs.

Investigating Network Problems and Network Troubleshooting

As internetworks continue to become distributed, offer higher bandwidths, and support more protocols, network managers must be prepared to adjust their network support departments and to purchase new analysis tools.

Distributed networks require companies to change the structure of centralized MIS departments. Individual locations need their own network management staff to handle user-related problems, while the headquarters location can be better equipped to analyze internetwork failures.

The development of high-bandwidth connectivity has reduced the economic life of existing network analysis and management equipment. When the typical WAN link was an analog circuit, for example, a network administrator suspecting a problem on that circuit would test it for compliance with analog transmission parameters, such as impulse noise, envelope delay distortion, and phase jitter. But today's digital circuits that constitute the high-bandwidth pipes require entirely different techniques to analyze completely different transmission parameters. For example, T1/T3 circuits must be tested for proper data framing and improperly generated signals, such as bipolar violations (BPVs), and special data encoding, such as B8ZS (bipolar with eight zero substitution). If the transmission medium is optical fiber, rather than twisted pairs or coaxial cable, the analyzer needs an optical rather than an electrical interface.

The following are some general guidelines that provide a framework to help you get started:

- **Define the problem.** You can't troubleshoot a problem that you can't clearly describe.
- **Develop a solution.** Proceed carefully and methodically to solve the problem.
- **Document your work.** You can learn from the past.
- **Disseminate the results.** Others can benefit from your experiences.

Network Management Tools

Network management tools are very complicated, and become more complicated as you increase the number of protocols that they must monitor. Multiprotocol internetworks will require more intelligent analyzers. Analyzers that once handled a single protocol suite, such as SNA, must now take care of several, such as SNA, DECnet, and TCP/IP. To understand this trend, you need a little background on how analyzers work and the direction in which they have been developing.

Using Protocol Analyzers

A protocol analyzer works as follows. The analyzer attaches to the internetwork in a passive mode and captures the information transmitted between various devices. This information can be divided into two categories:

- **Data**—The data comes from an end-user process, such as an electronic mail message.
- **Control**—The control information assures that the data transfer obeys the rules of the protocols.

For this reason, the control information is often called *protocol control information* (PCI), and it is unique to each protocol. Thus, if seven protocols were associated with a particular internetwork function, there would be seven unique PCI elements. These elements, usually called *headers*, are transmitted along with the data inside the Data Link Layer frame. The data to be transmitted originates at the Application Layer, and is therefore called *Application Data* (AD). The *Application Header* (AH) is then appended to the data, and that combination (AH + AD) is passed to the next lowest layer (that is, the Presentation Layer). The Presentation Layer treats this information (AH + AD) as its data, and appends its own header (the *Presentation Header*, or PH). The result is PH + AH + AD. The process continues until the entire frame is constructed with the appropriate PCI from each layer.

The protocol analyzer's job is simply to unravel the PCI and display it in a user-understandable format. However, as discussed later in this chapter, the unraveling process has become quite complex.

The capabilities of protocol analyzers have been evolving over time. First-generation analyzers were actually datascopes that simply decoded a datastream and produced a hexadecimal display on the CRT. They had no user-friendly interface. The second generation added analysis capabilities up to OSI Layer 3. They could decode bit-oriented protocols, and users could program them to perform various tests, based upon their troubleshooting requirements. These tests, for instance, might restrict the data captured to the communication from one specific workstation or one particular protocol, such as the Internet Protocol (IP). Third-generation analyzers can decode and process protocols up to and including OSI Layer 7 and provide a user-friendly interface that facilitates programming and report generation.

Fourth-generation protocol analyzers are better suited for handling complex network topologies consisting of LANs, MANs, and WANs. Some of the fourth-generation protocol analyzers have some Artificial Intelligence capability to suggest the existence of a problem and its possible solution. MANs and WANs encompass OSI Layers 1–3, although higher layer information, such as signaling or network management data, may also be present. LANs cover OSI Layers 1–7 (see Figure 41.1). A MAN/WAN analyzer must be able to decode the PCI at the Physical, Data Link, and Network Layers. Thus, it will test the way the packets traverse the communications subnetwork (Layers 1–3), but it won't decode the information contained within those packets. It is the end users on LAN workstations that are interested in the information inside the packets. Workstations run a network operating system, such as Novell's NetWare or Windows NT/2000, that include protocols up to and including Layer 7.

FIGURE 41.1

LAN and WAN analysis.

To properly diagnose a problem between a workstation on LAN A and a server on LAN B connected by the WAN, a LAN analyzer must decode those higher layers.

The testing requirements of LANs and WANs also differ because of the types of failures that typically occur. LAN failures tend to be repetitive, whereas WAN breakdowns may be one-time events. A final difference is the way the analyzer is physically attached to the LAN, MAN, or WAN. MAN/WAN analyzers are usually used in equipment rooms or central offices where space is limited. (For that reason, they are often designed for both vertical and horizontal use.) LAN analyzers are typically used on a desktop.

Expert Systems

In order to maintain good performance on complex internetworks, network analyzers must become increasingly intelligent. All analyzers contain quite a bit of embedded knowledge of interface characteristics, protocols, interactions between protocols, and so on. They use these to provide help screens, invoke test sequences, or extract protocol information on one port and use it with information extracted from another. But the smartest protocol analyzers (such as the fourth-generation protocol analyzers) are those that use expert systems.

True expert systems are able to use a set of rules, combined with their knowledge of the network and its operation, to diagnose and solve network problems. The expert system's knowledge comes from a variety of sources, including a theoretical database (for example, the IEEE standards by which the network should operate); a network-specific database (topological information regarding the network nodes); and the user's previous results and experiences. All the information then generates a hypothesis about the cause of the problem and a plan of action to resolve it. For example, an Ethernet with an abnormally high rate of collisions would infer further tests of the backbone cable and terminators, and eventually arrive at a conclusion.

Hewlett-Packard's LAN Analyzers meet the criteria of an expert system. Network General has an expert system known as the Expert Sniffer, which automatically identifies problems in real-time and suggests solutions based upon a combination of expert technologies. Other LAN vendors with plans for expert systems include Bytex and Wandel & Goltermann.

H-P's expert is named the Fault Finder. The user or the analyzer furnishes Fault Finder with a fault symptom and the analyzer develops a hypothesis based upon current network conditions and/or analyzer-generated tests. This process continues until the analyzer reaches a conclusion. If the process is inconclusive, the analyzer gives the user a list of potential problems and network symptoms to use in further troubleshooting. Because the expert system automates the hypothesis/testing cycle, it should minimize network downtime.

Because of the complex nature of WAN protocols, such as ISDN and Signaling System 7-SS7, third-generation WAN analyzers offer very powerful analysis features. For example, third-generation analyzers perform statistical analyses of the incoming datastream. A summary of these statistics at either the frame (OSI Layer 2) or packet (OSI Layer 3) level offers a quick diagnosis of the health of the WAN link; a low number of frames with CRC errors or few reject packets indicates a healthy link. Should errors occur, WAN protocol analyzers can help identify the cause by selectively examining the information on that high-speed link through a process known as *filtering*. For example, if only one workstation was experiencing a problem, the analyst could set a filter to capture only the data from that workstation.

PC-Based Analyzers

Intel Pentium microprocessors have brought the minicomputer power of the 1980s to the modern desktop. With their heavy-duty processing power, these lightweight units are ideal platforms upon which to build test equipment. The portability of laptop computers allows you to carry the analyzer to a remote site. The standardized bus (ISA, EISA, Micro Channel, or PCI) also allows you to easily add other devices, such as modems, for remote access. As a result, many of the analyzer manufacturers have chosen the PC as their hardware platform. The LAN analyzer manufacturers have traditionally supported PC-based systems because of their similarity to a network workstation. WAN analyzers are now basing their products on PCs as well.

When examining analyzers built on the PC platform, you need to ask two questions: How does the manufacturer define "PC-compatible," and how do you implement those capabilities? First, there's a difference between using a PC as the analyzer platform, and having PC capabilities built in to the analyzer itself. A number of vendors, including CXR/Digilog and ProTools, based their instrument on a laptop, luggable, or desktop computer. Cabletron Systems has an analyzer based on the Apple Macintosh. As a result, you can use these devices for other applications, such as word processing or spread-sheets, when you're not using them for network analysis. Other vendors, such as Wandel & Goltermann, use multiple processors: one for PC applications and another for network analysis. A third alternative, software supported by GN Navtel, allows any PC to analyze data captured by the analyzer. Other products allow you to use standard DOS disk drives for data storage, or an external output to a CRT or printer. Thus, you need to find out what a vendor means when you see the specification "PC-based."

The second issue is implementation: How do you turn your PC into an analyzer? You have three choices here as well. FTP Software's LAN analyzer is a standalone software product that you install on your own PC equipped with a LAN interface card. FTP offers versions of the software for various interface cards, such as 3Com Etherlink, Proteon ProNET, and so on. A second option is to purchase a combination hardware/software package and install it in a PC. WAN analyzers from Frederick Engineering and Progressive Computing use this approach. The third alternative, a complete turnkey system, is available from a number of LAN and WAN analyzer vendors, including CXR/Digilog Inc., Hewlett-Packard Company, Network General Corporation, and TTC/LP COM. Turnkey products provide better support because just one vendor is responsible for the system.

Alternatively, you can obtain protocol analyzers and their source code for free. One such example of a high-quality protocol analyzer that has been ported to Unix and Windows environments is Ethereal. For more information on this free protocol analyzer, consult `www.ethereal.com`.

Network Management Protocol Support

Volumes have been written about the need for network management standards to assist in the centralized management of complex internetworks. Two network management protocols that have been considered for this task are SNMP and CMIP. SNMP, is used widely within the TCP/IP community; and the OSI network management protocol, known as *Common Management Information Protocol* (CMIP). SNMP is the predominant standard. Although there is some support for CMIP—Tekelec supports CMIP for WANs, and AR/Telenex supports IBM's NetView, CMIP implementations are largely extinct these days.

SNMP's ability to decode network management protocols serves several purposes. Developers of SNMP Agents or Managers can test their code for accuracy by capturing the Agent-Manager information. The analyzer can also determine response time delays between an Agent report and an associated Manager response. Because management data consumes network bandwidth, the analyzer can also measure the percentage of network management information versus user traffic on the network.

SNMP can be decoded by Micro Technology, Novell for LANs, Kamputech, Wandel & Goltermann, and Network General for LAN/WANs.

Novell initially incorporated SNMP into a network probe called LANtern. LANtern attached to an Ethernet/IEEE 802.3 network, and uses SNMP to communicate with an SNMP-compliant network management console. The network itself provided the communication path between probe and console, and the probe is the SNMP agent. Because LANtern was an Ethernet network monitor, not a protocol analyzer, it collected network statistics such as collisions, CRC errors, and frame errors, but performs no frame decoding. Experience with LANtern, enabled Novell to contribute to the development of the RMON (Remote Monitoring) MIBs and RMON device standards.

Another LAN analyzer vendor, FTP Software, offers an interesting product, known as SNMP Tools, which is based on FTP's well-known product PC/TCP. SNMP Tools runs on any DOS PC and is supported by a large number of LAN interface cards. It also offers a development kit for custom SNMP applications.

Integration with Network Simulation/Modeling Tools

When networks were host-centric or confined to a single location, it was much easier to calculate delay and response time parameters and forecast network growth. The wide distribution of network resources has made predicting these network performance metrics more difficult. Performing an analysis of the current internetwork can help with these predictions.

Analyzers have always done an amazing job of collecting reams of data. But what do you do with all that information? Early analyzers provided a hardcopy ASCII output of the captured data. Later analyzers could convert the data into a spreadsheet or database file format for further analysis. For example, the spreadsheet could sort traffic on a LAN by source address and bill the appropriate department for network usage.

Most products in the LAN market today integrate the LAN analyzer with a LAN simulation or modeling software tool such as BONeS (ComDisco Systems, Inc., Foster City, CA) or LANSIM (InternetiX, Inc., Upper Marlboro, MD). Quintessential Solutions, Inc. (San Diego, CA), a developer of WAN simulation and modeling tools, offers products with the ability to input data from WAN analyzers. A typical application is modeling the response time of a polled SNA circuit. Given the actual polling or response time delays from the analyzer, the QSI software can predict the changes in these variables resulting from increases in traffic, adding applications, and so on.

Simulation/modeling software is useful for a number of purposes, including initial network design, reconfiguration or redesign, and stress testing. Numerous variables (which exceed 100, depending on the network under study) specifying the number and type of workstations, servers, protocols in use, traffic loads, and so on must be entered into the model. The value of these variables can change the outcome of the simulation significantly. For example, network response time is a function of the number of servers plus the number of users logically attached to each one. If response time degrades, the administrator might consider redistributing the users or adding servers. Rather than making an educated guess about the network's traffic measurements, using actual data from the analyzer allows the simulation to provide a much more accurate representation of the network's characteristics. This facilitates the interactive process of network design, growth, and redesign.

Bytex, Network General, and Spider Systems are among the LAN analyzer vendors that can export their data to one of the simulation/modeling tools mentioned. In the future, simulation/modeling software will be directly incorporated into LAN analyzers.

Setting Up SNMP

SNMP enables network administrators to remotely troubleshoot and monitor hubs, routers, and other devices. Using SNMP, you can find out information about remote devices without having to be physically present at the device itself.

SNMP can be a useful tool if understood and used properly. You can obtain various amounts of information on a wide variety of devices, depending on the type. Some examples of information accessible using SNMP include the following:

- The IP address of a router
- The number of open files
- The amount of hard drive space available
- The version number of the software running on the host

SNMP uses a distributed architecture design to facilitate its properties. This means that various parts of SNMP are spread throughout the network to complete the task of collecting and processing data to provide remote management.

Because SNMP is a distributed system, you can spread out the management of it in different locations so as not to overtax any one system, and for multiple management functionality.

The SNMP provided by Microsoft enables a machine running Windows NT/2000 to transfer its current condition to a computer running an SNMP management system. However, this is only the agent side, not the management tools.

Other management utilities are available that are not included in Windows NT/2000, including the following:

- IBM NetView
- Sun Net Manager
- Hewlett-Packard OpenView

Configuring SNMP on Windows

The SNMP service can be installed for the following reasons:

- You want to monitor TCP/IP with Performance Monitor.
- You want to monitor a Windows NT/2000–based system with a third-party application.

The following steps for installing the SNMP service assume that you already have TCP/IP installed and set up, and that you have administrative privileges to install and use SNMP.

Installing the SNMP Service

To install the SNMP service, follow these steps:

1. Open the Network dialog box and from the Services tab, click Add. The Select Network Service dialog box appears.
2. Choose the SNMP service and click OK.
3. Specify the location of the Microsoft Windows NY distribution files.
4. After the files are copied, the Microsoft SNMP Properties dialog box appears. Enter the Community Name and Trap Destination.
5. Click OK to close the SNMP Properties dialog box, and then click Close to exit the Network dialog box. When prompted, click Yes to restart your computer.

Installing the Protocol

The first step in working with SNMP is to install the protocol. The following is a step-by-step process to walk you through the installation of the protocol:

1. Open the Network dialog box, and click the Services tab.
2. Choose Add, select the SNMP Agent, click OK, and enter the source directory.
3. Choose Close on the Network Setting dialog box and restart your system when prompted.

Using SNMPUTIL to Test SNMP

In order to perform this test, you will need a copy of the SNMPUTIL, which can be found in the Windows NT Resource Kit. If you do not have the Resource Kit, you can also find SNMPUTIL on the Internet (however, the Windows NT/2000 Resource Kit is recommended).

You will want to increase the number of lines in the command prompt to support this test. To do this, click the Control Menu box in the upper-left corner of the window and select Properties. On the Layout tab, change the height value to a higher number, such as 300.

Then, follow these steps:

1. Start a command prompt.

2. Enter the following commands:
```
SNMPUTIL get 127.0.0.1 public
.1.3.6.1.4.1.77.1.2.2.0
SNMPUTIL get 127.0.0.1 public
.1.3.6.1.4.1.77.1.2.24.0
```

3. Verify the numbers that you received. To verify the first number, click the Services icon in the Control Panel and count the number of services that are started. (Or type **NET START** from the prompt and count the services listed.)

4. To verify the second number, open the User Manager for Domains and count the number of users.

5. In User Manager for Domains, add a test user. Switch to the command prompt, and enter the second SNMPUTIL command again (use the up arrow to repeat the command).

6. Verify that the user you added increased the number, and then enter the following command:
```
SNMPUTIL walk 127.0.0.1 public
.1.3.6.1.4.1.77.1.2.25
```
This should list the names of all users.

7. Click the Services icon from the Control Panel again. Stop the Server service. It will warn you that this will also stop the Computer Browser service; this is fine.

8. Re-enter the command:
```
SNMPUTIL get 127.0.0.1 public
.1.3.6.1.4.1.77.1.2.2
```

9. Verify that the services are not running, and then enter the following command:
```
SNMPUTIL walk 127.0.0.1 public
.1.3.6.1.4.1.77.1.2.3.1.1
```
The services that are running will be listed. Server and Computer Browser should not be included on the list.

Note

You are still able to access this information using the sockets interface even though the server service is stopped. Remember that the server service is a NetBIOS server. Because you are communicating over sockets directly, you are able to use the SNMP agent, which uses UDP port 161 directly.

10. Restart the server service and the Computer Browser service.

11. Enter the following optional command if you want a list of all the information in the LAN Manager MIB:

```
SNMPUTIL walk 127.0.0.1 public
.1.3.6.1.4.1.77
```

Configuring SNMP on Unix

Under Unix, protocol statements enable and disable protocols and set protocol options. There are protocol statements for SNMP, RIP, Hello, ICMP Redirect, EGP, and BGP. The structure of these statements falls into two categories: one structure for interior protocols and one for exterior protocols. SNMP is the only exception to this. The format of the snmp statement is

```
snmp yes | no | on | off
```

This command controls whether gated registers information with the SNMP daemon. SNMP is not a routing protocol and is not started by this command. You must run SNMP software independently. This statement only controls whether gated keeps the management software apprised of its status. Reporting is enabled by specifying yes or on (it doesn't matter which you use) and it is disabled with no or off.

SNMP Security Parameters

You can set several options that affect the security of the SNMP agent. By default, the agent will respond to any manager using the community name "public." Because this can be inside or outside your organization, you should at the very least change the community name.

The following sections cover available security options.

Send Authentication Trap

The Send Authentication Trap ends a trap to the configured management station if an attempt is made to access SNMP from a manager that is not from the same community or that is not on the Only Accept SNMP Packets From list.

Accepted Community Names

Accepted community names is a list of community names that the agent will respond to. When a manager sends a query, a community name is included.

Accept SNMP Packets from Any Host

Accept SNMP Packets from Any Host responds to any query from any management system in any community.

Only Accept SNMP Packets from These Hosts

Only Accept SNMP Packets from These Hosts responds to only the hosts listed so that you can only monitor the specified hosts and ignore data from other hosts.

SNMP Agents and Management

The two main parts to SNMP are the management station and the agent:

- The *management station* is the centralized location from which you can manage SNMP.

- The *agent* resides in the piece of equipment from which you are trying to extract data.

Each of these parts is discussed in the following sections.

The SNMP Management System

The management system is the key component for obtaining information from the client; you need at least one to even be able to use the SNMP service. The management system is responsible for asking the questions. As mentioned earlier, there are a certain number of questions it can ask each device, depending upon the type of device. The management system is a computer running one of the various software packages mentioned earlier (see Figure 41.2).

FIGURE 41.2

*Most of the com-
munications
between an agent
and a manage-
ment station are
started from the
management
station.*

There are also certain commands that can be given specifically at the management system. These generic commands are not directly specific to any type of management system:

- get—Requires a specific value. For example, it can query how many active sessions are open.

- get-next—Requests the next object's value. For example, you can query a client's ARP cache and then ask for each subsequent value.

- set—Changes the value on an object that has the properties of read-write. This command is not often used because of security considerations and the fact that the majority of objects have a read-only attribute.

Usually, you have only one management system running the SNMP service per group of hosts. This group is known as a community. Sometimes, however, you may want to have more. Following are some reasons for wanting more than one management station:

- You may want to have multiple management systems monitoring different parts of the same agents.

- There might be different management sites for one community.

- As the network grows and becomes more complex, you may need to help differentiate certain aspects of your community.

SNMP Agents on Windows

You have seen what the SNMP management side is responsible for and can specifically do. For the most part, the management side is the active component for getting information.

The SNMP agent, on the other hand, is responsible for complying with the requests and responding to the SNMP manager accordingly. Generally, the agent is a router, server, or hub. The agent is usually a passive component responding only to a direct query.

In one particular instance, however, the agent is the initiator, acting on its own without a direct query. This special instance involves a *trap*. A trap is set up from the management side on the agent; however, the management system does not need to go to the agent to find out whether the trap information has been tripped. The agent sends an alert to the management system telling it that the event has occurred.

In some cases you will configure other aspects of the SNMP agent. These settings set the type of devices that you will monitor and who is responsible for the system.

The options available are as follows:

- **Contact**—This is the contact name of the person you want alerted about conditions on this station—generally the user of the computer.

- **Location**—This is a descriptive field for the computer to help keep track of the system sending the alert.

- **Service**—The items in this box identify the types of connections and devices this agent will monitor. These include the following:
  - **Physical.** This should be used if this system is managing physical devices such as repeaters or hubs.
  - **Applications.** Set this if the Windows NT/2000 computer uses an application that uses TCP/IP. This should always be selected.
  - **Datalink/Subnetwork.** Selecting this indicates this system is managing a bridge.
  - **Internet.** This should be selected if the Windows NT computer acts as an IP router.
  - **End-to-End.** Set this if the Windows NT/2000 computer uses TCP/IP. Obviously, this should always be selected.

Any errors with SNMP will be recorded in the system log, which records any SNMP activity. Use Event Viewer to look at the errors and to find the problem and possible solutions.

SNMP Tools and Commands

Now that you've learned a little about the management system and agents, you can delve into the different databases that you can query with SNMP commands.

The data that the management system requests from an agent is contained in a *Management Information Base* (MIB). This is a list of values the management system can ask for. (The list of values depends on what type of device it is asking.) The MIB is the database of information that can be queried against.

A variety of MIB databases can be established. The MIB is stored on the SNMP agent and is similar to the Windows Registry in its hierarchical structure. These MIBs are available to both the agents and management system as a reference from which both can pull information.

The SNMP service is an additional component of Windows NT/2000 TCP/IP software. It includes the four supported MIBs; each is a dynamic-link library and can be loaded and unloaded as needed. It provides SNMP agent services to any TCP/IP host running SNMP management software. It also performs the following:

- Reports special happenings, such as traps, to multiple hosts.
- Responds to requests for information from multiple hosts.

- Sets up counters in Performance Monitor that can be used to monitor the TCP/IP performance.

- Uses hostnames and IP addresses to recognize which hosts it receives and requests information.

The SNMP utility does not come with Windows NT/2000, but it is included in Unix and does come with the Windows NT/2000 Resource Kit. Basically, it is a command-line management system utility. It checks that the SNMP service has been set up and is working correctly; you can also use it to make command calls. You cannot do full SNMP management from this utility; but, as you will see, you would not want to because of its complex syntax.

The following is the general syntax structure of the SNMP utility:

```
snmputil command agent community object_identifier_(OID)
```

The following are the commands you can use:

- WALK—Moves through the MIB branch identified by what you have placed in the `object_identifier`.

- GET—Returns the value of the item specified by the `object_identifier`.

- GETNEXT—Returns the value of the next object after the one specified by the `get` command.

To find out the time the WINS server service began, for example, (provided WINS is installed and the SNMP agent is running) query the WINS MIB with the following command:

C:\>snmputil getnext localhost public
.1.3.6.1.4.1.311.1.1.1.1

In this example, the first part refers to the Microsoft branch: .1.3.6.1.4.1.311 (or `iso.org.dod.internet.private.enterprise.microsoft`). The last part of the example refers to the specific MIB and object you are querying: .1.1.1.1 (or `.software.Wins.Par.ParWinsStartTime`). A returned value may look like the following:

```
Value = OCTET STRING ñ 01:17:22 on 11:23:1997.<0xa>
```

RMON and Related MIB Modules

The objects and events for RMON are contained in five MIB modules (see Table 41.1).

TABLE 41.1 RFCs Relating to RMON

MIB Module	Description
RMON-MIB	RFC 1757: Remote Network Monitoring Management Information Base (called RMON1; defines 203 objects and 2 events)
TOKEN-RING-RMON-MIB	RFC 1513: Token Ring Extensions to the Remote Network Monitoring MIB (called Token Ring extensions for RMON1; defines 181 objects)
RMON2-MIB	RFC 2021: Remote Network Monitoring Management Information Base Version 2 (called RMON2, but also includes extensions for RMON1; defines 268 objects)
HC-RMON-MIB	Internet-draft: Remote Network Monitoring Management Information Base for High Capacity Networks (called HC-RMON, and contains extensions for RMON1 and RMON2; defines 184 objects)
SMON-MIB	Internet-draft: Remote Network Monitoring MIB Extensions for Switched Networks (called SMON or SWITCH-RMON; defines 52 objects)

In all, almost 900 objects are defined in the RMON MIB modules. This is a large number. For example, only 56 objects are in the MIB module for transparent bridges, and only 110 objects in the MIB module for Ethernet repeaters. In addition to the RMON MIB modules, the document *Remote Network Monitoring MIB Protocol Identifiers* (RFC 2074) contains the definition of the specification language for protocol identifiers and the first version of a list of protocols. Please note that to apply RMON in your network you do not need to understand all of these objects.

Building Requirements

Following is a list of steps to take to develop a requirement matrix associated with the management of network components and functions.

Develop a Detailed List of Information

First, you'll want to develop a list of information attainable from each managed object. Describe in detail each piece of information, such as what the data element is, average versus actual, counter, raw integer, or a text message.

Present List to Support Organization

Take the list to the support organization responsible for that device function and have them decide what's pertinent to their way of doing business. Focus on information that will enhance their ability to accomplish their job in an easier manner.

Formulate Your Reporting Strategy

Formulate the reporting strategy for the device.

Determine Information Needed for Alarm Reporting (Realtime)

The following elements of information are pertinent to alarm reporting:

- Establish thresholds; for example, three counts in a one-hour time period.
- Establish the priority of the alarm and any thresholds associated with priority escalation of the alarm.
- Establish any diagnostic processes that could be run automatically or that the Help Desk could perform to make their job easier.
- Establish acceptable polling intervals (every five minutes, ten minutes, one hour, and so on).

Determine Information Needed for Monthly Reporting

The following elements of information are pertinent to monthly reporting:

- Availability of devices and services
- Usage and load

Determine Information Needed for Performance Tuning

What elements of information are pertinent to trending and performance tuning of network components and functions?

Look at ways to combine data elements or perform calculations on the data to make it more useful to the support organization.

Interview Management

Interview management to ensure the Network Management System is managing all areas pertinent to the business unit. This interview processes ensures that the solution that you are proposing will meet the organization needs.

As part of interacting with the organization management, you should keep in mind the following:

- Explain the role and objectives of the Network Management System.
- Increase productivity throughout the support organizations.
- Reduce the Mean Time to Repair times on the correction of problems.
- Provide a proactive approach to the detection and isolation of problems.
- Enable collaboration and the flow of information across support departments and sites.

Here is a checklist that will help you gather management requirements:

- Gather the requirements for the management of any function important to the business unit.
- Don't limit these functions to only SNMP-manageable devices.
- If the devices associated with a function have no intelligence whatsoever, go back to management later with a proposal to upgrade the devices.

Implement the Requirements

Implement the requirements. Focus each implementation toward each requirement while integrating the total system. The specific techniques for accomplishing this are discussed in the following sections.

Alert Support Organization to Monitoring

After implementation of each piece, notify the support organization associated with the managed object or system that monitoring has started.

Revisit Requirements

To ensure that the initial requirements are still valid during the life cycle of a network, you should revisit the requirements periodically. The following is a list of things to consider when revisiting requirements:

- At the first reporting period, go back and revisit the requirements with each support organization and management.

- Reestablish requirements if necessary.
- Be advised that the reports and types of data will change as each support organization becomes better informed.

Keep the Help Desk Informed

During implementation, focus the alarm messages toward the Help Desk. Its personnel are the front line of any MIS organization. Keeping them well informed of problems is paramount to the successful deployment of the Network Management System.

Test Alarms

Perform dry runs of alarms and the diagnostic steps associated with getting the problem on the road to resolution in a quick and efficient manner. Have the appropriate support organizations participate so that all diagnostic steps can be identified and included. Don't leave out any management notifications that may be necessary.

Train the Help Desk to Troubleshoot

Train the Help Desk to input troubleshooting procedures pertinent to their function into the diagnostics table. This can include anything from a user calling in with a problem with an application (for example, MS Word), to filling out forms for a specific service to be provided to an end user.

Document Diagnostic Procedures

The skills associated with the support organizations in one Management Functional Domain (MFD) may be different from another MFD. The gathering of diagnostic procedures allows a sharing of the wealth of knowledge across the enterprise. The diagnostics procedures are a knowledge base of information, by symptom, of problems and tasking and what needs to be accomplished to correct the problem. Having the skills of Desktop Support, Unix System Support, Network Support, and so on at the fingertips of Help Desk personnel increases their ability to logically react to problems as they occur. The Network Management System, as a total integrated system, must be modular and easy to expand and contract as the needs of the business change.

Simplify Element Management Systems (EMSs)

Element Management Systems, whether they are third-party products such as SunNet Manager, HP OpenView, NetView 6000, NetView, NetMaster, 3M TOPAZ, Larsecom's Integra-T, or in-house developed pollers, need to be easy to integrate into the whole system. Recognize that in the architecture, no EMS is really aware of another. Awareness across EMS's needs to be accomplished at a higher layer so that the EMS's can focus on their area of management within their MFD.

Relying on Artificial Intelligence

Functions such as Alarm Correlation, Diagnostics across EMS's, and so on can be accomplished using artificial intelligence principles within a relational database. Almost all manner of Manager products employ risk assessment of how likely a component is to break. The risk assessment is often done by an expert systems component. The inclusion of the expert system component drives up the cost because of the complexity of software. These types of decisions need to be accomplished through the support organizations within the MFD because these folks know the local environment better than any machine or personnel at another site. Doesn't the overall application serve its purpose better if it is more tightly integrated into the business units?

Expert systems still need to be applied, but at a much different level. Network General Distributed Sniffer Servers are an excellent application of expert systems technology. By analyzing the relationships of protocols, traffic, connections, and LAN control mechanisms, the DSS uses expert systems to sort out problems at a very low level before they become user-identifiable problems and cause degradation or downtime.

Additionally, artificial intelligence can be used to capture the heuristics of network behavior and help with the diagnostics. The information available from past alarms of similar problems associated with what was accomplished to isolate and correct the problem needs to be incorporated into the overall system.

Summary

This chapter has covered Simple Network Management Protocol as it relates to Network Management. As you have seen, SNMP is a very simple protocol that can be used to look at the information stored in a Management Information B2zase. This allows management software (such as HP's OpenView) to read information from a Windows NT/2000 or Unix system.

If you intend to use SNMP, you must purchase SNMP management software. SNMP can be installed whether you are using it directly or not; this is done to allow the Performance Monitor counters to function correctly when using Windows NT/2000.

The following list summarizes the key points in this chapter:

- You need to understand that the SNMP agent is only an agent, and only an SNMP Manager API (no software) is provided.

- You need to know the three commands that a manager can send an agent: `set`, `get`, and `get-next`.

- You need to know what a trap (event notification) is, and that this is sent from the agent.

- You need to know the five areas the agent can monitor and where each is used: physical, applications, datalink/subnetwork, Internet, and end-to-end.

- You need to know how to install the agent.

- You need to know how to configure an authentication trap.

- You need to know how to configure the community names and the addresses of the stations that will be acting as managers.

- You need to understand the structure of an MIB and which four MIBs come with Windows NT/2000: LAN Manager MIB II, Internet MIB II, DHCP MIB, and WINS MIB.

- You need to know that the SNMP agent must be installed to enable the Performance Monitor counters.

Many excellent products are available today that provide capabilities to manage not just hardware, but services and applications. The ways that these systems are implemented are also critical in that each management capability installed must match a business need for such a system. Additionally, these diverse systems must be integrated together and into the support organizations to achieve maximum effectiveness.

SNMP: The Network Management Protocol

by Tim Parker

The previous chapter discusses network management issues and the network management tools. This chapter presents a more detailed look at the *Simple Network Management Protocol* (SNMP), which is used to administer network devices and obtain information about peripherals. SNMP is used on many TCP/IP networks, especially larger ones, because it makes administration much easier. SNMP was also designed to enable intelligent peripherals to send messages about their own states to special SNMP server software, relaying details about error conditions or other problems that may occur. A network administrator can use SNMP to reconfigure and obtain statistics about any node on the network that is capable of dealing with SNMP, all from one location.

What Is SNMP?

The Simple Network Management Protocol was originally designed to provide a means of handling routers on a network. SNMP, although it is part of the TCP/IP family of protocols, is not dependent on IP. SNMP was designed to be protocol-independent (so it could run under IPX from Novell's SPX/IPX just as easily, for example), although the majority of SNMP installations use IP.

SNMP actually has three components, which are

- **Management Information Base (MIB):** A database containing status information
- **Structure and Identification of Management Information (SMI):** A specification that defines the entries in an MIB
- **Simple Network Management Protocol (SNMP):** The method of communicating between managed devices and servers

Peripherals that have SNMP capabilities built-in run a management agent, either loaded as part of a boot cycle or embedded in firmware in the device. These devices with SNMP agents are called by a variety of terms depending on the vendor, but they are known as SNMP-manageable or SNMP-managed devices. SNMP-compliant devices also have the code for SNMP incorporated into their software or firmware. When SNMP exists on a device, it is called a *managed device*.

SNMP-managed devices communicate with SNMP server software located somewhere on the network. The two ways the device talks to the server are *polling* and *interruption*. A polled device has the server communicate with the device, asking for its current condition or statistics. The polling is often done at regular intervals, with the server connecting to all the managed devices on the network. The problem with polling is that information is not always current, and network traffic rises with the number of managed devices and frequency of polling.

An interrupt-based SNMP system has the managed device send messages to the server when some conditions warrant it. This way, the server knows of any problems immediately—unless the device crashes, in which case notification must be from another device that tried to connect to the crashed device. Interrupt-based devices have their own problems, too. Primary among the problems is the need to assemble a message to the server, which can require a lot of CPU cycles, all of which are taken away from the device's normal task. This can cause bottlenecks and other problems on that device. If the message to be sent is large, as it would be if it contains a lot of statistics, the network can suffer a noticeable degradation while the message is assembled and transmitted.

If a major failure occurs somewhere on the network, such as a power grid going down and uninterruptible power supplies kicking in, each SNMP-managed device may try to send interrupt-driven messages to the server at the same time to report the problem. This can swamp the network and result in incorrect information at the server.

A combination of polling and interruption is often used to get by all these problems. The combination, called *trap-directed polling*, involves the server polling for statistics at intervals or when directed by the system administrator or on receiving an SNMP trap message. In addition, each SNMP-managed device can generate an interrupt message when certain conditions occur, but these tend to be more rigorously defined than in a pure interrupt-driven system. For example, if you use interrupt-only SNMP, a router may report load increases every 10 percent. If you use trap-directed polling, you will know the load from the regular polling and can instruct the router to send an interrupt only when a significant increase in load is experienced. After receiving an interrupt message with trap-directed polling, the server can further query the device for more details, if necessary.

An SNMP server software package can communicate with the SNMP agents and transfer or request a number of different types of information. Usually, the server will request statistics from the agent, including number of packets handled, status of the device, special conditions associated with the device type (such as out-of-paper indications or loss of connection from a modem), and processor load.

The server can send instructions to the agent to modify entries in its database (the Management Information Base). The server can also send thresholds or conditions under which the SNMP agent should generate an interrupt message to the server, such as when CPU load reaches 90 percent.

Communications between the server and agent are accomplished in a fairly straightforward manner, although they use the ASN.1 (Abstract Syntax Notation Rev 1) for message contents. For example, the server might send a "What is your current load" message and receive back a "75%" message. The agent never sends data to the server unless an interrupt is generated or a poll request is made. This means that some long-standing problems can exist without the SNMP server knowing about them, simply because a poll wasn't conducted or an interrupt generated.

Management Information Base

Every SNMP-managed device maintains a database that contains statistics and other data. This database is called a Management Information Base, or MIB. The MIB entries have four pieces of information in them: an object type, a syntax, an Access field, and a Status field. MIB entries are usually standardized by the protocols and follow strict formatting rules defined by *Abstract Syntax Notation One* (ASN.1).

The object type is the name of the particular entry, usually as a simple name. The syntax is the value type, such as a string or integer. Not all entries in an MIB will have a value. The Access field is used to define the level of access to the entry, normally defined by the values read-only, read/write, write-only, and not accessible. The Status field contains an indication of whether the entry in the MIB is mandatory (which means the managed device must implement the entry), optional (the managed device may implement the entry), deprecated (on its way out to being obsolete), or obsolete (not used).

Two types of MIB are in use, called MIB-1 and MIB-2. The structures are different. MIB-1 was used starting in 1988 and has 114 entries in the table, divided into groups. For a managed device to claim to be MIB-1–compatible, it must handle all the groups that are applicable to it. For example, a managed printer doesn't have to implement all the entries that deal with the *Exterior Gateway Protocol* (EGP), which is usually implemented only by routers and similar devices. Instead, to be MIB-1–compatible, it needs to address only those issues a printer has to deal with.

MIB-2 is a 1990 enhancement of MIB-1, made up of 171 entries in 10 groups. The additions expand on some of the basic group entries in MIB-1 and add three new groups. As with MIB-1, an SNMP device that claims to be MIB-2–compliant must implement all those groups applicable to that type of device. You will find many devices that are MIB-1–compliant but not MIB-2–compliant.

In addition to MIB-1 and MIB-2, several experimental MIBs are in use that add different groups and entries to the database. None of these have been widely adopted, although some show promise. Some MIBs have also been developed by individual corporations for their own use, and some vendors offer compatibility with these MIBs. For example, Hewlett-Packard developed an MIB for its own use that some SNMP-managed devices and software server packages support.

Using SNMP

The Simple Network Management Protocol itself has been through several iterations. Usually SNMP is used as an asynchronous client/server application, meaning that either the managed device or the SNMP server software can generate a message to the other and wait for a reply, if one is expected. These are packaged and handled by the network software (such as IP) as would be any other packet. SNMP uses UDP as a message transport protocol. UDP port 161 is used for all messages except traps, which arrive on UDP port 162. Agents receive their messages from the manager through the agent's UDP port 161.

The first major release of SNMP, SNMP v1, was designed for relatively simple operation, relatively easy implementation by device manufacturers, and good portability to operating systems. SNMP v1 supports only five kinds of operations between server and agent:

- `get`—Used to retrieve a single entry in the MIB
- `get-next`—Used to move through the MIB entries
- `get-response`—The response to a `get`
- `set`—Used to change MIB entries
- `trap`—Used to report interrupt conditions

When a request is sent, some of the fields in the SNMP entry will be left blank. These are filled in by the client and returned. This is an efficient method of transferring the question and answer in one block, eliminating complex look-up algorithms to find out what query a received answer applies to.

The `get` command, for example, is sent with the Type and Value fields in the message set to `NULL`. The client sends back a similar message with these two fields filled in (unless they don't apply, in which case a different error message is returned).

SNMPs v2 added new capabilities to the older SNMP version. One such capability that is useful for servers was the new `get-bulk` operation, with which a large number of MIB entries can be sent in one message. (SNMP v1 required multiple `get-next` queries.) In addition, SNMP v2 has much better security than SNMP v1, keeping unwanted intruders from monitoring the state or condition of managed devices. Both encryption and authentication are supported by SNMPv2. Of course, SNMPv2 was a more complex protocol and is not as widely used as SNMP v1. Because of political problems in the development of SNMP v2, SNMP v2 was never widely implemented. The current version of SNMP is version 3, and it includes support for IP version 6, as well as improved security and administration.

SNMP allows proxy management, which means that a device with an SNMP agent and MIB can communicate with other devices that do not have the full SNMP agent software. This proxy management makes it possible to control other devices through a connected machine by placing the device's MIB in the agent's memory. For example, a printer can be controlled through proxy management from a workstation acting as an SNMP agent, which also runs the proxy agent and MIB for the printer. Proxy management can be useful to offload some devices that are under heavy load.

Despite its widespread use, SNMP has a few disadvantages. The most important is its reliance on UDP. Because UDP is connectionless, there is no reliability inherent in messaging between server and agent. Another problem is that SNMP provides only a simple messaging protocol, so filtering messages cannot be performed. This increases the load on the receiving software. Finally, SNMP almost always uses polling to some degree, which consumes a considerable amount of bandwidth.

The SNMP manager handles the overall software and communications between the devices using the SNMP communications protocol. Support software provides a user interface, enabling a network manager to observe the condition of the overall system and individual components and monitor any specific network device.

Unix and SNMP

When dealing with a very large network, SNMP is often the only way for an administrator to know what's going on with the devices on the network, as well as to get warnings about problems. SNMP is bundled with every Unix version available, is quite simple to set up, and after a quite steep learning curve, can be effectively used to manage networks with thousands of devices on them. For those running Linux, the approach is exactly the same as that for Unix.

This section looks at how to set up SNMP on a typical Unix system. As you can probably imagine, a GUI-based SNMP management software package is a lot friendlier than a character-based system, so many Unix vendors have special add-in SNMP administration applications.

Setting Up SNMP Under Unix and Linux

Most Unix versions include both the client and server software as part of the operating system. The client software is executed through the snmpd daemon, which usually runs all the time when SNMP is used on the network. Normally, the snmpd daemon is started automatically when the system boots, controlled through the rc startup files. When

SNMP starts, the daemon reads a number of configuration files. On most SNMP agents, the files snmpd reads are

/etc/inet/snmpd.conf

/etc/inet/snmpd.comm

/etc/inet/snmpd.trap

The directories these files are under may be different for each Unix version, so you should check the filesystem for the proper location.

The snmpd.conf file contains four system MIB objects. Most of the time these objects are set during installation, but you may want to verify their contents. Here is a sample snmpd.conf file:

```
descr=SCO TCP/IP Runtime Release 2.0.0
objid=SCO.1.2.0.0
contact=Tim Parker  tparker@tpci.com
location=TPCI Int'l HQ, Richmond
```

In many snmpd.conf files, you will have to fill out the contact and location fields yourself (which define the contact user and physical location of the system), but the descr and objid fields should be left as they are. The variables defined in the snmpd.conf file correspond to MIB variables in this manner:

descr	sysDescr
objid	sysObjectID
contact	sysContact
location	sysLocation

The snmpd.comm (community) file is used to provide authentication information and a list of hosts that have access to the local database. Access by a remote machine to the local SNMP data is provided by including the remote machine's name in the snmpd.comm file. A sample snmpd.comm file looks like this:

```
accnting    0.0.0.0       READ
r_n_d    147.120.0.1     WRITE
public   0.0.0.0      read
interop  0.0.0.0      read
```

Each line in the snmpd.comm file has three fields: the community name, the IP address of the remote machine, and the privileges the community has. If the IP address is set to 0.0.0.0, any machine may communicate with that community name. The privileges can be READ for read-only, WRITE for read and write, and NONE to prevent access by that community. Read and write access are references to capabilities to change MIB data, not filesystems.

The snmpd.trap file specifies the name of hosts to whom a trap message must be sent when a critical event is noticed. A sample snmpd.trap file looks like this:

```
superduck 147.120.0.23   162
```

Each line in the snmpd.trap file has three fields: the name of the community, its IP address, and the UDP port to use to send traps.

SNMP Commands

Unix offers a number of SNMP-based commands for network administrators to obtain information from an MIB or an SNMP-compliant device. The exact commands vary a little depending on the implementation, but most SNMP systems support the commands shown in Table 42.1.

TABLE 42.1   SNMP Commands

Command	Description
getone	Uses the SNMP get command to retrieve a variable value
getnext	Uses the SNMP getnext command to retrieve the next variable value
getid	Retrieves the values for sysDescr, sysObjectID, and sysUpTime
getmany	Retrieves an entire group of MIB variables
snmpstat	Retrieves the contents of SNMP data structures
getroute	Retrieves routing information
setany	Uses the SNMP set command to set a variable value

Most of the SNMP commands require an argument that specifies the information to be set or retrieved. The output from some of the commands given in Table 42.1 is shown in the following extract from an SNMP machine on a small local area network:

```
$ getone merlin udpInDatagrams.0
Name: udpInDatagrams.0
Value: 6
$ getid merlin public
Name: sysDescr.0
Value: UNIX System V Release 4.3
Name: sysObjectID.0
Value: Lachman.1.4.1
Name: sysUpTime.0
Value: 62521
```

None of the SNMP commands can be called user-friendly because their responses are terse and sometimes difficult to analyze. For this reason, many GUI-based SNMP network management systems have become popular. The use of a graphical interface offers a more effective environment for the operation of SNMP functions and the presentation of the resulting management data.

The use of a GUI-based SNMP tool enables the presentation of full-color graphical displays that can be used to relay network operational statistics in real-time. These tools are often complex and expensive to implement; however, once established they can provide an essential source for network monitoring and device management.

One of the most useful features of SNMP is that it provides network devices with the capability to signal error conditions and performance problems. The use of a GUI management station makes it possible to graphically represent this information within topological network maps.

Windows and SNMP

Windows NT/2000/XP, Windows 9x/ME, and Windows 98 can all participate to some extent in SNMP. There are drivers available for each operating system that let you act as an agent on an SNMP reporting network, and some operating systems such as Windows NT/2000/XP and Windows 9x/ME support administration agents. The following sections take a quick look at each operating system to see how SNMP is used on them.

Windows NT/2000

Windows NT/2000 provides a set of SNMP monitoring services that can be installed as a standard service. Begin by launching the Network applet from the Control Panel, and choose the Services page tab. If SNMP Services does not appear on the list, click the Add button, then scroll down the list of services to SNMP Services and add it to your system. After reading a set of drivers from the distribution list, a window with three page tabs will appear in which you can add configuration information.

The first SNMP page, shown in Figure 42.1, is for the SNMP Administrator's contact information. The two fields at the top of the page are for the administrator's name and location. These fields are optional and don't have to be filled in, but doing so makes it easier for someone to find out who the SNMP administrator is across a network. The lower part of the window shows the services on which SNMP is to be used. The default values are the best set for most networks.

FIGURE 42.1

The SNMP Agent page tab.

The Traps page tab, shown in Figure 42.2, is used to enter the name of SNMP communities that are to be watched. Any community listed will be monitored for error traps. Usually, all machines on a network are members of the public community. If you do enter information into this page, it lets you specify an IP address for each community's SNMP monitoring device. This lets you route SNMP traps from a community called "research" to the research SNMP manager, for example.

FIGURE 42.2

The SNMP Traps page tab.

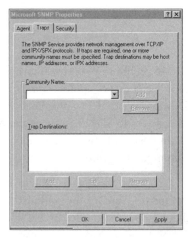

The last page tab in the SNMP Services window is the Security tab, shown in Figure 42.3. This window can be used to restrict access to the SNMP service based on community and console. The lower screen has two buttons that let you force SNMP to accept requests only from certain devices.

FIGURE 42.3

The SNMP Security page tab.

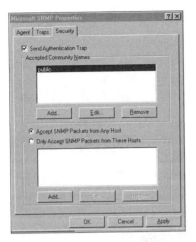

After this process is completed, Windows NT will reboot and the SNMP Services will be active.

Windows 9x/ME

A number of Windows 9x/ME SNMP agents are becoming available, mostly public domain or shareware, readily found using Web search engines. Windows SNMP agents tend to allow you to monitor networks, some report SNMP problems, and a few allow you to manage a network from a Windows platform.

One of the most popular Windows 9x/ME tools is NetGuardian, developed at the University of Lisbon. NetGuardian requires a TCP/IP stack or Trumpet WinSock. Usually distributed as a .ZIP file, NetGuardian unpacks into a directory and does not need linking into the Windows kernel or special loading of drivers. This makes it very easy to use (and ignore when you don't need it). One of the best features of NetGuardian is its interface, which is about as simple as you can get with a complex subject like SNMP.

The main window for NetGuardian is shown in Figure 42.4. The figure shows a network map with all the machines that NetGuardian knows about on the diagram. A big X through the machine means NetGuardian can't connect to it (which isn't surprising, because this is the default setup sent with the NetGuardian package and represents machines in Europe!). To have NetGuardian search your own network, you need to select the Discover option from the Net menu. This will display a window that asks for a range of IP addresses to search, as shown in Figure 42.5.

FIGURE **42.4**

The NetGuardian
window showing
a network map.

FIGURE **42.5**

When discovering
a network,
NetGuardian asks
for a range of IP
addresses.

After a check of each machine in the range you specify, NetGuardian shows the results in a new map. Figure 42.6 shows a simple network with only three machines reporting their presence. NetGuardian discovers machines on the network by pinging each address in the range you specify.

FIGURE **42.6**

The NetGuardian
network map with
three machines
reporting active
on a network.

Using the simple NetGuardian interface, an administrator (or a curious user) can check on machines that are active on the network, add or remove items from the network map, and rearrange network maps so they look different. The NetGuardian package is very easy to learn and use, and has a number of special features that many SNMP packages lack (such as the graphing of net performance, shown in Figure 42.7).

FIGURE 42.7

A graph of network performance from NetGuardian.

42

SNMP: THE
NETWORK
MANAGEMENT
PROTOCOL

> **Note**
>
> You can get a copy of NetGuardian from a number of places on the Web, or from anonymous FTP through ftp.fc.ul.pt in the directory /pub/networking/ snmp/netg*XXX*.zip, where *XXX* is the version number.

Summary

SNMP is a simple, effective method of managing network devices. It has grown in complexity and popularity since its inception in 1988 and is the management system of choice. The simple nature of SNMP is one of its major advantages because vendors of peripherals can incorporate SNMP capabilities into their devices with minimal effort. For the network administrator, though, SNMP is nothing short of a wonderful tool.

## CHAPTER 43

Securing TCP/IP Transmissions

by Anne Carasik

IN THIS CHAPTER

As much as networking is about having access, in today's world it's just as important to have security. You need to determine whether applications should be allowed access to network services based on the TCP port they use. Also, you can secure TCP/IP through *Virtual Private Networks* (VPNs) to create a secure tunnel without having to secure the application itself.

Defining Required Network Security

When you define a network security policy, you need to define what network traffic and what network applications you allow outbound and inbound (if any). Unless you have an absolute need (and it should be well-defined if you do), do not allow inbound network packets if you can avoid it. Too many "script kiddies" are out there who can download a script from a hacking site and easily access your network if you're not careful.

If you do allow inbound traffic, make sure you're extremely careful in monitoring the software running on the inbound port and make sure you make patches to the software as soon as it becomes available.

Another option you have is cryptographic applications such as Secure Shell, Secure Sockets Layer (SSL), and VPN products that allow you to have better authentication and encryption with public key ciphers. It's also a good solution for outbound traffic—you don't want people sending out unencrypted information like passwords to your business partner's site.

What Is Network Security?

Network security, in its simplest sense, can be defined as what network traffic is allowed in and out of a network. A network can be a subnet in a *Local Area Network* (LAN) or it can cover an entire region, such as a *Wide Area Network* (WAN).

One way to define network security is to segment a network to include *chokepoints*, such as a firewall or router. On a firewall or router, you can define what types of network traffic and network applications are allowed through the chokepoint.

A chokepoint works like a filter. It allows only certain network traffic through (inbound, outbound, or both). For example, e-mail is crucial for business. In a very simple network security policy, e-mail should be allowed inbound and outbound on port 25 for *Simple Mail Transfer Protocol* (SMTP). All other traffic should be blocked and not allowed through.

Figure 43.1 shows examples of various chokepoints.

FIGURE 43.1
*How chokepoints
separate various
networks.*

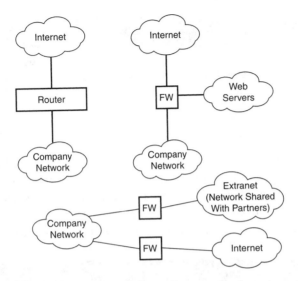

Why Is Network Security Important?

As the number of users on the Internet continues to grow, so does the need for security. Many more people and businesses are susceptible to an attack. The following are some of the reasons attacks occur:

- Someone wants to obtain sensitive information about you or your company.
- Someone is testing his penetration testing skills and decides to use you as a guinea pig.
- Because it's a fun thing to do.

Security Levels

Network security is also defined by access—who has it and who doesn't. With network security, certain users can have administrative privileges, whereas others have a general level of privileges that all users have.

There are also many levels of security between the administrators and the users. Some administrators have limited access to one system, whereas others may have access to several systems. For example, there may be an administrator for the development system, while someone else administers the firewalls.

Many operating systems, such as Unix and Windows NT/2000, have administrator accounts (on Unix, this is the root account) and general user accounts. These represent the two extremes of network security. Other levels of access include users with some administrator privileges but not others, and a general account such as guest.

43

SECURING TCP/IP
TRANSMISSIONS

> **Note**
>
> Be very careful adding accounts like "guest," which come by default with some Unix systems and Windows NT/2000. You'll want to disable them before you connect your system to the network, especially if you have critical information on it.

Some operating systems, such as HP-UX CMW (Compartmented Mode Workstation), which is used in the HP-UX Virtual Vault, use a compartmentalized version of HP-UX. Access is defined by four different levels, and there is no one administrator account. The administrator privileges are divided among several accounts. The four different levels are *system high*, *system low*, *system outside*, and *system inside*, as illustrated in Figure 43.2.

> **Note**
>
> Certain operating systems, like Windows NT/2000, automatically assign the "Everyone" group full control (read, write, delete, and execute) of items. Users should want to go in and redefine their permissions appropriately (such as removing "everyone" access). Also, administrators should do the same on critical system and network files.

FIGURE 43.2

The compartmentalized access for HP-UX CMW.

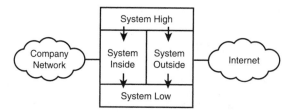

You can read down, and write to an equal level, but you cannot write or read up.

Within the four different levels, a user cannot write up but can read down. Reading and writing on the same level are permitted. For example, someone who is using his administrator account in the system low compartment cannot write to system high.

> **Note**
>
> For more information on the Virtual Vault, go to `http://www.hp.com/security/products/virtualvault`.

Passwords and Password Files

Passwords are the most common way to verify a user's access to an account. There are other means, including biometrics (which authenticates on physical attributes) and public key cryptography. However, most network authentication protocols and applications still use passwords.

The problem with passwords is that they are easy to bypass. Some password schemes do not have strong encryption mechanisms, and others allow ways to bypass the password mechanisms altogether. However, even if the password mechanisms are implemented properly, there are other problems.

Unfortunately, most passwords are easy to crack because users want something easy to remember. Many people will pick a password found in the dictionary or use their birthdate, phone number, dog's name, or something equally as easy to discover about them.

As a result, many administrators are requiring users to pick strong passwords. There is software available that will pick strong passwords or force people to use them.

A strong password includes the following:

- Alphanumeric characters (numbers and letters)
- Mixed cases (upper- and lowercase)
- Special characters (!@#$%^&*_-=+\|?/>)—adding <.,"':~`)

These decrease the likelihood that a password will be cracked in a relatively short time.

An example of a strong password is

```
%Ji928a*jpeijAjdkljW
```

The problem with this password, however, is that you couldn't remember it. You would have to write it down, which is a security risk in itself. Instead, you'll want to use a phrase that you remember and write it in a license plate fashion:

```
iLuv2c0mputePrimez!
```

This would not be easy for someone to crack with a dictionary attack.

> **Tip**
>
> Adding a space to your password also helps make it more secure.

Also, the time to change the password should be enforced. Many secure sites usually require a password change every 90 days. They also require that you do not reuse a password because that is a security risk as well.

If you want to see the value of strong passwords, run a test machine (without any critical information on it and remove it from the network) and create dummy user accounts. Make some passwords easy to crack, and others with different levels of strength. Software is available to allow you to test how long it will take to break a password. Table 43.1 shows you a list of some freeware password crackers you can use to test the value of your passwords.

TABLE 43.1   Password Crackers

Program	Location
Crack	`http://www.cs.purdue.edu/COAST`
L0phtcrack	`http://www.10pht.com`
John the Ripper	`http://www.openwall.com/john/`

Controlling Access to Passwords

Passwords should be stored in an encrypted file or database to prevent users from reading others' passwords and logging in to those accounts.

Passwords are stored in various locations depending on the operating system. Table 43.2 shows you the location of some password files.

TABLE 43.2   Location of Local Password Files on Different Operating Systems

Operating System	Password File Location
Windows NT	Registry
Unix	`/etc/passwd` or `/etc/shadow`

The permissions and ownership to the password files need to be set properly. For example, the password file on Unix should only be accessible by root, and if the passwords are shadowed, the shadow file should only be readable by root and not other users.

On more secure versions of Unix, such as the HP-UX CMW and the B1 Solaris, passwords are stored in a database or multiple files. This prevents someone from accessing one file and trying to crack all the passwords at one time.

Enforcing Network Security

Enforcing network security is always the biggest challenge because it involves getting users to agree to policies and follow them. Many people will not follow security policies if they do not benefit from them. However, ways exist to help you enforce and even improve your network security.

Types of Attacks

In the world of network security, there are several types of attacks, which are explained in the following sections.

Trojan Horses

Trojan horses are programs that are disguised as another program, but really get information for a hacker. For example, someone can substitute a fake network login program and obtain your username and password, and it just sends you error messages. After the fake program gets the information, it mails it to the attacker.

Trojan horses do not just gather information. They are really destructive programs that masquerade as benign ones. Trojan horses do not replicate themselves and are therefore not technically viruses. For example, a Trojan horse can masquerade as a Unix login where you try to log in and it prints out error messages. Each time you type your password, it is stored on the system for later access.

Backdoors

Backdoors are hidden in a program or operating system and are not known by the public, so someone can obtain access by overriding any security measures in place.

Denial of Service/Quality of Service

Denial of Service and Quality of Service attacks either bring down a network service completely (for example, a Web server) or slow it down considerably, affecting its performance and making users very unhappy.

Network Attacks

Network attacks include scanning ports for an opening. For example, port 5641 on Windows NT/2000 and Windows 9x is the PCAnywhere port. This port will prompt you for a username and password. As a result, someone can use brute force to get a password or username or obtain backdoor information from PCAnywhere.

Spoofing

Spoofing is pretending to be a user or host that you're not. One of the biggest problems that the Berkeley r-utilities have is that they can be easily tricked. The only thing that the r-utilities trust is the hostname, so they do not check to make sure the hostname is coming from the right place and the right machine.

The r-utilities can be tricked because hostname and username authentication can be easily faked. For example, you can change the hostname on a system on the outside to the same as a trusted system on the inside. Unfortunately, there is nothing that will check to make sure the system you connect from is the actual trusted system. You can spoof the hostname and trick the r-utilities that way.

> **Note**
>
> Today's routers have anti-spoofing mechanisms for IP addresses to help prevent this type of thing, but they do not affect the hostname. You can also define rules that do not allow the r-utilities to have traffic inbound as well.

Password Cracking

If someone is able to get hold of the password file or the NT/2000 registry, he can download freeware off the Internet and get password crackers. Provided the person has the time, he can eventually crack at least one of the passwords and obtain access to a computer.

Software Exploits and Buffer Overflows

A common method of attack today is to check a software program for an exploit, or a hole in the program, that allows someone to get root or administrator access from a program that does not panic when too much information is entered. This makes the program choke, and produces a memory dump. This type of exploit is known as a *buffer overflow*.

Many network applications, such as sendmail and NFS, have many exploits and are considered insecure network applications.

> **Note**
>
> There are other options for STMP in addition to sendmail, such as qmail, which is a secure mail server package. You can find out more about it at
> http://www.qmail.org/.

> Even though NFS is insecure and a necessity, there is an alternative known as Andrew File System (AFS). For more information on AFS, take a look at `http://www.faqs.org/faqs/afs-faq/`.

Improper Permissions

If a file on Unix or Windows NT/2000 has improper permissions, someone may have the ability to run a program as root (or Administrator) and either crash the system or open an application exploit. When an application is opened with improper permissions, someone can exploit the system and gain root or Administrator privileges.

If root or Administrator owns a file which others can write to, someone can change the contents of the file or application to give a local or remote user root or Administrator privileges without the root or administrator knowing.

Virus

A virus is a program that attaches itself to another program without anyone knowing. The sole purpose of a virus is to cause damage to a computer, including remapping the keyboard, destroying the contents to a hard drive, or wiping out only a particular type of file.

Many companies make antivirus software. The key to making the antvirus software work effectively is to make sure the virus profiles, or databases, are updated at least monthly.

However, the latest and greatest craze in the Internet is to declare every problem a virus. Many programs (such as Netbus and Back Orifice) that are Trojan horses and backdoors are considered viruses by the virus companies. Even though these programs technically are not viruses, virus companies do help detect and prevent a world of problems that would otherwise bring a system to its knees. Some organizations run more than one virus detection software in the hope that if one virus detection software cannot detect a virus, the others can.

Social Engineering

Social engineering, which is obtaining access by feigning you need access, is the hardest form of network security exploit to fight. Someone can con a system support person into giving him or her a password over the phone, thereby giving him or her access.

Social engineering also includes such methods as bribing or tricking employees into giving you their access information or leaving you alone with access to their computer. Another method involves pretending to be a delivery person to try to gain access to computers. The movies *Sneakers* and *Mission: Impossible* are both very good examples of social engineering to get access to a network.

43

SECURING TCP/IP
TRANSMISSIONS

Enforcing Network Security

This section shows you some of the things you can do to enforce your network security. Keep in mind that resources like time, people, and how much sleep you want play into how much enforcement you can actually do with your network security.

User Education and Re-Education

Believe it or not, education is the most important thing you can do to enforce your network security. You need to make sure that employees, both new and old, are familiar with your network security policy and that they believe in it. Provided they do and it becomes part of the corporate culture, then you can enforce things like securing passwords, keeping smart cards and private keys in secure locations, and making sure people don't share critical files.

Intrusion Detection Systems

Intrusion detection systems detect unusual network traffic including Denial of Service attacks and using uncommon packets like Windows OOB (Out of Bound packet) that can cause a system to crash. This can help you track down someone trying to attack your system. Table 43.3 shows some intrusion-detection systems available.

TABLE 43.3   Intrusion-Detection Systems

System	Location
Network Flight Recorder	http://www.nfr.com
RealSecure	http://www.iss.net
NetProwler	http://www.symantec.com

Penetration Testing

Penetration testing is breaking into your own network through known security holes. This is the most effective way to make sure your network is secure; however, it is also the most controversial because many hackers have become highly sought after by consulting firms that offer penetration testing services. Even if you don't use the consulting services, you should run penetration tests against your own system for a minimal check to make sure that no obvious holes exist in your network.

Plenty of software is available to help you with penetration testing. Many Web sites have hacker's code available for you to download and compile to test on your own system.

Many commercial and freeware programs are available from the security community as well. Table 43.4 lists some penetration testing software that is available.

TABLE 43.4   Penetration Testing Software

Software	Location
Internet Security Scanner	http://www.iss.net
SATAN	http://www.fish.com/satan/
Nessus	http://www.nessus.org
Cybercop	http://www.nai.com

File Integrity

One of the most fundamental ways to determine whether someone has gained access to your system is to check whether files have changed. Programs are available that can check whether the file system has changed or whether a file has been altered. This technique can help find what has been altered and whether a system administrator is changing the files or whether someone is really attacking the system. Table 43.5 shows some file integrity software that is available.

TABLE 43.5   File Integrity Software

Software	Location
Tripwire	http://www.tripwiresecurity.com
COPS	http://www.cerias.purdue.edu/coast/
Tiger	http://www.cerias.purdue.edu/coast/
System Scanner	http://www.iss.net

Log Monitoring

Log monitoring is the simplest and cheapest way to check for attacks. You look at your logs for strange activity. This, unfortunately, is also one of the most time-consuming and tedious things you can ever do. Another problem with checking your logs is that you cannot prove they have not been altered. If someone has gained administrator or root access to your computer, he or she has the ability to change the logs and cover his or her own tracks.

43

**SECURING TCP/IP
TRANSMISSIONS**

Configuring Applications

To ensure a secure network, you need to configure your applications properly and, if you can, securely. Properly configuring network applications is key to network security. Some important things to remember include the following:

- Only use applications you absolutely need.
- Turn off everything you don't need.
- Secure the applications you run as best as you can.
- Networks are designed for access. Anytime you allow network access, you create an opening to your network and thus risk allowing someone not meant to have access a way in.

The Internet Daemon and `/etc/inetd.conf`

Most of the applications on Unix can be turned off in `/etc/inetd.conf`. The `/etc/inetd.conf` file controls what network application daemons are run by the Internet super daemon, `inetd`.

> **Note**
>
> There is more information on `inetd` and `/etc/inetd.conf` in Chapter 39, "Protocol Configuration and Tuning."

A new system where the `/etc/inetd.conf` file has not been edited and configured may look like this:

```
#
# Authors:     Original taken from BSD Unix 4.3/TAHOE.
#              Fred N. van Kempen, <waltje@uwalt.nl.mugnet.org>
#
echo     stream    tcp    nowait    root      internal
echo     dgram     udp    wait      root    internal
discard    stream    tcp    nowait    root      internal
discard    dgram    udp    wait    root    internal
daytime    stream    tcp    nowait    root      internal
daytime    dgram    udp    wait    root    internal
chargen    stream    tcp    nowait    root      internal
chargen    dgram    udp    wait    root    internal
time    stream    tcp    nowait    root    internal
time    dgram    udp    wait      root    internal
```

```
# These are standard services.
#
ftp     stream  tcp   nowait root   /usr/sbin/tcpd   in.ftpd -l -a
telnet  stream  tcp   nowait root   /usr/sbin/tcpd   in.telnetd
#
# Shell, login, exec, comsat and talk are BSD protocols.
#
shell   stream  tcp   nowait   root   /usr/sbin/tcpd   in.rshd
login   stream  tcp   nowait   root   /usr/sbin/tcpd   in.rlogind
#exec   stream  tcp   nowait   root   /usr/sbin/tcpd   in.rexecd
#comsat dgram   udp   wait     root   /usr/sbin/tcpd   in.comsat
talk    dgram   udp   wait     root   /usr/sbin/tcpd   in.talkd
ntalk   dgram   udp   wait     root   /usr/sbin/tcpd   in.ntalkd
#dtalk  stream  tcp   waut     nobody /usr/sbin/tcpd        in.dtalkd
#
# Pop and imap mail services et al
#
#pop-2  stream  tcp     nowait root     /usr/sbin/tcpd      ipop2d
pop-3   stream  tcp     nowait root     /usr/sbin/tcpd      ipop3d
imap    stream  tcp     nowait root     /usr/sbin/tcpd      imapd
#
```

In this case, any service that does not have a comment (#) in front of it is an active network application that inetd runs. If you want to keep this system so that the only network application daemons running are FTP and Telnet, the new /etc/inetd.conf file looks like this:

```
#
# Authors:      Original taken from BSD Unix 4.3/TAHOE.
#         Fred N. van Kempen, <waltje@uwalt.nl.mugnet.org>
#
#echo          streamtcp  nowait   root   internal
#echo          dgramudp   wait         root   internal
#discard    streamtcp  nowait   root   internal
#discard    dgramudp   wait         root   internal
#daytime    streamtcp  nowait   root   internal
#daytime    dgramudp   wait         root   internal
#chargen    streamtcp  nowait   root   internal
#chargen    dgramudp   wait         root   internal
#time          streamtcp  nowait   root   internal
#time          dgramudp   wait         root   internal

# These are standard services.
#
ftp   stream   tcp   nowait   root   /usr/sbin/tcpd   in.ftpd -l -a
telnet  stream  tcp   nowait   root   /usr/sbin/tcpd   in.telnetd
#
# Shell, login, exec, comsat and talk are BSD protocols.
#
```

```
#shell   stream  tcp   nowait   root   /usr/sbin/tcpd   in.rshd
#login   stream  tcp   nowait   root   /usr/sbin/tcpd   in.rlogind
#exec    stream  tcp   nowait   root   /usr/sbin/tcpd   in.rexecd
#comsat  dgram   udp   wait     root   /usr/sbin/tcpd   in.comsat
#talk    dgram   udp   wait     root   /usr/sbin/tcpd   in.talkd
#ntalk   dgram   udp   wait     root   /usr/sbin/tcpd   in.ntalkd
#dtalk   stream  tcp   waut     nobody /usr/sbin/tcpd   in.dtalkd
#
# Pop and imap mail services et al
#
#pop-2   stream  tcp        nowait  root   /usr/sbin/tcpd   ipop2d
#pop-3   stream  tcp        nowait  root   /usr/sbin/tcpd   ipop3d
#imap    stream  tcp        nowait  root   /usr/sbin/tcpd   imapd
#
```

Now, with everything commented out, the only network application daemons running are FTP and Telnet. This means that known insecure applications like echo, login, shell, and finger are disabled and no one can connect to your computer using those services.

Note

Note that Telnet and FTP are not secure applications themselves. They send passwords in plain text, and they can be read by a packet sniffer.

Encryption Network Software

One of the best ways you can secure your TCP/IP transmissions is with encryption software. This includes Secure Sockets Layer (SSL), which is used to encrypt http traffic; Secure Shell (SSH), which is usually used to encrypt terminal and X traffic; and Virtual Private Network (VPN), which is used to create tunnels usually between two remote sites through the Internet or a client connecting to a main site through the Internet.

SSL and SSH can be used to create secure tunnels for other applications including POP3, IMAP, and FTP. When you use SSL or SSH, you use public keys (RSA or DSA, for example) for authenticating and usually symmetric ciphers for encryption (DES, triple DES, or IDEA).

VPNs are usually used to allow all insecure network traffic from one end to another. For example, file sharing, which is very insecure, can be secured by using VPNs without having to re-create the network application from the ground up.

> **Note**
>
> More information on SSH can be found at `http://www.employees.org/~satch/`
> `ssh/faq`. You can find more information on SSL at `http://psych.psy.uq.oz.au/`
> `~ftp/Crypto/`. For more information on VPNS, take a look at
> `http://www.vpnc.org`.

TCP Wrappers

Many network applications can be secured with TCP Wrappers. These Wrappers enable a way to track and limit access to network applications that are run by `inetd`. They also enable an audit trail and a way to control who has access to certain network applications like `finger`, `rsh`, and `ftp`.

In order to get a network application daemon to work with TCP Wrappers, you need to make sure that TCP Wrappers is installed and configured properly on your system. When you run a TCP application through TCP Wrappers, it is considered wrapped.

To install TCP Wrappers, just uncompress the tar archive and run `make`:

```
# gzip -dc tcp_wrappers-7.6.tar.gz | tar -xvf -
# cd tcp_wrappers-7.6
# make
```

Next, you'll need to follow the instructions for installing TCP Wrappers for your environment.

After that, you'll need to configure `/etc/inetd.conf`, `/etc/hosts.deny`, and `/etc/hosts.allow`. The two configuration files that TCP Wrappers used for access control are `/etc/hosts.allow` and `/etc/hosts.deny`. In order to use TCP Wrappers, you need to have the network application daemons run by the TCP Wrapper program, `tcpd`.

To add an entry for wrapped network application through `/etc/inetd.conf`, the basic format looks like this:

```
netappd      stream tcp      nowait  root     /usr/sbin/tcpd  netappd
```

This will fork a new process for `netappd` from `/etc/inetd.conf` on each request to Secure Shell (SSH).

Assume with the previous example that you still only want to run FTP and Telnet. To start an FTP wrapped daemon, the entry will change from

```
ftp    stream   tcp   nowait   root   /usr/sbin/in.ftpd   in.ftpd -l -a
```

43

to the following:

```
ftp    stream    tcp    nowait    root    /usr/sbin/tcpd    in.ftpd -l -a
```

You'll want to make sure your /etc/hosts.deny is set so no one can access your system through TCP Wrappers applications. This prevents any host not defined in /etc/hosts.allow from being allowed in. To keep everyone out except for those you specify, you'll want to put this entry in /etc/hosts.deny:

```
ALL : ALL
```

After creating your /etc/hosts.deny, you need to add entries for ftpd to /etc/hosts.allow. A simple /etc/hosts.allow file for a wrapped FTP and Telnet daemon looks something like this:

```
in.ftpd: example.com: allow
in.telnetd: example.com : allow
```

This will allow in only clients from the example.com. The basic format for the /etc/hosts.allow and /etc/hosts.deny looks like this:

```
deamons: clients: allow/deny
```

In the following example, you don't trust any clients from the evil.org domain. In this case, you would define your /etc/hosts.deny to look like this:

```
in.fingerd: evil.org: deny
```

> **Note**
>
> You can find more information about TCP Wrappers at ftp://ftp.porcupine.org/pub/security.

Using Ports and Trusted Ports

Ports are used by Unix and Windows NT/2000 services.

If someone runs a port scan and checks to see whether the port is open, usually he or she will check what type of application runs on that port. This port may be a backdoor or it may be a way to flood packets to the machine, thus bringing it to its knees in a Denial of Service attack.

Firewalls

A firewall is a chokepoint on a network that determines what types of network applications are allowed through. Most firewall products only work on TCP/IP networks, although other firewall products may work on other networks such as IPX.

Firewalls do provide logging functionality, so you can see which applications are being run and which ones are being dropped or blocked from going out or coming in to your network. Many firewalls have built-in definitions of what applications are allowed through.

> **Note**
>
> Just because a firewall allows insecure connections like NFS and Berkeley "r" commands through does not mean you should configure your firewall to do so.

A firewall is only as secure as you make it. You need to make sure you do not enable unsecure applications because they defeat the purpose of having a firewall.

Packet Filters

Packet filters check the packet to make sure it's going through an allowed port. The contents of the packet are not checked. For example, a router can be a packet filter that just lets packets go in and out through certain ports but does not check the content. Despite the fact that packet filters do not check the content of the packet, they are very quick and provide very fast performance.

Application Gateway

In addition to the port being checked, the packet itself is checked to make sure that the contents of the packet match the application it is trying to connect to. An application gateway checks everything on the packet, including the type of application it connects to. Because the application gateway has so much information on each packet to check, performance takes a considerable hit compared to a packet filter. This also prevents an application gateway from being very scalable.

Many application gateways provide additional functionality such as VPN support, work in conjunction with intrusion detection systems, and provide router management.

Application gateways have a difficult time detecting what application an encrypted packet for Secure Shell (SSH) or *Secure Sockets Layer* (SSL) connects to. In this case, the application gateway acts more like a packet filter.

Other Application Filters

Checkpoint, Novell's BorderManager, and Cisco PIX use *stateful inspection*, which is a hybrid of an application gateway and a packet filter. The inspection checks the contents of the packet, but not to the extent that an application gateway does.

> **Note**
>
> For more information on firewalls, see Chapter 20, "Firewalls."

Summary

When securing TCP/IP transmissions, it's important to define what TCP/IP traffic you need. It's also important to define a chokepoint, which is what will be a gatekeeper for allowing certain types of traffic in and out of your network.

You can also define which network services you want running. When you do this, you define which network applications need to be configured properly to make sure you secure your transmissions.

Even though most network applications are considered insecure, you can run network encryption applications such as Secure Shell, Secure Sockets Layer, and Virtual Private Networks. These applications will help protect you from someone eavesdropping or hijacking your session.

Troubleshooting Tools and Issues

by Bernard McCargo

Because most problems have a simple cause, developing a clear understanding of the problem often provides the solution. Unfortunately this is not always true, so this section begins to discuss the tools that can help you attack the most intractable problems. Many diagnostic tools are available, ranging from commercial systems with specialized hardware and software that may cost thousands of dollars, to free software available from the Internet. This chapter emphasizes free or "built-in" diagnostic tools.

There are a few reasons for this emphasis. First, a commercial system that costs thousands of dollars should be fully documented. Second, many administrators can't buy commercial diagnostic tools, but everyone has access to the free tools. Finally, most network problems can be solved using the free diagnostic software. Large networks probably need a commercial *time domain reflectometer* (TDR), but many smaller networks can make do with the publicly available diagnostic software.

The tools used in this chapter, and many more, are described in RFC 1147.

Monitoring Network Behavior

To approach a problem properly, you need a basic understanding of how to monitor the network. Without some type of third-party or built-in network monitoring system, troubleshooting network problems would be very time consuming.

Monitoring the network behavior allows you to perform preventative maintenance before a problem occurs. If a problem does occur, it provides you the ability to gather detailed information about exactly what's happening. When the problem is reported, review what was recorded on the network monitoring system. Find out which application failed. What is the remote host's name and IP address? What is the user's hostname and address? What error message was displayed? Try to verify the problem by having the user run the application while you talk him through it. If possible, duplicate the problem on your test system.

Standard Utilities

The standard utilities discussed in this chapter and throughout this book are

- `ifconfig`—Provides information about the basic configuration of the interface. It is useful for detecting bad IP addresses, incorrect subnet masks, and improper broadcast addresses. This tool is provided with Unix operating systems. The same tool is called `ipconfig` on Windows NT/2000 operating systems and `winipcfg` on Windows 9x operating systems.

- arp—Provides information about Ethernet/IP address translation. It can be used to detect systems on the local network that are configured with the wrong IP address. This tool exists on Windows and Unix systems.

- netstat—Provides a variety of information. It is commonly used to display detailed statistics about each network interface, network sockets, and the network routing table. This tool exists on Windows and Unix systems.

- ping—Indicates whether a remote host can be reached. ping also displays statistics about packet loss and delivery time.

- nslookup—Provides information about DNS name service.

- dig—Also provides information about name service, and is similar to nslookup. dig is available via anonymous ftp from venera.isi.edu in the file pub/dig.2.0.tar.Z.

- ripquery—Provides information about the contents of the RIP update packets being sent or received by your system. It is provided as part of the gated software package, but it does not require that you run gated. It will work with any system running RIP.

- traceroute—Tells you which route packets take going from your system to a remote system. Information about each hop is printed. It is available via anonymous ftp from ftp.ee.lbl.gov in the file traceroute.tar.Z. On Windows NT/2000, this is called tracert.

- etherfind—Analyzes the individual packets exchanged between hosts on a network. etherfind is a TCP/IP protocol analyzer that can examine the contents of packets, including their headers. It is most useful for analyzing protocol problems. It is the SunOS version of a program called tcpdump. tcpdump is available via anonymous ftp from ftp.ee.lbl.gov.

- ethereal—Analyzes the individual packets exchanged between hosts on a network. ethereal is a high-quality TCP/IP protocol analyzer that can examine the contents of packets, including their headers. This program has been ported to Windows and most Unix operating systems. For more information consult www.ethereal.com.

Each of these tools, even those covered earlier in the text, is used in this chapter. We start with ping, which is used in more troubleshooting situations than any other diagnostic tool.

44

TROUBLESHOOTING TOOLS AND ISSUES

Testing Basic Connectivity

The ping command tests whether a remote host can be reached from your computer. This simple function is extremely useful for testing the network connection, independent of the application in which the original problem was detected. ping allows you to determine whether further testing should be directed toward the network connection (the lower layers) or the application (the upper layers). If `ping` shows that packets can travel to the remote system and back, the user's problem is probably in the upper layers. If the packet can't make the round trip, lower protocol layers are probably at fault.

Frequently, a user reports a network problem by stating that he can't `telnet` (or `ftp`, or send e-mail, or whatever) to some remote host. He then immediately qualifies this statement with the announcement that it worked before. In cases like this, where the ability to connect to the remote host is in question, `ping` is a very useful tool.

Using the hostname provided by the user, `ping` the remote host. If your `ping` is successful, have the user `ping` the host. If the user's `ping` is also successful, concentrate your further analysis on the specific application with which the user is having trouble. Perhaps the user is attempting to `telnet` to a host that only provides anonymous `ftp`. Perhaps the host was down when the user tried his application. Have the user try it again, while you watch or listen to every detail of what he is doing. If he is doing everything right and the application still fails, detailed analysis of the application with `etherfind` and coordination with the remote system administrator may be needed.

If your `ping` is successful and the user's `ping` fails, concentrate testing on the user's system configuration, and on those things that are different about the user's path to the remote host, when compared to your path to the remote host.

If your `ping` fails, or the user's `ping` fails, pay close attention to any error messages. The error messages displayed by `ping` are helpful guides for planning further testing. The details of the messages may vary from implementation to implementation, but there are only a few basic types of errors:

- `unknown host`—The remote host's name cannot be resolved by name service into an IP address. The name servers could be at fault (either your local server or the remote system's server), the name could be incorrect, or something could be wrong with the network between your system and the remote server. If you know the remote host's IP address, try to `ping` that. If you can reach the host using its IP address, the problem is with name service. Use `nslookup` or `dig` to test the local and remote servers, and to check the accuracy of the hostname the user gave you.

- `network unreachable`—The local system does not have a route to the remote system. If the numeric IP address was used on the `ping` command line, re-enter the `ping` command using the local hostname. This eliminates the possibility that the IP address was entered incorrectly, or that you were given the wrong address. If a routing protocol is being used, make sure it is running and use `netstat` to check the routing table. If RIP is being used, use `ripquery` to check the contents of the RIP updates being received. If a static default route is being used, reinstall it. If everything seems fine on the host, check its default gateway for routing problems.

- no answer—The remote system did not respond. Most network utilities have some version of this message. Some ping implementations print the message 100% packet loss. telnet prints the message Connection timed out, and sendmail returns the error cannot connect. All of these errors mean the same thing. The local system has a route to the remote system, but it receives no response from the remote system to any of the packets it sends.

  There are many possible causes of this problem. The remote host may be down. Either the local or remote host may be configured incorrectly. A gateway or circuit between the local host and the remote host may be down. The remote host may have routing problems. Only additional testing can isolate the cause of the problem. Carefully check the local configuration using netstat and ifconfig. Check the route to the remote system with traceroute. Contact the administrator of the remote system and report the problem.

The tools mentioned in this section are discussed later in this chapter. However, before leaving ping, let's look more closely at the command and the statistics it displays.

The ping Command

The basic format of the ping command is

ping *host* [*packetsize*] [*count*]

host is the hostname or IP address of the remote host being tested. Use the hostname or address provided by the user in the trouble report.

packetsize defines the size in bytes of the test packets. This field is only required if the *count* field is going to be used. Use the default *packetsize* of 56 bytes.

count is the number of packets to be sent in the test. Use the *count* field, and set the value low. Otherwise, the ping command continues to send test packets until you interrupt it, usually by pressing Control+C (^C). Sending excessive numbers of test packets is not a good use of network bandwidth and system resources. Usually five packets are sufficient for a test.

To check that uunet.uu.net can be reached from workstation bernard, we send five 56-byte packets with the following command:

```
% ping -s uunet.uu.net 56 5
PING uunet.uu.net: 56 data bytes
64 bytes from uunet.UU.NET (137.39.1.2): icmp_seq=0. Time=14. ms
64 bytes from uunet.UU.NET (137.39.1.2): icmp_seq=0. Time=14. ms
64 bytes from uunet.UU.NET (137.39.1.2): icmp_seq=0. Time=14. ms
64 bytes from uunet.UU.NET (137.39.1.2): icmp_seq=0. Time=14. ms
64 bytes from uunet.UU.NET (137.39.1.2): icmp_seq=0. Time=14. ms
```

```
----uunet.UU.NET PING Statistics----
5 packets transmitted, 5 packets received, 0% packet loss
round-trip (ms) min/avg/max = 12/13/15
```

The -s option is included because bernard is a Sun workstation, and we want packet-by-packet statistics. Without the -s option, Sun's ping command would only print a summary line saying uunet.uu.net is alive. Other ping implementations do not require the -s option; they display the statistics by default.

This test shows an extremely good wide area network link to uunet.uu.net with no packet loss and fast response. The round trip between bernard and uunet.uu.net is taking an average of only 13 milliseconds. A small packet loss, and the round-trip times an order of magnitude higher, would be more normal for a connection made across a wide area network. The statistics displayed by the ping command can indicate low-level network problems. The key statistics are

- The sequence in which the packets are arriving, as shown by the ICMP sequence number (icmp_seq) displayed for each packet

- How long it takes a packet to make the round trip, which is displayed in milliseconds after the string time=

- The percentage of packets lost, which is displayed in a summary line at the end of the ping output

If the packet loss is high, the response time is very slow, or packets are arriving out of order, there could be a network hardware problem. If you see these conditions when communicating great distances on a wide area network, there is nothing to worry about. TCP/IP was designed to deal with unreliable networks, and some wide area networks suffer a lot of packet loss. But if you see these problems on a local area network, they indicate trouble.

On a local network cable segment the round-trip time should be near zero, there should be little or no packet loss, and the packets should arrive in order. If these things are not true, there is a problem with the network hardware. On an Ethernet the problem could be improper cable termination, a bad cable segment, or a bad piece of "active" hardware, such as a repeater or transceiver. Check the cable terminations first. They're easy to check; either there is a terminating resistor or there isn't, and it's a common problem, particularly if the cable ends in a work area where users have access to it.

A helpful tool for checking cable hardware problems is a *time domain reflectometer* (TDR). A TDR sends a signal down the cable and listens for the echoes the signal produces. These echoes are displayed on a small screen on the front of the tester. If the cable is not terminated, the signal display jumps to the top of the screen. A normal display shows only small spikes where the transceivers tap into the network. With a TDR, detecting a cable problem is easy.

The results of a simple ping test, even if the test is successful, can help you direct further testing toward the most likely causes of the problem. But other diagnostic tools are needed to examine the problem more closely and find the underlying cause.

> **Note**
>
> Under some systems such as Linux, the ping command does a reverse lookup of the target IP address. If DNS is not running, the ping command takes a long time because it waits for DNS to time out. The results of ping, in this case, are misleading because of the long delays reported due to DNS timeout. To eliminate this possibility, do a ping with the -n option, which suppresses name resolution.

Troubleshooting Network Access

The no answer and cannot connect errors indicate a problem in the lower layers of the network protocols. If the preliminary tests point to this type of problem, concentrate your testing on routing and on the network interface. Use the ifconfig, netstat, and arp commands to test the Network Access Layer.

Using the `ifconfig` Command

ifconfig checks the network interface configuration. Use this command to verify the user's configuration if the user's system has been recently configured, or if the user's system cannot reach the remote host while other systems on the same network can.

When ifconfig is entered with an interface name and no other arguments, it displays the current values assigned to that interface. For example, checking interface le0 on bernard gives this report:

```
% ifconfig le0
le0: flags=63<UP,BROADCAST,NOTRAILERS,RUNNING>
inet 128.66.12.2 netmask ffff0000  broadcast 128.66.0.0
```

The ifconfig command displays two lines of output. The first line of the display shows the interface's name and its characteristics. Check for the following characteristics:

- UP—The interface is enabled for use. If the interface is down, have the system's superuser bring up the interface with the ifconfig command (ifconfig le0 up). If the interface won't come up, replace the interface cable and try again. If it still fails, have the interface hardware checked.

- RUNNING—This interface is operational. If the interface is not running, the driver for this interface may not be properly installed. The system administrator should review all the steps necessary to install this interface, looking for errors or missed steps.

The second line of `ifconfig` output shows the IP address, the subnet mask (written in hexadecimal), and the broadcast address. Check these three fields to make sure the network interface is properly configured.

Using the `arp` Command

The `arp` command is used to analyze problems with IP-to-Ethernet address translation. The `arp` command has three useful options for troubleshooting:

> `-a`—Displays all ARP entries in the table.
>
> `-d` *hostname*—Deletes an entry from the ARP table.
>
> `-s` *hostname ether-address*—Adds a new entry to the table.

With these three options you can view the contents of the ARP table, delete a problem entry, and install a correct entry. The ability to install a corrected entry is useful in buying time while you look for a permanent fix.

Use `arp` if you suspect that incorrect entries are getting into the address resolution table. One clear indication of problems with the ARP table is a report that the wrong host responded to some command, such as `ftp` or `telnet`. Intermittent problems that affect only certain hosts can also indicate that the ARP table has been corrupted. ARP table problems are usually caused by two systems using the same IP address. The problems appear intermittent because the entry that appears in the table is the address of the host that responded quickest to the last ARP request. Sometimes the correct host responds first.

If you suspect that two systems are using the same IP address, display the address resolution table with the `arp -a` command. Here's an example:

```
% arp -a
bernard (128.66.12.2) at 8:0:20:b:4a:71
annette (128.66.12.1) at 8:0:20:e:aa:40
bernadette (128.66.12.3) at 0:0:93:e0:80:b1
```

Verifying that the IP and Ethernet address pairs are correct is easiest if you have a record of each host's correct Ethernet address. For this reason, you should record each host's Ethernet and IP address when it is added to your network. If you have such a record, you'll quickly see whether anything is wrong with the table.

If you don't have this type of record, the first three bytes of the Ethernet address can help you to detect a problem. The first three bytes of the address identify the equipment manufacturer. A list of these identifying prefixes is found in the Assigned Numbers RFC, in the section titled "Ethernet Vendor Address Components."

Table 44.1 lists several equipment manufacturers and their assigned prefixes. Using this information, we see that the first two ARP entries displayed in our example are Sun systems (8:0:20). If bernadette is also supposed to be a Sun, the 0:0:93 Proteon prefix indicates that a Proteon router has been mistakenly configured with bernadette's IP address.

TABLE 44.1   Vendor Ethernet Prefixes

Prefix	Manufacturer	Prefix	Manufacturer
00:00:0C	Cisco	08:00:0B	Unisys
00:00:0F	NeXT	08:00:10	AT&T
00:00:10	Sytek	08:00:11	Tektronix
00:00:1D	Cabletron	08:00:14	Excelan
00:00:65	Network General	08:00:1A	Data General
00:00:6B	MIPS	08:00:1B	Data General
00:00:77	MIPS	08:00:1E	Apollo
00:00:89	Cayman Systems	08:00:20	Sun
00:00:93	Proteon	08:00:25	CDC
00:00:A2	Wellfleet	08:00:2B	DEC
00:00:A7	NCD	08:00:38	Bull
00:00:A9	Network Systems	08:00:39	Spider Systems
00:00:C0	Western Digital	08:00:46	Sony
00:00:C9	Emulex	08:04:47	Sequent
00:80:2D	Xylogics Annex	08:00:5A	IBM
00:AA:00	Intel	08:00:69	Silicon Graphics
00:DD:00	Ungermann-Bass	08:00:6E	Excelan
00:DD:01	Ungermann-Bass	08:00:86	Imagen/QMS
02:07:01	MICOM/Interlan	08: 00:87	Xyplex terminal servers
02:60:8C	3Com	08:00:89	Kinetics
08:00:02	3Com (Bridge)	08:00:8B	Pyramid
08:00:03	ACC	08:00:90	Retix
08:00:05	Symbolics	AA:00:03	DEC
08:00:08	BBN	AA:00:04	DEC
08:00:09	Hewlett-Packard		

44

If neither checking a record of correct assignments nor checking the manufacturers' prefixes helps you identify the source of the errant ARP, try using `telnet` to connect to the IP address shown in the ARP entry. If the device supports `telnet`, the login banner might help you identify the incorrectly configured host.

Checking the Interface with `netstat`

If the primary tests lead you to suspect that the connection to the local area network is unreliable, the `netstat -i` command can provide useful information. The following example shows the output from the `netstat -i` command:

```
% netstat -i
Name Mtu   Net/Dest Address     Ipkts Ierrs Opkts Oerrs Collis Queue
le0 1500 family.com annette     442697 2    633524 2     50679  0
lo0 1536 loopback localhost  53040 0     53040   0    0       0
```

The line for the loopback interface, `lo0`, can be ignored. Only the line for the real network interface is significant, and only the last five fields on that line provide significant troubleshooting information.

Let's look at the last field first. There should be no packets queued (`Queue`) that cannot be transmitted. If the interface is up and running and the system cannot deliver packets to the network, suspect a bad drop cable or a bad interface. Replace the cable and see whether the problem goes away. If it doesn't, call the vendor for interface hardware repairs.

The input errors (`Ierrs`) and the output errors (`Oeers`) should be close to zero. Regardless of how much traffic has passed through this interface, 100 errors in either of these fields is high. High output errors could indicate a saturated local network or a bad physical connection between the host and the network. High input errors could indicate that the network is saturated, the local host is overloaded, or there is a physical network problem. Tools, such as `ping` statistics or a TDR, can help you determine whether it is a physical network problem. Evaluating the collision rate can help you determine whether the local Ethernet is saturated.

A high value in the collision field (`Collis`) is normal, but if the percentage of output packets that result in a collision is too high, it indicates that the network is saturated. Collision rates greater than 5 percent bear watching. If you consistently see high collision rates, and you see them among a broad sampling of systems on the network, you may need to subdivide the network to reduce traffic load.

Collision rates are a percentage of output packets. Don't use the total number of packets sent and received; just use `Opkts` and `Collis` when determining the collision rate. For example, the output in the earlier `netstat` example shows 50,679 collisions out of

633,424 outgoing packets. That's a collision rate of 8 percent. This sample network could be overworked; check the statistics on the other hosts on this network. If the other systems also show a high collision rate, consider subdividing this network.

Checking Routing

The `network unreachable` error message clearly indicates a routing problem. If the problem is in the local host's routing table, it is easy to detect and resolve. First, use `netstat -nr` and `grep` to see whether a valid route to your destination is installed in the routing table. This example checks for a specific route to network 128.8.0.0:

```
% netstat -nr | grep '128\.8\.0\.0'
128.8.0.0       26.20.0.16    UG    0    37    std0
```

This same test, run on a system that did not have this route in its routing table, would return no response at all. For example, a user reports that the network is down because he cannot `telnet` to `nic.ddn.mil`, and a `ping` test returns the following results:

```
% ping -s nic.ddn.mil 56 2
PING nic.ddn.mil: 56 data bytes
sendto: Network is unreachable
ping: wrote nic.ddn.mil 64 chars, ret=-1
sendto: Network is unreachable
ping: wrote nic.ddn.mil 64 chars, ret=-1

----nic.ddn.mil PING Statistics----
2 packets transmitted, 0 packets received, 100% packet loss
```

Based on the `network unreachable` error message, check the user's routing table. In our example, we're looking for a route to `nic.ddn.mil`. The IP address of `nic.ddn.mil` is 192.112.36.5, which is a Class C address. Remember that routes are network oriented. So we check for a route to network 192.112.36.0:

```
% netstat -nr | grep '192\.112\.36\.0'
%
```

This test shows that there is no specific route to 192.112.36.0. If a route was found, `grep` would display it. Because there's no specific route to the destination, remember to look for a default route. This example shows a successful check for a default route:

```
% netstat -nr | grep def
default    128.66.12.1    UG    0    101277    le0
```

If `netstat` shows the correct specific route, or a valid default route, the problem is not in the routing table. In that case, use `traceroute`, as described later in this chapter, to trace the route all the way to its destination.

If netstat doesn't return the expected route, it's a local routing problem. There are two ways to approach local routing problems, depending on whether the system uses static or dynamic routing. If you're using static routing, install the missing route using the route add command. Remember that most systems that use static routing rely on a default route, so the missing route could be the default route. Make sure that the startup files add the needed route to the table whenever the system reboots.

If you're using dynamic routing, make sure that the routing program is running. For example, the following command makes sure that gated is running:

```
% ps `cat /etc/gated.pid`
PID TT STAT  TIME COMMAND
27711 ? S    304:59 gated ñtep /etc/log/gated.log
```

If the correct routing daemon is not running, restart it and specify tracing. Tracing allows you to check for problems that might be causing the daemon to terminate abnormally. The next two sections discuss RIP updates and tracing routes.

Checking RIP Updates

If the routing daemon is running and the local system receives routing updates via Routing Information Protocol (RIP), use ripquery to check the updates received from your RIP suppliers. For example, to check the RIP updates being received from annette and bernadette, the bernard administrator enters the following command:

```
% ripquery -n -r annette bernadette
44 bytes from annette.family.com(128.66.12.1):
0.0.0.0, metric 3
26.0.0.0, metric 0
   264 bytes from bernadette.family.com(128.66.12.3):
128.66.5.0, metric 2
128.66.3.0, metric 2
     .
     .
     .
128.66.12.0, metric 2
128.66.13.0, metric 2
```

After an initial line identifying the gateway, ripquery shows the contents of the incoming RIP packets, one line per route. The first line of the preceding report indicates that ripquery received a response from annette. That line is followed by two lines for the two routes advertised by annette. annette advertises the default route (destination 0.0.0.0) with a metric of 3, and its direct route to Milnet (destination 26.0.0.0) with a metric of 0. Next, ripquery shows the routes advertised by bernadette. These are the routes to the other family-net subnets.

The two `ripquery` options used in this example are

- `-n`—Causes `ripquery` to display all output in numeric form. `ripquery` attempts to resolve all IP addresses to names if the `-n` option is not specified. Using the `-n` option is a good idea; it produces a cleaner display, and you don't waste time resolving names.

- `-r`—Directs `ripquery` to use the `RIP REQUEST` command, instead of the `RIP POLL` command, to query the RIP supplier. `RIP POLL` is not universally supported. You are more likely to get a successful response if you specify `-r` on the `ripquery` command line.

The routes returned in these updates should be the routes that you'd expect. If they are not, or if no routes are returned, check the configuration of the RIP suppliers. Routing configuration problems cause RIP suppliers to advertise routes that they shouldn't, or to fail to advertise the routes that they should. You can detect these problems only by applying your knowledge of your network configuration. You must know what is correct to detect what is wrong. Don't expect to see error messages or strange garbled routes.

Tracing Routes

If the local routing table and RIP suppliers are correct, the problem may be occurring some distance away from the local host. Remote routing problems can cause the `no answer` error message, as well as the `network unreachable` error message. But the `network unreachable` error message does not always mean a routing problem. It can literally mean that the remote network cannot be reached because something is down between the local host and the remote host destination. `traceroute` is the program that can help you locate these problems.

`traceroute` traces the route of UDP packets from the local host to a remote host. It prints the name (if it can be determined) and IP address of each gateway along the route to the remote host.

`traceroute` uses two techniques, small *time-to-live* (ttl) values and an invalid port number, to trace packets to their destination. `traceroute` sends out UDP packets with small ttl values to detect the intermediate gateways. The ttl values start at one and increase in increments of one for each group of three UDP packets sent. When a gateway receives a packet, it decrements the ttl. If the ttl is then zero, the packet is not forwarded and an ICMP `Time Exceeded` message is returned to the source of the packet. `traceroute` displays one line of output for each gateway from which it receives a `Time Exceeded` message.

When the destination host receives a packet from `traceroute`, it returns an ICMP `Unreachable Port` message. This happens because `traceroute` intentionally uses an

44

TROUBLESHOOTING TOOLS AND ISSUES

invalid port number (33434) to force this error. When `traceroute` receives the
`Unreachable Port` message, it knows that it has reached the destination host, and it
terminates the trace. In this way, `traceroute` is able to develop a list of the gateways,
starting at one hop away and increasing one hop at a time, until the remote host is reached.

The following example shows a `traceroute` to nic.ddn.mil from a system hanging
SURAnet. `traceroute` sends out three packets at each ttl value. If no response is
received to a packet, `traceroute` prints an (*). If a response is received, `traceroute`
displays the name and address of the gateway that responded, and the packet's round-trip
time in milliseconds.

```
% traceroute nic.ddn.mil
traceroute to nic.ddn.mil (192.112.36.5), 30 hops max, 40 byte packets
1  * pgw (129.6.80.254)  4 ms   3 ms
2  129.6.1.242 (129.6.1.242)   4 ms   4 ms   3 ms
3  129.6.2.252 (129.6.2.252)   5 ms   5 ms   4 ms
4  128.167.122.1 (128.167.122.1)   50 ms   6 ms   6 ms
5  * 192.80.214.247 (192.80.214.247)   96 ms   18 ms
6  129.140.9.10 (129.140.9.10)   18 ms   25 ms   15 ms
7  nsn.sura.net (192.80.214.253)   21 ms   18 ms   23 ms
8  GSI.NSN.NASA.GOV (128.161.252.2)   22 ms   34 ms   27 ms
9  NIC.DDN.MIL (192.112.36.5)   37 ms   29 ms   34 ms
```

This trace shows that eight intermediate gateways are involved, that packets are reliably
making the trip, and that round-trip travel time for packets from this host to nic.ddn.mil
is about 33 ms.

Variations and bugs in the implementation of ICMP on different types of gateways, and
the unpredictable nature of the path a datagram can take through a network, can cause
some odd displays. For this reason, you shouldn't examine the output of `traceroute` too
closely. The most important things in the `traceroute` output are

- Did the packet get to its destination?
- If not, where did it stop?

The following shows another trace of the path to nic.ddn.mil. This time the trace does
not go all the way through to the NIC.

```
% traceroute nic.ddn.mil
traceroute to nic.ddn.mil (192.112.36.5), 30 hops max, 40 byte packets
1  * pgw (129.6.80.254)  3 ms   3 ms
2  129.6.1.242 (129.6.1.242)   4 ms   4 ms   4 ms
3  129.6.2.252 (129.6.2.252)   5 ms   5 ms   4 ms
4  128.167.122.1 (128.167.122.1)   6 ms   6 ms   10 ms
5  enss.sura.net (192.80.214.248)   9 ms   6 ms   8 ms
6  t3-1.cnss58.t3.nsf.net (140.222.58.2)   10 ms   15 ms   13 ms
7  t3-0.enss142.t3.nsf.net (140.222.142.1)   13 ms   12 ms   12 ms
```

```
8  GSI.NSN.NASA.GOV (128.161.252.2)  22 ms  26 ms  21 ms
9  * * *
10* * *
      .
      .
      .
29* * *
30* * *
```

When `traceroute` fails to get packets through to the remote endsystem, the trace trails off, displaying a series of three asterisks at each hop count until the count reaches 30. If this happens, contact the administrator of the remote host you're trying to reach, and the administrator of the last gateway displayed in the trace. Describe the problem to them; they may be able to help. In our example, the last gateway that responded to our packets was `GSI.NSN.NASA.GOV`. We would contact this system administrator, and the administrator of `nic.ddn.mil`.

Checking Name Service

The server problems are indicated when the `unknown host` error message is returned by the user's application. Name server problems can usually be diagnosed with `nslookup` or `dig`. `dig` is an alternative tool with similar functionality to that of `nslookup`. Before looking at `dig`, let's take another look at `nslookup` and see how it is used to troubleshoot name service.

The three features of `nslookup` that we will cover are particularly important for troubleshooting remote name server problems. These features are its ability to

- Locate the authoritative servers for the remote domain using the `NS` query
- Obtain all records about the remote host using the `ANY` query
- Browse all entries in the remote zone using `nslookup`'s `ls` and `view` commands

When troubleshooting a remote server problem, directly query the authoritative servers returned by the `NS` query. Don't rely on information returned by non-authoritative servers. If the problems that have been reported are intermittent, query all the authoritative servers in turn and compare their answers. The remote servers returning different answers to the same query sometimes cause intermittent name server problems.

The `ANY` query returns all records about a host, thus giving the broadcast range of troubleshooting information. Simply knowing what information is (and isn't) available can solve a lot of problems. For example, if the query returns an MX record but no A record, it is easy to understand why the user couldn't `telnet` to that host! Many hosts are accessible to mail that are not accessible by other network services. In this case, the user is confused and is trying to use the remote host in an inappropriate manner.

If you are unable to locate any information about the hostname that the user gave you, perhaps the hostname is incorrect. Given that the hostname you gave is wrong, looking for the correct name is like trying to find a needle in a haystack. However, nslookup can help. Use nslookup's ls command to dump the remote zone file, and redirect the listing to a file. Then use nslookup's view command to browse through the file, looking for names similar to the one the user supplied. Many problems are caused by a mistaken hostname.

An alternative to nslookup for making a name service query is dig. dig queries are usually entered as single-line commands, whereas nslookup is usually run as an interactive session. But the dig command performs essentially the same function as nslookup. Which you use is mostly a matter of personal choice. They both work well.

As an example, we'll use dig to ask the root server aggie.nca&t.edu for the NS records for the jhu.edu domain. To do this, enter the following command:

```
% dig @aggie.nca&t.edu jhu.edu ns
```

In this example, @aggie.nca&t.edu is the server that is being queried. Name or IP address can identify the server. If you're troubleshooting a problem in a remote domain, specify an authoritative server for that domain. In this example we're asking for the names of servers for a top-level domain (jhu.edu), so we ask a root server.

Troubleshooting the Network Interface

Although there doesn't seem to be much at this layer, it is possible for things to go wrong at the bottom of the stack. There are basically four problems you might run into at this level:

- **Physical connectivity.** As with all networking, TCP/IP works better if it is plugged in. All networks require that the system be connected to the network, so always check the cable.

- **No IP address was assigned to the DHCP client.** This should be obvious to the user because a large message appears. There are two ways you can receive an IP address. You can statically configure an IP address, or you can dynamically obtain an IP address from a DHCP (Dynamic Host Configuration Protocol) server. However, you should always verify that an IP address is assigned by using the IFCONFIG utility in Unix, the WINIPCFG utility in Windows 9x, or the IPCONFIG utility in Windows NT/2000.

- **ARP problem.** If the address resolution protocol is not functioning properly, you will not be able to resolve an IP address to a MAC address. The ARP utility, described earlier in this chapter, allows you to verify the ability to resolve addresses.
- **Duplicate IP addresses are on the network.** Another problem you can run into occurs when two systems on the network share the same IP address. This is not supposed to happen; but if it does, your system may resolve the MAC address to one system at first and to the other the next time.

The only case in which you should have a problem with the ARP is if a static resolution is added to the ARP cache, which might be done for performance purposes. However, if the network adapter is changed in the system for which the IP address was entered, the mapping will cause problems. You can check for this problem using ARP.

Troubleshooting the Network (IP) Layer

As you should recall, the Internet Layer is responsible for the routing of packets. This is where you will need to carefully check the IP address, subnet mask, and default gateway. In addition to the configuration, there may be problems with the routing table or with a router somewhere between your system and the system you are attempting to communicate with.

TCP/IP Configuration Parameters

Three main parameters specify how TCP/IP is configured: the IP address, the subnet mask, and the default gateway, which is usually the router's interface to your particular segment. These parameters are configured in a Windows environment through the Protocols tab of the Network dialog box, as opposed to the command-line entry using ifconfig in a Unix environment. Although receiving an IP address from a DHCP server is possible, for the moment this discussion focuses on parameters that are manually configured.

The three TCP/IP parameters must be configured correctly or you will not be able to connect with TCP/IP. An incorrect configuration can result from typographical errors; if you type the wrong IP address, subnet mask, or default gateway, you may not connect properly or at all.

Whether the TCP/IP configuration parameters are wrong due to a typo or due to a mistaken number, the incorrect parameters affect communications. Different types of problems occur when the different parameters have a configuration error. Identifying and fixing the errors are covered in the following sections.

IP Address Configuration Problems

An incorrect TCP/IP address might not cause any problems. If you configure an IP address that is on the correct subnet and is not a duplicate, but it uses the wrong host ID, the client may be able to communicate just fine. If, however, the correct IP address has been entered in a static file or database that resolves hostnames to IP addresses, such as an LMHOSTS file or a DNS database file, there are going to be some communication problems. Typically, therefore, an incorrect IP address causes some problems.

Incorrect configuration of the TCP/IP parameters can cause different symptoms for each type of parameter. The following sections examine the effects that each TCP/IP parameter can have on IP communications.

IP Address

A TCP/IP address has two or possibly three components that uniquely identify the computer the address is assigned to. At the very least, the IP address specifies the network address and host address of the computer. Also, if you are subnetting, the third part of the address specifies the subnet address of the host.

Figure 44.1 shows the effect of an incorrect network address. In this example, the TCP/IP address assigned to a client is typed incorrectly. The address assigned to the client is 143.168.2.9, whereas the correct address was supposed to be 133.168.3.9. The network ID for the incorrect address is 143.168.x.x, whereas the network ID for the correct address should be 133.168.x.x.

With this incorrect address (143.168.3.9), the client is not able to communicate with any other TCP/IP hosts. Because the network address is incorrect, any packets this client sends will be routed to the wrong location.

If the incorrect host (143.168.3.9) sends a message to a local client (133.168.3.20), the TCP/IP configuration of the sending host indicates this is a remote address because it doesn't match the network address of the host initiating the communication. The packet won't ever reach the local client because the address 133.168.3.20 is interpreted as a remote address.

If a local client (133.168.3.6) sends a message to the incorrect host (143.168.3.9), the message never reaches its intended destination. The message is either routed (if the local client sends the message to the IP address as written) or it stays on the local subnet (if the local client sends it to what should have been the address, 133.168.3.9). If the message is routed, the incorrect client does not receive the message because it is on the same segment of the network as the local client. If the message is not routed, the message still does not reach the incorrect client because the IP address of the destination host (133.168.3.9) does not match the address as configured on the incorrect client (143.168.3.9).

FIGURE 44.1

An example of the effect of an incorrect IP address.

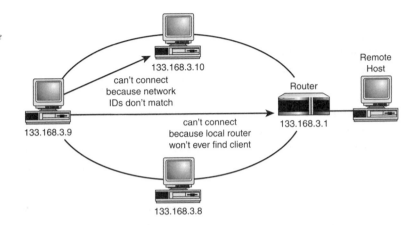

Figure 44.2 gives another example of an incorrect IP address. In this case, a Class A address is used (33.x.x.x). The subnet mask (255.255.0.0) indicates the second octet is being used to create subnets. In this case, even though the client has the same network address as the other clients on the same subnet, the client has a different subnet number because the address was typed incorrectly.

This time the incorrect address specifies the wrong subnet ID. The client 33.5.8.4 is on subnet 5 while the other clients on the subnet have the address 33.4.x.x. In this case, if the client 33.5.8.4 tries to contact other clients on the same subnet, the message is routed because the subnet ID doesn't match the subnet number of the source host. If the client 33.5.8.4 tries to send a message to a remote host, the message is routed; however, the message isn't returned to the client because the router doesn't handle subnet 5—it only handles subnet 4.

FIGURE 44.2

An example of the IP address returning an incorrect subnet ID.

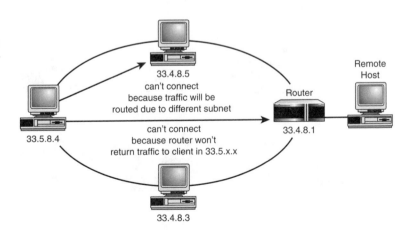

If a local client tries to send a message to 33.5.8.4, the message doesn't reach the client. If the local client uses the address as configured, the message is routed, which isn't the correct solution because the intended destination host is local. If the local client sends the message to what should have been the IP address, 33.5.8.4 doesn't receive the message because the IP address isn't configured correctly.

The last component of an IP address that can cause communication problems is the host address. An incorrect host address may not always cause a problem, however. In Figure 44.3, a local client has the wrong IP address, but only the host address portion of the address is wrong. The network address and subnet match the rest of the clients on the subnet.

In this case, if a client sends a message to the client with the incorrect address, the message still reaches the client. However, if someone tries to contact the client with what should have been the address, he cannot. In fact, he could contact another host that ended up with the address that was supposed to have been given to the original host.

If the original host ends up with the same IP address as another host through the configuration error, the first client to start up works, but the second client to start up may note the address conflict and not load the TCP/IP stack at all. In this case, the second client to start up isn't able to make any TCP/IP communications.

FIGURE 44.3

*An example
of the effect of an
incorrect IP
address giving the
wrong host ID.*

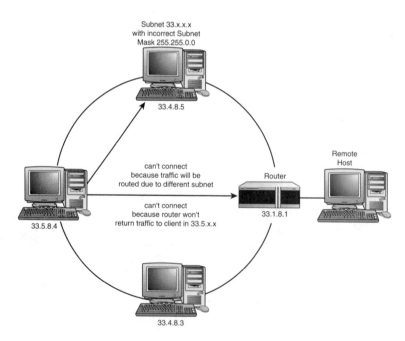

Another problem arises when the correct address is registered in static files, such as an LMHOSTS file or a DNS database. In this case, no one can communicate with this client by name because the name resolution for this host always returns the correct address, which can't be used to contact the host because the address has been typed incorrectly.

Basically, the problems you encounter with an incorrect host address are intermittent. However, if the host was configured to be a WINS client (using a Windows operating system, not Unix), the hostname is registered along with the incorrect address. Another WINS client trying to connect with this computer receives an accurate mapping for the hostname.

Subnet Mask

The subnet mask indicates which portion of the IP address specifies the network address and the host address. Also, the subnet mask can be used to divide part of what would have been the host address into subnets. If the subnet mask is not configured correctly, your clients may not be able to communicate at all, or you may see partial communication problems.

Figure 44.4 shows a subnet on a TCP/IP network that uses a Class B network address of 138.13.x.x. However, the third octet is used in this case for subnetting, so all the clients in the figure should be on subnet 4, as indicated by the common addresses 138.13.4.x.

Unfortunately, the subnet mask entered for one client is 255.255.0.0. When this client tries to communicate with other hosts on the same subnet, he should be able to contact them because the subnet mask indicates they are on the same subnet, which is correct. However, if the client tries to contact a host on another subnet, such as 138.13.3.x, the client fails.

In this case, the subnet mask still interprets the destination host to be on the same subnet, and the message is never routed. Because the destination host is on another subnet, the message never reaches the intended destination. The subnet mask is used to determine routing for outgoing communications, so the client with the incorrect subnet mask can receive incoming messages. However, when the client tries to return communications, the message isn't routed if the source host is on the same network but on a different subnet.

So, in actuality, the client really can establish communications with only one side of the conversation. Contacts with hosts outside the local network still work because they are routed.

FIGURE 44.4

Even if the IP address is right, the wrong subnet ID can be used because of the subnet mask.

Figure 44.5 shows a subnet mask that masks too many bits. In this case, the subnet mask is 255.255.255.0. However, the network designers had intended the subnet mask to be 255.255.240.0, with four bits of the third octet used for the subnet and four bits as part of the host address.

If the correctly configured client tries to send a message to a local host and the third octet is the same, the message is not routed and, thus, reaches the local client. However, if the local client has an address that differs in the last four bits of the third octet, the message is routed and never reaches its destination. If the incorrectly configured client tries to send a message to another client on another subnet, the message is routed because the third octet is different.

Problems with the subnet mask also lead to intermittent connections: Sometimes the connection works, sometimes it doesn't. The problems show up when the IP address of the destination host causes a packet to be routed when it shouldn't, or to remain local when it should be routed.

Default Gateway

The default gateway address is the address of the router—the gateway to the world beyond the local subnet. If a client's default gateway address is wrong, it can contact local hosts but is not able to communicate at all beyond the local subnet. It is possible for the incorrect client to receive a message because the default gateway is used only to send packets to other hosts. However, as soon as the incorrect client attempts to respond to the incoming message, the default gateway address doesn't work and the message doesn't reach the host that sent the original message.

FIGURE 44.5
Communication problems will occur if the subnet mask uses too many bits.

Troubleshooting TCP and UDP

There is little to worry about at the Transport Layer. If you can ping, your Transport Layer should be functioning properly. The only problem that you will normally have at this layer concerns the TCPWindowSize discussed in Chapter 9, "Overview of the IP Family of Protocols."

This problem will typically result in slow communication speed (similar to the 110-baud terminals used in the 1970s and '80s). However, if you have verified everything up to this point, a quick way to check TCPWindowSize (in Windows NT/2000, for example) is to open the Registry and see whether a Window Size entry exists. If you see an entry, make a note of the setting and then delete the value. This will reset the window size to its default.

Sockets Problems

Assuming that you have the correct IP address and protocol, and that you are able to find a route to the remote computer, it will need to be running the service you are looking for on the correct socket. If you are providing services to the network or trying to connect to a service on the network, you need to know which port number to use.

The *Internet Assigned Numbers Authority* (IANA) assigns the common port (socket) numbers; however, in some cases the service might use a different port. There is a file (described in the following section) that you will want to check to verify that the correct port is used. After you verify this, you can use the NETSTAT command to verify that the port is ready to receive data.

The Services File

Located in the `system32\drivers\etc` directory of Windows NT/2000 is a services file, which is used by most of the services that initialize the socket numbers they use when they initialize. The following is a small portion of a services file:

```
#

#   This file contains port numbers for well-known services as
# defined by RFC 1060 (Assigned Numbers).

#


#   Format:

#


#   <service name>    <port number>/<protocol>    [aliasesÖ]    [#<comment>]
#
echo            7/tcp

echo            7/udp

discard         9/tcp       sink null
discard         9/udp       sink null
systat          11/tcp

systat          11/udp      users

daytime         13/tcp

daytime         13/udp

netstat         15/tcp

qotd          17/tcp        quote

qotd          17/udp        quote

chargen         19/tcp        ttytst source

chargen         19/udp        ttytst source
ftp-data          20/tcp

ftp           21/tcp

telnet          23/tcp
```

```
smtp        25/tcp      mail

time        37/tcp      timeserver

time        37/udp      timeserver

rlp         39/udp      resource            #  resource location
name        42/tcp      nameserver
name        42/udp              nameserver
whois       43/tcp      nicname         #  usually to sri-nic
domain      53/tcp      nameserver      #  name-domain server
domain      53/udp      nameserver
nameserver  53/tcp      domain          #  name-domain server
nameserver  53/udp      domain
mtp         57/tcp              #  deprecated         bootp
67/udp              # boot program server        tftp    69/udp
```

If you are having problems with particular services, you should check this file if they are listed to make sure the correct port is used. If a service is not listed, you may need to add it so that the system knows which port to initialize the service on. (This is a normal text file that can be viewed and edited using either Edit or Notepad.)

Troubleshooting the Application Layer

Finally you come to the Application Layer, where you will want to verify communications. There are two main problems you may encounter at this layer: NetBIOS problems and name resolution problems. By far the most common problem will be name resolution problems, which affect both socket applications and NetBIOS applications. In the next sections, these name resolution problems will be reviewed.

Name Resolution Problems

If you have configured TCP/IP correctly and the protocol is installed and working, the problem with connectivity is probably due to errors in resolving hostnames. When you test connectivity with TCP/IP addresses, you are testing a lower level of connectivity than users generally use.

When users want to connect to a network resource—to map a drive to a server to connect to a Web site, for example—they usually refer to that server or Web site by its name rather than its TCP/IP address. In fact, users do not usually know the IP address of a particular server. The name used to establish a connection, however, must be resolved down to an IP address so that the networking software can make a connection.

After you've tested the IP connectivity, the next logical step is to check the resolution of a name down to its IP address. If a name cannot be resolved to its IP address, or if it is resolved to the wrong address, users will not be able to connect to the network resource with that name, even if they can connect to it using an IP address.

As you know, two types of computer names are used when communicating on a network: A NetBIOS name is assigned to a NetBIOS computer, such as a Windows NT/2000 server or a Windows 9x system; and a hostname is assigned to non-NetBIOS computers, such as a Unix server. In general, when using Microsoft networking to connect to a server for file sharing, print sharing, or applications, for example, you refer to that computer by its NetBIOS name. But when you execute a TCP/IP-specific command as you do when using FTP or a Web browser, you refer to that computer by its hostname.

Summary

Problems caused by bad TCP/IP configurations are much more common than problems caused by bad TCP/IP protocol implementations. Most of the problems you encounter will succumb to analysis using the simple tools we have already discussed. But on occasion, you may need to analyze the protocol interaction between two systems. In the worst case, you may need to analyze the packets in the data stream bit by bit.

Appendixes

IN THIS PART

RFCs and Standards

by Tim Parker

IN THIS APPENDIX

Most of the information about the TCP/IP protocol family is published as *Requests for Comments* (RFCs). RFCs define the various aspects of the protocol, the protocol's use, and the management of the protocol as a set of loosely coordinated notes.

There is a lot of useless information (mostly because it is system-specific or considerably outdated) in the RFCs, but there is also a wealth of detail. Unexpectedly, there is quite a bit of interesting and humorous reading in the RFCs, including several classic works such as "'Twas the Night Before Start-up" (RFC 968), "ARPAWOCKY" (RFC 527), and "TELNET Randomly-Lose Option" (RFC 748).

This appendix lists the important or interesting RFCs which readers may want to refer to. Instructions for accessing the RFCs are also included. This list is not complete; old and outdated RFCs have been dropped from the list.

Accessing RFCs

RFCs can be obtained in several ways, the easiest of which is electronically. Paper copies are available, upon request. Electronic copies are usually in ASCII format, although some are in PostScript format and require a PostScript interpreter to print them. Most RFCs obtained electronically don't have diagrams, figures, or pictures.

Accessing RFCs Through the Web

Many sites catalog RFCs on the World Wide Web. The easiest way to find them is to use a search engine with the search string "RFC". Most sites present simple lists of the RFCs in numerical order, but some do provide a breakdown of interesting subjects (although the lists tend not to be complete). For the official RFC index, visit the site
`http://www.rfc-editor.org`

Accessing RFCs Through FTP

RFCs can be obtained using FTP through the Internet *Network Information Center* (NIC) or one of several other FTP sites. Use FTP to access the NIC archive `NIC.DDN.MIL`. Use the user name `guest` and the password anonymous. RFCs can then be retrieved by using the FTP `get` command with the following format:

```
<RFC>RFC527.txt
```

Replace the `RFC527` portion with the number of the RFC required. You can only FTP into the NIC archive if you have access to a machine with Internet access.

Accessing RFCs Through Email

RFCs can be requested through electronic mail. Both the NIC and the NFSNET Network Service Center provide automated responses, returning the requested RFC. Both services read incoming electronic mail for keywords that indicate which RFC is required, as well as the sender's e-mail address, and then send back the RFC requested.

To obtain an RFC from the NIC, send a message with the subject field set to the RFC that you want. Mail it to `service@nic.ddn.mil`. If you want more information on obtaining information through the NIC e-mail system, send mail with the word `help` as the subject.

To obtain RFCs from the NFSNET Network Service Center, send a message with the first two lines like this:

```
REQUEST: RFC
TOPIC: 527
```

The first line specifies that you want an RFC and the second line gives the RFC number. Send the mail to `info-server@sh.cs.net`. For more information, set the topic to `help`.

Accessing Printed Copies of RFCs

You might not have access to electronic communications, so a preprinted copy of an RFC must be requested. To obtain a printed copy of any RFC, call the Network Information Center at 1-800-235-3155.

It is considered bad manners to make the NIC staff wait while you find which RFCs you want. Make a list first so your telephone conversation is short and succinct. The staff must answer many calls a day and are usually quite busy.

Useful RFCs Sorted by General Category

The list that follows includes most of the RFCs that provide either details of the protocols and their usage, or more general information about a particular subject to do with TCP/IP. There are many RFCs not included in this list, both because they have been superseded and are obsolete, or because they have nothing of interest to TCP/IP. The list is, admittedly, one chosen by the author of this book based on my own preferences. With that in mind, you might want to check the entire list of RFCs if you don't find what you are looking for.

General Information

RFC1340	"Assigned Numbers," Reynolds, J.K.; Postel, J.B.; 1992
RFC1360	"IAB Official Protocol Standards," Postel, J.B.; 1992
RFC1208	"Glossary of Networking Terms," Jacobsen, O.J.; Lynch, D.C.; 1991
RFC1180	"TCP/IP Tutorial," Socolofsky, T.J.; Kale, C.J.; 1991
RFC1178	"Choosing a Name For Your Computer," Libes, D.; 1990
RFC1175	"FYI on Where to Start: A Bibliography of Internetworking Information," Bowers, K.L.; LaQuey, T.L.; Reynolds, J.K.4 Reubicek, K.; Stahl, M.K.; Yuan, A; 1990
RFC1173	"Responsibilities of Host and Network Managers: A Summary of the 'Oral Tradition' of the Internet," vanBokkelen, J.; 1990
RFC1166	"Internet Numbers," Kirkpatrick, S.; Stahl, M.K.; Recker, M.; 1990
RFC1127	"Perspective on the Host Requirements RFCs," Braden, R.T.; 1989
RFC1123	"Requirements for Internet Hosts—Application and Support," Braden, R.T., ed; 1989
RFC1122	"Requirements for Internet Hosts—Communication Layers," Braden, R.T., ed; 1989
RFC1118	"Hitchhiker's Guide to the Internet," Krol, E.; 1989
RFC1011	"Official Internet Protocol," Reynolds, J.R.; Postel, J.B.; 1987
RFC1009	"Requirements for Internet Gateways," Braden, R.T.; Postel, J.B.; 1987
RFC980	"Protocol Document Order Information," Jacobsen, O.J.; Postel, J.B.; 1986

TCP and UDP

RFC1072	"TCP Extensions for Long-Delay Paths," Jacobson, V.; Braden, R.T.; 1988
RFC896	"Congestion Control in IP/TCP Internetworks," Nagle, J.; 1984
RFC879	"TCP Maximum Segment Size and Related Topics," Postel, J.B.; 1983

RFC813	"Window and Acknowledgment Strategy in TCP," Clark, D.D.; 1982
RFC793	"Transmission Control Protocol," Postel, J.B.; 1981
RFC768	"User Datagram Protocol," Postel, J.B.; 1980

IP and ICMP

RFC1219	"On the Assignment of Subnet Numbers," Tsuchiya, P.F.; 1991
RFC1112	"Host Extensions for IP Multicasting," Deering, S.E.; 1989
RFC1088	"Standard for the Transmission of IP Datagrams over NetBIOS Networks," McLaughlin, L.J.; 1989
RFC950	"Internet Standard Subnetting Procedure," Mogul, J.C.; Postel, J.B.; 1985
RFC932	"Subnetwork Addressing Schema," Clark, D.D.; 1985
RFC922	"Broadcasting Internet Datagrams in the Presence of Subnets," Mogul, J.C.; 1984
RFC919	"Broadcasting Internet Datagrams," Mogul, J.C.; 1984
RFC886	"Proposed Standard for Message Header Munging," Rose, M.T.; 1983
RFC815	"IP Datagram Reassembly Algorithms," Clark, D.D.; 1982
RFC814	"Name, Addresses, Ports, and Routes," Clark, D.D.; 1982
RFC792	"Internet Control Message Protocol," Postel, J.B.; 1981
RFC791	"Internet Protocol," Postel, J.B.; 1981
RFC781	"Specification of the Internet Protocol (IP) Timestamp Option," Su, Z.; 1981

Lower Layers

RFC1236	"IP to X.121 Address Mapping for DDN IP to X.121 Address Mapping for DDN," Morales, L.F. Jr.; 1991
RFC1220	"Point-to-Point Protocol Extensions for Bridging," Baker, F., ed.; 1991
RFC1209	"Transmission of IP Datagrams over the SMDS Service," Piscitello, D.M.; Lawrence, J.; 1991
RFC1201	"Transmitting IP Traffic over ARCNET Networks," Provan, D.; 1991

RFC1188	"Proposed Standard for the Transmission of IP Datagrams over FDDI Networks," Katz, D.; 1990
RFC1172	"Point-to-Point Protocol Initial Configuration Options," Perkins, D.; Hobby, R.; 1990
RFC1171	"Point-to-Point Protocol for the Transmission of Multi-Protocol Datagrams over Point-to-Point Links," Perkins, D.; 1990
RFC1149	"Standard for the Transmission of IP Datagrams on Avian Carriers," Waitzman, D.; 1990 (April 1 release!)
RFC1055	"Nonstandard for Transmission of IP Datagrams over Serial Lines: SLIP," Romkey, J.L.; 1988
RFC1044	"Internet Protocol on Network System's HYPERchannel: Protocol Specification," Hardwick, K.; Lekashman, J.; 1988
RFC1042	"Standard for the Transmission of IP Datagrams over IEEE 802 Networks," Postel, J.B.; Reynolds, J.K.; 1988
RFC1027	"Using ARP to Implement Transparent Subnet Gateways," Carl-Mitchell, S.; Quarterman, J.S.; 1987
RFC903	"Reverse Address Resolution Protocol," Finlayson, R.; Mann, T.; Mogul, J.C.; Theimer, M.; 1984
RFC895	"Standard for the Transmission of IP Datagrams over Experimental Ethernet Networks," Postel, J.B.; 1984
RFC894	"Standard for the Transmission of IP Datagrams over Ethernet Networks," Hornig, C.; 1984
RFC893	"Trailer Encapsulations," Leffler, S.; Karels, M.J.; 1984
RFC877	"Standard for the Transmission of IP Datagrams over Public Data Networks," Korb, J.T.; 1983

Bootstrapping

RFC1084	"BOOTP Vendor Information Extensions," Reynolds, J.K.; 1988
RFC951	"Bootstrap Protocol," Croft, W.J.; Gilmore, J.; 1985
RFC906	"Bootstrap Loading Using TFTP," Finlayson, R.; 1984

Domain Name System

| RFC1035 | "Domain Names—Implementation and Specification," Mockapetris, P.V.; 1987 |

RFC1034	"Domain Names—Concepts and Facilities," Mockapetris, P.V.; 1987
RFC1033	"Domain Administrators Operations Guide," Lottor, M.; 1987
RFC1032	"Domain Administrators Guide," Stahl, M.K.; 1987
RFC1101	"DNS Encoding of Network Names and Other Types," Mockapetris, P.V.; 1989
RFC974	"Mail Routing and the Domain System," Partridge, C.; 1986
RFC920	"Domain Requirements," Postel, J.B.; Reynolds, J.K.; 1984
RFC799	"Internet Name Domains," Mills, D.L.; 1981

File Transfer and File Access

RFC1094	"NFS: Network File System Protocol Specification," Sun; 1989
RFC1068	"Background File Transfer Program (BFTP)," DeSchon, A.L.; Braden, R. T.; 1988
RFC959	"File Transfer Protocol," Postel, J.B.; Reynolds, J.K.; 1985
RFC949	"FTP Unique-Named Store Command," Padlipsky, M.A.; 1985
RFC783	"TFTP Protocol (Revision 2)," Sollins, K.R.; 1981
RFC775	"Directory-Oriented FTP Commands," Mankins, D.; Franklin, D.; Owen, A.D.; 1980

Mail

RFC1341	"MIME (Multipurpose Internet Mail Extensions) Mechanisms for Specifying and Describing the Format of Internet Message Bodies," Borenstein, N.; Freed, N.; 1992
RFC1143	"Q Method of Implementing Telnet Option Negotiation," Bernstein, D.J.; 1990
RFC1090	"SMTP on X.25," Ullmann, R.; 1989
RFC1056	"PCMAIL: A Distributed Mail System for Personal Computers," Lambert, M.L.; 1988
RFC974	"Mail Routing and the Domain System," Partridge, C.; 1986
RFC822	"Standard for the Format of ARPA Internet Text Messages," Crocker, D.; 1982
RFC821	"Simple Mail Transfer Protocol," Postel, J.B.; 1982

A

RFCs AND STANDARDS

Routing Protocols

RFC1267	"A Border Gateway Protocol 3 (BGP-3)," Lougheed, K.; Rekhter, Y.; 1991
RFC1247	"OSPF Version 2," Moy, J.; 1991
RFC1222	"Advancing the NSFNET Routing Architecture," Braun, H.W.; Rekhter, Y. 1991
RFC1195	"Use of OSI IS-IS for Routing in TCP/IP and Dual Environments," Callon, R.W.; 1990
RFC1164	"Application of the Border Gateway Protocol in the Internet," Honig, J.C.; Katz, D.; Mathis, M.; Rekhter, Y.; Yu, J.Y.; 1990
RFC1163	"Border Gateway Protocol (BGP)," Lougheed, K.; Rekhter, Y.; 1990
RFC1074	"NSFNET Backbone SPF-based Interior Gateway Protocol," Rekhter, J.; 1988
RFC1058	"Routing Information Protocol," Hedrick, C.L.; 1988
RFC904	"Exterior Gateway Protocol Formal Specification," Mills, D.L.; 1984
RFC827	"Exterior Gateway Protocol (EGP)," Rosen, E.C.; 1982
RFC823	"DARPA Internet Gateway," Hinden, R.M.; Sheltzer, A.; 1982
RFC1136	"Administrative Domains and Routing Domains: A Model for Routing in the Internet," Hares, S.; Katz, D.; 1989
RFC911	"EGP Gateway under Berkeley Unix 4.2," Kirton, P.; 1984
RFC888	"STUB Exterior Gateway Protocol," Seamonson, L.; Rosen, E.C.; 1984

Routing Performance and Policy

RFC1254	"Gateway Congestion Control Survey," Mankin, A.; Ramakrishnan, K.K., eds.; 1991
RFC1246	"Experience with the OSPF Protocol," Moy, J., ed.; 1991
RFC1245	"OSPF Protocol Analysis," Moy, J., ed; 1991
RFC1125	"Policy Requirements for Inter-Administrative Domain Routing," Estrin, D.; 1989
RFC1124	"Policy Issues in Interconnecting Networks," Leiner, B.M.; 1989

| RFC1104 | "Models of Policy-Based Routing," Braun, H.W.; 1989 |
| RFC1102 | "Policy Routing in Internet Protocols," Clark, D.D.; 1989 |

Terminal Access

RFC1205	"5250 Telnet Interface," Chmielewski, P.; 1991
RFC1198	"FYI on the X Windows System," Scheifler, R.W.; 1991
RFC1184	"Telnet Linemode Option," Borman, D.A., ed.; 1990
RFC1091	"Telnet Terminal-Type Option," VanBokkelen, J.; 1989
RFC1080	"Telnet Remote Flow Control Option," Hedrick, C.L.; 1988
RFC1079	"Telnet Terminal Speed Option," Hedrick, C.L.; 1988
RFC1073	"Telnet Window Size Option," Waitzman, D.; 1988
RFC1053	"Telnet X.3 PAD Option," Levy, S; Jacobson, T.; 1988
RFC1043	"Telnet Data Entry Terminal Option: DODIIS Implementation," Yasuda, A.; Thompson, T.; 1988
RFC1041	"Telnet 3270 Regime Option," Rekhter, Y.; 1988
RFC1013	"X Window System Protocol, Version 11: Alpha Update," Scheifler, R.W.; 1987
RFC946	"Telnet Terminal Location Number Option," Nedved, R.; 1985
RFC933	"Output Marking Telnet Option," Silverman, S.; 1985
RFC885	"Telnet End of Record Option," Postel, J.B.; 1983
RFC861	"Telnet Extended Options: List Option," Postel, J.B.; Reynolds, J.K.; 1983
RFC860	"Telnet Timing Mark Option," Postel, J.B.; Reynolds, J.K.; 1983
RFC859	"Telnet Status Option," Postel, J.B.; Reynolds, J.R.; 1983
RFC858	"Telnet Suppress Go Ahead Option," Postel, J.B.; Reynolds, J.K.; 1983
RFC857	"Telnet Echo Option," Postel, J.B.; Reynolds, J.R.; 1983
RFC856	"Telnet Binary Transmission," Postel, J.B.; Reynolds, J.K.; 1983
RFC855	"Telnet Option Specifications," Postel, J.B.; Reynolds, J.K.; 1983
RFC854	"Telnet Protocol Specification," Postel, J.B.; Reynolds, J.K.; 1983

RFC779	"Telnet Send-Location Option," Killian, E.; 1981
RFC749	"Telnet SUPDUP-Output Option," Greenberg, B.; 1978
RFC736	"Telnet SUPDUP Option," Crispin, M.R.; 1977
RFC732	"Telnet Data Entry Terminal Option," Day, J.D.; 1977
RFC727	"Telnet Logout Option," Crispin, M.R.; 1977
RFC726	"Remote-Controlled Transmission and Echoing Telnet Option," Postel, J.B.; Crocker, D.; 1977
RFC698	"Telnet Extended ASCII Option," Mock, T.; 1975

Other Applications

RFC1196	"Finger User Information Protocol," Zimmerman. D.P.; 1990
RFC1179	"Line Printer Daemon Protocol," McLaughlin, L.; 1990
RFC1129	"Internet Time Synchronization: The Network Time Protocol," Mills, D.L.; 1989
RFC1119	"Network Time Protocol (Version 2) Specification and Implementation," Mills, D.L.; 1989
RFC1057	"RPC: Remote Procedure Call Protocol Specification: Version 2," Sun Microsystems, Inc.; 1988
RFC1014	"XDR: External Data Representation Standard," Sun Microsystems, Inc.; 1987
RFC954	"NICNAME/WHOIS," Harrenstien, K.; Stahl, M.K.; Feinler, E.J.; 1985
RFC868	"Time Protocol," Postel, J.B.; Harrenstien, K.; 1983
RFC867	"Daytime Protocol," Postel, J.B.; 1983
RFC866	"Active Users," Postel, J.B.; 1983
RFC865	"Quote of the Day Protocol," Postel, J.B.; 1983
RFC864	"Character Generator Protocol," Postel, J.B.; 1983
RFC863	"Discard Protocol," Postel, J.B.; 1983
RFC862	"Echo Protocol," Postel, J.B.; 1983

Network Management

| RFC1271 | "Remote Network Monitoring Management Information Base," Waldbusser, S.; 1991 |
| RFC1253 | "OSPE Version 2: Management Information Base," Baker, P.; Coltun, R.; 1991 |

RFC1243	"AppleTalk Management Information Base," 1991
RFC1239	"Reassignment of Experimental MIBs to Standard MIBs," Reynolds, J.K.; 1991
RFC1238	"CLNS MIB for Use with Connectionless Network Protocol (ISO 8473) and End System to Intermediate System (ISO 9542)," Satz, G.; 1991
RFC1233	"Definitions of Managed Objects for the DS3 Interface Type," Cox, T.A.; Tesink, K., eds.; 1991
RFC1232	"Definitions of Managed Objects for the DS1 Interface Type," Baker, F.; Kolb, C.P. eds.; 1991
RFC1231	"IEEE 802.5 Token Ring MIB," McCloghrie, K.; Fox, R.; Decker, E.; 1991
RFC1230	"IEEE 802.4 Token Bus MIB," McCloghrie, K.; Fox R.; 1991
RFC1229	"Extensions to the Generic-Interface MIB," McCloghrie, K., ed.; 1991
RFC1228	"SNMP-DPI: Simple Network Management Protocol Distributed Program Interface," Carpenter, G.; Wijnen, B.; 1991
RFC1227	"SNMP MUX Protocol and MIB," Rose, M.T.; 1991
RFC1224	"Techniques for Managing Asynchronously Generated Alerts," Steinberg, L.; 1991
RFC1215	"Convention for Defining Traps for Use with the SNMP," Rose, M.T., ed.; 1991
RFC1214	"OSI Internet Management: Management Information Base," LaBarre, L. ed.; 1991
RFC1213	"Management Information Base for Network Management of TCP/IP-Based Internets: MIB-II," McCloghrie, K.; Rose, M.T., eds.; 1991
RFC1212	"Concise MIB Definitions," Rose, M.T.; McCloghrie, K., eds.; 1991
RFC1187	"Bulk Table Retrieval with the SNMP," Rose, M.T.; McCloghrie, K.; Davin, J.R.; 1990
RFC1157	"Simple Network Management Protocol (SNMP)," Case, J.D.; Fedor, M.; Schoffstall, M.L.; Davin, C.; 1990
RFC1156	"Management Information Base for Network Management of TCP/IP-Based Internets," McGloghrie, K.; Rose, M.T.; 1990

RFC1155   "Structure and Identification of Management Information for TCP/IP-Based Internets," Rose, M.T.; McCloghrie, K.; 1990

RFC1147   "FYI on a Network Management Tool Catalog: Tools for Monitoring and Debugging TCP/IP Internets and Interconnected Devices," Stine, R.H.; ed.; 1990

RFC1089   "SNMP over Ethernet," Schoffstall, M.L.; Davin, C.; Fedor, M.; Case, J.D.; 1989

Tunneling

RFC1241   "Scheme for an Internet Encapsulation Protocol: Version 1"; 1991

RFC1234   "Tunneling IPX Traffic Through IP Networks," Provan, D.; 1991

RFC1088   "Standard for the Transmission of IP Datagrams over NetBIOS Networks," McLaughlin, L.J.; 1989

RFC1002   "Protocol Standard for a NetBIOS Service on a TCP/UDP Transport: Detailed Specifications," NetBIOS Working Group; 1987

RFC1001   "Protocol Standard for a NetBIOS Service on a TCP/UDP Transport: Concepts and Methods," NetBIOS Working Group; 1987

OSI

RFC1240   "OSI Connectionless Transport Services on Top of UDP: Version 1," Shue, C.; Haggerty, W.; Dobbins, K.; 1991

RFC1237   "Guidelines for OSI NSAP Allocation in the Internet," Gollela, R.; Gardner, E.P.; Callon, R.W.; 1991

RFC1169   "Explaining the Role of GOSIP," Cerf, V.G.; Mills, K.L.; 1990

Security

RFC1244   "Site Security Handbook"

RFC1115   "Privacy Enhancement for Internet Electronic Mail: Part III—Algorithms, Modes, and Identifiers [Draft]," Linn, J.; 1989

RFC1114   "Privacy Enhancement for Internet Electronic Mail: Part II—Certificate-Based Key Management [Draft]," Kent, S.T.; Linn, J.; 1989

RFC1113   "Privacy Enhancement for Internet Electronic Mail: Part I—Message Encipherment and Authentication Procedures [Draft]," Linn, J.; 1989

RFC1108   "Security Options for the Internet Protocol," 1991

Miscellaneous

RFC1251   "Who's Who in the Internet: Biographies of IAB, IESG and IRSG Members," Malkin, G.S.; 1991

RFC1207   "FYI on Questions and Answers: Answers to Commonly Asked 'Experienced Internet User' Questions," Malkin, G.S.; Marine, A.N.; Reynolds, J.K.; 1991

RFC1206   "FYI on Questions and Answers: Answers to Commonly Asked 'New Internet User' Questions," Malkin, G.S.; Marine, A.N.; 1991

List of RFCs by Number

For a list of all the RFCs in the RFC index check the Web site `http://www.rfc-editor.org` for the latest updates.

A

RFCs AND STANDARDS

Abbreviations and Acronyms

by Tim Parker

ABI   Application Binary Interface

ACB   Access Control Block

ACIA   Asynchronous Communications Interface Adapter

ACK   Acknowledgment

AD   Active Directory

AF   Address Family

AFP   AppleTalk Filing Protocol

AFS   Andrew File System

AIX   Advanced Interactive Executive (IBM Unix)

ANSI   American National Standards Institute

AOCE   Apple Open Collaborative Environment

API   Application Programming Interface

APPC   Advanced Program-to-Program Communications

APPN   Advanced Peer-to-Peer Networking

ARA   AppleTalk Remote Access

ARP   Address Resolution Protocol

ARPA   Advanced Research Projects Agency

AS   Autonomous System

ASA   American Standards Association

ASCII   American National Standard Code for Information Interchange

ASN.1   Abstract Syntax Notation One

ASPI   Advanced SCSI Programming Interface

ATM   Adobe Type Manager

ATM   Asynchronous Transfer Mode

AUI   Attachment Unit Interface

A/UX   Apple Unix

BBLT   Bus Block Transfer

B

BBN   Bolt, Beranek, and Newman, Incorporated

BER   Basic Encoding Rules

BER   Bit Error Rate

BGP   Border Gateway Protocol

BIOS   Basic Input/Output System

BISDN   Broadband ISDN (Integrated Services Digital Network)

BITBLT   Bit Block Transfer

BITNET   Because It's Time Network

BSD   Berkeley Software Distribution

CAMMU   Cache/Memory Management Unit

CBLT   Character Block Transfer

CCITT   Consultative Committee on International Telegraphy and Telephony (translated from French)

CDE   Common Desktop Environment

CDMA   Code Division Multiple Access

CLI   Call-Level Interface

CLI   Command-Line Interpreter

CMC   Common Messaging Calls

CMIP   Common Management Information Protocol

CMIS   Common Management Information Services

CMOT   Common Management Information Services and Protocol over TCP/IP

CORBA   Common Object Request Broker Architecture

COSE   Common Open Software Environment

CPU   Central Processing Unit

CRC   Cyclic Redundancy Check

CREN   Consortium for Research and Education Network

CSMA/CD   Carrier Sense Multiple Access with Collision Detection

CSNET   Computer Science Network

CUA   Common User Access

DARPA   Defense Advanced Research Projects Agency

DARPANET   Defense Advanced Research Projects Agency Network

DAT   Digital Audio Tape

DBMS   Database Management System

DCA   Defense Communications Agency

DCE   Data Circuit-terminating Equipment (also called Data Communications Equipment)

DCE   Distributed Computing Environment

DDBMS   Distributed DBMS (Database Management System)

DDE   Dynamic Data Exchange

DDN   Defense Data Network

DES   Data Encryption Standard

DFS   Distributed File Service

DHCP   Dynamic Host Configuration Protocol

DIF   Data Interchange Format

DIME   Dual Independent Map Encoding

DISA   Defense Information Systems Agency

DIX   Digital, Intel, and Xerox Ethernet Protocol

DLL   Dynamic Link Library

DLP   Data Link Protocol

DME   Distributed Management Environment

DNS   Domain Name System

DOE   Distributed Objects Everywhere

DSA   Directory System Agent

DSAP   Destination Service Access Point

DTE   Data Terminal Equipment

DTMF   Dual-Tone Multifrequency

DUA   Directory User Agent

DVI   Digital Video Interactive

EBCDIC   Extended Binary Coded Decimal Interchange Code

ECC   Error Correction Code

ECM   Error Correction Mode

EGP   Exterior Gateway Protocol

ENS   Enterprise Network Services

EOF   End of File

EOR   End of Record

ERLL   Enhanced Run Length Limited

ESDI   Enhanced Small Device Interface

FAT   File Allocation Table

FCS   Frame Check Sequence

FDDI   Fiber Distributed Data Interface

FIN   Final Segment

FTAM   File Transfer, Access, and Management

FTAM   File Transfer Access Method

FTP   File Transfer Protocol

GGP   Gateway-to-Gateway Protocol

GIF   Graphics Interchange Format

GOSIP   Government Open Systems Interconnection Profile

GPF   General Protection Fault

GPI   Graphics Programming Interface

GTF   Generalized Trace Facility

GUI   Graphical User Interface

HAL   Hardware Abstraction Layer

HDLC   High-level Data Link Control Protocol

HDX   Half Duplex

HFS   Hierarchical File System

HIPPI   High Performance Parallel Interface (also called HPPI)

HOB   High Order Byte

HPFS   High Performance File System

HPPI   High Performance Parallel Interface (also called HIPPI)

HTTP   Hypertext Transport Protocol

IAB   Internet Activities Board

IAB   Internet Architecture Board

IAC   Interapplication Communication

IAC   Interpret as Command

IANA   Internet Assigned Numbers Authority

ICMP   Internet Control Message Protocol

ID   Identifier

IDE   Integrated Drive Electronics

IEEE   Institute of Electrical and Electronic Engineers

IEN   Internet Engineering Notes

IESG   Internet Engineering Steering Group

IETF   Internet Engineering Task Force

IFF   Interchange File Format

IGMP   Internet Group Management Protocol

IGP   Interior Gateway Protocol

IMAP   Interactive Mail Access Protocol

INT   Interrupt

IP   Internet Protocol

IPC   Interprocess Communications

IPX/SPX   Internet Packet Exchange/Sequenced Packet Exchange

IRC   Interrupt Request Controller

IRQ   Interrupt Request

IRTF   Internet Research Task Force

ISDN   Integrated Services Digital Network

IS-IS   Intermediate System to Intermediate System Protocol

ISN   Initial Sequence Number

ISO   International Organization for Standardization

ISODE   ISO Development Environment

JPEG   Joint Photographic Experts Group

KB   Kilobyte (1024 bytes)

LAN   Local Area Network

LAPB   Link Access Procedures Balanced

LAPD   Link Access Procedures on the D-channel

LLC   Logical Link Control

LOB   Low Order Byte

LSB   Least Significant Bit (or Byte)

LSD   Least Significant Digit

MAC   Media Access Control

MAN   Metropolitan Area Network

MAPI   Messaging API (Application Programming Interface)

MAU   Medium Access Unit

MFC   Microsoft Foundation Classes

MFS   Macintosh File System

MHS   Message Handling Service

MIB   Management Information Base

MILNET   Military Network

MIME   Multipurpose Internet Mail Extensions

MNP   Microcom Networking Protocol

MSB   Most Significant Bit (or Byte)

MSS   Maximum Segment Size

MTA   Message Transfer Agent

MTU   Maximum Transmission Unit

MTU   Message Transfer Unit

MX   Mail Exchanger

NAU   Network Access Unit

NDIS   Network Driver Interface Specification

NDS   NetWare (or Novell) Directory Service

NETBIOS   Network Basic Input/Output System

NETBEUI   NetBIOS Extended User Interface

NFS   Network File System

NIC   Network Information Center

NIC   Network Interface Card

NIS   Network Information Service

NIST   National Institute of Standards and Technology

NIU   Network Interface Unit

NLM   NetWare Loadable Module

NMI   Nonmaskable Interrupt

NNTP   Network News Transport Protocol

NOS   Network Operating System

NREN   National Research and Education Network

NSAP   Network Service Access Point

NSFNET   National Science Foundation Network

NVT   Network Virtual Terminal

ODAPI   Open Database API (Application Programming Interface)

ODI   Open Datalink Interface

ONC   Open Network Computing

OSF   Open Software Foundation

OSI   Open Systems Interconnect

OSPF   Open Shortest Path First

PAD   Packet Assembly/Disassembly

PCMCIA   Personal Computer Memory Card International Association

PDU   Protocol Data Unit

PI   Protocol Interpreter

PING   Packet Internet Groper

POP   Post Office Protocol

POTS   Plain Old Telephone Service

PPP   Point-to-Point Protocol

QIC   Quarter-Inch Cartridge

RARP   Reverse Address Resolution Protocol

RFC   Request For Comment

RFS   Remote File System

RIP   Routing Information Protocol

RMON   Remote Network Monitor

RPC   Remote Procedure Call

RST   Reset

RTT   Round Trip Time

SAP   Service Access Point

SDLC   Synchronous Data Link Communication

SLIP   Serial Line Interface Protocol

SMDS   Switched Multimegabit Data Service

SMTP   Simple Mail Transfer Protocol

B

ABBREVIATIONS AND ACRONYMS

SNA   Systems Network Architecture

SNMP   Simple Network Management Protocol

SONET   Synchronous Optical Network

SPF   Shortest Path First

SSAP   Source Service Access Point

SSCP   System Services Control Point

SYN   Synchronizing Segment

TCB   Transmission Control Block

TCP   Transmission Control Protocol

TCP/IP   Transmission Control Protocol/Internet Protocol

TCU   Trunk Coupling Unit

TELNET   Terminal Networking

TFTP   Trivial File Transfer Protocol

TLI   Transport Layer Interface

TP4   OSI Transport Class 4

TSAP   Transport Service Access Point

TTL   Time-to-Live

UA   User Agent

UART   Universal Asynchronous Receiver/Transmitter

UDP   User Datagram Protocol

ULP   Upper Layer Protocol

URL   Uniform Resource Locator

UUCP   Unix-to-Unix Copy

WAN   Wide Area Network

WWW   World Wide Web

XDR   External Data Representation

XNS   Xerox Network Systems

INDEX

Hey, you've got enough worries.

Don't let IT training be one of them.

Get on the fast track to IT training at InformIT,
your total Information Technology training network.

 | **www.informit.com** | **SAMS**

■ Hundreds of timely articles on dozens of topics ■ Discounts on IT books from all our publishing partners, including Sams Publishing ■ Free, unabridged books from the InformIT Free Library ■ "Expert Q&A"—our live, online chat with IT experts ■ Faster, easier certification and training from our Web- or classroom-based training programs ■ Current IT news ■ Software downloads ■ Career-enhancing resources

InformIT is a registered trademark of Pearson. Copyright ©2001 by Pearson.
Copyright ©2001 by Sams Publishing.